STEALING
Puget Sound

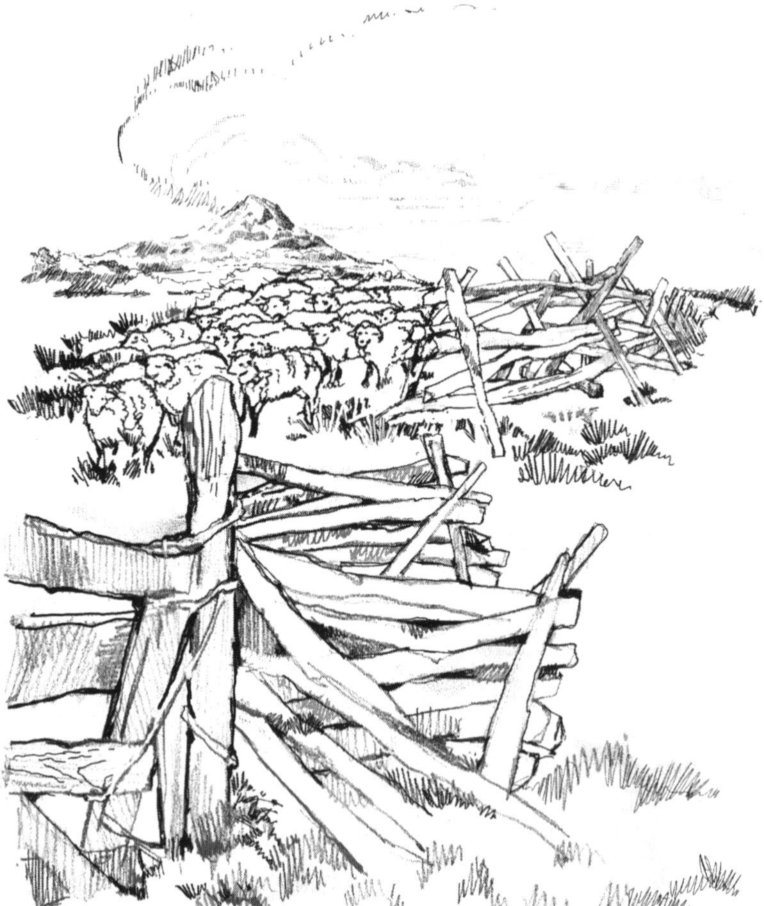

STEALING
Puget Sound

1832~1869

JERRY V. RAMSEY, PH.D.

Illustrated by Carol Ann Johnson

Published by
Doghouse Publishing
3800 Bridgeport Way West
Suite A-467
University Place, WA 98466

www.doghouse-publishing.com

Copyright © 2015 by Jerry V. Ramsey, Ph.D.

All rights reserved. No part of this book shall be reproduced, stored in a retrieval system, or transmitted by any person by any means, electronic, mechanical, photocopying, recording, or otherwise, without written permission from the publisher. No patent liability is assumed with respect to the use of information contained herein. Although every precaution has been taken in the preparation of this book, the publisher and author assume no responsibility for errors or omissions. Neither is any liability assumed for damages resulting from the use of information contained herein.

ISBN: 987-0-9846234-3-3
LCCN: 9846234-3-4

Note: This publication contains the opinions, ideas and research results of its author. It is assumed to provide helpful and informative material on the subject matter covered. It is sold with the understanding that the author and publisher are not engaged in rendering professional services in the book.

The author and the publisher specifically disclaim any responsibility of any liability, loss, risk, personal or otherwise, which is incurred as a consequence, directly or indirectly, of the use and application of any of the contents of this book.

Copy Editor: Darlyne A. Reiter
Illustrator: Carol Ann Johnson
CarolArt Web & Fine Arts www.csrolsrt-studio.com
Indexer: Darlyne A. Reiter
Cover and interior design by Kathryn E. Campbell
Proof Editors: Pamela Wray and Kathy Cunningham

Printed by Gorham Printing
3718 Mahoney Drive, Centralia, WA 98531
www.gorhamprinting.com

Printed in the United States of America

DEDICATIONS

*I dedicate this book to those who seek to learn more
about Puget Sound area history and to the
entire heritage community of the region.*

*I also dedicate this work to my wife,
Elaine Sigrid Perdue Ramsey,
for her encouragement and support
during all these years.*

Copies of this book are available from the author.
Wholesale purchases for retail re-sale are negotiable.

CONTENTS

Acknowledgments ... viii

Prologue ... x

Author's Note ... xi

First Footprints—A summary from prehistory to 1832 ... 1

Chronological Events ... 31

1832	First HBC Fur Traders arrive at Sequalitchew ... 37
1833	Nisqually House is built—Trading begins ... 47
1834	The Company roster and aggressive construction ... 65
1835	The HBC Steamship *Beaver* arrives ... 85
1836	Captain McNeill, an American, is hired ... 93
1837	Influenza strikes—Spanish cattle arrive ... 99
1838	Sheep, cattle and record-size potatoes ... 113
1839	Puget's Sound Agricultural Company formed ... 123
1840	Missionaries arrive, Governor Simpson visits ... 141
1841	Wilkes visits, palisades built, herds grow ... 153
1842	First American settlers marry & a baby is born ... 179
1843	Provisional government of Oregon ... 187
1844	Joseph Heath, 12,000 sheep, 10,000 cattle ... 197
1845	Newmarket, American grist mill, saw mill ... 205
1846	54-40 or Fight, Boundary set, British build more ... 213

1847	Fort Nisqually palisades built for security	231
1848	Territory of Oregon, PSAC world trade grows	237
1849	Huggins, US Army arrive at Fort Steilacoom	247
1850	Americans accuse Dr. Tolmie of arming Indians	263
1851	More American Settlers & Squatters	283
1852	Americans seize British ships and cargo	297
1853	Washington Territory created, Fort cattle killed	315
1854	Dr. Tolmie's new house, court hears squatters	343
1855	PSAC successful, Fur Brigade visits Fort Nisqually	357
1856	Indian Treaty War continues, Shop Sales slow	375
1857	Settlers squat on PSAC land, Huggins marries	393
1858	Americans hang Leschi, PSAC wins in court	399
1859	Pierce County records burn, Tolmie leaves	405
1860–2014	U.S. buys PSAC land, summary of events	413

Appendix Part One 423

Appendix Part Two 424

Appendix Part Three 428

Appendix Part Four 430

Index 433

LIST OF ILLUSTRATIONS

Sheep split-rail fence ii

Footsteps on the beach xiv

Beaver pelts dryed and baled 36

Squared timber building 46

Longhorn split-rail fence 67

S.S. *Beaver* load 84

Map of British Possessions 94

Cattle drive 103

Big sheep herd 119

Cabin and plow 129

Fort Nisqually palisade 140

Fort Nisqually palisage and blockhouse 162

Sheep and steer fence 180

Fence toward Mt. Rainier 193

Splitting cattle and sheep 201

Tall split-rail fence 204

Shooting cattle 214

Shipping dock 245

Cattle fence 253

Rifles and beaver traps in storehouse 262

Pasture fence before Mt. Rainier 289

Schooner 296

Treaty desk 314

Houseplans 342

Warehouse furs 356

Hudson's Bay Company store interior 374

Longhorn fence 392

Hanging execution site 400

Dead tree 404

The American flag 412

ACKNOWLEDGMENTS

All of the excellent illustrations contained here are commissioned originals by Carol Ann Johnson, copyright owner, and are used here by permission of the artist. Prints are available directly from the artist.[1]

A single map of Puget Sound Agricultural Company property is included in the work. It is a highly adapted version of the fine research done by Steven A. Anderson. Copyright originals are used here with his permission. Single copies of the map may be available for a fee from the mapmaker by special request.[2]

Darlyne Reiter, a diligent and gentle editor and indexer; Carol Ann Johnson, professional artist who can actually 'see' what I say; Dale Wirsing, a professional reporter, editor, and patient friend; Steve Anderson, who helped immensely and seemingly without effort; and Elaine Sigrid Perdue Ramsey who has been my companion, girlfriend, wife, critic, coach, mentor, boss, confidant, fellow conspirator, and wise teacher for fifty-two years.

Groups of people also helped write this book by being themselves and by being someone else, too. Local area re-enactors who present historically accurate personages at many events every year, while consistently 'time-travelling' to tell the story of the first European settlement on the shores of Puget Sound.

This is the mostly untold story of the historic period prior to the development of the City of Destiny, Tacoma, the western terminus of the second transcontinental railroad, which arrived less than four years after the British property had been purchased by the United States of America. One can only imagine the alternative history had the railroad arrived forty years earlier along with PSAC. Clearly the city would have developed differently with an established agri-business nucleus, operated by the largest commercial enterprise in the world. Most local history tells only the story of the industrial city that ultimately grew at the Pacific railhead.

Thank you, dear reader and local history buff, for purchasing my book. It has been a longtime effort, with many side trips and hardships. My wife Elaine developed a life threatening brain disorder just after the composition was begun. Needless to say, the manuscript was set aside, several times, to deal with her medical needs. So, ten years later, a book is born. I hope you like it. —JR

---

1 Johnson, Carol Ann, www.carolart-studio.com, 253-858-2378, carolart@centurytel.net
2 Anderson, Steven A., The History Place, 1008 Arendell Street, Morehead City, N.C. 252-247-7533

PROLOGUE

"Traders, preachers, adventurers and warriors throughout history have shaped and reshaped human interconnectedness and interdependence that continues today at ever increasing speed and ease. Globalization—from the lone trader carving a new trail to great expansive commercial enterprises —connects the cells of our bodies by invisible threads that stretch across continents and millennia. For better or worse we are bound together."[3]

---

3   Chandra, Navan, *Bound Together*, Yale University Press, New Haven & London, 2007

AUTHOR'S NOTE

It is widely recognized that primary source material relating to the historic period of Puget Sound between 1830 and 1860 is both sparse and frequently conflicting. Accordingly, any attempt to produce a reliable historical synthesis from these sources will almost inevitably be open to alternate interpretations, suggestions and analyses. The author has tried to produce a readable and carefully written account that effectively tackles a topic many predecessors have avoided or glossed over.

The primary source of the calendar central to the sequence of *Stealing Puget Sound: 1832-1869* comes from the undated transcription *Journal of Occurrences at Fort Nisqually, May 30, 1822 through September 27, 1859* by George Dickey.

The task of history-keepers is far more than simply recording facts. Those facts, and events that created them, must also be set in the correct historical context, highlighting scenes of unique interest that illuminate people, events, and places with the highest degree of accuracy. The goal here is to glean information, preserve it in a convenient form for now and the future. The search for rare data can become a marvelous obsession. The presentation of the results can pleasantly affect many people. This book is the genesis of a potentially impressive discussion.

Hudson's Bay Company was in supreme control of the land from the Arctic to the lower Columbia River, and from the Pacific Ocean to the Rockies for many years. British political interests were at stake as well as the fur trade in the era when Fort Nisqually was established. The remote outpost would grow over time into a substantial international business establishment. It would, in fact, become a huge agricultural business, with farms and ranches covering much of the prairies near Puget Sound, and stretching from the Cowlitz River banks to Vancouver Island. Before American political jurisdictions were established the British companies, centered at Fort Nisqually, would cover 161,000 acres, or 250 square miles,[4] in what is now Pierce County, with other sections in Thurston,

---

4   The entire land area of modern Pierce County is huge; extending from sea level to 14,411 feet at the peak of Mt. Rainier it also rises higher than any single county in the country. HBC land was roughly the western third of the 1,806 square miles of land. By comparison the State of Rhode Island covers 1,212 square miles. As noted PSAC farms and ranches extended well beyond present-day Pierce County boundaries.

Lewis, Cowlitz and San Juan Counties of Washington State, as well as large farmlands in British Columbia, Canada, along the Fraser River and on Vancouver Island.

Not included in this book are the 13 other trading posts scattered about 200 miles apart along the Pacific Coast from Spanish California to Russian Alaska and the Rocky Mountains to the Canadian Arctic Ocean. The southwestern section, the Columbia Department, was about one-fourth of the 1.5 million square miles of land granted by British Royal Charter in 1670 to the Hudson's Bay Company by King Charles, the Merry Monarch of England, Scotland, and Ireland.

A specific area occupied by Hudson's Bay Company (HBC) and Puget Sound Agricultural Company (PSAC) was, eventually, British real estate inside the boundaries of the contiguous territory of the United States of America. That real estate continued to be legally recognized as British property until 1870, well after the American Civil War, and three years after Alaska was purchased in 1867. Much of Pierce County, Washington Territory, was clearly a British corporation's land, consecrated by an international treaty[5] that was approved by the United States Congress, the British Parliament, Her Majesty the Queen and the President of the United States. The primary focus in this book is the British history on the shores of Puget Sound for the period 1832 to 1870, including the unethical and illegal means used by American civilian and legal authorities who tried to seize control by *Stealing Puget Sound*.

Let the discussion begin.

Jerry V. Ramsey, Ph.D.
Tacoma

---

5   Treaty between Her Majesty and the United States of America, for the Settlement of the Oregon Boundary in Regard to the Limits Westward of the Rocky Mountains, and also known as the Buchanan-Pakenham Treaty, particularly Articles III and IV.

STEALING
Puget Sound

1832-1869

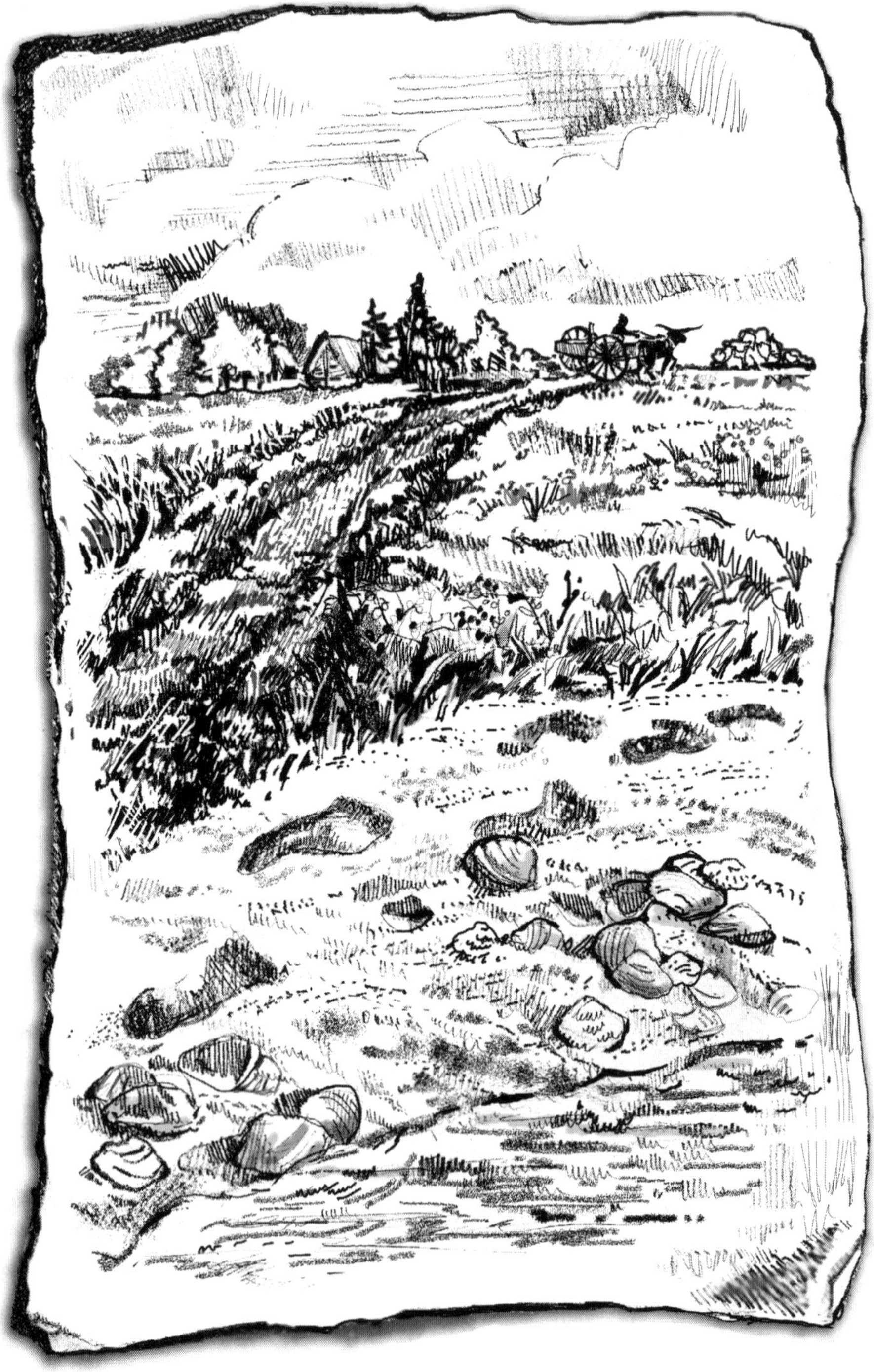

First Footprints

LONG BEFORE ANY human beings inhabited the area we know today as the Puget Sound Region, it was geologically created by tremendous volcanic episodes and plate-tectonic collisions occurring over many centuries. The Okanogan micro-continent smashed into the North American continent some 100 million years ago. That collision put the west coast of North America near what is now the Idaho-Washington border.

About 50 million years ago the North Cascades crashed very slowly into the North American continent widening the continent a bit more. Between 14 and 7 million years ago massive volcanic activity created what we call the Cascade Mountain Range. Vancouver Island and the San Juan Islands were formed about 15 million years ago, followed by the pushed-up Olympic plate. These plate movements, collisions, and other geologic activity continued for millions of years. During the Ice Age glacier ice was sometimes 2,000 feet thick coating what is now the Puget Sound region. As the ice moved, the land was gouged into huge ditches. Piles of earth were deposited forming the shorelines and islands of what is now Puget Sound.

American continental human habitation may have begun as early as 32,000 years ago, based on discoveries in southern Chile.[6]

The retreat of the Ice Age as the globe warmed gradually allowed humans to expand their habitat. Correspondingly, the oldest human remains in the Pacific Northwest are those of "Kennewick Man" found in 1997 near the city of that name along the Columbia River. That ancient skeleton has been "age dated" to about 8,500 years ago which corresponds well with the retreat of the Ice Age.[7]

About 10,000 years ago every part of the world was inhabited by humankind, except

---

6   Man, Charles C. 1491, *New Revelations of the Americas Before Columbus*, Alfred A. Knopf, New York, 2005.

7   Owsley, David, editor, *Kennewick Man: The Scientific Investigation of an Ancient American Skeleton*, Texas A & M University Press, as reported by Douglas Preston, *The Smithsonian Institution Magazine*, September, Washington, D.C., 2014 and on-line at http://www.smithsonianmag.com/history/kennewick-man-finally-freed-shar-his-secrets-180952462/?no-ist

Antarctica. Temperatures warmed everywhere, allowing the expansion of available human habitat. Global climate has continued to warm for 12,000 years, just as today's continents continue a seismic drift toward an ultimate, unknown future.

Human beings probably entered the Puget Sound basin in significant numbers a short time after the Osceola Mudflow, although they may have been in the area as early as the last stages of the ice age.[8] If humans were here it was in small and scattered population groups. Semi-permanent aboriginal homes and camps were eventually established in convenient places along fish-spawning rivers.

Mount Rainier sloughed off the Osceola Mudflow approximately 5,600 years ago; caused when the volcanic summit of Mount Rainier collapsed, taking 2,000 feet off the top of that grand mountain. Nearly a cubic mile of material flowed into what is now the Duwamish and White River Valleys. The massive avalanche of mud and rock moved at 12 to 15 miles per hour burying everything in its path for nearly fifty miles and raising the land level above the old water line of Puget Sound that had previously filled those valleys. About 500 years ago another, smaller mudflow buried some of those first human beings and their homes in the Puget Sound region.

An enormous earthquake shook the West Coast of North America on January 26, 1700, at about 9:00 PM Pacific Standard Time.[9] The epicenter was 60 to 70 miles out to sea on the ocean bottom. It sent a 33-foot-high tsunami racing across the Pacific Ocean. North American Indian legends and Japanese written records agree it was a cataclysmic event. The Washington coastline dropped three to six feet, according to the geologic record.

The "Orphan Tsunami" as it is called in Japan was caused by a magnitude 8.7 to 9.2 earthquake along a fault that stretches about 600 miles from British Columbia to California. It was a mega-thrust quake with an average slippage of about twenty meters. The earthquake created a tsunami that was at least 33 feet high and reached the island of Honshu 300 miles northeast of Tokyo ten hours later, completely devastating 600 miles of Japanese coastline. At Miho, 90 miles southwest of Tokyo, the tsunami wave toppled pine trees. The huge but diminishing waves came in seven times before 10 AM.

The earthquake-caused tsunami hit Kodiak, Alaska, where elders tell of ancestors spending the night in the cold hills. When they returned to the village site everything had been washed away. Children were taught to run to the hills if they felt an earthquake,

---

8   Ibid. On page 172–173, Mann writes, "The Western Hemisphere should perhaps no longer be described as the "New World." Britain… was empty until about 12,500 B.C., because it was still covered by glaciers. "…people were thriving from Alaska to Chile while much of northern Europe was still empty of mankind and its works."

9   Atwater, Brian F., et al, *The Orphan Tsunami of 1700—Japanese Clues to a Parent Earthquake in North America*, U.S. Geological Survey Professional Paper #1707, Washington, D.C. 2005.

or saw a large wave approaching.

The Yurok people of Northern California have stories of supernatural beings shaking and thundering along the coast to specific places showing evidence of the 1700 A.D. great earthquake. The Hoh and Quileute tribes along the Pacific shore of Washington have legends describing epic battles between supernatural beings that shake and jump to make the earth tremble, roiling the waters. A Makah legend tells the story of losing nearly everything during an earthquake and tsunami. According to verbal history a whale was left stranded on the beach as the sea retreated during the geologic event. Survivors' lives changed forever as they lost nearly every possession, including all of their stored food supplies. The stranded whale was butchered to save the Makah from starvation. The historic fact of the earthquake is the cultural justification for the internationally recognized and legally-approved Makah Indian whale hunts today.

The exact origin of the indigenous First People of what is now western Washington remains unclear. Most likely they came over the Cascades from the east or migrated from the north along the coastline. Language experts agree the Coast Salish language dialect spoken by most Puget Sound Native Americans (Lushootseed is a local variation of Coast Salish) is linguistically related to the Salish language dialect spoken by the people who lived between the Cascades and the Rockies.

The earliest non-aboriginals in the area were Spanish explorers sailing along the coast. On August 11, 1774, Juan Perez, commanding the *Santiago,* sighted and named Cerro Nevada de Santa Rosalia (Mount Olympus). Perez called the Pacific Northwest "Nueva Galicia" in reference to the Viceroyalty of New Spain (now Mexico and Central America).

On July 12, 1775, Juan Perez landed the *Santiago* in Grenville Bay (Grays Harbor) claiming Nueva Galicia for Spain. The first Europeans to set foot in what is now Washington State included Commander Bruno Hezeta, Father de la Sierra, Don Cristobal Revilla, surgeon Don Juan Gonzales and Captain Perez. Hezeta named the land Rada de Bucareli.

Later that day and a bit farther north a second ship, the *Sonora,* sent a party of seven unarmed crewmen ashore for fresh water and firewood. Quinault warriors massacred all seven then paddled toward the *Sonora.* The ship's commander ordered defensive cannon fire. Several Quinault were killed. Bodega named that battle scene Punta de los Martires. Martyrs Point is today called Point Grenville.

Five days later, on August 17, 1775 Hezeta, the first non-Indian to see the Columbia River, mapped what is now the mouth of the mighty Columbia. He named the northside cliff Cabo de San Roque (now Cape Disappointment). The mouth of the river he called Bahia de la Asuncion de Nuestra Senora. The south side of the river entrance he named Leafy Cape. Although there is no certainty that he knew it was a river mouth rather than a bay (Bahia), he probably had the good sense to test the water for potability, salinity and silt.

On March 7, 1778, English Captain Cook spotted the northwest coastline, naming it New Albion, an archaic name for the white cliffs of Great Britain. It was the second use of the name for the same general area; therefore the English reasoned they had the right to claim it all.[10] To further the English claim, on March 22, 1778, Captain James Cook specifically named Cape Flattery, the home of the Makah people.

Cook's claim was disputed vigorously by the Spanish, and the Russians who had probably been there. The Makah, Haida, Quinalt, and other Northwest First People were absolutely unaware of the eventual loss they would suffer and that history would deliver much of this land to others.

On July 6, 1788, English fur trader John Meares, commanding the Portuguese-flagged *Felice Adventurer* renamed the north side of the Columbia River entrance Cape Disappointment, because he could not see the river. He decided Hezeta had seen only a bay.

In 1789 less than a year after the mouth of the Columbia River was called a bay, General George Washington was inaugurated as the First President of the United States of America following the Revolutionary War of 1776. Generations of European people had lived on Eastern shores of North America for over 165 years by the time the Spanish arrived at Nootka. About eight generations of religious pilgrims' descendants were developing a distinctly "American" culture.

At that time, on the bountiful shores of Puget Sound, an equal number of Native American generations had developed another distinctive culture. Their culture was fifty generations older. Theirs was a holy land in the valleys and shadows of "the Mountain that was God."

The Spanish sailors, under Salvador Fidalgo, built the first foreign settlement in the Pacific Northwest at Neah Bay. The little fort bolstered Spanish claims, but in October 1790 the English Royal Navy was no longer occupied with fighting the American Revolution. The Spanish, fearful of the powerful, and suddenly available, English navy, signed the Nootka Treaty with England, which opened the north Pacific to English explorers and traders north of the 42nd parallel, the northern border of today's California.

In 1792, American Captain Robert Gray, English Captain George Vancouver and Spanish Captain Salvador Fidalgo were all exploring the region, each trying to take control of the area for their country. The Spanish were there because they had prior claim, and were ignoring the Nootka Treaty. The English were there because they had Nootka

---

10   It was the second use of the name New Albion. Sir Francis Drake, although he had not seen the North Pacific coast named it New Albion during his circumnavigation aboard the *Golden Hind*, 200 years earlier.

Treaty rights. The Americans were there because, well, just because.

The term "Manifest Destiny" had not yet entered the political lexicon of the nation, but the idea of a broad nation extending its borders across the entire continent was brewing in the minds of explorers and politicians.

Hezeta's well-documented report of a big river or bay has most often been credited to Robert Gray. The American actually sailed up the river 17 years after Hezeta's initial notice, proving that it was indeed a river. Gray named the river after his ship, the *Columbia Rediviva*, which crossed the treacherous sand bar on May 11, 1792. Gray traded with the local inhabitants using the Indian Chinook trade language. He learned the Indians called the river Wimahl, meaning Big River.

Archaeologists have documented human activity along the Wimahl for more than 10,000 years, giving credence, carved in stone, to the idea of ancient Indian settlements. Gray came into contact with the Clatsop and the Chinook people. They lived in perhaps fifty villages along the river banks. The Clatsop and the Chinook operated a very complex material-trading culture. The Columbia River area was, perhaps, the most heavily populated and naturally rich areas north of Mexico.

In Europe during the early 18th century, no proper gentleman would appear in public without a proper hat. The very best hat was made of felted beaver fur. Demand for a beaver-felted hat was high. The European beaver was trapped to extinction when the Hudson's Bay Company discovered the rich fur resources of North America. During the heyday of the beaver fur trade, 100,000 beaver were consumed annually for the hats of the European dandies. The European explorers were happy to be the vanguard of the fur trade business.

Captain Robert Gray conducted a brisk trade, indicating fair prices were experienced by both side of the exchange. Gray collected 150 otter and 300 precious beaver pelts and many other land animal skins. Gray also obtained full casks of fresh water, five types of salmon prepared in various forms, wapato, camas, berries, meat, and other edibles in trade. Gray paid for these purchases with manufactured metal goods that were not otherwise available along the Columbia.[11] The Northwest fur trade business had begun in earnest.

---

11   It was one of those non-Indian trading ships that brought smallpox and other diseases, to the native population in the 1770s. An estimated 11,000 Indians were killed by smallpox along the Washington-Oregon coast during a 100–years span. Measles, influenza, syphilis and other diseases took an estimated toll of 28,000. By 1850 there were approximately only 900 survivors in Columbia River and Coastal communities that conservatively had numbered over 50,000 previously. Puget Sound Indians were devastated by smallpox in 1836-37, by measles in 1847-48, and again by measles in 1862. It is now also recognized that some diseases passed from Indians to whites during these trading exchanges.

After eight days of trading, Gray cached some coins under a pine tree on the north bank, and claimed the entire drainage area of the Columbia River for the United States of America. This cache was a significant argument for American claims to the north side of the Columbia many years later.

The Indians, the aboriginal First People of Puget Sound—called "Whulge" in the Coast Salish language—continued living almost completely unaware of the foreign visitors only one hundred miles away along the ocean shore. The strangers were moving closer and had been doing so for over 200 years, but the people had not yet met face to face.

Villages along the shores of Whulge most often bore the name of the nearby freshwater stream or a larger river in close proximity. The people called themselves by the name of the village and added the suffix "people of," such as the Sequalitchew Nisquallyabsch. They were the people of the village named Sequalitchew and the river named Nisqually.

There was no comprehensive name, at the time, for all of the people of Whulge, although Salish is now often used because it is the name of the root language spoken by most tribes. There was a sense of social and linguistic unity, but without any political institution, or territorial hierarchy. Each village had a fundamental clan-like social structure and territorial claim, but lacked the integrated internal political hierarchy of a modern nation state.

The character of the people of any village, their affiliations with individuals in other villages, and their aggregate affiliations were the determining factors for levels of social and political influence over others. Affiliations, bonds, marriages, adoptions, alliances, coalitions, associations, compacts, conquests, and connections among kinsmen changed from time to time. Changes came about under varying circumstances, often overlapping with new combinations of political and social structure.

There were links that tied tribes together, creating unions of sorts, but often the links were short of political alliances. They maintained an affinity with independence, a relationship with liberation. They had a mutual understanding, respect, and acceptance for traditions, legends, folklore, customs, beliefs, and practices of others, including white people. For instance certain songs were 'owned' by a family, tribe, or chief; others might sing the song, but the owner was always asked for permission first. In similar fashion berry patches or fishing spots in certain seasons were 'owned,' but were shared in specific, often subtle ways, such as at the end of the day or after the owner was finished.

The English language lacks adequate terminology to describe all of the intricate social and cultural relationships of the First People clans and tribes of Whulge.

There were villages, large or small, permanent or temporary, near the mouth of every freshwater stream flowing into Puget Sound. Most were built to be unseen from passing, and potentially enemy, canoes. Escape routes were carefully planned. In addition there were numerous allied villages farther upstream on nearly every tributary, as well as temporary "camp" sites regularly occupied seasonally for hunting and gathering work.

Below is a sample of some of the well-documented villages of southern Puget Sound.[12] Many of these villages seem to have had close affiliations with the Sequalitchew Nisqually village near where the first South Puget Sound Native American contact with Europeans occurred. All spoke a dialect of the Salish language, specifically tribal dialects like the Lushootseed language. Chinook was a near-universal, but very limited trade jargon known throughout the Pacific Northwest.

Some Known Puyallup-Nisqually Villages:[13]

1. Se-qual-it-chew—at the mouth of Sequalitchew Creek and possibly applied to homes at the mouth of the Nisqually River and Medicine Creek (McAllister Creek). This village was not of particular importance, as the Nisqually were primarily an up-river people who also fished salt water. HBC Fort Nisqually located here 1832 elevating Sequalitchew to trade status.

2. Toot-sehts-awh'lh—Near the mouth of the Nisqually River (See #1)

3. Sho-dab-dab—McAllister Creek, Medicine Creek, or She-nah-num, Mit-suk-we (See #1) Considered a place of shaman power with ill effects which were often attributed to whites. (See # 1)

4. N's-qually—DuPont Creek confluence with Sequalitchew Creek (See #1)

5. S'Gukugwa-Muck Creek confluence with Nisqually River.

6. Kwod-kwool-Mashel Creek village on the high land above the confluence of the Mashel and Nisqually Rivers was distinctly Nisqually as home of Leschi, but related to the Sahaptin (Interior Salish) Yakima of the Columbia River plateau.

7. Yo-wahisa-Clear Creek confluence with the Nisqually (perhaps the largest village at the time of the Medicine Creek Treaty signing in 1854).

8. Sitschahlabsh at Budd Inlet (Olympia)

9. South Bay (See # 8)

---

12 Smith, Marian W., *The Puyallup–Nisqually*, Columbia University Press, New York, 1940.

13 Department of Public Works & Government Services (Canada) Native American Place Names Map by DPWGS, Reference File L, produced October 17, 2006.

10. Henderson Inlet (See #8)

11. Mud Bay (associated with the Upper Chehalis villages)

12. Oyster Bay or Totten Inlet

13. Arcadia (A very large village that commanded the outlets of Budd Inlet, Mud Bay, Oyster Bay, and Shelton Inlet).

14. Coulter Creek

15. Mason Creek at Allyn

16. Glen Cove

17. Minter Creek closely associated with Glencove

18. Burley Lagoon closely allied with # 16 & 17

19. Stehrsasamish at Tumwater Falls.

20. Puyallup River mouth (then near 15th and Dock Street in Tacoma). This settlement may have been four or five semi-separate villages located in very close proximity, including longhouses near 24th and Pacific. Sweat houses were located on the nearby boot-shaped mudflats. Nicholas Delin would build the first immigrant home and lumber mill near here in 1852 while some employees stole the sweat house for a home.

21. Clay Creek and First Creek, near the Emerald Queen Casino east of Portland Avenue.

22. Wapato Creek

23. Clark's Creek off the Hylebos Waterway

24. Stuck River confluence with the Puyallup River. This village had familial connections with the White River and Duwamish River Indian villages as well as with the Nisqually.

25. Carbon River confluence with the Puyallup near Orting. This village had familial connections to the people at Nisqually.

26. Voight Creek where it enters the Carbon River

27. Cole Creek where it enters South Prairie Creek. This village had ties to Green River villages of the Muckleshoot People, and even the Snoqualmie People.

28. Gig Harbor, the main village was at the mouth of Donkey Creek at the head of the bay and a satellite village at nearby Crescent Valley Creek.

29. Wollochet Bay, an overflow of the population from Gig Harbor village.

30. Quartermaster Harbor may have been occupied by a wandering or banished Skagit family.

31. Sawamish at Oyster Bay on Totten Island. The name refers only to the inlet.

32. Skwai-aitl or Skwaiatl located on Mud Bay, Eld Inlet. People here were closely related to Nisqually and Upper Chehalis. It may have been a transitional village.

33. Sahehwamush or Sahewabsh, located at Arcadia, had command of the outlets of Budd Inlet, Oyster Bay and Shelton Inlet. The village extended to all those areas.

34. Unknown name—village opposite Shelton at Munson Point and allied with the village at Arcadia on the south side of Hammersley Inlet.

35. Sch-tal-a-cop (aka Kiawalamsain)—Steilacoom at Chambers Creek

36. Tsa-tsat-we—Clover Creek, aka Tlithlow

37. Spa-nu-eh—Spanaway Lake, likely a root gathering place associated with #38

38. Chet-teh—Near Parkland, likely near Brookdale Golf course / Clover Creek

39. Bau-kum—JBLM at Fort Lewis

40. Yi-cax-tal—JBLM at Fort Lewis

41. Nis-jucs-wa—JBLM at Fort Lewis

42. Mit-suk-wie—along upper Mit-suk-wie (Medicine) Creek

43. Dop-shet—along the Nisqually River near Yelm (Yellem) Prairie

44. Tse-alum fishing station, exact location is unknown

45. Keh-cuis-duts fishing station, exact location unknown

46. Horn Creek fishing station

47. Day Island lagoon fishing, hunting station. Vertical nets were used to capture migrating waterfowl as they settled into the lagoon waters.[14]

---

14 In 1966 the United States Land Claim Commission acknowledged the Puyallup Tribe Land Claim as it existed prior to the Medicine Creek Treaty of 1854. "*The Puyallup Tribe of Indians was in possession of the occupied land from time immemorial. That land is enclosed beginning at Gibson Point on Fox Island, thence to Kapowsin, to Lake George, to the crest of the Mountain, to Fairfax, to Wilkinson, to Lake Tapps, to Pacific City, to Midway, to Three Tree Point, to Ollala, to Burley, to Vaughn, To Home, to Devil's Passage on the south side of McNeil Island to Sunset Beach at Steilacoom, then to the beginning point on Fox Island.*"

There were ten or twelve villages that were specifically Puyallup, and some that were exclusively Nisqually. The Steilacoom Band[15] was possibly related to the Nisqually or Puyallup Tribes. The Steilacoom Band today claims as many as 600 members in five bands at seven village sites independent of Nisqually and Puyallup tribes. The principal Steilacoom village was at Steilacoom River (now Chambers Creek) near where the town of Steilacoom developed. There were three other villages along Clover Creek near Sastuck that may have been Steilacoom. Other villages, at Spa-nu-eh on Spanaway Lake, and Tlithlow on Murray Creek, were possibly Steilacoom villages or the Puyallup-Nisqually group. Some people today are certain the Steilacoom were a distinct tribe that did not become recognized by a signatory treaty as a distinct tribe.

These First People of Whulge, the inland sea that would be called Puget Sound, were unaware, in any real sense, of the world beyond the relatively small geographic area they occupied. Soon the European demand for fashionable beaver felt hats would impact every aspect of their lives.

In continental Europe men's hats became a status symbol, indicating the owner's authority, importance, and even heritage and social rank. The finest felted hats were made using animal fur. Felted beaver fur was preferred for high-quality hats from about 1500 in England. The craze for beaver top hats exploded in the 1600s. The wild beaver produced the best quality fur. The animal was hunted to near-extinction throughout Europe in the 1700s.

The dense fur of a beaver produces a durable, waterproof felt with a lustrous sheen. The best hats were made from pelts with the "guard hairs" removed, leaving the luxuriously soft and downy "under fur." Indians often made robes of beaver pelts, wearing the soft fur against their skin. This practice naturally removed the guard hairs in a short time. Robes of beaver fur with the guard hairs removed brought the highest prices in trade to European fur traders.

Good English hatters could make nine hats per week. It was a thirty-six step process involving five teams of men and women, secret formulas, exclusive procedures and heavy metal poisoning. Mercuric oxide was used to remove the fibers from the beaver skin. The process attacked the human nervous system creating actual "Mad Hatters."

At the peak of popularity, a single well-made beaver hat could command a price equal to six month's wages for a skilled worker. Hats were inherited by the second and third generations of even wealthy men.

While Europeans were obsessed with vainly stylish beaver hats, the Nisqually people

---

15 Steilacoom band was not considered as a separate tribe by the early settlers in any known document.

were quite happy to trade locally-abundant natural materials with nearby and distant people for needed goods and services. Bands of Nisqually people occupied land along the Nisqually River watershed for at least 5,000, perhaps ten thousand, years. At the confluence of the Nisqually River and streams such as the Muck and the Mashel, the Nisqually people built permanent villages of huge cedar plank long houses. A single cedar plank long house accommodated as many as eight multi-generational and extended families. At various times of the year the Nisqually people moved to different areas to obtain various foods from nature's bounty; salmon, shellfish, roots, berries, deer, elk, bear, and beaver among other things. The Nisqually habitat movements were not unlike today's "snow birds" traveling to Arizona for the winter.

Sequalitchew Creek drains a portion of the natural prairie land between the Nisqually River and the Puyallup River. There are numerous lakes in the drainage area, today known as Fort Lake, American Lake, Sequalitchew Lake, Spanaway Lake, Wapato Lake, Lake Charlton, Steilacoom Lake, and grasslands in communities today known as Lakewood, University Place, Fort Lewis, McChord, Hilltop, Spanaway, Parkland, Elk Plain, Graham, Frederickson, South Tacoma, Fern Hill, Larchmont, Midland, Summit, and others.

The Nisqually of Sequalitchew Creek were generally thriving in the early 19th century. They were among the wealthiest aboriginal people of any place on earth because of nature's bounty and the mild climate of the Puget Sound area. They lived at the mouth of the bountiful Sequalitchew Creek for too many generations to count. The banks of the small creek were thick with blackberry vines, swamp grass, and cattails. The inland higher ground near the creek was also thick with bountiful prairie grasses, forest patches, lakes and other creeks. All of the water courses teemed with spawning salmon five times a year and the saltwater shores offered clams, oysters, mussels and seaweed.

The Sequalitchew village was on the broad gradual slope of shore, below a steep embankment.[16] The beach provided an abundance of shellfish, while the saltwater inland sea at their front door offered over 200 varieties of fish and shellfish, including six varieties of salmon. The sky provided a huge variety of birds for meat and feathers. In later years, people would express the abundant richness of the area by saying, "The table is set when the tide is out." In addition, it was the best opportunity to obtain the world's largest clam, the geoduck. Spelled in a facsimile of the native Nisqually Lushootseed language it is the "gwiduhg".[17]

---

16 That shoreline, between low tide and the high bank, was completely eliminated by the introduction of the railroad along the edge of Puget Sound in 1913.

17 http://www.lushootseed.net

The lives of these people centered on the sea and its rich offerings, especially salmon. Located near the mouth of Sequalitchew Creek, the salt and fresh waters offered a variety of fish. There were specific places nearby for traditional processing of salmon, clams, and oysters, all of which were prized trade items. The Nisqually were tool makers, too. To process the sea life they built stone, bone, wood and fiber implements such as baskets, arrows, spears, weights, nets, traps, and weirs. They built solid cedar dugout canoes and cedar long houses, as well.

Nisqually villages were scattered along the entire length of the river from the mouth to the snow line at the Nisqually Glacier on Mount Rainier. Remnants have been found by archeologists at Muck Creek, Mashel, and other places. The Puget Sound waterways, were the "highways" of these people, who traveled extensively. Trails led over the Cascades, but more importantly, the waterways led to hundreds of villages along the shores of Puget Sound, to Vancouver Island, and even to the Inside Passage to Alaska and the Queen Charlotte Islands and the Pacific Coast. A classic trade route was down the sound to Black Lake, the Black River to the Chehalis River, and to Grays Harbor and Pacific shores.

Fishing was the primary occupation of the Nisqually people and their neighbors. They built elaborate fish traps to capture salmon returning to spawn. A door in the fish trap was opened as the tide came in and the fish swam upstream. As the tide changed the door was closed, trapping the fish in shallow water for relatively easy harvest.

No one knows for certain today, but perhaps 75 people lived in the little Sequalitchew Creek village[18] which consisted of only two substantial cedar plank buildings. These "long houses" were built with thick plank walls, split from tall straight cedar trees. The planks were stacked on edge between vertical poles. A roof of overlapping cedar planks was laid over the walls and a strong center beam. A small smoke hole was opened using a long pole to slide a plank aside near the center of the roof. These two houses, perhaps 100 feet long and 30 feet wide, were typical of the long houses built in many villages on the shores of the inland sea.

The entry doors of the two nicely-decorated homes faced each other across a narrow open breezeway. Both doorways were thus protected from the predominant southwesterly winds and the nearly ceaseless winter rains. A back doorway was probably hidden from outside view. It was used as an escape route in the event of an enemy raid.

A community fire burned slowly and continuously in that breezeway between the buildings. Six to eight extended families of the Sequalitchew Nisqually were comfortably

---

18 In the census of 1838-39, 258 Nisquallys were counted. Ruby, Robert H. and Brown, Johsua, "A Guide to Indians Tribes of the Northwest" Oklahoma University Press, Norman, OK 1986.

accommodated in these two sturdy longhouses. There was probably about 9,000 square feet of floor space, with certain apartment areas designated for individual families. There were storage shelves and cupboards on the walls for the dozens of handmade baskets, wooden bowls, utensils, cooking tools, blankets, and other possessions. Hunting implements and fishing nets were piled under the bottom shelves. Bedding mats, animal fur and woven cedar blankets were stored near each family's small, sunken cooking fire. Dried food hung from the ceiling and from racks dividing family spaces.

The people of the Whulge were quite wealthy by worldwide standards of the day, with plenty of human comforts including portable summer homes that could be carried inland and upstream to fishing spots claimed by each clan. Ownership was recognized by ancient traditions. These summer dwellings were mostly constructed of woven cattail matting over cedar poles. All of their possessions could be packed and carried by individuals and horses on relatively short notice. Primarily used in summer weather, the portable homes could also be used by relatives visiting from over the mountains. The cattail mats were often used for carpet-like floor coverings inside the big long houses, too.

Much of the wealth of the Sequalitchew Nisqually and their neighbors came from nature's "super market" near the front doors of their sturdy homes. The sandy beach and the waters of the Whulge provided seafood items. The ancient forests provided cedar for housing, canoes, clothing, and tools. The grassland prairies yielded edible roots and other plant life. Animals and birds were harvested in wide varieties. The dietary mainstay and cultural foundation was the salmon. The one resource they were unable to exploit was metal ores.

The ancestors of the Nisqually people, the Squalli-absch, are said to have migrated perhaps 10,000 years ago from the Great Basin, over the Cascades to the area known today as the Skate Creek basin, just south of the Nisqually watershed. A major village by the time Europeans arrived was near the confluence of the Mashel and Nisqually Rivers.

Conflict appears to have been rare among the neighboring people of the Whulge, but it did occur occasionally. About 1825 the Nisqually and other people of the Whulge were attacked by the Cowichan from the southwest coast of Vancouver Island. The Nisqually and their allies suffered heavy losses. There was no interest in war among the Nisqually after that disaster. Thirty years later, the Nisquallys had nearly forgotten how to choose a war chief.

The Nisqually were an entrepreneurial trading nation. They bought, sold and traded nearly any available item with strangers, friends and relatives far and near. Among the favorite traders were the people of thirteen or so local area villages. They were all descendants of the First People to immigrate to the region. Some trade items were purchased from, and sold to the people of the hot dry lands east of the mountains. The extensive interchange of the Native American trade system was very efficient and very wide, ranging to what is now the Rockies, Alaska, Canada and California. Individuals are known to have traveled far and wide.[19]

The Sequalitchew Nisqually did not use money as a medium of exchange or even as a store of value. But everything was "for sale" at the right bargaining price. Their simple trading system had been in use for centuries, in many cultures worldwide. It worked well. Buyers and sellers would offer one item for another, then "haggle" over the "price" until an agreement was made to trade one item for another. Often the difficulty was to provide the "change" to equalize the value of the major items traded. An animal skin could be traded for a salmon, if the correct number of beads or pretty shells was added to the animal skin to equalize the value of the salmon.

Another means of exchange among the Native Americans of the Northwest was the potlatch. The potlatch featured the giving of gifts to the guests at a party. Huge celebrations were held to give thanks for a good harvest of wild berries or to welcome the returning salmon. There were also potlatches for weddings, healings, births and dying. Wealthy people, or those who wanted to be thought of as wealthy, gave gifts to others. It was important to show generosity, even extravagance. It was so important that often during a potlatch everything a person owned would be given away. Everyone, of course, had the full knowledge that soon there would be another potlatch, redistributing all those gifts and the wealth once again.

The material culture of the Salish people has been overlooked in history and art until relatively recent times. The more glamorous carvings and paintings of the northern tribes grabbed more attention. Recently, however, the woven clothing of the Salish has attracted collectors and museums.

Salish men's and women's blankets, shirts, dresses, bags and mats have patterns that are elegant, subtle, and display beautiful workmanship. The materials used included canine wool, mountain goat wool, fireweed fluff, milkweed, cattail heads, and cotton grass. Each material was gathered, prepared, and stored at various times of the year for use when enough of the stuff had been collected to make a garment.

Yellow dye came from the bark of the Oregon grape. Lichen produced yellow-green to lavender hues. Red was obtained from Alder bark and black came from the black mud in salt marshes. Clothing was utilitarian, but also decorative. The clothing with the nicest patterns was used for special occasions such as naming ceremonies, funerals,

---

19   Anderson, Steve A, *Angus McDonald of the Great Divide: The Uncommon Life of a Fur Trader, 1816-1889*. The book includes the story a family trek from Montana to the Sea of Cortez, p 23, 24 & 38.

potlatches, memorials, and to welcome visitors. It was a sign of respect to others to wear the very best regalia.

Baskets, mats, room dividers, fishing nets, hats, and wall hangings were also hand woven by the Salish craftsmen and women. Some mats were so tightly woven that they were used as coverings over their temporary homes during camping, hunting and trading trips.

Formal schools with classrooms did not exist among the Nisqually. Children were taught by something like a "home school method" during regular activities of the family. Traditions were especially important and were repeated during story telling around the evening fire. History was a story to be told and retold until learned verbatim. Skills were demonstrated and practiced daily until they became second nature. Once the youngster had learned enough to tell the story, catch the salmon, dig the clam, weave the basket, cook the food, etc., adulthood could begin.

The Nisqually Deity was Dokibatt, the Changer, who was the son of a human woman and a star. They believed Dokibatt and Coyote, the trickster, had much to do with the existence of the world. Dokibatt was believed to have created everything from language to roots and berries. He removed life from stones, made the insects small and less harmful. Dokibatt taught the Nisquallys how to make fire, clothing, fish traps, and medicines.

The Puyallup, Steilacoom, Squaxin, Muckleshoot, Duwamish and other people of the Whulge were related to the Nisqually linguistically and culturally, but were distinctively different "nations" politically. The Steilacoom people resided primarily along what are now Chambers Creek and Steilacoom Creek. The Puyallup people lived mostly along the banks of the river that bears their name today, although some lived on Vashon Island and Gig Harbor. Even the Nisqually were somewhat divided with villages at the mouth of the river and at various locations upstream at Mashel, Muck, and other spots. These people and others all utilized Puget Sound as a great highway. All Native American groups along the Whulge also took advantage of the numerous nearby prairies for gathering plants and grazing their horses. The prairies were tended each summer with small fires designed to burn off the dead grasses and keep the forests from encroaching. The ashes tended to enrich the meager soil, as well.

Horses were probably introduced to the Puget Sound area around 1740. One horse trail through the Cascade Mountains reached the southern end of Lake Washington, another came almost directly over Naches Pass to the Puyallup River Valley. This trail is sometimes called the Longmire Trail as the pioneer Longmire family used this route from Walla Walla to Puget Sound. For them it was the final leg of the Oregon Trail.

Naches Pass is about 50 miles from Puget Sound and reaches an altitude of 4,920 feet on the northern flank of Mt. Rainier. The trail links the headwaters of the Naches River east of the Cascades and the Greenwater River on the western slopes. While it is very steep in places, confounding the early settlers with heavy wagons, the Native Americans of the south Puget Sound area used it as a horse trail as a great trade advantage. Native American trails were very well used. Often the bed of the track was several feet deeper than the surrounding soil simply from repeated use of the centuries. These trails were easily recognized, and followed, even by strangers. They were the 'freeways' and arterial highways of the time and certainly added to travel corridors of rivers, streams, and the saltwater sound.

Native people of the region showed little inclination to organize politically beyond the residents of their winter villages. This developed into hundreds of groups living in their own ways, developing their own traditions over a long time. It is impossible to speak of a single people, society, or even culture among Washington's native first people. Nearly every river had its people.[20]

The Sequalitchew Nisqually remained completely unaware that in far-away parts of the world explorers yearned to see distant places. Eventually, British explorers reached Whulge and changed its name to Puget Sound. European encroachment into the world of the Whulge began with the explorations of 1792. The United States of America was barely sixteen year old.

It was in April 29, 1792,[21] when English Captain George Vancouver visited the inland sea aboard the *Discovery* and the *Chatham*, fine sea-going vessels out of London. Vancouver was the first European to rename places near the homes of the Sequalitchew Nisqually. Takhoma became Mount Rainier. Vancouver continued the tradition begun by Christopher Columbus, by calling the Sequalitchew Nisqually people "Indians" when they finally met.

Vancouver saw skeletal remains scattered along Puget Sound beaches. He concluded that the area had recently experienced an epidemic. He also observed that native groups possessed horses. These two things, horses and disease, produced a social revolution and severely depopulated the region, respectively.[22]

That first meeting came shortly after Captain Vancouver sent a launch and a cutter commanded by Lt. Peter Puget south through the Tacoma Narrows. Puget made his way south then west around Point Fosdick to enter Wollochet Bay. Some Indians were

---

20   Buerge, David M. and Rochester, Junius, *Roots and Branches, The Religious Heritage of Washington State*, Church Council of Greater Seattle, Seattle, WA 1988.
21   On May 11, 1792, American Captain Robert Gray sailed into the Columbia River.
22   Ibid. Page 4.

collecting clams on the beach. The clam diggers fled to the safety of the forest as the strangers approached. Some other Indian men, following in a canoe, were soon convinced the strangers meant no harm. Traditional trading gestures began. The Europeans offered colorful buttons and beads. The Indians offered fresh clams in trade. The strangers wanted the Indians' bows and arrows, but that trade was not made. Prudent traders do not relinquish their means of personal defense to total strangers.

The next day the strange hairy white-skinned men fired their personal weapons at some crows. The Indians named the strangers "pooh-pooh men" in imitation of the sound of the guns heard from a distance. The term was not meant to insult the explorers.

It was during this first exploration that Peter Puget and his crew met the Sequalitchew Nisqually. Puget and his crew explored the western reaches of Puget Sound, then turned northward near the Nisqually River. Beyond the tide flats and saltwater marsh lands at the mouth of the Nisqually, some local Indian canoes joined the launch and cutter. Showing no fear and behaving peacefully, the local paddlers came alongside the European ships offering to trade. Peter Puget wrote in his journal,

> "Commerce was therefore established for their Different Articles which was carried on with the Strictest Honesty and Apparent satisfaction of both parties."[23]

The Nisqually traded local furs for European-manufactured metal and glass items; the international business of the fur trade had commenced on Puget Sound. Both groups were curious about the "new" people they had encountered. Soon basic economic activity took precedence. Both groups were friendly, even learning a few words of the others' language. World trade was used for peaceful purposes.

Another group of explorers came from the United States to the Northwest—if not to Puget Sound—the U.S. Army Corps of Discovery (1805) led by Captains Meriwether Lewis and William Clark. They came overland and along the Columbia River. This group stretched the American claim to all of the territory from the Rockies to the Pacific Ocean and from Russian Alaska to Spanish California. These newcomers did not see all of that territory, and certainly did not approach Puget Sound, but the political effect of their "Voyage of Discovery" was enormous.

John Jacob Astor, an immigrant American businessman, bolstered the American claim when his employees established a trading post at Astoria in March 1811. His little outpost, set on the southern bank at the mouth of the Columbia River, collected furs from the Clatsop and Chinook, but still no more new people came north to the Whulge.

---

23 Ibid, Page 4

Historians call the territory between the Rockies and the Pacific, 42 and 54 degrees north, by the name "Oregon," but disagree on the origin and meaning of the word. After the 18th century it was valuable and vast real estate coveted by Spain, Russia, England, and the United States. Never mind the mostly gentle people who lived there as their ancestors had for at least 10,000 years. As a comparison, the Egyptian Pyramids were built only 5,000 years ago, and the Christian era began only about 2,000 years ago.

Gradually, the English and the Americans became foremost in the "possession" game played with Old Oregon as the prize for the winner. Both countries sent traders to the area by sea and overland. In 1818, to avoid a military conflict that neither country wanted, the Americans and the English agreed to jointly occupy the Oregon region with all rights equally granted to each other. Through diplomatic means and other treaties the Russians and the Spanish were excluded completely from the territory by the Americans and the British. The Spanish held California. The Russians controlled Alaska. The Americans and English, with the Joint Occupancy Treaty of 1818, shared the natural bounty of the vast Old Oregon region. American citizens and subjects of the King of England were free to roam, trade, live anywhere they chose in the enormous land between the Rocky Mountains, the Pacific Ocean, Russian America (Alaska's southern point at 54 degrees and 40 minutes north), and Spanish California (stretching to 42 degrees north).

The Hudson's Bay Company (HBC), was chartered in England on May 2, 1670, by English King Charles II. It was officially known as "The Governor and Company and Adventurers of England Trading in the Hudson Bay." Over 7,000 hand-scribed words were written on five sheepskin parchments stating the new company's goals, fur trading, mineral exploitation, and finding a northwest passage. In the course of time the Company established hundreds of fur trade posts all across northern North America. The real estate encompassed 3.8 million square kilometers of land. The HBC became the *de facto* government across North America before any European states or the United States laid claim to any of the territories. The HBC was the largest landowner in the world, i.e., about 15% of North America was legally Rupert's Land, completely disregarding all native ownership.

In October 1671, the first HBC fur ships from North America arrived in London. Two fur actions were held at Garraway's Coffee House near the Royal Exchange on January 24, 1672. They were "candle auctions" and made lots of money. Candle auctions were conducted in two different ways. One was by using a one-inch-tall candle which was lit by the first bid. When the candle guttered out the last high bidder secured the goods. The other method was to stick a pin in a candle. The winner of the goods was the last bidder before the pin fell out. Auctions at Garraway's Coffee House were always noisy, gala affairs drawing the wealthy elite of English society. Even Prince Rupert was often seen there with his compatriots, the Duke of York and poet John Dryden.

In 1821 Napoleon Bonaparte died in exile at Saint Helena, and the population of the entire United States was only 9.6 million.[24] Today Washington State has over 7 million people.

It was also the year that the Hudson's Bay Company merged with the North West Company, with the HBC surviving. An extraordinary man was selected to manage the huge new Hudson's Bay Company. George Simpson, a short red-headed clerk in his thirties, was from London, He contracted with HBC in 1820. His first assignment was at Fort Wedderburn in Athabasca, a fur trade post in what is now Alberta, Canada. Five years later, he was appointed governor of all HBC operations. He earned the nickname, The Little Emperor, while ruling one of the largest commercial empires on earth.

When he was only 28 years old, George Simpson was sent to Athabasca. He was there to implement the merger of the North West Company and the HBC. Soon Simpson was appointed co-governor and then grabbed the opportunity to put his personal stamp on the company's dealings for the next forty years. He slashed staff, closed poorly performing posts, downsized and rationalized, always with a keen eye on the bottom-line profits. He wanted to see things for himself and in doing so forced many speed records for travel in North America. As Governor, he never paddled a canoe, put up a tent, saddled a horse, or cooked a meal. Although small of stature, he drove his men mercilessly.

While he demanded efficiency and order, his personal life was a mess. He was called "severe and most repulsive" by his cousin and secretary for seven years. He had one mistress after another across Britain and Canada before he married in 1820.

Simpson believed the HBC was something of an extension of Britain, continually making the political case for Britain, and therefore HBC control.

With the merger the HBC became the largest, as well as the oldest, corporation in the world. Its nearest rival had been the North West Company out of Montreal. The North West Company had expanded to the Pacific Coast by taking over the American-owned Pacific Fur Company post at Astoria. The merger was sudden. As the surviving entity, the HBC was indeed huge in monopolized geographic land area alone. The original 3.8 million square kilometers of real estate grew to 7.8 million square kilometers of North America. The HBC controlled all but the fringes of North America. There were only the 13 American states along the Atlantic seaboard, the former French colonies along the St. Lawrence River and Great Lakes, Spanish claims in the Southwest, and Russian-America

---

24 The population of Washington State in 2014 was estimated at 6.9 million according to the United States Census Bureau.

along the coast and islands of what is now Alaska. A serious game of "Fur Trade Monopoly" became the actual business practice.

The singular object of this expansive business was the beaver pelt. The North American beaver is the second-largest rodent in the world. It can weigh in at about 70 pounds and measure over four feet long with a broad 12 inch tail. It has huge chisel-like teeth that grow constantly if not worn down by gnawing on trees.

Beavers build lodges with underwater entrances to very complex interiors that include feeding rooms, warm dry sleeping nests, secret escape holes and ventilation systems for constant fresh air. Their bedding consists of soft grasses and twigs that are changed regularly for the five or six inhabitants. Exteriors are plastered with mud, making an outer shell that animal enemies cannot break.

The water level of the pond surrounding the beaver lodge is controlled by a network of beaver-built dams and canals. The dams are constructed of sticks, rocks, and mud and can be massive. The canals are designed by these engineers of nature to divert water to more useful locations and provide easy transportation routes. Beaver's diversion ditches have been measured at five feet wide, three feet deep, and 36 feet long.

While the Hudson's Bay Company was building hundreds of trading posts across North America, none of the individual establishments meant much, directly, to the Sequalitchew Nisqually. Travel and trade kept the news current for the Nisqually. They knew foreigners were moving closer, making European and American manufactured trade goods more available through indirect trade, but the people of the Whulge still saw no more of the white men.

Every trapper, native or not, needed equipment so every man was given, usually on loan, all the gear he would need to survive and return with abundant furs. Each trapper was provided an 'outfit' that generally included a rifle, a horse or mule, and six or eight steel traps that cost about six dollars each. The trap was the most important tool because it caught the beavers.

Many designs were used for beaver traps, all essentially the same: the mechanism was intended to catch beavers without damage to the precious fur skin. Traps had semicircular or squared-off jaws. Some had sharp teeth, most were flat-edged. To use the traps one was required to spread the jaws wide open, forcing the two thick elbow-shaped bands of steel that served as the spring mechanism to compress. These bands were held in place under great tension by a metal rod called a dog, connected to the flat steel pan.

When a beaver stepped on the pan, the dog released the jaws which snapped shut very quickly with tremendous force trapping the beaver's foot or lower leg. The trapper placed the mechanism in about six inches of water near the edge of the pond, with the five-foot-long anchor chain attached to a wooden stake pounded into the bottom of the pond in much deeper water. To attract the beaver to the trap for the fatal move a pungent mixture of castoreum,[25] and other ingredients (spices, camphor, juniper oil) called 'medicine' was smeared on a twig inches above the water line about a foot from the trap. When the trap grabbed the beaver's leg the animal reacted naturally by diving into deeper water. Unable to free himself the beaver drowned being pulled under by the weight of the trap and chain.

Most trappers were rarely out of debt to their employers. Annual supplies and tools of the trade were provided, on loan, every year or 'outfit' as HBC records reveal. When the season was complete, all debts were paid from the financial return earned. Frequently, the gains were equal to the debt plus a little more which was often consumed at the annual Brigade Encampment or Rendezvous. Trappers then took "on account" the trade goods and supplies necessary for the next "outfit" of trapping season after being out of debt only a few days at most.

The Sequalitchew Nisqually conducted extensive trade with other tribes for many commodities as did other Native First People across the continent. The beaver was used for food, clothing, and medicine, but it was not central to the Nisqually culture. The Nisqually sold cedar products and fish and fish oil to friends east of the Cascade Mountains. The beaver was not the most important trade item around Puget Sound before the arrival of the Europeans. The Nisqually were a canoe people but also the horse people of Puget Sound because of their close trade with the Yakama [sic] over the Naches Trail.

European fur traders often married local women wherever they built fur trade posts. This practice sealed relationships at the family level as well as creating solid economic, political, and mercantile alignments. The European-manufactured trade products were of a high quality not otherwise available to those who willingly, often eagerly, traded away animal pelts. Prices were reasonable, fair, and always negotiated. Nothing was ever traded without complete agreement of both parties to the transaction. Sometimes bargaining took days, with many free incentives offered to "sweeten" the deal. (Today's shoppers often look for the "free offer" or "rebate" that goes with the purchase of some "one-day-sale" item.) Neither buyers nor sellers have an advantage, or the other party walks away. Europeans only wanted high-quality furs, available by setting traps. Those traps were of European manufacture, often available free to an Indian fur trapper who agreed to return in due time with many pelts. Northwest Indians agreed with these economic and social

---

25 Castoreum is the exudates from the castor sacs of the North American Beaver. It is a yellow secretion, combined with the beaver's urine, used in marking territory. Castoreum is a safe food additive often referenced as "natural flavoring" in lists of ingredients.

terms that led to a higher standard of living, and sometimes a spouse and children, also.

The European fur traders were extremely outnumbered, therefore very careful to trade fairly. Spoiled or inferior goods were easily recognized by the shrewd and experienced Indian trader. The whites could have been physically overwhelmed at any moment. Indian fur traders were also cautious, knowing the Europeans had superior weapons and could, at least briefly, defend themselves. Adversarial relationships were avoided by both sides for their mutual and peaceful benefit.

The trading process was not much different than today's shopping trip. Purchasers are wary of "special deals," yet enticed by bargains. Sellers want to make a profit and will not sell below costs. Together, a price acceptable to both sides is reached or there is no sale. You would not return to a store where you felt cheated, and neither would the Indian or the European fur trader.

In 1824, the HBC replaced the former American fur trade post at Astoria on the south side of mouth of the Columbia River with a new post named Fort Vancouver[26] located 100 miles upstream on the north bank of the river. Additional fur trade posts had already been established along rivers and streams all the way from Hudson's Bay at the Arctic Circle and the Great Lakes in the East.

Hudson's Bay Company Governor Sir George Simpson assigned Doctor John McLoughlin to Fort George in 1824. It was McLoughlin who selected the former Jolie Prairie site for the new Fort Vancouver. French voyageurs working for the company had changed the name of the site from the original Chinook name Skatcutxat (Mud Turtles).

This new post was designed to accomplish several things. It would put HBC on the North shore of the Columbia River in an effort to solidify British claims on the north side of the river. The site was more difficult to service from overseas, but it was level and fertile. Within fifteen years, Fort Vancouver was surrounded by 2,500 acres of fenced gardens, orchards, and fields. It was almost completely self-sufficient with horses, cattle, sheep, and hogs. A village outside the palisades grew to about 300 men, who worked for the fort, and their families.

Buildings went up fast under McLoughlin's direction. By March they had two merchandise warehouses and a 13-foot high perimeter palisade installed. Voyageurs using two flat-bottomed rafts moved the sundry cargo upstream 100 miles through heavy winter rains in multiple round trips. Their cargo included trade goods, living supplies, two small cannons, 32 cattle, 17 pigs and horses.

HBC Governor George Simpson smashed a bottle of rum on the flag pole after

---

26 A list of Hudson's Bay Company trading posts built west of the Rockies is presented in the Appendix. This list may be a useful reference while reading the text.

running up the HBC banner in March 19, 1825. It was a formal christening of the place that would be headquarters for the Hudson's Bay Company for nearly 25 years. Simpson said:

> "In Behalf of the Honorable Hudson's Bay Company I hereby name this establishment Fort Vancouver, God save King George the 4th. The object of naming it after that distinguished navigator is to identify our soil and trade with his discovery of the River and Coast on behalf of Great Britain."[27]

Simpson's claims for Vancouver's discoveries were greatly exaggerated. Of course the Chinook people had lived there for centuries, and the first non-Indians to visit were American Robert Gray and his crew aboard the good ship *Columbia*, thus the name of the river.

A few hundred miles north of Fort Vancouver, an aboriginal battle of epic proportions took place. For ages the Indians of the North raided the more peaceful aborigines of the Whulge. These raids were often devastating to the local population. Most often women and children were captured—kidnapped really—and made slaves. Little defense was offered, and almost never a counter attack. That is why the Cowichan Raid led by Suquamish Chief Kitsap is so remarkable. Usually the sight of a Cowichan raiding party of dozens of large war canoes was enough to send the Suquamish, S'Klallam, Duwamish, Puyallup, and Nisqually and other tribes fleeing to the forest. Villages were regularly destroyed by the raiders.

Dr. Tolmie's estimation, after talking with people involved, estimated the date of the epic battle at Dungeness Spit at 1825. Chief Kitsap organized the various tribes who were fed up with the Cowichan raids. They launched, perhaps, 200 war canoes, paddles to Vancouver Island (near the future Victoria). Kitsap and his loyal warriors systematically encircled nearly every Cowichan camp and village. The Cowichan males of fighting age were missing. Kitsap ordered all of the old people killed and the women and children taken captive.

The Indians of Puget Sound crossed the Strait of Juan de Fuca into the fog covering Dungeness Spit. The Cowichan warriors were on the spit celebrating a recent successful raid. They were singing and dancing, and did not see Kitsap and the 200 canoes arrive in the fog. When the fog lifted, the Kitsap men were seen landing his forces with all of his captives. Kitsap ordered each and every one of the Cowichan captives killed in full

---

[27] Crutchfield, James A., *It Happened in Washington*, Morris Book Publishing, LLC, 2008, Guilford, Connecticut., p.25.

view of the Cowichan warriors. In turn the Cowichans killed all of their captives, too.

A full battle ensued with the Kitsap forces triumphantly defeating their northern enemy. Some say Chief Kitsap was able to heal his own serious wounds, because he was a very powerful "medicine man."[28]

In December, a few months before the christening of Fort Vancouver in March 1825, John Work, a young Irish clerk employed by Hudson's Bay Company, recorded a journey in his diary. That trip, led by Scotsman James McMillan, took a small group of HBC men from Fort Vancouver, intent on building a trading post on the Fraser River. First, they needed to find a satisfactory route from the Columbia River to Puget Sound.[29] Probably they followed a number of existing Indian trails.

We know from John Work's diary that the 1824 explorers followed the coastline from the Columbia River to Gray's Harbor then turned inland on the Chehalis River to the shallow Black River. It was hardly navigable as it was clogged with natural debris. Downed trees and snags lay everywhere. It was a miserable trip, taken during cold, heavy December rains. The party struggled through the necessary portages until they finally reached Puget Sound at Mud Bay, near today's Olympia. These 41 men are credited as the first white men to approach the calm waters of Puget Sound by land, that is, without an ocean-going ship. They arrived 32 years after the "pooh-pooh" men of Peter Puget's crew had arrived by sea from the north. The Nisqually were well aware of the trade possibilities these men represented.

Work recorded the rainy evening of December 6, 1824:

> "...passed a house...saw two Indians in a canoe... stopped at a little village of the (Sequalitchew) Nisqually Nation."[30]

This village probably stood at the mouth of what is now called Chambers Creek where the Steilacoom-Nisqually lived or at the outfall of the Sequalitchew Creek.

The sulphur friction match was invented in 1827, the same year that the HBC established Fort Langley. Fraser River was a rich salmon stream, but furs were the prerequisite product sought. It was soon realized that a more direct route between Fort Vancouver and Fort Langley would be required. The new route went from Fort Vancouver, downstream

---

28 Chief Kitsap was recognized in 1857 when local settlers named a new county after him.

29 They may have followed some of the trails used by Jean Baptiste Ouvré, an Astorian fur trader who, according to the Fort Nisqually *Journal of Occurrences* had the "temerity of naming the Duwamish River after himself" (Ouvré's River) when he was assigned to Fort Nisqually in 1833.

30 Work, John, "Journal of John Work, November and December, 1824", *The Washington Historical Quarterly*, Vol. III, No.3, July, 1912, pp. 198-228.

on the Columbia River to the Cowlitz River, then up that stream to a convenient landing where, over time, a trail was opened across the scattered prairies to Puget Sound.[31] The Cowlitz Portage eventually became the main road between three important Hudson's Bay Company posts, connecting Columbia Department headquarters of the HBC and the yet to be built PSAC headquarters at Fort Nisqually.

Along that route, in 1828, Simon Plomondon staked out a farm of his own.[32] He was leaving service with Hudson's Bay Company to settle on his own farm. He was the first of several HBC servants who would eventually build a substantial settlement at Cowlitz Landing (Toledo, Washington). Plomondon, a French Canadian, first saw the Cowlitz Prairie in 1816. Later, he was encouraged to settle there by Dr. McLoughlin. Plomondon married She-ne-wah, daughter of Chief Schanewah of the Cowlitz tribe, in 1829. Upon the death of his father-in-law, Plomondon inherited the right of leadership in the Cowlitz tribe; as the husband of the dead chief's daughter. She-ne-wah died in April 1827 when her fourth child was born. Simon Plomondon produced five more children with his second wife, Emilie Marie Bernier. They were not Americans, but they were settlers—on what would become British sovereign territory, until Americans took over.

The HBC men in the Work-McMillan's brigade were eager to trade and learn. The first contact between Nisqually and HBC men resulted in interesting exchanges with both sides benefiting as in any economic transaction. HBC men were able to hire guides who were skilled in the ways of Puget Sound. The Indians were paid well in goods they could never dream of owning before the two groups met. The new Cowlitz route was clearly more serviceable than the ocean shore-Black River route. It was also only a fourteen- to seventeen-day journey to the Sequalitchew village.

The Nisqually Indian economy improved markedly after the gift-giving and trade with HBC men began. Geography had given the Sequalitchew a slight advantage over other nearby tribes. Mostly, HBC men passed by the Steilacoom, Squaxin, Puyallup, Muckleshoot, Snohomish and other tribes when passing through Whulge. This was not a purposeful slight, only a business plan carried out. The fur traders could have stopped at the Muckleshoot homeland on what we call the Green and White Rivers today. The Muckleshoot people called the White "Stuck River" (and so do some moderns). "Stuck" derives from the Muckleshoot word "stuckum" which means "big fish." The fur traders wanted furs more than they wanted fish. It may have been as simple as that.

Passing HBC men not only stopped to rest near the Sequalitchew, but traded furs

---

31 The Cowlitz Portage followed nearly the same route as Interstate 5 does today.
32 Toledo History Committee, *The Toledo Community Story*, The Toledo Parent Teacher Organization, Toledo, WA 1976.

there, hired guides, and purchased canoes and horses. The Nisqually gained prestige among the tribes of the area because of their connection with the British traders. Friendship that implied some major advantages, assistance in time of need or turmoil, perhaps even insider knowledge of newly-arrived trade goods inventory from Europe. There was also the chance of being the "middle man" of an extended trade system.

The item Indian traders prized most was the "HBC point blanket." The point designation referred to the size and weight of the blanket. It had indigo blue lines woven into the fabric. A full point measured 14 centimeters (5.51 inches). A half point was half as long. The best quality blanket had six points, the poorest was one point. Each full point represented one large male beaver pelt.

The first HBC trade blankets were hand-woven by master craftsmen working for Thomas Empson Witney of Oxfordshire, England. Later blankets were mass-produced on complex machines using wool from England, Wales, New Zealand, and India. HBC blankets are still a very tight water-resistant weave. The blankets are strong, warm, and soft. The white three-point blanket had, and has, a series of colored bands of distinctive bright colors of indigo, green, red, and yellow. It has become as much the icon of Canada as the beaver or the maple leaf. More points in the blanket meant a more luxurious, warmer, heavier, and occasionally larger-sized blanket.

Nearly all North American Indians traded beaver pelts to Europeans. Eric Jay Dolin in his excellent history of the fur trade business explained the process of producing a quality beaver pelt for trade.[33]

> "The Indians employed many hunting methods in their pursuit of beaver. They used traps on land and nets in the water, baited with wood the beavers ate. Sometimes the Indians' dogs would catch the beavers. Indians would also damage parts of the dam, shoot the beavers with arrows and spears when they came to mend the breach, or, if the pond was frozen over, the hunters might kill the beaver by taking advantage of its need for air. If it wasn't, they used a 'curved stick' and their club to grab the beaver and smash its skull.
>
> The dead beavers were then given to the Indian women to be skinned, a relatively tedious job that began with cutting off the beaver's legs at their base, then slitting the animal from the underside of the chin to the tail. Starting at the edges, the pelt was slowly sheared and pulled away from the body, making every effort to cut off as much of the meat and fat as possible. After cleaning and preparation, the oval pelts would travel one of two paths. Many were cut

---

33 Dolin, Eric Jay, *Fur, Fortune and Empire, The Epic History of the Fur Trade in America*, W.W. Norton and Company, New York, and London, 2010.

> into rectangular pieces and stitched together...then worn as robes for a year or more before being traded to the Europeans. This coat beaver, or 'castor gras' as the French called it, was the most valuable because nearly all of the pelt's guard hairs—which stick out beyond the soft undercoat,—were removed...(by) the constant friction between the pelt and the Indian's body. As an added bonus the Indian's perspiration thickened the remaining hairs, making them easier to felt and giving them a lustrous sheen.
>
> Pelts incorporated into robes were stretched on branch hoops, using animal sinews threaded through the edges, and dried.... The pelt was scraped to remove the last vestiges of meat or fat and dried some more. When finally removed from the stretcher it was stiff as a board and ready for trade. Such pelts were called parchment beaver or "castor sac" and were of lesser value.... No matter how the pelts were prepared, it was extremely important that it be done properly, (to avoid) maggot or moth infestation, rendering the pelt worthless."

As things sometimes go, after that first encounter with overland fur traders another eight years would pass with only occasional visits to the Nisqually by traders commuting between Fort Vancouver and Fort Langley. The English had taken to sailing their ships directly to each fort, bypassing Puget Sound. Indian hopes for a more lucrative connection between HBC and Nisqually traders were revived on April 8, 1832, however.

The place called Oregon Country was taking shape on the world stage. In 1818 the United States and Britain had agreed during the Anglo-American Convention to joint occupancy of the very ill-defined Oregon Country. Also in 1818 the Adams-Onis Treaty (USA & Spain) established the northern boundary at the 42nd parallel for a state in New Spain called California. That treaty agreement held even when New Spain became Mexico after the revolution in 1821.

The 1825 Anglo-Russian treaty was signed by diplomats from Great Britain and Russia concerning the southern end of Russian Territory for what is now Alaska. The Russians agreed to a demarcation line at 54 degrees and 40 minutes north. This treaty left in doubt all rights to fish, hunt, and trade south of that line and north of Spanish California.

The "Convention between the United States of America and His Majesty the Emperor of all Russians, relative to the navigating, fishing, hunting, etc. in the Pacific Ocean" was signed on April 12, 1824, and ratified on January 11, 1825. This agreement halted Russian political expansion into North America.

Finally, the four sides of Oregon Country were clearly defined by international treaties or physical demarcations. The Pacific Ocean and the Rocky Mountains formed the eastern and western borders, while the Spanish and Russian treaties signified the north and south edges of Oregon Country. The Joint Occupancy Treaty of 1821 allowed British and Americans equal legal access to Oregon Country. HBC called it the Columbia Department.

In 1824, Dr. McLoughlin ordered a new Fort Vancouver to be built on the north side of the Columbia River. It would be the HBC headquarters for the next 22 years. At its peak of power Fort Vancouver and McLoughlin controlled 34 outposts, 24 ports, 6 ships, and at least 600 employees scattered across the Columbia Department, or Old Oregon..

John McLoughlin was soon thinking about his own future as well. In 1829, only five years after the opening of Fort Vancouver, he laid personal claim to the "Falls of the Willamette" well south of the Columbia. The "Father of Oregon" could not foresee that Americans would settle there in large numbers, negate his legitimate claim, and treat him with less respect than one might expect after a beneficent reign as "king" of Old Oregon. He would eventually retire at Oregon City where his grave remained unmarked for decades in an American cemetery.

―――

Aboriginal people came from the plains east of the mountains in the early days, perhaps 10,000 years ago. Indians say it was long before the advent of white people that they roamed over the mountains to settle on the Nisqually Plains. History, myth, or legend… it really doesn't matter as the event was long, long ago.[34]

The Squally people lived along a fast-moving steam they called the Squally River. The north bank fell abruptly to the river's edge from the wide plains and prairies to the north and west. This bank, several hundred feet high in most places, afforded fine natural protection from enemies bold enough to attempt invasion from that direction. Some had tried, but were quickly routed with few left to tell of their defeat.

Northerners occasionally succeeded with small parties raiding the Squally Tribal homeland to carry away captives to become slaves, but these raids came by canoe parties. There came a time when the raids were no longer tolerated. A bold chief of the 'Squally' called his people together and presented a plan to stop the northern raids completely.

Henry Sicade has written some of the history of the Nisqually people[35]. He takes the story from here quoting an elder of the Nisqually:

> *Our enemies from the cold and snowy land are many; but we are better fighters than they. This you know, we are plains people; but we understand the*

―――

[34] It was the Neolithic Era, when cultivation of wheat began and Jericho was built. Writing was invented about 5,500 years ago.

[35] Henry Sicade's story was transcribed by Bonney, William P., *History of Pierce County, Volume One*, Pioneer Historical Publishing Company, Chicago, 1927.

canoe mode of traveling. Have we not been able to ride the rapids, the whirlpools and the treacherous streams? Why not challenge them to a great battle on the water; let them fight us in their own way. Is there a coward among you who would not fight for his native land? Then I say to you, if there is such among you, he can move away, just as far as he likes out of harm's way. He will not be hereafter a member of our people; we have no room for him among us.

I propose to build a fleet of canoes to meet the enemy on the salt water and give them battle; a fight to decide whether we are to be made slaves and do their bidding forever; or they will hereafter never molest us and we live in peace in our fair land..

The young men... at the big meeting under oak trees rose up and as one gave a great cheer, for they stood ready to fight... but the older men would have to build the canoes and paddles.

For months all over the river bottoms and up the mountain streams, the great forests gave up the best cedar trees for... the great fleet. At the Squally flats there were received many basketsful of red paint from the natural paint banks at the head of Hood Canal, to give the final touches to the war canoes. From sunrise to dusk a constant drill kept all busy and there were different races and different maneuvers on the water.

Finally all was ready. Watchers were placed on the (high) steep banks of Maury Island to prevent surprise (attacks).... a big smoky fire would signal the approach of a fair sized party; a very large party of invaders would give rise to five or more smoky fires to give the alarm.

One fair day there were smokes arising from steep banks all the way down (the Sound), telling the Squally that the enemy in countless numbers was coming, choking the Sound with hundreds of giant war canoes. With fair winds and tide, masts up for sails, the warriors from the land of snow came around the point (Defiance) unconcerned, singing as though going to a party, keeping time with their paddles, standing up, whirling in unison, the bright sun shining on those red painted paddles, reflecting like an immense mirror.

The Squally chief was constantly drilling his men for the decisive combat. [using] bows and spears and only elk hide shields... they put out to meet the numerous, confident foe. Squally war canoes were laden down with boulders, common ordinary large rocks; but each canoe carried at least two stalwart warriors who had practiced pitching these rocks until their aim was true and threw with great force.[36] *Other [paddlers] were to 'operate' the canoe straight at*

---

36 Modern baseball pitchers have been clocked by radar as throwing baseballs at near 100 miles per hour. Many baseball batters have been injured in that friendly game.

the enemy's line. Orders were to given to encircle the whole fleet before giving battle. No quarters were asked or expected. Much to the astonishment of the invaders, no instruments of war were in sight; those plains people could paddle so gracefully, the enemy waited to see how the [Squally] would fight. On they came, working in unison [without] a spoken word. [Suddenly] a great cheer was given and up stood the big brawny Squally. Before the invaders knew, big rocks were hurled which crushed their war canoes... they were helplessly swimming and...drowning. Darkness saved a few of the invaders who escaped to tell of their utter defeat.

The tide and wind brought thousands of bodies to the beaches and none were buried.

The old 'Squally' story teller would solemnly warn young ones that someday they might be called to defend the Squally lands and waters. The Squally remembered their forefathers and expected to fight if need be.

The aboriginal name Squally came from the tops of the flowers and various herbs and roots which grew abundantly and annually in the area. These flowers were beautiful to behold, especially when the wind blew, causing a wavy motion. The Squally named themselves after the beautiful natural phenomena.

The French voyageurs changed the spelled name to 'Nezsqually' and the Yankees changed it to Nisqually.[37]

The Nisqually occupied about twenty-seven hundred square miles of land in the southern Puget Sound area when the first Europeans arrived. That territory encompasses almost all of Pierce County including Mt. Rainier, all of Thurston County, and large portions of Lewis, Grays Harbor, and Mason Counties. Apparently the Nisqually culture dominated the other regional tribes. Their language, a Salish tongue called Lushootseed, was spoken by nearly all tribes in Western Washington. The Nisqually may have been arbiters of disputes in distant places. Even the mighty Hudson's Bay Company deferred to the Nisqually headman of Sequalitchew Village, Lahalet, for some decisions.

---

[37] Bonney, W.P., *History of Pierce County, Volume One*, Pioneer Historical Publishing Company, Chicago, 1927.

Chronological Events

1543
Bartlome Ferrelo, commander of a Spanish sailing expedition exploring western North America, sighted the coast.

1592
Apostolos Valerianos, a Greek sailing for the Spanish (Juan de Fuca was his Spanish name), is reputed to have discovered the Strait of Juan de Fuca.

1602
Vizcaino, another Spanish explorer, sailed along the Pacific coastline of North America.

1774
Juan Perez sighted and named Mount Sierra de Santa Rosalia (now Mount Olympus).

1775
Bruno Heceta and Juan de Bodega y Quadra landed on Washington's coast near Point Grenville, claiming the land for Spain.

1778
Captain James Cook, English navigator, sailed into and named the Strait of Juan de Fuca. Cook charted the coast from 44 degrees north to 70 degrees north. He rested for a month at Nootka Sound.

1788
Captain John Meares, English trader, and William Douglas, flying both the English and Portuguese flags for protection, renamed Mt. Olympus, and named Cape Disappointment. His crew built the first ship on the northwestern coast at Nootka.

1788
Captain Robert Gray commanding the *Lady Washington* and John Kendrick commanding the *Columbia* arrived in the PNW. They were American fur traders.

1789
Estevan Martinez, a Spanish navigator, entered Nootka Sound, captured British ships, and claimed the land for Spain.

1790
Francisco Eliza' fortified Nootka and claimed Neah Bay for Spain, building a small farm there. Manuel Quimper explored the San Juan Islands.

1791
Francisco Eliza sent an exploring expedition from Discovery Bay to Bellingham Bay.

May 11, 1792
Captain Robert Gray carried the American flag around the world and discovered the mouth of the Columbia River and Gray's Harbor.

1792
Captain George Vancouver discovered, named, and with Peter Puget, explored Puget Sound.

1794
Spain made restitution for British property seized at Nootka. All claims to the region were relinquished, leaving the United States and Great Britain with claims.

1803
The United States purchased the Louisiana Territory from France, increasing interest in Oregon Country. Spain had a previous claim to the land that was administered by France. The French sold Louisiana Territory for $15 million dollars.

1805
The Meriwether Lewis and William Clark Expedition successfully crossed the Rocky Mountains with the guidance of Sacajawea. They reached the north-side mouth of the Columbia River in November, strengthening the United States claim to the region.

1810
The North West Fur Company (English) built Spokane House (nine miles northwest of Spokane)—the first white settlement in what is now Washington State.

1811
Pacific Fur Company, owned by American John Jacob Astor, built Fort Astoria and Fort Okanogan.

1811
Englishman David Thompson explored Kettle Falls (in present-day Washington State) on the Columbia River, and the Snake River (now in Washington, Oregon and Idaho) claiming them for England.

1812
Fort Spokane was built by Astor's Pacific Fur Company to compete with the North West Company. War (of 1812) was declared between the United States and Great Britain.

1813
John Jacob Astor sold the Pacific Fur Company, including Fort Astoria and Fort Okanogan to the North West Company

1814
Treaty of Ghent ended the War of 1812 but did not solve the dispute over Oregon Country.

1818
Fort Nez Perce (Fort Walla Walla) built by the North West Company. Joint occupancy policy agreed to by the U.S. and Great Britain for a period of ten years.

1819
In the Treaty of Florida, Spain agreed to relinquish all claims to Oregon Country.

1821
Hudson's Bay Company absorbed the North West Company, taking all of its trading posts and all employees, except three deemed unsuitable. Peter Skene Ogden, one of the three, fought the decision in London, appearing before the HBC Board of Governors to personally appeal his case. He is believed to have said he would win his job back or end up in the prison down the street from HBC headquarters. Years later, Skene served on the HBC Columbia Department Board of Management.

1824
John Work travelling from Fort Vancouver to the Fraser River to locate a site for a new trading post wrote: *"In the evening passed the Nisqually River which falls in from a pretty large bay. The shores are steep and built of a compound of clay, gravel. They are covered with woods, principally pine, to the water's edge. In several places the wood appears pretty clear and not much chocked with under wood."* Near the Nisqually River Work noted "Sequalitchew Creek" which seems to be of S'Klallam dialect meaning "the face is marked" in reference to dark facial markings on the fish of that creek.

Work also:

> "Stopped at another little river where there was a village of the Nisqually Nation consisting of six houses, these are miserable habitations constructed of poles and planks covered with mats. We were detained 1½ hours at this village getting two men and a woman, wife of one of them, to act as interpreters and guides for us."

On his return trip Work wrote:

> "Embarked a little after 4 o'clock in the afternoon at our guides' village which is called Chilacoom."

1825
Fort Vancouver was built on the north side of the Columbia River to replace Fort William (Fort Astoria) on orders of Doctor John McLoughlin, factor of the Hudson's Bay Company. Fort Colville was built to augment Fort Okanogan and replace Spokane House.

1826
Dr. McLoughlin's men built a water-powered sawmill, school and library, and planted an orchard at Fort Vancouver.

1827
The Joint Occupancy Treaty between the Unites States and Great Britain was extended indefinitely, but one year of notice was required to modify the pact.

1828
Alexander McKenzie and four other fur traders ventured north from Fort Vancouver as far as Whidbey Island on Puget Sound. S'Klallam warriors viciously murdered the European traders. Before long before HBC retaliated, by opening fire with broadside cannons from a British gunboat. The cannon-fire killed most of the S'Klallam people residing in a village near the entrance to Hood Canal. The S'Klallam or "Strong People" had been feared by tribes of Puget Sound for, perhaps, centuries.

1829
Fort Vancouver was nearly re-built. A sailing ship named *Vancouver* was built to facilitate trade to the Hawaiian Islands. Three hundred Hawaiians (Kanaka) were hired to work at Fort Vancouver.

1831

Former U.S. President John Quincy Adams took his seat as an elected member of the U.S. House of Representatives. Nat Turner revolted. Cyrus McCormick invented the reaper.

1832

President Andrew Jackson was re-elected. Martin Van Buren was elected Vice President, and the Federal Department of Indian Affairs was established.

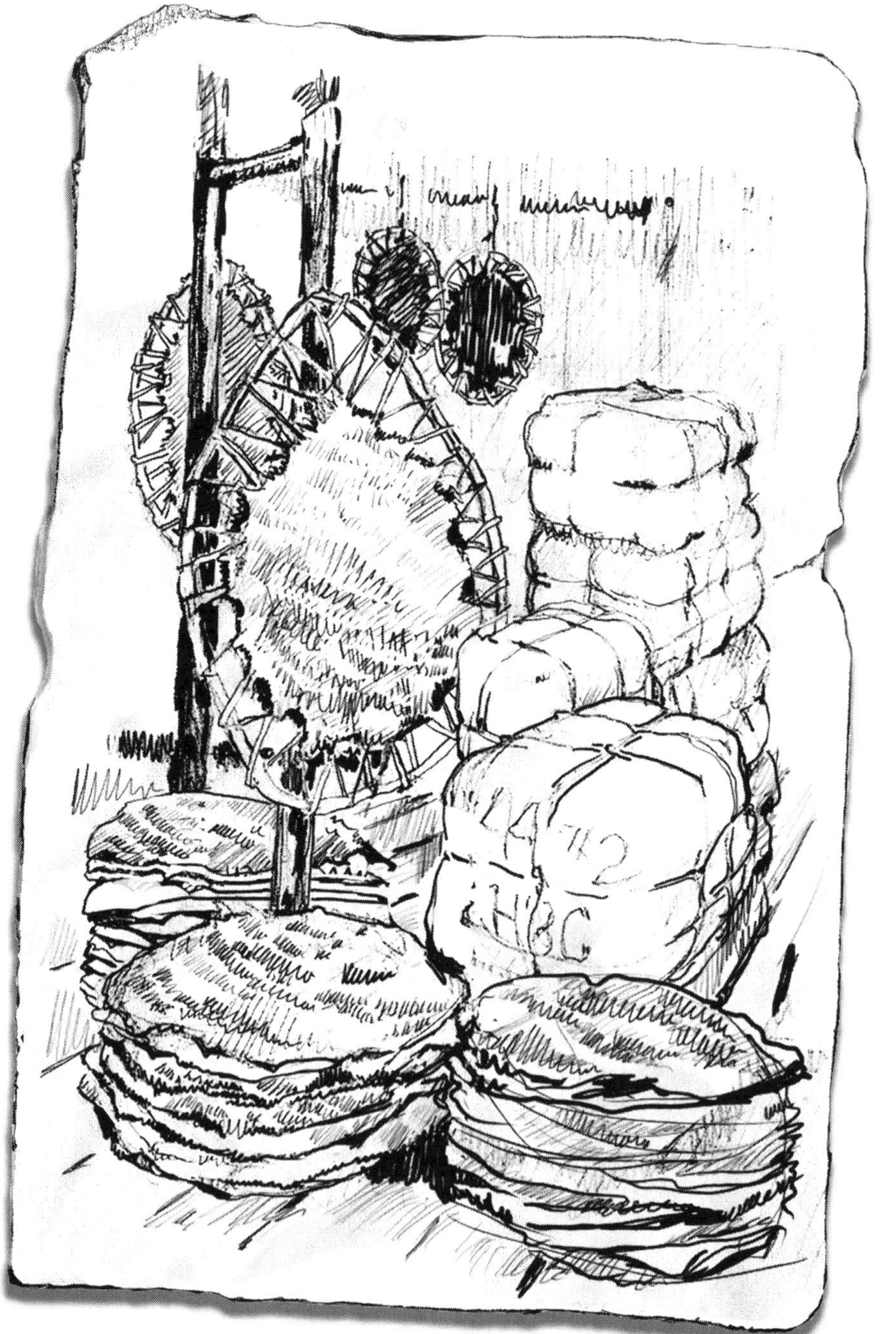

1832

TO GET A SENSE of the era we note some people, places and events around the world.

Captain Benjamin Louis Eulalie de Bonneville, a French-born officer in the United States Army, began an exploration expedition in early 1832, leaving Missouri with 110 men. With the intention of traveling overland to Fort Vancouver, the party included Nathaniel Jarvis Wyeth, a shipping magnate from Cambridge, Massachusetts. The men trekked along what eventually became the Oregon Trail, arriving at Fort Vancouver on October 29, 1832. Wyeth was rebuffed, politely but firmly, by Doctor McLoughlin. The good doctor eventually forbade any trade with Bonneville at that time.

At the Walla Walla River confluence with the Columbia, Bonneville saw only Indians who were loyal to the Hudson's Bay Company (HBC) fur traders. Rejected and dejected by the British presence, Bonneville returned east in April 1835.

In 1831 four Nez Perce Indians[38] from Idaho, west of the Rockies, arrived in St. Louis to inquire about the white man's religion, about which they had heard from Lewis and Clark. Within a few months the idea of the Oregon Methodist Mission was developed.[39]

Reverend Jason Lee, a recent graduate of Boston's Wilbraham Academy, was chosen to lead the Methodist Mission to Oregon on March 22, 1833. By September 5, 1834 the Methodist Missionaries, traveling with Nathaniel J. Wyeth's second party of 70 men, 250 horses, mules, and cattle, arrived at Fort Vancouver on the Columbia River.

In 1832, President Jackson was winding up his first term in Washington, D.C. He labeled his practice of rewarding political supporters with government jobs "reform". In the Senate William Marcy put it this way; "To the victor belong the spoils of the enemy." Cartoonist Thomas Nast depicted Jackson atop a pig that symbolized the Civil Service system.

Scientific advances in agriculture and industry increased the need for workers in

---

38 Their names were Black Eagle, Man of the Morning, Rabbit Skin Leggings, and No Horns on the Head according to http://www.timetracts.com/Homepage.htm

39 It was not until 1836 that Reverend Henry Spaulding and his wife, Eliza, came to the Nez Perce with the Bible.

the Southern States, resulting in nearly 25 percent increase in the price of a strong, healthy slave. In Connecticut, free Negroes were admitted to the Methodist Wesleyan University in 1832.

On a cold rocky shore of Puget Sound in November, 1832, thirteen European men ate a mostly cold meal. Chief Trader Archibald McDonald, on orders from Dr. McLoughlin, looked seriously for a site to erect a new fur trade establishment on Puget Sound as an extension of Fort Langley. It would be called Nisqually House, an outpost far across the oceans at the very far western edge of an enormous continent. It would be completely self-reliant. The thirteen Europeans would be outnumbered by, perhaps, 10,000 mostly friendly native Coast Salish.

The Europeans easily made friends with the Squalli-absch (Nisqually Indians) who inhabited the small village at Sequalitchew Creek. McDonald and his men stayed for twelve days. Sequalitchew Village consisted of two substantial cedar plank longhouses built as the homes for several related families of the Sequalitchew branch of the Nisqually Tribe, a Coast Salish linguistic group.

Legend told the Nisqually people that their ancestors came from the Great Basin, crossed the Cascade Mountains and settled at Skate Creek, just south of the Nisqually River watershed's southern edge. Later a major village with, perhaps, 500 people was developed at the confluence of the Mashel River and the Nisqually River. Other villages also began to appear as the population grew. The Sequalitchew Village was newer than many of the others, but was still very old. It was the custom of the very friendly Nisqually to welcome new people and visitors as equals. Thus the Europeans were welcomed.

The HBC planned Nisqually House to become "the principal establishment in the Columbia"[40] Department with a deep water seaport that would avoid the deadly Columbia River bar. Fort Vancouver was to be abandoned eventually in favor of this new place.

Archibald McDonald and most of his men returned to Fort Vancouver for Christmas with their families. A seasoned fur trader, Jean Baptiste Ouvré, and only two other men spent the winter of 1832-1833 in a single 15 x 20 foot squared-timber home on the south side of Sequalitchew Creek.

The winter months were not severe in terms of weather, but supplies were short and the neighbors were potentially dangerous. The three fur traders were outnumbered. Trade was nearly impossible as Ouvré had nothing to trade that the Native Americans did not already possess. Fish and shellfish were abundant, and the Nisqually gave permission to exploit the resource, but Ouvré and the men were not good fishermen, they

---

40 Cole, Jean Murray, Editor, *This Blessed Wilderness*, UBC Press, Vancouver, 2001.

traded for sustenance.

Nisqually House would soon become Fort Nisqually. In a few years it would house the Puget Sound Agricultural Company, a huge agri-business of major international impact.

British and Hudson's Bay Company political thinking behind the new post at Nisqually was that the eventual boundary between the United States and British land claims would run along the Columbia River. British opinion held that Puget Sound would be safely in British territory. The HBC post on the Columbia (Fort Vancouver) would "hold" the north bank for the British. An international treaty would necessarily deal with those American claims to the entire Columbia, by right of Captain Gray's discovery, and the very first "permanent" establishment at Fort Astoria.

As early as 1818, when the HBC established Fort Walla Walla, the United States had offered to divide the Oregon Country along the 49th parallel. The British had refused that offer, countering with a line along the Columbia River west of the Rockies. The U.S. rejected the British-proposed line in 1818, 1824, 1826, 1843, and 1845.

The vast Oregon Country stretched along the Pacific Coast, from Spanish land in the south, to Russian property in the north and inland to the Rockies, a region of 443,000 square miles. American proposals to split the area would give the U.S. 286,541 square miles and the British would have 157,330 square miles of territory. The British negotiators rejected the U.S. offer because it gave the larger and better portion where the Americans had only Gray's discovery claim, Lewis and Clark's trek, John Jacob Astor's[41] failed Fort Astoria.

The British countered with their claim to possess all of Oregon offering evidence of British ownership. They pointed, somewhat feebly, to Fort William (1812), which was actually Fort Astoria (1811) and to Fort Vancouver (1824), as well as to hundreds of trappers all over the entire region, from Spanish California to Russian Alaska.

American claims were politically animated in the Democrat Party campaign cries of 1844. They were motivated by patriotic, perhaps jingoistic[42] "Manifest Destiny[43]" slogans

---

41 Astor was born Johann Jakob Astor (1763-1848) in Germany. He came to the USA after the American Revolution, became a business magnate, merchant, investor, and the first multi-millionaire in the United States. His Pacific Fur Company built Fort Astoria in 1811. It was the first United States community on the west coast.

42 Jingoism is patriotism in the form of aggressive foreign policy, usually referring to threats against peace with other countries. It shows excessive bias in favor of one's own perceived national superiority.

43 Only 29 years later the City of Tacoma would claim the nickname "City of Destiny" as the western terminus of America's second transcontinental railroad line. The nickname Manifest Destiny is working with jingoistic local boosters.

like "Fifty-four Forty or Fight." The first slogan expected the country to grow by some divine manifest fate to include the entire continent. The second rally cry referred to the latitudinal, and treaty lines that bound the Spanish at the 42nd parallel and the Russians at 54 degrees and 40 minutes line. All land between those lines was "ours," according to the Democrats' ambitious campaign. With the election going to the Democrats, the possibility of war for territory was very real.

The Treaty of Ghent[44] in 1818 provided for joint occupancy of Oregon. The British were clearly dominant all across Oregon Country, until the arrival of American Missionaries in 1834. Joint occupancy allowed the Americans back in the territorial claim game.

The spot selected for Fort Nisqually was a few yards south of the Sequalitchew Nisqually village, on the upper edge of the rocky shore, above high tide on a sandy bank of Puget Sound. McDonald and his men were planning the grand opening of a new store. Imagine the excitement among the Nisqually, for they would be the new customers and employees of this fantastic new store, with wonderful imported goods of the highest quality which were never before available locally.

It took McDonald's crew only 12 days to build another 15 x 20 foot structure with 12" wide walls of squared timber under a sturdy cedar-bark roof. They filled the rough-and-ready establishment with a generous supply of trade blankets and other trade goods, but more importantly, several kegs of potatoes and garden vegetable seeds, in anticipation of long-term settlement and survival. Jean Baptiste Ouvré and two others were left in charge when the building was completed on April 20, 1833. Meanwhile, McDonald took the other crew members north 175 miles to Fort Langley, on the Fraser River.

A short half-mile inland, the Nisqually Plains stretched across open grassland interspersed with clumps of Garry oak trees, sparkling lakes, and bordered with heavy timber near rivers to the north and the south. The gravelly prairie held a quarter million acres of rich grassland capable of supporting many thousand head of livestock. The Nisqually Plains was a marked contrast to the dense forests in much of the region. The grassland was like a park of open land, with rivulets, lakes, natural and native roads, with splendid scenery stretching across the miles to the majestic mountain they called Tahoma. The mostly un-forested area of what is now Pierce County covered some 250 square miles, between the Nisqually and Puyallup Rivers, and from near the shore of Puget Sound to the foothills of the Cascade Mountains.

Imagine one's spirits rising, as the scene of tranquil content spreads before one's eyes.

---

44 Treaty of Ghent, Flanders, ended the War of 1812 between the USA and the United Kingdom, Great Britain, and Ireland, and restored relations between the two.

The urge to sit and rest awhile, even if not tired, was compelling to many before and since 1833. (Like thousands of others—perhaps the reader—stayed for a lifetime after a brief encounter with the region). Imagine sitting under one of the old Garry oak trees, even if they were not that old, it was a rare sight. These oak trees are scarce near Puget Sound, for these are the Garry oak (*Quercus garrymana*[45]), not the same as the ones found three thousand miles away in Maryland. It was named after Nicholas Garry who assisted David Douglas during Pacific Northwest explorations in the 1820s. He never saw these groves at Puget Sound, but they are the same tree known colloquially as the Oregon white oak.

The Garry oaks thrive on the south facing slopes, in the driest areas of what is now Western Washington. They thrived at the Mima Mounds, Weir Prairie, Lakewood, Steilacoom, South Tacoma, and Joint Base Lewis/McChord (JBLM). A combination of gravelly soil, rich grasses, beautiful wildflowers, grazing wild animals, and Garry Oak trees dominated plains areas of the South Sound region.

Garry oak trees are extremely slow growing, but may reach 90 feet tall, and might take 280 years to produce a trunk 18 inches in diameter. When the first Europeans arrived at the prairies above the Sequalitchew village, many Garry oak trunks were in the four-foot diameter range. The new people at Sequalitchew saw the trees for their value as furniture, flooring, structural support, firewood, fencing material, and as ship-building material.

Indians often burned the prairie grasslands to protect the wild bulbs of the camas—an important food source—and to keep the ever-encroaching Douglas fir trees at bay. The fire-resistant Garry oak survived to feed squirrels and the Salish tribes with fresh acorns every year.

Jean Baptiste Ouvré and his companions were resourceful fur traders. The Sequalitchew were delighted to be chosen for the new trade post of the most powerful international corporation in the world. Coincidentally, HBC operated from London, the capital of the most powerful nation in the world. Although the Indians were unaware of the effect HBC would have on their lives and their culture, it felt good to be the people nearest to the only source of new imported products that would be offered for trade. It was as if Costco or WalMart had moved into the area, to the delight of cost-conscious consumers.

The three men planted potatoes and other vegetable seeds as the weather turned to a glorious spring on Puget Sound. The men hunted wild game for meat when they

---

45 Garry oak is generally short, with a thick trunk. It has a hard grayish-black bark with deep grooves and narrow horizontal furrows which create an almost mosaic pattern. The narrow limbs seem to struggle away from the trunk. The silhouette at night against a stormy sky is often used as a scene in a scary movie.

could, and traded for fish and fowl with Indian merchants. Ouvré and his companions may have been lonely, however, they were experienced fur traders accustomed to being alone and outnumbered in an unknown land.

No one knows for certain, but chances are other "new" people came from time-to-time by land and sea to the shores of Whulge during the 100 centuries of human habitation. Gradually all were acculturated into the dominant resident culture. Within a couple of generations, each new group assimilated. The Nisqually, like most of the Salish people, were not war-like, often hiding or running away to avoid battles or capture. They were gentle fish and shellfish gatherers. There was no reason for the Nisqually to think the whites behaved much differently, because they had obviously come in peace to trade.

In 1832, Nisqually whites were far outnumbered by more than 5,000 Indians to less than two dozen whites. It had now been 41 years since the first "pooh-pooh" men led by Captain Vancouver and Peter Puget came peacefully to the land and waters ruled by Mount Tahoma. Native Americans made many good trades, and no bad things had happened. The new whites clearly wanted to stay, learn the local Salish and Chinook languages, perhaps take a wife and raise a family. It was as it had always been on the Whulge. Newcomers were welcome additions to the Sequalitchew community, because they brought with them new ideas, new tools, and new trade items. Nisqually people could adapt to new people and new ways, to enrich their culture.

The "Company of Adventurers Trading out of the Hudson's Bay"[46] and beyond had a distinct "company culture" to match the official name. It was surely based on the British military model, but included aspects of royalty, military, business structures, including racial, gender, and class divisions, along with specialized division of labor described by Adam Smith in 1776.[47]

Many of the attitudes and practices of the Company, indeed the entire Western society of the 19th Century, would be considered at minimum prejudicial and racist today. While the Fort Nisqually Living History Museum certainly does not endorse the centuries-old practices, those practices are depicted by reenactors for historical accuracy and educational purposes.

The Company's four distinctly stratified socio-economic and ethnic divisions crossed many national boundaries. British (Irish, Scots, and English), French-Canadians, Native Americans (Iroquois, Nisqually, Puyallup, Cowlitz, Chehalis, and others), Hawaiians (Sandwich Islanders at the time), Métis (mixed heritage European and Native American

---

46 This was the legal name of the HBC according to the Royal Charter signed in 1670.

47 Smith, Adam, *An Inquiry into the Nature and Causes of the Wealth of Nations,* reprint by The Easton Press, Norwalk Connecticut, 1991. The publication date of the original book was in 1776.

(First People), and a few West Indians worked at Fort Nisqually. Even some American settlers, discharged soldiers, and sailors were employed by the Company. Each of these people were represented in the four socio-economic classes of the Company, i.e., Proprietors, Commissioned Officers, Servants, and Charges.

The Proprietor class was occupied exclusively by English men who lived in London, who hired (primarily) Scots as managers at local posts. The Scots, in turn, hired French-Canadians, some Iroquois and Métis, Kanakas from the Sandwich Islands, and Native Americans (mostly Nisqually at Fort Nisqually) to do the physical "day" labor.

One could easily recognize a sub-class; that of "day laborer," which was most often filled by female Indian farm laborers, who were paid in trade goods at the end of the work day. These people were hired under a specific verbal contract for certain services and for a mutually-agreed-upon payment. Typical jobs varied from two weeks for shearing sheep, to a fall harvest, which might take several months of back-breaking hand labor.

The workers were also paid for animal pelts brought into the trade shop. The terms of the engagement were up to the trapper. He negotiated his remuneration during every trading session. Many Indian trappers and traders adopted European-style clothing styles and trim, since they were often paid with clothing and other European goods. Not many months passed before most Nisqually were fully clothed in HBC garments or fabric.

The Sandwich Islanders were called "Kanakas" or sometimes "Hawaiians" by the British. These men were hired on two- or three-year contracts for heavy labor, and on occasion as cooks. The brown-skinned Islanders with thick black hair added more ethnic diversity to the region, as many married local Native American women.[48]

Skilled laborers were most-often English, Irish, Scottish, Métis, French-Canadian, and American. These people ranked higher on the social class scale than the more abundant unskilled local laborers. Most of them were tradesmen specializing in blacksmithing, carpentry, cooperage (barrel making), and other skills, including swimming and diving. They received the best wages, although still well below the earnings of the upper classes. These craftsmen were transferred by the Company at a moment's notice. They carried a tool box, called a cassette, with them at all times. The cassette contained the tools of their trade and most of their worldly belongings. Their value to the company, and to their own well-being, was the transferability of the skills and the man. These men and their families enjoyed many more sundries than unskilled laborers. Skilled laborers often bought earthenware pots, mugs, and plates in bright colors. Their living quarters were more decorative, with affordable items, though not as fine as the comparable items one

---

48   There are many descendants of the original Kanaka immigrants living today.

would find in an upper class home.

Dr. McLoughlin occasionally had guests for lavish formal dinners at his home in Fort Vancouver. One of those guests was an American merchant ship captain and fur trader—Captain William Henry McNeill. He was an employee of Bryant and Sturgis Company of Boston. He traded from his ship, the *Llama*, all along the North Pacific coast. McNeill was recognized by American and British competitors as the most formidable trader of all. He had all but eliminated American competition by negotiating exclusive trade agreements among the tribes. McNeill loaded his ship with "wooden soldiers, jumping jacks, little wagons, whistles, and funniest of all, squeaking cats and dogs."[49] He sold his enticing cargo piece by piece for precious furs easily collected by the First People, the aboriginal natives who knew the land and the sea as well as the animals.

McLoughlin wanted to meet the man who was taking so much business along the coast. When the *Llama* arrived on the Columbia River, the Indians bought a great number of the toys from McNeill. They had a great time with the little wagons on the beach. The dog and cat toys entertained the Indians for hours. They went into laughing fits over the jumping-jacks and toy soldiers. They loved the whistles!

HBC traders concentrated on beads, mirrors, cloth, and feather decorations. The 'redmen' were suddenly deaf to their traditional offers of trade. McLoughlin silently admitted defeat. He purchased McNeill's ship and the entire cargo! Then McLoughlin hired McNeill and his crew to operate the vessel for the HBC.[50]

On Wednesday, August 29, 1832 the log of the *Llama* recorded that at:

"*11 AM, fired 3 salutes of seven guns… hald [sic] down the American colors and hoisted the English Middle…so ends the Voyage*" of the American vessel *Llama*.

Next was the beginning of the log of the HBC *Llama*. It was, also, the genesis of an illustrious lifetime career for Captain William Henry McNeill with Hudson's Bay Company. McNeill would play a strategic role at Fort Nisqually and other posts. He would earn the highest rank of any American in service to Hudson's Bay Company.

McNeill was clearly the most successful trader on the North Pacific coast. McNeill fancied himself the leader of HBC "Marine Department," which McLoughlin never officially acknowledged. In fact, McLoughlin worked for years to build a land-based system of trading posts to replace the "expensive" ships. Fort Nisqually became the southernmost dock, the "home port" of the little fleet of fur trade ships, lead by McNeill. Aided

---

49 Parrish, Philip H., *Before the Covered Wagon*, Binsford and Mort Publishers, Portland, Oregon, 1931.

50 McNeill was clever. He sold the ship, thus gaining a commission. He sold the cargo for another commission, then hired his own crew to operate the ship he just sold after being hired as the 'new' captain.

by the new HBC Steamship *Beaver,* McNeill would increase his contributions to the fur trade industry, his status in the HBC, as well as his personal income.

For the most part, 1832 was a long, uneventful year for the few Europeans in Old Oregon. It was not realized at the time for the historic significance 1832 eventually would hold. To the Puget Sound area (and in some ways the entire West Coast) this year was equivalent to 1620 at Plymouth Rock or 1607 at Jamestown. It was the beginning of a new "colony" of Europeans. It was only 56 years after the American Revolution brought political independence to a new nation, but 340 years after Columbus first sailed to a New World.

But the Americans were coming. The American Fur Company built a fur trading outpost on the upper Missouri River: they called it Fort McKenzie. It was also the year that American George Catlin went up the Missouri to the headwaters. It was less than one year before the Spaniard Maximillan explored the length of the Missouri River for Spanish Mexico.

In June, Asian cholera struck Quebec, killing about 6,000 people of Lower Canada, and for the first time the song "America" was sung publicly on July 4, 1832.

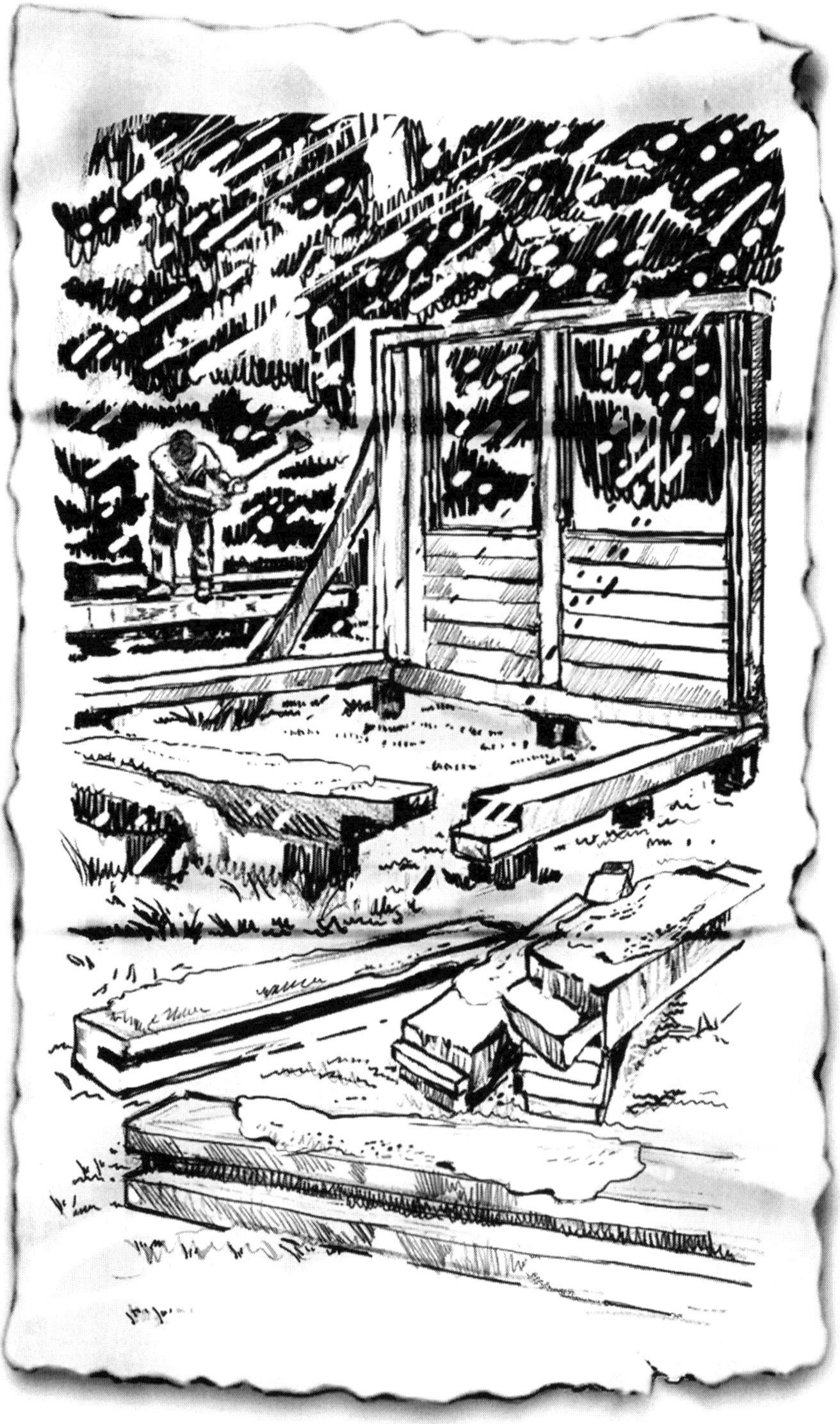

1833

WHILE ENGLISHMAN JOHN BALL began teaching the Métis children at Fort Vancouver, Fort Nisqually improvements were under construction, directed by Archibald McDonald, for the Hudson's Bay Company.

American settlers in San Felipe de Austin, Texas, adjourned a three-day meeting on April 3, 1833, agreeing to seek Texas independence from Mexico. In August, 1833 Mexico demanded that all Missions in California drop their Roman Catholic religious affiliations.

On September 1, New York City, publisher Benjamin Day produced America's first penny newspaper. It was four pages of topical politics, editorials, human interest stories, and sensational accounts of crime and horror.

In Grand Detour, Illinois, 29-year-old John Deere developed a remarkable steel-blade plow that could cut, and turn over, the dense soils of the Midwest. Previous plows were mostly based on the Thomas Jefferson design, suited for the lighter soils of the East.

The world's longest railroad at 136 miles was completed near Hamburg, South Carolina.

The Society of Friends opened the first Quaker College in Haverford, Pennsylvania, while Joseph Walker travelled overland to Mexican California under orders from Captain Bonneville.

In Washington D.C., the Treasury Building burned. The fire did not prevent President Jackson from ordering the Treasury Secretary to withdraw all federal funds from the Second Bank of the United States. The Treasurer refused to do as he was ordered, so Jackson fired him, replaced him, and carried out the shift of funds to the Girard Bank of Philadelphia. Soon the Second Bank was without funds and out of business.

Fur trader Archibald McDonald returned to the simple settlement at Nisqually on Sequalitchew Creek, near the shores of Puget Sound.[51] He arrived on Thursday, May 30, 1833 after 14 days of very difficult travel on roadless land from Fort Vancouver. Fourteen men, four fully-loaded oxen wagons, and four equally-loaded horse wagons arrived at the grassy plains where Mount Tacoma seemed so near. There were only a series of Native

---

51 Today the site is within the City of DuPont, Washington.

American horse trails across the hills and grassy plains near what is now Interstate Five (I-5). McDonald expected to meet the schooner *Vancouver* at Puget Sound. It held a cargo-hold full of European trade goods, seed potatoes, peas, and other provisions. McDonald and his brigade were permanently relocating to the neighborhood of the Sequalitchew Nisqually.[52] Imagine the excitement among the Nisqually for the grand opening of this new trade store! They would be the closest customers, and the first employees hired. Employee discounts were expected.

McDonald augmented Ouvré's existing three-man Fort Nisqually crew. Four of McDonald's men were assigned to Fort Langley on the Fraser River, but the others increased the Fort Nisqually population to 11 hands, and—temporarily—two gentlemen. McDonald had brought with him from Fort Vancouver a young Gentleman Class surgeon from Scotland who was not counted with the laborers. His name was Dr. William Fraser Tolmie.

Twenty-one-year-old Tolmie earned his License in Surgery in 1832. Tolmie studied anatomy, surgery, and dissection. He spoke English, Scottish, French, Latin, and later learned Chinook and Lushootseed. He was hired in London as Surgeon for Hudson's Bay Company. His first assignments were at Fort McLoughlin and Fort Simpson, fur trade posts in the far north near the Russian America Company at 54 degrees north. Tolmie was born in Inverness, Scotland, on February 3, 1812, received his primary private schooling in Edinburgh. His diary reveals his practical habit of reading and writing about medical matters and observing various medical procedures, as well as interests in botany, religion, political science, and current events.

Tolmie signed on to serve as Physician and Surgeon, departing almost immediately from Gravesend, England, on September 15, 1832, bound for the Northwest Coast of North America, aboard the *Ganymede*. He arrived half way around the world on the Columbia River at Fort Vancouver on May 1.

Tolmie was listed as a "Licentiate," however, that was not a title for students of the Faculty of Physicians and Surgeons of Glasgow University. A Licentiate could only be earned at Cambridge University, and only in surgical medicine. Since Tolmie attended Glasgow University earning the title Surgeon, his training was (apparently) equivalent to a Cambridge's "Licentiate." Though clearly not of the rigorous classroom and hospital residency requirements expected today, Tolmie's education was certainly common practice for potential surgical students of Glasgow University in 1832. His title, whether "Licentiate" or Surgeon, probably fits well between a modern BA and MD.

---

52 More correctly called Squalli-Absch, which means "people of the river" in Lushootseed.

Tolmie was clearly a doctor by the standards of early 1830s England or America. The HBC considered him to be a surgeon, paying him accordingly with his very first employment contract.

The primary expectation of any surgeon in the early 19th century was speed. A good surgeon was expected to remove an injured limb, stop the bleeding to save the patient's life, and do it quickly. The surgeon was charged with simultaneously cutting the flesh and bone, while finding and clamping the affected arteries. In their haste many surgeons of lesser skills not only lost the patient, but also lost their own, or a helper's, fingers.

Tolmie was scheduled to leave Fort Nisqually on the northbound company schooner *Vancouver* ten days after his arrival. However, it was delayed by slack winds. By the end of May, McDonald was deploring the circumstance of the missing supply ship. The workmen were kept busy constructing a small farm house at the edge of the plain, above the steep, high bank. On the beach, at least one half-mile downhill from the trading house, a simple dock and small float were completed. The house on the plains was indispensable, because it would be home for the lead shepherd near the small livestock herd pasturing on the open plain.

Hudson's Bay Company transferred McDonald to Fort Langley, and sent Chief Trader Francis Herron to take charge of Nisqually House. One of his first projects was to cut a diagonal oxen road into the slope of the hill, from the beach to the prairie above the bluff. It was the first man-made road near Puget Sound. It was truly a "road," as opposed to a "trail" because there was no natural surface contour resembling anything like a road or a trail. Men with shovels and ox wagons removed and reshaped the slope. The road created a ledge angling up the face of the bluff above Puget Sound waters.[53]

Dr. Tolmie, with no official duties, was restless. On June 29, 1833, Mr. Herron agreed to go along with Tolmie on a "botanizing" expedition. Tolmie was following the lead of the famous David Douglas, who was already collecting northwest plant samples for the leading British botanists. Douglas, also a Scot, collected thousands of specimens of northwest plants, including the Douglas fir that now bears his name. Tolmie's name also appears on some plants, examples of which are still growing in the Royal British Gardens in London.[54] This botanizing jaunt was planned as a simple tour of the nearby

---

[53] The Historic Oxen Road was utterly wiped out with the coming of the railroad in the 1870s. The entire hillside was regarded to provide a foundation for a sturdy gravel bed for the wooden ties and steel rails.

[54] The Piggyback Plant (*Tolmiea menziesii*), Tolmie's saxifrage (*Saxifraga tolmiei*), Tolmie's onion (*Allium tolmie*), Tolmie's star-tulip (*Calochortus tolmiei*), and (*Carex Tolmiei*), and a bird (*Oporornis tolmie*), a Warbler, are named for Dr. William Fraser Tolmie's discoveries.

countryside, with three company employees on foot for the two gentlemen on horseback. Tolmie continues the story:

> *While thus engaged, our three attendants. McKie, Brown, and Peter Tahi, the Islander, felt the earth under them shake violently at least twice, Brown exclaimed first, and seemed much alarmed. He and McKie were on their knees at the time and felt violently lifted up, the sensations of Peter I could not ascertain. Mr. Herron and I did not perceive anything remarkable. This happened at 20 minutes from 2.... On returning to the fort we learnt that the shock had been felt there, the boards in the floor of the house rattling together. The Indians were much struck and said, "Chief Herron's medicine is strong. He has gone up the hill to shake the grounds".... The steep and broken faces eastward of the islands in the sound render it probable that they have been severed from the main shore by an earthquake.*[55]

The weather was very dry during the summer of 1833. Hunting was difficult. Fishing was nearly non-existent. The supply ship, *Vancouver*, was very late. There was little trade activity, because there was no inventory of trade goods, even though Indian customers were eagerly visiting the place daily.

Archibald McDonald and Dr. Tolmie explored the mud flats and low saltwater estuary near the mouth of the Nisqually River by canoe. The area was pronounced pleasing to the eye, very dry and sterile at that season. Eventually Tolmie would have a cattle pasture located there.

Concerns for the supply ship grew. Sailing ships were to be the lifeline to the European fur traders. Herron and Tolmie decided to take a canoe and six men to search for the *Vancouver*, somewhere to the north on Puget Sound. Leaving James Rindale, a cooper, in charge of the grounds, and Pierre Charles to manage the work crews, McDonald and Tolmie departed. Their hired Indian oarsmen, rowed steadily, reaching Point Orchard on June 6th, and Hood Canal on the 7th, Port Townshend[56] on the 8th, and Whidby Island on the 9th. The hungry men purchased some dog meat, having eaten all of their supplies of meat, grains, and peas. At Point Partridge they finally spotted the schooner a few miles ahead.

---

55   Tolmie, William Fraser, *The Journals of William Fraser Tolmie, Physician and Fur Trader*, Mitchell Press, Ltd., Vancouver, 1963.

56   These places were named by Captain Vancouver as geographic spots. Some later became towns with similarly spelled names when Americans settled there. Whidbey Island was named for Joseph Whidby, who circumnavigated the island in 1792, but was changed to Whidbey by Americans.

Captain Ryan explained that a light breeze and a flood tide were the total locomotion from the Pacific through the Straits of Juan de Fuca, and Admiralty Inlet to Puget Sound. The Indians in villages all along the way to the South Sound were anxious to trade some fine beaver pelts, but found the offering prices too low on board the *Vancouver*.

Finally the winds picked up, becoming somewhat sprightly. At 11 o'clock on the night of June 10, 1833, the *Vancouver* anchored offshore, within sight of the little trade house at Sequalitchew Creek.

Three hours before anchoring at Fort Nisqually, around eight o'clock, the ship had received news by express canoe of a serious accident at the Fort. Pierre Charles had nearly severed his foot with a broad axe. He was bleeding seriously and fainting. Doctor Tolmie was dispatched instantly on his first "house call" directly back to Fort Nisqually!

Six seamen pulled on the oars of the captain's shore boat, delivering the doctor to treat the dreadful, life-threatening gash in Pierre Charles' foot. The newly-arrived doctor, assigned to Fort Simpson and Fort McLoughlin in the far north, would be delayed for several months at Fort Nisqually to treat Pierre Charles' life-threatening injury.

The contents of Dr. Tolmie's medical valise will likely never be exactly known. Suppositions can be made from other available sources about what a typical doctor of the era may have carried to administer to patients. First, the bag was probably black leather with a carrying handle and, perhaps, a metal latch. In later years, the contents one could expect the valise might carry: an ophthalmoscope and an otoscope. These devices are used to examine the retina of the eye and the ear drum, respectively. The ophthalmoscope was invented in 1847, gaining wide use by 1851. The otoscope was most often sold with the ophthalmoscope. There is no evidence that Tolmie ever ordered either instrument, but may have purchased them while on leave in 1841.

Tolmie may have owned a trephine for surgically cutting bones, a device used as much as 2,000 years ago to remove a circular disk of cranial bone. The procedure could relieve pressure, reveal an underlying problem, or assist in the removal of broken bone fragments.

The medical professional in Doctor Tolmie's day did not have the support of comprehensive medical systems consisting of pharmacies, ambulances, hospitals, helicopters, or even nurses. For the most part, he had to be prepared for anything and everything. The doctor may have carried some sort of tongue depressor, reflex hammer, pins and brushes to test sensory nerves, and a head mirror to reflect the ambient light from a candle to the patent. He undoubtedly carried a scalpel or two, and obstetrical forceps for delivering frontier babies.

The doctor probably had glass suction cups for treating lung disease, and assorted slings, splints, and cloth bandages. A good doctor always carried some medicines, such as they were, in his black bag. These might have included mercury and arsenic compounds for fighting infections, laudanum (opium) for pain, plus various herbal compounds, leeches, salves, and whiskey to treat the patient, the family, or even himself.

Undoubtedly, Dr. Tolmie's bag contained a wide variety of surgical instruments, including suture materials, needles, hemostats for clipping off blood vessels, along with various probes, and maybe extra long forceps for removing bullets and other foreign objects. Frontier doctors had to deal with everything modern medicine deals with, but without much experience.

When the *Vancouver* finally pulled ashore at Fort Nisqually, McDonald noted that there was a good deal of activity. Fully-loaded and occupied Indian canoes were arriving by sea, along with horses and riders by the dozen. Two plows had been hard at work that day behind four oxen on the endless plain. This activity was a very uncommon scene in Indian country. It was, after all, a very new establishment, with only two crude square-timber buildings.

With all hands on shore pulling lines, the big schooner was brought within a few feet of the gravelly shore. An anchor and a shore boat were dropped to the water. Once the cargo was offloaded to the landing, it was only a few paces up the beach to the storehouse above high water. The cargo included a bale of heavy HBC blankets, ten traps, ten flintlock guns and ammunition, some blue duffle, capotes, baize, fine cotton shirts, and tobacco. The Indians were disappointed: they were shopping for feathers, rum, molasses, beads, and hats. Trading began in a few hours, however, with 90 skins crossing the trade store counter. Within days, distant riders and canoe paddlers brought in 290 more skins. Fort Nisqually was apparently a success.

It was a happy time for the trade store operators and the customers. Trade was brisk. Buyers and sellers were happy to profit so easily. Plus, the really good news was that a second supply ship, the *Cadboro*, was expected in a few days. She would have even more trade goods for sale.

Doctor Tolmie and Pierre Charles were otherwise occupied. The axe wound to Charles foot was massive and life-threatening. The axe had cut through the upper part of Pierre's left foot, from the instep to the toes, and nearly half of the blade was through the middle part of his foot. It extended from

> "his astralus [sic] in the ancle [sic] joint...(to the) extremity of the great and second toe—metatarsal bones being probably sliced."[57]

---

57 Tolmie, William Fraser, *Physician and Fur Trader, The Journal of William Fraser Tolmie*, Mitchell Press Limited, Vancouver B.C., Canada,

Tolmie decided that since the injury was *"of no ordinary description"* he was obliged to interfere with company plans for his work assignment to Fort McLoughlin.

Tolmie had great difficulty, even on the second day, in stopping the hemorrhaging when he examined the wound. He administered one gram of opium and two grams of calomel. The danger of infection was tremendous. Most men died of wounds like Pierre's, some even less severe, with no antibiotics and only rudimentary pain killers.

Four days later, on June 14th, McDonald agreed with Tolmie, respecting the doctor's professional attendance to his patient. There was no hesitation on the subject, due to the dangerous state of the patient. Tolmie's baggage and personal belongings were removed from the schooner. He would remain at Fort Nisqually for the entire summer of 1833. Tolmie's official HBC assignment would wait.

The laboring-class men of Fort Nisqually were not preoccupied with the injuries to Pierre Charles, nor were they totally occupied with the many customers at the new trade store. By mid-June crops planted in the early spring were "showing", Tolmie recorded:

> *"The potatoes were greatly improved by the rains of Monday and Tuesday & also the carrots and turnips—a pen has been formed near the tent of Pierre Charles, the superintendent of works, in which the oxen were enclosed & nearer the bank of the (creek) substantial house of red pine, but which wanted a roof for its completion. The space occupied by this infant establishment is perhaps 100 square yards, & it is enclosed on all sides by tall pines except towards the NE, where it is open to the boundless & picturesque prairie. It was gratifying to witness this; the first step towards colonization & the calm stillness of the gloaming was well calculated to excite pleasing sensations."*[58]

Potatoes, peas, carrots, turnips, radishes, corn, and cabbage were sprouting. Due attention was accorded the crops to keep the wild varmints away and provide the ditches necessary for irrigation waterways. Root cellars were dug for eventual preservation of the produce for winter use.

Young Doctor Tolmie, a temporary resident of a very new establishment in a very foreign land, suddenly found himself temporarily in charge of the place. After all, he could read and write. Literacy gave him automatic English Gentleman rank and full HBC authority. As the only other member of the Gentleman Class present, McDonald left Tolmie to rule with full authority as he took leave on June 20, 1833. McDonald was fully aware that his replacement would arrive in a few days (June 27, 1833), but he trusted

---

58 ibid.

young Tolmie's leadership instincts for those seven days.

The first business at Fort Nisqually garnered 380 very valuable furs collected at the tiny outpost. The furs were carried by three horses to Fort Vancouver, under McDonald's leadership. McDonald knew his replacement, Chief Trader Charles Herron, would arrive soon aboard the schooner *Cadboro*. But Tolmie was thrust temporarily into the leadership role. Tolmie would run the place until Herron arrived, all the while caring for his severely injured patient, Pierre Charles.

The biggest problem Tolmie faced was the low inventory of trade goods. The traders had sold almost all the inventory to obtain the furs McDonald was transporting southward. However, the situation was more serious: the men faced a survival problem with equally-low food supplies. Pierre Charles, an excellent marksman, was the most experienced hunter in the small group. He had brought in three very fine elk and a deer a short time earlier. It was no small service for hard-working men. And now, with Pierre Charles incapable of even walking, food supplies were diminishing rapidly. Luckily, with McDonald and his assistants gone, the demands were slightly reduced.

Tolmie, as the man in charge, instituted a new policy, which did not satisfy the hunger each man was facing: Tolmie demanded the observance of Sunday as a day of rest and religious instruction. Reading Tolmie's journal, we learn of his very extensive reading habits. That Sunday morning in June 1833, Tolmie rose at 5 am "reading Cowper's Poem on Charity until about 8 am".[59] He held services for the men of his command and the local Indians. Mostly he told them of Christian thinking and read Bible verses.

His Sunday observance policy affected not only the men of Fort Nisqually, but the Nisqually, Puyallup, Squaxin, and other nearby tribes. The religious aspect of the policy began a long and difficult acculturation in religious practices. Soon enough, the gradual British-favored policy would be replaced by an abrupt American treaty-signing process that imposed an emotionally wrenching transition, tearing traditional tribal sinews apart.

Closing the store on Sundays, Tolmie reduced consumer demand at the Trade Store by one seventh. To further reduce food consumption at the fort, and help transport the valuable furs, McDonald took Gilbert Powers and two Sandwich Islanders (Kanakas) with him on the overland journey to Fort Vancouver. Tolmie was left with a small crew of assistants. Pierre Charles, in his sickbed but in an improving state, James Rindale, J.B. Ouvré and four others remained at Fort Nisqually. They were literally surrounded by thousands of Indians. Only goodwill obtained through fair trades kept the outnumbered new people safe.

---

59   Ibid., p. 201.

Tolmie received explicit instructions from McDonald regarding how the business should be conducted after his departure. *Trade Blotter* notes and Journal entries were to be made for every single transaction, disbursement, return and trade for furs, provisions and necessities. He was to supervise the building of a frame house for the laboring men. It was placed between Pierre's canvas tent/shed at the south end of the store. Pickets were installed in front of both buildings, leaving only a narrow path between them and the high water mark. A gate was placed in the middle of the front line of pickets nearest the water. Fort Nisqually was secure.

The young surgeon often set out to collect plant specimens. Tolmie had learned at Glasgow University that plants were the primary source of possible new medicines. He was usually on horseback with three "attendants:" McKie, Brown, and Tahi (a Sandwich Islander "Kanaka"). To maintain his status, a proper Gentleman needs European-style attendants.

As their temporary leader, Tolmie kept the men busy with regular daily tasks, "jobbing about the place". One of the vexing problems was the tendency of the oxen to wander unless working or constantly attended by one of the men. A somewhat ineffective device was tried. They yoked the oxen together while feeding, then kept the yoke in place. At least that prevented them from going different directions.

McDonald's replacement, Chief Trader Francis Herron, arrived aboard the *Vancouver* on Thursday, June 27, 1833 (actually two days before the earthquake), aboard the supply ship *Vancouver*. Trading began immediately and in earnest. Altogether, Tolmie counted 66 furs and skins taken in during his short tenure of six days. With an experienced trader and ample goods for sale, the company netted 90 furs of all kinds that first day after the *Vancouver* was unloaded. Each prime beaver pelt sold for one 2½ point blanket, which was the most popular trade item.

Chief Trader Herron's first known personal entry in the *Journal*, made through July 11th, says the men were set to work clearing away brush in a forty foot square at the top of the bank to build a temporary trading fort. This location is now referred to as the 1833 historic site.

Herron, from Northern Ireland, was described by Tolmie as tall and stout, with *"a striking resemblance to my father."* Herron had a low opinion of Archibald McDonald, his predecessor. Herron was certain that McDonald manipulated an assignment to Fort Colville, outing Herron from that well-established and comfortable post. Herron was greatly disappointed at being assigned to undeveloped Fort Nisqually, on the rainy side of the Cascade Mountains.

The Europeans were nervous because of the more demanding trades Herron had made and the changes to the established routines. The store had a huge and desirable inventory. Herron changed sleeping arrangements to accommodate his family. He created, then converted, some available space in the store to a bedroom for his wife and Pierre Charles' wife. Tolmie was left alone and not at ease. He loaded five guns, placed them in the corner, loading a rifle, gun, and pistol at the head of his bed. Tolmie gave his dog to James Rendall,[60] who was told to bunk with William Brown and John McKay (pronounced McKie and sometimes spelled that way).

Nature augmented their fears on June 29, 1833, when the earth shook violently at least twice at around 1:40 pm, according to James Rendall's pocket watch. The Indians were convinced that the new Chief Trader was a powerful man. He had gone to the hills to shake the ground.

Herron was still not pleased with the physical location of Fort Nisqually. He decided to move everything to the "Shoots River" (De Chutes). On June 30, the move commenced. Herron took a leaking boat filled with some building materials to construct a small shed. Three large canoes were loaded with provisions and manned by Indians under the command of Ouvré. A raft of logs was dispatched, too. Bourshaw went overland with the oxen team. Tolmie sent his trunk, gingham bucket, and three reams of brown botanizing paper, but stayed behind to read his Bible. A Scottish Gentleman HBC visitor was not expected to participate in physical work.

Within two days Herron changed his mind again. On July 3rd the move was reversed. One S'Klallam Leader-Chief, from the northern tip of the Kitsap Peninsula, refused to travel any further south than Nisqually. He was a producer of an abundance of beaver pelts, and a valuable customer. The S'Klallam (Strong People) lived in at least 15 villages containing approximately 1,500 individuals.

Herron decided to return to the original site to please this serious customer. By July 4th Herron had his home in the building originally intended for the men. One of the three open bays became a mess hall of sorts, and the other was his private family bedroom. Nisqually-style reed mats created "walls" between the apartments.

Herron was still unhappy. He sat all day July 7 with Tolmie. He wanted to quit the HBC service. His difficulty was deciding on a place to retire. On July 8th, Herron decided to move the Fort 20 miles north. He sent Tolmie on a three-day site-evaluation safari. Tolmie reported "unfavorably" on all possible sites north from Nisqually to today's Elliott

---

60 James Rendall was a long time cooper from Fort Langley who became a short-timer at Fort Nisqually, assisting with the care of Pierre Charles' injury. He returned to Kirkness, Orkney, in 1846. http://www.fortlangley.ca/JamesRendall.html

Bay, on the highly populated Duwamish River.

On July 15 Tolmie was sent to examine a site upstream along Sequalitchew Creek. He recommended a spot 200 yards from the small Sequalitchew Lake, on the border of the plain where a path emerged eastward from the shoreline forest.

The new Chief Trader surveyed the area. He found a swampy area slightly more than 1¼ miles from the beach trade store. The spot was ideal for pasturage of the oxen. Once the swamp was drained adjacent to about twelve acres of natural meadow land, some simple farming could begin. These two areas would become the basis of unforeseen farming and ranching business. The superlative attraction of the location was the nearby fresh, clear water of Sequalitchew Creek.

Herron employed his men to deconstruct the storehouse and build another dwelling house. With the help of 23 Indians, the store inventory was carried up to the new location. By 8 pm, the old store was completely dismantled. Before breakfast the next day, all of the materials and inventory were moved. The Indian laborers and company servants were paid 10 charges of ammunition and 8 inches of tobacco to dismantle the original building and reassemble it in the new location.

The newly rebuilt house faced eastward toward Mount Tacoma. It measured 48x20 feet and was divided into three apartments: one for Herron's family, one for the commercial store, and one for the men.

Temporarily, Tolmie was granted 10 feet, more than half, of the store space. His status as HBC Gentleman gave him this privacy. He carpeted it with reed mats and hung red baize[61] on the walls. The wall-hanging was meant more for insulation against open cracks in the walls than as decoration. On July 18th, the vacated buildings that remained at the beach site were occupied by Indians.

A grass fire broke out on July 17th, consuming everything in its path for several miles in every direction. It was all grassland, punctuated occasionally by clumps of Garry oak. The new buildings were saved from the flames, as the wind blew away from the structures.[62]

On Friday, July 20, 1833 Doctor Tolmie was visited by Chilalucum, Chief of the Snoqualmies. Tolmie, trying to increase the customer base of the tiny store, gave the Chief a *"capote and a pair of trowsers for his general good conduct"* and asked Chilalucum to visit the S'Klallams. Chilalucum was to invite that tribe to return to trade at Fort Nisqually's

---

61   A coarse woolen fabric, now often used to cover billiards tables and casino gaming tables.
62   The Nisqually annually set fire to burn off the dry grasses, encouraging new green grass growth which lured forest animals out of the forests. Their arson strategy was to enable easier autumn hunting.

original location near Sequalitchew Creek.

Five days later the S'Klallam arrived with furs to trade, interrupting Tolmie's reading of *Moore's Irish Melodies*. On Sunday, while Tolmie read the *Book of Acts* and *Paley's Theology*, a horse went missing. A fruitless search was undertaken for the animal and the thief. After three days, the *Journal of Occurrences* states that a suspect thief was also absent from the area.

The peas and corn crops were sprouting in July, but the potatoes sprouts were still to be seen. Cabbages, onions, and corn were transplanted to a fertile edge of the small lake. Tolmie estimated 500 to 600 arable acres in the nearby meadow. He found some ripe fruit (*Galteria shallon*[63]) in the woods near the lush meadowlands.

The beaver trade continued with visiting customers from Snoqualmie, Soquamish, Payallipa, Chechellis, Kachet, Nuamish, Nisqually, Squaxin[64] bands. They brought bundles as large as 50 to as small as two pelts. Soon the inventory of trade goods was low again, leaving little choice for the Indian customers. On July 27th, a band of S'Klallams arrived in two huge war canoes carrying 40 Thuanok men. These frustrated customers either waited for new supplies, or carried their furs away with plans to return later.

The wait was not long. New trade goods arrived overland along the Cowlitz Trail from Fort Vancouver. Along with the regular and usual items for the trade, this shipment included 300 Hudson's Bay Company blankets, the premium item from the Indian point of view. Trade was very brisk.

By August 2nd the men completed packing 457 beaver and otter skins into 90–pound packs for transport to Fort Vancouver. The very next day some three hundred Indians from four tribes arrived at the fledgling Fort Nisqually. These Indian traders sold their furs with careful deliberation, discussion, and bargaining. It took three days for Chief Trader Herron to collect 205 more skins in trade for blankets and other goods.

The men of the Fort were busy with the daily tasks of surviving on the frontier. Two men were sawing pickets for fencing. Two others were squaring timbers for a new farm dwelling house. Pierre Charles had recovered sufficiently to supervise most of the work with the aid of his crutches. Some six hundred bundles of natural hay had been cut and stacked near the marsh.

With trade goods inventory and supplies running low again, it was good news that the old trader Ouvré brought on the 14th. He reported that the schooner *Cadboro* was

---

63 *Galteria shallon* is Latin for Salal, a leathery-leaved shrub in the heather family. Salal has edible sweet berries and young leaves. It was a significant food source for Native Americans. It is used as a sweetener, to thicken salmon eggs, flavor fish soup, and to counter the tartness of Oregon-Grapes.

64 Spelling of tribal names is as found in the HBC *Journal of Occurrences*.

spotted in Puyallup Bay (today's Commencement Bay). The *Cadboro* brought news that the *Ganymede* was expected at Fort Vancouver soon with more supplies from London. The news of these expected supplies, and the power projected by the ship's presence, gave Herron the advantage he felt he needed to raise prices in the trade store. The new price was announced as two beaver skins for a 2½ point blanket. The old price was one prime beaver pelt for a two point blanket.

Actually, the new price had been set by the Board of Governors of the HBC in London some months earlier. The timing and circumstance of announcing the price at the point of sale was entirely up to the local establishment. For quite some time the new prices were a sticking point during bargaining. Little trading was accomplished for several days. The idea of a "fixed price" was difficult for Indian fur traders who always bargained for the best "deal."

September 1833[65] saw a throng of Indians on the grounds of Fort Nisqually, even though few were willing to trade at the higher price. With little trade activity, the Fort laborers were kept busy with the erection of another new larger 20'x30' trade store. This construction took several days with all of the men involved, save for two who were stacking hay and Doctor Tolmie who was again "botanizing" for plants from which new medicines might be concocted. He collected many previously unknown plants for English scientists to study. Some plants even ended in Kew Gardens, London's exclusive Botanical gardens[66].

Thursday, August 29, 1833, Doctor Tolmie set out on another botanizing excursion toward Mount Tacoma. He did not return until September 5th but brought back a stimulating variety of plant specimens. Tolmie hired a Nisqually man named Lachelet as his guide for a serious trip to Mt. Rainier. He rented three horses from Lachelet's friends. The plan was to ride one and use the other two as pack animals to carry his bedroll, food supplies, and plant specimens he intended to collect. They planned for the trip to take four days, according to Lachelet comments.

There was a tremendous thunderstorm on the planned day of departure. The Indians and horses did not show up until the next day. Departure was further delayed with packing and finalizing arrangements for the trip. At last, about 3 pm, the expedition

---

65 On September 10, 1833, the brig *Tuscany* docked in Calcutta, India. She carried 100 tons of crystal clear ice, cut from the winter ponds of Massachusetts. The tropical British colony in Calcutta was seeing inroads of American entrepreneurs Frederic Tudor and Nathaniel J. Wyeth of Boston, the world's first "Ice Merchants".

66 The Royal Botanical Gardens at Kew are located 10 miles from central London along the Thames River.

was underway.

Lachelet was paid a blanket, his nephew Lashima received ammunition. Others on the trip were not paid, but Nuckalkat and Quillhiamish of the Puyallup Tribe of Indians were welcomed by the Doctor for their knowledge of the terrain to be traversed and the fresh meat they might provide the whole party. These extra men considered it to be a hunting trip, expecting to shoot some elk, and deer. They were so positive of a successful hunt that they had already promised the animal fat to their friends.

Tolmie was impressed with the natural beauty of the area as they crossed the grassy prairies[67] and the flood plain of the Puyallup River Valley. After a delicious salal salad supper, they spent the first night sleeping in drizzling rain.

As he slept under a large pine tree for some limited protection from the rain, Tolmie was suddenly attacked by a large decayed tree branch that fell, hitting his leg and inflicting some injury. Although bruised, he was able to proceed.

The party got underway again at dawn on Friday, August 30. Later they had breakfast of bread, salal leaves and berries, and dried cockles with a small piece of venison. In Europe, a Gentleman of his stature would refer to those accompanying him on an excursion as "attendants," but here Tolmie labeled them companions. Perhaps this is a glimpse of the doctor's personal sense of human equality, regardless of rank, race, or station of life in the pre-Victorian Era.

With the drizzle continuing to fall on the travelers, they met some Tekatat Indians in a small village of three families. Tolmie, the trader, immediately acquired some dried meat in exchange for some ammunition balls and some finger rings. The Tekatats insisted on feeding the travelers, as was their custom. Lachelet insisted that the custom was to eat a great amount, promising to fast later. Two large kettles were filled with stew meat and bouillon. The travelers quickly emptied the kettles to please their hosts, as well as fill their own bellies.

The Tolmie Party moved on in the heavy mist, through dense thickets and occasional prairies. They descended into the valley, proceeded upstream, and crossed the Puyallup River several times as it meandered. About 7 pm they came upon a cedar plank house near a dry part of the river bed. Here Tolmie examined the water, declaring it "impregnated with white clay".

The Puyallup River continues to this day delivering the "white clay" sediment eroding from the Cascade Mountains. Even casual observers notice the distinct tan color demarcation of Puyallup River water entering the darker blue water of Commencement Bay.

---

67 Ten miles southwest of Fort Nisqually they crossed enormous natural prairies. Some 2,929 acres of those prairies would become the site of McChord Air Force Base in the 1940s.

From the beginning Lahalet—also known as T'ck-wen-tom—had tried to discourage Tolmie from ascending to the snow line of Mount Rainier. He tried again that evening before the entire group rested for the night, again unsuccessfully.

Freshly-caught salmon trout were prepared for breakfast on Saturday, August 31st. Quillhiamish left a stick standing in the ground with the fish gills attached. It was a sign to other travelers that fish could be caught at that spot. Better, but not great weather moved them into a day of intense travel through cedar and pine forests with uneven ground. They necessarily crossed the river several times seeking the least resistance from nature. Tolmie admitted his endurance to be inferior to that of his companions. The Indians led the way "at a smart trot which obliges me to rest," Tolmie said. His bruised leg was not mentioned.

Northwest rain poured down that Sunday. Tolmie was discouraged by the rain and diminishing provisions. For breakfast they ate dried venison, meat boiled in a cedar basket with hot stones. Tolmie traded his HBC blanket, which he used as a coat during daytime travel, for a capote that had an ownership that included, at one time or another, almost every Nisqually. The capote was warmer, but not drier, than the blanket. Along with the rain the intrepid explorers crossed and recrossed the Puyallup several times. The men were wet to the bone. Supper consisted of berries warmed in a small kettle.

Tolmie and his companions found a dry spot along the bank of the river to get some rest. The current had eroded a portion of the bank to form an overhanging shelf with a very rugged shore. Tolmie called it a "troglodytic mansion".

Monday dawned with more optimism. Blue skies revealed the snowy peak that was their objective. Tolmie and his companions crossed three miles of steep river valley toward the lofty peak. They ascended toward the spot with the most apparent snow. The mountain seemed to evade them.

While resting on a grassy mound near several dead trees, Tolmie took his afternoon tea. A few hours later, the explorers reached the snow line. Quickly they were ankle deep in the cold white stuff. Tolmie, Lachelet, and Nuckalkat set out for the summit, clearly unaware they were still miles away from the 14,411 foot peak. It was the first time a white person had approached Mount Tacoma. Tolmie undoubtedly climbed higher that day than any other person before him.

On Monday, September 2, 1833, the Tolmie Botanizing Expedition reached its goal. The doctor had collected a vasculum[68] full of plants at the snow line. He recorded:

---

68 A vasculum is a kind of case or box used by botanists to carry specimens as they are collected. It is a flattened cylindrical metal case with a lengthwise opening. It is lined with moist cloth to maintain a cool, humid environment. The vasculum is carried by a horizontal strap so specimens lie flat inside.

> The air temperatures "at the base 54 degrees—at the summit of ascent 47 degrees."

Tolmie's reference to "the summit" has been misinterpreted by some as meaning the full summit of Mount Tacoma. He was referring to the highest point of his personal ascent, possibly to the snow line at Tolmie Peak, on the north side of the mountain. That prominence has been named after the HBC doctor in recognition of the significant pioneer explorer of Mount Tahoma, as the Indians had called the mountain for centuries.

Tuesday brought heavy rain. The small party of botanizers and hunters slept that night on a woody islet of the Puyallup River. Before sunrise the wind shifted and a heavy frost set in. Tolmie sent Quilliash back to the snow line to measure the air temperature. In the sparkling sunshine above the clouds the temperature was 33 degrees. As the clouds cleared, Tolmie looked south-south-east from his campsite. "Mount Rainier appeared surprisingly splendid and magnificent."

The fatigued Tolmie party had a tedious four-day journey ahead as they walked over the river and through the woods and across the prairies. They reached the Tekatats who again provided a feast, this time of boiled elk and salmon berries. Tolmie pushed on, completing his botanizing adventure to Mount Rainier on Saturday, September 7, 1833.

While Tolmie was away botanizing, the new Chief Factor, Francis Herron, made known his displeasure of the entire site along Sequalitchew Creek. He was of the opinion that a more northerly site would be better for business. Herron ordered a reconnaissance of Whidbey Island, then announced to the Indians his intention to move. Stunned by the abrupt announcement after the shipping delays, Indians of the south sound declared they would not go north to trade. It was from the far north that their enemies came. The northern tribes raided the south sound villages for wives and slaves. To be forced to trade in northern lands was far too dangerous. They refused to discuss the proposal. Herron soon relented and immediately began to adjust the local site to better meet the needs of the Company and the desire of their customers.

From September 22, to November 13, 1833, Chief Factor Herron was delivering the accumulated fur to Fort Vancouver. Tolmie was in charge, again, at Fort Nisqually. He recorded many interesting facts about Fort Nisqually and his new friends. He told of his friendship with La-ha-let, a *"gigantic man"* of the Nisqually Nation. At one point Tolmie engaged his friend in a contest of the "putting stone" (shot put). Tolmie was evidently the more practiced in the traditional Scottish sport[69] bettering his larger friend's throw

---
69 The Scottish Stone Put event is similar to the modern shot put, but uses a large 20 to 26 pound "Braemer Stone," which is thrown from a standing position with one hand cradling it in the neck until released.

by half a yard.

Stories began to circulate among the Indians of the arrival of an American fur trade ship on Puget Sound. The story said the Americans, or "Bostons," were offering better prices than the new "fixed price" offered by HBC. A lack of a monopoly would bring about a competitive price reduction. Fort Nisqually held the price after deciding the Indian story was cleverly fabricated to affect prices.

In October, Chief Factor Herron had all of the men squaring logs except Pierre Charles, who was advised by his doctor to refrain from work, even though his severe foot injury was healing nicely. Pickets were being installed to link the front corners of the house and the store. This would provide a small courtyard and some privacy, as well as protection in case of an attack. Soon 200 pieces, each about 10 feet long, were squared and ready for direct use. It was a good thing. As the Nisqually began to move to their fall fishing habitation for the purpose of laying in a stock of salmon for the winter, a violent wind laid prostrate the pickets in front of the store. Some laborers were set to work digging a deeper trench and resetting the pickets. Others were building wheels and a wagon, perhaps the first wheeled vehicle in the Puget Sound region.

On October 15, 1833 Doctor Tolmie wrote in his journal,

> *"A fine view of Tuchoma, or Mt. Rainier, appearing in relief against the cloudless firmament."*[70]

The Fort was finally taking a recognizable shape by November. Men were building a pit saw and some chimneys for their homes. Clay was collected from a nearby island (probably Ketron) to make bricks and mortar. The fireplaces helped fend off the typical damp, cool winter. With the sawn wood from the saw pit they even built some furniture, the first country-made furniture in the area.

During trading hours at the store, only a few Indian customers were allowed to enter the store at any one time. Others were allowed into the courtyard in front of the store. If more customers arrived they were enclosed in the courtyard in front of the laborer's dwelling. Indians were never allowed into HBC men's private living quarters with the new arrangement.

The possibility of a raid, or an attack, seemed very real. It seems that a S'Klallam Chief's son was slain by an HBC employee, Mr. McLeod, at some other place. The S'Klallam were rumored to be planning to seek revenge by attacking Fort Nisqually.

---

70 Large, R. G. editor, *The Journals of William Tolmie, Physician and Fur Trader*, p. 242, Mitchell Press Limited, Vancouver, B.C. Canada, 1963.

Security was at least as relevant to the fur traders as it is to modern merchants, with door locks and video cameras.

Doctor Tolmie's first serious patient, Pierre Charles, was recovering nicely. He was back to work, and that was what really counted. On December 12, Doctor William Fraser Tolmie left Fort Nisqually aboard the HBC ship *Cadboro*, destined for Fort McLoughlin on Milbanke Sound. In only five months at Milbanke, Tolmie was instrumental in moving the Company trade post to the new Fort Simpson location. The new site proved to be a more profitable (and defendable) location. Those assignments also provided a great deal of experience to Tolmie. He didn't realize how well the experience would serve him at Fort Nisqually, or that he would return ten years in his future.

1834

AMERICAN WILLIAM SUBLETTE built Fort Laramie just as the Rocky Mountain Fur Company was absorbed into the American Fur Company. Fort Laramie soon became a useful spot for Oregon Trail travelers.

Reverend Jason Lee, an American Methodist Missionary, arrived at Fort Vancouver after traversing the route soon to be widely known as the Oregon Trail. He was cordially greeted by Dr. McLoughlin, who politely encouraged the preacher to build his intended Methodist Mission south of the Columbia River in the Willamette River Valley.

President Jackson ordered federal troops to halt the riot of Irish immigrant workers on the Chesapeake and Ohio Canal. He was the first President to use the U.S. army in a labor dispute.

Riots broke out in Philadelphia and New York after large anti-slavery meetings were held. In Philadelphia, 31 houses and two churches were condemned when citizens voted to reimburse the black owners for the damage done by the rioters. A town meeting condemned the white rioters and the noise coming out of the Negro churches.

An anti-Catholic riot destroyed a convent and school in Charlestown, Massachusetts in August. False rumors of a woman being held against her will apparently caused the riot.

On June 30, Congress passed a law that made all land west of the Mississippi River "Indian Country" except the states of Missouri, Louisiana, and the Territory of Arkansas. President Jackson said, "The Aborigines" can learn the "arts of civilization" and "attest to the humanity and justice of this government." Jackson was the US President who forced the Cherokee Removal, often called the Trail of Tears.

Cyrus McCormick was granted a patent for an automatic grain-reaping machine. Farmers who saw it said it would reduce their reliance on seasonal labor. In Illinois, a struggling twenty-five-year-old attorney named Abraham Lincoln enjoyed an election victory as he began a term in the Illinois Assembly.

A slight departure, here, to provide the reader with a sense of the organization of the

Hudson's Bay Company. By a contract drawn up with the power of law, the company most often confined an employee to a particular location for a set number of years. Young men were hired for a specific term of years and a particular service and stipend. The most frequent term of years was seven, and then often renewed by another seven years. The hiring and contracting process could weed out the more ordinary men.

Literate young clerks (HBC Governor George Simpson called them "semi-literate") often had charge of the daily mercantile aspects of the Indian trade store. They were required to have the skills necessary for detailed record keeping in journals and jotters, the account books and spreadsheets of the era. HBC demanded they obey first, then learn to command. In time, a clerk could be assigned to a first-rate establishment as a fur trader and eventually achieve the social rank of a Gentleman.

The Gentlemen lived in comfort and were nearly always Scots, or at least Irish or English. Being the greatest in the land, they could do pretty much as they pleased. They often commanded territory far in excess of the land area of the monarch of his original homeland. While all buildings and property belonged to the Company, the Gentlemen always took the most favorable houses, apartments, or tents. In a canoe, they were always in the center and without a paddle. Their abodes were often divided into rooms for specific purposes, while clerks resided in the corner of a store house, and laborers often slept on the ground. The uniform of the Gentlemen was the most fashionable: a beaver top hat, wool trousers, and a great coat, with fine linen shirt and tie or cravat. Their boots were often handmade to exact size for each foot. The Gentlemen could please themselves with hunting, fishing, pleasure rides in the countryside, and other joyous pastimes. The Gentlemen must never degrade themselves with even the simplest physical labor. Their basic human needs were met by efforts of others. They were the object of attraction and admiration. They had free use of tobacco, imported beverages, and the envy of the lower classes and the local maidens. Gentlemen of the fur trade lived a life of luxury and longevity seldom equaled in any society. Gentlemen often retired to their origins with very few outliving their substantial means.

Voyageurs constituted a significant segment of the fur trade population, and deserved no less praise. They were the canoe men, the backbone of communication and commerce. Most were French Canadian. They glorified arduous labor, enduring hardship as a badge of honor. While the Gentleman sat in the center, Voyageurs paddled the birch bark canoe to the most remote locations in mere days. Voyageurs could move a fully loaded 1,000 pound canoe on the Columbia to Lake Superior 1,000 miles in 100 days.

The next social or ethnic class to note is native Sandwich Islanders. Also known as Kanaka, the Owyhee (Hawaii) people were honest, trustworthy, loyal, courageous,

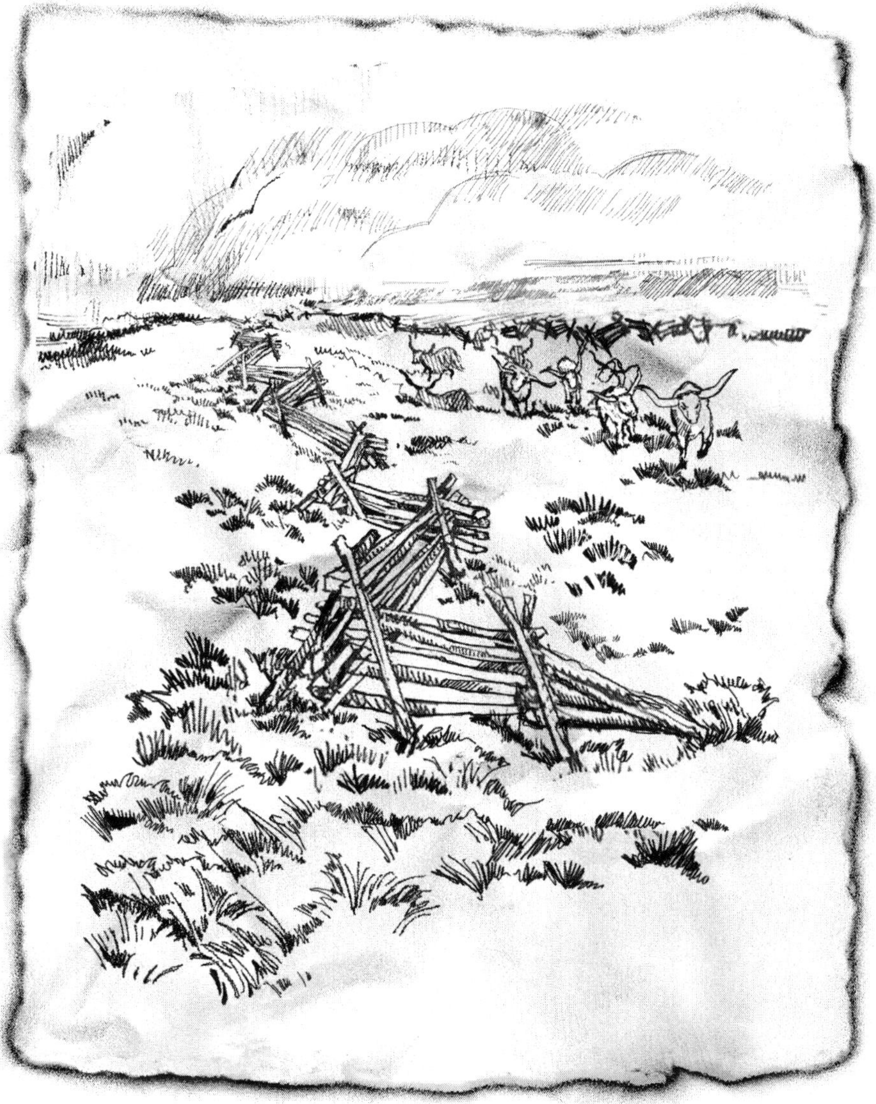

and willing to perform industrious physical tasks. As excellent swimmers, they saved Company effects and men in many perilous situations. It is said that it was nearly impossible to drown if a single Kanaka was nearby. This class was most often paid little more than mere food and clothing, an insignificant expense that kept them in consideration at contract signing times. Kanakas always exhibited a fidelity and zeal to protect and provide for the Gentlemen's welfare. They were not wanting in personal courage. In conflict situations, the Kanaka were always ready to rush the enemy, but never qualified for any rank of company leader.

In the earliest years of the Columbia fur trade, nearly one third of the HBC employees were Iroquois from the Montreal area. They had great skill as voyageurs, trappers, and traders, but were somewhat fickle, sullen, and indolent. There are accounts of cowardice and treachery to add to their independent streak, as well. Too often the Iroquois trader gave away company trade goods to gain favor of, or even purchase, a particularly attractive young female. Iroquois seldom rose in rank in the company.

Another group of fur trade participants was the Métis. They were the mixed race offspring of European and Indian unions. Bay men were encouraged to make alliances with local Indians to garner business advantages, but some of those alliances were strictly personal. Native women were often officially hired as cooks, couriers, or outdoor drudges and day laborers in the fields. The vigilance of these women was often instrumental in the safety of the forts. They were attached to the men of the fort and often they also attached their Indian families to the fort. Many Gentlemen had a "country wife," as a Native American marriage partner was labeled.

Perhaps the most unfortunate individuals in the fur trade business were the Gentlemen's sons. Often indulged, seldom taught industry or frugality, the son was nevertheless a Gentleman, too. Those sons who became employed in the fur trade most often knew more of mischief and less of the required skills.

Account ledgers and trade blotter rosters provide a sense of the national and ethnic population diversity that existed at Fort Nisqually in 1833-34:

1833

Silvin Bourgeau—French Canadian
Herea—French Canadian
Louis Segohaneuchtal (Sagohanenchto)—Iroquois
Archibald McDonald—Fur Trader

1834

John McKay—English
Pierre Charles—French Canadian
William Brown—English
Charles Proulx—English
Jean Baptiste Ouvré—French Canadian
Francis Herron, Chief Trader—English
Dominique Farron—French Canadian
Pierre Martineau—French Canadian
Anawaskum McDonald—Métis (Indian/Scot)
Simon Plomondeau (Plomondon)—French Canadian
Hereea (Hiria, Herea)—French Canadian
Peter Tai (Tahi)—Kanaka
William Kittson (Guillaume)—French/English
Charles Herron[71]—English

Life at Fort Nisqually continued as it began only a year or so earlier. The diversity of the mixed nationalities and ethnicities of HBC engages (contracted workmen) was an advantage that had not been planned. It seems someone among the group was always suited to the various tasks. The Trader, Chief Trader, Factor, or Chief Factor at most HBC establishments was a Scot, an Irishman, or an Englishman. Always stern with employees and customers, he acted in the manner of a superior military officer. His power of command was unequalled and seldom challenged—never successfully—by laboring class men. He was in turn challenged by an equally tough tribal potentate, usually a Chief or Shaman who commanded, and demanded, respect as the local royalty.

Most Native American Chiefs considered themselves equal, if not superior, to any simple foreign trader. The Nisqually leaders were not "Indian Chiefs," but were considered leaders of a culture, while the visiting traders were lowly salesmen. Neither could ever turn off their command arrogance, even in the face of equal arrogance. Both developed a toughness that was understood, yet fair. Potential conflict was often avoided by the firmness of the initial cultural contact, which was focused on trade. Violence was never desirable, not inevitable, but nearly always an ultimate resort. One side had a few men with overwhelming weapons, while the other had enormous numbers with

---

71 Fort Nisqually *Indian Shop Blotter*, March 1, 1834-June 30, 1836, transcribed and restructured by Steve A. Anderson, 2008, unpublished manuscript.

primitive weapons.

Many times the Chief Trader sent a surrogate among the tribes to deal with trouble. The ethnic diversity of HBC men worked in favor of this tactic. For example, a Métis individual might smooth over a potential conflict, where a self-righteous Scot could have aggravated the situation. Sometimes a Kanaka employee was selected for the job because he had a local wife. A French Canadian voyageur with experiences in many different tribal groups might have a solution to the disagreement. Customers and merchants wanted to reach agreements for the economic improvement of both positions.

Sometimes the roles were reversed. In these instances, HBC men were the consumers, and the Indians became the merchant suppliers. HBC Traders needed food, guides, transportation, labor, as well as allied protection from more hostile Indians. These services could be had if the price was right. These trades worked well.

As is the case today, neither side of any trade transaction would feel "cheated" more than once. If someone cheated, there was often instant retaliation: sometimes violent efforts were needed to regain "fairness." Most often all traders dealt intelligently with their counterparts. Both sides gained what they wanted from the trades, or there would be no trade. Today we operate the same way. If prices are too high we seek other sources or products to fill our needs. If retailers need more customers, they frequently reduce prices. Even "one day sales" tend to increase transactions. Gifts were offered in the Fur Trade era, just as today we are offered "free" inducements to shop.

One of the difficulties of the inter-cultural trade occurred when the *Cadboro* was unloaded in the fall of 1833. Some 30 Nisqually and Snoqamish men were hired to assist in stevedoring the barrels and boxes of supplies and trade goods from the hold of the schooner. Three hundred blankets were in that shipment. Part of the pay offered and accepted by the temporary longshoremen was a generous portion of rum, freshly delivered in a handsome cask. Rum led directly to a fight between La-ha-let and two Snoqamish men. HBC employee William Ouvré, a French-Canadian Métis, finally broke up the drunken fight. Ouvré may have had some insight that helped him quell the quarrel. Rum was probably the only villain, giving courage to the combatants to raise a smoldering grievance. Thereafter, at Fort Nisqually, rum was seldom used as a reward for hard work. Furthermore, no one was paid until the task was completed.

Construction of the corner bastions began on January 3, 1834 as a simple security measure. There was no military threat to the place, but Chief Factor Herron wasted no time after allowing a New Year's Day "blowout similar to that which they had on Christmas, which afforded them ample enjoyment." After each of those holiday parties the men were not required to work, as they were rather indisposed. The upper floors of the bastions, when the buildings were completed, were frequently used as jails to hold drunken or sobering employees.

Sawing, squaring, hauling, and everything necessary for the preparation of timbers for construction was the order of the day—every day. That winter there was little fur trade, but lots of rain, snow, frost, sleet, and rather disagreeable weather. The work was miserable. Herron claimed little was completed, most of poor quality. Some of the wood for the bastions was from the small oak groves on the Steilacoom prairie.

Some of their time was spent cutting the necessary firewood and roofing the dwelling house with cedar. Men were ill in 1834: winter colds and flu had them sick to incapacity. As an alternative employment, Herron sent five men to Fort Langley for some supplies that should have been retrieved earlier.

Today Fort Nisqually Living History Museum at Point Defiance Park often receives donations of support. Captain McNeill, according to the 1834 *Journal of Occurrences*, made such a gift to the new enterprise. On June 12, 1834, McNeill donated

"a couple of iron pins and about one fathom of Bower Cable Chain[72]"

The circle of generosity continues today when tax advantaged donations are made to the Fort Nisqually Foundation.

In the middle of January, 1834, Fort Nisqually had two feet of snow on the ground. Due to the heavy snow, only 15 beaver had been traded. The Big House received an exterior cedar bark covering for insulation. Temperatures were low, so much of the daily work time was spent cutting and hauling firewood.

Five hunters could not find targets, as the temperatures dropped even lower. They killed only one deer and ate it all, except one leg joint, before returning to the Fort. Finally the cold weather broke on January 31st with welcome rain and a severe "hurricane wind".

An Indian came to the Fort with the bad news that a ship was wrecked on Cape Flattery, at the extreme northwest corner of what is now Washington State[73]. He had a piece of very thin (rice) paper with unintelligible markings on it. The verbal story said that all hands perished except four, who were captured and held as slaves by the Makah. News like this was often discounted as an attempt to put pressure on the trade price for beaver. Herron's bargaining did not budge. The price was "fixed" at two prime beaver pelts for a single two-point wool HBC blanket. In a few years the price would rise to

---

72 The Bower anchor, carried in the bow, is attached to the ship by a chain, cable, or rope.

73 The nautical distance between Nisqually and Cape Flattery is about 250 miles. The overland distance is about 175 paved highway miles today.

double that, and Indian traders saw the two-beaver price as prohibitory of a good trade.

The scrap of paper and the verbal word of the shipwreck were sent to Fort Vancouver, where a force of thirty men was organized to rescue the sailors from slavery. The winter weather returned with a vengeance in February. About a foot of snow fell overnight on the 16th, after a week of heavy rain and high winds. The rescue force was turned back by the weather, distance, and vicious undergrowth along the simple trails to Cape Flattery.

Grizzled old Jeanne Baptiste Ouvré was sent out to trade, toward the New Dungeness village along the Straits of Juan de Fuca. He returned with a few skins and some welcome fresh venison. Everyone had a full day's ration as a treat. Ouvré also reported on the shipwreck story. He said it was a "pure fabrication" according to the "Chlallum" (S'Klallam Tribe), who occupied villages along the Straits.

Ouvré and Brown were sent on a trading expedition to Ouvré's (Duwamish)[74] River. Others returned from Fort Langley with some supplies, but not all that Herron had requested. Herron also complained that the supplies were "rather damp." Pierre Charles, sufficiently recovered from the foot injury, led a hunting party that finally found some success, returning with eight deer. Finally they had a larder of food, even though the snow was still at least half a foot deep.

Herron put the men to work cutting fence rails, while the S'Klallams came in with about fifty small beaver to trade. As the ground grew bare of snow, baby George Herron was born to Chief Factor Francis Herron and his wife Rosette. Little is known of this event, since the Journal pages from the spring of 1834 are missing.

Francis Herron did not like his Fort Nisqually assignment from the beginning. He said his assignment at Fort Nisqually was "not an enviable one." He continued:

> "...with (only) seven most miserable hands, the refuse of the country, I had on the bare beach to raise the tariff two fold. I think... Puget Sound will not answer as a substitute for Fort Vancouver as projected..."

That discussion was aimed at the location of Fort Vancouver, on the Columbia, where ships were regularly lost crossing the bar at the mouth. One argument said that a more northerly location could provide safer shipping and eliminate either Langley or Nisqually with a single site on Whidby Island.[75] Eventually a site on Vancouver Island was selected as the new HBC headquarters, but it took another ten years.

---

74 See Anderson, Steve, *Ouvré's River*, Renton Historical Society Newsletter (Historical Fiction)
75 Eventually a site called Fort Camosun was chosen, renamed Fort Albert, on Vancouver Island. Erected in 1843, it was again renamed Fort Victoria, in honor of the young new queen of England in 1846.

1834

Francis Herron came to the HBC as a clerk in 1810. He was promoted to Trader in 1828. After only a few months, he left Fort Nisqually forever. On March 2, 1834, Herron took his wife Josette (Josephet) and baby George to the Willamette Valley. Notes in the *Indian Trade Shop Blotter* indicate that Herron put William Brown in charge of the place, with provisions to supply Ouvré with fur trade goods to continue the business. It seems to have been a hasty departure. There were no further entries in the *Journal of Occurrences* between March 2 and May, 1834. Herron wanted out. His replacement would not arrive until mid-May, 77 days with illiterate Brown in charge.

Herron promptly took complete leave of the Company until 1838, when he returned to Fort Vancouver to be confronted by Dr. McLoughlin. In addition to his Fort Nisqually family, it was revealed that Herron had another wife and family at Norway House in Canada. His Canadian children were already 12 and 17 years old by 1834.

It was a difficult time to be in charge at Fort Nisqually. Upon Herron's departure, twenty-four year old William Brown took command by default, it seems. He hailed from Sandwick[76] on Scotland's Orkney Island, but was a laborer at seven HBC locations in Canada before working at Fort Vancouver and Langley. Now, at Fort Nisqually, Brown was recovering from severe intermittent fever. Pierre Charles was recovering from a life-threatening axe injury to his foot. The Indian customers were protesting increased prices for trade goods. In fact, the Indians became a bit belligerent, which brought apprehension among the somewhat leaderless men of the fort.

Herron was officially replaced at Fort Nisqually by a third CEO, William Kittson, who took command on May 18, 1834, only one year after Archibald McDonald established the outpost. By comparison, keep in mind that a round trip to the London Headquarters of the Hudson's Bay Company could take nearly two years in the 1830s. Changing leadership had a detrimental effect on the new trading post.

The roster listed only nine Company men assigned to Fort Nisqually when William Kittson arrived. The roster included old-time trapper Jeanne Baptiste Ouvré, the recently injured Pierre Charles, William Brown, Simon Plomondon, Louis Sagohanenchata, Silvan Boutgeau, Anawescum McDonald, John McKee, and Tai.

Kittson immediately ordered the kitchen torn down and rebuilt. He also demanded a "large house" often referred to as the "Tyee House" because it was occupied by the Tyee, or chief of the fur traders. The kitchen needed a "better situation." Only the kitchen and the Tyee[77] Gentleman's dwelling had wooden floors, the store and the men's dwelling

---

76 Sandwick is Old Norse, meaning "Sand Bay." It is a parish on the west coast of Mainland, Orkney, four miles north of Stromness, Scotland.

77 Tyee is Chinook jargon for elder brother, senior, boss, leader, chief, or a king salmon of large size.

got by with dirt floors. The Tyee House had two rooms, a dining room and a bedroom. Later a small second bedroom was added to the south side. The dining room measured 15x12 feet. It was used to entertain guests.

Squaring timbers and building chimneys began immediately. Soon Kittson had the men plastering and whitewashing walls, installing flooring and securing roofs. When the kitchen was finished, Kittson called it a "farmer's cottage" then claimed it for his home.

While expecting the brig *Llama*[78] to arrive with supplies from England, Kittson took inventory. With extreme detail he itemized 184 specific varieties of furs, 12 fresh salmon, and 300 pounds of venison while the men "cleaned up about the place."

Finally, the *Llama*, Captain William Henry McNeill, arrived at Fort Nisqually on June 11, 1834. McNeill had been in the Trans-Pacific trade business (northwest furs and Sandwich Island sandal wood) for fifteen years working for a Boston company, Bryant & Sturgis. He was a formidable fur trader, personally taking at least 10% of the entire American fur business on the Northwest Coast.

McNeill was at the Nass River when HBC gentlemen Peter Skene Ogden and George Simpson tried to negotiate with the Russian American Fur Company for an agreement to allow British access up river to the interior territory. The Russians could not seem to grasp the words of several languages used by the HBC negotiators. It was difficult for the British to see the American, McNeill, successfully trading with the Russians in English.

Simpson ordered Chief Factor Dr. John McLoughlin to meet McNeill, offering him employment. It was a strategy of reducing the formidable competition by tuning McNeill into an HBC man. The meeting occurred at Fort Vancouver, but the deal was not complete until McNeill sailed to the Sandwich Islands. In Hawaii the Bryant and Sturgis Company agent, Charles H. Hammatt, had been ordered to close all business in the islands for the company. The Yankee traders were getting out of the Pacific Trade business, because unrest among Hawaiian natives was destroying the sandalwood trade. The *Llama* was for sale.

Captain McNeill bargained with the HBC representative, Duncan Finlayson. McNeill wanted a sale price of $6,500, which would include his commission. Peter Skene Ogden had objected to one of McNeill's crew, but McLoughlin liked the man. To counter the objection, McNeill pointed out that his crew had collected 5,600 furs on a single voyage to the Pacific Northwest Coast. He could easily return to the competitive venture.

---

78 *Lama* was the spelling of the ship's name in all of the log books signed by Captain McNeill. The actual name of the ship used the more traditional spelling of *Llama*. McNeill always refrained from using the double letters, even though his own name, when correctly spelled, ended in the same double letters. Wilkes named McNeil Island, which is actually, and officially, misspelled.

McNeill received a personal commission for the sale of his cargo, and another commission for the sale of the ship. He persuaded McLoughlin to increase his salary and hire his crew. McNeill got a new employer, doing exactly what he had been doing, with the same men, in the same places, and for more money. He was a shrewd trader indeed.

McNeill's arrival at Fort Nisqually renewed the story of a shipwreck on Cape Flattery. McNeill confirmed the truth of the Indian story by sailing there. He picked up two Japanese sailors from the Makah. There was still another Japanese sailor amongst the Indians. McNeill demanded that he be brought forward, but the poor fellow had been sold inland. McNeill expected to pick him up on the return of the *Llama* to the coast, and he did. The Japanese sailors were only teenagers. They were taken to Fort Vancouver, where they were taught some rudimentary English before being sent to England. Eventually they tried to return to Japan, a closed society, but were rejected as contaminated by the outside world. They lived the rest of their lives in Hong Kong.

In the school classroom at Fort Vancouver was teenager Ranald McDonald,[79] son of a fur trader. He too, was a teenager. He learned enough of the Japanese language to actually enter Japan successfully, as the first Westerner to do so.

The ship arriving at Fort Nisqually was loaded with different cargo than the place had ever received. There were live cattle on board. Not a huge herd, but three cows, three calves, and a bull that made some enormous changes at Fort Nisqually. First among the changes were the injuries from one particularly wild and wicked long horn beast. She kicked William Brown in *"the testicles and nearly killed two more men,"* and broke John McKee's thumb before she was successfully landed. Brown and McKee were laid up for at least a week with their injuries.

The remaining cargo was offloaded without incident. These cows were lean, nearly wild, Spanish longhorns. They would be used as work animals when trained to the plow. The men then loaded five horses destined for Fort Langley, possibly the first live animal exports from Fort Nisqually. Peter Tai, the Kanaka, was reassigned to Fort Langley.

More and more local Indians were hired for day labor jobs. Some women were put to work in the potato and vegetable patches removing weeds. Men were hired to help gather cedar bark for roofs, others were hired to hunt. One full cask of venison was salted for winter use.

In June, reports of "raging ague" were coming from distant quarters. Ague is a very serious, sharp malaria-like malady, marked by periods of acute fever, extreme chills, and sweating at regular intervals. It is sometimes called a "shivering fever fit." People were

---

79   Ranald McDonald is buried near Colville, WA.

known to die from its effects. There was no cure, and virtually no successful treatment in the 19th century.

Another disease common to fur traders was contracted from the cooking or drinking water drawn downstream from a beaver dam. The daily stew, a cup of delicious cold water from a seemingly clean, clear mountain stream, could carry a potent colony of giardia[80] parasites. An infestation would give the hardiest fur trader a severe case of very uncomfortable diarrhea for many days.

Contaminated cooking utensils could have transmitted the relatively limited diarrheal disease, campylobater.[81] It is still the most common food poisoning, but it can be treated with antibiotics today.

Perhaps the worst of the water borne diseases was the bacterium Vibrio[82] cholera, the source of the cholera disease. Ingestion of that particular bacterium could kill a previously healthy fur trader within hours. Thousands were, in fact, killed by this disease in the Old West. It is still feared today in areas where water supplies have been compromised by natural disasters. President James K. Polk died of cholera in Nashville, Tennessee, on June 15, 1849, some sixteen years after Fort Nisqually was begun.

There were, and still are, many other deadly types of food poisoning, including botulism, mushroom poisoning, and ecoli. Suffice it to say there were no authorities to recall contaminated food, and little in the way of medicines to protect the fur traders.

July was very productive in 1834 at Fort Nisqually. The new house was up and occupied. It had a solid floor and a cedar roof enclosing 32 x 18 feet, with a post foundation that lifted the floor two feet off the ground. It had at least two chimneys. The men were quite proud of their accomplishment, and very comfortable.

William Kittson, Chief Trader at Fort Nisqually, had laboriously spent weeks packing furs for ocean transport. He expected the *Llama* to return, but received a message saying that since Fort Nisqually had no potatoes to spare, the ship would proceed on to Fort Vancouver. Kittson went to work immediately repacking the furs into smaller 90 pound bales for horse-back overland transport to Fort Vancouver. Already he had in excess of 960 skins of various types. It took three men and four horses to carry the 8

---

80 Giardia is a protozoan parasite that reproduces in the human intestines once ingested with contaminated food, soil, or water.

81 Campylobater, meaning twisted bacteria is an infectious disease caused by bacteria that are Gram-negative, spiral, and microaerophilic with a corkscrew appearance. It is a cause of spontaneous abortions in cattle and sheep, as well as in humans. It is often transmitted by contaminated water. Symptoms include dysentery, cramps, fever and pain lasting five to seven days.

82 Vibrio cholera was discovered in 1854 by Filippo Pacini, but not publicized until 1885, too late for the number one killer of Oregon Trail victims of the disease (1849-1852).

1834

ninety-pound packs over the portage to the Cowlitz River.

The next building to be constructed was the Indian hall. It was nearly finished when Kittson demanded it be taken down "in order to get it done better." By July the men were plastering the walls and smoothing the floor on an acceptable finished project.

During July, 1834, the Journal at Fort Nisqually reflects an unusual amount of non-business commentary. It was almost gossip. It seems that Simon Plomondon, one of the laborers, was married to a local Indian woman of the Nisqually or Cowlitz clan. She was seriously ill that summer, and several notes are included in the business records. She would have none of the white man's medicine, preferring to be *"glowed by her countrymen."* She gave away all of her property, depended on tribal doctors, then finally asked for medicines from Kittson. Even after using Kittson's remedy, full credit for the relief was given to the tribal doctors.

Construction of a new dwelling house and a new plough were begun before July was gone. Suddenly word arrived via La-Ha-Let that the Rocky Mountain fur brigade had passed on horseback through Yakima Indian lands in mid-month. The brigade was destined for Fort Vancouver. A great rendezvous was planned for late summer, when all fur traders and trappers congregated to turn in the furs collected during the winter and spring. The fur men would have one great party for a few days, collecting new supplies and trade goods before striking out again for the always-elusive perfect fur. Each fur trader would arrive with a fortune in furs, sell them to the HBC, then spend their annual earnings buying new supplies and trade goods. What little profit might have been made was quickly spent, or lost, drinking and gambling.

The extensive Fort Nisqually farm was finally taking shape.[83] Indians, mostly women, were assisting in the potato and pea patches. Initially, it took five men and "the women" to harvest 16% of the pea crop. Increasing the crew to six crews of five men and women got the harvesting 100% completed in three days. Thrashing and drying took them well into August.

The very important Paleilah Plain pasturage-land stretched from the southwest corner of today's University Place to Meadow Park, Oakbrook, and Steilacoom golf courses eastward (across Tacoma) to the Puyallup River. It was a relatively flat, treeless, somewhat undulating grassy tableland that continued north past modern day Mt. Tahoma High School and Wapato Lake, across all of South Tacoma and Nalley Valley to Tacoma's Old Town and Hilltop, including the ridge above the Tacoma Dome at McKinley Hill, and south to Spanaway, Parkland, Graham, Elk Plain and beyond the Roy "Y" at state highway seven to Mount Rainier. Nearly all of Joint Base Lewis McChord is on this plain.

---

[83] By 1846, the British-owned Puget Sound Agricultural Company ranches and farmlands would encompass 250 square miles of western Pierce County, with headquarters at Fort Nisqually.

The vast plains, covering about 250 square miles of land in what is now western Pierce County, were kept clear of encroaching forests by intentional, seasonal controlled burning of the grasses in the late summer. Indians had begun the practice perhaps centuries before. Clearing the prairies of dead growth allowed a new grass crop to rise, green and nutritious. From this vast grassland the Nisqually, Puyallup, and others harvested vegetable sprouts, roots, bulbs, berries, and nuts. The most important, perhaps, were the bracken, camas, wapato, acorns, and more. Grazing game animals easily found the fresh fodder and became easy prey for native hunters. The natural food supply in the region was so abundant that south Puget Sound aboriginal people developed the only sedentary hunter-gatherer society that has ever existed. These natural grassland plains were valuable for sheep and cattle ranches, in the HBC view.

Final harvest totals for 1834, the first of many, were impressive. The freshly dried peas filled 35 nine-gallon kegs, approximately 315 gallons. It was more than a three-fold increase on the 100 gallons of seed planted. The trade store business that season purchased 358 various pelts, 910 pounds of venison, five horses, and a colt.

When, in August, twenty-four S'Klallams in three huge war canoes came to Fort Nisqually, they appeared to be a fierce and frightful war party, probably led by Chief Lughkynum. A warning alarm was sounded. The Nisqually people fled. To escape was their best means of defense. The vision of any S'Klallam war party on Puget Sound always forced area native residents into a defensive position. All of the Fort's men were called in by signal cannon fire.

The S'Klallam warriors were responsible for a vicious attack on HBC fur trader Alexander McKenzie and four men on Whidbey Island in 1828. Although armed, Fort Nisqually was built for peaceful fur trade. The palisade and bastions were for retail store safety, not military security. Cautiously Kittson gave the S'Klallam chief a pipe and some tobacco, promising to trade the next day. Meanwhile he ordered all the men to be "about the place" on "account of safety during the S'Klallams" visit. None of the Fort's wary men normally carried guns, but at this point weapons were loaded and handy, just in case.

The S'Klallams were expecting to trade one prime beaver fur for one HBC wool blanket. Kittson informed the S'Klallam that the price was higher. The trade could not be consummated at the new rate, so Kittson closed the store, turning the reluctant customers out. They immediately began haranguing protest speeches, which Kittson ignored, paying "no attention to their ill humor." Finally, on the third day of their visit the S'Klallams decided to trade at Kittson's prices, and offered 98 high-quality beaver skins. In the end, the ever-fierce S'Klallams did not destroy Fort Nisqually or enslave the village at Sequalitchew, as had been feared. After some months had passed peacefully, the

S'Klallams became welcomed regular customers at the little HBC fur trade store.

A few days later, a large party of Oh-qua-mish or Sin-no-oh-mish Indians pitched camp nearby to gather acorns and berries. They asked Kittson on Sunday for instructions as to what was proper in regard to our Divine Being. After his lessons they held a devotional dance "for without it they would think very little of what we say to them." Kittson was able to gather 20 beaver skins from the Sin-no-oh-mish before preaching another Sunday lesson.

While the men were covering the dwelling houses with cedar bark (300 pieces on one building) the visiting Indian population continued to grow. About 300 people from eight different tribes were at Fort Nisqually by late August. Only one incident seems to have upset Kittson. A Chief, Babillard, got into a scrape with the Chief Trader. Old Ouvré had warned Kittson of this fellow's ill temper and troublesome ways. Kittson sent the poor man running in fright. Kittson carried a Brass Bludgeon.

Sunday, August 3, 1834, found 250 peaceable Indians gathered for another sermon. Kittson spoke in the Flat Head Salish dialect. His remarks were translated by "the Chief Frenchman," a Skalatchet Indian who dressed strictly in European style and sported a heavy beard. He spoke the "Spokan" language, as did former Chief Trader Herron's wife. The men of the fort and the visiting Indians "were attentive to their devotions," according to the notes in the daily *Journal of Occurrences*.

On September 15, 1834, Reverend Jason Lee, accompanied by Nathaniel Wyeth and leading a cadre of Methodist missionary workers, arrived at Fort Vancouver. Dr. John McLoughlin extended great hospitality to the weary travelers, who had been on the trail since the previous April. The Methodist Mission to Oregon had its inception in 1831, when four Nez Perce men arrived in St. Louis asking for information about religion. Jason Lee had a sense of Christian citizenship that would encompass many projects that had never before been regarded as part of missionary work. Lee's detractors and critics often cited his "non-missionary work" among the non-native settlers.

As the September fair weather and cool nights approached, all the men of Fort Nisqually were, for the first time, secure in their own dwellings. With a good wagon hauling hay, Simon Plomondon was making stairs for the dwelling entrances, some tables and cupboards. The regular tasks continued, of course. Water and firewood needed to be collected, along with more bark for roofing repairs. Fence rails needed to be split. Fields needed to be ploughed. The barley needed to be pulled, the wheat planted, and a stable or cow barn had to be erected. A tree stump that "was in our way" was easily removed with the help of some gun powder.

While some Indians were gathering acorns, two teenage boys decided to take HBC horses for a joy ride. It was the same as a "stolen car joy ride" today. When he caught them, Kittson gave the lads a "drubbing" a mild punishment for horse thieves, in Kittson's world.

With up to 200 Indians attending Kittson's Sunday worship services, it seemed a good time for a Nisqually woman, La Grande Bish, to marry a lad of the So-qua-mish tribe. The drumming and dancing went on late into the night, earning loud complaints from tired farm hands.

As the fall season moved into the Puget Sound area, the men were working at the same tasks that had occupied them for many weeks. Ploughing the pea and potato fields was of utmost importance. Many hours were spent keeping the cows from the piles of harvested potatoes. It was frustrating. The animals loved the taste of fresh potatoes. Pickets were cut to fence off sections of the fields. A double fence was also built between the facing corners of the trade store and men's dwelling, to create a courtyard for more privacy and security.

On Thursday, October 9, 1834, Fort Nisqually was visited by the American brig *Eagle*. It was said to be loaded with sundry articles and settlers headed to the Willamette. They intended to begin salting salmon. These Americans did not trade furs. Some Makah Indians apparently escorted the *Eagle* to Fort Nisqually. The Makah traded some beaver skins and seventy fathoms of Hyquas[84], the highly prized sea shells used for necklaces and other ornamentations.

The ploughing continued on the days when they could find the oxen. Some men were sawing wheels and boards for another wagon. Others were building a store counter. Still others were digging a root cellar and placing boards on the walls, ceiling and floor. Potatoes and other root crops were to be stored there, away from hungry cows. A total of 13 kegs of potatoes were grown from eight kegs of seed, a 62% return. It was a comfortable, nearly outstanding, increase. Five kegs could be consumed during the coming seasons, before the next harvest.

Plomondon and his family, along with J.B. Perrault, his Indian wife, and her slave, were reassigned to Fort Vancouver. Fort Nisqually's work force was reduced to only six European men and Kittson. The spaces between the palisade irregular pickets were filled in by placing another small pole in each gap. This closed the view of peeping eyes and made the men feel more secure, while being still outnumbered by thousands.

The stable was completed in November. Pack saddles and a wheel barrow were built.

---

84 Great value was placed on Haiqua shells. The best are two inches long in the form of a hollow tube ¼ inch in diameter. One shell could be had for 40 large China glass beads, or three HBC 2½ point blankets.

More pickets were installed to fence off another small building. A new building would provide overnight accommodations outside the stockades for Indian visitors and other strangers coming from a distance. Communication with Fort Vancouver expressed anxiety about the non-arrival if the supply ship *Dryad*. The overland express had arrived from York Factory, in the Canadian far north, but the European supplies were not at hand.

Operating orders did not change. Fort Nisqually would continue to grow as the collection point for furs from the north coast and as a source of food production. Nearly every HBC outpost, from Puget Sound to Russian America to the Rockies expected, and needed, food supplies produced at Fort Nisqually.

While the fort's men were planting apple trees in hot boxes in a little orchard near the Fort[85], the Indians were catching the fall salmon run, and trading for other food supplies at the fort. Besides some fine salmon they also brought in several hundred pounds of venison, shellfish, and various fowl. Kittson triumphantly proclaimed, "We are living off the fat of the land." But he sent the men to cut more firewood anyway. Winter would be upon them in no time.

Simon Plomondon was the first non-Indian settler in what is now Southwest Washington.[86] Plomondon is also the first white man to become an "Indian" Chief after marrying into the Cowlitz tribe. Plomondon was sent by HBC upstream by boat along the Cowlitz River, many years before any other whites arrived. Plomondon lived there when his first child was born at Cowlitz in 1821. We also know that several of the Plomondon children were adults when John R. Jackson settled nearby on Jackson Prairie. When the boundary question was settled Plomondon automatically became an American citizen, based on his long time-residence.

Simon Plomondon was a long-time employee of HBC. He established Cowlitz Farm on the Cowlitz Prairie before the Puget Sound Agricultural Company (PSAC) was formed. The PSAC eventually incorporated the Cowlitz Farms into the company properties.

He was a giant of a man, standing six feet two, strong and straight as an arrow. It is said that Simon married very young and many times. There are many descendants, and many stories of the exploits of Simon, his good reputation, and his fair dealings

---

85   First planted in 1834 at the old fort, the trees were transplanted. Cuttings from these trees were grafted at the Fort Nisqually Living History Museum in 2000, and planted in the nearby meadow of Point Defiance Park in Tacoma.

86   Michael Cottoneer (Cottonier) was the first "official and legal" American land owner claiming a spot at the Cowlitz Landing in 1834, at least 13 years after Plomondon arrived there to build Plomondon's Farm, which became the PSAC Cowlitz Farm in HBC records.

with new settlers. There are records of his marriage to Henrietta Pillefier on July 10, 1848 at St. Paul, Oregon. She was the niece of Archbishop Francis Norbert Blanchet, and of Bishop A.M.A. Blanchet. A son, named Francis Norbert Plomondon, was born at Cowlitz prairie in 1850.

Plomondon's Cowlitz Farm was, in the beginning, just a farm. Today we would call it a ranch because of the size. It covered four square miles of land along the northern bank of the Cowlitz River, northeast of today's Toledo, Washington. It became an HBC farm in the late 1830s. Its fields produced 10,000 bushels of wheat annually. It fed 100 head of dairy cattle and 500 ewes. Horses and beef cattle were pastured and other food crops were produced in similar abundance.

South of the Columbia River, a Methodist Mission was established by Jason Lee and Daniel Lee. Dr. McLoughlin wrote to England requesting an Anglican priest from the Church of England. Reverend Herbert Beaver and his wife Jane responded to the call. They were horrified to learn of the marriage practices in Old Oregon. They were especially disturbed by the interracial "country" marriage. Mrs. McLoughlin was an Ojibwa. James Douglas had married a Cree woman. All of the clerks and servants had married similarly.

Reverend Beaver made his racial-purity opinion well known, creating ill feeling among the Indian wives, certainly, but also among their white husbands. McLoughlin fell into a rage, chased the preacher from Fort Vancouver, caning him all the way.

Later, with a cooler head, McLoughlin apologized, but Beaver was having none of it. The Reverend and Mrs. Beaver departed for England on the very next homeward bound ship.

As Fort Nisqually closed out the account books for 1834, fatigued men and oxen had ploughed hundreds of acres of farm land with equipment that constantly needed repairs. The men cut 1100 fence poles that needed to be split into rails. Most of the Indians were off to winter quarters, the rail splitting would be done by six lone men at Fort Nisqually.

Kittson was exasperated by the theft of the iron parts from Captain McNeill's little shore boat, a Captain's Gig that Fort Nisqually used as often as the captain did. Thieves took the anchor, chain, and oar locks. All would bring good prices in trade at other places. Kittson vowed to "give the villains a good drubbing" with his famous Brass Bludgeon.

At Christmas, Kittson *"allowed the best that I had"* as gifts. Each man got a duck, some venison, and a half pint of rum at his Christmas Regale. Most of the following week was spent gathering dung and spreading it to fertilize the acres of potato and pea fields. McDonald built a couple of chairs and Kittson traded for a nice Indian canoe to replace the shore boat now without its essential iron parts. To celebrate the New Year, called

"Hogmanay" by the Scots, Kittson allowed the men to sip a share of the Company rum.

In sharp contrast, 1834 saw more than 1,000 Packet steamers moving vast amounts of cargo along the Mississippi River. Steam boats were the dominant mode of travel and provided extensive commerce in that region for the next 50 years. Fort Nisqually was about a 15-days walk by land, and nearly two weeks by sea, from any other establishment reasonably connected to the rest of the world.

[84]

1835

THE YEAR OPENED as Reverend Marcus Whitman and Reverend Samuel Spaulding prepared to head west. Texas declared the right to secede from Mexico, and Samuel Colt received the patent for a single barrel revolver and a rifle.

Whitman and Spaulding made a historic decision to take their wives along on the mission to the Nez Perce. Narcissa Whitman and Eliza Spaulding are the first white women to cross the American continent.

The Texas Declaration of Independence led to the death of Davy Crockett.

The aggressive construction program begun in 1834 at Fort Nisqually by Alexander Kittson continued in the New Year. The hearty crew built a 25x50 foot barn, and hauled some 700 pieces of cedar bark from the Nisqually delta to roof it. They also built a small grain storehouse, a milk barn, and a pig sty, along with a couple of wagons and ploughs. By July 13 the third bastion was completed. This one was at the main gate, to provide "some order for defence" [sic] according to Francis Herron's[87] journal.

The animal population grew with the addition of a small herd from Fort Vancouver. This time the animals were driven overland, in perhaps the first cattle drive in the Pacific Northwest. Four cows and their calves, then four oxen, were added to the bovine collection, which now counted ten cows. Five new plough horses were put to work immediately.

The barley, wheat, and oat fields were harvested using the horses and wagons. Then the winter wheat fields were ploughed and planted. Indian women were hired to dig the potatoes and store them in the cellars.

Just as many Indian customers visited Fort Nisqually's trade store in 1835 as had during the previous two years combined. Herron usually listed specific names of customers arriving to trade. These individuals included 'The Frenchman' of the Sinahomish, Quay-aye-mal, the Chickay-lits Chief, Can-La-Fer-Quoy, Si-yah-ish-soot, as well as La-Ha-Let

---

87 Francis Herron served at a number of HBC posts. He was born in Donegal, County Donegal, Ireland in 1794. He married twice: first Josephite Boucher Clarke, then Isabella Chalifoux.

of the Nisqually, the man who had befriended Dr. Tolmie.

La-Ha-Let had four wives and at least two daughters by 1835. One of his daughters was hired for domestic chores in Herron's home. Each of his four wives bore a child in 1835. Herron frowned upon the Salish practice of flattening foreheads of soft-skull infants to increase the royal status of a baby. He feared that they might die from the practice, although he made no journal entry recording a single death as a result of the ancient practice.

Some Indians were hired as company workers, others for a specific task or job, while others were regularly utilized as domestic workers for long periods. Generally, individuals controlled the circumstances of their employment, while the HBC men controlled the pay rate. There were more Indian people willing to work than were needed at most times of the year. The Native Americans of the South Sound were remarkable in their ready acceptance of European culture. The economic term "surplus labor" would seem to apply.

Kittson hired a young Indian lad to guide him to a lake nearby, about five miles long and at least one-half mile wide. First they followed the zig-zag course of Sequalitchew Creek, to mile-long Sequalitchew Lake. From there it is a portage of 300 yards to the bigger lake. (American Lake would get its name from the Methodist Missionaries and U.S. Navy Lt. Charles Wilkes). Kittson described it as *"a beautiful sheet of clear water, with four small islands"*. On the largest of the islands Kittson carved his name, presumably on a tree. The geese were numerous, but not the fish. Kittson said, *"I cannot tell the kind of fish in this lake..."*

Many times Indians were hired to paddle canoes and transport people and goods. Chief Factor John Work, with a brigade of fur trappers, passed through Puget's Sound in 1824. He was destined to trade further to the North. In 1835 he made a second visit to the South Sound. The plan was for him to travel south from Fort Langley on the Fraser River aboard Captain McNeill's *Llama*. As it happens on Puget Sound, the lack of winds made the voyage impossible. John Work was put ashore at today's Port Townshend, which was still an Indian village, not yet a town. It had been named to honor a British subject who had never been there. The *Llama* could not fight the lingering morning fog, the afternoon tides, and lack of wind. Earlier, two canoes had been towed behind the ship for John Work, but heavy seas along the coast had destroyed them.

John Work, an experienced and clever trader, was able to purchase two sturdy Indian canoes at Port Townshend. They were promptly loaded with peas, potatoes, and other supplies destined for Fort Nisqually. John Work insisted from the outset of the voyage that the supply items bound to Fort Vancouver should be taken around by way of the Pacific, not overland from Fort Nisqually. Mr. Work hired Native American canoe paddlers as guides at Port Townshend for the remaining 90 miles to Fort Nisqually. The first night the boats were secured high on the beach, and the men bedded down for the night.

Moonlight revealed a new problem. The tide had receded more than 300 feet, leaving the very sturdy, very heavy, cedar canoes very high and dry. Nearly twelve hours would pass before the tide was high enough to re-float Work's newly purchased canoes. Finally arriving at Fort Nisqually after another nine hours of constant paddling by his skilled Indian crew, Work delivered the Fort Nisqually supplies on October 20. He had departed from Fort Langley on the 8th. Work would not arrive at Fort Vancouver over the Cowlitz Portage until October 24th, with ten 90 pound packs of Fort Nisqually furs. The four-day portage via the Cowlitz brought more difficulties. Mr. Work and his men noted the strong fall salmon runs and, without complaint, they mentioned the heavy wet snowfall that drenched the travelers and iced their pathway on the last days of their 16-day struggle to cover the 300 mile journey.[88]

Sir George Simpson, Governor of HBC, described Chief Factor John Work as "… a queer-looking fellow of Clownish manner and address, nevertheless he is a shrewd sensible man." Work was born in Ireland, and joined the Company in 1814. He was promoted to Chief Trader in 1830 and to Chief Factor in 1857. At a future date, John Work would become father-in-law to Doctor William Frazier Tolmie.

Captain McNeill took John Work as a passenger aboard the *Llama*,[89] for the journey north, from Fort Vancouver to Milbanke Sound. By that time, Doctor Tolmie had already arrived and settled in at Fort McLoughlin, on Milbanke Sound. It was, perhaps, the first meeting of the three men. Almost certainly, McNeill had not met Tolmie previously, but Work and McNeill may have had previous differences of opinion. Certainly their command styles were not compatible.

John Work expressed surprise at the length of time McNeill took in preparation for the voyage to Milbanke Sound. Work was anxious to move, as land brigades moved with little regard for weather conditions. They were going to the HBC trading post named for Dr. McLoughlin where Doctor Tolmie was assigned. Work again expressed concern at the delay that McNeill insisted on before crossing the Columbia Bar. McNeill was worried by the danger created by a strong westerly gale. He was determined to hold the ship at anchor in Baker's Bay to allow the storm to blow itself out. John Work, quite impatient to be underway, went ashore to personally assess the conditions at the Columbia Bar from shore side. He returned to the ship thoroughly convinced, by McNeill and the fierce Pacific breakers, of the necessity of perhaps several-days delay to allow the sea to settle to a level safe enough for a reasonably hazardous passage.

---

88 Today we travel on international freeways to cover the distance in less than six hours.

89 Captain McNeill spelled the name of his ship with one L, but insisted that his own name had two.

Now that Mr. Work agreed with McNeill's previous decision, McNeill ordered all hands to their duty stations. McNeill took the *Llama* across the treacherous Columbia bar less than forty-eight hours after he had decided to not do that very thing until much later. McNeill simply would not allow Work, a decidedly landlubber, to determine any course of action for his ship.

The *Llama* proceeded to cover 160 miles in the next 24 hours, arriving only eight remarkable days later at Milbanke Sound. The *Llama* fairly flew through the open waters of the Pacific, pushed by the strong western gale. McNeill may have been motivated to complete the journey as the only way to rid himself of Mr. Work's "sailor's opinions." Actually, McNeill found the favorable winds of a typical Pacific southwester, which he had been utilizing for sixteen years, since 1919, when he was First Mate of the *Paragon*.

Dr. Tolmie reported the arrival of the *Llama* in his diary. He hired an Indian crew to paddle a canoe out to the ship. As they neared the *Llama*, a blinding snow storm caused McNeill to turn from the shore while Tolmie turned back, finally finding refuge on the rocky beach. He seems somewhat prudish as he writes "...*passed the most uncomfortable night under an inverted canoe, where red man and whites were all promiscuously huddled together...*"

The dinner discussion the next day was primarily the difficulty John Work was having as he tried to get the men of Fort McLoughlin to re-engage at the fort. They objected to the dreary spot. They objected to the 80 percent Indian smoke-cured salmon diet. They objected to the fresh salmon, which was of poor quality. They objected to the American fur traders buying Indian furs at a higher price. Work's re-enlistment talk turned into a general gripe session.

Work had the same difficulties at Fort Simpson. He saw firsthand the difficulties of American competition in the fur markets. In his diary Work describes the general crew discontent and treachery along with his own gripes about uncharted rocks, rigging repairs, lack of fresh food, and continuous threat of Indian attack.

McNeill explained that the *HMS Vancouver* had been plundered by the Haida. The captain had abandoned ship when it was apparent to him that the enormous force of Indians on the shore would kill everyone on board. The ship ran aground and broke up. McNeill also explained that the "enormous force" was only eight Indian men. They had lit dozens of fires to deceive the Captain of the *Vancouver* into thinking the beach was occupied by a great force ready to attack.

McNeill left John Work at Fort Simpson while the *Llama* dogged the three American ships in the North Pacific. The season was successful for McNeill and HBC Marine Department. Fort Nisqually offloaded 144 sea otter furs and 4,500 other furs collected along the Inside Passage, all the way to the Russian settlements at Sitka and New Archangel, Alaska.

On the return voyage, the *Llama* stopped at Point Roberts. Here, Work took the ship's long boats up the Fraser River to Fort Langley. He planned to collect the furs at that post and return to Point Roberts with the fur packs loaded in Indian cedar canoes. Work somehow damaged both of the long boats. In fact, the boats were no longer sea worthy or repairable. He sent word by land to McNeill, insisting on being rescued. With great seamanship, McNeill navigated the *Llama* upstream to the rescue. In fact, McNeill took the *Llama* well beyond the rescue point. He sailed all the way to Fort Langley, arriving on October 2, 1835.

Captain McNeill accomplished the task with the much larger *Llama*. Work had been unable to complete the job with two very maneuverable shore boats. The fur packs were reloaded, along with Work, and taken to Fort Nisqually, ending a ten-month trading voyage, and perhaps a sterling feud. The Irish Gentleman Fur Trader (Work) and the American Sea Captain Fur Trader (McNeill) saw the end of an era. The new age of steam power was approaching at breakneck speed.[90]

Both McNeill and Work would remain on the North Pacific shores the remainder of their lives, residing in or near Victoria. McNeill sought to bring his "spinster" sister from Boston to raise his twin daughters, born in 1853. His beloved Matilda, of the Nishga tribe, died during childbirth. Work, who also married a Native American woman, found he was bound by that union to reside in the area where interracial marriages were acceptable. He detested the HBC Columbia Department, the geographic area contested by the Americans and the British, saying it was a "cursed country" as well as a "barbarous country." It had a high human mortality rate due to syphilis, tuberculosis, smallpox, and intermittent fever (malaria, perhaps aggravated by typhus). John Work was struck with intermittent fever in 1833. He nearly died as he was "reduced to a perfect skeleton and could scarcely walk."[91]

In London, England, near the banks of the Thames, specifications were drafted for the *SS Beaver*. It was to be a small paddle steamship. She would work as a traveling factory, independent of wind and tide. She would enter every bay and backwater, every creek and cove, along the rocky Pacific shore to collect furs from the most isolated Indian communities. Easily as important, she could navigate the large bays and rivers with

---

90 In 1820 there were 69 steam ships operating regular schedules on American rivers.
91 Gibson, James R. *Farming the Frontier, The Agricultural Opening of the Oregon Country, 1786-1846*, University of British Columbia Press, Vancouver, 1985.

speed and precision. The plan called for the *SS Beaver* to be armed along military lines and operated to enforce "Company Regulations."

Near London, at Blackwall, the firm of Green, Wigrams and Green (GWG) was commissioned to build hulls for the steamer *Beaver* and the sailing barque *Columbia*. A second contract was awarded to GWG for the masts, yards, and rigging. The steam machinery was built by Boulton and Watt over 100 miles away in Soho, near Birmingham.[92]

The price of the *Beaver* as a sailor, sans power, was only £3162. The steam machinery increased the total construction cost to £7662 (about $13,147 U.S Dollars). John McLoughlin objected to the excessive expenditure and even the idea of a Marine Department. McLoughlin opposed the cargo space lost to machinery and the high cost of operating such a vessel to be wasteful. Land-based fur trade forts cost much less in all comparisons.

The *Beaver* was designed to sail initially as a three-mast schooner. There could never have been enough fuel on board for even the first leg of the trans-world voyage. All of the steam engine machinery was installed. All of the paddle wheels, stations, rails and bulwarks were fitted, finished and completed as necessary for a schooner. All could be removed, replaced or adjusted after arrival on the Columbia River.

On August 29, 1835, the *SS Beaver*, without steam, set sail from Gravesend under command of Captain David Home, and in the company of the *Columbia*. The *Beaver* arrived at Fort Vancouver on April 10, 1836.[93] Her engine, boilers and paddlewheels were reassembled and reinstalled. At 4 p.m. on May 16 the steamship lived up to her name as her boilers were fired up. *The SS Beaver* was the first steam-powered vessel on the Pacific Coast of North America.[94] On May 25, 1836 the *Beaver* crossed the Colombia River bar, never to return to Fort Vancouver. Her home port for the next seventeen years would be Fort Nisqually on the southern reaches of Puget Sound.[95]

Then, just as Fort Nisqually and the *SS Beaver* formed an operational partnership, the fur trade began a steep decline in relevance. The trade continued, and continues today, but in diminished scope and significance. Chinese silk entered the European hat

---

92 James Watt is often considered the father of steam power engines.

93 The *SS Beaver* was not the first steamer on the Pacific Ocean. She was, in fact, the third. The first to arrive on any Pacific waters was the *SS Telica*. She arrived at Guayaquil, Ecuador, South America, in 1825. She had traversed the Atlantic under sail and wind with her boilers to be fully installed at Guayaquil.

94 If truth be known *The SS Beaver* was the first steam-powered machinery of any kind on the North Pacific Ocean or Puget Sound.

95 The first Russian steamboat on the North Pacific was the *SS Sitka*. She appeared at San Francisco Bay in 1849, but sank there after only four months service. She was salvaged and spent her remaining days as the American owned *SS Rainbow*.

market to compete with the best beaver-pelt felt hats. Silk hats had a certain sheen and durability, but the low price made the difference. Silk hats were of the same high quality as beaver hats, but about one-third the price at retail sales.

This competition came suddenly, just as the scarcity of wild beavers was increasing. Beaver pelts were becoming more difficult to extract from the wilderness. With more difficulties in production, one should expect higher costs would be passed on to the retail

NOTES CONCERNING STEAMSHIPS

In 1831 the second steamer on the Pacific arrived, unannounced, at Sydney, Australia. The *SS Sophia Jane* arrived under steam power from England. The 251-ton *SS Sophia Jane* served in the South Pacific for many years.

HBC-owned *SS Otter*, sister ship to the *SS Beaver*, arrived at Victoria in 1852. She was a screw-drive vessel of 222 tons, 122 feet long, but only drew 2 feet of water. During the Puget Sound Indian War the *SS Otter* was leased at $300 per day by the U.S. Government as a warship.

The *SS Otter* was joined in the fur trade by the *SS Sea Bird* in 1858.

The first regularly scheduled steamship line on the Pacific was the Pacific Mail Company which began service from Panama to San Francisco in 1849. Three side-wheelers, the *SS California, SS Oregon, and SS Panama* carried gold prospectors paying $1,000 for the trip.

The first steamboat built on the North Pacific was the *SS Lot Whitcomb*, named for the owner and builder in 1850. After four years service she was sold to California owners who re-named her the *SS Annie Abernathy* working the Sacramento River Trade.

The *SS Fairy* arrived on Puget Sound in 1853 as cargo on board a sail boat from San Francisco. She was too small to hazard an ocean voyage on her own power. Her home port was Olympia, but had regular runs to Elliott Bay. Often as she rounded Alki Point she would roll on her side, with one side-wheel paddle completely out of the water. Perhaps that was the reason her boiler exploded off the Fort Nisqually roadstead landing on October 21, 1857. Dr. Tolmie treated the injured, but no life was lost as a result of the accident.

The above notes are from: Benson, Richard M., *Steamships and Motor Ships of the West Coast*, Bonanza Books, New York, 1968.

purchaser. Silk top hats were cheaper to purchase, but held similar social value to the consumer. The effects were felt all the way to Nisqually. There was more talk of increased farming and ranching operations for the two-year-old establishment.

1836

ON JUNE 18, 1836 the Hudson's Bay Company steamship *SS Beaver* departed from Fort Vancouver. Veteran Captain David Home, after sufficient sea trials (including some "party cruises" with ladies along for the rides) sailed out of the Columbia River, never to return. The *Beaver* would call Fort Nisqually homeport, not Fort Vancouver, after a fur gathering expedition to Milbanke Sound and all points between. Milbanke Sound is between the north end of Vancouver Island and the south end of Haida Gwai (Queen Charlotte Islands), on the northern coast of British Columbia.

On November 12, Fort Nisqually men were much surprised by the arrival of the *SS Beaver*. The fog had only slightly delayed the steamer.[96] Sailing vessels were often delayed by fog, tides, and lack of wind.

Four-year-old Fort Nisqually had perhaps twenty European workers. The Indian population was still very large in comparison, despite the depletion by diseases. In Spanish California, a division in population groups was beginning. Many people of mixed Spanish, Mexican and Indian blood were beginning to call themselves Californio. A 1836 Los Angeles census found 2,228 people divided ethnically as 500 "tame Indians," 46 foreigners, of which 22 were called Americans. This is an interesting comparison of population numbers that signifies nothing, but still interesting.

Captain McNeill made his last trading voyage as Master of the *Llama* in 1836. Taking command of the *SS Beaver*, McNeill used the winter months to familiarize himself with steamship operations. At Fort Simpson, Captain Home began his retirement, and McNeill began his most successful and famous career move, as Master Mariner of the HBC *SS Beaver*.

Captain Home is usually described as benevolent. Captain McNeill, on the other hand, left no doubt that he was the master. He worked hard, with enterprising efficiency,

---

96 The *SS Beaver* continued to steam up and down the Pacific Northwest coast, under various owners and for various jobs, until she was wrecked on the rocks near Vancouver, British Columbia. A stone masonry and bronze marker in Stanley Park remembers the incident.

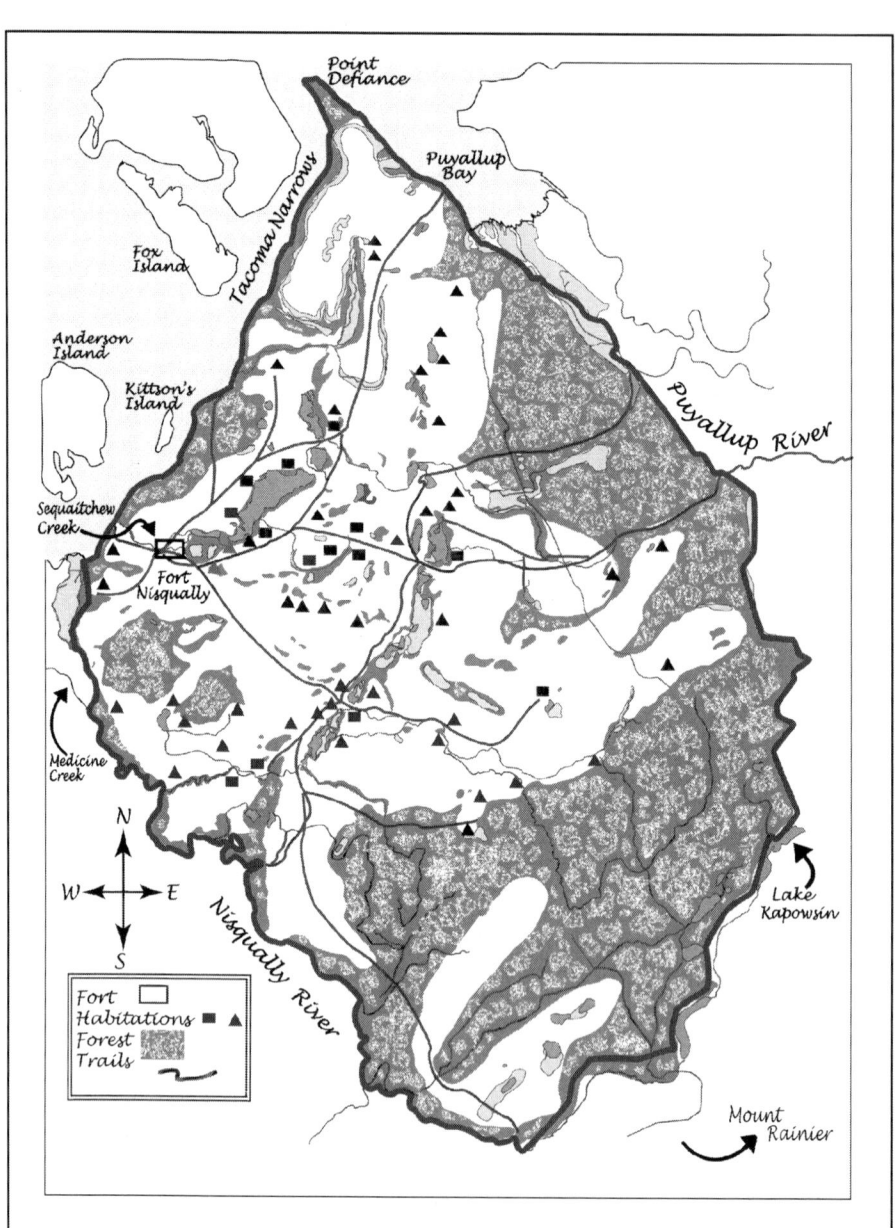

An Accurate "Map of British Possessions Bounded by the Puyallup and Nisqually Rivers, Oregon Territory, as Occupied by the Hudson's Bay Company and Puget's Sound Agricultural Company in the Year of Our Lord Eighteen Hundred and Fiftytwo showing In Different Manner all the Prairies, Rivers, Swamps, Marshes, Bays, Creeks, Harbors, With Roads and Indian Villages and Paths as well as Sheep and Cattle Stations and Parks, the Boudary Lines, the whole delineated from Actual Surveys by John B. Capman, William Tolmie, Edwards Huggins and Others" (Including © Steve A. Anderson, used by permission.)

running the crew with an iron hand, with the approval of HBC Governor James Douglas. McNeill was known to punish men on the spot with his cane for abusive language. Two crew members were punished with 24 lashes each for failing to load fuel wood. His first year in command, McNeill logged 5,640 kilometers collecting a record number of beaver pelts.

McNeill spent five months, from April through August, visiting coastal Indian villages at Kigarney, Nass, Clement, Cossack Harbour, Seal Harbour, Calamity Bay, McLoughlin Bay, Milbanke Sound, Active Cove, Kyumpt Harbour, and Nahwitti, purchasing 1,574 furs. This tremendous haul was deposited at Fort Nisqually, a triumph for what McNeill called the "marine department" of the HBC. It was an outstanding return even for McNeill, already a skilled master trader. In London, HBC Governor George Simpson was certainly impressed. At Fort Vancouver, John McLoughlin was upset because he had long favored land-based trading posts to the ships that Simpson favored. It was a dispute that lasted until McLoughlin's retirement.

Like its animal namesake, the *SS Beaver* had a voracious appetite for wood. She steamed two-hundred-thirty miles on her first day of trading. She reached Milbanke Sound with 30 crewmen on board. The six axe-men cut and loaded 40 cords of fuel wood in two days. That fuel was burned completely in one day. Apparently the boiler engineers learned some efficient procedures with experience. Later reports say that 26 cords of firewood could last the *Beaver* three or four days. Fuel economy was an inexact science even then, with claims made more or less as a political move, either for the new innovation, or against the terrible machine.

William Kittson was in charge at Fort Nisqually, having relieved Francis Herron. Kittson was born in what is now Canada about 1793. He served in the War of 1812. His employment with the North West Company (NWC) out of Montreal sent him to various posts, Colville being his location at the time of the NWC-HBC fur company merger. HBC soon sent him to replace Herron at Nisqually. His wife, Helen Kittson, was a Métis daughter of Finian McDonald. Her linguistic skills made her of great assistance in dealing with native populations west of the Rockies. William and Helen Kittson had two children, Pierre and Jules, when they arrived at Fort Nisqually. Two more Kittson children would be born, and die, at Fort Nisqually.

In early 1836, William Kittson was dealing with a serious epidemic. March was not a good month, especially for the Indians. Kittson blamed "… *their living bad.*" When he reported that five were unwell with sore throats. He gave La-ha-let a purge of a concoction of Dovers powder to save him. An 18-year-old woman rejected Kittson's elixir, but died of her affliction. A second girl took the medicine, but died five days later. One

Indian family moved closer to the fort's medicine man, putting themselves under the fur trader's care. Kittson's healing powers consisted of a dose of Dovers powder, a warm foot bath, and a neck blister.

Another Indian died, according to Kittson, when suddenly dowsed with cold water following a long, hot steam bath. Others experienced improving health after two weeks of suffering. Many of the young ones bounced back more quickly than the adults. However, one mother died suddenly, and soon her baby followed her to the grave. One man lost his entire family, five children and a wife. Kittson complained they would not follow his medical advice.

While we know some information about William Kittson's family, we do not know it all. We do know his Indian wife Helen gave birth on July 25, 1836 to their third child. Only three baptismal records exist, but there were five Kittson children. Pierre Charles was born April 6, 1832, and Jules may have been older. The new baby was named Eloise Jemima. Two of the Kittson children died during the epidemic of 1837.

The farm and ranch work continued, even with sick employees. The animals and the crops knew nothing of the human difficulties. At mid October the morning fog was thick, but wheat was sowed, potatoes dug, and fruits picked. The general yield was up from 1835. The men even found time to repair the gallery along the palisade behind the kitchen.

The 10 kegs of potato seed had yielded 42 kegs of the staple crop in October. Many potato fields were yet to be worked. There were also many meals during the summer months that included freshly-dug potatoes not included in the official reports. Sowing one wheat crop followed directly on the heels of the harvest of the next. The fur trade was falling off. By mid-October Fort Nisqually collected a total of 255 furs, but not one was a prime beaver. The men enjoyed the meat of eight animals brought in by Nisqually hunters.

Work continued, of course, around the growing agri-business. Anawascum, a loyal, skilled Nisqually, was building window frames, while Henry, another loyal native worker, was harrowing a wheat field. Still other Nisqually men and women were still harvesting the huge potato crop in late October. One particular field produced 157 kegs, from 16 kegs of seed potatoes, almost ten times the original investment. Other fields gave up 13 kegs, 34 kegs, 22 kegs, proving the place to be a success in producing potatoes.[97]

On Thursday, October 20th Kittson reported *"The sun appears with a black spot on*

---

97 One keg is said to contain 12.76 Imperial Gallons liquid measure. A keg stands 23 or 24 inches tall, with a diameter of 16 or 17 inches. One can only estimate the potatoes in a standard size keg at 160 pounds. This particular harvest probably garnered 36,000 pounds of spuds.

its western edge." He could observe this phenomenon without eye damage because of the thick smoke in the air. The Indians had the prairies ablaze annually, releasing the thick black smoke while burning off the dry grasses and assisting nature's new growth of fresh grass and delicious camas[98] root crops. Camas roots were a staple in native people's diet. Camas is harvested when the beautiful blue-purple flowers wilt. The root bulbs are pit-roasted or boiled. Sweeter than a sweet potato, the bulbs can be pounded into a flour when dried. There were once immense spreads of camas across the grassland plains around Puget Sound. The only human attention given to the camas was the annual ritual burning of the summer dry meadow vegetation.

At the end of October, five beaver were traded from a Pool-yal-lap trapper/trader/hunter. The man reported the abundance of wild fowl, suggesting a hunting party was in order. HBC men were soon living on some fat ducks and fatter geese. The records indicate 164 ducks and 60 geese were probably devoured during the final days of 1836 by Kittson and his nine HBC men.

The oxen were exhausted and the ploughs were "out of order" that autumn season. Meal time talk was centered on the need for a millstone. Mr. Walker took Louis, an Indian, to the Chute River in search of a proper millstone. Only one stone met the approximate size and shape criteria for a millstone. Walker found a large granite boulder, an erratic left by glaciers centuries before. After the application of a great deal of labor to reshape the stone and move it to a desirable location, the millstone served their needs.

Kittson ordered the trade shop exterior covered with new boards, and the old kitchen was remodeled into a new stable. The tired oxen were employed again harvesting barley and oats. Then the fields were sowed and harrowed over with the same hard-working oxen.

Even though there was a reduction in the fur trade, the numbers looked better by the end of the month. Sixty-four large beaver were added to the October report. Other HBC posts in the Columbia District were reporting a diminished native beaver trade. HBC policy along the Snake River was to trap out all the beaver to discourage the Americans from the territory. The company policy of sustainable crop yields was not working anywhere in the Columbia District except at Fort Nisqually.

One speculates on the reason for the slight decline in "fur revenue" at Nisqually, Vancouver, and other west coast sites. It may have been related to the spread of smallpox among the Indians during the winter of 1836–37. It was not an "epidemic" in the classic

---

98 *Camassia quamash* is native to much of the West. It is known as Camas, Quamash, Indian Hyacinth, and Wild Hyacinth. It grows perennially in moist meadows. Long basal leaves emerge in spring, then produce a multi-flower stem up to 50 inches tall. The flowers are white to deep purple, and often color entire meadows.

sense, but it was deadly. Estimates of the number of victims vary widely. There was no accurate method of counting a census in general, let alone counting the number who died in remote villages and camps. Often individuals were counted more than once, not in a subversive plan, nor by accident. Some could be counted as the spouse, while another tribe might count the same individual as a son or daughter. Extended families connecting distant communities could also have been completely unaware of a smallpox death. Finally, in many cases the Indians were not interested in counting the dead. They were often more interested in accounting for the death, expecting a "death price" to be paid by someone, responsible or not.

Dr. and Mrs. Marcus Whitman established an American Board Christian Missionary at Wailatpu, near Walla Walla. The Reverend and Mrs. H. H. Spaulding built another mission at Lapwai, in eastern Nez Perce country. Roman Catholic priests Blanchet and Demers took posts at Fort Walla Walla, and later in the Willamette Valley. In addition, a Belgian Jesuit, Pierre Jean de Smet, campaigned among the Salish, along the Columbia and Kootenay Rivers.

Nevertheless, Doctor John McLoughlin may have realized his empire was at the beginning of a brilliant sunset. Fort Umpqua was established in southern Oregon, near the present town of Elkton. The site had been selected by Jean Baptiste Gagnier about a year earlier. The location was at the crossroads of the Coos River, Elk Creek and the Umpqua River, along with ancient trails forming convenient travel routes to and from Ash Valley.

Fort Umpqua, along the river of the same name in (now) southern Oregon, was much like Fort Nisqually in size and manpower, but unlike Fort Nisqually, Fort Umpqua closed completely in 1854 after being moved and rebuilt several times. It was finally located roughly 40 miles east of the Oregon coast (at Reedsport), and forty miles west of today's Cottage Grove, just outside Elkton on the Umpqua River.[99] It never housed more than 13 HBC men, and averaged five or six. It contained "three or four" log huts built on three sides of a square. All were covered with a cedar bark façade. A twelve-foot high stockade surrounded the establishment. Two bastions erected in opposite corners commanded all sides for defense of the place, but still Umpqua was twice besieged by Indians [100] and burned down in 1851.

---

99 In 2008 a replica of Fort Umpqua was built to commemorate the historic site.
100 http://fortwiki.com/Fort_Umpqua

1837

IN THE SPRING of 1837, another severe influenza epidemic struck. The spread of smallpox began to decrease, and cases of Asiatic cholera were increasing. Most of the Fort employees complained of sore throats and colds. Beginning as early as February, nearly every laborer was listed as sick for at least a day or two. Indian children and the employee's families were the first to feel ill. Death was common and swift, whether the cause was influenza or smallpox.

Financial panic in 1837 adversely affected the fur trade. Investors in the eastern United States began using their funds to purchase cheaper used Indian buffalo robes as the smallpox along the upper Missouri killed thousands of Indians.

In March a new Fort Nisqually cow shed was nearing completion. The oats, barley, and potato seeds were planted. The splitting of fence rails and firewood continued. A new and serious quarrel developed between two hired Indians, leading to attempted murder. Details are sketchy, but we know from the *Journal of Daily Occurrences* that Kittson was the peacemaker. HBC officers, in the absence of any law enforcement, acted as sheriff, prosecutor, defense attorney, judge, and jury. Under the HBC Charter of 1670, the highest-ranking HBC man had the responsibility to maintain law and order as he saw fit.

Kittson's men expanded the farm by plowing another three acres for growing pea crops. Kittson couldn't stop the small pox epidemic, no matter how powerful his charter might have been. Smallpox was very serious and continued unabated.

Kittson sent urgent messages by courier down the Cowlitz Portage Trail calling for medical assistance, but it arrived too late for many. Most of the people in the region were sick in May, 1837. So many children were suffering that Kittson formally asked for help from "The Depot," meaning Fort Vancouver and Doctor Tolmie. Before the emergency medical team arrived, the disease took the life of Kittson's son and several others close to the establishment.

On May 12, Kittson said the sick men were doing very little work and the children were suffering, even his five-year-old son. Two days later the Kittson boy died at "...*3/4 past nine...on Sunday May 14, 1837."* The little boy was buried on the bluff near the prairie at the site chosen for the New Fort, one of the first buried in what is now called the "Old Fort Cemetery".[101] The record does not reveal his exact burying place. After the funeral Kittson gave the men some time off. Most of them, even Kittson, were very ill.

Finally, on May 17, Doctor Tolmie arrived. Tolmie stepped into Fort Nisqually at 6:30 PM after a grueling 56½-hour trek from the Columbia River. Kittson tells of gathering 20 leeches from Sequalitchew Lake at the Doctor's request. They were used for bloodletting and as a trade item with Fort Vancouver, as the proper kind could not be found near the Columbia River.

Tolmie began inoculations with cowpox vaccine as soon as he arrived. He feared another outbreak of smallpox, which had already reached epidemic numbers along the Columbia River. Tolmie also began treating the sick for the devastating intermittent fever and influenza. Illness was taking an extreme toll among the Indians.

It was also in May that three hens were brought to Fort Nisqually. They were the first chickens in what is now Pierce County. They were brought from Cowlitz Landing by Simon Plomondon, the first settler/farmer in what is now western Washington. The first rooster did not arrive until June. Plomondon was a retired HBC employee who settled along the Cowlitz River at a spot where the soil was dark and fertile, and the river's navigability ended. It was the perfect place to develop a retirement farm and still keep in touch with the travelers of the Company.

At Fort Nisqually on June 28, Kittson's older daughter died of smallpox. She was buried next to her brother, after only six days of illness. At this point, Kittson decided to send his wife and remaining children to Fort Vancouver. Tolmie continued for many days to inoculate all who would submit to his needle. Thirty-five mostly Indian names are recorded in a list of those receiving inoculations.

Spring weather seemed to clear the air. Finally the epidemic was over. Tolmie returned to his regular post at Fort Vancouver, The Scotchman had performed his medical magic at Fort Nisqually a second time. Years before, he had saved Pierre Charles' foot, and his certain death, after a severe axe blade accident. Now he was off to other places, a warm westerly wind following him down the Cowlitz trail, as the sun set on a fine spring day on Puget Sound.

The employee roster at Fort Nisqually in June 1837 included Louis (Lewis), an Iroquois, Mowat, Anawascum, Dominique, Quenelle, Williams, Cowie, Walker, Ouvré, and Kittson. These men had annual contracts, we presume, as was the practice across all

---

101   It is located near Center Drive in du Pont, Washington.

HBC sites. Other employees were assigned to the Marine Department, and still others (mostly Native Americans) were employed as "day labor," working only for a day's pay.

Just three HBC men stayed at Fort Nisqually in February during the epidemic. The others were dispatched on the "Langley and Nisqually Express" brigade to Fort Vancouver, carrying some 3900 furs of various kinds, destined for Europe. A big work crew was not needed at Fort Nisqually that winter, as the milk cows were dry. The three men who remained tended the vegetables (radishes, peas, potatoes, cresses, turnips, and cabbage) and chopped the daily requirement of fire wood. Hauling dung from the sheep and cattle pens was a regular chore, as long as the hand cart was serviceable. Many fields were fertilized by a natural method, i.e., by setting rail fencing as a "sheep fold" for the night.

A band of 30 Cowlitz Indians came by, but spent their time with La-Ha-Let and the Frenchman, probably gambling. Kittson was disappointed in the lack of trading. Both men were honored to receive long twelve fathom strings of Hyqua, the delicate cylindrical sea shell they so valued. The Cowlitz seemed to be in a "Potlatch mood" until a large contingent of Sinahomish traders arrived.

Soon the well-outnumbered HBC was in the middle of a quarrel between angry Sinnahomish and Cowlitz over the death of three Sinnohmish. One of the deceased was a valuable Sinnahomish fur trader. Kittson gave many gifts to the trader's family to reinforce the Company's friendship, offset the quarrel, and encourage the fur trade. He gave away a calico shirt, material for leggings, 15 balls and powder, and two fathoms of Hyqua shells in an attempt to regain the peace.

Five days later, the quarrel was suddenly over and trading was restored. Kittson remembered the size of the gathering as filling six giant cedar forty-foot war canoes. There could have been as many as 125 to 150 people, with their trade goods and supplies, conveyed in those ocean-going canoes. When the Express crew returned after the Indian quarrel, the HBC men went back to ploughing fields.

The 1837 inventory of horses and cows showed a growing herd of both animals. The fifteen horses were all named somewhat descriptively as "La Petite Rouge Pauline" as were the cows. The calves were not named, but journal entries carried individual descriptions, including gender and birth date. The cows produced exactly one calf each, doubling the herd to twenty in one season.

Repairs were needed on the dung cart. Anawiscum had been hauling dung for days when the cart head broke where the oxen were hitched to the cart. Without the head, a man would have to pull the cart. Anawiscum quickly improvised a substitute head using a piece of iron chain with a hook. The dung hauling resumed until the snow fell on the Thursday before Good Friday.

To celebrate Easter as a Christian Holiday, Kittson gave the men "some meat with grease" to eat as part of the observance of rest and fasting. He said;

> "Where ever I am in charge, the men shall be made to observe the Sabbath as recommended by our creed."

Two- and one-half gallons of corn, seeds, and many more gallons of melon, pumpkin, cucumber, and other seeds were in the ground by April 1st. That didn't end the planting, however. More than twenty bushels of peas were planted in early April. Thirty-seven bushels of potato seeds, six bushels of barley, five bushels of oats, and some Indian corn also went in the ground that month. The soon-to-be-officially-created Puget Sound Agricultural Company (PSAC) was growing already—crops, herds and flocks, at least.

Puget Sound Agricultural Company was more than just an idea. Crops and herds were growing at Fort Nisqually, while legal paperwork and investors in London anticipated growing profits. Soon a new corporation would be listed on the London Stock Exchange.[102]

All of this planting created the need for more fencing materials, while a new small guest house needed lumber. It was built for the increasing number of visiting customers. A second guest house, built soon after the first, would also allow separate quarters for warring or hostile tribes. New fence gates were built and installed, along with a new fort gate door. It was a human-size door built into the big wagon-size gates. One individual could pass through the big fort gate by simply using the door.

Kittson shot a dog that had been attacking the goats. The dog belonged to a deceased wife of Plomondon. There seemed to be no protest, and routine work continued.

Chimney repairs required two men to dig up the clay (probably from a nearby island), and others to actually fix the chimneys. Some men were helping a cow deliver a new black calf, while a much-needed horse would expire in another month.

By mid-May, another new building was underway. The timbers were squared and bark siding was collected. The squared timbers were stacked Canadian post-and-beam style to fill the walls of the new building. The growing farming enterprise needed the shelter and storage capacity the new granary would offer at harvest time.

Kittson seemed mostly pleased with the place, but felt the work was "getting along slowly," in his words. For every step forward there was an occasional step backward. The horse keeper, Sou-cat, suddenly quit his job. He was off to find better pay elsewhere. Then

---

102 The Puget Sound Agricultural Company was listed on the London Stock Exchange for nearly one hundred years, 1838 to 1934.

another valuable horse died even before another horse keeper could be hired. The new man hired was Tun-sind, a local Nisqually, presumably better qualified by experience and interest. Most Nisqually were well acquainted with the Yakama horse-breeders east of the Cascade Mountains.

Ploughing continued almost daily. The oxen were paired into three teams for Mowat, Le Pain, and Williams. Typically the men ploughed for half a day, then cleared weeds, hoed vegetables, or otherwise "worked about the place." It was said the oxen needed the afternoon rest.

A most grisly job one day was to salvage as much meat as possible from the carcass of a goat killed by wolves. Nothing was wasted, especially if it could be eaten or traded. The Indians were willing to offer fresh and smoked salmon, to supplement the goat carcass, and other food stuff for the Fort's trade goods.

The Fort Nisqually population increased again when the men returned from delivering the furs to Fort Vancouver. It was good timing, because the cows were coming into milking season again. A new gallery was needed, and as always, new fences were required to better protect the goats, pigs, and crops. Some feral dogs injured two fattening piglets. Again, trade meat was offered, but at a punishing price. It is likely that the offending dogs were killed.

After weeks of hard labor, the place was looking comfortable. The dwelling house was whitewashed, the ploughing and seeding was completed, and fields were even showing green sprouts under the gentle June rains. That didn't mean the work was finished. Anawiscum was repairing a canoe, 120 squared-timber pieces were stacked for another new stable, fence rails had been split but needed to be stacked, while milking, cooking, firewood gathering, and fur trading continued without pause.

Kittson reported that the men had cut and stacked 40 cords[103] of firewood in anticipation of the arrival of the *SS Beaver*. The steamer would require nearly all of the firewood for its next voyage. Much of the work was done despite the fact that all were still ill, and many Indians and their children were dying.

The *SS Beaver*, under command of Captain William Henry McNeill, sailed away from Fort Simpson on March 10, 1837,[104] and arrived at Fort Nisqually for the first time on July

---

103 One cord of firewood corresponds to a stack ranked and well-stowed measuring four feet high, eight feet long, and four feet deep, making 128 cubic feet. Forty cords would be 5,120 cubic feet in volume.

104 McNeill's *Llama* was sold in Hawaii for $5,000 on behalf of the Company. The new captain, John Bancroft, hired a crew of indians from the village of Kigarney to hunt sea otter off California. Kigarney (or Kygarnie) is a village of the Kaigani (First People) closely related to Haida (First People) of (formerly) Queen Charlotte Islands, now the Haida Gwaii. The crew mutinied, killing Bancroft and his wife, after taking control of the ship in 1838.

12, 1837. It was not a speedy trip because the job was to collect furs along the route. On his 122-day maiden voyage as Master Mariner of the steamship, McNeill collected 2,346 pelts, a 49% increase over his returns aboard the *Llama* during the previous outstanding year. (Another comparison point: Fort Langley and Fort Nisqually combined purchased about 2,900 furs over the entire winter).

European sailing ships had supplied Fort Vancouver and worked the Pacific Coast since the days of discovery. Most were not part of HBC. Most were competitors in the fur business or whalers from the United States. A few were from Russia or Spain.

Among HBC vessels were 24-ton brig *Nereide*, 70-ton schooner *Cadboro*, brig *Eagle*, 145-ton brig *Llama*, 213-ton *Ganymede, Colombia, Vancouver, William and Ann*, and *Isabel*. These ships were not in service simultaneously. In fact, some replaced others on the list. Some were sunk or wrecked, like the *William and Ann*, and the *Isabella*. After more than 40 years of service, even the venerable *SS Beaver* eventually floundered on the rocks near Vancouver, B.C. Most of the ships sold when their usefulness to HBC waned.

In 1833 the so-called HBC Marine Department consisted of five vessels assigned exclusively to the coastal trade. The *Columbia* and the *SS Beaver* arrived in 1836, boosting HBC coastal trade Marine Department to seven ships.

A partially successful "triangle trade" of goods from the Pacific Northwest to the Sandwich Islands (Hawaii) to China or California was tried. Timber and salmon from the Pacific Northwest sold well in the Sandwich Islands, while manufactured goods sold well along the coast. Furs sold exclusively at auction in England.

Once in service, *SS Beaver* didn't leave the coastal trade and never returned to the Columbia River. She was one of the smallest on the roster, at 101 feet, four inches, but easily the most powerful, with modern steam engines and matching side paddle wheels. She had the speed and physical adroitness the others lacked entirely. She could turn in a circle within her own length, for example, by simply reversing one of the side paddle wheels. She could also travel in reverse, which was nearly impossible for sailing ships.

The illnesses that had plagued Fort Nisqually in the spring lay quiet for a time, and then it returned forcefully in late June. On July first, Kittson sent his wife and remaining children to Fort Vancouver for a cowpox vaccine, to inoculate them against the sickness. Soon the vaccine was available at Fort Nisqually. It was delivered aboard the *Cadboro*, under Captain Brotchie, which had arrived on the same day as *SS Beaver*. Women and children were inoculated first. HBC employees were next, and by the end of the month Kittson had inoculated 20 Indians of three tribes.

Captain McNeill and a horse brigade took the portage southward to Fort Vancouver with the furs he had collected from Fort Simpson. Returning to Fort Nisqually, he found

Kittson's family celebrating a happy reunion, as the surviving family members. The little steamer pushed off with a flood tide at 4:00 AM on Thursday, July 24, 1837. McNeill was headed for the northern coastal trade, where he would ply the waters for many years.

In 1837 the HBC Board of Governors in London formally established the agricultural extension of the Company by issuing new stock shares for the Puget Sound Agricultural Company. It had been long talked about by Governor George Simpson and Chief Factor John McLoughlin, but finally decisions were made with the needed capital in place.

Puget Sound Agricultural Company was formed as a subsidiary of HBC. Initially, only officers and employees of the Company were allowed to purchase shares. This new company took over existing properties, built many new farms and ranches in the area, including substantial stations at named locations, such as the upper Cowlitz, Tlithlow, Treehatchee, Old Muck, New Muck, Kul-Kul-eh, Spanueh, Elk Plain, Belle Vue Farms on San Juan Island and S'Gukugwas. Nearly all were settlements initiated, perhaps centuries before, by aboriginal ancestors of the Nisqually, Puyallup and other tribes, then modified for international agri-business.

Archaeologists have identified approximately 250 sites of ancient and modern human activity in the Puget Sound region by the mid-19th Century. The list includes ancient Indian villages, along with PSAC trading posts, fishing camps, trails, roads, corrals, herding huts, homesteads, farms, horse corrals, sheep pens, pig pens, and other outposts of the earliest British pioneers.[105] The British PSAC acted on the Treaty of Joint Occupancy, while Americans did not.

The goal for the PSAC was to completely supply the basic human needs for food, clothing, and shelter for all Company employees throughout the Columbia Department. Fort Nisqually as PSAC grew in importance and ability to meet the stated goals, but never quite reached the "finish line," which was constantly moving. Given more time, less international political interference, and less turmoil in local government, the farms and ranches of the PSAC could have provided far greater yields. What PSAC was able to accomplish still remains an amazing achievement.

Historians have frequently referred to the large scale PSAC posts as *"a series of Great Farms.... raising ... fine crops..."*, which demonstrated the agricultural possibilities of the region. Unfortunately for the British, the demonstration indirectly promoted American interest in western homesteading, i.e., an American demand for free farmland. United States politicians began using the term "Manifest Destiny" to describe the bold dream of extending American borders "coast to coast" including Mexico, Canada, Central

---

105 "Archaeology at Fort Lewis, Protecting Our Past", undated United States Army pamphlet, Environmental and Natural Resources Division, Cultural Resources Office, Fort Lewis, Washington.

America, and even the Philippine Islands.

The first thing the new PSAC needed was more livestock. There were as yet no beef cattle at Fort Nisqually, and few at Fort Vancouver. In May, three chickens were brought to Fort Nisqually from the Cowlitz. They were procured from Plomondon, as was a rooster that joined the hens in June. Domestic poultry and eggs quickly became welcome new menu items.

Here the story swings to an American who comes to the rescue of the British Hudson's Bay Company. To tell the true tale, we need to revert for a moment to the winter of 1834–35, when Ewing Young, an American fur trapper of some renown in the Southwest, had settled on the east side of the Willamette River, at Champoeg in Old Oregon. In 1829 several former HBC trappers had chosen to settle west of the river, too. Champoeg[106] was beginning to look like a town.

To set the stage, it was a mild winter in 1834–35, with little snow and an early planting season beginning. Mr. Ewing Young did some trapping in the Oregon Cascade Mountains, but had also fenced his horses and sowed a garden near some log cabins that had been built by HBC trappers. Life was not as hard here as it had been for Young when he lived in the desert southwest. There was a plentiful variety of fish and wild game nearby and he had the beginnings of a more sedentary agricultural life.

By 1836, Young had expanded his land holdings into a full-fledged ranch, with a saw mill. He learned that another American, Nathaniel Wyeth, had been unsuccessful competing with the mighty HBC. Young had been selling furs to Wyeth for several years, because Dr. McLoughlin would not accept Young's business, labeling Young an "opposition competitor" (that is, an American). Young, in return, said that the absolute authority exercised by McLoughlin was "tyrannizing oppression," treating Americans with "more disdain than any American of feeling can support." [107] That report is Young's words, according to McLoughlin.

Many trappers were fond of wine and whiskey, often making their own beverages which were essentially unavailable from Fort Vancouver. Young felt challenged and eager to compete with HBC in any way possible. Failure of Wyeth's fur business seemed to be an opportunity for Young, the "retired" American fur trapper. Young bought the large iron cauldron that Wyeth had used to pickle salmon, intending to build a distillery to

---

106 Champoeg is (pronounced sham-POO-ee) is a Kalapuyan word referring to a local plant.
107 Holmes, Kenneth L, *Ewing Young, Master Trapper*, Binsford & Mort Publishers, Portland, OR, 1967

compete directly with McLoughlin's meager "moonshine" availability.[108]

The American Methodist Missionaries, led by Reverend Jason Lee, already settled in the Willamette Valley by 1834, were opposed to the erection of any distillery, and the sale or use of liquor in any form. John Wesley, founder of the Methodist movement, prohibited the use of wine in communion services, so as to not tempt those with a weakness for alcohol. That practice continues today in United Methodist churches.

On February 11, 1836, long before Young actually built a still, eighteen mission members signed a pledge to "save this rising settlement from the curse of intemperance."[109] Accordingly, a meeting of the newly formed Oregon Temperance Society was organized on January 2, 1837. All trappers were formally asked to stop their undesirable business. As an inducement to stop production of liquor, the Society offered to reimburse Young $51, plus some wheat, for losses he might incur by ceasing operations. There was no immediate reply. Young had to evaluate this cash offer. The plot changed quickly, as a lucrative cattle deal developed.

Entering the stage now is Lt. William A. Slacum, U.S. Navy, a personal representative of President Andrew Jackson of the United States. Slacum was aboard the brig *Loriot* which had just arrived on the Columbia. Slacum was sent by the president to study "conditions" in Oregon Country. After meeting with McLoughlin, Slacum visited Reverend Lee, and later met with Young. Ignoring the issue of the distillery business, Slacum came to the conclusion that the Willamette Valley Americans were in need of some cattle. It was a valid conclusion, as HBC cattle were unavailable, or were extremely high priced, to discourage American settlement.

It had long been HBC policy to only loan cattle from the small herd at Fort Vancouver. McLoughlin would not sell a single cow. He refused to even sell meat to ship captains, naval officers, former employees, and of course, any Americans. McLoughlin declared that only 3 bulls, 23 cows, 5 heifers and 9 steers were available, while he and HBC had need for nearly one hundred oxen to do the work of the farm. All cattle loaned were expected to be returned at some future date. All of the offspring from the loaned cattle were to be brought to Fort Vancouver after weaning.

Slacum, Young, and Lee discussed the abundance of available cattle in Spanish California. They could be purchased for $3 per head. A meeting was called for January 12, 1837, at the Oregon Methodist Mission to develop a plan to acquire cattle. This delighted

---

108 Ibid, A letter to London Headquarters from McLoughlin, dated October 31, 1837, *'As to Distilling, I began to distill in 33, but by '36 finding the bad effects it had in our affairs gave it over… we distilled about 300 Gallons.'*

109 Ibid; An entry in the Mission Record book for that day.

Slacum and Young, providing competition they could present to McLoughlin. The idea delighted Lee, because the American settlers could purchase less expensive cattle.

The Willamette Cattle Company was formed with Young as the leader. Eleven investors contributed $399.79 to the venture. It was an enormous sum of cash. Young decided to forego building the alcohol distillery. He publicly refused the money offered to close the enterprise that had never produced a drop of elixir. He thanked the Temperance Society, then privately accepted $50 credit at the Mission Store on October 10, 1838 "for one large kettle." Make of these facts what you will.

More money came to the Cattle Company from other sources, too. Lee invested $624 on behalf of the Methodist Mission, a transaction that was strictly prohibited by the Methodist hierarchy. The investment would eventually lead to Reverend Lee's dismissal from the Mission.

Slacum reported to President Jackson his personal advance of $500. Interestingly, John McLoughlin invested $558, while Duncan Finlayson and James Douglas, each of HBC, put up $300. The total capital of the Willamette Cattle Company was $2,381.79.

On January 18, 1837, the *Loriot* sailed for Spanish California. After waiting 22 days for a violent gale at the Columbia Bar to subside, Captain Brotchie of the *Nereide*, Captain McNeill, of the *Llama*, the U.S. Navy's Slacum aboard the *Loriot*, agreed that the sea had calmed enough to attempt a bar-crossing exit. The crews of all three ships were anxious to set sail after the long delay.

After an uneventful journey down the coast, the *Loriot* anchored March 1 at Whaler's Harbor, on the north side of San Francisco Bay, across from Yerba Buena. Here the HBC had a handsome two-story trading post. After a great deal of "administrative confusion" and "sharp altercations" with the Spanish authorities and cattle sellers, the great cattle drive began. They had purchased 729 head of the "wildest kind possible." Perhaps because they were so wild, they planned to drive the cattle overland to Oregon and Puget Sound, rather than risk disaster at sea.

That historic cattle drive of 1837 probably began in Spanish California, near Fresno,[110] and eventually reached the Willamette Valley.

While small numbers of surplus cattle have always been driven to markets, the first recorded large Texas cattle drive occurred in 1846,[111] nine years after the more arduous cattle drive from California to Puget Sound. Edward Piper herded 1,000 head of cattle

---

110 It was Fresno, or Sacramento, or Vacaville. Accounts disagree. Chances are the cattle were acquired at all of these places to compile the herd, 630 of which survived the overland trek to the Willamette Valley in 1837. Author's observation.

111 The Online Handbook of Texas, http://www.tshaonline.org

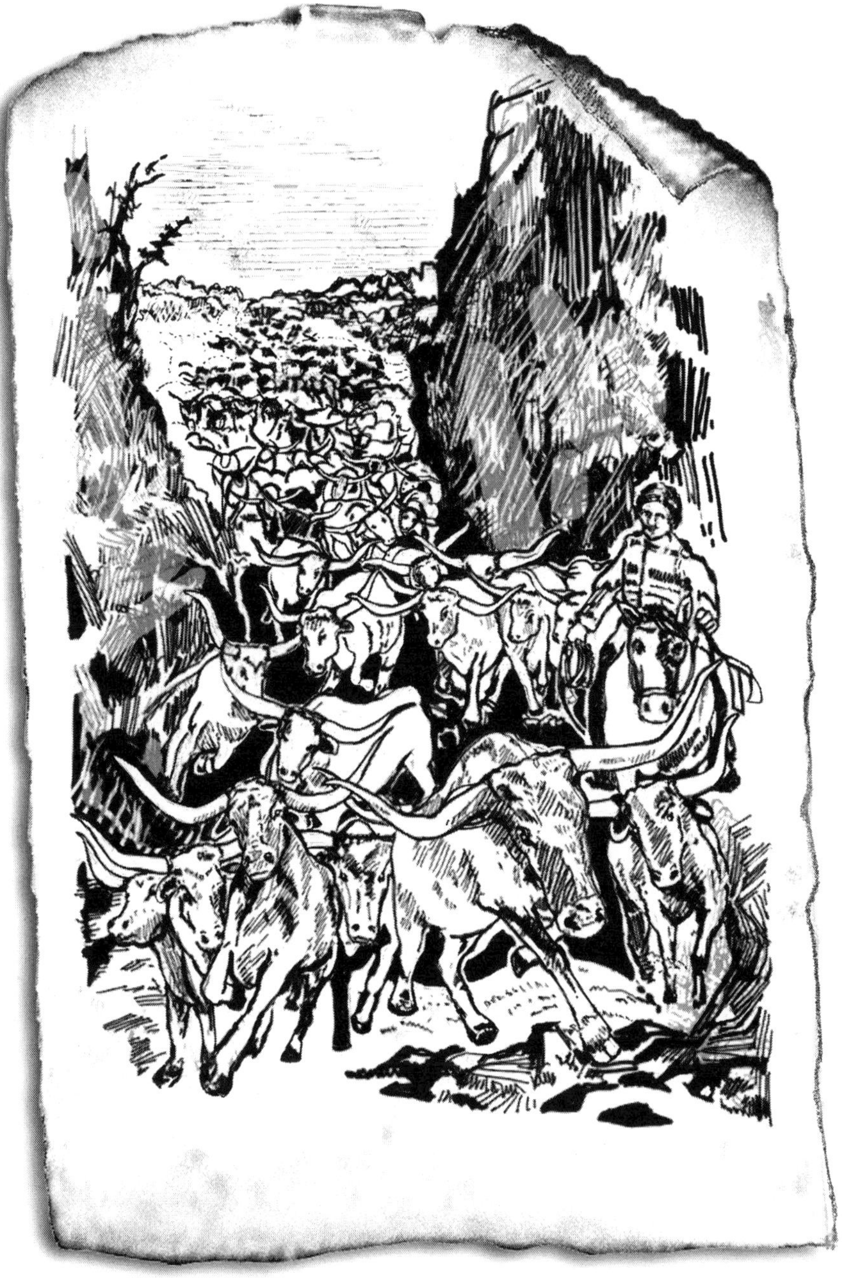

1,000 miles, from Texas to Ohio,[112] without mountains to cross. In contrast, Young drove 729 cows 880 miles from California to Puget Sound over rugged mountain trails.

The temperatures in the Sacramento Valley at noon on July 27, 1837, must have been searing. The valley was certainly parched and uninviting. Malaria had ravaged the Indians in the valley. Hundreds of Indians were dead or dying. Too often, birds of prey were seen feasting on the uncovered corpses.

Crossing the San Joaquin River proved to be an almost impossible task. Young's herd reached the southern bank on June 25, and crossed the last animal twenty-five days later, on July 20, 1837. Some animals were lost, but replacements were purchased from a nearby Pueblo.

The last week in August saw the herd begin to ascend the Siskiyou Mountains, near the present-day freeway ascent towards Redding. It was a harrowing trek. The terrain was brushy, very steep, with some water, but no grass.

They were following portions of trails blazed several years earlier by the Hudson's Bay Fur Trade Horse Brigade lead by Michel Laframboise. That party had found no beaver, but hunted for food along the way. The American cattle drovers[113] had an exponentially more difficult task, with over 700 head of cattle to move. The drovers often quarreled among themselves. Young was a very strong-willed and forceful leader. The cattle and men were hungry and weary, growing more so with each step. Every inch of progress was contested, tedious, and dusty.

By August 29 they had lost 49 animals. The herd was moved only in short marches, each day stopping frequently to feed, water, and rest the animals and the men. Still, some of the men were on the edge of endurance and patience. When the drovers met two Indians along the Rogue River Valley (near Medford today), the Indians were shot and killed at short range without provocation. Young immediately censured the act and condemned the men who did it. They next day other drovers got into a knife fight among themselves, with some resulting serious injuries, but no fatality. Indians did not attack the cattle train directly, but did shoot cattle, as hunters do. On one occasion, Indians shot Young's horse. Fortunately, they had spare horses.

The herd was moved up the trail approximately where Interstate 5 and/or U.S. Highway 99 cross the Umpqua watershed, then down into the Willamette Valley. The men directed the herd to the west side of the valley, to avoid crossing the many Willamette

---

112 Ibid. Earlier, much smaller cattle herds were driven from East Texas to New Orleans.

113 Ewing Young's cattle drovers were Philip Leget Edwards, Calvin Tibbets, John Turner, William J. Bailey, George Gay, Lawrence Carmichael, Pierre de Puis, B. Williams, and Emert Ergnette. http://en.wkipedia.org/woki/Ewing_Yomng

tributaries that flow out of the Cascade Mountains east of the river.

It was early October, nearly three months on the trail, when the motley herd arrived at the Willamette Valley southern-most settlements. McLoughlin acknowledged the arrival on the tenth with a letter to Lee expressing his happiness over the safe arrival of the cattle drovers and the new herd.

The roundtrip had taken nine months and brought 630 head of lean, mean Spanish longhorn heifers to the Oregon Country. The animals had cost the investors $8.30 per head. The quality of the animals was described as *"better than no cattle at all."*

The American settlers returned one cow for each one McLoughlin had earlier loaned. It was often not the same animal, of course. Spanish longhorn beasts were often sent in place of the nicely tame and broken bovines McLoughlin had loaned in such miserly fashion. McLoughlin did not object, so long as he received the same quantity of animals as he had loaned.

Ewing Young's entrepreneurial efforts had made himself the wealthiest man in Old Oregon. American competition was at the HBC doorstep in the form of a fur trader turned cowboy who threatened to sell whiskey.

On April 23, 1841, only four years after the first cattle drive, John McLoughlin wrote to Alexander Caulfield Anderson at Fort Nisqually about a newly arrived HBC herd. He wrote "*...began to break-in the wild cows to mild, broke in thirty in the season...*"[114] Most of the 1841 cattle-drive animals were on their way to Puget Sound Agricultural Company pastures near Fort Nisqually. Eventually the herd grew into an unmanaged, and unmanageable, throng of ten thousand huge beasts grazing contentedly on land that became Pierce County.

In the fall of 1837 PSAC ploughing, squaring, and chopping continued daily as the butchering began. They butchered some hogs on November 6, 1837. On the 7th two carcasses were dressed out at 166 pounds and 323 pounds, "*the fattest one ever killed here,*" Kittson recalled. Twenty-eight pounds of salt-cured ham were sent to Captain McNeill and crew aboard the *SS Beaver*. The remaining meat was salted and packed in barrels for later use at Fort Nisqually.

The sailors aboard the steamer were allowed shore leave whenever the ship was in a safe port like Fort Nisqually. The seamen were fond of horse racing and gambling games. They would borrow Indian horses to race across the countryside, betting on the outcome, while the engineers and wood choppers were busy at work. The latter were gathering fuel for the hungry engines, while the engineers were overhauling the boilers. The soot,

---

114   Ibid, On-Line Handbook of Texas, page 135.

ash, and clinkers had to be removed from the fireboxes and flues to keep the boiler apparatus as efficient as possible. It was a dirty and thankless job, especially resented when the sailors were playing games and riding horses for pleasure.

Snow fell the November morning of the departure of the SS *Beaver*. The men of the Fort expected the ship to deliver some letters outbound to the next ship she would encounter. They could not hope for a reply for at least a year, or perhaps two.

On December 6, the Chief Trader wrote that Chief See-yat had murdered an Indian doctor.

"*There was much talk about the affair amongst the Soquamish tribe. I wish they would determine on shooting the villain.*"

Later Kittson wrote:

> *Challicum with a party of his Indians cast up, put a few skins in the store and left us for a visit to the Saw-aye-waw-mish to buy articles for the death of a So-qua-mish shot by the villain See-yat, the latter having got a gun from the Saw-aye-waw-mish and with it committed murder.*"

Apparently See-yat changed his ways after his baptism, becoming very friendly to whites.

On December 21st, about one o'clock in the morning,

"*a couple of shocks of earthquake were felt. The second made us jump in our beds throughout the Fort.*"

Apparently there was no damage done. The next day the men were about their jobs without another mention of the quaking.

1837 ended with the fur trade business calculations showing an increase in large black bear pelts and deer skins, but a decrease in all other furs traded including the highly valued Beaver. The trade business brought in 30 gallons of whale oil for the first time. Most American merchant ships had shifted from the otter hunt to whale hunting because the fur trade was so depressed. Whale oil was the fuel of the economy in the mid nineteenth century. Chief Trader Kittson proudly reported that the fence around the gentlemen's vegetable garden was secure and the winter firewood stack was nearly complete.

1838

SAMUEL MORSE AND ALFRED VAIL gave the first successful public demonstration of the telegraph in Morristown, New Jersey, in 1838. It would be many years before any messages arrived at Fort Nisqually by the new technology. Sometimes it seemed like there was nothing but work to do.

January at Fort Nisqually began with a lack of New Year treats, the Scot tradition of celebrating Hogmanay. William Kittson refused to reward what he called "bad conduct" and "disobeying orders." No one received the traditional "regale" to celebrate the renewal of the calendar. Besides, the soon-to-arrive steamer required refueling, dung needed to be hauled, tons of hay needed to be cut, and wheat needed thrashing. For four days straight there was "no change in our work," as Kittson remarked in the *Journal of Occurrences*.

While Princess Victoria (1819–1901) became Queen of Great Britain in 1837, by 1838 beaver pelt prices were dropping rapidly in the face of stiff competition. At the same time, the fur trade business in London was facing competition from cheaper Chinese silk made into top hats. The fur trade business meant work at Fort Nisqually, as more bands of Indians from more distant homes came with furs to trade. Some of the customer groups visiting Fort Nisqually in 1838 were:

> Cle-cat-tats, Sin-no-whom-mish, eight canoes of Skay-waw-mish, four more canoes of Su-nook-que-le-mish, S'Klallam, Upper Nisqually, Nisqually, Pool-yal-laps, Scock-se-nate-mish, Holth-nuh-mish, Sah-saps, Saw-aye-waw-mish, So-qua-mish, and by land Cowlitz and twenty Yac-kah-mah.

Some of the individuals to visit were:

> Chief Saw-wham-mish, the Big Belly Chief Klallune, La-ha-let, Thom-mas-chum, Wyaseo, the widow of Louis, Lashimiere, the Red Head and his father, Challacum, See-yat the murderer, and Sin-ne-tee-aye with his family.

All of these Native American names are presented as hand written in the *Journal of Occurrences* at the time. Many phonetic spellings and actual linguistic renditions are more correctly presented today.

A complete and accurate roster of individuals residing at or near Fort Nisqually remains unfound, making it difficult to recreate from historical records. We can, however, obtain from the *Indian Trade Shop Blotter* (the sales ledger or accounts book) a list of customers. This book was handwritten, of course, and contains the details of transactions between the store and every customer. Probably all of the many customers purchased and sold "on account" without the use of any currency other than the items brought in to trade. It was a barter system, to be sure, but with set values applied to each item in every transaction. Some of the individuals who did business at the company store according to recent research include:[115]

> Jean Baptiste Ouvré, French Canadian, shop man, experienced fur trader
> John Bull, English laborer
> Joseph Pin, English laborer
> John Dunn, English laborer
> James Scarborough, English, HBC Ship's First Mate
> William McNeill, American, HBC Ship's Captain
> Louis Latour, French Canadian
> Jean Baptiste La Fleur, French Canadian
> John Aucock, English Laborer
> Michel, Indian laborer
> Abraham Le Pain, French Canadian laborer
> Charles Borgeau, French Canadian Laborer
> Owyhee, Hawaiian laborer
> Adam Gunn, English laborer
> Oliver Dauphine, French Canadian, Fort Simpson laborer
> Paul Haus, Orkney Islander, Fort Simpson laborer
> Charles Sagogetsta, Iroquois Indian laborer
> Ka'I, Hawaiian laborer
> Elee-ay-nay, Nisqually Indian fur trader
> La-ha-let, Nisqually Indian Chief
> YTanatacow, Nisqually Indian fur trader and father of Leschi
> Leschi, Nisqually Indian farmer/horse breeder-trader/Chief

---

115 Anderson, Steve A., in an email message January 16, 2009, based on transcribed pages of the *Indian Trade Shop Blotter*: February, 1838-January, 1839, Nisqually Papers, FN 1247 Volume 2, Soliday Collection, Huntington Library, San Mateo, California.

Some of the palisade posts were replaced as the wood was rotting in the damp Pacific Northwest climate. Mid-January saw the typical variety of snow, rain, fair skies, and delightful weather at some point almost every day. The weather allowed the streamer fuel wood to be cut, collected, split, and stacked into 38 cords. With that in mind, 38 cords of fuel for the steamer would mean a pile four feet high by four feet wide by 304 feet long, containing 4,864 cubic feet of fire wood. The little steamer was only 109 feet long. After loading the fuel there was little room for the 30 crew members, their gear, provisions, and normal trade goods.

The chimney of the Indian hall was torn down and rebuilt in a three-day effort while the Indians were away at their winter homes. Of course it snowed overnight, making the job all the more urgent. Still there was time to slaughter five fattened pigs and get the meat salted and stored in barrels. The pork meat weighed in at 1002 pounds of salted meat, plus eight fresh hams and 16 fresh cheeks that would be consumed within the day. Farm produce totals were just as impressive. Six bushels of barley, 20 of corn, 35 of oats, 100 of peas, 113 of wheat, and a whopping 385 bushels of potatoes were stored in the root cellars.

On February 11, 1838, S'Klallams brought news that a ship had visited the Clasits (Clatsop?) tribe, who lived along the Columbia River.[116] The white people on board the vessel purchased land for the purpose of making a settlement. A few days later Cowlitz Indians came with the news that Captain Home and four sailors, formerly of the *SS Beaver*, and were drowned in the Columbia, at Baker Bay in a shoreboat under sail.

Physical danger was waiting at every turn. Kittson and two men went to retrieve some fence rails split in 1835. While leading the oxen wagon down a steep incline, the heavy load shifted ever-so-slightly, causing the beasts to panic. Suddenly, moving at near full speed, one 2,000 pound animal ran over Kittson's rump, flattening him face down in the muddy dirt and rocks. He received no serious injuries, but in his words, *"got a few rubs from the stones."* His dignity may have been injured. One can imagine the guffaws from his closest helpers.

Another danger came from the wolves. Typically the hungry wild animals would not attack humans, but were fearless against young colts. One colt was wounded in the leg, while another died, unable to fight another late April wolf attack.

It is slow work to till a field with draft horses or oxen and only a few plows. In the

---

116 The Clatsop are a small Chinookan-speaking Native American tribe inhabiting the area of present-day Oregon near the Columbia River and south of Tillamook. Clatsop (La t cap) was the name of a single village, meaning "place of dried salmon." Lewis and Clark's Corps of Discovery made contact with them.

customary damp April of 1838 the large swamp had been drained, but the weather was still cold. Stay at the work for long was difficult without a warming break near the small fire at the edge of the former swamp. It was eerily quiet and somewhat of a spectacle to see the green swampy field gently turning over behind the plow to reveal the rows of rich deep brown earth, the color of wet cocoa powder.

In the coming days and months, the eight or so acres of that early PSAC planting would turn into neat furrows, producing as much as 150,000 pounds of fresh fruits and vegetables. At first it would be almost exclusively potatoes, later many other root crops and grains would be produced. All of the fresh produce would be distributed directly to the traders at Fort Nisqually or other HBC outposts as a portion of their compensation.

It was not long before the Sequalitchew were watching, then helping, then hired to work a day, and eventually becoming regular day laborers in the PSAC farms. More swamps were drained, adding more fertile fields to plow, plant, and harvest. The Nisqually were instrumental in the farm and ranch expansion.

New buildings and new births were the natural order, as spring construction continued on a pig pen, three barns, and the fence lines. The pig pen was 60 feet by 18 feet with fourteen foundation posts. It was one of three new buildings erected that spring of 1838. A calf and a litter of kittens were born, while Kittson was successful in persuading a hen to sit on five of her own chicken eggs and five duck eggs. All of the precious eggs apparently hatched without difficulty.

While a steamship on the Mississippi River completed the run from Louisville to New Orleans in only six days, it took a little longer for news to arrive at Fort Nisqually. On June 8 Kittson learned the February 4th news from England. He wrote in the official journal, *"King William 4th died...Queen Victoria is on the throne."* He also learned of the births, deaths, and promotions of HBC officials near and far.

The men at Fort Nisqually were employed as before. The routine was setting in for another summer. Ouvré,[117] with at least two men, was on a trading expedition to the Duwamish River villages. Kittson sent McDonald, Le Pain, Latour, and John Bull to the fields with two *"lazy Owhyhees."*

Often HBC men were temporarily transferred to other posts for specific duties. Existing records do not reveal when they arrived, but a man named St. Martin, along with other men on loan from Fort Vancouver, were sent back to the Columbia in mid-summer.

---

117 First names are generally omitted here, as was the practice in the original *Journal of Occurrences* and *Indian Accounts Book*, which were written as company reports, not as historic fact. Many Indian names were simply made up by the store clerk. All were spelled in very imprecise and inaccurate phonetic style.

Anawascum was building a wheelbarrow and a cradle scythe, while periodically repairing the plough. A Yakama horse keeper left his post, allowing the horses to scatter. He was punished and forced to help retrieve the animals. Mundane farming tasks continued to typify the summer days.

A momentous event occurred at the end of July. The *Nereide*, Captain Brotche, was sighted off the small island that would someday be known at Ketron, but was now called Kittson. Every man was called to the shore to assist with the landing. It took the whole day for the tide and winds to cooperate in bringing the ship near enough to cast her anchor. The *Nereide* carried a precious cargo of live sheep from San Francisco. Of the 800 head of sheep which started the voyage from Spanish California, only 634 survived the trip. It was certainly a significant increase in the Fort Nisqually flock, however. Kittson hired two "Indian Lads" to watch over the sheep and the potato fields, while HBC men harvested peas, wheat, oats, turnips, etc. Most of the Indians were away picking berries.

In August, Kittson received word that the cattle expected after an overland cattle drive from California to Fort Vancouver had been abandoned after an attack by the Shasta Indians in southern Oregon. PSAC would mount a successful Spanish cattle drive from California in a few years. It would be longer, more dangerous, and well before the famous Texas cattle-drives began.

September 18, 1838, was another momentous and special day. At 10:20 AM and the next 2 hours and 43 minutes, the people of Puget Sound experienced a partial eclipse of the sun. Kittson made a smoked glass to make direct observation possible. He was very satisfied with his makeshift tool, but the "*Indians were much afraid and could not make out the cause of the matter.*"

Later news reports told Kittson that there was "civil commotion" in the Snake Country, where a second Fort Boise was being built. Probably the eclipse and the new construction combined to create the reported commotion.

The fine weather of October allowed much work to be accomplished, none of it new to the laborers. They were thrashing wheat and peas, digging up potatoes for days and days. Saddles were repaired and additional firewood cut and split, but these jobs were as routine as herding sheep had become. The herd was large enough now that three men were assigned the task, and more fence work was necessary. Every week or so, the split-rail fences were moved to create the same sort of overnight corral again and again. The purpose was to protect the herd, while also fertilizing a patch of ground where crops could be planted.

An old Nisqually Indian fur trader named Skthon-la-tum (called Gross-pied by the Europeans) was "*on his dying bed*" for seven days before passing. There was no word of his illness, or the cause of death. He was eulogized briefly as *"at one time a good trapper."* Kittson provided a HBC blanket to cover the body for burial.

The Fort Nisqually pit sawyers[118] were very productive. In a twenty-day period they turned out 1,236 board feet of 8'x10" planks, averaging over 7' each, plus many slabs of bark. Kittson tallied the boards as "171 pieces." Quite a "pile" of lumber produced with human sweat and muscle.

The pork production of PSAC was up considerably in 1838. On October 24th Kittson reported eight hogs butchered, "weighted and salted down." The total was an impressive 1,207 pounds of pork. The single largest animal weighed 277 pounds and the smallest at 109 pounds.

As a matter of interest and comparison, the largest PSAC potato recorded was 2½ pounds according to the *Journal of Occurrences*...

The pork production was impressive, but so was the general meat production. Some 366 of nature's creatures were either hunted or traded at Fort Nisqually for the meat. The list included salmon, geese, ducks, cranes, deer, and elk. Whale oil continued to come in as a trade item, particularly from the S'Klallam, who probably acquired it from the Makah.

Fort Nisqually men had no airplanes, trains, or automobiles to meet or to take them away. They could not know of the outer-world until somehow its news came to them. The steamer *Beaver* could bring bits of "news" from other places more frequently than any other conveyance. With a passenger on the freight-laden ship, the outer world could be very briefly glimpsed.

The men seldom missed a steamboat arrival, even in the earliest hours of the night or day. Nothing struck their imagination more than the appearance of the *SS Beaver* approaching out of the night, out of the fog, the bow headed directly at them like no sailboat dared. From the Indians' point of view, the roaring furnace with fiery eyes and thick black smoke surging from the stack, belching, coughing, with the hot steam escaping made the *Beaver* seem like a giant 100 foot-long sea monster. It was a scene to impress the poet and the superstitious.

In early November the steamer somehow found its way through the heavy fog to offloaded bales of collected pelts. According to Captain McNeill, First Mate Mr. Stouddard, and Chief Trader John Work, traveling as a passenger, the news of the coast was good. (That was the glimpse of news the lonely men needed at the foreign outpost on

---

118 A saw pit was dug under a place where a log was to be sawn, allowing for one man to work from below while a second worked the saw from above the log. Many logs were far too large to move from the forest without being sawn.

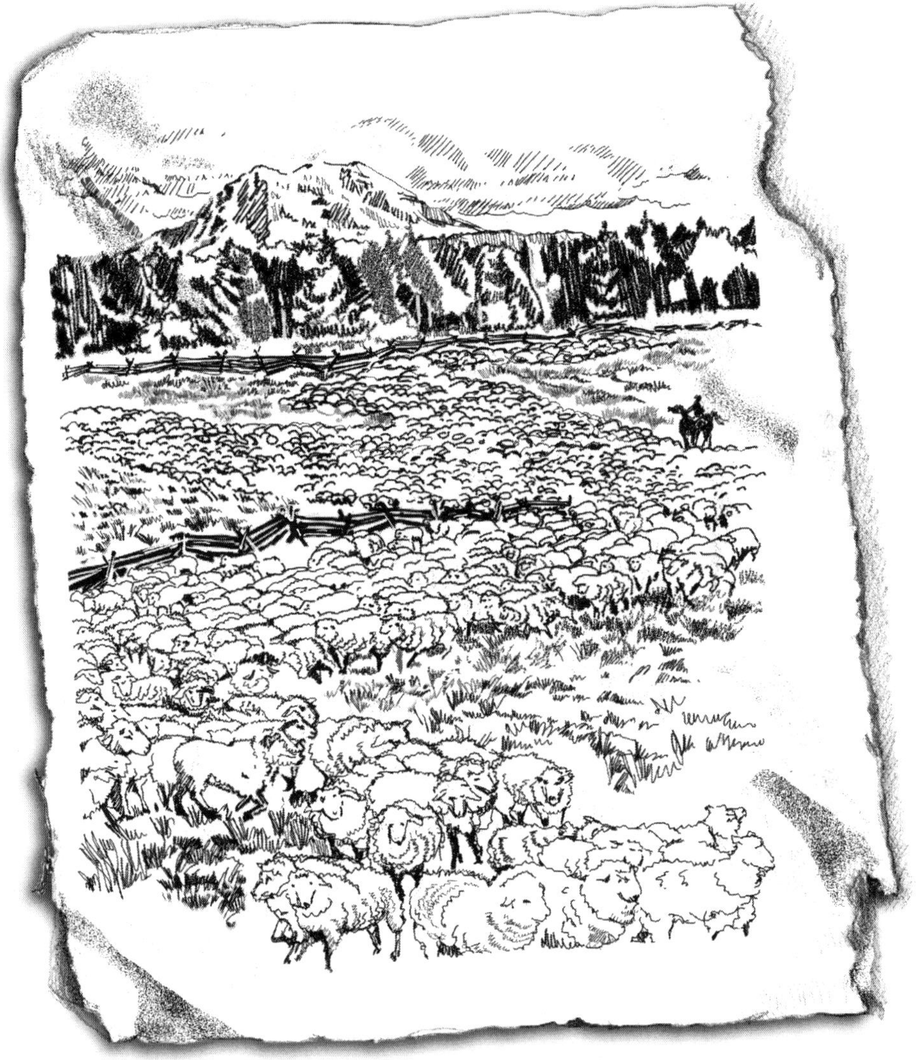

the edge of Puget Sound). McNeill, Work and four men immediately took the Cowlitz Portage to Fort Vancouver, delivering the fur cargo as a horse-back brigade. Woodcutters began gathering and loading cords of fuel for the boilers at day break. The sailors rested after a long voyage, while the engineers cleaned the boilers of spent wood ash and clinkers, and refilled the water tanks.

At Fort Vancouver things were different when the fur packers arrived. Doctor John McLoughlin was gone. He had begun a long anticipated leave of absence in the spring of 1838. At the director's meeting in London, McLoughlin pointed out his added responsibilities of administering the PSAC accounts and the newly leased Russian territories (Alaska Panhandle area) to the already heavy burden of the fur trade business in the Columbia Department of HBC that he operated from Fort Vancouver. The Governor and Committee were very impressed with his descriptive workload. They agreed to a salary of £500[119] per year for the new responsibilities, in addition to his earnings as Chief Factor.

While in London, McLoughlin learned that on July 3, 1838, PSAC shares[120] were finally made available to the stockholders, Directors, and Gentlemen of the HBC. At about the same time a company policy was established to treat religious missionaries with respect, courtesy, and a piece of ground for a church and sustaining crops.

To extend the Oregon Methodist Mission of the Willamette Valley, Reverend Jason Lee chose a site at Nisqually on September 29, 1834. Lee assigned Reverend David Leslie to Nisqually, along with William Holden Wilson, a carpenter at the Oregon Methodist Mission, to build the amenities for a mission, home, and school. The place would house an ordained minister, his family, and a teacher.

Reverend Jason Lee saw great potential for missionary work in Old Oregon Country as part of the American political destiny. Lee was not the first American to reach the area. As we have seen, Captain Robert Gray (1792) came by sea, and Captains Meriwether Lewis and William Clark came overland (1803–1805). The Winship brothers set up a trading post in 1810. Not much is written about these men because their enterprise faded quickly in the face of native opposition and nature's challenges. Nature came in the form of a devastating flood. Indian pilfering depleted the inventory of trade goods at the Winship's trading post.

German immigrant John Jacob Astor's Fort Astoria was built in 1811. The men of the Canadian North West Company arrived there in 1812, among them John Baptiste Ouvré, who was probably the first white man to visit Puget Sound by land. It is believed that

---

119 Purchasing power of about $30,000 today.
120 See the Washington Historical Quarterly article by Leonard A. Wrinsch, a downloadable PDF at journals.lib.washington.edu/index.php/WHQ/article/…/8572/7607

trapper and trader Ouvré ventured far and wide from Astoria in search of the precious "soft gold" beaver pelts.

Fort Astoria changed hands from American to British and back again during the War of 1812. It was renamed Fort George during the British takeover, but eventually was acquired by the HBC after the merger of the venerable Company and the North West Company in 1821. By 1824 it was virtually closed in favor of the new Fort Vancouver, 200 navigable miles upstream on the North bank of the Columbia.

Reverend Lee was aware of this bit of history as he pressed Chief Factor McLoughlin for true "joint occupancy" north, as well as south, of the mighty river. He campaigned by letter for more Methodist Missionaries to join him in occupying all parts of the Oregon Country, including the Puget Sound area. His reasoning was based on missionary work: his politics worked toward fulfilling America's dream of Manifest Destiny. Exactly when Reverend Lee visited Fort Nisqually is uncertain, but sometime during early 1838 he selected a site about a half mile east of the fort's primary buildings to construct a mission house and school.

With reinforcements approved and already traveling west, Lee returned to the East recruiting more religious leaders. The Reverend Leslie and Mr. Willson began construction of the Nisqually Methodist Mission house. The exact location selected for the Mission was along the south side of Sequalitchew Creek,[121] above the bluff, southeast of American Lake, at the western edge of the vast prairies that stretched through what is today DuPont, Fort Lewis, University Place, McChord Air Force Base, Tacoma, Parkland, Spanaway, and on to Elk Plain and even to Muck Creek at Roy.

Reverend Jason Lee, with full knowledge of (and probably with assistance from) William Kittson, selected the site for the Nisqually Methodist Mission. With the creation of the PSAC, Fort Nisqually needed to move the center of operations from the beach and the edge of the bluff above Puget Sound, to the prairies. The actual move would not occur for some years, but planning had apparently begun. The Mission would be well suited to the spot north of the little Sequalitchew Creek. Kittson's selected new fort site was south of the creek, perhaps 200 yards from the mission property.

William Holden Willson earned his passage to Oregon as a ship's carpenter. He studied medicine and assisted the ship's doctor during the voyage. He has been described as somewhat eccentric for his nearly consuming passion for cats and tobacco. Once in Oregon he continued the practiced frontier medicine. Apparently he learned his limited medical skills well in practical situations. He may have also learned some medical skills

---

121 An historic marker sits along the current Sequalitchew Creek Trail, a few yards from the Dupont city hall, where the well-marked trail begins. It is a short, mostly paved, trail to the water's edge.

from relatives who operated a pharmacy in New England. As most "doctors" in the 19th century, he had no formal schooling beyond some tutoring by other, mostly self educated doctors.

Willson's credentials should not be taken as a derogatory description. In fact, most of the "Colonels" and "Captains," even "Generals" who crossed the Oregon Trail took their titles after being elected to leadership positions for the journey, not for having earned them. It was a practice developed by local militia during the Civil War to determine leadership positions. Lincoln and Grant were both elected "captains" at early points in their careers. Doctors were titled much in the same way.

Reverend David Leslie, his wife, and three children were among the first of the Methodists in Oregon. Leslie was, in fact, in charge of the Willamette Methodist Mission (1838–1840) while Reverend Lee was in the east recruiting more help for the huge task of missionary work. As an administrator and jack-of-all-trades, his reports to the American Board of Missions during his tenure reveal a great deal of history.

Reverend Leslie was unanimously elected by the settlers in the Willamette Valley to the position of "Willamette Valley Justice of the Peace and Chairman of the Committee," which would formalize a provisional government for Oregon Country. It was a direct challenge to Dr. John McLoughlin's (HBC) views. McLoughlin also saw Leslie as responsible for the aggressive anti-Hudson's Bay Company petition circulated in 1838.

While more missionaries were being escorted to the Willamette Valley by the Hudson's Bay Company, Charles Dickens was enjoying the success of his novels *Oliver Twist* and *Nicolas Nickleby*. Shares of PSAC stock were legally and formally issued in London.

1839

ON FEBRUARY 27 1839, a committee of the Hudson's Bay Company met at Hudson's Bay House (London) to discuss *"a prospectus for the formation of an association to be styled the "Puget's Sound Agricultural Company..."*[122] The prospectus detailed the objects of the company and was favorably received by the gentlemen present. They expected that a significant branch of the HBC could be created while *"improving the conditions of the native Indians and other persons habiting that remote country..."* [123]

A resolution was passed to permit the PSAC to *"carry on contemplated operations"* with assistance and support from the HBC. The new company would raise *"flocks and herds on an extensive scale"* and produce *"Wool, Hides, and Tallow for the British market"* and agricultural produce for the Columbia District. The association was capitalized at £200,000 with 2,000 shares. The prospectus was issued on March 20, 1839.

PSAC management the first year consisted of Sir George Simpson, Henry Pelly[124], and Deputy Governor Andrew Colvile, with annual elections thereafter. These three held controlling interest with twenty shares apiece. Plans were also made to incorporate the PSAC to seek a land grant. It was a contingency plan based on the possibility of the HBC license cancellation. Sir George Simpson wrote:

> *We are strengthening that claim to it (the territory)...by forming the nucleus of a colony through the establishment of farms and the settlement of some of our retired officers and servants as agriculturalist.*[125]

---

122 Wrinch, Leonard A., in the Washington Historical Quarterly (undated) quoting from his Master's Thesis on "The Land Policy of Vancouver Island, 1849—1866" at the University of British Columbia, in which Winch quoted the "Minutes of a Committee" document in the British Columbia Archives, Victoria, B.B., Envelope E P 316 (undated).

123 IBID.

124 Henry Pelly was the son of Sir John Pelly, Director of Hudson's Bay Company.

125 http://www.hbcheritage.ca/hbcheritage/history/businesws/other/pugetsound

A circular, with the prospectus enclosed, was distributed to officers and clerks throughout the Northwest to invite individuals to purchase stock in the company. It can safely be assumed that a monopoly of shares was held by Gentleman employees of the HBC.[126] Dr. John McLoughlin, as the manager of the Columbia Department for the HBC, sent a dispatch detailing the establishment of a PSAC farm at Cowlitz, and a ranch at Nisqually. Crops were to be planted on "as much land as convenient with the least possible delay" to relieve the HBC of the Agricultural Produce Contract with the Russian American Company." McLoughlin expected that setters from England would soon be sent. He said that Nisqually lands would be used primarily for rearing of flocks and herds of sheep and cattle. Some ground at Nisqually would be cultivated to provide animal fodder and some for local human consumption. Animals were to be imported from Spanish California (Bona Ventura), conveyed by sea from Yerba Buena, and overland by a cattle and sheep drive planned for the coming trapping expedition of 1841. McLoughlin expected about 1,000 young cows.

Coincidentally, there was a formal trade agreement between Russian American Fur Company and Hudson's Bay Company concluded in Hamburg on February 6, which probably expedited the PSAC formation. For ten years HBC had been trying to establish friendly relations with the Russian company. One assumes the effort was made to assure a market, although the Russians were never mentioned in HBC minutes. Governor Simpson's signature appears on both the Russian trade agreement and the document launching the PSAC. Nisqually, it was hoped, could supply beef to the Russians and wool to the English.

With its position on Puget Sound, the businesses at Nisqually promised to offer virtually unlimited quantities of various commodities. There was only one obstacle, the aggressive American immigrant seeking to seize the one essential ingredient. That one essential was the monopoly on the arable and pasture land north of the Columbia River and west of the Cascade Mountains.

The importance of the Russian contract can be surmised by the quantities of produce involved only two years later. Fort Nisqually shipped 8,400 bushels of wheat sold at five shillings per bushel, and 17,920 pounds of butter, at sixpence a pound.[127] Actual 1839 commodities production at Fort Nisqually (PSAC) included:[128]

---

126 In a list of stockholders containing 155 names, 86 were HBC men, according to the B.C. Archives' Library staff member. People other than HBC employees also held stock in the HBC. The list is undated, but is believed to originate between 1860 and 1876.

127 Wheat sold at five shillings per bushel. 8,400 bushels sold for $10,500. Six pence equals about ten cents, so the butter sold for about $1792.00. http://www.baldwin.co.uk/PRDF22/ Press Release 5 Jun 2013.

128 Stuart Walter Henry, *Some Aspects of the Life of William Fraser Tolmie,* Unpublished Thesis, University of British Columbia, Vancouver, September, 1948.

160 cwt wheat
130 cwt peas
130 cwt grits & barley
300 cwt salted beef
160 cwt salted butter
30 cwt pork hams

Personnel assigned to the PSAC farms were:[129]

At Cowlitz Farms	At Nisqually Farms
1 Principal Farmer	1 Clerk in charge
1 Principal Shepherd	1 Ploughman [sic]
2 Assistant Shepherds	1 Rough Carpenter
6 Ploughmen	4 European Herdsmen
1 Blacksmith	2 Indian Herdsmen
1 Assistant Blacksmith	
2 Canadian Laboring Servants	
10 Canadian Laborers	
2 Rough Carpenters	

The original intention in forming PSAC was to select indentured servants, or tenant farmers, under the complete control of the watchful eyes of the company to settle on 1,000 acre farms. The company expected to control leasing, as well as select the individuals from a long line of eager applicants. Another source of ready labor was to be supplied from the Red River Settlement in Rupert's Land, near present-day Winnipeg, Manitoba. The actual Red River originates in present-day North Dakota, flowing northward through about 395 miles of the United States, then some 160 miles into Canada.

McLoughlin presented details for closely regulated tenant farmers from England and the Red River. The details were probably perfectly designed for potential English arrivals, and not so much for the Métis of the Red River. The conditions of settlement were, however, in extreme contrast to the American settlers' entrepreneurialism and unexpected aggressiveness to obtain "free land."

HBC strategy was to formally notify American squatters of trespassing. In Chief Factor James Douglas' words:

> "…to warn off all new comers, in a pleasant way, and keep always on the right side of the law."[130]

---

129 Winch, Leonard A., *Washington Historical Quarterly*, undated, photocopy in author's possession.

130 http://www.hbcheritage.ca/history

The company kept detailed records, copies of all letters and notices, so that at some later date the legal process might allow damage claims by the beleaguered English businesses.

HBC encouraged settlement north of the Columbia River, but held the best land for the farming enterprise. British settlers were expected to comply with strict contracts that favored the company. Farmers could expect 1,000 acres of lease land, 20 cows, one bull, 500 sheep, 8 oxen, 6 horses, and a few pigs. Leases were to run five years, with provisions provided by the company until crops were harvested. At the end of the lease all land and buildings would revert to the company, along with half of the increase of the livestock. This tenant farmer contract was typical of the era, except for the Americans, who got free land south of the river.

Fort Nisqually's first three months of 1839 were about as routine and monotonous as any had been. There was always something in need of attention no matter what the grand plans might entail. The sheep herds were growing. The prized "Red Cow" sadly lost her calf shortly after birth, but other cows were expected to increase the herd that spring. Horse stock could be increased or decreased almost at will, simply by trading with the very skillful and successful Nisqually horse traders, such as Leschi, who[131] had "connections" with the Yakima horse traders east of the Cascades. Considerable labor during the year went into curing many pounds of mutton and beef, filling casks with the salted meat, then loading it aboard vessels for shipment to Russian America. The meat fulfilled much of the PSAC contract with the Russian American Fur Trade Company at Sitka.

On October 9, 1838 through May 21, 1839, a speed record for news delivery was established at Nisqually. The notable achievement was accomplished when a ship sailed around Cape Horn, South America, to the Columbia River, in less than eight months. Of course, a roundtrip to London was expected to take more than twice that long. In spite of the distances involved, the connections were becoming more frequent. Local and regional travel helped to scatter the news, too.

Chief Trader Kittson ventured to Fort Vancouver and Fort Langley, while his men planted the spring crops, tended the animals and the Trade Store. While at Vancouver, he was probably informed of the legal formation of the Puget Sound Agricultural Company (PSAC) to be located at Fort Nisqually and Cowlitz Farms. He was also instructed as to the treatment of the American Missionaries as decreed by the London Governors of the Hudson's Bay Company. It was important to know the policies, as Fort Nisqually

---

131 Leschi should not be called a "Chief" as he was not one until the Medicine Creek Treaty written by Governor Isaac Stevens so declared. Most historians agree the Nisqually did not use the title. Author notes.

was about to have some new neighbors. This important news did circulate in spite of distances.

One bit of that news was about the Methodist Church, but it was not only newsworthy within its own institutional infancy. The missionary zeal that John Wesley preached was the news of Methodism in the early 19th Century. Success came when the Methodist Church in America was officially organized in 1784, in Baltimore. By 1839 it was spreading all across America. When the Wesley brothers returned to England, they were convinced of the failure of their mission to America. It was a church that John Wesley, its "founder," never joined. He preferred the government-approved, therefore "official" Church of England.

The Oregon Methodist Mission constructed along the Willamette River was initiated in 1832, a year before the construction of Fort Nisqually began. The Fort was still subject to some indecision about a permanent location in 1834, even after construction had begun at Sequalitchew Creek. The British fur traders were well aware of the Methodist preacher's efforts to establish an American religious presence on the Pacific Coast. It was only a matter of time before they would expand upstream along the Columbia to build a mission at The Dalles, and then to the north on the shores of Puget Sound.

Sometime in late 1838, Jason Lee, leader of the six year old Willamette Oregon Methodist Mission, selected the first Christian mission site on Puget Sound. It was near the fresh water of Sequalitchew Creek, at the edge of a vast prairie, upstream from the old Nisqually Indian village and the new Hudson's Bay Company fur trader's post. Fort Nisqually was relocated to a site opposite the Methodist's creekside spot nearly three years later.

Methodist missionary Reverend David Leslie was temporarily assigned to the new mission site at Nisqually. He left his wife and three daughters at the Willamette Mission, arriving with only a carpenter, William Holden Willson, at Fort Nisqually on April 10, 1839.[132] They were greeted warmly, but formally, by William Kittson, the HBC Trader and Supervisor of the fledgling Puget Sound Agricultural Company at Fort Nisqually. A bevy of curious Nisqually were also present.

Leslie and Willson were the first American citizens, however described (missionaries? settlers? pioneers? immigrants?) to live in the Puget Sound basin. These American pioneers arrived more than five years before the famous "First Americans" of the Bush-Simmons party of 1845, and six years before the Boundary Treaty officially declared the area as American land. At the time of these Methodist arrivals, the original, but revised,

---

[132] Methodists occupied the Fort Nisqually Methodist Mission from April 10, 1839 until September 1, 1842, a total of three years and five months. Author's calculations.

1818 international treaty proclaimed all of Old Oregon to be Joint Occupancy Territory for the British and the Americans.

Rev. Leslie and Mr. Willson immediately built a home and a school. It was two years before Congress sent the famed U.S. Navy Exploring Expedition from the United States around Antarctica and across the Pacific to Puget Sound.[133] Growing public pressure to explore the west pushed congressional policy for naval research to follow the U.S. Corps of Discovery, led by Lewis and Clark thirty-five years earlier. A petition, with extreme accusation against the British was sent by 67 Oregonians for U.S. jurisdiction and protection to the Secretary of War.

Willson had boarded the *Hamilton* in 1836, on the Atlantic seaboard. He was bound for Oregon Country, by way of the Sandwich Islands. Doctor Elijah White[134] was one of his traveling companions. Willson had begun medical training in New England pharmacies, and continued training with Dr. White. Willson's medical education was typical of the era, as most medical instruction came from practicing doctors. Many frontier doctors had significantly less training than Willson received during the long sea passage and five month layover in the Islands. Willson studied Dr. White's books earnestly. The teacher–student relationship continued aboard the *Diana*, while re-crossing the Pacific, bringing them to Fort Vancouver in late April, 1837.

The *Fort Nisqually Journal of Occurrences* details the historic events of April 10, 1839, when Americans first put down roots and began constructing a firm foundation on the bluff near the shores of Puget Sound. With great ceremony, and the full cooperation and assistance of the Fort Nisqually men, the Methodists began to collect the construction materials they would need. As if to recognize and reinforce the English-American Joint Occupancy Treaty in effect at the time, the first tree was felled, with some ceremonial festivity. American Willson swung the first ax, while (Canadian) Kittson struck the last in great symbolic cooperation, toppling the first tree for the American Methodist Mission. Then Kittson, with dripping diplomacy, suggested that the preacher's broad ax should be sharpened… on the Fort Nisqually grinding wheel, of course.

That first building stood alone for nearly two years at the edge of the grassy plain in full view of Mt. Tacoma.

---

133 Job Carr, often called the first Tacoma settler, arrived in 1864. Nicolas Delin opened his sawmill in what is now Tacoma on April 1, 1852. Author's observations.

134 White was an agent for the U.S. government in Oregon while acting as a Missionary with Rev. Jason Lee. Animosity developed between the two men, resulting in White's departure and later return with a wagon train of 112 settlers in 18 wagons in 1842. White became the official Indian agent of the U.S. government and a leader in the Oregon Provisional Government by 1843. .http//en.wikipedia.org/wiki/Elijah_White

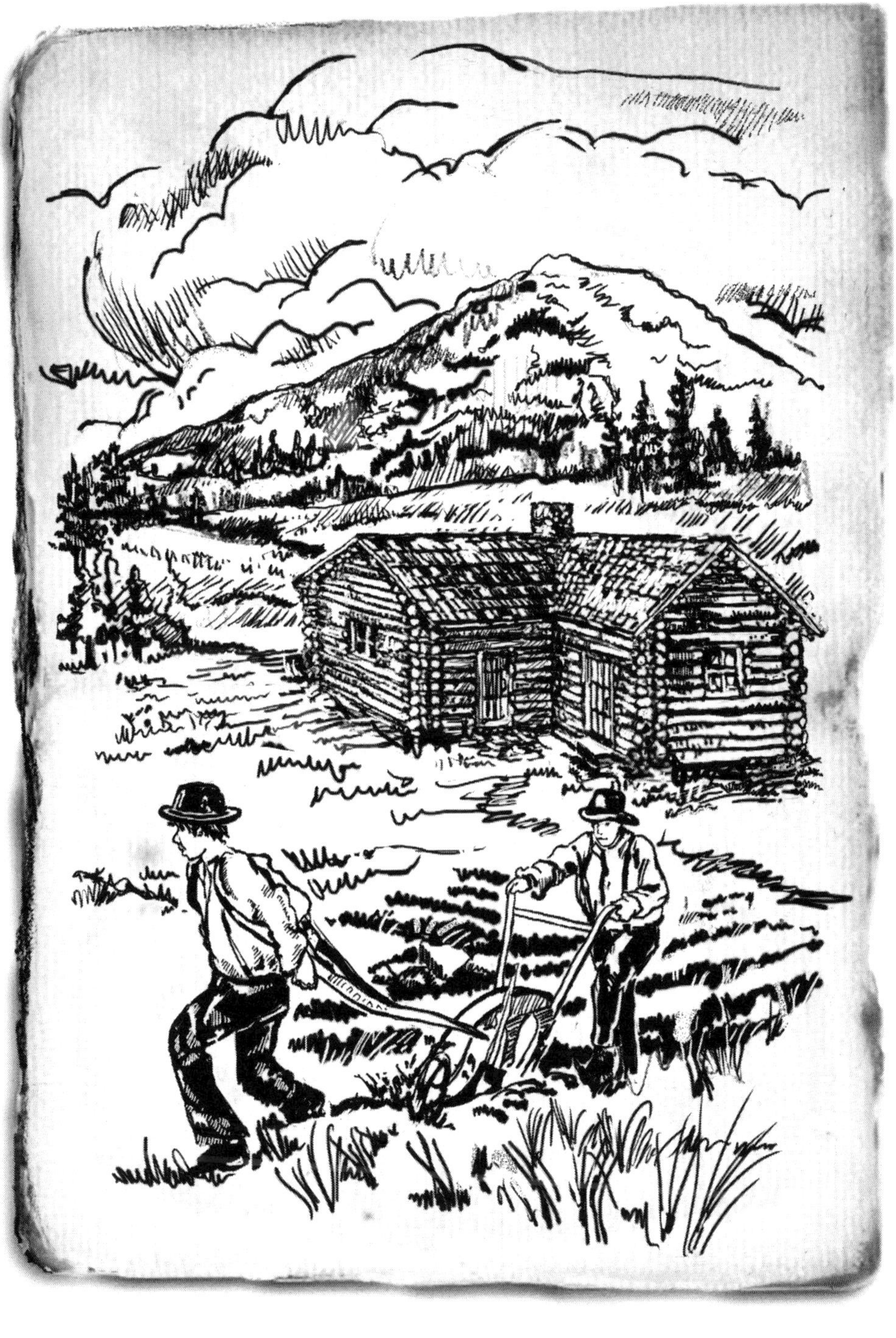

Willson positioned the Nisqually Methodist Mission house upstream, and much closer to fresh water than either the existing fort or the Indian village. Nearby fir trees, at the very edge of the prairie, were readily available for walls and fences. The very rocky soil, while not prime, was adequate for the needs of the tiny Methodist community. The prairie, with a clear vista of Mt. Tacoma, would soon be called the American Plain. It is not far from what is now called American Lake. The early influence of these very first American pioneers is still felt today in the city of Dupont. Today, City Hall is practically next door to the mission site.

There is little doubt that the Americans selected the site after consultation with Chief Trader Kittson. They were certainly aware of Kittson's plans to move the main Fort Nisqually buildings from the bluff and beach to the inland prairie and nearer to fresh water. The relocation was, no doubt, tied to the revised business plan developed in London to incorporate PSAC. Eventually Fort Nisqually and the PSAC agri-business would occupy 161,000 acres, for enormous farming and ranching activities. The Methodist home, school, and gardens probably occupied no more than a couple of acres, at most, along the northern side of Sequalitchew Creek.

Fort Nisqually and PSAC faced absolutely no business competition from the Methodists, but religious competition for the Methodists was coming. Many earlier requests by the fur traders for Roman Catholic priests to come west of the Rockies were ignored. But the arrival of the Methodists stirred the Catholics in the east to fund missionaries of their own.

Years earlier several Iroquois Indians from New York had followed Hudson's Bay Fur Traders westward, first into the Great Lakes Region, then the Canadian prairies. Often both the Europeans and the Iroquois married into local tribes. It was no different when the Iroquois reached the Rockies, the Bitterroot Mountains, or Puget Sound. They regaled their newly adopted families with tales of the east. The stories included legends of "Black Robes," that is, white men who wore black gowns, carried golden crucifixes, and remained wifeless after vowing to spread the word of the Great Spirit who granted life after death. The stories had great appeal to the Indians because they, too, had oral traditions that closely matched the Iroquois interpretations of Christianity.

The advance of Catholicism was a challenge to Protestant Americans. Foreign missions had been a mainstay of protestant faith from its earliest days. Sending missionaries to Oregon Country was different only in that this territory had the potential to become part of the country's manifest destiny, that politician's dream of a vast nation stretching from ocean to ocean, and perhaps isthmus to the Arctic, too. So with political support and ambition, Oregon Missions began.

At about 11 AM on April 21, 1839, possibly during Reverend Leslie's first Methodist Sunday Sermon at the Nisqually Mission, Father Demers of the Roman Catholic Church arrived. It was only eleven days after the Methodists arrival at Fort Nisqually, a clear competitive challenge quickly organized.[135] Reverend Leslie emphasized the Bible, in all probability, urging the Indians in attendance to learn to read the stories of Christianity. Father Demers probably told the story of Christ with the help of an interpreter, who closely matched the Iroquois versions already familiar to the Nisqually people. Reading is often a difficult process, while hearing an oral tale is easy and it "fit" well in the Nisqually tradition. One experience was enchanting, perhaps, while the other was considerably more labor-intensive.

1839 was the year the St. Francis Mission was established on the Cowlitz Prairie to convert the Indians and serve the spiritual needs of the five fur traders who lived there with their Indian wives and children.[136] Father Francis Norbert Blanchet planted the first cross and celebrated the first mass, but it was Father Modeste Demers who erected a small log chapel and a priest's dwelling. He also laid out a cemetery before his departure. It was left to one of his successors, Father Richard, to build the first Catholic mission school more than two decades later.

Jesuit society contributions to American life were significant. They were active from the first Spanish and French explorer–missionary expeditions. Father Pierre–Jean DeSmet, a charismatic missionary, helped broker peace between Sitting Bull and the U.S. Army before he arrived at Puget Sound.

While the Methodists at Nisqually were engaged in only their second regular Sunday worship services at the new mission, Father Demers and his Indian entourage were warmly greeted by the fur traders at Fort Nisqually. Demers traveled with representatives of some twenty-two tribes of Indians. Today we might call them "Groupies," but there was an advantage to having many Indian supporters as the priest entered a village.

John and Charles Wesley, founders of the Methodist Society, never separated from the Church of England, and were never "members' of the Methodist Church. They were

---

135 Coast Salish are believed to have traded for crucifixes and rosaries with Spanish explorers in 1774-75, according to the Catholic Encyclopedia, The Encyclopedia Press, 1913, and in 1907 by Robert Appleton Company, 1907. French Canadian fur traders probably kept the memory alive after the first contact, until the arrival of Father Demers in 1839. Methodists do not use jewelry beads or crucifixes, but the Indians were attracted to the simple shiny symbols. It was a disadvantage the Methodists could not overcome.

136 The five families were led by James Birnie, George Roberts, Simon Plomondon, Marcel Bernier, and Antonie Gobar. All five were employed by or retired from the HBC. All were married to Indian women except Roberts. Author's notes.

intent on creating a "Society" within the official Anglican Church of England, their homeland, when they brought the Methodist Society to America. It took many years for the "Society" movement to become an organized church in America. The Methodist Missionary system is still an important part of the United Methodist Church in the 21st Century.

Historically, Methodist men traditionally dressed in very conservative long sleeve shirts, dark waistcoats, and trousers for the weekday sweat equity work of building a home and school. It was a "method" of displaying, or witnessing, personal faith in God. Every day except Sunday they were engaged in serious physical labor and farm work. Methodists sang only hymns, did not dance or play games, and certainly did not gamble or drink alcohol of any kind. Even Holy Communion was practiced strictly and exclusively with unfermented juice of the grape.[137] Alcohol in wine was rejected because of the temptations it offered. The frontier Methodist lifestyle was austere in the extreme by today's standards.

No Methodist preacher ever claimed to have an exclusive direct connection to God. In fact every person, they believe, could pray to God without the intercession of any other person, especially a priest or other clergy. Confessions were generally private conversations between a person and God. Only when a sin was publicly known did a person feel compelled to confess that sin publicly. Public confessions were offered in open church meetings when forgiveness was asked of the public as well as of God.

Alternatively, the Roman Catholic priest wore traditional black robes. He performed a ceremonial and rhythmic Latin canticle. Puget Sound Indians saw that Father Demers[138] offered mystery and magic, with timeless rhythms and undulating incantations in a hushed candlelit room. Kittson provided the room, and therefore *"official fur trader sanctions"* inside Fort Nisqually. The Catholic rituals and oral histories appealed to the Nisqually, many say, for they also used ceremonial garb, rituals, and rhythmic chants. The similarities were uncanny, in stark contrast to the Methodists.

The Methodists offered less than subtle back-breaking farm and construction work, too. They sang solemn hymns and read English language Bibles as they witnessed for their faith strictly by example. They did not have the obvious approval of Trader Kittson

---

137 Thomas Bramwell Welch and his son Charles processed the first "unfermented wine" to use during Methodist Church communion services. Welch developed a pasteurization process that halted fermentation. *"An Outline History of the Wesleyan Church,"* 4th edition Indianapolis, Indiana. Wesley Press, 1990, p. 68.

138 Demers began a Chinook Jargon dictionary that was not completed until 1867 by Father Blanchard, and not published until 1871 by L. N. St. Onge.

that the Catholic Priest enjoyed, and certainly not the "inside" accommodations. Methodists were easily identified as "outsiders," foreigners, "Boston men" who were "different" and less accepted than Roman Catholic missionaries. The latter seemed like old friends of the Iroquois, voyageurs, and French-Canadian HBC men, so by extension became new friends of the Nisqually.

Undaunted, the two American Methodist pioneers continued their construction work at Nisqually, proudly preparing a place for the recently appointed Methodist preacher, his wife and children as well as a young female school teacher. The Methodists repudiated all that they considered ostentatious ritual and ceremony. Their religious ceremony was very frugal and very fundamental, performed by preacher and layman alike, most often in equal measure.

The Catholic priest performed the rituals of baptism, marriage, and confession, as did the Methodists, but with great dramatic performance and rhythmic Latin poetry during his 12-day visit. He left Nisqually on May 2, 1839, with his coterie of adherents intact as any camp followers had ever been.

The more practical Methodists turned the soil and planted garden crops. Without a plow or draft animals, the prairie sod was broken by strong backs and hand blisters, only to find rocky alluvial dirt virtually unworthy of farming. The Methodists put great stock in being a "witness" for their faith. The Greek word "*martys*," from which English derives martyr, means "witness for faith." The martyr is one who suffers for his faith, that is, provides an opportunity for others to witness the depth of his devotion to God. Thus these hard working men were demonstrating their devotion, and trusted in the belief that divine revelation, or realization, would somehow ultimately prevail among the Native Americans through Methodist example or witness. That philosophy was working all across America, as Methodist churches saw ever-increasing membership numbers for over a century, well into the 1950s. The Methodist philosophy was tailor made for the American culture of the era. It was almost completely alien to the Indian culture of that period.

Willson and Leslie planted a kitchen garden large enough to feed themselves and the men, women, and children who would soon occupy the little colonial outpost. The Methodist School was expected to enroll the children of the fort and the Indian village for elementary instruction in reading. The crops planted in April were harvested before winter, then stored. There had to be enough laid away for the two men to stay the winter and feed the six hungry replacements in the coming spring and summer before new crops could be grown for a second harvest in 1840.

Four years after the Nisqually Methodist Mission began, the journal of a Presbyterian missionary, Thomas J. Farnham, was published. It was commissioned by Horace Greely in an effort to publicize the Oregon Trail. Farnham related his experience with the Presbyterian Missionaries among the Nez Perce:

> "I attended the Indian school to-day. Mrs. Whitman is an indefatigable instructress. The children read in monosyllables… repeat a number of hymns…. They learn music readily.
>
> The course pursued by Dr. Whitman and other Missionaries to improve the Indians is to teach them… Fixed grammatical rules…opening to them the Arts and Religion of civilized nations
>
> At 10 o'clock the Indians had assembled for worship in the open air. The exercises were in the Presbyterian form: the invocation, the hymn, the prayer, the hymn, the sermon, a prayer, a hymn, the blessing; all in the Indian Tongue.[139]

The Farnham journal tells the story of many mission locations in significant ways.

In late August, 1839, while the Methodists (preacher Leslie and carpenter Willson) continued to hold regular Sunday services for the Indians, harvest their crops, and store the yield for winter, a second Catholic priest visited Fort Nisqually. Father Blanchet received a warm welcome from William Kittson, who generously provided a house for the priest to live in during his short visit. Blanchet performed in much the same way that Demers had for a few days four months earlier. Speaking in the Chinook Jargon trade language, Nisqually people were baptized and married by the priest. Mass was said in Latin, however, with soothing ritual and ceremony.

The Methodists offered their simple ceremony, austere by comparison, along with the struggle of some back-breaking work during a rigorous daily continuum of life. The civil, yet intensely earnest, Christian competition continued politely. Willson, a surprisingly literate carpenter who had studied medicine, served as the legal observer (by signing his name) at two Catholic weddings at Fort Nisqually. Why the devout Methodist was chosen to witness Catholic ceremonies is anybody's guess, but the fact that he could read and write may have been a major factor. Few fort employees beyond the leadership were literate. Kittson may have been the only literate HBC man at Fort Nisqually at that time. None of the local Indians could read or write.

William Holden Willson was born in Massachusetts of English ancestry. As a youngster, he learned carpentry skills. He stood five feet, ten inches in height. Contemporaries

---

139 Farnham, Thomas J. "An 1839 Wagon Train Journal of Travels in the Great Western Prairies, the Anahuac and Rocky Mountains and in the Oregon Territory," Greely & Mc Elrath, Tribune Building, New York, 1843. Reprint by Northwest Interpretive Association, Bracken Hill Press, Monroe, Oregon.

described him as cheerful, sympathetic, and affectionate. He was fond of telling old sea stories from his days as a ship's carpenter on an American Whaler out of Boston to the North Atlantic. One of Willson's peculiar characteristics was his almost childish affection for cats. He talked to them as if they were human. That is not a bad thing, just noteworthy.

Willson was also fond of tobacco, a near-universal trait among men of the fur trade era. Willson is known to have studied medicine at every practical opportunity. It was a difficult task, as medical colleges did not exist then as we know them today. Textbooks were rare. With carpentry and limited medical skills, the Reverend Jason Lee offered William Holden Willson a position (July 28, 1836) in the secular department of the Methodist Missions in Oregon Country. Willson would be hired as a carpenter, with higher aspirations and potential.

Later, Lee expressed some concern over Willson's practice of medicine. Lee wrote that Willson could bring *"...some of us...to an untimely grave."*[140] But then, Lee had no personal medical training of his own, and the Mission certainly needed some sort of additional medical skills. Absent of choice, Willson was the doctor.

An enormous opportunity for the Puget Sound Agricultural Company came in 1839 when the Russian–American Fur Company allowed British ships to travel across a section of Russian coastline at Glacier Bay (Alaska). The British wanted access to the interior for the beaver fur trade available there. The Russians were having difficulty feeding their people at Sitka due to the short growing season at that northern latitude. Both companies were monopolies protected by their governments. So while the governments fought a war in the Crimean and Black Sea, the capitalist fur companies traded food for furs and made geographic compromises.

It is interesting to note that Doctor Tolmie, while residing at Fort Simpson, was following the occurrences at Nisqually. On January 9, 1839, Tolmie had written directly to the Methodist Missionaries endorsing the Americans to endeavor working at Fort Nisqually:

> *"What a promising field for missionary enterprise Nisqually and Fort Langley present. Schools...at these places would...elevate [sic] the Physical and Moral Condition of the Natives, and could be carried on at moderate expense*[141].*"*

---

140 Lee to corresponding secretary (Willamette Falls, March 39 1843) Loewenberg, Robert J., *Equality on the Oregon Frontier, Jason Lee and the Methodist Mission, 1834-1843.* University of Washington Press, Seattle, 1976.

141 Tolmie, W.F. *"The Journals of William Fraser Tolmie, Physician and Fur Trader,* "Mitchell Press Limited, Vancouver, Canada, 1963.

He also sent personal *"compliments to Mrs. Leslie, and the ladies and gentlemen of the Mission."*

At Fort Nisqually during the spring, summer and fall of 1839, Willson and Leslie built, plowed, and planted in preparation for the already expanding Nisqually Methodist Mission. They first built a structure 18' x 12' of simple chinked log walls with a split cedar shingle roof, with smooth flat floor boards, presumably cut at the Fort Nisqually pit saw, (although Leslie and certainly Willson were quite capable of smoothing floor boards with hand tools). Completion of the first Mission House in the late spring gave the men the opportunity to erect an 18' x 20' school addition to one side of the original dwelling house. With a total of about 935 square feet of living space, with wooden floors, the Mission was becoming quite comfortable, even by frontier standards.

Willson and Leslie proceeded to surround the acreage near Mission House, school, and vegetable tracts with a solid nine foot-high fir-post fence of timbers set in a hand-dug trench several feet deep. They planted crops of peas, potatoes, carrots, onions, turnips, etc., in the glacial till soil. They were fully aware of the need for the garden produce to sustain them over the winter. Knowing that a family of growing children would soon arrive probably motivated the preservation of a great deal of food supplies. In the next spring (1840) they expanded their vegetable garden two-fold.

Meanwhile, at nearby Fort Nisqually, Kittson and his men received word of the contract with the Russian fur traders at Sitka, Russian America. Fort Nisqually and PSAC had plenty of work ahead. The 10-year contract provided the Russians with butter, ham, salted beef, wheat, flour, and other food supplies to be produced at Fort Nisqually by the Puget Sound Agricultural Company. It was an agreement extending to 1850. This contract helped eliminate American fur trade, supply ships, and even whalers from the North Pacific, while it expanded the export market for HBC and PSAC.

The farms and ranches of PSAC would be built on the prairies stretching from the Columbia to Puget Sound along the Cowlitz Portage. The trail was sometimes called the Mountain Portage, but is really a trail crossing a series of rolling hills between parallel streams generally flowing westward from the Cascade Mountains to the Pacific Ocean. Along the Cowlitz Trail, the traveler of 1839 found considerable coniferous forest lands interspersed with more abundant grassy openings. These "plains" or "prairies" amounted to some eighteen places along the 60 miles trail. In terms of area the prairies totaled perhaps 6,000 acres in the southern portion. Those prairies north of midway were each fifteen to twenty miles long, and five to fifteen miles wide. Later Dr. Tolmie would state that the Puget

Sound Company occupied... "*160 square miles of predominately prairie land.*"[142]

Eventually the Cowlitz Farm was about a mile wide and four miles long. The topsoil along the river was fifteen inches deep over clay subsoil. Farming commenced on the Cowlitz Prairies in 1833, when retired HBC French Canadian *engages* cultivated some farmland. Company farming began in the fall of 1838. By the spring of 1840 approximately 600 acres had been plowed, several houses built, and considerable livestock brought to the prairies. By 1846 over 1,400 acres were enclosed and subdivided with fencing and ditches. Some sheep flocks were grazing well beyond the original pastures, on public land, according to PSAC claims documented on the Boundary Treaty evidence. An animal census counted only 800 cattle, 1,000 sheep, 120 horses, and 300 large hogs, but stock rearing was much larger at Fort Nisqually.

The Cowlitz farm employed 24 men and a supervisor for full-time work, with "a large number" of Indian men and women on a part-time basis. Indians were paid approximately £4 to £8 per year plus provisions. The British shepherds were paid £35 per annum plus provisions and housing.

The first sheep to arrive at Fort Nisqually were brought aboard the *Neride*, from San Francisco, in 1838. She delivered 634 head, having lost 166 in passage. In 1840 another California shipload arrived, with only 350 of the 700 sheep Fort Nisqually had purchased. Losing half of the animals doubled the actual cost

Fulfilling the Russian contract was a staggering undertaking. It was so big some of its terms were impossible for the Puget Sound Agricultural Company to meet, and too ambitious for any single company in the world to fulfill at the time. One clause required eight tons of butter delivered annually to Sitka. Apparently five tons was the largest single butter shipment recorded. Even when two additional dairies were established at Fort Langley, and all the inland posts sent their cows to Fort Nisqually, the production was insufficient to fully complete that aspect of the contract.

London officials of Puget Sound Agricultural Company expected to expand operations with wage laborers and sharecroppers, but such workers did not exist around Puget Sound. Chief Factor James Douglas, in a letter to George Simpson, called it:

> "*A grievous burden... imposed on the agriculture of this portion of America, by the impossibility of finding labourers, exactly in the season they are wanted, with the option of dismissing them at pleasure.*"

---

142 Modern estimates place the Puget Sound Agricultural Company farm and ranch acreage at 253 square miles of land, mostly in (now) western Pierce County.

McLoughlin developed the concept of PSAC as early as 1832, but nothing happened until he was attending the London Governors meeting in 1839. It was then that HBC signed the contract with the Russian American Company to supply the great quantities of agricultural supplies to Russian settlements in Russian America (Alaska).

Legally, PSAC was an independent corporation, with carefully designed and worded stock certificates for the shareholders. The fact was, however, nearly all the shares issued were purchased by the Officers and Gentlemen of the Hudson's Bay Company. They envisioned a large export operation that would supply far more of the world's needs, not just the needs of Russian America Company. They expected an export trade to the entire world as was being done from East India. And it nearly happened.

Fort Nisqually and PSAC exported food to all HBC operations west of the Rockies. The enterprise also sent to the European auction houses many ship loads of furs, hides, hooves and horns. Other products went to the Russians, the Californians, the Sandwich Islanders, and, perhaps indirectly, to the Chinese, and thus the rest of the world. The PSAC was certainly a big operation for the time period. At its peak, the Company controlled 12,000 head of sheep, 10,000 head of cattle, at least 600 milk cows, 300 to 500 horses, numerous oxen, swine, and fowl, at nearly two dozen sites on 161,000 acres of land, in what is now Pierce and Thurston Counties. There were outstations in the San Juan Islands, called Belle Vue Farms, and Longacres on Vancouver Island, near Fort Victoria. It still may not have been big enough to accomplish everything dreamed by the London Governors.

On May 2, 1839 Kittson records that the posts for the southwest bastion were installed. It had been quite difficult. It was not the most severe difficulty of the day, for a message arrived revealing that Father Demers had lost six budget-letters he was asked to deliver to Dr. McLoughlin at Fort Vancouver. Kittson went to work immediately creating new reports from the copies always kept at Fort Nisqually. The reports to McLoughlin would be late.

Mr. Willson, the Methodist carpenter, learned a frontier lesson from a "scamp." It seems that Willson hired an Indian to help with some of the work, but the fellow demanded payment before he would do anything. Willson paid him in advance, expecting a day's work, but the fellow shammed illness in order to visit his gambling friends. Willson worked without help for a while.

May was sheep-shearing month. Indian women did most of the shearing work, while the men herded the animals through a tobacco-slurry behind a small dam in Sequalitchew Creek. The slurry was designed to kill the vermin embedded in the wool before shearing. The job must have been messy and smelly, but the difficult first day saw 23 rams shorn of their valuable wool. The next four days saw 163, 189, 117, 116 sheep sheared, respectively.

The fur trade was brisk, while the loose wool was washed in the creek. A total of 4,091 furs were purchased at Fort Nisqually in May, 1839. It was the same month that Kittson and Helene were married. Two of their children, Pierre and Jules, born of a "country wedding," were baptized by Father Demers.

In August Father Francis Norbert Blanchet visited Fort Nisqually. The priest, clad in his traditional black robe, spoke to the gathering of local Indians, his touring entourage, and HBC employees, especially the French Canadian voyageurs.

Meanwhile, at Fort Vancouver, an American named William Cannon built the first flour mill in the Columbia District for Dr. McLoughlin.

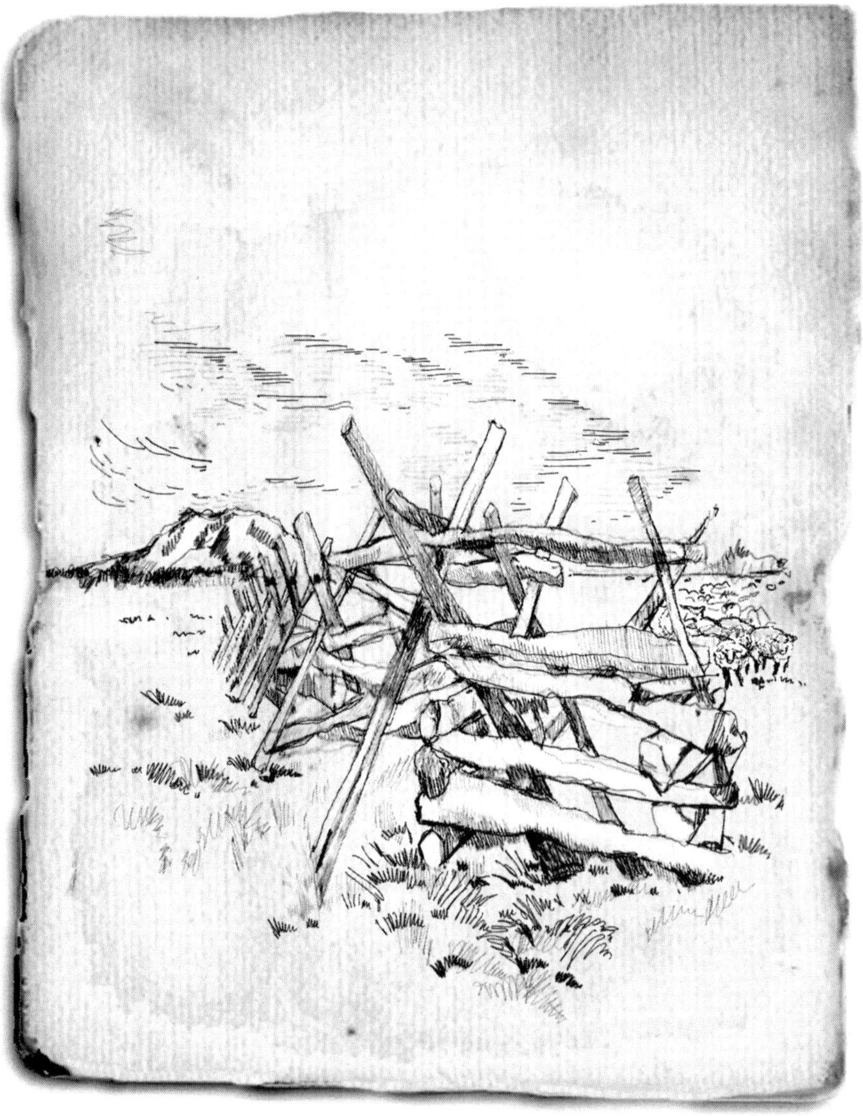

1840

BRITAIN'S QUEEN VICTORIA married Prince Albert of Saxe-Coburg and Gotha. It was a marriage that would last, as well as the beginning of the true Victorian Era.

By 1840 the price of beaver pelts had declined to the point that the American fur trappers' rendezvous system was no longer viable. They had met annually at a rendezvous to replenish their supplies and party for a few days. The streams had been trapped to near extinction. The Rocky Mountain trapping system was abandoned.

The last fur trade caravan to leave the settlements of Missouri headed for the Rockies with Jim Bridger, Andrew Drips, and Henry Fraeb leading the way. Father Pierre Jean DeSmet performed the first Catholic mass in Wyoming during this last trip to the fur traders' rendezvous.

Robert "Doctor" Newell and Joseph Lafayette Meek were free trappers. They worked for none of the big trading companies, but were independent trappers. They traded their furs for supplies at the annual rendezvous in the Rocky Mountains. Both men married Nez Perce women and had growing families when they decided a permanent home might provide some advantages for their wives and children. With three wagons, the families left Fort Hall (Idaho) destined for the Willamette Valley settlements. No one had ever traveled by wagon overland to Oregon. Theirs were the first, reaching the HBC trading post at Walla Walla in September.

Newell had guided some missionaries to Fort Hall. They continued on horseback, giving the wagons to Newell as payment for his guide services. Fort Hall was the farthest westward that anyone had ever taken wagons before the Newell and Meek families came along. They knew it would be difficult. "Doctor" Newell described the conditions:

> ...we began to realize the difficult task before us...(the) sage was higher than the mules backs... seeing our animals begin to fail, we began to lighten up, finally threw away our wagon beds ... all the consolation we had was that we broke the first sage on the road... In rather reduced state we arrived at Dr. Marcus Whitman's mission station in the Walla Walla Valley...we were (also) kindly

received by Mr. P. C. Pambrun, Chief Trader of the Hudson's Bay Company, and superintendent of the post.

The two Oregon Trail families arrived at the Willamette Valley on a cold day in December. Spring would see more and more wagons follow their tracks westward. The 2,000 mile trek across the continent was the longest overland journey to Old Oregon Country American settlers would attempt. Perhaps 10 percent of the travelers died along the trail. Some called it the "world's longest graveyard." In was closer to fact than hyperbole. On average, it is estimated that one body is buried every 80 yards of the trail. That is, of course, assuming that all who died were properly buried. Some were lost in swollen rivers, and no one knows how many died in total isolation away from the wagon trains, therefore never having been buried at all.

There were 114 white American citizens counted in all of Oregon Country in the 1840 census. The population soared when 51 more Methodist Missionaries arrived. They were the reinforcements eagerly anticipated by the Mission staff.

Among the new arrivals were the Reverend John P. Richmond[143], MD, his wife America (Walker) Richmond, and three children. Their difficult journey took them by wagon from Jacksonville Station, Illinois to the muddy lake front village of Chicago. They sailed across the Great Lakes to the Erie Canal, where they transferred to a mule-pulled barge to the Hudson River. Transferring again to a river boat, they finally arrived in New York City. During a brief layover in New York, Mrs. Richmond gave birth to her third child, which she named Oregon. Almost immediately, the family, now numbering six, departed from New York aboard the *Lausanne* for a voyage around Cape Horn to the Sandwich Islands, then to the Columbia River. Baby Oregon spent most of his first year at sea nursing at his mother's breast.

The *Lausanne* carried all the Methodist reinforcements from New York to Rio de Janeiro, Cape Horn, Valparaiso, the Sandwich Islands (also known as the Kingdom of Hawaii) and eventually to the Columbia River. From Fort Vancouver, the Richmond family was transported by rented canoe to the Cowlitz River Landing, (note: the Landing was many miles upstream on the river. The Landing was a "place") where they climbed aboard rented horses for the 140 mile rough overland portage to Puget Sound. These

---

143 John Plaster Richmond of Schuyler County, Ill, was born in Middletown, Fredrick County, Maryland. He was the son of Francis Preston Richmond and Susanna (Stottlemeyer) Richmond. John later became an Illinois Senator (1849-1852, 1859-60), a member of the Illinois House of Representatives (1855-56), a Presidential Elector, delegate to the Illinois constitutional convention, and finally Schuyler County Postmaster 1862. He died in South Dakota August 28, 1865. www.http://findagrave.com

hardy pioneers, with all of their worldly possessions, needed 17 horses for the last leg of a 15,000 mile trek.

The Richmond family was accompanied, as planned, by Miss Chloe Aurelia Clark, a twenty year old school teacher from Windsor, Connecticut. It was thirty-seven days after landing at Fort Vancouver when the Richmond family and Clark finally arrived at the assigned spot at Puget Sound on July 10, 1840. Reverend Leslie and William Willson had been there for 15 months. All of them were five years ahead of all subsequent American settlers at Puget Sound.[144] America Richmond's next child, Francis Richmond, was born at Nisqually. Francis was the first baby born to American citizens living in (now) Western Washington. On February 28, 1841, Francis celebrated his sixth birthday.

In May, 1840, after a short visit of less than ten months, Father Blanchet left the Christian proselytizing around the fort to the Methodist's permanent missionaries... He reported to Fort Vancouver that Kittson was bedridden and quite ill. By the fall of the year Fort Nisqually's highest ranking Gentleman of the fur trade was forced by his severe illness to seek medical help at Fort Vancouver. Even with better medical care, William Kittson's condition did not improve. By December 25, 1841, he would be dead. He was 47 years old.

Born in Canada in 1793, William Kittson was adopted by George Kittson of Sorel, Quebec. He served in the Canadian Voltigeurs in the War of 1812, leaving the service as a Second Lieutenant. He was hired as an apprentice clerk by the North West Company in 1817. In 1818 he was sent to Fort Walla Walla, then to Spokane House. After the merger of North West Company and the HBC, he joined Peter Skene Ogden on the Snake River expedition of 1824-25. Kittson was placed in charge of the Kooteney Post during 1826-29 and 1831-1834, with an interval at Flathead Post. He was one of the founders of the Colville and Fort Nisqually facilities where he managed the trading and farming during 1834-40. He was instrumental in separating the fur trade of Fort Nisqually from the agricultural activities of the Puget Sound Agriculture Company.

Kittson was cordial to the Methodist missionaries and welcoming to the Catholic priests. He was partial to the Catholics, based on his personal beliefs, but fair to both religious traditions as represented at the Fort. After his death, the Methodist Mission at Nisqually continued, but the Catholic priests departed for Fort Vancouver before Kittson gave up his command at Fort Nisqually

The soil was almost worthless for farming where the Methodist Mission was situated.

---

144 The Bush-Simmons group of thirty-one arrived at Puget Sound in 1845. The first child born to the Bush-Simmons party, Lewis Nesqually Bush, arrived on December 25, 1847. ;EWIS Nesqually Bush was the first Black American born at Puget Sound. http://www.histroylink.org

The exact site was chosen cooperatively by Reverend Jason Lee and William Kittson. Only a thin layer of topsoil covered the extensive gravel left by the ancient glaciers of the ice age. The rocky soil was soon exhausted when planted with food crops. It required a great deal of rain, more than fell in a typical summer, or extensive irrigation, to bring a crop to maturity.

Reverend Richmond did not enlist in the Oregon Mission project to be a farmer, and certainly not a farmer unable to feed his family adequately. He had expected, and anticipated, the aggravated inconveniences of frontier living. He had even anticipated a difficult acclimatizing process for a wife of southern origin with small children. He had also expected to raise the vegetable crops for their daily consumption. He was pleased to rent a cow from HBC at Fort Nisqually and purchase meat from the Trade Store. He had expected to hunt for some meat and came prepared to bring it home from the foothills of the Cascades. He was not prepared for the naturally depleted, and physically aggravating, glacial till soils of Steilacoom Prairie that would test his limited farming talents.

The Indians, especially the Nisqually, were friendly and very helpful. The Puyallup-Nisqually culture had a tradition of accepting trade and newcomers, as well as immigrants, with friendly intent. They recognized some of the limitations of these heartland newcomers. As a trading people they also realized they had some things to gain by the cultural contact. The midwestern preachers had much to learn regarding the local seafood. Indians helped them gather oysters, mussels, clams, crabs, and salmon. The missionaries purchased venison, bear, ducks, geese and swans. The Americans learned to eat camas and wild cabbage roots, dried salal, and abundant seafood. In return, the Methodist missionaries taught simple root-vegetable farming methods.[145]

Alexander Caulfield Anderson was sent to Fort Nisqually in October 1840 to manage the place temporarily. Anderson was only 27, quite young for the responsibility of commanding a fur trade post and the Puget Sound Agricultural Company. Anderson remained in charge at Fort Nisqually only until the fall of 1842, when Angus McDonald returned to take over the management role.

Anderson was guided during much of his tenure at Fort Nisqually by Captain William

---

145 An incomplete list of Native American wild foods of the Puget Sound region include: Hazelnuts, acorns, blackcap raspberry, cranberry, elderberry, huckleberry, salal, salmonberry, service berry, soapberry, thimbleberry. Wild black berry, wild strawberry, bitter cherry, chokeberry, crabapple, currant, gooseberry, wild plumb, wild rose, cat-tail, cow parsnip (parsley), fiddlehead ferns, firewood ferns, horsetail shoots, nettles, spruce shoots, wild lettuce (spring beauty & violet), watercress, camas, biscuit root (wild carrot), bracken fern root, lily roots, Pacific cinquefoil, spring bank clover, Wapato (swamp) potato, wild onion, bedstraw, sugar maple, mustard, kelp, chickweed, dandelion greens, lamb's quarters, clams, fish eggs, geoduck, muscles, barnacles, oysters, shrimp, crab, seal, octopus, salmon, smelt, halibut, ling cod, sturgeon, trout, duck, grouse, deer, elk, and bear. Author's notes and personal recollections.

Henry McNeill. Although McNeill was an American, he was a loyal HBC gentleman. He headed the self styled "Marine Department" which operated out of Fort Nisqually as the southernmost port of a string of fur trade posts extending to Russian America (Alaska). Furs were collected along the Inside Passage both northbound and southbound on somewhat regularly scheduled voyages. McNeill, aboard the *SS Beaver* and other vessels, was quite skilled at collecting valuable sea otter and beaver pelts. Often the Marine Department equaled or bested the take of the inland posts. All pelts collected by the ships were brought to Fort Nisqually for transport to Fort Vancouver and on to London.

During the period of Anderson's leadership at Fort Nisqually, Chief Factor James Douglas was in charge at Fort Vancouver, while Dr. John McLoughlin was on leave in England. Douglas began an inspection tour of all northern posts at Fort Nisqually on April 29, 1840. Fort Nisqually was first and last on the tour schedule because the steamer *SS Beaver* based its operations there. Douglas, as the only passenger, would travel in style, and with speed, aboard the *SS Beaver*.

Official Fort Nisqually Journal records are missing for much of the period from 1839 to 1846, but other sources help to fill some gaps. We know, for instance, that Sir George Simpson also visited Fort Nisqually in 1840. He sketched a "Map of Puget Sound to the Cowlitz River, 1840" that was sent to the London Governors. Douglas also drew a map. His map was a "Sketch of Prairie Land about Nisqually, 1841." Both maps were used during the Boundary Commission hearings to determine the boundary between American and British land claims.

Another "big event" at Nisqually, just after the inspection tour, was the complete overhaul of the *SS Beaver* with Captain William Henry McNeill in command. It took almost two years to complete the overhaul which included, among other things, the total removal and replacement of her rusted-out boilers and huge sections of rotted wooden decking, and even a deck-support beam. The new boilers did not arrive from England until May, 1841. Meanwhile, the sailors, engineers, and woodcutters found seventeen rotted planks and one inferior beam to replace.

The men also constructed a Lighter[146] of about 150 tons to be towed behind the steamer. The ingenious plan was to increase the efficiency of the steamer by increasing her load capacity nearly two-fold. The schematic plan and blueprints for the Lighter were brought from England aboard the *Prince Albert*. The Lighter was soon considered part and parcel of the *Beaver*, towed everywhere without any material hindrance or inconvenience and considerable advantage. This policy made the steamer more fuel-efficient

---

146 A Lighter is a type of unpowered barge, moved only by a powered ship.

as the Lighter was the perfect place to carry the many cords of necessary fuel wood, or alternatively to safely carry the precious fur cargo.

McNeill directed the ship's crew to help the Fort Nisqually men build a large warehouse on the beach to replace the one Francis Herron removed to the plains in 1833. This building made offloading supply ships a much easier task. All cargo could be stored immediately and securely as it came ashore. Previously, with the storehouse on the plain, all cargo was hauled ashore, then up the oxen-road to the inland warehouse building to be stored. The process was simplified with the larger, more strategically located facility on the beach.

There are historians who picture the Methodist carpenter, William Willson, differently than the historical account relied on here. That account was written by his granddaughter, based on his wife's diary.[147] It is admittedly not a primary source, but everyone has the right to interpret history. Some castigate Willson for an event not easily explained even in today's less strict social sensibilities.

It seems that Willson, as a simple carpenter with some medical skills, working for missionaries is (today) held to a moral standard different than the fur traders working for European capitalists. The fur men often took another "country wife" at seemingly every opportunity. The practice was encouraged by HBC to help seal business deals with tribal leaders who happened to be fathers of eligible daughters. Willson, on the other hand, was married only once, and never took a country wife, yet is labeled a philanderer.

Reverend Leslie of the Willamette Methodist Mission recognized a shortage of housing after the sudden influx of the new Methodist reinforcements. There was also a lack of any means to quickly build a new dwelling before winter set in. The community had one house where Willson, a single man, was living alone. Although he had been hired as a carpenter, he had studied medicine enough to be a frontier doctor. His dual skills were clearly valuable to the Methodist community. He also had aspiration to be a preacher. That was his political Achilles heel.

Margaret Smith was a single young lady among the reinforcements who, of course, could not build her own home, and did not have the means to hire the work done. Margaret Jewett Smith, of Sagas, Massachusetts, had dedicated herself at age seventeen to Christian service. Even though she was not a Methodist, by age 25 she was offered a position as a teacher at the Oregon Methodist Mission. Margaret was apparently quite shy. She confessed in her semi-autobiographical account to being "almost afraid to be seen speaking to an Indian man on account of being single". Her concern may have had roots in Puritan

---

147 Gill, Frances, *Chloe Dusts Her Mantle*, The Press of the Pioneers, Inc. N.Y. 1935.

religious law at Plymouth Colony, Massachusetts, where living alone was strictly prohibited by Church law. Solitude among the Puritans was seen as breeding ground for sin and anti-social behavior. Puritan women were treated with tremendous severity.

Shy or not, Margaret was also fiercely independent. She was difficult, argumentative, and narrow-minded in her interpretation of proper Christian living conditions. Margaret was not a pleasant companion. She harbored some resentment at the household tasks she was asked to perform by Reverend David Leslie and his family, who shared the journey west. Margaret felt that she was treated as a servant to Mrs. Leslie, and resented that situation.

Upon arrival at the Oregon Mission, there was no teaching position or home immediately available for Margaret. While in continuous dispute with Leslie, Jason Lee forced her to hire herself out as a housekeeper to make a living for herself. She resided for several months in the house of Dr. Elijah White, his wife and children, as a hired washer woman and seamstress. She resented this situation and treatment much as a modern teenager might.

At Reverend Leslie's urging, Willson finally offered to share his home with Margaret. Leslie suggested that the two single people make the best of the available frontier habitations together. A blanket could be strung between sides of the cabin to provide privacy. There was still a problem, Margaret complained. She adamantly declined Willson's offer of free housing, as it would be improper for her to live in the same house while unmarried to her house mate. She suddenly reversed her opinion when she learned of a letter Willson had sent to the east seeking a "mail-order" bride.

Willson, trying to take his pastor's practical advice in a difficult situation, offered to marry Margaret in March, 1838, shortly after his letter was delivered in Indiana. She flatly refused his proposal of a practical marriage because it lacked her need for romance and affection. Willson was clearly disinclined to offer either romance or affection to this difficult woman.

Willson's open public letter seeking a bride was probably addressed to the father of any potential wife in the East inviting any recipient to come west to become his bride. Reverend Jason Lee hand carried the letter to Illinois, which was the hot spot for missionary recruitment. Letters such as Willson's were not uncommon in the 19th and even the 20th century. The potential wives were often called "mail order brides."[148]

---

148 Seattle's famous Mercer Girls all arrived under similar open invitation. Some called them prostitutes. They became wives of the loggers and lumbermen of Elliott Bay. This author's grandfather sought, and got, a second wife in exactly this manner after his first wife passed away in the early 20th Century. Today people use the internet to meet other singles.

Willson never received a reply from any potential "mail order bride" after his single open letter was hand carried by Rev Lee to the midwest. Reverend Leslie, at the Willamette Mission, was aware of Willson's letter and the lack of a response. He urged Margaret and Willson to occupy Willson's house as a practical matter. The practicality was that Margaret would leave Leslie's home.

In June, three months after rejecting Willson's marriage offer, Margaret decided to accept Willson's suggestion and Leslie's urging, citing the necessity of innocent, but practical, cohabitation before winter. Willson urged Margaret during the winter of 1838-39 to agree to an immediate marriage. Margaret refused to marry him until there was proof that the letter of proposal had been withdrawn. Willson could not retrieve the letter already sent, of course.

A letter of retraction could not have been delivered to all of those who had seen, or heard of the initial letter seeking a bride. It was also impossible to intercept that letter before Jason Lee had passed it around among fathers of potential brides at various Methodist meetings halfway across the continent.

Margaret's terms were difficult, indeed. The "couple", instead, began what she described as a "purely platonic and practical" cohabitation, with the encouragement and blessings of Rev. Leslie. Margaret later wrote that:

> "Willson argued that they were already living together as husband and wife except they were denying themselves of an important and blessed benefit of holy wedlock..."

Even when encouraged by Rev. Leslie, Margaret refused to marry Willson. Her diary says;

> "Boarding with him for several months has given me an opportunity to become thoroughly acquainted with him, and many circumstances have given me an extreme dislike of him."

Margaret denied that they had reached the slightest level of intimacy,[149] a claim Willson also vehemently declared. Wilson's love of his cat, his tobacco, and his endless storytelling may have had additional negative effects on Margaret's opinion of him.

This certainly put the good Reverend Leslie in an awkward position, as some

---

149 Margaret Jewett Bailey, *The Grains: or Passages in the life of Ruth Rover, with Occasional Pictures of Oregon, Natural and Moral*. Portland, Carter & Austin, 1854, as quoted by Emma Milliken "Romance on the Frontier, The True Story of William Holden Willson and Chloe Aurelia Clark" in *Occurrences Journal of Northwest History During the Fur Trade* Vol. XX, No. 4 Fall 2002.,

historians have said, because he had urged their original cohabitation, without marriage, as a practical housing matter. He probably had some hope that the two would eventually become compatible. Finally Leslie, in a personal effort to save face, urged both of them to quickly and publicly confess and repent their sins. This simple solution would have also had the convenient additional benefit of absolving Leslie of any complicity.

Margaret and Willson both refused to confess anything, but both were trapped, betrayed by their trusted clergyman. They were without independent (non-mission) employment prospects and utterly dependent on the Methodist Mission for all of the necessities of life; shelter, sustenance, and certainly social acceptance. As outcasts from the Mission, neither could have survived in Old Oregon.

Margaret continued to adamantly refuse to confess any sin, protesting absolute and complete innocence.

Willson soon saw an opportunity when Leslie made an offer. The very job he had been denied when he joined the Methodist Mission was in the offing. Hired as a simple carpenter for the Mission, his lack of religious education and "preacher" training prevented the possibility of ever preaching. Reverend Leslie offered clerical forgiveness, if Willson confessed publicly to his "sins" while living with Margaret. Forgiveness would reopen all of Willson's personal opportunities for advancement at the Mission.

Willson decided it was prudent, (politically correct, if you will) given the impossible situation he found himself in, to confess as Leslie had requested. It was a "no contest confession" because he could not "prove" his innocence. He found it useful to actually confess on many public occasions, with loud lamentations. He was always visibly tearful in his repentance performances. His sincere efforts developed a sympathetic audience. His tactic soon worked in his favor. Willson was publicly forgiven by Reverend Leslie and subsequently, with Reverend Leslie's generous ordained support, Willson became a leading light among the licensed preachers at the Oregon Methodist Mission.

Margaret, on the other hand, while steadfastly denying any sinful behavior, was emotionally abused by the religious community. She was shunned and shamed by the Mission Methodists, all while she continued to publicly proclaim her absolute innocence.

Eventually even Margaret's innocent resolve collapsed. She finally succumbed to the pressure confessing her sins, as required, by Reverend Leslie. Almost immediately, on March 4, 1839, she married Dr. William J. Bailey. It was another "politically correct" decision, but this time motivated by potential romance. Still there was no wedding dress, no wedding supper, and no public celebration of marriage. She described the solemn ceremony as "dismal as a funeral." Margaret did not get the romance and affection she so desired. Divorce solved the dilemma.

Less than one year later, Margaret married Francis Waddle. She continued to be difficult and argumentative, even with her new husband, self-describing her 15 year marriage to Bailey as continuously unhappy. Her second marriage ended in divorce three years later, as well. Margaret Jewett Smith Bailey Waddle died in Seattle, alone in bitter and destitute circumstances in 1882. She left no children.

William Willson, on the other hand, led a remarkably happy life. Even though he had confessed first, Wilson was still single for seventeen months after Margaret married her first husband. When Willson did marry, it was to Chloe Aurelia Clark. She became his one-and-only, lifetime companion, a young lady he met at the Nisqually Methodist Mission.

Methodist Missionaries William Holden Willson and Chloe Aurelia Clark met for the first time in July, 1840,[150] more than a year after Margaret's first wedding. Clark had just arrived at Nisqually from Vancouver where the *Lausanne* discharged the Methodist reinforcement missionaries that Reverend Jason Lee had recruited in the East. She was hired as a teacher, and in short order was quickly assigned to the Nisqually Mission. Willson was already at Nisqually working in the capacity for which he was originally hired, as carpenter/builder of the physical structures for the Nisqually Mission house and school.

The following story is abridged from a recollection published as "Chloe Dusts Her Mantle."[151]

> *During one of her early days at Nisqually, Chloe slipped, spraining her wrist, while fetching a bucket of fresh water from Sequalitchew creek. Willson, somewhat the "frontier doctor," fashioned a splint to help reduce the swelling in Chloe's wrist. He used short willow switches and strips of cotton cloth that had been soaked in boiling water. He wrapped the wrist and fitted a cotton cloth triangle into a sling around her neck to support the injured arm and relieve the pain. His "doctoring" was no doubt inspected by the real doctor, as Reverend Richmond was a trained M.D. Some have said Willson, a man with a passion for cats and tobacco, was perhaps better at handling wooden splints than human souls.*

The Willson-Clark courtship was simple. They lived in the same mission buildings, ate most meals with the Richmond family, and endeavored to complete mission work as

---

150 Gill, Frances, *Chloe Dusts Her Mantle*, The Press of the Pioneers, Inc., New York, 1935. This is an historical fiction account written as if a granddaughter was recording the memories of her grandmother. .

151 Gill, Frances, *Chloe Dusts Her Mantel*, The Press of the Pioneers, Inc., New York, 1935.

coworkers. There were few opportunities for formal East Coast style, courtship rituals at the mission: an occasional walk to collect wild leaves for a salad, sincere, straight forward conversations about her Connecticut home some 200 miles from his, in New Hampshire, big ambitions, personal plans, their mutual faith. She explained that the famous western explorer William Clark was not a relative, as far as she knew.

Willson talked of politics and the British fur traders who desired a wild country because the skins and pelts they traded for were worth so much money. He explained it was in the British interest to hinder the missionaries, if they could. He even said the fur traders hated the missionaries. They felt, he said, that Americans like Chloe would educate the Indians to their full human potential, ruining the subservient role assigned so successfully by the British fur traders. The education that Chloe had come so far to provide would destroy the native fur trade, he said, even as it saved souls. The profit motive was working against her noble endeavor.

Slowly Chloe saw positive changes in the children enrolled in her classes. She had nearly 50 names in the roll book. School was open five days every week, but attendance was sporadic, and not a single student had altered their basic nature. Many were learning English words, however. They were also appreciative of the hardworking Methodists. The little settlement was 15 months old and progress was being made. A community was being built. Success was still in the future, if ever there could be success in such a speculative venture.

The Nisqually Indians apparently liked the dietary variety offered by the Methodist's vegetable garden, especially the potatoes. Indian-owned potato crops sprouted along with the missionary gardens. They often traded local wild foodstuff with the missionaries. Years later, the Methodists would often reminisce about the local Native Americans seeking a bargain in garden produce.

The first protestant marriage ceremony of an American couple in what is now Washington was held on August 16, 1840, at the Nisqually Methodist Mission. William Holden Willson and Miss Chloe Aurelia Clark were married by Reverend Doctor John P. Richmond. Their happy and loyal marriage lasted sixteen years, terminated only by Willson's death on April 17, 1856. Willson's greatest civic accomplishment was probably developing the street plan for Oregon City. Chloe Aurelia Clark Willson passed on in 1907, after nearly half of a century of service as first a missionary, then as the founding professor at the Oregon Institute in 1842, which became Willamette University in 1852.

In the winter of 1840-41, Alexander Simpson, the HBC governor's cousin, purchased 3,670 ewes and 661 cows in California. He paid $2 each for the sheep and up to $6 for each cow. The herd was driven overland from central California to Puget Sound by thirty drovers. It may have been the very first large overland cattle/sheep drive in North America.[152] It was an arduous three months of following Indian trails, and no trails, through mostly mountainous unmarked, unmapped and hostile landscape. Some 470 sheep and 110 cows were lost, mostly crossing rivers, mountains and ravines. Following this historic cattle drive the Nisqually Farm animal population increased by a remarkable 3,200 sheep and 551 cows that spring. In early 1842 another cattle herd was assembled at Forts Colvile, Okanagan, and Nez Perce. Some 283 head were driven through the Yakima Valley and over the Cascade Mountains through White Pass to the Nisqually Farms. It was another precedent-setting cattle/sheep drive.

These animals joined the breeding stock imported from England on annual shipments. Six pairs of purebred Leicester and Merino sheep, and two Scottish shepherds (and their herding sheep dogs?) arrived on the barque *Columbia* in 1839. In 1840 twenty-four more head of the same high quality breeding sheep arrived from London.

London was a city connected to 1,881 miles of railroad tracks in 1840. North American railroads would not reach Puget Sound for another 33 years before Tacoma would be chosen as the western terminus of the railroad. It would be a few more years before that first transcontinental train actually arrived.

---

152 The great cattle drives of Texas and the mid-west began in the 1860s.

1841

UPPER CANADA AND Lower Canada were proclaimed united under an Act of Union passed by the British Parliament in 1841. Both were originally created by the Constitutional Act of 1791. The names refer to the relative positions beside the St. Lawrence River, one being up stream and the other downstream. The Colony of British Columbia was not brought onto the Canadian Confederation until 1871, after some pressure was exerted for the colony to join the USA along with Alaska.

In 1837 the herds at Fort Nisqually, still in Joint Occupancy Old Oregon, grew after what may have been the largest and longest North American sheep/cattle drive[153] to that date. The natural propagation increased the size of the Nisqually herd by double in 1842, and doubled it again by 1846. Every year saw a substantial increase in the size of the herds and flocks from the 1841 totals of 2,342 sheep, 649 cattle, and 12 horses. Nearly all of the cattle were offspring of the very first cattle drive from California in 1841. Smaller herds of cattle were driven from HBC posts at Colville and Vancouver, as well.

In the 1830s, enterprising American men brought the first few California horses and cows to the Willamette Valley. The overland route they used was really a disconnected set of local trails. Ewing Young headed the outfit that brought the first few animals—150 horses and mules—on what became known as the Siskiyou Trail. His route connected ancient Native American trails, Hudson's Bay Company hunter/trapper trails, and natural animal pathways between the Central Valley of California and the Willamette Valley. It passed from the Sacramento Canyon to a trail beside the lofty Castle Crags, near Mount Shasta. The inhospitable route crawled through the ferruginous water at Soda Springs and the deep ravines of the Rogue River Valley.

---

153 In 1837 Ewing Young and an all American crew drove 630 head of Spanish Long Horn cattle from California to the Willamette Valley as the Willamette Cattle Company. The roster of drivers included William A Slocum, Philip Leget Edwards, Calvin Tibbets, John Turner, William J. Bailey, George Gay, Lawrence Carmichael, Pierre De Puis, B. Williams and Emert Ergnette. It is unknown how many animals survived the 600 mile trek. End of the Oregon Trail Museum PDF www.endoftheoregontrailsmuseum.org

The almost unthinkable trek was undertaken in 1841 by the Puget Sound Agriculture Company men. It crossed 725 miles of wilderness along the Siskiyou Trail from Mexican-California rancheros to Puget Sound prairies. It cut a swath that much of U.S Highway 99 and Interstate 5 freeway follow today, but followed disconnected Native American trails. Those foot trails wound their way through river valleys and over mountain passes. Most likely the earliest European visitors were HBC trappers and hunters in the 1820s searching for the elusive beaver. Alexander McLeod led the California Brigade through the Willamette, Umpqua, Rogue, Shasta, Klamath, Siuslaw and Sacramento Rivers in 1826 and 1828. The highest summit along the trail is 4,310 feet at Siskiyou Summit. Other HBC trappers known to have used the trail included Michel Laframboise and Peter Skene Ogden.

During the historic 1841 cattle and sheep drive, the animals and the herders faced starvation, drought, and hostile, hungry natives who were also defensive of territory that had been theirs for centuries. Much of the time the herders were actually lost, but always searching for a trail north. One can only imagine their travails. They could only move short distances each day, occasionally backtracking to gain an unforeseen better route. They were in the brushy mountains for weeks, exchanging one steep ravine for another during long laborious days. The herdsmen's bones must have ached. Their voices surely grew hoarse from shouting at the animals and each other. Imagine their lungs, painful from the thinner air at high altitudes. Simple calculations seem to indicate that they progressed 6 to 8 miles each day, if they were capable of any steady daily movements. Most likely some days speed was not a consideration. Survival was foremost.

PSAC ranch and farm production probably netted $8,000—$10,000 in the 1840-46 years. In 1841 alone PSAC produced 7,000 bushels of wheat to sell. In 1840 some 20,000 pounds of raw wool was shipped to the London auction houses. Exactly 361,130 pounds of wheat was sold at Kamchatka, Russia, while the Russian Fur Traders at Sitka purchased an additional 8,400 bushels each year under the contract signed in the 1830s. Investors received a minimum 5% dividend from PSAC each year (1844-1854) with a bonus dividend of up to 10% when an extra 10 tons of wheat went to Kamchatka.[154]

The sheep-breeding stock at Fort Nisqually was carefully managed to produce a "better" animal. Some imported English Leicester rams were crossed with the poor quality California Merino ewes. The flocks were shifted for grazing daily, folded nightly in pens ("sheep parks") which were moved regularly to "manure" the land for the eventual crop planting.

---

154 HBC Archives D.4/125:63

The entire flock was moved every three months around the vast open Nisqually Plains (Joint Base Lewis McChord area) to the bluff above the Puyallup River Valley (Tacoma's Hilltop) until 1844. The large sheep heard (once counting 12,000 animals) was divided into eight self-contained flocks that were rotated semi-annually through 161,000 acres of natural grazing ranges. Great care was taken to prevent over grazing any pasture, which could completely destroy a pasture. PSAC was designed to be a long-term company.[155] With so much invested, and at risk, the company was very protective of the grasslands. Later Americans would claim HBC had, in fact, over-grazed the land in a propaganda effort to diminish the value of the real estate the Americans coveted so dearly.

In the early 1840s PSAC head herdsmen were a Mr. Lewis, a Scot who lived near the flocks in a "house on wheels,"[156] and John Montgomery, an illiterate Scot who was the first non-native settler at Spa-nu-eh (Spanaway). Shepherds who lived in the temporary huts-on-wheels were easily moved. Montgomery built a permanent country home for his wife and child[157]. Lambing lasted about six weeks every spring and shearing began shortly after the lambing was complete.

The cattle were also penned at night, mainly as protection from wolves. The cows, except for the milk cows (numbers range up to 600), were also moved to new grass weekly, but kept on the Dairy Plain. This allowed the cows a bit of learning to be driven and provided the farm with close-by fertilized vegetable gardens. Suckling calves were left with the milk cows. The ones being milked were cared for at the main dairy, about five miles from the actual fort at the Dairy Plain on land now occupied by the U.S. Army base (JBLM).

Back at Fort Nisqually landing, the *SS Beaver* needed extensive repairs. She had been launched in 1835 and served well as the first steamer on the North Pacific, but now she needed some serious attention. Fort Nisqually landing provided the best location for a makeshift shipyard.

---

155 The PSAC was incorporated in 1838 at the London Stock Exchange. It was listed continuously until 1934, when the last real estate near Victoria, British Columbia, Canada was sold for urban development. Perhaps coincidentally the Young Men's Business Club of Tacoma instigated the move of historic building once belonging to the PSAC to Tacoma's Point Defiance Park. There a replica reconstruction of the original Fort Nisqually was built using those two old buildings as central features of the Fort Nisqually Living History Museum. See articles in the *Tacoma Times* and the *News-Tribune* for Sep 4, 1934.

156 Gibson, James R., *Farming the Frontier, The Agricultural Opening of the Oregon Country, 1786–1846*, University of British Columbia Press, Vancouver, 1985.

157 Montgomery eventually became an American citizen before legally claiming his farm under American Donation Land Claim laws.

One of the *Beaver's* unneeded and impractical masts was removed to reduce the overall weight of the vessel. Neither of the masts was ever used to operate sails after the engines moved her along. The redundant and removed mast remained stored at the Fort for years, just in case. Such was the sailor's faith in steam. Edward Huggins admitted 57 years later to having the mast cut into boards at a nearby American sawmill. As a nineteenth century conservationist, he salvaged the Mizzen top of the mast to make souvenir walking sticks for himself and friends.

The original hardwood decking of the *Beaver* was completely removed in 1841 and replaced with red pine[158] planks, a fine quality material for ship's decking because of its naturally thick gum, or resin. Very rare red pine groves grew at Muck and Hillhurst.[159] The English ship builders considered it to be a handsome quality wood. Its resin made a fine chewing gum, too. The red pine is also known as western yellow pine. While it is not common west of the Cascades it is often found to the east of that range. It can grow to 200 feet or more, with a trunk up to eight feet in diameter.

The trees for the new decking were whip-sawn by hand labor of the *SS Beaver* woodcutters who normally rough-cut only fuel wood into pieces three feet in length and piled above tidewater on convenient beaches between Fort Nisqually and Stikeen (Alaska). Thirty cords could move her 230 miles, or the sailing distance from Fort Nisqually to Fort Victoria. John Work said she could carry enough fire wood for three or four days travel.

Other ship's parts for the *Beaver* were from very diverse forests, indeed. Her keel was made of elm, the stern and post stern were of British oak. The exterior hull, overlaid with copper sheeting, was of that same hearty British oak and her original decking of African teak.

The *Beaver* was described as a "comical looking tub," but her paddles were well formed. The stern looked like a "dry goods box cut square in half." There was "nothing of a clipper in her" but she could clip along at ten miles an hour, faster than any clipper ship before a fresh wind. She had splendid, state-of-the art high technology steam machinery designed by none other than James Watt, the Scottish inventor whose skills were fundamental to the Industrial Revolution. Watt's partnership with Matthew Boulton made both highly successful and wealthy men.

---

158 Red pine is *Pinus poderosa*, and also known as Western Yellow Pine, Bull Pine, Blackjack Pine; it can grow to 200 feet with a diameter of 10 feet, but is not common in Western Washington. It has a variable habitat in temperate climates worldwide. http://en.wikipedia.org

159 Hillhurst was located along what is now a railroad route five miles south of Lakeview six miles southwest of Spanaway, and nine miles north-northwest of Roy, within the current Fort Lewis Military Reservation. Unpublished map by Steven A. Anderson

1841

While the *Beaver* was under repair and refitting, Captain McNeill was often a guest at the Methodist Mission. Rev. Richmond was a gracious host inviting McNeill, his wife and children, to dine with Chloe and William Willson, America Richmond, and her children. At one point the Captain asked that his Métis children be baptized. The preacher did as had been his missionary practice among the Cherokees and the Nisqually, and later the Dakotas.

On May 11, 1841, Lt. Charles Wilkes[160] arrived at Fort Nisqually. Wilkes was U.S Navy Commander of the United States Exploring Expedition[161] sent by the United States Congress (1838) to explore the world from Antarctica and the South Seas to the North Pacific, Puget Sound, the Columbia River, that is the Joint Occupancy Country of Old Oregon. The "Ex. Ex.," as it was called, was the navy's (political and scientific) version of the US Army Corps of Discovery (the Lewis and Clark Expedition).

Earlier, on May 2, 1841, Wilkes sent a message to Fort Nisqually that a sea pilot was needed at the entrance of the Strait of Juan de Fuca. The Indian courier returned with William Heath, brother of Joseph Heath and the lone British settler at Steilacoom. William was employed as navigator aboard Captain McNeill's *SS Beaver*. He piloted the *Porpoise* and the *Vincennes* to the southern end of Puget Sound, anchoring the *Vincennes* and the *Porpoise* at the mouth of Sequalitchew Creek. Along the way, Wilkes had already begun exploring, surveying, charting, and naming the shorelines and islands he encountered.

Upon dropping anchor at Fort Nisqually that beautiful morning in May, Wilkes was welcomed by Alexander C. Anderson, Captain William McNeill, and the Methodist Missionaries Richmond, Willson and their families. All of these people, except Anderson, were American, but Anderson offered a fine meal at his home inside the fort. McNeill asked for and received Wilkes' manpower assistance with the steam boiler installation project aboard the *Beaver*. The Methodists offered Lt. Wilkes some old fashioned American cooking and a family home atmosphere to be enjoyed many times in the months to come.

Wilkes responded to the hospitality of the local residents with an elegant officers'

---

160 *Charles Wilkes*, Encyclopedia of World Biography, 2004. Charles Wilkes was the son of John de Pointhieu Wilkes and Mary Seton. When his mother died in 1801 Charles was cared for by various female relatives among who was His aunt, Elizabeth Seton, canonized by Pope Paul VI in 1975 as the first Roman Catholic American saint. Seton Hall University was named for her.

161 Barkan, Frances B. *The Wilkes Expedition: Puget Sound and Oregon Country*, Washington State Capital Museum, 1987. Congress passed the Naval Appropriations Bill on May 14, 1836 authorizing President Andrew Jackson to "send out a surveying and exploring expedition" which reached Cape Flattery on April 29, 1841.

mess aboard the *Vincennes* for Anderson, McNeill, the preachers, and their families. He also commented on the rosy cheeks of the first white children he had seen in months. In his official journals, Wilkes described the physical appearance of Fort Nisqually:

> *It is constructed of Pickets some 20 feet high, quadrangular in shape, with Bastions at each corner covering less than an acre. It was of sufficient size however, to accommodate the initial establishment, but this having become but one of the HBC farms, they found it much contracted. There is indeed, as I am informed, little or no necessity for defence [sic] now, the Indians few in number some 60 to 100 and perfectly peaceable. The fort is in this shape.* [A rectangular drawing of the fort was included] *The bastions thus serve the whole side and the defenders being entirely under cover are enabled to fight against great odds. Besides having the bastions the galleries extend all around the pickets. I was shown their garden in which among other things are the peas about eight inches in height. Strawberries are still in full blossom and will be ripe in a few days.*[162]

Wilkes further described Fort Nisqually and PSAC operations. He noted grain fields, large barns, sheepfolds, agricultural implement, and workers engaged in cattle husbandry. The operation included seventy milk cows, from whose milk cheese and butter were made. James Steel, from England in 1839, served a two-year contract as clerk and dairyman. Cattle were grazing at least four miles from the Fort to the north, south and east, while sheep folds were at least seven miles to the east. The dairy was on the northeast edge of Lake Sequalitchew, in an area later known as the Dairy Plain. Wilkes also noted several hundred head of cattle, crops of wheat, peas, oats and potatoes. Outlying farms were actually PSAC sheep and cattle stations operated by John Montgomery as Spaneuh (Spanaway) Farm Manager, John McLeod, Manager of Whyatchie Farm near Wyatchew Lake, and John Edgar the Steilacoom (River) Farm Manger. Edward Heath leased PSAC land for his 100-acre farm west of Steilacoom. The others were employees of PSAC.

The heart of PSAC operations was on the north side of Sequalitchew Creek. There barns, cultivated fields, and sheep folds dated from the earliest days of PSAC. Walking eastward from the core of PSAC activity one would encounter dwellings, storehouses, and an enclosed stockade for cattle operations. Further along were large structures identified as, "Horse Pen," "Round Pen," "Slaughter House," and a series of long pens each terminating at Sequalitchew Creek, allowing all of the stock to have easy access to drinking water. Three large barns were most likely used to store grain. There was a piggery, a

---

162 Wilkes, Charles, Narrative of the United States Exploring Expedition during the Years 1838, 1839, 1840, 1841, 1842, Philadelphia; Lea & Blanchard, 1845, Five volumes; pp 411-413, Vol. 4.

[158]

sheep shearing barn, large calf pens, and an enclosure on the south bank beside a dam where sheep were washed.

To the south were cultivated fields, former swamps drained and planted with potatoes. The large garden area ran along the creek bank. A rail fence enclosed about 220 cultivated acres. Crops included wheat, oats, barley, peas, potatoes, turnips, and colewart, along with timothy and clover for the animals. The emphasis at PSAC was on livestock as the highest priority.

Commander Wilkes ordered the construction of two log buildings on the bluff above Sequalitchew Creek, overlooking the waters of Puget Sound. The structures were immediately called "Wilkes Observatory." The exact site for his observation station is at Latitude 47 degrees, 07 minutes, 12 seconds north, and at Longitude 122 degrees, 38 minutes, 15 seconds west. On the bluff just to the south of Sequalitchew Creek, the crew erected a sextant and telescope to determine their exact location by astrological, navigational observations and calculations. They also observed and recorded the weather for the ships' logs. Maps, charts, and voluminous reports were developed based on the calculations at the Wilkes Observatory for the United States Government. The fact that the HBC developed few maps of their Columbia Department helped the Americans later to establish boundaries between British and United States claims to Old Oregon.

Plans were made to send the brig *Porpoise* to conduct a hydrographic survey of all waters of Admiralty Inlet, Hood Canal, and Puget Sound, beginning at Commencement Bay. The brig's long, narrow shore boats (often called gigs) were perfect for the endeavor led by August Ludlow Case, memorialized by Case Inlet.

Wilkes expedition Midshipman August Ludlow Case wrote in his journal to describe some of what he saw it at Fort Nisqually in 1841.

> *The Puget's Sound Land Company as the HBC have a farm and several hundred head of cattle and sheep here... servants hired by the company & bound by the most rigid rules.... areas laid down in wheat, oak, peas, potatoes... cattle and sheep all looked well and I was told increased rapidly...they are of the California breed, the sheep mixed with the English.*
>
> *Near the fort lived Dr. Richmond, an American attached to the Methodist Mission—he has built himself a house & takes possession of a large plain which he has named "Richmond's Plain" and is living very comfortably. He does little or nothing in his profession saying when asked about it: "Nothing could be done with the Indians" and having been convinced he is correct, remains here drawing his salary for the good old women at home.*
>
> *The company steamer 'Beaver"...makes this place... headquarters. She is*

kept as a dispatch vessel to carry supplies to the north forts & to collect furs inside Vancouver's Island.[163]

Midshipman Case also described the Nisqually clan:

> *...a small tribe inhabiting the plains in the vicinity and the headwaters of the Sound. They [have] flattened heads... and acknowledge no Chief. They have a dialect of their own although most of them speak the Chinook trading language [too]. Their master residences are built of logs roofed with boards... contain several families.... and generally situated near a spring or near water.*
>
> *They own a good many horses & generally ride at the top of a horse. Their dress consists of a hunting shirt, trousers and moccasins made of deer hide, shirts and trousers from the fort... a blanket according to the wealth of the wearer. The women wear frocks of deer skin or calico ... some of these highly ornamented and looked very well when clean.*
>
> *They were tolerably good looking, middle sized and very indolent.... they give a shirt...(for) two chaws of tobacco... as a consequence of our giving such prices the gentlemen at the fort have gone without salmon...*[164]

Wilkes' journal included a description of the general area surrounding Fort Nisqually:

> *The anchorage off Nisqually is very contracted in consequence of the rapid shelving of the bank that soon drops off into deep water. The shore rises abruptly to a height of about two hundred feet, and on the top of the ascent is an extended plain, covered with pine, oak, and ash trees scattered here and there so as to form a park-like scene. The hill-side is mounted by a well-constructed road of easy ascent. From the summit of the road the view is beautiful, over the sound and its many islands, with Mount Olympus covered with snow for a background. Fort Nisqually, with its out-buildings and enclosure, stands back about half a mile from the edge of the table land.*

Other Wilkes Expedition exploration plans included sending a survey crew with Lt. Robert Johnson to the interior, across the Cascade Mountains. A third survey crew led by Midshipman Henry Eld went south and west along the Chehalis River to Gray's Harbor. Finally, Wilkes led a fourth crew down the Cowlitz River to Fort Vancouver, where, he learned later, a ship in his fleet was destroyed at the mouth of the Columbia. When the

---

163 Blumenthal, Richard W., editor, *Charles Wilkes and the Exploration of Inland Washington Waters*, McFarland & Company, Inc, Publishers, Jefferson, N/C, 2009.

164 Ibid

Peacock went down, all hands were saved, but thousands of scientific specimens were forever lost. Those specimens were collected all across the South Pacific and Antarctica. It was a disastrous blow to the expedition.

The survey crew Eld Inlet[165] consisted of eight men and Lt. George Colvocoresses. Colvos Passage was named for him. Their task was to explore and map the mostly water route from Black Lake (today West Olympia) to the Black River, and further to the Chehalis River and Gray's Harbor. They apparently hired an Indian guide, a "Squaw Chief of the Sachal tribe."[166] The tribe was more likely "Tsatsal," but even that spelling does not find footing in most histories. One speculator suggests that she was Cowlitz-Nisqually.

When the explorers' light shore boats floundered in the heavy four-foot wind waves of Gray's Harbor the same Indian lady came to the rescue, delivering the eight seasoned sailors in her sturdy cedar dugout to a safe and secure landing across the bay. No lives were lost and all of the precious instruments were protected. The primary source story of this remarkable woman is recorded only in the Colvocoresses log on file at the National Archives in Washington, D.C.

Puget Sound Native Americans were canoe people. That is the clans along the shores of Puget Sound were closely related to fishing and water transport. Wilkes, however, commented on the Puget Sound Native Americans and their horsemanship:

> *...the Indians were clothed in worn out European costumes... with a few ribbons and cock's feathers stuck in their caps... not unpleasing...The management of their horses is truly surprising... those (horses) that a foreigner or pale face would be unable to get off to a walk they will mount and proceed with speed without the aid of spur or anything but a small switch... the usual bridle is simply a piece of rope fastened to the under jaw which (is) all sufficient for the management of the most refractory horses...*[167]

The Nisqually were closely related and intermarried with the Yakima, who were "horse people' on the dry plains east of the Cascade Mountains. Leschi, of the Nisqually, was the son of a Nisqually-Yakima marriage who became a great horse trader and leader of the Nisqually.

W. D. Brakenridge was a horticulturist on the Wilkes Expedition. After exploring the

---

165 Eld Inlet was named by Charles Wilkes for Midshipman Henry Eld. Phillips, James W., *Washington State Place Names,* University of Washington Press 1971.

166 Taylor, Paul, "An Adventure on Black River" Columbia Magazine, Winter 2007-08, p. 3-5

167 Meany, Edmund S. *Diary of Wilkes in the Northwest,* Washington Historical Quarterly, Vol. 16, No. 1-4, January to October 1925, pp. 55-58.

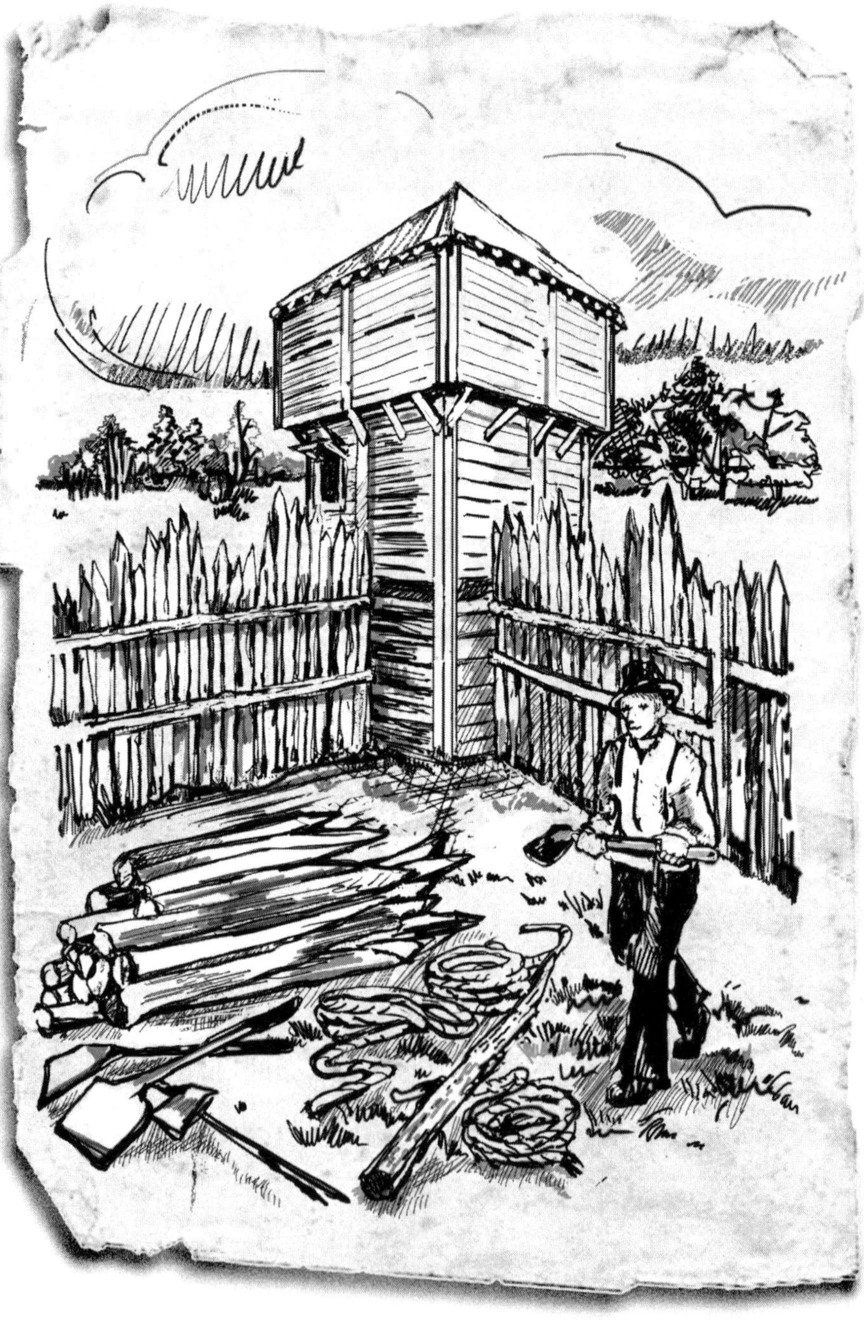

prairies around Fort Nisqually, he wrote this 1841 report which was added to the official documents of the Expedition:

> "Fort Nisqually lays inland a good half mile from the Bay on the plains or margin of extensive prairies which stretch back into the interior 15 or 20 miles. Right above the quay or landing place is a high bank along the face of which a good road has been formed through the bush towards the Fort: the Company has got as dairy about three miles out from the Fort: In the way of which I fell in with some Sandwich Islanders busy plowing land for potatoes. In the same field a quantity of Peas, Oats, & Wheat looked well. The soil was light brown earth, intermixed with a goodly portion of gravel and stones. Such soil required a great deal of rain during the summer to bring a crop of grain to perfection. The plains were at this season one complete set of flowers… intersected with and broken in upon by belts or clumps of spruce trees, with a dense undergrowth… scattered oaks … Near several of the fresh water lakes I observed two kinds of ash (tree)… solitary examples of Yew… a wood the Natives prefer for making their bows . ."[168]

On May 17, *Porpoise* Master George Sinclair began a detailed survey of Puget Sound at a place he appropriately named Commencement Bay. Earlier Wilkes had written "I do not consider the bay a desirable anchorage," but then Wilkes was referring to Elliott Bay, not Commencement Bay.

The *Porpoise* was 224 tons, 88 feet-long two-mast ship rigged as a brigantine. She carried 65 men. Two boats were sent to explore the area. Wilkes named hundreds of islands and physical features of the area. Significant to Fort Nisqually, Anderson Island was named after Alexander C. Anderson, the man in charge when Wilkes arrived. Nearby McNeil Island was named after the venerable commander of the *SS Beaver*, Captain William Henry McNeill. It is interesting to note that Wilkes, or his scribe, failed to use the double letter spelling used by McNeill. Two very prominent geography features, Mount Rainier and Mount Saint Helens, retained the names Captain Vancouver gave them almost exactly 39 years earlier. Native people called Mt. Rainier, "Takhoma" or "Tak-o-bet" (the mountain that was God). Mt. St. Helens was known as Louwala-Clough (Smoking Mountain) until Captain George Vancouver renamed it to honor the British Ambassador to Spain, Alleyne Fitzherbert, who held the regal title of Baron St. Helens.[169]

The Wilkes Expedition began with six ships in 1838, sailing from Norfolk, Virginia.

---

168 Wilkes, Charles, op cit.

169 U.S. Geological Survey Web Site, www.usgs.gov/ 2004

The orders were to explore the Pacific Ocean, chart Antarctica, the South Pacific, Central Pacific, San Francisco Bay, and Puget Sound. The expedition had been three years at sea by the time Wilkes' fleet reached Puget Sound. They lost only one ship, the *Peacock*, which went down at the mouth of the Columbia River. The other vessels were the flagship *Vincennes, Porpoise, Relief, Sea Gull,* and *Flying Fish*.

The *Peacock* crew was saved, with only one injury. Much of the supplies and scientific instruments were also saved. The scientific specimens were completely lost. American Methodist missionaries from Point Adams provided replacement tents and food. HBC offered space for a temporary camp at Fort George (Astoria). The crew erected the flag from the *Peacock*, and named their campsite "Peacockville."

Immediately Wilkes negotiated the purchase of an HBC ship, the *Thomas Perkins*, renamed the *Oregon*. The crew set to work exploring the Columbia upriver to the Cascades. They conducted the first hydrographic survey of the river reinforcing American claims based on Captain Robert Gray's discovery of the river.

Often trade negotiations were more difficult. On June 12, 1841, midshipman Augustus L. Case and a crew were surveying Hood Canal. After several days it became apparent that the crew needed more food than had been packed for the expedition. Case tried to engage a couple of Indians to return to Nisqually with a letter requesting a canoe load of bread. An old Indian man persuaded the other Indians that the price Case offered was not enough. The Indians would not go for the offered pay. Later that same day Case found a creek at the head of Hood Canal. He crossed the portage of two and one-half miles to Puget Sound. There he hired an Indian to take two crewmen back to Nisqually for the needed bread.

Due to the portage, it should be noted that the canoe trip from that spot was considerably shorter than the water route Case originally proposed for the same price utilizing the full length of Hood Canal. The old Indian was, of course, aware of the two distances, thereby driving a hard bargain.

The Navy mess cooks could drive a hard bargain, too. Nisqually Indians with fresh venison to trade were turned away when they asked a price in ammunition higher than the chef was willing to pay. Fort Nisqually beef was the chef's choice.

Official government-sponsored American Independence celebration was held for the first time on the Pacific coast by U.S. Navy sailors, Marines, and American citizens on Monday, July 5, 1841. It was a great party held on the American Plain on the shores of American Lake near the British Fort Nisqually. Of course, the main entree was a great American-style beef barbecue. As the first official government agency (U.S. Navy) sponsored-celebration of American Independence on the west coast of North America, it was regarded as "Manifest Destiny." The one day delay was made to not interfere with the Sabbath celebrated solemnly at the Nisqually Methodist Mission and the ship's chapel.

Wilkes had made a calculated political move. He was, of course, aware that his expedition leadership was a political appointment meant to bolster those who favored the idea of American Manifest Destiny—a claim for the entire continent. Wilkes had already met with the American settlers in the Willamette Valley. That area was secure from British territorial claims. Puget's Sound was not at all securely American, with only the two American families settled there. But, it was not clearly British territory either. Joint Occupancy rules still applied around Puget's Sound. Wilkes needed to assure his political supporters in congress of the eventual American possession of land north of the Columbia River, west of the Rockies. American Independence Day provided the perfect opportunity to establish an American face to Puget's Sound, even if it came only on the 5th of July.

The Methodists were in complete agreement with Wilkes concerning the idea of a grand celebration. The pious clergymen declined to celebrate on the exact date, important as it was, the Fourth of July being the Sabbath. The barbecue waited until Monday. And it was a glorious day at that. Doctor McLoughlin was invited, even expected, but did not arrive until Tuesday. That tardiness may have been a political statement of his own, to arrive after the American excitement was subdued, thereby reclaiming a bit of British "ownership" of the region when the welcoming committee greeted his arrival.

Lt. Wilkes and Dr. Richmond planned a full day of feasting and oratory for the expected crowd. The audience included the two Methodist families, the entire ships' complement of sailors and marines, the Fort Nisqually men, and most of the nearby Indians. Altogether about 500 people attended this grand party. After all it was a unique thing in the world. No other country at that time had ever gained complete political and economic independence and liberty from any colonial power.

The day began with the warm sun rising in a clear blue sky. The Mountain was gleaming in the brightness. After reveille and the usual morning chores, Wilkes ordered a twenty-six gun salute, consecutively sounding one blast form a cannon for each of the twenty-six states in the union. The crows and seagulls complained loudly, but the Indians instinctively understood there would be a party.

By ten o'clock the crew of the *Vincennes* had formed a formal parade line-of-march behind the fife and drum. The starboard watch filed onto the parade ground in starched white uniforms, followed by the marines in stiff dress blues. The larboard[170] watch fell in

---

170 Larboard was a British term in reference to the starboard side of the ship. The term probably was influenced by Middle English terms implying to the left, to load, laden, to board a ship at the dock. Port was finally adopted by the British Navy in 1844. Larboard is used here as the author's choice.

line wearing their crisp dress white uniforms. The brass howitzer was rolled, and dragged, along by the gunnery crew throwing their shoulders into the task.

The American civilian families were the next entry in the parade. Reverend Richmond wore his freshly pressed black wool suit as he led his wife and their flock of freshly scrubbed children. Finally the U.S. Navy officers not assigned to a watch proudly fell into line.

The Indians walked along behind them with no recognizable formation, more spectators than parade participants. There were at least several hundred Native Americans, mostly dressed in trade shirts and trousers, their finest hats festooned with elaborate feathers. They mostly wore the European style clothing available at the Fort Nisqually Trade Store. The European cultural invasion was rapidly infiltrating and replacing the Native American culture.

The parade passed by the scrub oak of the vast prairie. They saw late blooming wild rhododendron, poison oak, salal, Oregon grape, giant Douglas fir and western red cedar on the short trek. As the naval parade marched by the Fort Nisqually palisades, the Americans gave three cheers. HBC people cheered back, as the American military men moved out onto the plain four abreast singing "Yankee Doodle." All day the Americans continued their deliberately provocative display of American patriotism. With a stem-wider speech by Reverend Richmond declared the eventuality of a completely American Oregon. Following Monday afternoon this prairie grassland would be known as the American Plain, even in the Fort journals.

Independence Day had created an American "claim." A nearby lake was renamed American Lake, after America Richmond and the country she came from.[171] The only Americans north of the Columbia lived there; all nine of them. Those first settlers were supported financially by the Methodist Episcopal Board of Missions. Now they were supported emotionally, politically, and militarily by the U.S. Navy. It was a fact of great significance to the supporters of Manifest Destiny that Americans on Puget Sound were successful. It helped, too, that the newer Mission buildings were more substantial and solid than the Old Fort, according to Wilkes reports.

To be specific, the American civilians were led by twenty-nine year old Reverend Doctor John Richmond, a bespectacled Marylander who had earned college degrees in medicine and theology. He was accompanied by his wife Amelia, or "America" as

---

171 In 1916 The Pierce County Board of Commissioners authorized $2 Million to purchase 87,000 acres for a military cantonment. On January 6, 1917 the land that became Camp Lewis (now Joint Base Lewis McChord). On January 3, 1923 the War Department Secretary of the U.S. Army leased 377 acres for the Veterans Hospital at American Lake, arguably the most beautiful setting of all Veterans Hospitals. www.historylink,org

she was called, an attractive dark-haired former widow, and their children. Amelia was 'with child' during the Independence Day celebration. Her fifth child would be born the next February.

Captain Wilkes commented on the Richmond children:

> Here I found Mrs. Richmond...(who) has four fine, rosy and fat children, whose appearance speaks volumes for the health of the climate.

Also in the American party were newlywed Chloe A. Clark Willson and her husband William Holden Willson. The Navy crewmen cheered again as the Richmond and Willson families marched onto the picnic grounds between the little Sequalitchew Lake and larger Spootsylth Lake (now named American Lake).

The site for the big celebration was suggested by the Indians. They had always raced horses along the flat prairie land, while using a slight rise near some oak trees as a spectator area. This day the spectator area would be a perfect shaded location for the many picnic tables.

Preparations had begun the day before. The ship's commissary had purchased a bullock[172] from the Company herd. They drove it to the chosen site before slaughtering it beside the freshly dug roasting pit. John Sac, a Maori, was the official chef for the Navy ship. He fashioned a spit, or cross-rod, to hold whole carcass over the fire pit. The iron rod hung suspended between two selected trees. The sailors connected a ship's mechanical windlass to the spit. The beef kept turning over the trench of hot alder coals for twenty-four hours. Bread was baking nearby in portable field ovens. The tables, brought from the ship, the fort, and the Mission were placed along the lake shore near the spot where the sailors and marines had planted five stands of U.S.A. and navy colors, while the marines ceremoniously stacked their rifle pyramids. Canvas and blankets were spread over the ground on top of a bed of fir boughs. Mrs. Richmond brought a nice lace cloth to dress her family table.

The parade halted, then with the order "Fall Out" the little community held first official American Fourth of July celebration and picnic west of the Rockies.

Some sailors raced on rented Indian ponies across the six miles of open prairie. Indians cheered the horse races and taught the Americans a gambling game using bones. Some sailors and marines played an early version football, while others enjoyed corner ball (an early type of baseball). Still others danced to a fiddler's tunes on a large door removed from the ship and laid flat on the ground.

---

172 A bullock is a castrated young male bovine, a bull or steer that is not yet trained as an ox or draft animal. Author notes.

Apparently the fiddle had never been seen by the Nisqually people before. They were curious as to how the box could make so many different sounds. After careful, and repeated examination they learned it was hollow, then decided the devil inside was invisible.

The Indians partied that day as well. One of the games the Indians taught to the sailors was a gambling game they called Swuckulst. The game of Swuckulst is played mostly in winter before an open fire when the nights are long and the weather bad. The game can last for weeks at a time. It is usually played by two tribes who select their best players. Both sides put their treasures in two piles on the floor. It is a very simple game, but played amidst great noise and excitement, and resembles the old fashioned English game of "Button, Button, Who's Got the Button?"

The players seat themselves on each side of a large mat or blanket about 12 feet long by 3 or 4 feet wide. The buttons with which they play are usually round wooden discs about the size of a silver dollar and are covered with shredded bark to hide the color of the discs; a broad counter is placed before the marker, several small wooden sticks lay crosswise to mark the plays or points. All the goods to be gambled are piled on the floor in someone's guarded possession before the game commences.

The scorer, or marker, is seated in the middle and the players at each end. The game then starts by a player taking a number of the discs, one of which is brightly colored, and proceeds to cover each disc with the shredded bark, then shuffles them all together and divides them into two piles. Taking a pile in each hand he holds them high over his head. His opponent proceeds to guess which hand the colored disc is in. After his guess is made the discs in the hand guessed are laid on the mat, so all may see if the colored disc was in that hand. If the guess was a good one, the side guessing right scores a point. [173]

The game is nearly endless, with exhaustion often declaring the winner.

At precisely noon Wilkes ordered the marines into formation for ten rounds of musket fire and another twenty-six gun salute from the brass Howitzer, one blast for each state of the union. After several loud shots, Quarter Gunner Daniel Whitehorn rammed home a new Howitzer powder cartridge. It was instantly ignited by the debris of earlier shots smoldering inside. The explosion destroyed Whitehorn's left hand. The ships' surgeon, after a second consulting opinion from the missionary Doctor Richmond, recommended immediate amputation.

The accident put a gloom over the festivities for a while. "Men of war are somewhat familiar with such scenes," Wilkes said to the crowd. Whitehorn was carried by litter to

---

173 Anonymous, *Pacific Coast Historical Almanac, 1931*, Pacific Savings and Loan Association, Tacoma, page 3.

the *Vincennes* to have the wound cleaned. He was treated for pain and the prevention of tetanus. Amazingly, Whitehorn adamantly refused the recommended amputation surgery. He was carefully bandaged, but never recovered the use of his hand. Soon after the Expedition returned to the States, Whitehorn was given a Navy medical discharge and lifetime pension.

Wilkes' thermometer registered 120°F in the early afternoon. Perhaps some of the hot air was created by the speeches and ceremony. The Reverend Dr. Richmond led off with a prayer, the sergeant of the marines read aloud the Declaration of Independence. Captain Wilkes read some Biblical scripture. Another sergeant led the audience in singing "My Country 'Tis of Thee" and the "Star Spangled Banner".

Reverend Doctor John P. Richmond, wearing his thick "bottle bottom" spectacles, read a speech loaded with Yankee patriotism, a full load of jingoism[174], and his prophetic confidence in an American future for the Puget Sound area. It was a remarkably insightful oration. Here is part of Richman's prophetic speech:

> *We entertain the belief that the whole of this magnificent country, so rich in the bounties of nature, is destined to become a part of the American Republic.*
>
> *The time will come when these hills and valleys will be peopled by our enterprising countrymen, and when they will contain cities and farms and manufacturing establishments, and when the benefits of home and civil life will be enjoyed by the people.*
>
> *They will assemble on the 4th of July, as we have done today, and renew their fidelity to the principles of liberty embodied in 'The Declaration of Independence' that we have heard read here today.*
>
> *The future years will witness wonderful things in the settlement, growth and development of the United States, and especially of this coast. This growth may embrace the advance of our dominion to the frozen regions of the North, and south to the narrow strip of land that separates us from the lower half of the American continent.*
>
> *In this new world there is sure to arise one of the greatest nations of the earth. Your names and mine may not appear in the records, but those of our descendants will.*
>
> *The industrious founders of the American Republic declared against the union of Church and State; in this they did well, yet it is undeniably true that the world's civilization today is inseparably connected with the religion of*

---

174 Jingoism is extreme nationalism in the form of aggressive, or belligerent, chauvinistic patriotism. *Merriam Webster's Collegiate Dictionary, 10th Edition,* 1977, 1993, Merriam-Webster Inc.

Christ, and it could not survive if the Christ-like and the spirit were eliminated from it. Our mission to these children of the forest is, to teach them the truth of the gospel, that they shall be fitted for the responsibilities of intelligent Christian citizenship. We are here to assist in laying the foundation stones of a great commonwealth on these Pacific shores.[175]

One preeminent factor in securing American political supremacy on the Pacific coast was the work of Reverend Jason Lee and his representative at Nisqually, Reverend Dr. John P. Richmond. The Navy Exploration Expedition (Ex. Ex.) under Captain Wilkes was a matter of secondary moment at the time, even though many politicians considered the Ex. Ex. to be an auxiliary U.S. government sponsored movement to support and strengthen the civilian colonial work undertaken by the Methodist Mission. Lee's Methodist Mission also had congressional approval. Is it any wonder, given the mass American belief in "Manifest Destiny," that modern cities would spring up a few miles from this spot less than 10 years later?[176] Thirty-two years later (1873) the second transcontinental railroad reached Tacoma, the "City of Destiny."

These efforts, one under Jason Lee and the other under Captain Wilkes, were contemporaneous events planned and developed by people with the similar high aspirations. Congress granted government financial assistance when Jason Lee chartered the *Lausanne*, then, with further appropriations, Congress authorized the Wilkes Expedition. Assisting one and commissioning the other reveals the political purpose of securing the occupancy and control of Oregon Country as far north of California as possible.

Dr. Richmond first took up the recruiting work begun by Lee. In time the Richmond family joined the westward movement, taking the arduous sea route up Lake Michigan, through Lakes Superior, Huron, and Erie, then through the recently opened Erie Canal to Hudson River and New York City. They sailed the North Atlantic, Caribbean Sea, and the South Atlantic before traversing the Straights of Magellan. Entering the South Pacific they sailed directly to the Sandwich Islands, then to the Columbia River. Finally they loaded themselves and their belongings on seventeen horses to traverse the extreme

---

175 President of the Day, R. L. McCormick, President Washington State Historical Society, Under the auspices of the Pierce County Pioneer Society, assisted by The Washington State historical Society, The Washington State Pioneer Society, The Daughters of the American Revolution, The Sons of the American Revolution, The Loyal Legion and the G.A.R. *Commemorative Celebration at Sequalitchew Lake, Pierce County, Washington, July 5, 1906 at 2 O'clock.*. Pierce County Pioneer Association, 1906.

176 Newmarket (Tumwater) was founded in 1846 by Michael Simmons and George Bush. Nicholas Delin built a sawmill at the head of Commencement Bay in 1852, according to Hunt, Herbert, *Tacoma, Its History and Builders, A Half Century of Activity, Volume I*, The S .J. Clarke Publishing Company, 1961. Tacoma Historical Society Press, Tacoma, Washington, reprint 2005.

wilderness of Puget Sound.

Forty-three years later Dr. Richmond wrote for the Tacoma News[177] to explain the dual purpose of the Methodist Mission to Nisqually and all of Old Oregon:

> *Very few persons seem to comprehend the logic or purpose of the Board of Missions in sending a large number of men and women into Oregon. The contravening claims of the United States and the British Government were held in abeyance by the treaties of joint occupancy until 1846. The Hudson's Bay Company and its subsidiary organization, the Puget Sound Agricultural Company, had stretched their... occupation over the territory and were urging the British Government to hold fast to the country. They had sheep and herds of cattle, dairy farms with shepherds, herders and servants to conduct them.*
>
> *In 1824 the Russian Government recognized the claim of the United States to the country south of 54 degrees 40 minutes north latitude. In 1827 a treaty of joint occupancy was entered upon between the United States and British Governments.*
>
> *Under conditions of things the Hudson Bay Company had full sway. Their jurisdiction was acknowledged by their servants and employees. They had British laws, with officers and magistrates to enforce them. On the other hand the American missionaries and settlers had no protection of law, until they themselves created a provisional government.*
>
> *...the Missionary Society of the Methodist Church labored to establish a foundation of proper influences and principles that would be helpful to the emigrants.*
>
> *In the meantime they were to use every appliance available for the betterment of the Indians. My part of the work was to represent American citizenship and American enterprise on Puget Sound. I had no complaints to make against the Hudson Bay Company in the matter of hospitality. But I wish it distinctly understood that they received proper compensation for the favors shown, and the help granted. On the contrary, I could not be impressed with the conviction that I was regarded as an intruder.*

Captain Wilkes, on his visit to the Columbia River in the summer of 1841, learned of the plight of some Americans who had been refused passage on the HBC *Cadboro* bound for California. The Americans, Joseph Gales, Felix Hathaway, and three others were planning to purchase cattle to resell in Oregon... HBC declined to allow their passage on a company ship in an effort to prevent competition in the cattle business.

---

177 Richmond, John P., correspondence to the *Tacoma News*, April 8, 1884.

Gales and Hathaway proceeded to build their own boat on Wapato Island near the mouth of the Willamette River. They named their craft *The Star of Oregon*. The first ship built in Old Oregon would fly the stars and stripes.

Captain Wilkes saw the almost finished craft and tested Gales' knowledge of navigation. Gales received his Ships Master credentials immediately. Wilkes also gave him a United States flag, an ensign, a compass, a log line, glasses, an anchor, and a hawser 140 fathoms long. Only five days later the wind brought the new American merchant vessel to San Francisco. *The Star of Oregon* returned with a full load of cattle for sale to American farmers, in direct competition with the mighty HBC.

Near the end of August, 1841, Lt. Wilkes met Sir George Simpson, North American Governor for the Hudson's Bay Company at Fort Vancouver. Simpson was bound for an around the world tour, including a stop at Fort Nisqually. Wilkes was headed for the Willamette Valley to tell the American settlers that the time had not yet arrived to establish a civil government in Oregon.

Wilkes told Simpson he intended to recommend that the U.S. claim all of the Pacific Coast to 54 degrees 40 minutes north. Simpson was not sympathetic to the idea, of course. He recommended that the British Foreign Office not allow any boundary that was north of the Columbia River. The two men were solemnly cordial with each other while their warships sat off shore The Wilkes Expedition left the Columbia sailing south on October 9, 1841. Simpson went north to Puget's Sound. He, in a day-long conversation with Dr. Richmond, again solemnly explained the British political position and the prospects of British settlers coming from the Red River, before resuming his world tour through Sitka, the Russian America fur trade post.

The American Missionaries were discouraged by Simpson's confident rhetoric, but held on for another year. Mrs. Richmond was already two months pregnant. Their crops were harvested and stored. The Chloe's Mission school continued with sporadic attendance by nearly fifty Indian children and Richmond's four, in one classroom. Sunday services were conducted with typically sparse attendance. American settlers would not arrive for another four years, eventually fulfilling Dr. Richmond's prediction of an American triumph on Puget Sound.

In late September, 1841 a party of twenty-three families (116 people)[178] emigrated from the Red River colony in what is now Manitoba, North Dakota, and Minnesota. This immigration is usually ascribed to Governor George Simpson of the Hudson's Bay

---

178 Three babies were born on the trail and one family apparently turned back. Gibson, James R. *Farming the Frontier, The Agricultural Opening of the Oregon Country, 1786—1846,* University of British Columbia Press, Vancouver, 1985.

Company, but was not solely his doing. The HBC Governor and Committee, with approval of their fellow London investors, sent a letter to Dr. McLoughlin dated December 31, 1839, suggesting that 20 families from the Selkirk Settlement on the Red River should be encouraged to migrate west to reduce the difficulties created by the increasingly large population at the Red River. It was certainly part of a political scheme to populate the western lands with citizens of Canada, and therefore subjects of England. They came overland, across the Canadian Rockies, most likely following the voyagers' watery trails to Fort Vancouver, then north along the Cowlitz Trail to Nisqually.

They were generally young and active, but at least one 75 year-old was following her son to his new home. Her name was "Saskatchewan," which was also the name of her birthplace. The three youngest Red River settlers were born on the trail, slowing progress of the trekkers by only a few hours each. Every family had two, sometimes three, carts as well as horses, cattle and dogs. The carts were covered with canvas awnings to protect the women and children from the sun and rain. The entire caravan was over a mile in length when they travelled single file. Often they moved side-by-side to avoid some of the dust stirred up by the wheels and hooves. This procedure meant each of the three columns required one leading cart to 'break' the road less trail for 6,253 kilometer (3,885 miles).

Fourteen families (seventy-seven people) located satisfactory farmlands at Nisqually. Seven other families took farms on their own account outside PSAC jurisdiction, but accepted advances of seed and implements from HBC. The Red River settlers were promised that each family would receive 10 pounds sterling in advance. They would have a guide and would receive goods, horses and provisions along the way. At Puget Sound they were promised houses, barns, fenced fields, farm implements, seed, 15 cows, one bull, on ram and oxen or horses. In return the farmers would deliver to HBC one-half of the yearly crops for five years and after five years they would deliver to HBC one-half of the increased animal herds.

John Flett was a member of the Red River settler's brigade. Later, after the Treaty of 1846, he became an American citizen and was often annoyed by the phrases "American born" and "first American child" that most historians and Reverend Richmond used. He was most annoyed by the fact that the Methodists eventually concentrated their efforts in the Willamette Valley instead of at Nisqually. John Flett once said;

"I have a bible that Dr. Richmond gave me in 1841, that I prize much. It has been my companion for many years. I wish I could present the public something that the 'first missionary' left in this country besides this book."[179] [180]

The migrants arrived on October 13, 1841 at Fort Vancouver. The Red River Settlers were immediately told that the Company would not help them at all. The Company blatantly broke the agreement. Only 13 of the 23 families decided to venture on to Nisqually in spite of the lack of HBC support. In fact, only 22 of the 80 Red River Settlers actually came to Nisqually. The others settled in Fort Spokane, the Cowlitz Valley, the Willamette Valley, and even California.

Only a few months after the first celebration of American Independence, the Fourth of July, those twenty-two English subjects, Red River Settlers all, were taken to the American Plain along Steilacoom Creek. It was a short walk to the Methodist Mission, out beyond the barbeque spit, the football field, the corner ball pitch, the horse racetrack, and the fateful spot where the Howitzer drew American blood while proclaiming American Independence. It was a long walk to Fort Nisqually. The Methodist Mission was soon surrounded by nominally hostile people: French-Canadian Catholics from Red River and Puget Sound Indians. None of these nearby neighbors physically threatened the Americans, but all were prepared to establish and support a political threat. The American Methodists at Nisqually were, to say the least, very uncomfortable with their

---

179 Bagley, Clarence, *The Acquisition and Pioneering of Old Oregon*, Ye Galleon Press, Fairfield, WA, reprint 1975.

180 By today's standards nearly all non-Indian settlers who came after 1841 to Whulge were brutally regressive with severe racial biases. While most earlier fur traders and mountain men married Native Americans and raised families, most of the later settlers verbally impaled Native Americans with cruel epithets, regarding the entire population as "savages," "children of nature," "low-browed," "superstitious souls," "dirty fish-eaters" and "Pagan," among other racially derogatory phrases, all of it ingrained in the European genteel aristocracy and the American "political religion" of the Oregon Trail and Manifest Destiny. An example of the racial attitudes of the time can be seen in this rare published passage written in 1884 by a respected historian: *"It has always seemed to me that the heaviest penalty the servants of the Hudson's Bay Company were obliged to pay for the wealth and authority advancement gave them, was the wives they were expected to marry and the progeny they would rear. What greater happiness to the Father, what greater benefit to mankind than noble children. I could never understand how such men as John McLoughlin, James Doulas, (Peter Skene) Ogden, (Roderick) Finlayson, (John) Work and (William F.) Tolmie and the rest could endure the thought of having their name and honors descend to such degenerate posterity. Surely they were possessed of sufficient intelligence to know that by giving their children Indian or half-breed mothers, their own Scotch, Irish, or English blood would be greatly debased, and hence they were doing all concerned a great wrong. Perish all the Hudson's Bay Company thrice over, I would say, sooner than bring into being offspring subject to such a curse."*—Hubert Howe Bancroft, *History of the Northwest Coast*, 2 volumes, The History Company, New York, 1884, II, 650-51.

old and new neighbors. This mission was turning out quite differently than the idealistic portrayals imagined by those mid-west American religious recruiters.

John Flett, that prominent Red River settler, claims to have received wheat seed, potatoes, and some iron, with which he built his own plow, from the HBC through Fort Nisqually. There was much discontent among the Red River settlers who received virtually nothing. John Flett and his brothers James, David, and William departed from Nisqually in June, 1842. After planting only a single spring crop, they gave up before summer. These settlers had been at Nisqually less than eight months when they quit the place. By the fall of 1843, after less than a two year tenancy, the last of the Red River settlers were gone from Nisqually. It was only one year after the American Methodists departure, but still two full years before the first so-called first Americans. Simmons and Bush, arrived in October, 1845.

Some Red River settlers did not even try farming under PSAC supervision. They struck off for themselves, taking land along the Cowlitz River. Had there been no other farming land available, these families would have had to comply with PSAC contracts. Probably the most serious objection the non-compliant settlers had was the quality of the soil on Nisqually plains. While ideal for pastures, it is not rich in nutrients needed for farming. The other objection expressed by the Red River immigrants was the 'indentured servant" language of the contract. HBC records also blame the failure on poor soil, poor crops, and exorbitant costs with little or no returns. Legal action taken by some settlers was eventually dismissed by the American courts.

Of course the question of national sovereignty of the region was a huge factor working to the advantage of HBC and PSAC until 1846. Many would-be American settlers were reluctant to risk losing their farms if the boundary was to be along the Columbia River where the British were certain the line would eventually be located.

Following the harvest of 1841, A. C. Anderson took some men, English, Scotch, French-Canadian, Kanakas, Indians, and Métis to collect cattle from other HBC posts east of the Cascades. He would consolidate all of the HBC animals on the plains and prairies of Nisqually for the PSAC. They crossed at the Sinahomish [sic] pass following an ancient Indian trail. They noted that on the way east the trail would require "a good deal of labor to make it passable" for herds on the return trip. They met the first herd of cattle in the "Yachimah" [sic] valley. Since the herd was larger than Anderson had expected, he hired some Yakima Indians to assist in driving the cattle over the mountains. This Yakima 'alliance' had an added advantage. It tended to reduce the chances of hostile actions by other surrounding tribes, as well.

After organizing the cattle drive, Anderson and one man left the herd, returning to

Nisqually for supplies and even more men. With the augmented "cowboy" drovers the cattle drive was completed with only a few lost strays. Perhaps many of the stray cattle found their way to Nisqually, or back to their home range, by following the trail left by the herd. More likely the stray cattle fell to predators.

The even larger California cattle herd arrived as the Yakima herd settled in at Nisqually. Some new ewes (female sheep) were introduced to Nisqually at the same time. The California herd was purchased by HBC Chief Factor James Douglas. It might be noted that the great Texas cattle drives began some twenty-four years later.

Between 1835 and 1841, the herds and flocks at Fort Nisqually grew in number and quality. It was in 1841 when HBC officially transferred the agricultural property at Fort Nisqually to the Puget's Sound Agricultural Company. Considerable research has been done[181] to reveal the animal populations at the new PSAC farms. From as few as 11 cattle in 1835, the herd grew to 50 in 1840. The horse herd went from 6 to 61 in 1843. There were 36 hogs in 1843 and some 16 poultry, presumably of several types. The shepherd included 728 head, with at least nine goats roaming the grounds.

In 1841, Fort Nisqually men were milking two hundred cows with several hundred more "beef" cattle on the open range. Immediate efforts were undertaken to improve the milking breed with some animals imported from England. The farms were beginning to return good yields as well. One year, some 15,000 bushels of grain were shipped to the Russians by the Puget Sound Agricultural Company. Butter and cheese also went to the Russians, while hides, horns, tallow, bones, and wool were sent to England. The animals needed little feed, as they were basically free-range animals. The business was quite profitable for the company. Using the profits wisely, the company purchased the best European breeds, including Merino, from the farms of England to continue the improvement of the herds.

Having been recently Knighted, Sir George Simpson journeyed around the world in 1841-42, stopping at nearly every Hudson's Bay Company post in North America. Fort Nisqually was not left out, and in fact merited two visits. He first arrived at Fort Nisqually on Saturday, September 4, 1841 with an entourage of some 27 men, including some Kanakas and Chinooks. His return visit was simply to pass through in order to continue his circumnavigation of the globe from Fort Vancouver.

Simpson apparently learned all he could from the mild mannered missionary about Methodism, as well as American political plans north of the Columbia River. On the other hand, in his report to London, Simpson scarcely mentions the encounter. His

---

181 Gibson, James R., Farming the Frontier, The Agricultural Opening of the Oregon Country, 1786—1846, University of British Columbia Press, Vancouver 1985.

notes say, "...*we remained for six and thirty hours,... visiting Dr. Richmond, an American missionary stationed in the neighborhood.*"[182] Clearly, it seems, Richmond was informed of the plans for Red River settlers to occupy the area.

On Monday, September 6th, the Simpson party embarked on the *SS Beaver* with a seven gun salute. By the next morning Captain McNeill had already shown Simpson the keen advantages of the steamship and the excellent harbor at the southern tip of Vancouver Island, beyond what would someday be called Ogden Point after Peter Skene Ogden. Fort Victoria was built on the inner harbor two years later. It would become HBC headquarters displacing Fort Vancouver and replacing Fort Nisqually farms.

By the end of the month Simpson had diplomatically called on the Russians at Fort Stikeen and all HBC posts along the labyrinth of waterways forming the Inside Passage. Simpson passed through Fort Nisqually the second time in somewhat of a whirlwind that took him on to the Golden Gate at the Presidio of San Francisco under the Spanish command of Prado Mesa. Simpson was losing his sight in 1841 and may have been suffering from syphilis,[183] but his business sense was still intact. The Spanish were good trade partners.

Simpson ordered Forts McLoughlin, Stikine, and Taku to be closed and completely dismantled. He had planned to drive all of the Americans from Oregon Country by depleting the beaver population, thereby eliminating the American desire to cross the Rockies. The British fur trade was a success when viewed as a mission to destroy the competition. American ships no longer traded fur with the Russians at Sitka. It was also a success because the Russians were not disappointed, and the prices were not higher than those of California. HBC netted between $8,000 and $10,000 annually on the commodities in the Russian contract according to Dugald McTavish, a Company man, testifying before the British and American Joint Commission in 1866.[184] To further support the assertion that PSAC was a success, consider that the Puget Sound Agricultural Company was not dissolved until 1934, after nearly a century in operation.[185] Its headquarters were moved to the outskirts of Fort Victoria and it continued operations for nearly a century without changing its mane or business plan. It simply operated beyond the country of its origin.

---

182 Bagley, Clarence B. The Acquisition and Pioneering of Old Oregon, In the Beginning, Ye Galleon Press, Fairfield, WA, 1982.

183 Huch, Barbara, et al, *Exploring the Fur Trade Routes of North America*, Heartland, Winnipeg, 2002.

184 Gibson, James R., Farming the Frontier, The Agricultural Opening of the Oregon Country, 1786—1846, University of British Columbia Press, Vancouver, 1985.

185 Your author asserts that the rescue of two historic Fort Nisqually / PSAC buildings in 1933 was partially motivated by the news of the day concerning the demise of PSAC in 1934.

McLoughlin's vision of a string of land-based fur trading posts along the coastline to Russian America was dashed. Simpson's whirlwind tour resulted in his order to close all but one of the northern coastal posts. Simpson further declared that the coastal furs would be collected by the *Beaver*, the company's steamer. Simpson ordered the fur be brought to Fort Nisqually until a new headquarters could be built on Vancouver Island to replace Fort Vancouver on the Columbia.

McLoughlin was furious. He presented every argument he could to save Fort Vancouver on the Columbia. He even traveled to London to argue the point with the stockholders. To make matters between the two men even worse, Simpson ruled that the murder of McLoughlin's 23-year-old son was the direct result of the young man's own actions. This decision protected Simpson from the charge that he had assigned young John before he was well enough trained for the position. The older McLoughlin spent much of the following years trying to clear his son's name and prove Simpson wrong.[186] The disagreements over the coastal trade posts and his son's death created a complete rift between McLoughlin and HBC as run by Simpson. McLoughlin even renounced his British heritage becoming a naturalized American citizen. He retired, and rests eternally in Oregon City.

---

186 Doctor John McLoughlin retired in 1846, to Oregon City, where he died heartbroken September 3, 1857. Holman, F.(1910) John McLoughlin in *The Catholic Encyclopedia*, New York: Robert Appleton Company,

1842

CHLOE CLARK WILLSON may have given birth prematurely in early February, 1842. There is no evidence beyond historical fiction. Any premature infant had little chance of survival on the frontier. Historical fiction gives the child little reference, no name, and no certain place of burial, except generally at the Nisqually Methodist Mission grounds. The information is sketchy at best, and not to be relied upon for historical accuracy.

However, it is known that a surviving baby was born at the Nisqually Methodist Mission. Francis Richmond, son of Reverend Dr. John P. Richmond and America (Amelia) Walker Talley Richmond, was born on February 28, 1842. Francis was the first surviving United States American child born north of the Columbia River and the second child born to the Richmond family since leaving Illinois. The older sibling, named "Oregon," was born aboard a ship in New York harbor before the family arrived in Old Oregon, but after they departed Illinois.

This newest little baby created quite a stir among the Nisqually people. He was very fair skinned and had very white hair. An Indian man became infatuated with the bright white-skinned, black-eyed baby. First the Indian man made efforts to purchase the infant by barter and trade. Realizing the futility of that endeavor, he proceeded to abduct the baby.

On the fateful day of the kidnapping, Dr. Richmond had gone to the Fort, leaving America in the main room of their house with domestic duties. The baby was in a cradle in the bedroom, while the other children were "off on a ramble" in the fenced yard. America had her 'mother's ear' carefully tuned to her infant. She heard a rustling and a slight cry from the baby. She hurried to the cradle to find it empty and the back door open. She saw through the window the infatuated Indian man, with the baby in his arms, heading over the prairie toward the Indian village beyond the Fort.

She seized the loaded rifle, which was always at hand above the front door, aimed carefully at the fleeing Indian. She is reported to have been a dead shot. Before she squeezed the trigger the Indian man saw her. He turned holding the baby between them

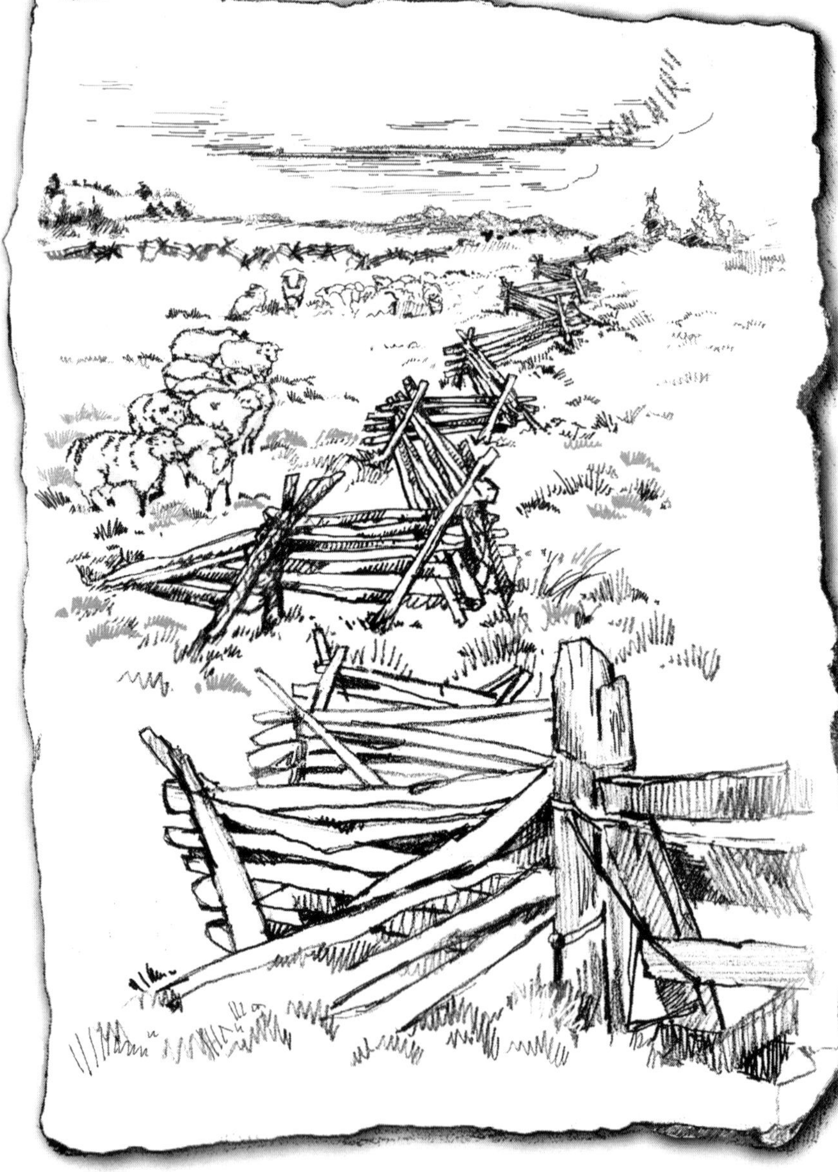

as he continued to move backward and away from the Mission House. She immediately began to run directly toward the kidnapper stealing her baby. She could not close the gap between them much, nor could the Indian expand the space in his desperate attempt to escape.

The Indian rounded a corner of the Fort Nisqually palisade. At that very moment Dr. Richmond came up behind the rascal. Richmond knocked the offender down with his walking cane. America arrived at the spot, handed the gun to her husband, and picked up baby Francis. The Indian seized the good doctor's cane and grabbed for the gun. After a considerable struggle, Doctor Richmond gained the upper hand, again knocking the kidnapper down. The kidnapper made his escape as the parents turned attention to their uninjured, now terrified, precious infant.

Dr. Richmond immediately reported the incident to the officers at Fort Nisqually. A comprehensive search was made for the culprit, with all hands participating in the manhunt. After several hours the kidnapper was found concealed under a large woven reed mat. His head and face were bruised and swollen from his earlier confrontation with the baby's father. Dr. Richmond, a forgiving man of faith, interceded for the kidnapper who was let off with light punishment.

On other occasions, according to Fort Nisqually records, the same Indian was discovered prowling around suspiciously and taken into custody by Fort employees for other minor indiscretions.

Mrs. Chloe A. Clark Willson was transferred from the Nisqually Methodist Mission, by the authority of Rev. Jason Lee. Reverend Richmond was not happy to see her go. Just as she was the first teacher in what was to become Pierce County, she became the first teacher of the Oregon Institute in the Willamette Valley. The Methodist Church established the "Oregon Institute" on March 15, 1842, near Salem. She was, therefore, the first American teacher of American children at the first American school of higher education (post high school) west of the Rocky Mountains.

She left the Nisqually Mission when it was nearly 3½ years old. Chloe Clark's long tenure at Nisqually was not typical for Methodist Missionaries worldwide, many serving a mission for only one year. Nearly all 22 of the civilian Red River families were already gone from Nisqually by the time of the departure of Chloe Clark Willson and her husband, William. Most of the Red River settlers stayed less than eight months following their October arrival. The last family departed in June 1842.

It is speculation to wonder if one important factor for the Red River settlers' decision to depart Nisqually may have been the re-assignment of the only teacher at Nisqually. They had been promised so much by HBC, and had so little delivered, that losing the one bright prospect of a teacher for their children, may have been huge in their eyes.

Three months after the last Red River family departed, on September 1, 1842, Dr. Richmond decided to close the Nisqually Methodist Mission. It had operated for three years and five months. Richmond returned to his home church in Illinois, fully expecting the Oregon Methodist Mission to replace him at Nisqually.

Of the eight original Methodist pastors who came to the Oregon Mission with the Richmond family, five died in harness, so to speak. Only three pastors, Richmond being one, returned to the States to serve established churches. They returned to the regular church rotation policy established by John Wesley, the itinerate preacher who founded the Methodist Society in America. That rotation policy still serves Methodism today. Pastors are transferred frequently, often against their personal wishes and the desires of the parishioners. Richmond's departure from Nisqually was not unusual.

The Oregon Methodist Mission under Reverend Lee's leadership, was becoming increasingly secular. They opened many farms, a gristmill, and sawmill in 1842. Jason Lee and Daniel Lee expended over $100,000 on operations and compensation. The Mission Board disagreed with Lee's entrepreneurial activities. Financial support was withdrawn.

Rev. Jason Lee was removed from his mission position in 1843. His brother, Rev. Daniel Lee, was removed in 1844. Other Oregon Mission positions were simply eliminated by the American Board of Missions when pastors died or departed.

The decision to not replace Rev. Richmond, or the school teacher at the Nisqually Mission, was similar to the decisions to not replace Reverend Jason Lee. None of those missionary pastors who died, nor those assigned to missions at Clatsop and Umpqua, were replaced. The Missionary Era in Oregon was over.

All Old Oregon Methodist Mission enterprises and real-land holdings were sold (except for churches and parsonages). The sale generated $30,000. The American Mission Board decisions were probably prompted as much by church politics east of the Rockies as by economics in the west. Other Oregon Missions were launched by a "corporate combine" created by Congregational, Presbyterian, and Dutch Reformed denominations. Their first Missionary was Dr. Marcus Whitman, who would die in the so-called massacre of 1847.

The ultimate decision regarding the Nisqually Methodist Mission was made a few days after the Richmond family departed Nisqually along the rugged Cowlitz Trail, destined for the Columbia River. An arson fire burned the little Methodist Mission House and School. Later Doctor McLoughlin wrote to the staff at Fort Nisqually concerning the arsonist:

I am sorry to hear that the Indians have burnt Dr. Richmond's house. Every endeavor ought to be made to give the perpetrator a good fright so as to prevent others from doing the same thing; I say give them a good fright, as I would not be justified, perhaps, in giving him corporeal [sic] punishment, and if I knew who it was, and did not do so, it might induce the Indians to do the like again; our policy, therefore, is not to find who did it but to make noise about it so as to frighten the Indians from doing the like."[187]

With an HBC policy so clearly lacking in support, the Methodists were not inclined to rebuild at Nisqually. HBC continued to be the only "authority" in all of Old Oregon, including Puget Sound, until the Boundary Commission ruled on the border dispute. That was still years away. All across North America, HBC was known for 'enforcing" order, even turning cannons to utterly destroy entire villages where a single individual had offended the Company. Finding the arsonist might have been an easy task. Most likely the actual arsonist was known by the men of the Fort, a possibility no one wants to consider, even when the arson actually supported the overriding Company objective of keeping Americans south of the Columbia River.

Today, guilt is often decided on the basis of means, motive and opportunity. HBC certainly had all three in more abundance than the Nisqually people. There is no evidence to support another contention, but blaming an Indian was admittedly convenient for Hudson's Bay Company. There is no known instance of the Nisqually Indians ever using arson as a weapon, but they didn't write their own history.

W. H. Gray of Salem, Oregon attributed the Indian unrest to HBC and Catholic priests, who were, in his words;

"aggressive though working undercover to discredit American missions and settlements" saying it was a *"deep-laid scheme to rid the country of protestant missionaries and American settlers. The Protestant missions in the country were greatly annoyed by the unreasonable and threatening conduct of the Indians about their stations… becoming disheartened and discouraged, and were beginning to abandon their operations."*[188]

Through all of their writings the Methodists acknowledge and emphasize their great obligations to the officers of Hudson's Bay Company. They always mention the generous

---

187 Bagley, Clarence, *The Acquisition and Pioneering of Old Oregon*, YE Galleon Press, Fairfield, WA, 1924, reprint 1982.

188 Gray, W. H. *History of Oregon"* Charter title "Efforts to Destroy the Missions" pp 365

hospitality, uniform courtesy, and considerate acts of kindness. Still, in those same writings one finds a vein of resentment, even unfriendliness and ingratitude.[189] HBC did not hide the official Company contempt for American intrusion into the Joint Occupancy of Old Oregon.

History, obviously, is a continuing debate between competing ideas and interpretations. Those with the power to control rival versions of historic events are often able to marginalize, or even define, public understanding. This is a disadvantage many tribes are still working to overcome.

Richmond's cooking stove was still aboard ship for transport from New York. Eventually it was transferred to McNeill's *SS Beaver*. There it remained, destined for the Nisqually Mission, but never arriving until after the missionary's departure. The final disposition of the cooking stove is unknown. McNeill's notes only inquire as to what was to be done with it. After a half-world tour, the stove never reached the Richmond family at Nisqually. Was this another 'hindrance' by HBC?

The Reverend Dr. John P. Richmond was born on August 7, 1811 in Middleton Maryland and died at age 84 on August 28, 1895. He was a remarkable man by nearly any standard. He graduated from a Philadelphia Medical College at the age of twenty. He was licensed to preach by the Methodist Church at age twenty-three and assigned to the Choctaw Mission where he met and married the widow America Walker Talley. Her deceased husband had been the Superintendent of the Methodist Choctaw Mission.

Upon leaving the Choctaw, Richmond was next assigned to the Methodist Itinerant Ministry in Illinois. With saddlebags on horseback he traveled a large territory across mostly road-less lands to preach at twenty-six churches during every three-week period. From Illinois he was assigned to a church in Jacksonville, Mississippi, and from there he volunteered for the Oregon Methodist Mission.

The Nisqually Methodist Mission operated as a part of the Oregon Methodist Mission for nearly three and one-half years. Following his service there, Richmond was assigned to Springfield, Quincy, and other points in Illinois. While Abraham Lincoln was in the lower house, Richmond was elected and served in the Illinois Senate. While serving in the lower chamber, Richmond was elected Speaker of the House. He was also selected by the Illinois Electoral College to cast the state's vote for President in 1856. He was a delegate to two Illinois state constitutional conventions and for eight years served as state superintendent of schools. By 1874 Rev. Richmond was living in Tyndall, Bon Homme County, Dakota Territory with his son Francis, who was the child born, and kidnapped,

---

189 Clarence Bagley said, "There seems some excuse for it". p. 133 *"The Acquisition of Old Oregon"*

at Nisqually. They were living not far from the Red River where the so called "Red River Settlers" of Steilacoom originated.

In Old Oregon, the single Roman Catholic Mission farm at St. Paul on the Willamette failed economically. Although records are fragmentary, only 400 bushels of wheat and 280 bushels of coarse grain were produced in 1842. The St. Francis Mission, as it was called, produced 650 bushels of grain and employed thirteen volunteer workmen, with one paid overseer. St. Mary's Mission among the Flathead in the Rockies, by comparison, had twelve log houses and abundant crops. The St. Igantius Mission (Idaho) constructed fifteen buildings and planted three hundred acres. None of these missions survived long due to a variety of physical obstacles and Indian indifference to the Christian message.

The Protestant missionaries were more successful as farmers than the Roman Catholic priests because they were less itinerant, more settled, and occupying better farm land. The "black robe" Catholics were the more successful religious proselytizers. The celibate priests could live near or among the Indians, while the missionaries with wives and children expected more family protection and privacy. They had a lighter burden during travel. The ceremonial aspect of the Catholic liturgy seems to have had a greater appeal than the quiet austerity of fundamental Protestant church service.

The tribes were heavily influenced by the mixed blood French-Canadian fur trappers. The Métis were well aware of what had happened to the Indian tribes in the East. Many were determined to prevent the same thing from happening again in the West. The more literate voyageurs, with extensive trade contacts and far ranging experiences, informed Puget Sound Indians of the potential for cultural destruction.

By 1850 all of the missions, Wesleyan Methodist, Congregational-Presbyterian, and Roman Catholic, were essentially abandoned. One bit of missionary zeal stuck. Farming literally took root among the Indians of Puget Sound, encouraged by HBC. The most successful adoption of farming was the complete acceptance of the potato. Cultivation of the potato was consistent with the Indian root-gathering culture. The potato diffused rapidly. Indians near Fort Nisqually were raising their own potato crops in 1839, when the Methodist Missionaries arrived. Lt. Charles Wilkes reported in 1841 that the Indians raised "extremely fine" potatoes in "great abundance." It was, he said, a large portion of their diet.

On September 10, 1842, HBC barque *Columbia* departed London bound for Fort Vancouver. She carried a cargo of trade goods and a passenger returning from a year-long furlough to England. Dr. William Fraser Tolmie, physician and fur trader, was returning to the Pacific Northwest Coast via the Atlantic, Pacific, and Hawaii. He would soon be assigned to Fort Nisqually. Tolmie had been granted a leave of absence in 1841, during which time he traveled home, via London, to Scotland, and to Paris for more medical training. After his leave he fully expected to be assigned to Yerba Buena, California.

Hudson's Bay Company operated a post there, in what is now San Francisco, for several years. In 1841 James Douglas of HBC established a trading post there, in a large building on the water's edge. The place was a wholesale store, selling goods from Oregon (salmon, lumber, and British manufactured items), while purchasing hides and tallow. The post also served to improve British (and HBC) relations with the Spanish California government. The HBC store in Yerba Buena was sold in 1846, two years before the California Gold Rush.[190]

---

190 The author donated an oil painting of the original 1841 HBC store in Yerba Buena. The art work hangs in the Fort Nisqually Living History Museum Research Library, Tacoma, Washington.

1843

DURING TOLMIE'S VOYAGE HOME, the world was astonished by the appearance of The Great Comet of 1843. Tolmie made no mention of the phenomenon, but Chief Factor James Douglas certainly did. He was living temporarily aboard SS Beaver while supervising the construction of Fort Victoria at a small bay the Indians called "Camosack" (also Camosun and later Victoria Harbor). On the evening of March 17, 1843, Douglas saw the comet clearly over the Olympic Mountains to the south.

> *I saw a luminous streak in the heavens… which lasted from dusk until 9 o'clock, when the moon rose and obscured it. It's highest altitude was at Betelguix in Orion, due south from the position we occupied at the time of its appearance, and extended from thence, in a continuous line to the south west point of the horizon, forming an arc of about 90 degrees. And (Betelguix) its breadth was (unreadable number here) arcs and it diminished gradually towards the south west horizon. We cannot account for this phenomenon, unless we may suppose that it is produced by the reflection of the waters in the Straits of de Fuca, although it is difficult to account for its existence on any such principle.*[191]

A letter from London to Dr. John McLoughlin at Fort Vancouver with instructions to assign Doctor William Fraser Tolmie to Fort Nisqually was dated December 21, 1842. Tolmie was contracted to combine the duties of his medical profession with those of Indian Fur Trader at Fort Nisqually for the Hudson's Bay Company. Soon he would be Superintendent of the farming operations of the Puget Sound Agricultural Company, as well. London Directors allowed a salary of up to £300 per year. They also estimated the need for fifteen men at Nisqually, and fourteen more at Cowlitz, to carry on the business of the two companies. By 1844 there were fifty-six men at each place, with

---

191 The Great Comet of 1843 formally designated C/1843 D1, was a long-period comet. It could be observed in broad daylight over a period of 45 days. *Great Comets of History*, Yeomans, Donald K., Jet propulsion Laboratory, California Institute of Technology, 2011.

considerable work still left undone or deferred. Settlers, who were expected to fill the labor gaps, chose to work elsewhere. HBC and PSAC employees had little choice as to where they would work or what they would do. In 1842, unskilled laborers were typically paid about £20 per annum.

Marcus Whitman, missionary and farmer at Wailatpu, in what is now eastern Washington, traveled from the northwest to Boston between October 1842 and March 30, 1843. His was an overland journey that sought financial assistance and publicized the Old Oregon Country as a place for American settlers. The political dream of Manifest Destiny began as a smoldering idea, boosted by the Methodist Missionaries, the Wilkes Expedition, and American merchant ships' reports of northwest profits.

The first major increase in the American settler's Oregon Country population was followed, on May 2, 1843, by the formation of a provisional government. The aim was self-rule, and it challenged the Hudson's Bay Company, which had operated a de facto British "government" in the region since the 1818 Treaty of Joint Occupancy.

The Provisional Government of Oregon convened its first legislative body on June 18, 1844. The first election was held on June 3, 1845, with 480 votes cast. HBC did not challenge the new government that existed for a short time independently of both the United States and Britain.

One thousand settlers and 1,000 head of cattle embarked on the Oregon Trail from Independence, Missouri on May 22, 1843. It was the "Great Emigration," one year after the first modest party of American settlers made the long journey overland to Old Oregon.

The British were settling in Oregon, too. Captain James Scarborough, of Essex, England, established a farm on Chinook Point, where Chief Concomly and his six wives once lived. The area became known as Scarborough (later Scarboro) Hill. Scarborough served HBC for 20 years. He crossed the Columbia River bar in 1830 aboard the *Isabella* as second mate and boatswain.[192]

Hudson's Bay Company, feeling pressure from the influx of Americans, negotiated with the First Nations of Vancouver Island to allow the construction of a new trading post. Soon Fort Victoria was built and under the management of James Douglas, who had been an able assistant to Dr. John McLoughlin at Fort Vancouver. Soon a town emerged around the fort, becoming the center for trade and commerce for the British on the Pacific side of North America. About the same time, the British Royal Navy began

---

192 After the U.S. Congress passed the Donation Land Law in 1850, Scarborough ended up with 643 acres that, in 1898, became the U.S. Army's Fort Columbia, then a Washington State Park in 1950. Author's notes.

development of Esquimalt, a nearby bay, as a western base for British Gun Boats known as the "Flying Squadron."

With the town of Victoria growing, the Navy recruiting, the fur trade business morphing into a broad-based consumer oriented enterprise, and the discovery of gold on the mainland, law enforcement was lacking. Victoria was a rough and tumble town, growing exponentially with new settlers, gold seekers, and adventurers. The growth in Victoria would continue for over a decade before some changes were made. We will pick up that part of the story again in 1851.

On November 15, 1843, John McLoughlin sent a message to the HBC London office that announced he had assigned Dr. Tolmie to Fort Nisqually, with the Company rank of Indian Fur Trader. The British were more convinced than ever of the inevitability of all the joint occupancy Oregon Country land north of the Columbia River was to become British land exclusively. The American Methodist Mission had pulled up stakes at Fort Nisqually, and the Wilkes Expedition had not resulted in an immediate influx of American settlers north of the Columbia. It all seemed clear that Britain had won the prized land west of the Rockies and north of the Columbia.

HBC outposts across the region needed a reliable source of food not supplied from London. Fur traders were notoriously poor farmers. Some outposts were nearly starved during the coldest winters. The need for reliable local sources of food was abundantly apparent as early as 1838. Puget Sound Agricultural Company was formed to concentrate the farming and ranching activities needed to sustain all HBC trading posts in the entire Columbia Department. It was also thought that the growth of a second international corporation would immunize the area from politically adventurous Americans and potential new settlers. At least that was the thinking in London. They were convinced that the eventual boundary would follow the Columbia River to the sea.

The new Indian Fur Trader at Nisqually, Doctor William Fraser Tolmie, you will remember, was temporarily at Fort Nisqually in 1833, just as it was opening for business. He remained there several months longer than expected or intended, with a personal and professional compulsion to treat a severely injured worker before moving on to his assigned northern coastal post at Fort McLoughlin.

While at Fort McLoughlin, Dr. Tolmie supervised the closure of Fort Simpson's original fur trade post and the successful opening at another safer site. During the closure and reopening of these two sites, both were extremely vulnerable to pilfering, if not outright attack. His second official assignment was at Fort Vancouver, where Tolmie served in a medical capacity that ranged far from that post into the southern Willamette Valley, north to the Cowlitz River Valley, and even to the Nisqually plains occasionally. All the while, Tolmie continued to pursue his interests in botany and agriculture as an avocation. He also took the time to begin learning some Indian languages, while teaching a young Indian boy to read English.

William Fraser Tolmie seemed well-suited to the new assignment at Fort Nisqually. His instructions were to expand the business of the place through PSAC. He first moved the main buildings one mile inland to the prairie, and then developed 1,500 acres of cultivated crop land. Over the years he developed huge herds of 10,000 to 12,000 sheep, 6,000 to 10,000 cattle, and expanded the reach of Indian trading partners, establishing regular trade with the Yakima and Kli-ki-tat people east of the Cascades. Within the next six years Tolmie would supervise the annual arrival of 250 fur-laden pack horses at Fort Nisqually for the annual Brigade Encampment.[193] Nearly all Horse Brigade fur trade business was conducted east of the Cascade Mountains. Each pack horse carried two packs of 90 pounds each. Simple math reveals that more than eleven tons of supplies were sent outbound in late August, while the same approximate tonnage of furs came west each summer. Each year also saw a huge influx of furs from the Marine Department. The *SS Beaver* collected huge totals along the Pacific Coast from Indian villages, HBC trading posts, and from the Russian traders at Sitka.

Tolmie's assignment to Fort Nisqually was a change of plans. His selection as Superintendent of the Puget Sound Agricultural Company was a strategic move. PSAC planned to sell agriculture produce by contract with the Russian-America Fur Company in Sitka. The contract would seek to allow British fur traders access to the interior of what is now British Columbia. In return for that access, HBC would provide essential food supplies from PSAC at Fort Nisqually. Tolmie had some cursory experience with the Russians while he worked close by at Fort Simpson.

As the Superintendent of the Puget Sound Agricultural Company's international operations, Tolmie essentially ended his medical practice. With PSAC resting entirely on his shoulders, this patient, tactful man no longer had the medical responsibilities of his original contract with Hudson's Bay Company. Eventually he became an unabridged businessman, harassed by American settlers who chafed at the fences around large tracts of desirable corporate lands.

Part of the business plan for Puget Sound Agricultural Company was to eliminate the occasional appearance of Russian ships along the coast. They were traversing between

---

193 By inference the 250 pack horses bearing furs could have carried some 45,000 pounds of the precious soft gold. If a prime "made beaver" weighed one pound, and all 45,000 pounds were of that quality, the Company could have sold the season's take for an estimated $126,000 that year. Author's calculations.

Fort Ross, in Spanish California, and the Russian Fur Company headquarters at Sitka.

The main Russian settlement, in what is now Alaska, was established in 1799 with aboriginal Shee Atka. The word "shee" means "people of" while "atka" meant the "seaward side" of Tlingit Island. Over time, the name Shee Atka was contracted to Sitka. Not long after his arrival, manager Alexander Baranov of the Russian American Fur Company constructed a fort on a promontory at the harbor. Native people had long revered that exact spot as sacred. The Tlingit's protested immediately. Resistance became outright hostility, which rapidly grew to violence. In 1802 nearly all of these Russians were killed.

Alexander Andreevich Baranov was born in 1747 at Kargopol, Russia. He became a successful merchant at Irkutsk, Siberia, but was lured to Alaska by the fur trading industry. By 1799 he was manager of the very profitable and influential Russian American Company. He was overseer of Alaska, the Aleutian and Kurile Islands, where seals and sea otters abounded.

Baranov organized Alaskan hunters to hunt as far as the coast of California, where Fort Ross was established. He ruled in Alaska for 28 years before his death in 1819.

Two years after the 1802 massacre at Sitka, Alexander Baranov retaliated during a six-day war the Tlingit had no hope of winning. They faced the enormous advantage of Russian firepower. The Russian cannons utterly destroyed the Tlingit village. The native town was renamed New Archangel. In 1842, Bishop Innocent, of the Russian Orthodox Church (Ivan Veniaminov), built his home and chapel on the site of the Kiksadi Clan. Soon nearly all signs of native habitation were completely gone. On the sacred hilltop, later known as Castle Hill, a castle-like structure was built in 1837. The fur trade from this place became the most profitable in the world.[194]

In 1838 Puget Sound Agricultural Company consummated the contract to sell food supplies to the Russian American Company in return for sea otter pelts. The contract allowed the Russians to close Fort Ross in California. They sold the site to John Sutter, an American rancher in Spanish California. Sutter did not want the land so much as the equipment at Fort Ross. The Spanish were somewhat stingy in allowing Sutter to purchase the equipment needed to successfully run a large ranch. The Russian equipment, wagons, fur and hide presses, oxen yokes, and surplus iron parts were quite valuable to Sutter.

The Russians no longer needed to sail along the North American coast to and from Fort Ross. This brought some satisfaction to the British, as well. They had eliminated

---

[194] By mid-century, over-hunting had diminished the sea otter take. On October 18, 1867 the Russians sold Alaska to the Americans. Clause-M. Naske; Herman E. Slotnik, *Alaska: A History of the 49th State,* University of Oklahoma Press, 1994.

the American seaborn fur trade, too. Americans had turned to whaling, where there was no competition.

Another benefit to the British contract with the Russians was limited British access to the interior of the northern Columbia Department, through Russian territory along a narrow strip of coastal land that today forms the Alaska Panhandle. British fur traders were allowed to pass through if they did not trade directly with the coastal tribes in Russian territory.

To summarize the PSAC–Russian Fur Company contract: The Russians would receive food and give up Fort Ross. The British would be paid in sea otter furs and have access to the interior lands, with the added benefit of no Russians sailing along the west coast. HBC was in good shape. The difficulty of producing substantial amounts of food was, seemingly, a small matter.

Immediately after the farming and ranching business was officially transferred to PSAC, Fort Nisqually was almost completely physically moved from the original spot near the bluff above the ship's landing, to a site about a mile inland, near fresh water. It was on the edge of the prairie, with a clear view of Mt. Rainier. It was on the southern banks of Sequalitchew Creek, almost directly across from the ashes of the burned out Methodist Mission. Many of the company's cultivated fields and pasture lands were already located in the vicinity.

A small log-and-mud dam was constructed across Sequalitchew Creek to impound water for the washing of sheep. The water had to be shallow enough for the sheep to climb out after being driven into the pond. Workers poured raw tobacco in the water as a disinfectant to kill the insects living as parasites in the sheep's wool. It was a cheap, if messy, operation, which the animals did not enjoy. The men may not have relished this essential work much either.

All of the usable construction timbers from the first site buildings were moved to the new location, as time allowed, while regular farming and ranching operations continued daily. The move to the new location was an extensive project. Some of the work was not completed for years. The northwest bastion was not built until 1848, when the palisades were erected for protection from a potential Sinahomish threat. Some of the old buildings were left in place as the new fort took over operations. Several new structures were built, including the officers' house, the men's dwelling, and a two-story storehouse. More buildings were built in subsequent years, as needed, by the ever-expanding business.

Several buildings were moved, as was Tolmie's little cabin-like home. It was called the Tyee House because "Tyee" is the Chinook word for Chief. It was probably about 18 feet by 12 feet, with only a dining (front) room and a bedroom. It would soon prove to

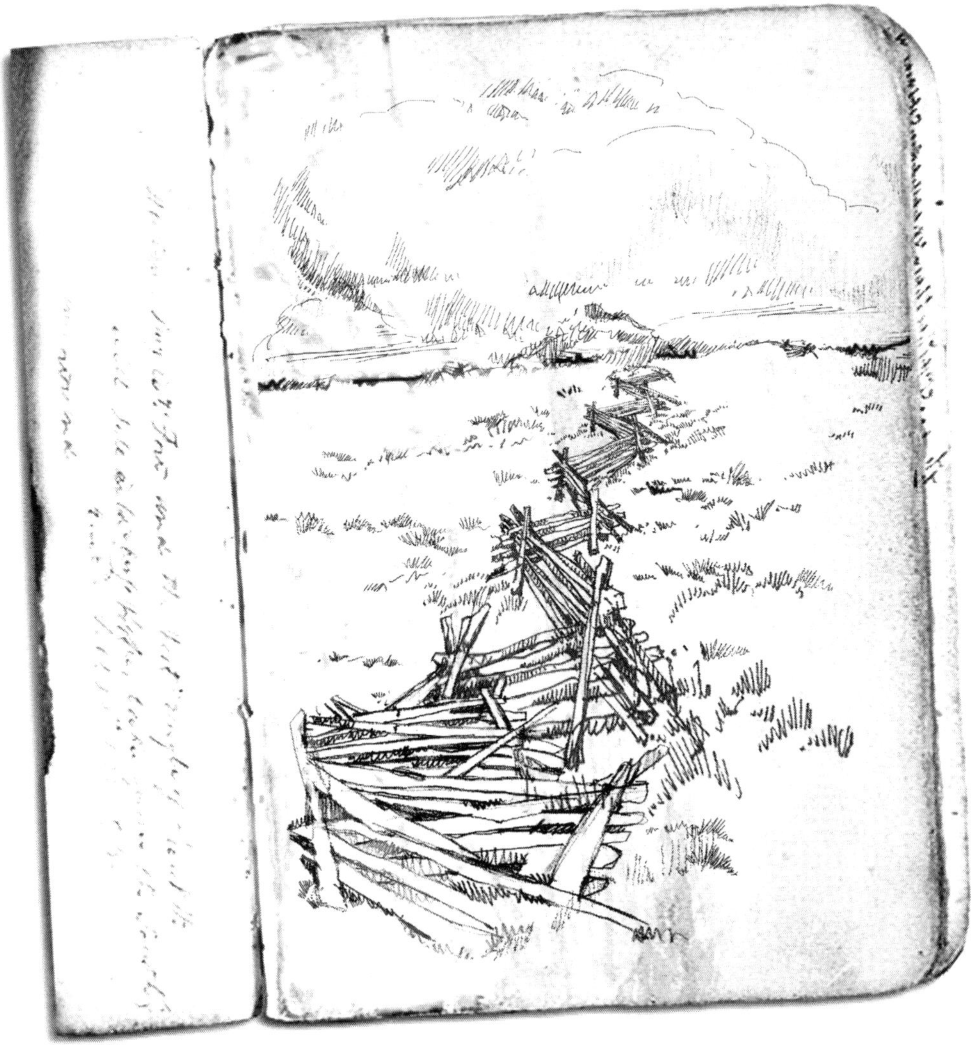

be too small as the Tolmie family grew.

A new Nisqually Village began to grow almost immediately as the Fort operations were moved. Nearly 300 Nisqually began camping, later building, on the north side of Sequalitchew Creek. They were anxious to be close to the action, close to the trade store, close to the employment center of the area.

Jason Lee, the leader of the Methodist Missionaries in Oregon, became the father of a little girl in 1842. Mrs. Lee died, a complication of the birth, one month after the baby was born. Rev. Lee continued his work as a single parent. In 1843 he was returning to the east when he learned he had been fired by the American Mission Board without a hearing. It was less than a year after Reverend Richmond closed the Nisqually Mission. Lee continued on his journey to New York, arriving in May, 1844. He was given the opportunity to plead his case before the Mission Board, but his appeal was too late. Church politics made that clear. He soon developed intestinal blockages and lung disease. He died on March 12, 1845. The Methodist Mission to Oregon Country quickly became a secular settlement, which led eventually to American statehood.

The Methodist Mission is credited with developing an economy based on cattle, and starting an American maritime trade with the east coast and Hawaii. The settlement led, in the end, to the boundary between Oregon and British claims.

Because of the Oregon Missions, including Congregationalists, Presbyterians, Dutch Reformed, and Methodists, a problem was solved peacefully. Reverend Jason Lee and Dr. John McLoughlin, though not always agreeing, led the movements to the solution without the two great English-speaking nations reverting to war. Lee and McLoughlin struggled selflessly with deliberate plans for conversion, preservation, and protection of Indians, and others, so that the Oregon Question was resolved peacefully. They were kind, single-hearted men acting with the purest motives. They did the foundation work. The structure of the Oregon Country was about to be built. It was undecided whether Old Oregon would become an independent country, a set of U.S. states, provinces of the British Empire, or a vicious political split.

Old Oregon was growing. There was a tremendous overland migration to Oregon that began slowly in 1843. A fledgling republic was formed in the Willamette Valley when the "Provisional Government" was set up by a vote of 52 to 50. They drafted a constitution called The Organic Act. The existing laws of Iowa were adopted in whole, with little modification. There was a considerable effort to seek formal recognition and authority from the United States. Most of the leading participants were previously connected to the old Methodist Mission.

Section seventeen of the Oregon Organic Act created the Land Claims committee, with powers to designate, record, and perhaps most significantly, limit the number and size of land claims. It required that all claims be surveyed and recorded with the committee. It also prevented speculation, fostered a community of farmers, and prohibited land claims by religious missions. The Methodists lost control of great stretches of farm land. Married couples could claim 640 acres at no cost. No legal "proof" of marriage was needed. It is believed that many "couples" were created for the convenience of land acquisition. Today those land claims are the only "record" of some early marriages, except for the records of the Methodist preachers and Catholic priests.

The prospects for PSAC continued to grow, too. Agricultural exports were sent to Russian Alaska, Spanish Yerba Buena (San Francisco), The Sandwich Islands (Hawaii), and London. Local PSA Company farms, called stations, were developed at Muck (near Roy), Spa-nu-eh (at the south end of Spanaway Lake), at Sastuc (between American and Spanaway Lakes), Tenalquot (across the Nisqually River in Lacey), Tlithlow (east of American Lake) Elk Plain (southeast of Spanaway Lake) and several others.

Each station had significant cattle herds and sheep flocks. Sheep pens were built to contain the sheep. These "sheep folds" provided some safety from marauding animal predators. The pens were moved frequently to conserve the plant life and to fertilize yet another spot of ground. The main objective was to create great herds of cattle and great flocks of sheep. Both were accomplished, as we shall see, at later dates.

As the Company expanded the herds and the land area to operate, the need for more workers increased as well. More and more Nisqually people, and others, were hired to tend the animals and crops. Most Nisquallys continued to live in their traditional homes, but a significant number were no longer gathering oysters and clams. Fishing remained their principle activity. Canoes were best maintained, and utilized, at the beach, not upland.

In 1843, Fort Nisqually and Puget Sound Agricultural Company had about 10 square miles under control as grazing and farming lands, for 1,396 cattle and 5,043 sheep. Several hundred acres were cultivated. Six years later, the animal census counted 12,419 head of sheep, including Southdown, Cheviot, Leicester, Merino purebreds, and crossbred animals.

The cattle herd numbers also increased. Spanish longhorns from Mexican California were crossbred with English cattle. The dominant Spanish cattle absorbed the English strain, leaving a "wild" cattle herd on the plains. Those animals provided a minimum of meat, and no milk. Oxen, pigs, riding and working horses were also bred at PSAC. The hogs provided the much needed meat and lard.

Each year PSAC grew spring wheat, winter wheat, barley, oats, buckwheat, peas, potatoes, turnips, colewort, flax, clover, and timothy. All crops were planted in a careful sequence, to assure ripening would not occur simultaneously for all crops. For instance, peas were planted before March 20 and matured only 120 days later, when it was possible to plant another pea crop. Oats, therefore, had to be planted before April 20 to ripen 137 days later... Spring wheat ripened in 127 days, while barley was due in only 103 days.

This careful attention to crop maturation led to yields of 100,000 bushels of wheat, 2,000 bushels of peas, 2,500 bushels of potatoes. Wheat weighed in at twenty bushels per acre and up to sixty-eight pounds per bushel. An "excellent" label was applied for both quantity and quality. Another measure of success was the "increase" based on the amount of seed used. In 1843, grain yielded sevenfold, peas fourfold, and potatoes produced eleven times the seed used.

While PSAC sold 6,000 bushels of wheat to HBC annually, the production was insufficient to meet the additional contract demands with the Russians. PSAC was expected to produce 8,400 bushels of wheat yearly for the Russian American Fur Company. Shortfalls were made up by purchasing commodities from the Willamette settlers and even California, to meet the contract demands. Sometimes the available supplies allowed HBC sales (an extra ten tons in 1842) to hungry folks at Kamchatka on the Asian mainland.

PSAC, through HBC, sold a variety of food stuff to the Russians. Included in the "shopping list" more often than not, were wheat, flour, biscuits, potatoes, oats, peas, pork, beef, pickles, dried apples, and molasses. In 1843 alone, 5,448 pounds of butter was produced for the Russians.

1844

JOSEPH THOMAS HEATH was born in 1805, the eldest of 13 children. As an adult, his passion was gambling on horse races. He lost his own and much of the family fortune. One of his brothers, William, was the British Commander (First Officer) of the *Cowlitz*, sailing from London to the Pacific Northwest coast, under the command of American Captain William Henry McNeill. Joseph Heath became a 38-year-old passenger who paid £20 Sterling for his passage in August 1843. The family insisted that he change his ways in the New World as a tenant farmer.

Heath arrived at Nisqually in June of 1844, when his brother's career was set. Joseph's younger brother William had been hired by HBC in 1832 as an able-bodied seaman already promoted to First Mate of the *Cowlitz*. Unlike William, the unmarried Joseph was a gentleman-farmer, helping the English populate the Puget Sound region. His noble words were not matched by quick action. Heath needed some encouragement even after he arrived in the Pacific Northwest. He resided as a guest at Fort Vancouver for 16 months (until December 13, 1844) before finally leasing 640 acres at Steilacoom.

Heath selected a spot along the Steilacoom River (Chambers Creek); seemingly undeterred by the failure of the Red River settlers at the very same site. He met with Dr. Tolmie at Fort Nisqually before choosing this property six miles from the fort. A Red River farmer had left a crude cabin and some split rail fencing.

On the original contract signed in London, Joseph Heath agreed to pay rent, 50% of the annual profits, and 5% interest on all advanced supplies, including food stuff, seeds, salmon, flour, grease, potatoes, and any other provisions to be purchased from Hudson's Bay Post at Fort Nisqually. It was a contract guaranteed to achieve failure, or at maximum, perpetual servitude. By design he would never be out of debt to the company.

As he took up residence, Heath built himself a bed, a table, two stools and lined the interior walls of his crude rented abode with Indian woven cedar bark mats to calm the wind whistling between the log walls. In the next five years, Heath would transform the place with a new house, a granary, a smokehouse, and several small out-buildings with the inexpensive labor of local Indians. Inside his home, he constructed a cupboard, a dresser, and furnished the cabin with a ship's mess table purchased from the crew of the *Fisgard*.

It was arduous work to transform the wild prairies into a working, and profitable, farm. With the help of those ever-present local Indians, hired for day labor, Heath enclosed 170 acres and planted 60 of those acres in wheat. Dr. Tolmie allowed him some sheep and cattle, with the contract stipulation that 50% of the profit would go to PSAC each year.

Heath seldom seemed to appreciate the work "his Indians" did on his farm. The fact is the Indians did most of the work. They were readily available to pick weeds, gather peas, sort, cut, and plant potatoes, harvest the crop, and tend the sheep. He hired some for domestic work, too. Women washed, ironed and cooked. He paid them all in blankets, shirts, needles, and similar trade goods, which he in turn had purchased at retail prices on credit, with 5% annual interest, at Fort Nisqually's Trade Store.

Before Heath arrived at Nisqually, Dr. Tolmie reported that HBC occupied ten square miles of prairie with 1,396 cattle, 5,043 sheep, and several hundred acres under cultivation. In that same report Tolmie claimed 13 Red River families were settled at Steilacoom, Muck Creek, and Spanaway. Some of that report was almost instantly out of date. Most of the Red River settlers departed for the Willamette Valley shortly after their original arrival, and long before Heath moved in.

Heath's early accounts tell of the difficulty of creating enough vegetable produce to feed himself and his employees. Protecting the animals and crops from predators was extremely difficult, according to his diary. He was facing the same situation faced by the Methodist Missionaries and the Red River settlers. Heath often had difficulty keeping his Indian employees from fighting each other over trivial matters, too. In addition, singular responsibilities fell on his shoulders because he was alone. He relished the infrequent visits from his brother, William, and the more frequent visits from his landlord, Dr. Tolmie.

Many of the Steilacoom Indians moved their lodges to be near the new farmer, creating the essence of a new village at his door step. He regularly traded for birds, ducks, deer, trout, salmon, and other food stuff they offered in barter. Heath was happy for the companionship and ready labor, but there were problems. The Indian dogs were nearly as difficult as the wolves and coyotes. The hungry animals often took advantage of Heath's meager flock of sheep.

Indian gambling games are often quite loud, especially the ones that continued all night. Heath complained of lost sleep during Indian funerals as well. The wailing during these tribal affairs was disruptive. He didn't like the Indian habit of "borrowing" tools and household supplies. It was difficult to enforce "law and order," and Heath, somehow, saw it as his responsibility. Occasionally, Heath offended an employee while trying to maintain a semblance of English personal privacy. You see, Heath had a habit of closing his doors and locking them. This was not the Indian way.

While the Methodist Missionaries, Richmond and Willson, did the farm work for their own families as a religious example, or witness, for the Indians to emulate, Joseph Heath was more inclined to hire Indian workers to weed, gather, cut, plant, and sort the produce of his fields and tend to his animals and household. Heath's goal was to get the work done as needed, using hired hands. The Missionaries intended to teach the Indians how to become independent farmers, rather than servant class workers, as was the English practice. The account books for the little Heath farm included an English name given to each individual Indian hired by Heath. He was quite busy managing his hired helpers, with little time to depart from the perception of his self-imposed "Gentleman Farmer" identity.

Heath suffered from extreme loneliness and a malady that historians find difficult to diagnose through the great distances of time. It may have been nearly anything between chronic indigestion and heart disease. His diary mentions the enjoyment of Sunday dinners with the Tolmie family, and occasional visits from other HBC/PSAC employees, such as John Edgar and John Ross and their families.

Heath's many complaints against the Company went unresolved. His requested supplies were often late, delivered in smaller portions than expected. Often supplies were inadequate, inferior, or unavailable. Heath wrote;

> *Am not well treated; they want to pawn off on me the refuge of everything. I will not bear it any longer."*[195]

His implied threat was never carried out. He had virtually no "leverage," as the contract was written with no recourse. He was so far in debt that securing passage, even aboard an outgoing cargo ship, was impossible.

Many of the early American immigrants to Oregon Country expressed a determination to settle north of the Columbia River in direct opposition to the policies imposed by Dr. McLoughlin at Fort Vancouver. Nearly all were turned south by the determined McLoughlin. In December, a party led by Michael Simmons started for Puget Sound. They found the travel extremely difficult in the winter months. They returned to winter at Vancouver while making elaborate plans to occupy the area near Tumwater Falls, on the Deschutes River above Budd Inlet.

---

[195] Heath, Joseph Thomas, *Memoirs of Nisqually*, Ye Galleon Press, Fairfield, WA 1979.

Nearly seven thousand pounds of wool were sent to England in 1844 from Fort Nisqually. Shearing season was part of the yearly work done mostly by the day to day employees, that is, the Indians. It was difficult work, done in a primitive manner. The shepherds drove a small flock into a tobacco-slurry pool. The animals would dutifully thrash around, getting completely soaked with the toxic juices. With dripping wet wool each sheep finally followed compatriots out the other side of the creek into the hands of waiting Indian women. At this point the wool was doomed to be removed from the sheep. A team of two wranglers forced each sheep to its back haunches. Sheep, you see, relax completely when put on their backs. Shearing commenced. Hand shears, like large scissors, flew at the valuable wool. In minutes an entire flock was shorn.

Shearing work was most often done inside, or at least near a large storehouse, called—for the moment at least—the shearing-house. Here the women sat on Indian mats working in pairs. One would take the hind part of the animal, the other taking the fore part. Although the animal would not struggle a great deal, the legs were tied as a safeguard against escape. Many of the shearers were quite skillful; others caused the poor helpless brute to be badly mangled.

Sheep were most often kept in bands of 500 or so, which were often further divided into flocks of 20 animals for easier management. Each band had two men as herders, under the supervision of a Company contract employee as shepherd for several bands. The shepherd resided at the out-station. Those in charge of a band stayed with the band day and night, often sleeping on the ground. On occasion it was necessary to fend off prowling wolves. One Indian reported that a wolf actually woke him one night licking the man's sweaty face.

Hudson's Bay people kept tight control on the use of the prairie lands. They did things in a prudent and methodical manner, business-like, to preserve the natural grasses for future seasons. Animals were also divided into smaller flocks of 150-200, then forced into an enclosure formed by portable fencing rails. This enclosure might hold the animals for several nights to adequately fertilize the soil. The flock would be released from the corral to the broader plains when the field was ready for the plough. The term for this operation was "parking," which was designed to gather manure in strategic locations while simultaneously providing a protective measure for the broader grasslands that could be over-grazed.

The bluish-green grass covered the land completely, unlike the bunch grass east of the Cascades, where half of the ground lies barren. Even in the driest season the bunch grass was thick enough on the prairies around Fort Nisqually to protect the roots, if the sheep were prevented from causing serious root damage.

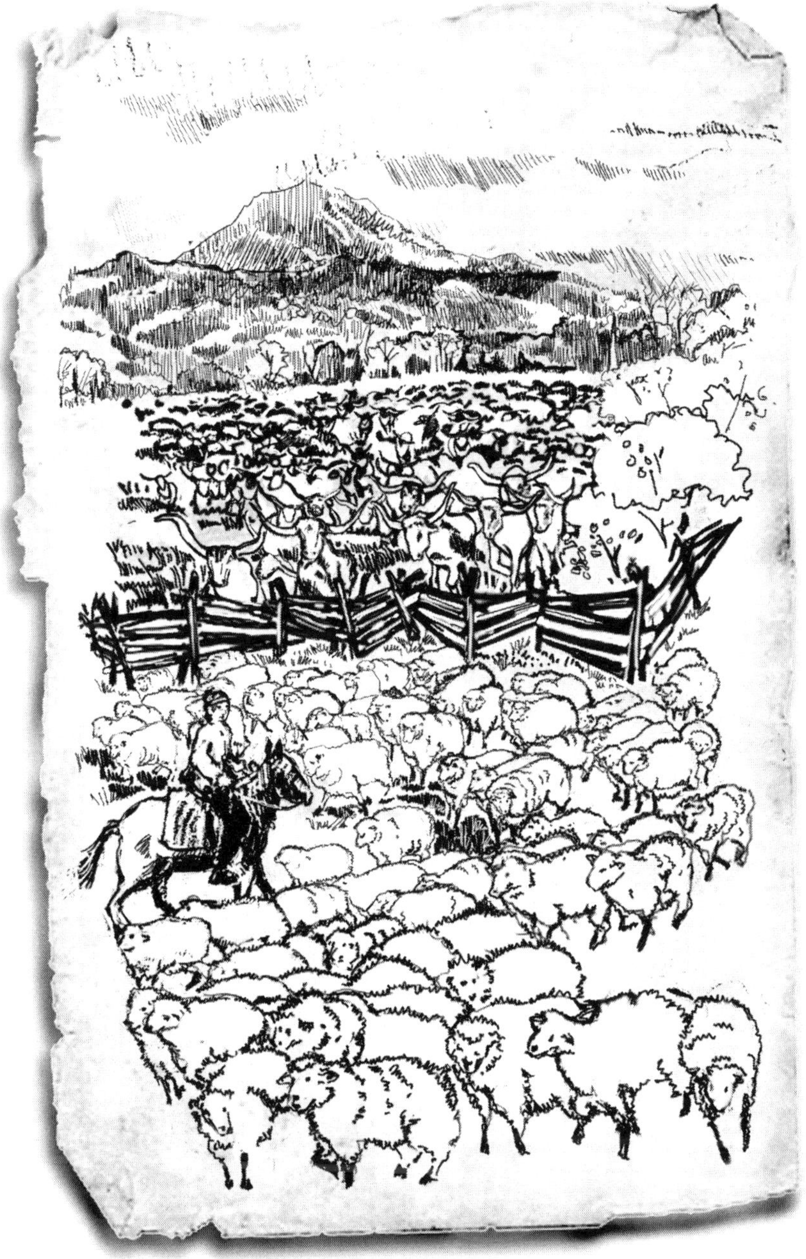

"...bunch-grass grew in great abundance, and though dry, retained its nutritious properties instead of losing them like other grasses in the autumn."[96]

Within a few years, the mostly unfenced herds of thousands of wild cattle, more thousands of sheep, plus huge fields of potatoes and acres of other crops, caused friction with the American settlers seeking to wrest the area from the Brits. There was enough acreage on HBC and PSAC land to provide thousands of settlers the land-grant farms promised by their United States government. The open rangeland, however, was not included in the land grant legislation. Soon farmers were illegally hunting and killing any steer on the open range. This made the entire herd even wilder, and forced Dr. Tolmie to seek legal recompense. The situation had the potential to spiral out of control.

Tolmie's impulse was always to do a good turn simply for the sake of it. He attended the birth of American Ezra Meeker's first child without hesitation. The Dr. was no longer operating a medical practice, and the request came from a total stranger, an American at that, but he responded at great personal inconvenience without a fee or the expectation of ever seeing the Meeker family again. However, according to Ezra Meeker;

"That first acquaintance ripened into a friendship life-long. Tolmie was a noble man, with noble impulses,"[97]

When the American settlers came, all thoughtful care of the wild grass ended. While PSAC grazed up to 12,000 head of sheep and 10,000 head of cattle, the settlers soon expected the land to support at least 30,000 head of sheep alone. The settler animals were scattered over the prairies during the spring and summer, with devastating impact. The sheep were left too long at any one location, eating grasses to the root, exposing the thin soil. This gave the grass seeds and the roots literally no chance under the hot sun and drying winds of a Puget Sound July or August. Those few weeks were crucial to survival for even the sturdy bunch grass. In a few years, worthless crab grass and weeds had taken the place of the nutritious natural prairie bunch grass.

Joseph Heath's journal pages are missing for the last half of 1844. From the Fort's records we learn that Heath and Tolmie were challenged by threats from Snoqualmie Indians. The threats were so menacing to Heath that he appealed to Fort Nisqually for assistance. Three company employees were sent to spend the nights with Heath. That alone was enough for the visiting band to leave, although the unrest continued for a week.

---

[96] Washington, Irving, *The Adventures of Captain Bonneville*, Boston, Twayne Publishers, 1977

[97] Meeker, Ezra, Pioneer Reminiscences of Puget Sound, The tragedy of Leschi, Lowman & Hanford, Seattle, WA 1905.

1844

The Nisqually people celebrated the Snoqualmie departure. They held nightly feasting and dancing on the beach. Their celebrations eventually led to the death of two men. That was serious, but Tolmie was more upset by the butchering of two choice oxen eaten during the festivities. While five Indians were involved in the slaughter, only two were caught. Tolmie *"Flogged the thieves at the cat's tail and imprisoned them in the bastion."* according to the company records. There were no further Indian troubles that season.

Another annoyance creeping up on the Company was far more serious. American settlers were coming north of the Columbia River. One American, still far away in Maine, would be instrumental in the development of the Old Oregon Country. That American was Lieutenant Isaac Stevens, a young West Point graduate, who built the first Fort Knox, named for Major General Henry Knox, the first Secretary of War during the American Revolution. The fort is constructed of stone and protects the Penobscot River Valley in Maine.

Stevens is the same man who died (1862) in the American Civil War as a Union Army Brigadier General, at the Battle of Chantilly, Virginia. He was eventually appointed Governor of Washington Territory (1853), but in 1844 he was an Army officer in a survey office in Washington, D.C. His journey to Puget Sound had not yet begun.

Russians were coming, though. New Archangel, in Russian America, was established in 1844. A secure presence was finally developed for the Russian fur trade when the Russian Orthodox Church was built in Sitka. The Cathedral of Saint Michael the Archangel was built in 1844, and became the seat of the Russian Orthodox Diocese governing all of North America. The cathedral still contains the Sitka Madonna, Our Lady of Sitka and other priceless icons.[198]

---

[198] After a fire in 1966 the cathedral was rebuilt. Most of the original icons and furnishings were saved from the inferno by Sitka residents. Today, tourist visits are led by Russian Orthodox priests.

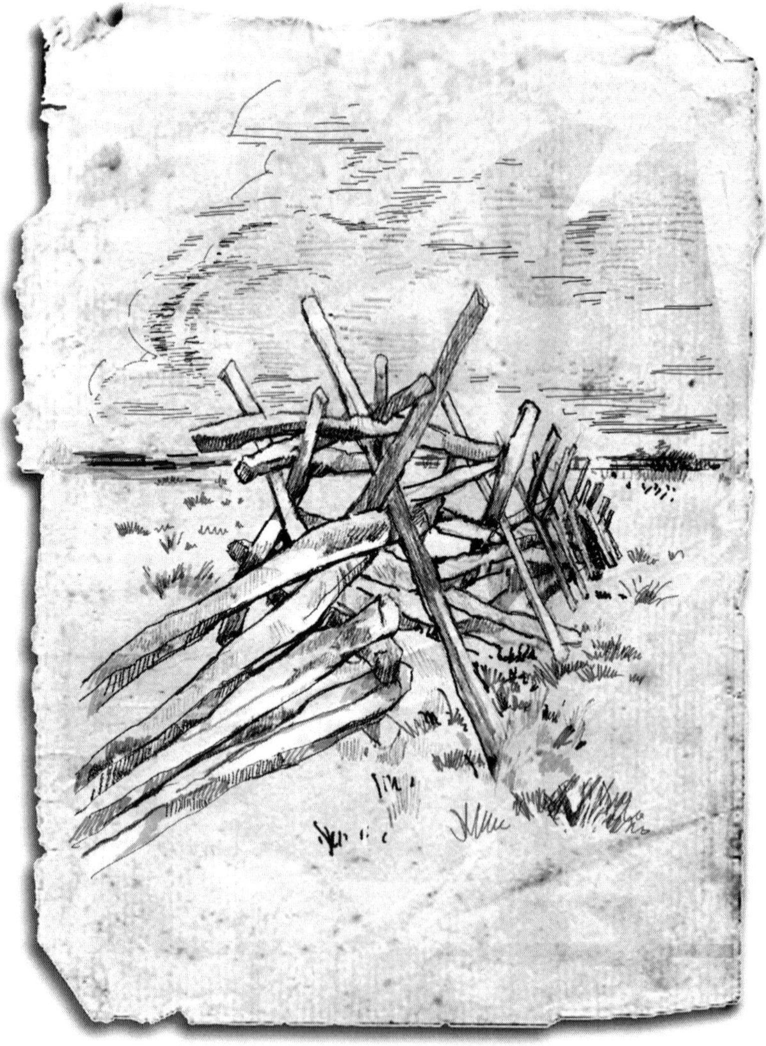

1845

THE BRITISH MERCHANT shipping industry expanded rapidly in the 1830s, due largely to the vast increase in corn imports. The short-lived shipbuilding boom augmented the need for Canadian timber carriers crossing the Atlantic. So many ships were built that the inevitable sharp depreciation of ship values came in 1843. Ship owners suffered badly as they anxiously sought employment for their vessels. Mortgages foreclosed in such numbers that Parliament tried to save the shipping industry with taxpayer money.

A discovery of huge supplies of bird guano on two islands, one near Peru, and the other off South West Africa, eventually saved British shipping. From 1842 through 1852, single ships carried as much as 1,500 tons of guano back to Liverpool and Glasgow. The guano sold for nine pounds per ton. The Admiralty reported that upwards of 294,486 tons of raw guano was available off Africa.

The Great Irish Potato Famine began in 1843, lasting through 1852 in most of Ireland and Scotland. The failing potato crop in Ayrshire, County Ayr, Scotland, was one area saved by the literal spreading of African guano. Although much of the agriculture of southwest Scotland was saved, inadvertently, by the depression in the British shipping industry, it was not enough to halt the emigration of one million people.

Bernard DeVoto, historian and author of "Year of Decision, 1846,"[199] may have been off by one year. Certainly great political decisions were made in 1846, as DeVoto stated, but in 1845 many citizens of the United States made the decision to trek westward to Oregon Country. Some even made the brave decision to continue north of the Columbia River, into British-held land, as well.

In personal dealings, the Americans and the British generally got along well. In 1845, with negotiations over which country would ultimately control Oregon Country, the British twelve-gun sloop *Modeste* was sent to Fort Vancouver. It tied up at the HBC dock on the Columbia River, remaining there until the dispute was settled by the Treaty of 1846. American settlers welcomed the sailors of the *Modeste*. There were many social events

---

199 DeVoto, Bernard, *Year of Decision, 1846*, Little, Brown & Company, Boston, 1943.

hosted by both sides, but the most important aspect of the interaction was the best of all. The Crown had sent a barrel of silver coins, as American dollars, minted for foreign trade. The *Modeste* sailors and officers were paid with these coins, which were soon in general circulation in Oregon Country. The reduced silver content was of no concern for the cash-poor Oregon economy. It was real money to replace paper or barter transactions.

After a few investigative ventures north of the Columbia, a small settler party was organized to defy HBC's ban on American settlement near Puget Sound. In October, Michael Troutman Simmons, with five other families and two unmarried men, settled at and around Tumwater, about 15 miles southwest of Fort Nisqually. From that day on, many historians have proclaimed the Simmons party the FIRST American settlers on Puget Sound, even though the American Missionaries from Illinois and New England built their homes at Nisqually six years earlier, living there for three years and five months. Those historians completely disregard the lives of nine American people (five of them children, one a newborn citizen) who lived through four planting-to-harvest seasons. They lived in what is now Pierce County, from early April, 1839, to September, 1842.

The historical record shows that Reverend David Leslie, William Willson, Chloe Clark Willson, Reverend John P. Richmond, America Talley Richmond, the four Richmond children (including Francis, who was born at Nisqually, and baby Oregon Richmond who was born in New York during the journey to Nisqually) all settled at Nisqually before any other Americans lived north of the Columbia River, including the so-called first American settlers of the Simmons Party. The fact is, Simmons followed the same trail from Cowlitz Landing that the Methodists settlers had used more than six years earlier.

Most historians say Simmons and his group can rightfully claim they were the first "permanent American settlers who came overland" to Puget Sound. The Methodist Missionaries were not "permanent" settlers, and they came by sea and overland, but the Methodist Church they served at Puget Sound is "permanent." It should be noted that the first non-mission church building in what is now Pierce County was constructed by a Methodist congregation in Steilacoom, a direct connection to the Nisqually Methodist Mission, which was founded by the Methodist Church of North America. Further, historians often argue that Fort Nisqually wasn't "permanent" either.

The earliest efforts of McDonald, Anderson, the Red River settlers, Tolmie, Heath, Leslie, Willson, Richmond, Flett, even Balch, at Steilacoom, as well as others, should not be dismissed from history or discredited for having "discontinuous" tenures.

It was the Nisqually Methodist Mission that actually broke the Hudson's Bay Company ban against American settlements north of the Columbia River, not Simmons, who gets the credit from most historians. It is true that HBC officials considered the Simmons',

American settlement as much more than a simple annoyance of some protestant Missionaries. They actually feared armed conflict with the "wild and armed Americans," who settled in and claimed land or directly competed in the fur trade. That was a threat never offered by the mild-mannered Methodist Missionaries. The Wilkes Expedition was a highly armed U.S. Navy fleet, including a squadron of Marines, but its ostensible purpose was scientific in nature, thereby posing little threat to the fur trade business, but bolstering the American ideal of Manifest Destiny.

In fact, Simmons and the other American settlers of 1845 appealed to Washington, D.C. for U.S. military assistance, but were told to protect themselves. Thus the settlers prepared for armed conflict, becoming "wild and armed Americans," as described by the Brits. Perhaps it was the American constitutional right to bear arms that bothered "John Bull," as the Americans referred to subjects[200] of the crown. The Americans armed themselves and prepared to use their weapons against any perceived threat: Indian, British, or claim-jumper. In that era, the English were hated and distrusted by most Americans. Those countries had already fought two wars in seventy years. Both wars pitted English soldiers against the great efforts of American civilians.

Colonel Simmons was ambitious. He built the first of many business-type improvements in the Olympia area. Tumwater was called New Market in the beginning. Simmons and his partners build the first gristmill and the first sawmill on Puget Sound. He was the first merchant, the first postmaster, and served in legal capacities in three different forms of government. He was a delegate to two conventions seeking territorial status. Simmons married Elizabeth Kindred, of Clay County, Iowa, in 1835. The marriage produced two daughters, Charlotte and Kittie. Michael Troutman Simmons died in 1867 at age 53, at Drew's Prairie, in what is now Thurston County.

American civilians took a hard line against the British and the Indians. Their view was diametrically opposed to the HBC view. Americans felt a God-given right to all the land they needed or wanted, and would take no opposition from those they considered "foreigners" or "savages," even when those words easily described themselves. Americans had a history of seizing land from Native Americans, who were the majority population in the beginning. Settling the Puget Sound area was a continuation of a ruthless, ongoing land grab, justified by the belief it was their God-given right to "smite the enemies of the Lord." They believed that it was against the laws of God that so much land should be left idle, when American Christians wanted it to raise their bread. The United States Army was called upon to defend this type of settler.

---

200 Americans are citizens, while people of British nationality were subjects of the Crown until 1949. Author's notes.

British who worked for the Hudson's Bay Company and the Puget Sound Agricultural Company, were regarded a bit better by the Americans if they were Christians. Americans had a healthy respect for the Scots and Brits, but remembered the country had fought two wars against the very same people in 1776 and 1812. Many Americans were "ready" for another fight.

Indians saw similarities in the Scots and their own culture. They wore similar garments: Scottish kilts and Indian cedar skirts. Scots had clans: Indians had tribes. They both had chiefs. HBC was not interested in occupying land: commercial trade was their interest. Indians were also traders. None of these similarities existed for the American settlers. Native Americans called the Americans "Boston" men, and the British were labeled "King George" men. They knew the differences.

One exceptional settler was the aforementioned lonely British gentleman, Joseph Heath. His few visitors were mostly local Indians who worked for him. Many who were from far away regions became his biggest concerns. They were American visitors who tramped across his farm, with complete disregard for his unfenced crops and property. They were searching for the ideal land to occupy as a homestead, while ignoring the Heath farm. Americans also ignored Fort Nisqually farms, ranches and outstations, on 161,000 acres of Puget Sound Agricultural Company land that stretched across what is now western Pierce County. That land had been guaranteed to the British in the Boundary Treaty of 1846. America could gain control of all British real estate in Washington Territory only by purchasing the British land rights. Hudson's Bay Company valued the land at $2,000,000, and expected that amount through the treaty language.

A few other British farmers were also occupying land in the region. They were all connected in some way to Fort Nisqually/PSAC/HBC operations. For example the families of John Montgomery, John Edgar, and John Ross lived relatively nearby. All farmed PSAC land as contracted servants of the Company. Some became American naturalized citizens to gain personal ownership of their farms.

John Edgar and his Indian wife lived on the south side of the Nisqually River, on the Yelm Prairie near the Stony Ford crossing on the Cowlitz Trail. Theirs was a tenant farm similar to the Heath property. John Edgar worked for the company as a shepherd, but lived on rented farmland.

John Ross maintained another tenant farm for the Company. He was the son of HBC Chief Trader Charles George Ross. Two brothers, Walter and Charles, also worked for the Company at Fort Nisqually. When Charles George Ross passed away at Fort Victoria in 1844 his wife, Isabella, came to live with her adult sons, bringing along several of her younger children. Isabella visited socially with Joseph Heath quite often, but there was never a hint of romance.

The Ross farm, known as Rossville, was located about two miles southwest of Fort Nisqually, at a place the Indians called "Wiscum." His crops were described by Joseph's brother, Thomas Heath, as;

> "excellent, far surpassing any at Nisqually... had it not been for the misquitos.

Nearby there were many oak trees. An American testifying for the Land Claims Committee some years later called them

> "...oaks like we on the Atlantic call scrub-oaks."

John Montgomery was instrumental in the farming and ranching activities of PSAC, especially near Spanaway Lake, where he eventually obtained farm land of his own, after becoming a naturalized American citizen.

The daily Trade Journal for Fort Nisqually is missing for the crucial years of the 1840s. However, the Fort Nisqually *Trade Blotter* records do still exist. On December 4, 1845 the *Trade Blotter* reveals that an Indian was paid to ferry Chief Factor James Douglas and his party across the Nisqually River. The ferry toll was 30 charges of ammunition, four #19 fishhooks, and two feet of twisted tobacco. Another entry in that same *Trade Blotter*, this time calculated in dollars and cents, lists $2/3$ of a foot of tobacco and a pipe for 25 cents.

The Indians of the Pacific Northwest were not doing well. Primitive people seldom thrive when impatient immigrants shoulder them aside. In the seventeen-year period from 1828 to 1945, the Indian population of Old Oregon fell from an estimated 100,000 to less than 20,000 individuals. The Indian population suffered, percentage wise, as much as the population of Europe had suffered during the Black Plague. Every Indian village became a burial place.

One first-person report from 1831, a narrative based on disease among the First People, is by John K. Townsend. He states:[201]

> *The depopulation has been truly fearful. Probably there does not now exist one (Indian) where five years ago there were a hundred...the only evidence of the existence of the Indian is an occasional miserable wigwam with a few wretched, half starved occupants.*

Indians, as well as Americans, continued to cause problems for PSAC by rustling cattle. The sick, starving natives made a big impact on company livestock in the winters

---

201 Parrish, Philip H. *Before the Covered Wagon*, Binsford & Mort, Portland Oregon, 1931.

of 1841-42 and 1844-45. Predatory wolves and cougars took their toll as well. As early as 1842, a member of the U.S. Exploring Expedition noted that wolves were very numerous and destructive of the sheep herds. In 1844, at least ten sheep, eight pigs, and two horses were killed by wolves at Nisqually. In January, 1845, a settler reported that wolves were being driven from the mountains by the heavy snow. The predatory kills in 1845 amounted to twelve sheep one night and twenty more another night. It should be noted that eagles occasionally took lambs. In an effort to combat the predators, Nisqually herdsmen were "authorized to kill" wolves in 1841–42. The trade store raised the price paid for wolf skins. In eighteen months they had bagged more than 100 wolves.

Disease also harmed PSAC business. In March 1842, scab struck the sheep, killing at least 140 head. More than 500 more died of the disease in the wet winter of 1842–43. Prices in London were depressed for Nisqually wool in 1845 because of the scab. In 1845 Braxy, an intestinal inflammation, killed ninety-nine sheep at Nisqually. More losses, however, came from insufficient tending of the animals. Animals strayed, fell over cliffs, drowned, or died of exhaustion after being moved in attempts to find healthier fields.

In the face of the staggering losses, the animal populations continued to increase. There were 573 ewes at Nisqually in 1845, some entering old age. Shearing production sent 8,621 pounds of wool to London in 1845, bringing 8 pence per pound. The 1845 shipment was even better at 11,845 pounds of wool, bringing 10¼ pence per pound. 1846 saw still another increase, to 14,642 pounds of wool that sold for another 8 pence per pound.

Puget Sound Agricultural Company was not able to reach its full potential because it never attracted enough British settlers to provide the requisite labor. The company successfully operated into the 20th century, but had people come in sufficient numbers to hold the land politically, as was the HBC plan, and contribute to the output, storage and transport of the farm product, the Puget Sound region might have remained in the hands of a British corporation.

In 1845, George Simpson, governor of Hudson's Bay Company in North America, with the complete support of Sir Robert Peel, British Prime Minster and Foreign Minister, sent a pair of undercover agents

> "...to gain a general knowledge of the capabilities of the Oregon territory in a military point of view in order that we may be enabled to act immediately and with effect in the defense of our rights in that quarter, should those rights be infringed by any hostile aggression or encroachment on the part of the United States."[202]

---

202 Morgan, Murray C., "Murray's People, a Collection of Essays, Henry Warre and Merwin Vavasour, British Spies" *Tacoma News Tribune*, December 9, 1973.

A fifty-gun British frigate was on her way to the Straits of Juan de Fuca to give comfort to the British fur traders, and intimidate the Yankees, who had recently elected President James K. Polk on a platform calling for the "clear and unquestionable" claim to all of Oregon from the Rockies to the Pacific, and from the Russian territory in Alaska to the Mexican lands in California.

Dressed as civilians, Lt. Henry J. Warre and Lt. M. Vavasour crossed the Canadian Rockies secretly evaluating the possibility of defending British lands in Old Oregon from an American invasion. Warre was aide de camp to the Governor of Canada, and Vavasour served in the Royal Engineers. They were instructed to assume the roles of gentlemen searching for the pleasures of field sports and scientific research. Warre had considerable talent with a sketch book and watercolors. Warre sketched and painted many scenes throughout the Pacific Northwest, including a fine illustration of Fort Nisqually. All of the sketches and water colors depicted common scenes and militarily strategic background areas. While Warre sketched, Vavasour talked with locals, gathering information about the Indians, the Americans, and their attitudes toward the English.

The spies spent like the wealthy gentlemen travelers they were expected to be when they arrived at Fort Vancouver. They purchased the highest quality beaver hats, frock coats, vests, tweed trousers, shirts, and fancy handkerchiefs. They were fond of personal comfort, too. They purchased the best pipes, tobacco, wines, whiskey, and a quantity of extract of roses.

In the spring of 1846 their report was forwarded to England from Montreal. In it the spies detailed information about Fort Nisqually that is unavailable in other forms. They described an;

> "....Excellent stream of water near the (new) Fort at all seasons (has) no wells. About one mile from and near the head of (navigation on) Puget Sound, and two miles from the Nisqually River, on the right bank, (is an) anchorage for ships of any burden. The site of Old Fort Nisqually is about (a) half mile from the shore. The position was removed on account of the difficulty of obtaining water.
> Men: 20
> Sheep: 5795
> Horses: 193
> Cattle: 1857
> Acres under cultivation: 100
> Description of Buildings: One large warehouse, one large and one small dwelling house; Accommodations for about 50 men; the ground is dry, the situation fine for camping; There are also several large barns and farm buildings

where temporary accommodations might be obtained for about 100 men.

Nature of the Country and Means of defense; Incapable of making any defense; The buildings are not even surrounded by pickets; The post is situated at the head of an extensive plain; The Oak and Pine timber is magnificent; From this point troops might be forwarded a distance of 60 miles to the Cowlitz River and from thence to any part of the (Oregon) Country."[203]

The report of the British spies arrived after Prime Minister Peel had already decided to yield the land south of the 49th parallel to the Americans. Warre's sketches were eventually published as *"Sketch of a Journey Across the Continent of North America from Canada to the Oregon Territory and the Pacific Ocean."* He didn't mention that he was spying on Americans while sketching. The spy reports still gather dust in the Public Records office in London.

---

[203] From "Papers relative to the Expedition of Lieuts. Warre & Vavasour to the Oregon Country" Hudson's Bay Company Archives, Winnipeg. (P.R.O.) F.O.5, Vol. 457

1846

INTERESTING THINGS HAPPENED around the world in 1846. It has been called the "Year of Decision." The first publicly known use of ether on a surgery patient was performed in Boston in October. It was that same October that snow marooned 80 members of the Donner Party in the Sierra Nevada Mountains. In September the three-day battle of Monterey ended when General Pedro de Ampudia surrendered to brevet Major General Zachary Taylor. California was instantly "American."

Elias Howe, Jr. patented the first sewing machine in 1846. His device used an eye-pointed needle, two strands of thread, and a shuttle to create a lock stitch. It would be many years before the machine saw the American western frontier.[204]

After nearly three decades of "joint occupancy" of the Oregon Country and the Columbia Department, farming, fishing, lumbering, and some manufacturing were well established industries. Most of this success was attributed to Hudson's Bay Company and the Puget's Sound Agricultural Company. Enough was being produced in each of the industries to export some for sale in Russian America, the Sandwich Islands, California, and of course London, England.

American President James K. Polk came from the established settlements in North Carolina and Tennessee. He was a protégé of Andrew Jackson, but was "small of stature and lacked the skills and traits of a natural leader."[205] He represented an extraordinarily dynamic country with people who were willing to take bold risks to get ahead in life. Polk's political enemies were clearly against expansion of the country, but most Americans were cheered by the president's sense of Manifest Destiny. Many would even say they

---

[204] Walter Hunt invented a stitching machine between 1833 and 1834, 12 years before Elias Howe secured a patent. Hunt's invention introduced the eye pointed needle and the interlocking stitch. He was unsuccessful in selling his machine according to Frederick L. Lewton's book: *The Servant in the House: A Brief History of the Sewing Machine*, as referred to in the History Channel Magazine, March / April 2008.

[205] Merry, Robert W., *A Country of Vast Designs, James K. Polk, the Mexican War and the Conquest of the American Continent*, Simon & Shuster, New York, 2009

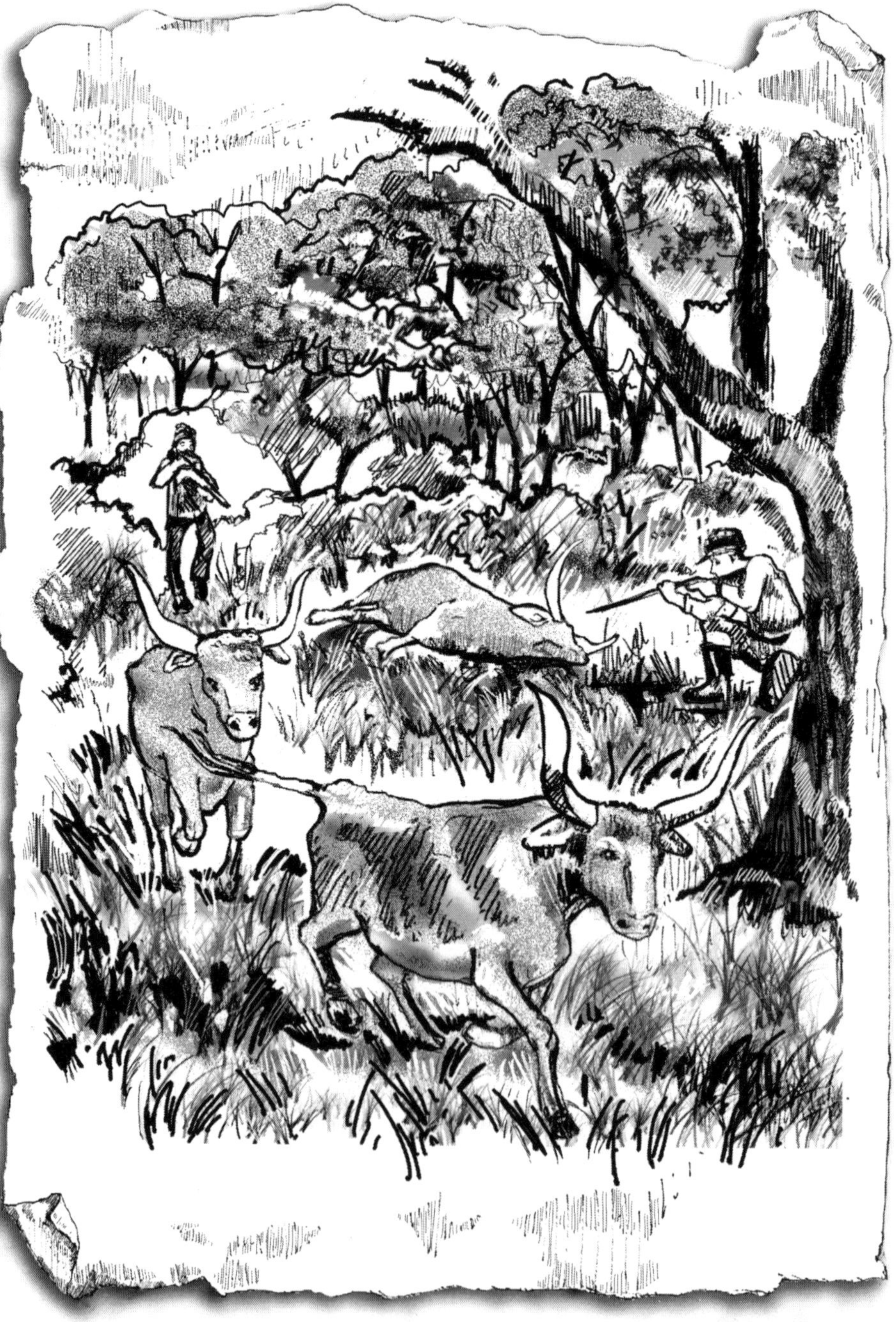

were ready to make better use of the continent than any of their predecessors, Indian, Mexican, English, Russian, or Spanish.

Today, Polk's Mexican War has become a defining American sin. Today that war is considered by the accepted general opinion to have been a power grab of exploitation of a weaker nation, beaten into submission. Even at the time, Ulysses S. Grant called the Mexican War the most unjust war ever waged.

Reality observes that Polk did not act in a vacuum. He did not dodge the most compelling issue of his time, but worked hard expanding the size of the country by more than one third. He added what are now the states of Washington, Oregon, California, Idaho, Texas, Nevada, New Mexico, Utah, Arizona, and a part of Colorado. This additional territory made America a Pacific nation, too, and eventually the most powerful nation on earth.

Polk's administration set out to accomplish four things: settle the Old Oregon question, acquire California, create an independent treasury, and lower import tariffs. He did this by risking war with England, winning a war with Mexico, and acting with extraordinary political will. He died a spent man only four months after leaving office.

The boundary question between the USA and British North America west of the Rockies was settled. Fort Nisqually, clearly in foreign territory, would be bought out by the U.S. government in due time. HBC and PSAC had only to 'hold on' until final payment was forth-coming. Moving livestock and men north became a priority, but business would continue right up to the final day.

Here American settlers would, for the first time in the westward expansion of the nation, confront an international culture. Here they met a society much different from those contacted across the Great Plains. Yes, there were Native Americans as expected, but also British subjects who considered themselves somewhat special. They were a proud people who were friendly, but very business-like. After all, they were employed by the oldest and largest corporation in the world, operating out of London, the center of capitalism and enterprise. True, the British were far from their government, but closer by sea than the Americans to their homeland.

It was an interesting world. Almost Garden of Eden for the Indians before Europeans arrived with wealth and commodities never dreamt of around Puget Sound. Nobody worked too hard. There was a great deal of work to do, but where six men might complete the job, there were often 20 available. The ranches and farms were large, as were the herds. There was still time for music, dancing, and horseback races. Pay was more generous than any Native Americans had ever experienced. Often they were compensated with clothing and commodities heretofore unavailable. Living was simple. Eating was easy, with tremendous amounts of food available. Nobody really wanted for anything.

Then the Americans—the "Boston men"—began to infiltrate the scene, bringing an unstated conflict, or at least extreme economic enmity and competition, while claiming Indian land without considering just compensation.

English cultural influence was in evidence in the Northwest. When Captain Thomas Baillie tied up the *Modeste* at the Vancouver dock in October 1845, culture was aboard. The ship was there to calm the tense situation between American settlers and the British entrepreneurs. An exercise in togetherness brought about the first performance of Gilbert and Sullivan's *H.M.S. Pinafore*. Crew members of the *Modeste*, sailors all, became actors and musicians. The small orchestra included a violin, flute, and bagpipes. Among the plays produced were *Love in a Village*, *The Mock Doctor*, and *The Mayor of Garrat*. The winter of 1847 saw settlers' daughters replace sailors who had been playing feminine roles.

At Cowlitz Farms, the first brick kiln north of the Columbia was operational on the Plomondon farm. It would be another year before the first sawmill was also operating there. Prior to 1844, HBC and PSAC had allowed only seven families to settle north of the Columbia River. Five of those families were connected with the company. James Birnie and George Roberts lived at Cathlamet; Simon Plomondon, Marcel Bernier, and Antonie Gobar lived at Cowlitz, near the company farms. The two families not connected to HBC were the Richmond and Willson families, who lived at the Nisqually Methodist Mission from 1839 to 1842.

A group of company officers, apparently led by Dr. William Fraser Tolmie, laid out extensive plans for houses, barns, and fences at Cowlitz. Cattle and sheep were brought from California and sheep from England were cross-bred to improve the strain. Skilled farmers and shepherds were brought from the old country. Certainly local Indians, French-Canadians, Kanakas, and Indian laborers from Fort Vancouver were hired.

Charles Forrest was the first to keep records at Cowlitz in a manuscript volume. Other records were kept by his successor, George B. Roberts, after December 1846. Roberts turned the record-keeping over to Henry Peers in 1851. Most of the notes these men wrote were about trouble and disaster.

Roberts remembered measles in 1847-48. The disease "struck down every one; man, woman, and child" indicating a very high mortality rate.

Roberts was at Cowlitz because of his own illness in 1831. As a graduate of the Greenwich Royal Naval School, the 17-year-old naval officer was aboard the bark *Ganymede* when she called at Fort George (before it was completely closed in favor of Fort Vancouver). Roberts was soon taken ill with ague. He was transferred to the *Cadboro* and remained there until transferred again to become an assistant to James Douglas[206] in February 1832. His skill with the French language and quick study of Indian languages made him quite useful, because those were the common languages at that place at that time. Roberts claimed the Frenchmen he encountered were the Canadian version, rather than the European version.[207] Roberts had spent one more year at sea with his naval school companions, traveling north all the way to the Stikine River in 1834. He transferred back to shore duty as a teacher and successor to S.H. Smith, an American school master at Fort Vancouver, who "ran off with the old baker's Indian wife." There were 50 children of several races and nationalities enrolled in that school at the time.

Before he replaced Charles Forrest at Cowlitz, while still assigned at Fort Vancouver, Roberts returned to London on leave from duty. While there he married Martha Cable, a first cousin, before returning to Fort Vancouver with his new bride. Their son was born August 1, 1845, the second white child born in what would become Clarke County, Washington. Roberts resumed his duties, now at Cowlitz, only two weeks after the child was born. His wife became a celebrity, or perhaps a curiosity, among the local Native American population. Mrs. Roberts was the first white woman who lived anywhere near Fort Vancouver, even for a short time. Indian wives (including McLoughlin's) never appeared at the table with their white husbands. This difficult social situation was overcome by Mrs. Roberts' tact and graciousness. She was able to reduce a racial apartheid situation to a societal quirk, but still often eating alone or with her child.

After 28 years of "joint occupancy" of the Oregon Country, Great Britain surrendered all claims to the land south of the 49th parallel. They signed the Treaty of Oregon on June 15, 1846. That treaty, however, contained some interesting articles protecting large British agricultural business land holdings.

Several things tipped the balance against the British efforts to hold the entire region. First was the establishment of Methodist Missions, followed by the rapid immigration of American settlers into the Willamette River Valley. Those new Oregonians created an independent "provisional government" in 1843. American politicians (mostly eastern state Democrats) were shouting "Fifty-Four Forty or Fight!" a slogan referring to the southern boundary of the Russian settlements in what is now Alaska. President Polk sent

---

206 Sir James Douglas (also known as the Black Douglas) was born in Guyana to John Douglas, a Scottish planter and Martha Ann Telfer, a Creole from Barbados. Douglas was HBC officer, Governor of Vancouver Island, and Governor of British Columbia. *Dictionary of Canadian Biography Online, Vol X 1871-1889* http://www.biographi.ca

207 Toledo History Committee, *The Toledo Community Story,* The Toledo Parent—Teacher Organization, Toledo, WA 1976.

James Garfield to Britain to negotiate a treaty to finally end the joint occupancy policy. It was a peaceful retreat for Great Britain, one that Americans could accept. On August 14, 1848, congress formally established Oregon Territory, while continuing to allow, by treaty, British land holdings within the Territory.

In October, Edmund Sylvester and Levi Lathrop Smith staked a joint claim to 320 acres on Budd Inlet, at a place the Squaxin called Cheetwoot, or "Bear," because the high tide shoreline resembled a bear. Cheetwoot was a winter home site for the Squaxin for untold years, perhaps centuries. Smith named the place Smithfield. Sylvester settled on Chambers Prairie near Fort Nisqually[208] at first, but soon inherited Smith's cabin and land share. In a short four years Smithfield became a dedicated town called Olympia. However, Fort Nisqually still reined as the supreme source of European manufactured goods available on Puget's Sound.

In December, 1846 there were only two settlements marked on the maps north of Fort Vancouver in what is now the United States: Cowlitz Farms and Fort Nisqually. The journal entries at Fort Nisqually resume in 1846 after a lapse of a few missing pages.[209] There was considerable activity: building construction at the prairie site for instance, during the time of the missing journal pages. Perhaps someday a diligent researcher will discover heretofore unknown copies of those precious pages. There were 29 laborers (up from 17 in 1845), 48 Indian employees, and three Gentlemen at Fort Nisqually in 1846. The three gents were Chief Trader William Tolmie, Trader James Sangster, and Walter Ross, the clerk in charge of the daily journal and the Sales Shop.

The animal population was impressive in 1846, too. PSAC counted 10,578 sheep, 3,063 cattle, 343 horses, plus pigs, mules, and poultry. The sheep produced a total of 16,569 pounds of wool, and 1,926 sheepskins. The cows produced 158 hides and 431 horns.

PSAC saw its first profit in 1844—about £1,577. That would have been about $7,601 in US dollars in 1844 (or around $51,454,640 in today's dollars). It was enough for PSAC Directors in London to declare a 5% dividend for shareholders. Annual dividends of 5–10% continued to be paid to shareholders until 1854. Losses began with the encroachment of American settlers after 1853. HBC covered PSAC losses (totaling £37,400 over 16 years) until the claims against the United States were paid in 1869. After 1870, PSAC easily became solvent again. Moving the business to Vancouver Island proved to be a

---

208 Levi Lathrop Smith was elected to the Oregon Territorial Legislature in 1848, but fell out of a canoe, possibly from an attack of epilepsy, and drowned in route to the first session. Http:// www.findagrave.com

209 Those pages have not been found by any researchers. Speculation abounds, but during the boundary settlement hearings some pages may have been used in testimony. Author's opinion.

successful business decision. The most profitable year for PSAC was 1845 when it netted £2,220 (about $72,434,560 today).[210]

Consider, too, that PSAC was also designed to undercut prices, offered by Americans who could also sell to the Russians. If the Americans could be driven out of the marketplace, (and eventually they were) HBC monopoly could be extended once again. HBC charged the Russians for "shipping and handling" all cargoes sent from Puget's Sound. The rate was only £10 per ton of cargo, but high enough that the Russians chartered supply vessels of their own. Even so, HBC profited by nearly £4000 in 1844 alone. HBC called the monopolistic trade along the Pacific Coast "tranquil" once the Americans gave up and Russian cooperation was secured.

On June 15, the International Boundary Treaty of 1846 established the border between American and British claimed lands west of the Rockies along the 49th parallel. It extinguished the Treaty of 1818 that allowed joint occupancy of the region. Hudson's Bay Company and Puget Sound Agricultural Company business interests south of the border were specifically protected by the treaty. The British companies were allowed to operate south of the 49th parallel until such time as the land areas, including improvements, were purchased outright by the United States government. This meant that British rule applied on all British real estate property parcels (even if totally unmarked) south of the treaty line, and that American law governed all other lands. It was confusing and frustrating to most American settlers, educated and informed or not.

Dr. John McLoughlin resigned from Hudson's Bay Company on May 20, 1846, after 21 years at the helm of the Columbia Department and Caledonia District. Only 26 days later the southern portion of the land McLoughlin had ruled became part of the United States, and so did McLoughlin. He made his new home with the Americans in Oregon City, where he had the earliest private claim on the falls of the Willamette River. McLoughlin would be harassed by unforgiving, and under appreciative Americans, who prevented his efforts to actively own, or even utilize, the falls. He died eleven years later (in 1857) at age 73, and lies near his friend Peter Skene Ogden in an Oregon City public cemetery above the Willamette River Falls. The Americans forgot (or ignored) the generosity of McLoughlin, as they had the contributions of Ogden. McLoughlin and Ogden were the men who fed and clothed so many Americans after their miraculous survival of the Oregon Trail hardships and the Whitman Massacre.

The HBC Pacific Coast headquarters were moved to Fort Victoria on Vancouver's

---

210 Historic currency exchange rates were found at http:// www.measuringgrowth.comukcompare/—a Google search for Historic Currency Exchange revealed "How Much is that? EH.NET" http://eh.net.hmit/

Island in 1846. James Douglas, formerly of the Board of Management at Fort Vancouver, was put in charge of all company affairs west of the Rockies. He would also soon become Governor of the colony of British Columbia after appointment by the Queen. Fort Nisqually and Puget Sound Agricultural Company continued as the de facto heart of HBC south of the border. It was a failing heart in need of a transplant.

Imagine the land between the Puyallup and Nisqually Rivers, between the sound and the mountains. Because of the wording of the Boundary Treaty, some 161,000 acres of that land remained "British" even when completely surrounded by the lands of the United States of America. Those acres were still under British ownership and control when Pierce County was formed in 1853. That real estate continued to be British until 1870. Twenty-four years after signing the Treaty of 1846, the U.S. Congress finally got around to appropriating the funds for the purchase mandated by international treaty. In defense of Congress, they did have to deal with the demise of a political party, a slavery problem, a Civil War, and the assassination of President Abraham Lincoln. In 1846 the U.S. government, led by President James K. Polk and political slogans like "Fifty-Four Forty or Fight," had a war with Mexico, expanded The United States into California and the Southwest. Fort Nisqually land claim disputes would wait for "Manifest Destiny" to play out.

By 1846 PSAC had farms and ranches scattered across the Pacific Northwest south of the 49th parallel. PSAC had expanded beyond the Fort Nisqually neighborhood. The main farms and ranches totaling 161,000 acres were in the vicinity of Fort Nisqually, but PSAC was widespread. Operating along the Cowlitz River, as well as (now) Pierce County, at outstations, cattle farms, ranches, sheep farms, crop farms, pastures, corrals, sheep pens, and dairy farms. There were fields and camps of one sort or another at named locations such as:

Old Fort, Wiscum, Tilithlow, Spanaway (or Spa-nu-eh), Muck Creek, Old Muck, Red House Plains, Edgar's Place, Cold Spring, Poplar Park, Turnip Park, Aspin Field, Lake Squally, Stuck, (along the Douglas River), Sastuc, Tenalquot, Mallard Hallow, Eilowhallis, Whyatchie, Paleilah (the southern portion of University Place), Millar's Lake, the American Plain, and Round Plain just south of the central establishment (now Dupont, Washington).

In January 1846, an animal census was undertaken at Fort Nisqually. The exact numbers are obscure in the *Journal of Occurrences*, but we do know that 3,770 head of longhorn cattle were rounded up.[211] Mr. Work, Tolmie's father-in-law, was instrumental as

---

[211] At peak production the Puget Sound Agricultural Company at Fort Nisqually had, it is believed, about 12,000 head of sheep, 10,000 head of cattle, 600 dairy cows, 600 horses, twenty oxen, plus dozens of other farm animals including pigs, turkeys, chickens, goats, and probably a considerable population of dogs. Exact figures are impossible as the numbers changed from day to day as animals were born or butchered. https://journals.lib.washington.edu/index

leader of the crew that included Tolmie, Montgomery, Edgar, and McLeod. Later, Latour and three Canadian axemen (Boulanger, Paquet, and Lucier) were sent to "protect" the land near Millar's Lake from being claimed by American Nelson Cook. They built a hut there, a second one on the sandy plain beyond the Nisqually River, and another one on a claim taken at the northwest extremity of the American Plain. Undoubtedly there were more built that were not entered into the record. These huts were designed to support HBC/PSAC ownership by "occupying" the land. Apparently the herds of animals, tended by at least one man, were inadequate to satisfy Americans eager to claim free land.

While the nearby swampland frogs were croaking in the mild February weather, Fort Nisqually laborers were installing a new floor and door in the Trade Store, butchering three beef carcasses, making cart wheels and shutters, filling butter kegs, salting beef for shipment, squaring oak for Fort Stikine, and slaughtering 12 head of beef cattle before selling four live cows to some American customers. Those Americans also bought coffee, sugar, and molasses from the Fort Trade Store.

Tamattutaiah reported that the Cowlitz portage was now passable, the high waters of winter had subsided. The knowledge induced a new "spring" garden, field, and pasture endeavors, but Murdock, McLoed, Robillard, Bayfield, Lhussich, and Sanders were given an afternoon off. They were told to prepare for reassignment at Fort Victoria. Downsizing at Fort Nisqually had begun. The "accounts" of furs shipped from Fort Nisqually were prepared for Forts Victoria, Langley, and Nisqually and the *S.S. Beaver*.

The men remaining at Fort Nisqually squared wood for a new barn wall, thrashed peas, cleared brush and rubbish from Mallard Hollow, butchered pigs, made more new wheels, sowed peas, packed beef casks, made pickles, filled barrels, salted pork, erected a calf shed, repaired fences, enclosed some Timothy fields, and brought in 23 milk cows, then loaded many cords of firewood for the steamer's voracious boilers.

Dr. Tolmie's skills were put to work on the medical front when a sailor named Michael fell sick and sought treatment. At about this time Mr. Lambert, the engineer on the Steamer, came to reside (actually retire) at Fort Nisqually. Lambert was suffering from chronic rheumatism and severe dysentery. The Company would generously allow his leisure years to be spent at Fort Nisqually.

Americans Sylvester and Smith arrived from Willamette Falls after ten days travel. They, along with Simmons, Jones, and another American, purchased supplies before they were off to visit Mr. Heath at Steilacoom Plain. Most often Americans visiting Heath were actually searching for information about available land in the area.[212]

PSAC was receiving livestock and farm produce from other HBC Indian trade posts at Fort George, Chinook, Pillar Rock, Cape Disappointment, Fort Umpqua, Fort Nez Perce, Fort Boise, Fort Hall, Fort Okanogan, Fort Colvile, Kootemai Post, Champoeg, and Coweeman. The total livestock population numbers at the peak of success of the Puget Sound Agricultural Company are impressive. There were some 12,000 head of sheep, 10,000 head of longhorn Spanish cattle, 600 horses, 300 milk cows, and uncounted pigs, goats, chickens, turkeys and oxen. There are few Texas cowboy cattle ranches that could match the PSAC animal population in the 1840s.

PSAC cultivated thousands of acres of crop lands and maintained thousands more acres as pasture and grazing lands. Potatoes and peas were staple crops. The acreage was enormous at the peak of activity. Tons of food supplies were produced. Wheat, barley, oats, corn and other grains were devoured by the men and animals. At one point 5,000 pounds of butter was delivered in one shipment from Fort Nisqually to the Russian–American fur trade post at New Archangel (Sitka) as part of the trade agreement. Actually, except for the cargo of butter, there is nothing remarkable about that shipment. Every ship carried hundreds of tons of cargo to the Russian-American Company.

The men of Fort Nisqually were squaring battens for the store, dressing three-foot long shingles, sawing boards for the Big House roof, felling trees near Mallard Hallow, and finally placing the shingles and battens on the store. Slocum was making candles for the *SS Beaver*. Lucier and Boulanger squared 20 feet long sawpit logs, while Bastian, Michael, and an Indian work gang repaired the road to the beach. Latour was getting the wheat trodden and sowing eleven bushels of oat seed.

By the time the wedder lambs were finished, spring showers had set in, but the pitsaw needed to be replaced. Wiscum got the digging duty in the chilly spring rain.

The pressure on the fort by encroaching American settlers was being noticed during daily activities. Some of the cattle could not be driven away from Douglas River where they were vulnerable to poaching, so Bastain was sent to bring home a wagonload of meat. The presumption was that the meat would cooperate more than the live cows. John Montgomery, as marksman, went along to slaughter the animals. They brought in three carcasses of beef, but reported there were another 12 that should be on the target list. By the end of the week, a dozen more cattle were slaughtered for their valuable meat, tallow,

---

212 Often the *Journal of Occurrences* does not reveal first names. Indians did not often have two names at the same time. European company employees were well known, and most often only informally noted in the record books. American customers were often hostile. Minimum records were adequate. Researchers are encouraged to determine accurate full names for the historical record.

hides, horns, and hooves. Even the bones would be used in stew pots. Any "leftovers" would go straight to compost.

In addition to the beef, Montgomery and Bastain brought home news of marauding Indians. They reported seeing a beach feast that ended in a squabble and the death of Eilowhalis, a Nisqually friend. Apparently the deadly fight was with two Swahsinamish about a gun.

Some Americans came from the settlement called Newmarket (Olympia) to the Fort at dinner time to purchase some fresh beef and other groceries. Each purchased a bullock, some coffee, sugar, and molasses. As a superb businessman, Tolmie invited them to stay for dinner. They didn't depart until after dinner the next day, and after spending that second day negotiating the price of four head of live cattle. Tolmie found the proper incentives to complete the sale. The little live herd of Spanish longhorn cattle moved down the trail with the Americans. Dr. Tolmie may have disliked people who squatted on PSAC land, but that was no reason to decline business transactions at the end of the day.

Potatoes and peas priced at about $7.00 a sack later in the week attracted two other Americans who were disappointed that they, also, would have to wait a day for the beef cattle they wanted. But they were off with two handsome beef carcasses before midday on that sunny afternoon. Apparently Tolmie was unable to strike a second bargain for additional live animals.

Dr. Tolmie learned during his conversations with his American customers that some land claims had been taken along the Puyallup River. He rode out to inspect the area, reporting to the *Journal of Occurrences* that "the grasses in that quarter were much less pastured than along the Nisqually range." Apparently those settlers had few grazing animals.

The men were building new casks for a beef shipment, filling the casks with salted meat. The steamer took 22 casks of salted beef, two casks for crew consumption, when the little ship cast off in early March, Captain Dodd in command. They carried a stubborn live bullock to Fort Victoria, too.

Dr. Tolmie, always the amateur botanist, noticed a wild bee and the smell of syngenesious plants in flower. He went to investigate with two men, while two more men departed from Fort Nisqually. Angus McDonald and John Macrae had completed the terms of their HBC contracts. They were on their way home to Europe, via Fort Vancouver, then up the Columbia, with the York Factory Express, a canoe party designed to travel fast and furiously to the post on Hudson's Bay. They had to arrive there before winter ice and storms closed the sea passages.

The Indian crew began digging up potatoes in March, first 9 bushels, then 5 bushels, then 11 bushels, all cut and replanted about eight inches apart. The next crop was begun before the current crop was completely harvested.

They were also sowing Timothy (a European grass) where wheat had been harvested. It was an early example of crop rotation. The science of crop rotation had to be taught to American farmers a century later to reduce the effects of the Dust Bowl.

One morning in mid-March some Indians were caught skinning one of the Fort's best work oxen. They took flight immediately upon being discovered. Tolmie organized an armed party, sending Latour and Michael to organize another. The first posse went overland to the site and searched from there for the culprits. Latour's group went by canoe along the beach, cutting off that escape route. Neither party was fortunate enough to find the culprits.

By noon all of the men were hungry and tired, so Tolmie ordered a fine dinner, after which the parties set out again. This time they were able to secure two of the five men in their canoes, carrying the greater part of a third oxen they had appropriated without permission. They also found the bones and head of the oxen killed in the morning. Tolmie flogged the thieves with the cart's tail and imprisoned them in the bastions. After a week, Qunasapam paid a rifle and a pistol to gain the liberation of the oxen-butchering thieves.

During February, March, April, and May, the men of Fort Nisqually laid the foundation for another barn, expedited the lambing, ploughed many of the fields, planted peas and coleseed (a mustard family forage crop sometimes used for its oil) and at Whyatchie, built a cheese press for the dairy at Paleilah.

The men fitted binders on a barn, completed the framework for another barn, elevating the posts and beams during frosty February weather. They squared the rafters, planted more potatoes, taught Joseph Heath the cheese making process, spread dung in rows two feet apart to fertilize the fields, sawed the flooring planks for the new barn, completed the slaughter of the old ewe flock, took the young wedders[213] to a potential potato patch for manuring the ground, cleared the last of the trees out of Mallard Hollow, drained the swamp at Mallard Hollow, erected a house at McCleod's new station, split hundreds of fence rails, harrowed the wheat after the women weeded the fields, collected ashes for soap, washed and sheared half of the Merino sheep (their fleeces were in superior condition, weighing 2 pounds each), commenced hoeing the beans, and traded for some furs.

Tolmie's Indian housekeeper at the time, Jock Hapalks, was accidentally shot by Lahalet's son Tilsalewa while visiting old friends in the Nisqually village. Dr. Tolmie was

---

213 Wedders are castrated male sheep. The word is part of the sheep-keeping lexicon of this very ancient craft. http://www.memindex.com

unable to save the man from his wounds. He died and was interred the next day. Tolmie was not blamed for the death. He was appreciated for the medical attention he provided.

Joseph Heath's farm at Steilacoom was considerably less successful than the PSAC acreage. By June 27, 1846, Heath was severely in debt, owing the Company 387 pounds 9 shillings, 8 pence (at a time when a pound sterling was equal to about three American dollars). He had fenced some 170 acres, planting 60 in wheat, while using the remainder for grazing sheep.[214]

The International Boundary Treaty was signed on June 15, 1846. It would be well into autumn before the news reached Puget Sound. The situation remained "unsettled" with English foreign policy and Oregon Provisional government at opposition.

Dr. Tolmie and Dr. McLoughlin pledged loyalty and allegiance to the Oregon provisional government when it was formed in an effort to reduce tensions. The ploy didn't work. They also asked for protection from the English Crown, whose foreign policy was revised about this time to include the protection of English business interests around the globe, and led to hundreds of little wars in the extended Empire.

Still, it was somewhat sudden when the *H.M.S. Fisgard* appeared at Nisqually Landing (May 16, 1846, Captain Duntze). The steamer *SS Cormorant* paid two visits in the next five months. The British sloop-of-war *H.M.S. Modeste* anchored in the Columbia River off Fort Vancouver. Then the British sent the *H.M.S. Constance, H.M.S. Pandora,* and the *H.M.S. Herald* to survey the Strait of Juan de Fuca and Esquimalt Harbor. The four British ships had manpower that exceeded the total American population of Old Oregon, and fire power to easily level every house and barn within range before any marines would be expected to land. It was an overwhelming force, and very visible gunboat diplomacy. That sometimes brutal foreign policy would soon extend unmercifully to the First Peoples of Vancouver Island and the Inside Passage, all the way to the Russian America frontier and nearly to the twentieth century.

Marines from the *Fisgard* immediately went to work converting the unused Fort Nisqually storage building on the beach into a temporary barracks. Their ship anchored only a shore boat away off Ketron Island, easily visible from Steilacoom City. Soon an exchange of social visits found the officers of the ship at Tolmie's little house, or at Heath's place, with both becoming dinner guests of the *Fisgard* officers' mess. The British social scene was a mirror of old England.

Captain Duntze requested that the entire fort contingent observe Queen Victoria's

---

214 Heath's farm was located where Western State Hospital, the Historic Fort Steilacoom buildings and Fort Steilacoom Park in the City of Lakewood are located today. Heath, Joseph, *Memoirs of Nisqually*, Ye Galleon Press, Fairfield, Washington, 1979

birthday with a "ball" at the waterside store. At least 100 Royal Marines and sailors were present to dance with the women of the fort area, all of mixed or full Indian blood.

Captain Duntze used the stay at Fort Nisqually to find a "timber suitable for a flagstaff." He "allowed' some sailors to assist the hoeing and planting of potatoes. It was a gentleman sailor's acknowledgement of the cost of the shindig and the new flagstaff.

June 8, 1846, the *Modeste*, with Captain Baillie, arrived. Baillie Invited Doctor Tolmie to dine on board that evening with Lt. Drake, Mr. Montgomery, and Mr. and Mrs. Peers from Cowlitz Farm. The next day Captain Duntze renamed Steilacoom Bay. He called it Fisgardita Cove, escorting Tolmie on the ship's launch of the same name to the little cove. They returned to Fort Nisqually by way of the American Trail, across the American Plain (named for the Americans at the Methodist Mission by Captain Wilkes of the U.S. Exploratory Expedition in 1841).

A packet of mail arrived at Fort Nisqually from Victoria. The mail had been delivered by the *Norman Morrison* recently from London and Oahu. Most of the mail was addressed "For Vancouver," so it was sent off immediately. Meanwhile, the marines and sailors celebrated Waterloo Day with horse races and other English diversions on the Round Plain just south of the Fort.

Farm animals were gradually being removed from Fort Nisqually to populate the Puget Sound Agricultural Company farms of Vancouver Island (near Fort Victoria), and the San Juan Islands. Mr. Cholmondeley, from Fort Victoria, arrived in his boat to pick up 21 sheep for the move. Lt. Patterson, of the *Fisgard*, agreed to move another 21 sheep in the ship's launch as well. Moving 42 sheep was only a slight change in the animal population. Several thousand animals were slowly moving out of the Puget Sound area.

American settler Michael Simmons built the first grist mill on Puget Sound at Tumwater in 1846. The millstones were chiseled out of erratic granite boulders left by the glaciers and found on the beach. Americans were slowing making their mark on the landscape of the Puget Sound area.

September 27 brought a fierce storm rolling in from the Pacific. It was one of those rare, but severe, autumn blasts of wind, rain, thunder and lightning. Most of the land-based population weathered the day fairly well, but the *H.M.S. Fisgard* was struck by a tremendous lightning bolt. The clap of thunder was louder than a blast of any broadside cannon. It knocked down crew members assigned to deck watch, splintering the main mast. There were no injuries, and all the commotion was over in a few minutes, but the *Fisgard* desperately needed repairs. Nature's energy struck the lightning conductor and saved the ship and crew from a disaster. There was some fusing and separation of copper sheeting plates.

The splintered main mast was quickly repaired with a local timber. Fortunately an isolated red pine forest near Muck Creek provided a wide variety of sturdy trees to provide the raw material for a new mast. Ship's carpenters and Nisqually woodsmen went to work on the task immediately. Soon the debris was cleared and a new mast stood tall above the deck.

Near bedtime on August 13, 1846, an Indian boy came running to Joseph Heath's little cabin. The boy excitedly exclaimed that a sailor was in need of help at Steilacoom Bay. It seems that two sailors had borrowed, or rented, Indian horses for the day, and upon returning found themselves on the beach north of the little bay and the Steilacoom Indian Village. Rather than climb the steep cliff, go inland a mile or two, then cross the little river safely, these sailors tried to cross the Bay on horseback. While the stream did not provide a threatening flow, the tide was treacherous. One (perhaps both) fell (or decided to swim) from their steeds as they crossed the deep, swirling waters of the treacherous bay.

The Indian boy who had alerted Heath also alerted the nearby Steilacoom townspeople. A rescue party was hastily organized and a search began. One sailor was dragged from the water alive. One was not. The missing sailor, a musician from the *Fisgard* band, was presumed to have drowned, and his body was never recovered. The funeral was held at 4:00 PM on Saturday, July 15, 1846, with a complete contingent of the officers and crewmembers present for the solemn naval service.

On August 31st Mr. Frampton, purser of the *Cormorant*, passed away after a long illness. There was no other mention of the man in the *Journal of Occurrences* before or after his funeral and burial at Fort Nisqually on September 1, 1846.

Early on the second day of September, the *HMS Fisgard's* guns were blazing. It was simply target practice, but the clear intimidation exercise continued all day. The men of Fort Nisqually continued the neverending work of running the establishment. Harvest season brought a short holiday on September 4th when the band from the *Fisgard* performed for a "merry dance". Another "holiday" was declared on October 1st after the noontime dinner. Grand racing was the order of the day at 2 PM. It all "came off with great spirit."

Some 1,089 bushels of potatoes (estimated at fifty ponds each, totaling about 54,500 pounds of spuds) were gathered by mid-October. Most of the crop was sent to Fort Victoria after seed potatoes were hand-picked from the piles. Other crops were carried in for packaging, storage, or immediate use at the Fort, or on the ships in the harbor. Cattle were slaughtered more frequently, and live sheep and cattle were loaded aboard the *Beaver* for transfer to Fort Victoria farms. Still more potatoes were brought in from

Muck, McLeod's, Edgar's, Montgomery's, and other farms.

Since Dr. Tolmie ordered the herd size reduced, sixty-six head of cattle were killed for meat. Of course, the animal slaughter meant other jobs. Men were employed in the slaughter house, skinning, butchering, cutting and salting the beef, melting the tallow, scraping and drying the hides, horns, and hooves. More people had the jobs of packing the meat and tallow for distribution in the greater area, while hides, hooves and horns were packed for export to London. Those cattle products would go to the auction houses, as the sheep's wool did. It would be months before the men would know what their work was worth.

The Treaty of 1846 delineated the "possessory rights" of HBC and PSAC. The treaty, as approved by Congress and the President, demanded that the individual American land claims had to be withdrawn in favor of the Hudson's Bay Company's prior possessions. Nine former HBC employees who had registered land claims with the Americans were forced to relinquish that land under the treaty because they had become Americans. All "settlers" who "squatted" on Puget Sound Company lands were sent a letter from D. Tolmie stating:

> "You are trespassing on the lands of the Puget Sound Agricultural Company, by the treaty ratified in July 1846 between Great Britain and the United States."[215]

HBC and PSAC were greatly disappointed in the so-called Oregon Treaty. It would, the companies complained, require the abandonment (after purchase by the U.S. government) of seventeen thriving HBC establishments south of the 49th parallel boundary. Many American settlers, on the other hand, felt the Company had no reason to expect more. Some resented the payment. Most resented the delay caused by the slow action of Congress.

The two companies had agreed to sell their rights and property, including improvements, south of the United States borders. HBC Governor Simpson set an offering price at $2,000,000 US. A sales agent was engaged in 1848, two years after the treaty was signed, but it would be another 22 years before final settlements could be reached. Fort Nisqually and PSAC continued operations as usual, except for the fact that British Frigate *Fisgard* was often anchored at the landing as, at least, symbolic protection against American aggression and encroachment. Americans had no naval equivalent north of California, but did have soldiers at Fort Steilacoom.

Before the news of the Boundary Treaty signing reached Fort Nisqually, the place was

---

215 Meeker, Ezra, *The Busy Life of Eighty Years"* p. 151, Lowman & Hanford, 1916, Seattle, WA

visited by no less than five heavily armed British ships, all with formidable weaponry. When news of the treaty arrived, the *S. S. Cormorant* towed the *H.M.S. Fisgard* out to deeper water near Ketron Island, where she anchored for months.

Mr. Sangster arrived from Fort Vancouver on November 19th to take charge of Fort Nisqually. Dr. Tolmie was ordered to report to Fort Vancouver temporarily. He returned on the 31st, and remained in charge twelve more years.

Many American soldiers were having a hard time as winter approached in late 1846. To earn some credit at the Fort Nisqually Trade Store, some brought in cedar shingles to trade for essentials and sundries. The *Journal of Occurrences* notes that 16 thousand were brought in one day, while 18 thousand on another day. After 12 inches of snow fell on December 13th, two Americans brought in another three-thousand cedar shingles. By January the piles of shingles were nearing 40,000 all together. There was no market for shingles, save Fort Nisqually and a generous Factor willing to bend a little for his fellow men in some distress, even if they were Americans. It was a humanitarian decision made in 1846, the "year of decision."

Britain was very concerned about losing Oregon Country. In early 1846 they sent British military officers to spy on the Americans' preparedness. They were to act as civilians looking for adventure, while actually examining the mouth of the Columbia for fortifications. Of course they found none, but wrote a report suggesting the installation of gun batteries at Cape Disappointment, Point Adams, and at Tongue Point near Astoria. Their report was dated June 16, 1846, one day after Britain had signed the treaty surrendering forever any claim to Old Oregon.

The first great San Francisco fire was two years in the future. In time Tolmie would find that market for cedar shingles.

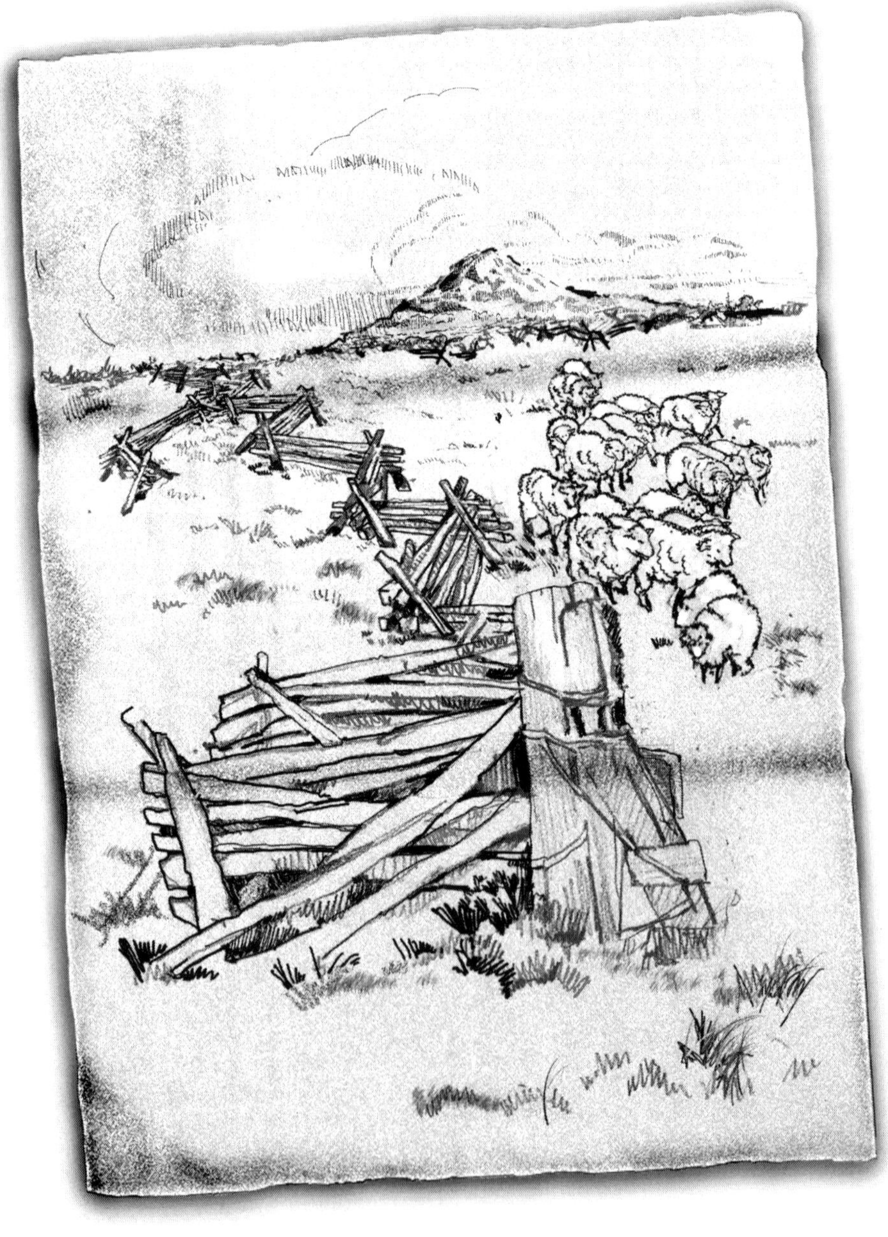

1847

THE BOUNDARY WAS established by international treaty between what would become Canada and the USA in 1846, but it was on September 14, 1847 that the Rio Grande was named the southern border of the states. General Winfield Scott raised the US flag over the Hall of Montezuma. The treaty ending the Mexican-American War granted California and all of Mexico's territory north of the Rio Grande to the United States.

The people of Fort Nisqually celebrated their eleventh local New Year in different ways throughout the day, but gathered for a Scottish Hogmanay[216] (First Foot) dance in the evening. It was mostly rainy, but a hard frost called a halt to ploughing toward the end of the week, so the men were engaged in changing sheep parks, butchering hogs, packing salted beef, and dressing mutton. The stables were cleared and the fields spread with manure. The winnowing machine was fitted with brand new boards, but the new wood was green. The green planks had to be replaced with dry cedar to avoid problems later when the green lumber dried.

Strong winter winds with snow and ice kept the workers inside during the second week of January. There was plenty to do: thrashing peas, cutting firewood, curing the ham and bacon. The eight to twelve inches of snow didn't slow the squaring of timber for the John Ross house, however.

With the thermometer registering minus 5½ degrees, a bundle of letters was prepared for Fort Vancouver. An American, Mr. Alderman, and Cowlitz Jack agreed to carry the letters, traveling on foot. It must have been a difficult journey. The weather was so poor that thirteen old ewes died of the cold before another six inches of snow fell. Cowlitz Jack returned to Fort Nisqually in mid-February. He and Alderman were severely frostbitten at Mud Mountain. Both of Jack's feet were badly injured. Only one of Alderman's was hurt, so he continued on with the mail. Jack returned to report his situation and seek medical help. It was several weeks before Jack could walk again.

---

216 Hogmanay is an ancient Scottish celebration of blessing or protecting the household and livestock in the next year. Author's notes.

Sheep continued to die at the rate of five or six per night until a quick thaw brought warmer rain toward the end of January. The warmer weather brought a "large gang of Americans" to the trade store and more personnel changes. Mathew Nelson Cook was sent to replace McLeod, who had completed his HBC contract.

Michael Simmons, the American who built the first grist mill, formed a partnership to build the first lumber mill on Puget Sound, at Tumwater Falls on the Deschutes River. There was a growing lumber market in San Francisco.

Hand squared timbers were still the favored construction material at Fort Nisqually. The bastions and palisades at two corners, surrounding the most important buildings at Fort Nisqually, were being erected to forestall a rumored threat. The threat was ever so vague. There might be an Indian attack, but probably not. The Indians were happily employed in the farming and ranching operations. The bigger threat might have been the Americans. They all had guns, and most did not like the British, but were often customers at the trade store. A third threat was more sinister. A measles epidemic had spread among the Puget Sound Indians, creating a great deal of serious illness and deadly unrest. Possessing limited immune systems, many Native Americans lost their lives to the measles.

Fort Nisqually had experienced no "Indian Problems" during the 14 years it had been in operation. The place was a store where the sellers wanted to maintain positive relationships with eager repeat customers. Hostile attitudes were extinguished with commercial zeal. However, there was a rumored threat of attack from the north by the Sinahomish in retaliation for the measles epidemic brought by Whites (without specification as to which Whites). The rumor held that the Sinahomish planned to set fire to the roof of the various houses at Fort Nisqually. They would shoot the men as they tried to extinguish the flames. Dr. McLoughlin, at Fort Vancouver, ordered Fort Nisqually enclosed with palisades and bastions for the first time. McLoughlin felt that trouble, if it started at all, would come from Indians from afar, who might party too much after successful fur trades, or possibly from the Americans, who were always armed, it seemed.

Fort Victoria was built near the Songhee people, who had the potential to be troublesome and violent. That HBC post had high palisades and bastions from the start of construction in 1843. Fort Vancouver and Fort Langley were also fortified from their beginnings. Only when American settlers began to build near Puget Sound, and after Marcus Whitman's American Mission at Wailatpu was attacked, did anyone feel compelled to fortify Fort Nisqually. It was without enclosing walls for most of the 36 years of operation. The local Nisqually, Steilacoom, Squaxin, Puyallup, and Muckleshoot tribes were not warlike. They were all wealthy by nature's bounty and willing to trade. Their culture was based on economic efforts, not conquests.

The bastions were constructed of heavy Douglas fir logs with tenons[217] mortised into them. The whole was pinned with oak pegs, some three feet long, driven into holes bored through both pieces. It was strong construction. In the bastions were housed the three signal cannons employed at Fort Nisqually. Until the "defensive mode" was adopted, the cannons were used strictly to signal arriving and departing ships in the time-honored traditional manner of the British Navy and merchant fleet. These cannon were actually small swivel guns capable of firing a one-pound ball with limited range. The bastions, once built, kept a supply of musketoons and blunderbusses, flintlocks, and muskets. HBC traders always kept these weapons handy at any frontier fur trade post. The bastions became a *defacto* armory, completely out of character for the place in previous years. The palisades soon fell into disrepair. Within 10 years the remaining material was salvaged only for firewood.

By the end of March, the frogs were again croaking and the weather showed some glimpses of sunshine. Ploughing was a daily task for at least two men and horses. Ten bushels of peas were planted before the arrival of the schooner *Cadboro*. The ship became wind-bound near the Snoquamish Village, but the mail arrived by express canoe.

When the *Cadboro* finally dropped anchor at Nisqually, she was quickly offloaded, discharging huge quantities of flour and other cargo destined for the trade shop. The outgoing cargo of furs and food stuff was quickly loaded, as well. The ship made her departure after two full days at the landing.

Sastuc Station was one of the sheep-ranching sites about ten miles from the fort.[218] As early as 1837 some sheep were grazing there under the watchful eyes of Kanakas, French-Canadians, or Scots. Gradually more local Nisqually were also employed at the sheep stations. Many men were needed to drive the animals into safe overnight sheep folds. The sheep fold was a portable fence enclosure made of split cedar rails. To protect the sheep from wild predators, and give the men a little time to sleep, the sheep fold became necessary. It had the added benefit of containing the sheep offal in a concentrated location for later collection and delivery to fertilize the field crops.

Shepherds were reporting the loss of sheep. Dr. Tolmie organized a posse to search

---

217 A tenon is a projection of the end of a piece of lumber shaped for insertion into a mortise to make a joint without use of nails or screws. A mortise is usually a rectangular cavity in a piece of lumber designed to receive a tenon, thus forming a joint. http://en.wikipedia.org

218 Sastuc Station was located near what is now the eastern boundary of McChord Air Force Base, immediately west of Spanaway Loop Road. Unpublished writings of Gary Fuller Reese *The Mossback*, June 21, 1984.

for sheep thieves. Ross, Wren, Bastian, and Deane were armed on horseback when they left at 10 AM, March 4th. John Edgar organized another party and planned to meet Tolmie at the end of the road still under construction east of Puyallup, through Natchez Pass. From that high point the joint posse planned to round up the rogues in the Puyallup Valley.

Tolmie and his men, with a show of force, had no trouble catching two of the culprits. Both were taken to the top floor of a bastion. The ladder was removed and the only door locked. The suspects were in complete limbo. One more suspect was brought in about noon the next day by Toelass, a friendly Nisqually. Tolmie had all three sheep thieves tied up and flogged, then were returned to the bastion. Three days later the oldest of the prisoners was set free after he promised to pay, in beaver pelts, for his theft. The next day the other thieves were put to work in PSAC farm fields to work off their debt.

Puget Sound could be a violent place in the 1840s. Shortly after Dr. Tolmie's posse captured the sheep thieves, a war canoe from the north attacked, killed the crew and pillaged a Puyallup fishing canoe on Puget Sound. Tolmie's HBC fur trader justice seems mild in comparison. The construction of palisades and bastions seemed like a good idea, too.

Americans were seldom deterred by the violence. A group of them stopped at Fort Nisqually to purchase supplies for an exploring expedition to the Straits of Juan de Fuca. They were intent on finding a suitable place for a settlement.[219]

Captain Wynter, Master of the HBC barque *Cowlitz* sailed from England with the news of the boundary agreement in March. The news had the location of the line incorrect, but that detail didn't matter. "Yankees were arriving daily in good numbers to have a look at the country," according to the journalist at Fort Nisqually. One of those Americans was Paul Kane, an American artist. Another was Mr. Sangster who arrived from Fort Vancouver with the correct news of the boundary line. It was established at the 49th parallel, after all.

Numbers indicate the ongoing work at or near Fort Nisqually. During one week the journal records three yoke of oxen hauling shingles, 24 bushels of potatoes planted, then 18 bushels, then another 24 bushels, two yoke of oxen hauling 3 foot long cedar shingles, three bushels of peas, 39 more bushels of potatoes, with houses being built on every spot an American land claim might be expected. And then there are the words

---

[219] In 1862 the first American settlers took up residence among in the S'Klallam villages of Tse-wit-zen and I'e-nis. Tse-wit-zen is the location of the "largest prehistoric Indian village and burial ground found in the United States." According to the U.S. Army Corps of Engineers in 2003. The place was occupied for about 2,700 years, but wiped out by smallpox by about 1835.

that signify a great deal of labor. "Slocum and the strong Indians sent to cut wood (because) the steamer *Beaver* arrived last night," according to the Fort Nisqually journalist. In a newly built kiln at Simon Plomondon's farm near the Cowlitz River, two men (S. Hancock and A.B. Rabbeson) are said to have made the first brick in what is now the State Of Washington.[220]

The first United States-issued postage stamps were available in 1847. They were in black and brown ink, depicting likenesses of George Washington and Benjamin Franklin. The black ink Washington sold for 10 cents, while the brown ink Franklin went for only five cents.

American postal officials issued private contracts for mail service to the Pacific coast in 1847. Letters were shipped to Panama, carried across the isthmus by burro, and then shipped north to San Francisco. Later in the year, the first six sacks of mail actually arrived safely at Astoria's new post office. This delivery system would not improve again until 1855.

Not to be outdone by the new U.S. postage stamps, Mexico's highly unstable government issued a new silver-dollar-sized five peso coin. It featured a magnificent portrait of Cuauhtemoc, the last Aztec emperor. The classic silver coin was produced for only two years. The Mexican-American War began on the southern border of Texas April 25, 1846, and ended on September 14, 1847. During those 17 months, the casualties of the war were extremely high. In this aspect, the war was the most disastrous in American military history. The impact was felt in both the United States and Mexico. Mexico ceded California and New Mexico, and recognized U.S. sovereignty over Texas. Mexico lost 1.2 million square miles of territory. The United States agreed to pay $15 million for the Mexican civilian claims of damage.

The American War with Mexico also established the intent of President James K. Polk to take by force, if necessary, any and all land considered part of America's Manifest Destiny. The British were well aware of the political effect in the Pacific Northwest.

Fourteen died in the Whitman Massacre at Wailatpu on November 29, 1847. It was the site of the Christian mission on the Walla Walla River established by Doctor Marcus Whitman and his wife Narcissa (Prentiss) Whitman. The mission served the Indians religiously, but also became an important rest stop for the Oregon Trail immigrants. The American Board of Missions was the same organization that called the Methodist Missions at Willamette, The Dalles, and Nisqually.

Whitman built a farm and gristmill, but in 1844 Indians burned it. Whitman re-built

---

220 Toledo History Committee, *The Toledo Community Story,* The Toledo Parent-Teacher Organization, Toledo, WA 1976.

the operation 20 miles away and added a lumber mill. The settlement's population grew to over 50 people by 1847, primarily because of the Oregon Trail and Indian orphans who were left to live with Whitman.

Several people were taken hostage by the Cayuse, who felt that Dr. Whitman was using his medical powers to kill Indians. Over 200 Cayuse died of measles, but only after taking Dr. Whitman's medicine. The Cayuse were certain it was the medicine that caused the deaths. They felt righteous in killing the person who had misused his spirit power. In effect it was a revenge that resulted in the massacre of fourteen people. Ironically two of the hostages died of measles.

The hostages were finally rescued by Peter Skene Ogden of HBC Board of Management at Fort Vancouver. At his personal expense, Ogden took over 3000 pounds of supplest; blankets, shirts, guns, ammunition, from the trade store at Fort Vancouver to buy the freedom of the American hostages. He was never compensated, or truly thanked, for his personal expenditures, or even the rescue.

The only response in Oregon Territory was to raise an army of Oregon Volunteers, who scattered the Cayuse into the mountains. In 1850 six Cayuse surrendered, were tried, convicted, and hanged by the U.S. Marshall, Joe Meek. The Cayuse tribe eventually lost its identity and language. The Cayuse people and culture dissolved into other tribes.

Pressure was being brought on Congress to formalize the political organization of Oregon Territory. People wanted army protection and formal political government. The region had become "American" in 1846. Now, two years later, little political structure existed.

1848

IN 1848 THE TALLEST BUILDINGS in New York were church steeples, but the city was linked to Chicago by telegraph, as the great rush for California gold was set to begin. Fifteen years after Chicago was founded, Manhattan Island was assessed for tax purposes at slightly more than sixty million dollars total.

In Seneca Falls, New York, some 300 people convened at the Wesleyan Methodist Church to "discuss the social, civil, and religious condition and rights of" women. Elizabeth Cady Stanton, Lucretia Mott, and three other women organized the meeting that declared "…all men and women had been created equal." One of the eleven resolutions they adopted in the *Declaration of Sentiments* demanded the right for women to vote. Seventy-two years later, women were finally allowed to vote when the 19th Amendment guaranteed women's suffrage.

Also in 1848, President James K. Polk triggered the Gold Rush of '49 by confirming that gold had been found in California. People in Oregon had heard this news first. Some were already among the 80,000 flocking to the gold fields. Puget Sound entrepreneurs supplied food, hardware, clothing, lumber, and other building material. Many ships originally destined for Oregon were diverted to California.

Still, in the Pacific Northwest, very few Americans had settled north of the Columbia River, even after the four-year-old settlement of the Nisqually Methodist Mission and the boundary line decision. British holdings of Fort Nisqually and Puget Sound Agricultural Company had already been operating for sixteen years.

Actually, the number of American settlements was diminishing. In August, 1848, Thomas Glasgow and Antonio B. Rabbeson, both with HBC connections and American ambitions, were forced to abandon their small farms on Whidbey Island. Puget Sound area Indians, probably of the Duwamish, Snoqualmie, and Snohomish tribes, were instrumental in convincing the two men to reestablish themselves nearer the protection of the farms at Nisqually.

American settlers Edmund Sylvester and Levi L. Smith claimed land where Olympia now stands to form Newmarket, only ten miles south of Fort Nisqually. Another American community, Tumwater, was already three years old and not far south of Newmarket. Still further south was HBC Cowlitz farm, established at the head of navigation on the Cowlitz River in 1837 by Simon Plomondon.

Except for occasional show of force by the Native Americans from the north, there had been no hostile incidents, and little reason for security concerns. Nevertheless, in 1848 the English Navy *Cormorant,* a steam-powered paddle-wheel gun-boat mounting six 32-pound guns, was anchored for several months off Fort Nisqually as protection for English business interests. It was ostensibly and officially sent to protect HBC from attack by First People, but the real effect was on the Americans in nearby Tumwater. The talk of the town was the British warship in regard to settlers' perceived rights to the very desirable Fort Nisqually ranches and farmland.

With apparently no reason to build them, on January 2nd construction was begun on the Fort's northwest bastion, the first of two to be built. We don't have much detail about the actual construction work, but there is a nearly daily mention in the *Trade Blotter,* which seems to signify that some sort of Indian day-labor was employed. At least one "fort Indian," a fellow named Dadyamki, was employed "looking after the cedar logs at the beach." By the 22nd of January, the men were "fitting the Northwest Bastion door"—a significant final construction act followed by the 'click' of a padlock.

There is no connection between increased security at Fort Nisqually fur-trade enterprise and the conclusion of the Mexican War, which gave the United States considerable land west of the Rockies. There were insignificant concerns about local security, and the unlikely American expansion of international hostilities, but the bastions were built.

In addition to the bastions and palisade construction, the January fur trade was fairly busy with several days of "brisk trading". Customers included Salalasal and his people, Hoiyah, Dadyamki, Chief Lahalet, Lame Peter, and an American named John Chambers, who bought sundries.

Early February had somewhat brisk trade as well. Dadyamki was back, Mr. Ross made several purchases with cash, and a large group of Skagit and Snoqualmie people brought in five large beaver skins. They camped overnight outside the new palisades. Several American settlers also came for business. Mr. Wunch and Mr. Ford paid cash, Misters Collins, Andrew Chambers, and Joseph Allard did not, but Mr. Jones, Jr. offered American coins. Joseph Heath stopped by, but apparently bought nothing, seeking only some brief companionship. Indians who traded in February included Qunasapam, two Cowlitz, and a Skagit whose family had the measles. Luschchyach, Yanactow, and a party of four Klickitats brought letters from Father Blanchet's Yakama [sic] Valley Roman

Catholic Mission. Sometimes Indians traded with cedar boards, as Kytahanum did on March 17th, or rented horses to the Fort, as did Lahalet and Laveille Steilacoom.

Other Americans trading at Fort Nisqually in early 1848 included Mr. Collins, William Packwood, George Washington Bush, Charles Eaton, both elder and younger John Chambers, and Richard Slocum, who brought in 111 fence rails to trade. Thomas Linklater, Mr. Shearer, and Mr. Cheezer all bought sundries, sometimes paying with labor, as did many Indians, but Americans brought much cash to the Trade Shop. By the end of April there was $35 in gold and silver coins secured in the seldom used safe.

The *SS Beaver* departed Fort Nisqually five days before Easter, with many of Joseph Heath's farm tools. He sent ploughs, muck forks, and axes for repair and sharpening at Fort Victoria. Apparently the simple grinding wheel and blacksmith shop at Fort Nisqually was inadequate for the needed repairs. Perhaps only the Victoria shop had the capacity to take on more work. Another theory suggests that the tools at Heath's place were not treated with considerable care.

In the early spring, construction of the second bastion at the southeast corner of the central campus was undertaken. Other work continued apace with trading, as primary, and agriculture, as a secondary venture. The trade blotter mentions every single transaction, its minute details of price, commodity, purchaser's name, labor traded, inventory implications, etc. The blotter even lists many "gifts" or rewards for good customers.

One day in June, the Trade Store paid workers with:

> *58 yards of cloth, a quarter pound of thread, 20 charges of ammunition, six inches of tobacco, two blankets, nine handkerchiefs, and ten pounds of flour. For this bounty the place received 18 furs, 15 handmade baskets, 17 handmade mats, a woven leather strap, and considerable labor. Indians had been hired to shear sheep, plough and sow oats, thrash wheat, plant carrots, onions, peas, beans, cabbage, and more. They slaughtered cattle, constructed buildings, winnowed wheat, cleared ground of brush, drained swamps, loaned horses, and paddled canoes to deliver mail and more. Occasionally a horse rented by Fort Nisqually was injured or died in service. That horse was purchased, then, to compensate the owner for the value of the horse.*

On November 5, 1848, Newmarket settlers gathered to oppose a long used PSAC pasture on the south side of the Nisqually River. It was a wonderful and luxurious graze for longhorned Spanish cattle, but the Americans bitterly opposed the British occupancy. They approved a resolution, or memorial, to require that the Spanish cattle be withdrawn, or suffer unmentioned reprisal. Dr. Tolmie bowed to public opinion. The offending herds were removed in the stipulated time.

The Americans (incorrectly) assumed the Company had no rights within the Oregon territory after the boundary settlement. In fact, they were certain that any action by the Company which interfered with any American was unjust. The mysterious distinction between 'actual settler' and PSAC was clear in the American politic. To Americans, the Company was a monstrous, soulless foreign giant deserving contempt and even combat, if necessary. It was impossible to counter that attitude. After all, Tolmie was British, and he did represent an alien company. Plus, the Americans had the argument of increasing force of numbers.

John Chambers took advantage of the popular sentiment six months later. Chambers staked out a claim for himself and his son at the mouth of the Nisqually, then with an 'in-your-face" effort built a sawmill at Steilacoom (now Chambers) Bay. Tolmie warned him off several times, but Chambers refused to move.[221]

There were times when the Trade Shop gave away gifts. A Skagit Indian was "loaned" a blanket when he announced that his family was laid up with the measles. The blanket probably was never returned, but its value was undoubtedly paid at some future date in trade or favor. Lahalet's wives had been working in the fields for five-and-a-half months when they finally received full payment in late June. The Fort's Indian Trader wanted to see the job completed before payment would be offered. Too often a small payment would result in no work until the worker needed something from the Trade Store.

On June 18, 1848, the hardware for the stockade gates was prepared for shipment to Fort Nisqually.[222] The Fort Victoria forge and blacksmith had just completed the iron work for the hinges, latches, and locks, which were ordered sometime earlier. Security at Fort Nisqually was much more assured, with the bastions, palisades, and locks. Installation was just in time.

A large trading party of Snoqualmies and Sinahomish arrived in late July, "gratifying us with the number and quality of their skins." They sold to Fort Nisqually ten beaver, two deer, one black bear, and several deer skins. The visitors stayed to enjoy their new purchases, remaining in the neighborhood several days.

By the fourth day of trading, Tolmie had to put the Company's men and Indian employees under arms, as some "Saltwater Indians" (Skywamish and Snoquamick) were

---

221 Tolmie frequently delivered notices of trespass to all squatters (Chambers, Lamie, Wren, McLeod, Dougherty, Smith, Bradley, Brownfield, and others) on Company lands. Notes from the Fort Nisqually *Journal of Occurrences*, 1848.

222 Roderick Finlayson to William F. Tolmie, 18 June 1848, Bagley Collection, University of Washington, as reported by Steve Anderson in the *Transcription of the Trade Blotters*, unpublished, 2005

selling slaves who were relatives of the local people. The visitors were "rather numerous" showing "an indication to make fresh captures, threatening "murderous intent," chasing a Nisqually right up to the Establishment, where he obtained shelter. Tolmie said, "On witnessing our demonstrations, the Strangers soon retired to their encampment beyond our gunshot range."[223] The entire affair was without bloodshed, but it certainly was a tense situation, especially with the palisades not yet completed.

On July 1st the men, probably led by Charles Wren, began construction on the stockade, or palisades,[224] to connect the bastions and surround the most important central buildings of Fort Nisqually. Earlier they placed one of the two padlocks available at Fort Nisqually on that bastion entry-door. The other padlock was probably already employed on the large storehouse door.

The installation of the vertical posts was simple. A trench was dug, and the former tree trunks were positioned in an upright position as they had grown. The loose soil left after digging the trench was returned to hold the posts in place. The palisade posts were placed so that a single row would have left gaps between each upright, so an additional pole was placed in the gap. The line of the palisade was, therefore, somewhat ragged but very effective as a device for shielding the interior from view and access. The tops of the palisade posts were not cut at the same height. Expedience demanded a quick, not pretty, installation. The tree was inserted into service at whatever length it arrived from the nearby forest.

All seemed to quiet down as August rolled around. Yakama Indians arrived from east of the Cascades with nine prime beaver. It was a Sunday when some Sinahomish and Suquamish insisted on trading. Dr. Tolmie's order to observe the Sabbath was relaxed in view of the "impressive trading stock" offered by the Indians. The Company took in 11 beaver, 4 otter, 20 bladders of oil and a variety of other skins. This "justified the trouble of it all," that is, the extra work of opening the shop on a Sunday.

Occasionally a trade listed in the *Trade Blotter* looks interesting, but there is no explanation. The entry for Tuesday, August 8, 1848, seems to have a story: "Pere Cherouze purchased the old steel mill for a sound, stout gelding." Alas, there is no further information to tell us of the "old steel mill" or of its purchaser.

In late August, a story does arrive, however. The *H.M.S. Pandora*, anchored at the Nisqually Landing under the command of Lieutenant Commander James Wood, Royal Navy. The *Pandora*, a Packet Brig, was part of a team that included the *H.M.S. Herald*, but

---

223 Anderson, Steve, *Trade Blotter* transcription, unpublished 2005.

224 Anderson, Steve, unpublished transcript of the Fort Nisqually "*Blotter*", 2005

that ship goes unmentioned in the journals, blotters, and diaries of the time. The ship's surgeon for both vessels was Doctor James Gordon, R.N., of Portsmouth, England.[225]

Dr. Gordon apparently expressed to Joseph Heath a desire to go hunting. It seems that Heath sent an Indian to guide Gordon across the Round Plain (through what is now the Tillicum-JBLM[226] area) to some prospective hunting grounds. The doctor either dismissed his guide, or the guide misunderstood the assignment. Soon the doctor was alone, on his own, in an unfamiliar area of a strange land. He was lost.

By late evening Heath was concerned for his new friend. Word was sent to Dr. Tolmie that Gordon had not returned as expected. Tolmie was equally concerned, so a dual search party was organized. One part of the search effort began at Fort Nisqually, while Heath organized the second party of searchers from Steilacoom.

Dr. Gordon was obviously in need of food and water before nightfall. The man was not found that first evening. The second day brought a beefed up search party together for a concerted effort to find the poor man. The searchers knew he was armed for hunting, but completely without provisions for overnight, let alone a second day.

To make matters worse, there were rumors of northern tribes organizing a raid to wipe out the white population in the South Sound area. Anxiety was running high among the searchers. Dr. Gordon had little chance of survival should he stumble upon an advancing hostile band.

On the morning of the third day (Sunday, August 20), the searchers found Gordon a few hundred yards from where he had last been seen. He was exhausted, dirty, hungry, and wore only the torn and tattered clothing he put on three days before. He could barely speak. His hands, face, and exposed parts of his body were severely swollen by the mosquito bites he had suffered. His only food during the ordeal was some berries he had found somewhere between the Round Plain and the Puyallup River.

Gordon was safely returned to Fort Nisqually. His August ordeal on the prairies near Fort Nisqually was over.[227]

---

[225] Portsmouth is the site of the Royal Naval Museum and the Royal Marine's Museum. The city remains a major dockyard for the Royal Navy, 64 miles from London. Notes collected during the author's visit, 1986.

[226] JBLM is Joint Base Lewis McChord, a U.S. military installation now occupying only a portion of former HBC/PSAC land, as seen on a map of western Pierce County depicting the former and the latter. Anderson, Steve A., *Columbia Magazine, Washington State History Museum*, Winter, 2011-12, page 24.

[227] Anderson, Steve A., *Of Gold Silver and Lost Surgeons: Her Majesty's Packet Brig "Pandora" Visits Nisqually, August 1848,* 2005 monograph. This story is made possible by the outstanding research of Steve Anderson, former Director of Fort Nisqually Historic site.

A few days before Doctor Gordon's adventure began, on August 14, 1848, President James K. Polk signed the "Oregon Territorial Organic Act." The law created the Territory of Oregon, defined as

> "that part of the Territory of the United States which lies west of the summit of the Rocky Mountains, North of the forty-second degree of North latitude, known as the Territory of Oregon."

All Fort Nisqually and PSAC land was clearly inside the Oregon Territory of the United States.

Toward the end of August Dr. Tolmie decided that having the HMS *Pandora* at the landing provided a great opportunity to have a large amount of accumulated cash, gold, and silver transported to Victoria offices of the Company. So while the biscuits, beef, mutton, and sundries were loaded to provision the ship, a secure bag was placed under the care of Captain Wood. The money would eventually reach London headquarters of the Hudson's Bay Company.

While the supply ship *Cadboro* and HMS *Pandora* were at dockside, the men of Fort Nisqually and the ship's crews may have celebrated Harvest Home. It was a holiday brought from the old country. It included target shooting and horse racing, music, dancing, and other pastimes and ceremonies, similar to the German Oktoberfest. Harvest Home has been described as a celebration of completion of the heavy autumn season work.

Once Her Majesty's ship and crew were assigned their stevedoring [sic] tasks, Captain Wood and the officers were treated to a day tour of the very new American settlement called Newmarket, at Budd Inlet. Dr. Tolmie was the well-qualified tour guide. Perhaps some of the expense incurred in anticipation of the Home Harvest Holiday was as a result of this excursion. Within five days of the departure of the *Pandora* from the Fort Nisqually landing, it was again active when the *Cadboro* anchored at the roadstead. Two Indian canoes were hired to offload the schooner. Nisqually landing was often a busy port of call.

September clients at the trade store revealed more American names, along with some familiar and new Indian customers. Mrs. Adam Beinston bought sundries on Saturday, while Yanatacow sold otter skins in a quantity or quality high enough to have the store opened just for him on Sunday.

Nisqually William was there with his people offering an impressive 13 furs to trade. Later a large party of Sinahomish sold skins for yard goods, while Thomas Linklater bought sundries. Squally brought letters from Cowlitz and Skagit Chief S'Neitlam traded 30 skins. The Suquamish and Sinahomish visited the fort again. Luschchyach brought skins, but three other Indians brought two horses to compensate for the ox they were guilty of stealing and killing. Later Baptiste came in to identify a fourth Indian, Tom, as another guilty party.

To give the reader a deeper sense of the activities of the clerk at the trade store, below is a complete list of the items taken in on a typical day—Sunday, October 1, 1848:

12 trout	
6 deer skins	**Then to complete the**
5 pair moccasins	**day, the outgoing goods:**
4 large beaver	203 charges of ammunition
2 midsized beaver	3 Kirby hooks
1 small beaver	8 fathoms of grey cotton
1 lynx	2 green three point blankets
8 fresh salmon	3 flints
Indian labor	

Most of the ammunition was in payment to Indian workers who dug up potatoes on company land, where McLeod was the overseer. While the above list was for a Sunday, most of the time the Sabbath was a day of rest. It is unknown why the trade store was active on this particular day.

Other items coming into the store included baskets, trout, bear skins, straps, elk hides, raccoon skins, dried salmon, and even sinews. Outgoing items included cotton shirts, winter shirts, a square headed axe, cod fish hooks, a broken wood framed mirror, common beads, a tin kettle, tobacco twists and plugs, thimbles, thread, and vermillion. Sometimes items were shipped to Victoria. Among those items on Saturday October 21st were 167 pounds of flat bar iron. The idea was to have the iron made into two iron cartwheels and new wicket gate hinges.

Contact with Cowlitz Farms seemed somewhat limited in 1848, but not without reason. Superintendent George Roberts regularly reported failures, troubles, and illnesses. An epidemic of measles devastated the region in 1848, only to be followed by an outbreak of typhoid in 1849. The fever took its toll, including Mrs. Roberts (in July 1850). She was the first white woman buried in what is now western Washington. Not long after her internment, the remains of the Roberts' two daughters, 18 and 20 years old, were laid

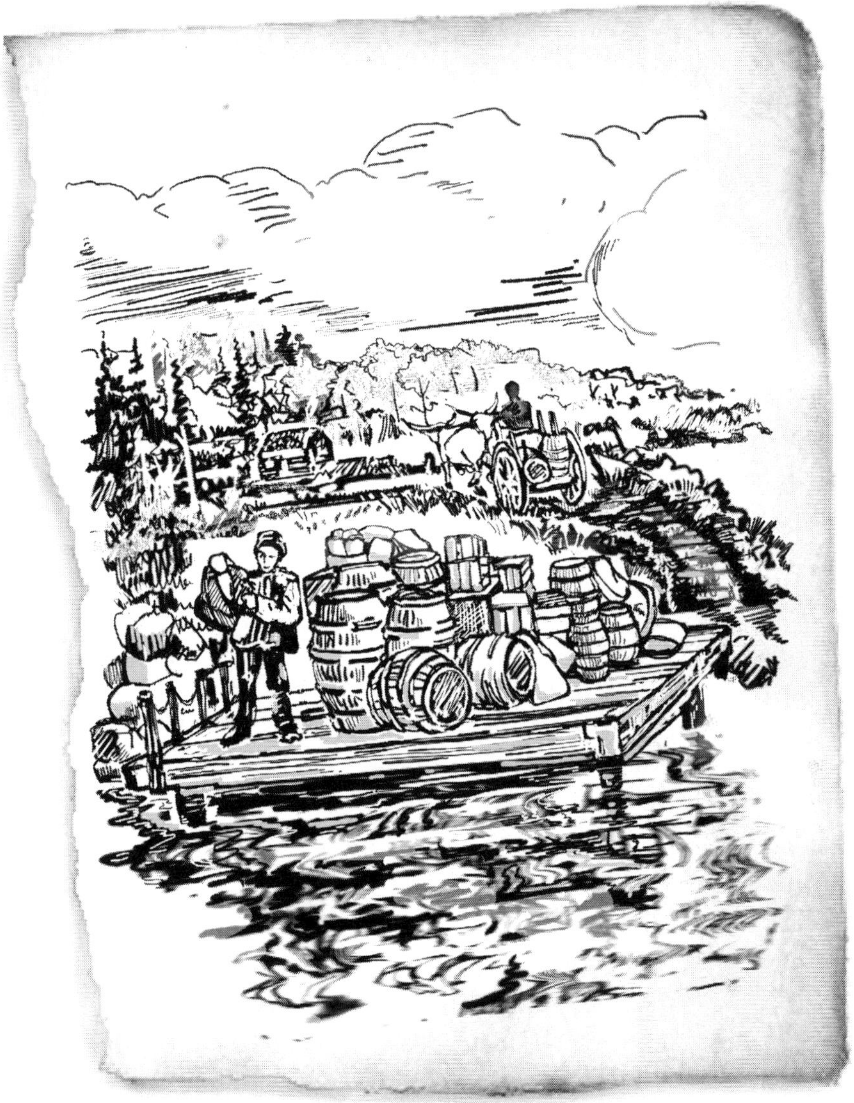

beside that of their mother.[228]

On August 14, 1848 Congress, laboring under the sweltering humidity of a typical Washington, D.C. summer, finally created the Territory of Oregon. Oregon citizens had organized their own "Provisional Government" in 1843. The United States gained sovereignty in the region (Oregon, Washington, Idaho) in 1846. President James K. Polk appointed General Joseph Lane of Indiana as governor. The Territorial Legislature designated the area around Puget Sound as Lewis County, without organizing any court system. But finally, more than a year after the Cayuse had killed 14 people at the Whitman Mission; the politicians formalized a territorial government.

In California, the sleepy Spanish town of Yerba Buena had become San Francisco, with a booming 800 residents. The city had not yet experienced the gold rush or the half-dozen fires that would destroy the place several times between 1849 and 1852.

Dr. Tolmie realized that American settlers in the area of Fort Nisqually needed jobs to be able to purchase goods at the Fort Nisqually store. He offered to pay men to split cedar shingles. He stacked the bundles of shingles wherever there was an open space around the Fort. At one point it is believed that Tolmie had over 100,000 bundles of cedar shingles on hand. Every bundle had resulted in some worker making a necessary purchase at the trade store. As yet there was no large market for the shingles. Local people could simply split their own shingles. Extra shingles bought commodities at Fort Nisqually. It was almost making your own money.

Tolmie proved to be a marketing wizard. When San Francisco began to burn, his shingles were sold there for a very handsome profit (about 70%). Tolmie's shingles were very popular in the City by the Bay until the Spring Valley Water Company emerged as the dominant water provider. An effective fire-fighting tool killed the market for Nisqually shingles in 1858, when Spring Valley constructed a reservoir and pipeline for all of San Francisco.

This cedar shingle export was just one of the products sent from Fort Nisqually that opened the way for the enormous international trade empire that characterized Puget Sound 150 years into the future. Tacoma alone would have 100 sawmills.

---

228 Toledo History Committee, *The Toledo Community Story*, The Toledo Parent-Teacher Organization, Toledo, WA 1976. Roberts later married Laura Winston, and on her passing, he married Mary Gray Snider. Each marriage produced children.

1849

A FLOOD OF immigrants arrived on the west coast following the discovery of gold on the American River, California, by carpenter James W. Marshall. The flood of immigrants was barely noticed at Fort Nisqually, until the economic impact was felt. The thousands of Forty Niners needed supplies, some of which could be sent from Fort Nisqually. Water- and steam-powered saw lumber mills sprang up around Puget Sound in the next few years.

Fort Nisqually was a "teenager" in 1849, actually over 16 years old, when the first American beaver trap lines were set up at False Dungeness (now Port Angeles). John Sutherland and John Everett strung lines between two lakes (now Lake Crescent and Lake Everett). They took their furs directly to Fort Victoria, only 17 miles away, across the Strait of Juan de Fuca, to trade for potatoes and other supplies. Port Angeles got her name from Don Francisco Eliza in 1791, when the Spanish explorer dubbed the place "Puerto de Nuestra Senora de Los Angeles."

The Russians gave Fort Nisqually some relief when they eliminated some requirements for potatoes and other foodstuff from one clause of the PSAC contract. It may have been too late to completely save the Puget Sound Agricultural Company from hard times about to begin. PSAC had operated at Fort Nisqually from July 3, 1839. Prosperity lasted until 1853, when it began to find its farmlands and ranches were being occupied by American settlers—illegal squatters, in fact. The company found itself surrounded by a foreign land politically. Each year became more difficult for the Company, as the men spent more and more time and manpower protecting the farms and ranches from squatters and livestock poachers. The pioneer American courts often sided with the illegal squatters, who were often not punished. Poachers simply shot the PSAC longhorn cattle as if they were wild forest animals instead of domestic herds. The local legal system ignored the treaty rights of the British. Those rights were ratified by Congress and signed by the president, but most citizens saw only "John Bull," the cartoon personification of everything bad about Great Britain just as "Uncle Sam" was everything good about America.

Englishman Joseph Heath's sheep produced wool of poor quality (according to the London auctioneers in 1848). Heath died of loneliness and physical (heart?) ailments on March 7, 1849. He had, by age 44, cultivated fields and built several farm buildings, including a nice home, on the rocky soils and rough timbers of Steilacoom Prairie. Heath was helped by his "people," the Cowlitz Indians. His tenure at Steilacoom was less than 51 months, only ten months longer than the Methodist Missionaries. The remainder of Heath's farm was simply absorbed by PSAC, as was the Methodist Mission grounds. His estate was settled by the Company with the few proceeds sent to Heath's brother William and other surviving family members in England.[229]

In early March 1849 the weather was mild around Puget Sound. The men of Fort Nisqually anxiously sowed the fields with oats, while others winnowed the winter wheat crop. The schooner *Cadboro*, Captain Sangster, brought more supplies and trade goods. Two men, Linklater and Nelson, traded jobs at Tenalquot during the lambing season. No reason was given in the Journals for the personnel shift.

It took six Indian men with Slocum and Kalama to load the *Cadboro* with cargo destined for London, while another six men were sent to skin several dead cattle on the prairie. Many had died from starvation. Some cattle may have been shot by American settlers. The winter was hard on the grasses, even harder on the nearly wild cattle that ate those grasses. The men counted 526 wedders when finally delivering fodder to the plains for the sheep herds.

Frogs were croaking the arrival of spring the day before five inches of snow fell on March 23rd. It was too warm for winter's return, however. Most of the white stuff had disappeared by noon. It was still enough "winter" for three Sinahomish Indians to kill a PSAC cow near the salt marshes at the mouth of the Nisqually River. They felt the need for fresh meat, and "winter" gave them an excuse.

A party of Fort men was sent to collect payment for the butchered cow. The Indians said it was found dead, and offered the head as evidence that it had not been shot. The Fort's men seized a gun anyway, saying the cow's throat had been cut. It was apparently a healthy, fat cow before it died. The gun was kept as payment.

Edward Huggins, a 17-year-old arrived on the northwest coast aboard the *Norman Morrison*. He became the right-hand man to Dr. Tolmie. Huggins continued to work at Nisqually and outstations in the area for the rest of his working life. Later he homesteaded, as a naturalized American citizen on the very same property after the fort closed. Eventually he retired and sold the land.[230]

---

229 Heath, Joseph Thomas, *Memoirs of Nisqually*, Fairfield, Washington, 1979.
230 In 1906 the DuPont Company paid $43,000 to Edward Huggins for the old Nisqually land. Crooks, Drew W., *The Story of DuPont Village*, www.dupontmuseum.com

In 1849 some Indians were restless. After some significant success driving farmers from Whidby Island, another confrontation was instigated. About noon on May 1st a large party of heavily armed Snoqualmie[231] and Skeywamish (Skykomish) arrived on the beach near the Sequalitchew village.

The horn at Fort Nisqually normally sounded to signal the noon meal. Because it was not noontime, the horn signal worked as a distress warning. Immediately all working Indians and their friends in the nearby Nisqually Village ran to the Fort, bringing with them every weapon or farm tool they could carry.

Although they were outnumbered, about one hundred Snoqualmies and Skeywhamish advanced up the oxen road toward the Fort. Some went to Lahalet's lodge, but the greater number gathered at the water gate near Sequalitchew Creek. Soon all of them were at the gate, wildly clamoring for justice.

When asked about their intentions in such numbers, they replied that they heard that young Lahalet, who married a daughter of one of their chiefs, was beating her brutally. They proclaimed to have no intention of harming any whites.

Chief Patakynum was invited into the Fort, through the water gate. He and others were given tobacco to smoke in the pipe of peace. They were also offered an empty lodge for shelter and comfort. Inside the Fort, armed men were stationed strategically around the perimeter, with two on the gate. One man tried to round up all of the fearful Nisqually for protection.

Suddenly a gunshot rang out. Nisqually Gohome had fired in jest. Four or five Snoqualmies rushed the gate, provoked no doubt by the shot. Snoqualmie Cussass, one of the more aggressive, rudely pushed Gohome, who was standing between the gate's posts. Cussass was told to keep quiet, but answered insultingly and was immediately put out of the Fort. Copass cocked his gun and drew a dagger, making threats to anyone near him.

Wren was called into the Fort from his position near the outside of the bastion, but the gate was closing as he approached, so it was reopened. As Wren entered the gate he seized one of the Snoqualmies guns. A scuffle ensued, preventing the full closure of the gate. Cussass pointed his gun at Huggins, who ordered him out and to be quiet. Huggins responded in kind, aiming directly at Cussass.

Wren twisted his gun, and with the butt end struck a Snoqualmie named Quillawowt. One of the Chiefs fired at him, but instantly Huggins fired as well. Tolmie's shot missed the target, hit another, and a good many shots followed. The gate was closed. The men of

---

231 "Snoqualmie," in the Coast Salish language, probably means "moon," The Snoqualmie Tribe of Indians is therefore "People of the Moon." Today many people hike the trails near Snoqualmie Pass in the Cascade mountains to see a magnificent display of the full moon on a warm summer night.

the Fort gained their assigned positions with weapons at the ready, just as the attacking Indians took flight at full speed toward their canoes.

Chief Patakynum somehow escaped unseen after the gate was closed. Apparently Lahalet showed him the way out.

Two Americans, Leander C. Wallace and a man only known in the records as Lewis, were unfortunately outside the palisade when the gate closed. They may have felt secure from harm as Americans, and not belonging to the Fort, remained outside. They did not respond to the call for all hands to come in and shut the gate. But, blocked out, they did not heed the warning or the invitation.

It was said that Cussass was the one who shot Wallace. Lewis was almost unhurt, as a ball went through his vest, one through his trousers, and one grazed his left arm. Segeass received a flesh wound in the neck. Later, he died of an infected wound. A Skeywamish Medicine Man was killed, and another Snoqualmie wounded in the shoulder.

Apparently three other Indians died during the squabble outside Fort Nisqually's gates. The Fort's *Trade Blotter* notes that a death price was paid in the form of blankets to the families of Stzeeass, Lashanugh, and Skeywhamish. Two were apparently killed by the Snoqualmies, but one may have been shot by Thibeault, one of the Fort's employees guarding the gate. One 2½ point blanket came from the PSAC account, and the others from the fur trade account.

It was certain that the War Party did not come to attack Fort Nisqually. They may have had some other objective in view other than the story about Lahalet. Probably the idea was to make a commotion and kidnap as many women and children of the Nisquallys as they could catch.

When the tobacco was passed out to make peace, none of the Indians would smoke until Wren smoked and chewed in their presence. They feared it was poisoned. That fear was probably given to them by the Indians of the South Sound as an attempt to keep the warlike tribes away. The Snoqualmies and Skeywhamish were the terror of all the tribes south of the Soquamish. Nisquallys would have helped whites to attack the northern tribes.

With a watch posted for the night and as Wallace was being buried, a dispatch was sent to Governor Lane and another to Fort Vancouver. Fort Vancouver sent two kegs of gun powder, but no lead. The disturbance led to the arrival of the US Army later in the year.

Dr. Tolmie, writing from Cowlitz, sent a letter and a counterfeit American dollar bill found by Mr. Roberts in the Cowlitz cash box. All cash at the Fort was carefully examined with two more American bills were found to be counterfeit. No suspect was mentioned in any of the reports. There apparently was no legal recourse, either.

Dr. Tolmie may have been at Fort Vancouver, perhaps near the Cowlitz Farms, on the occasion of the arrival of the United States Army in the northwest. On May 13, 1849, Companies L and M of the First Artillery arrived to establish an army post at Vancouver. Over time it was called variously Columbia Barracks, Fort Vancouver Military Reserve, and Vancouver Barracks.[232] It was located on the north bank of the Columbia River, on the ridge above the British fur trade post called Fort Vancouver. The two establishments were never "the same place," as modern tourist often surmise.

An artillery company from Vancouver Barracks was sent to Fort Steilacoom under the command of Captain B. F. Hill. It was the first company of United States soldiers stationed at Puget Sound. The Fort Steilacoom U.S. Army Post was established on the land Joseph Heath had occupied. Dr. Tolmie leased 20 acres to the U.S. Army for fifty dollars per month.

Years later, Ezra Meeker described Fort Steilacoom as

> "a camp of a company of United States soldiers in wooden shells of houses and log cabins...Dr. Tolmie, Chief Factor at the Puget Sound Agricultural Company at Fort Nisqually, quickly seized the opportunity to demand rent from the United States for the occupancy of the site, of six hundred a year and actually received it for 15 years."[233]

A few days had passed since the violent incident, "the killing of Wallace," when Huptickynum of the Snoqualmie Tribe came by to express his personal regret at the foolish behavior of the creators of the disturbance. He resolved to have nothing to do with the guilty Snoqualmies. Similarly, S'Neitlam, of the Scadgets, came to exculpate himself. He made the best excuse possible for holding a gun and a knife on the leader of the whites. With that came a note from Simmons, the leader of the American settlers, giving credence to the rumors of an invasion planned by the Snoqualmies.

Was it simple coincidence that William McNeill, from Victoria, arrived by eight-man canoe with the message that the *HMS Inconstant*, with 36 guns, was in the harbor at Esquimalt near Victoria? Captain Shepherd ordered the news spread far and wide. That news seems to have had a calming effect.

The Territorial Legislature finally got around to creating a court at Fort Steilacoom.

---

[232] Fort Vancouver remained active in reduced form until 2011, when it was officially turned over to the National Park Service. *A Bittersweet Handoff.* Von Lunen, Jacques, *The Columbian*, Vancouver, WA, pp. C1, 3, May 29, 2012

[233] Meeker, *Busy Life of 85 Years*, pp 79,80, Hunt's History of Tacoma, Chicago, 1916

On October 1, 1849, Chief Justice James P. Bryant, in the absences of any appointment for a district court judge, gaveled the proceedings of a grand jury to order. An indictment charging six Snoqualmies with murder was returned. Bryant appointed an attorney for the accused men.

The trial convened the next day and found two men, Cusass and Quillalwowt, guilty of the murder of Leander Wallace. The jury of American settlers also found four others not guilty. One was found to be a slave to Patakynum, who was not even present on the day of the altercation.

U.S. Marshall Joe Meek hanged Cusass and Quillalwowt the next day. These were the first two legal executions in the history of Washington. The U.S. Army had previously offered 80 blankets to Chief Patakynum as an inducement and reward to name the responsible parties. After the convictions, the bounty was paid. Justice Bryant included the blankets, travel costs, and juror's fees in the total trial cost of $2,379.54.

Still, in spite of the trial, some old misdemeanors were repeated. Gohome was robbed of a Company gun, an axe, and all of his provisions when on a voyage to Victoria. He was robbed by Scadgets led by S'Neitlam. Orders were immediately made to meet S'Neitlam with indifference on his next visit to the trade store.

News arrived that Chief Factor William Douglas was coming to the Fort. Immediately a new four poster bedstead was built for Douglas's use. Wren was finishing the bedstead when a letter arrived from Governor Lane dated May 17, 1849. He requested that the Trade Store stop selling ball and powder to the hostile Indians. Lane addressed part of the letter directly to the Chiefs. Dr. Tolmie read it aloud and translated for the natives assembled about the establishment. Mr. McAllister stood by as the witness for Governor Lane. The letter informed the Indians and the British alike that the American War Steamer *Massachusetts* had arrived at Vancouver with 150 artillerymen. Additionally, 600 Royal Dragoons were en route overland. They could be expected in August.

All the while the men of Fort Nisqually continued their daily chores. Swamp land soil was broken, new fur press construction continued, three flocks of sheep were washed and sheared, 14 bushes of potatoes were planted, and the kitchen garden seed, recently received from London, were sprouting nicely. Wren and Kalama built a new oak table to be used during Chief Factor Douglas' visit. Sheep shearing continued daily. Two new Catholic priests, Fathers Ricard and Lempit, arrived at Fort Nisqually, expecting to meet Douglas.

Planting crops and killing cattle continued well into the spring. Cattle not killed by the Company faced the same fate at the hands of the Indians and the Americans. At least the Company could market the meat, hides, hooves, horns, blood, and bones if the

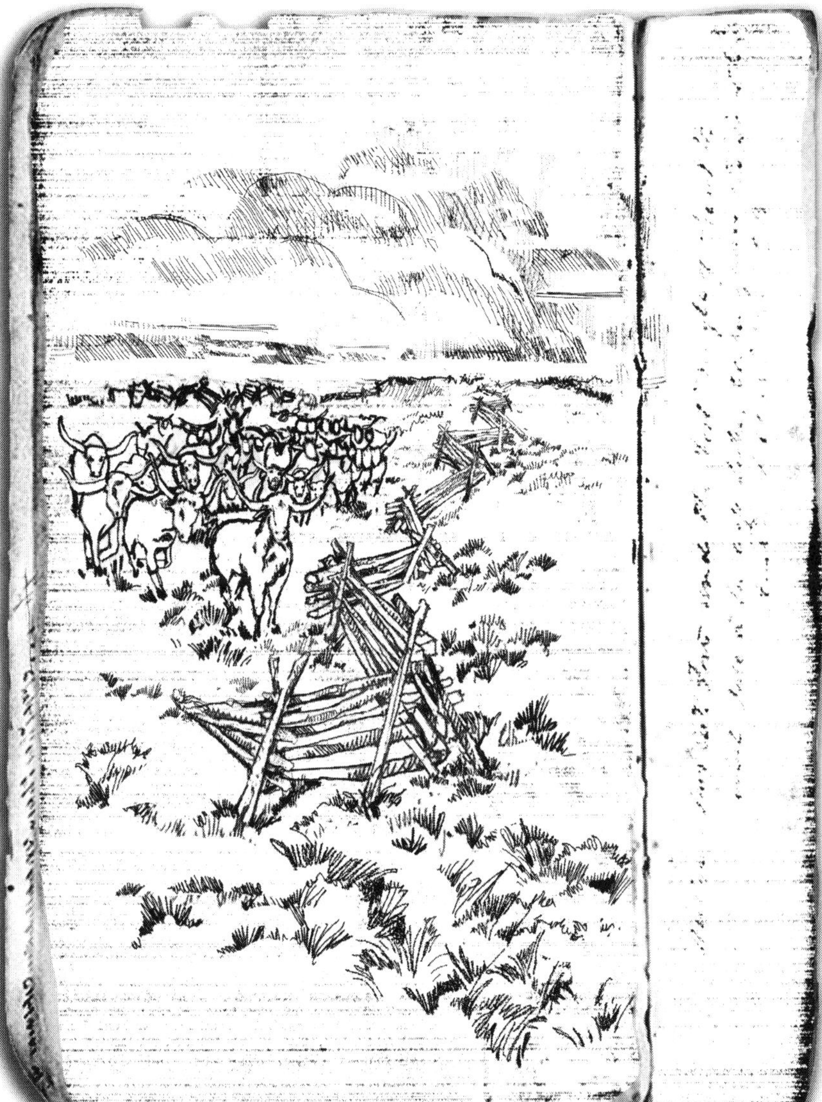

harvest was organized by the Company men. They found seven cattle hopelessly mired in the mud at Squally Lake. Two valuable working oxen were extricated and brought in. One with a broken leg was killed for meat. Nothing more could be done for the hapless five cows that remained stuck in the mud, without danger to the men.

Even with so many new events, the British were not all in "retreat" from the advancing Americans and increasingly hostile Indians. This was a case of a hard core Victorian morality struggling against the potential anarchy of vice and violence. Most of the Europeans, and even the Americans, were illiterate, but they knew their King James Bible and some of Shakespeare. Their minds were made up to advance civilization as they saw it.

On PSAC farms potatoes were planted for the first time at Mallard Hollow. A new foundation was laid for a new oven under the old Indian shed. Thibeault, Adam, and Lowe brought in some milk cows that had wandered away. The Soquamish traded 19 fur skins, so Wren began enlarging the old wool-press shed to make room for a new fur press.

Americans were sometimes helpful. Wren was having some difficulty converting the wool press to a larger fur press, so Glasgow, an American, was called in for assistance and consultation. After a hearty breakfast, the two men had the press in fine working order. They had packed a full bale of furs by nightfall. The next day Glasgow and Wren, with the help of two of the Islanders, made and installed a windlass for raising the inner extremity of the press lever. Other improvements had the press answering its call in fine fashion.

The 25th of May opened with a refreshing shower at sunrise. Three oxen were butchered on the expectation that Douglas and his traveling party would soon arrive. About 2 PM Mr. Chief Factor Douglas rode into the Fort on horseback accompanied by his three oldest daughters. They were followed by a parade of five wagons containing several cases of gold dust, many bales of furs and Douglas's personal property. Mrs. Douglas and the two younger children were in the last wagon, accompanied by Mr. MacArthur and W. Ross. That afternoon the population increased by at least fourteen at the Fort.

There were no slackers that night at Fort Nisqually. The Cowlitz wagons were offloaded and reloaded overnight. Douglas's cargo was replaced with 58 bushels of wheat, and the Cowlitz men were paid $40 for the work they had done, and were about to do, in transporting the Douglas family to the Fort and returning to the Cowlitz with saleable wheat. Dr. Tolmie estimated that the wheat would sell for 20 cents per bushel at Cowlitz, a higher price than possible at Nisqually at the time.

The Schooner *Cadboro* pulled up to the Nisqually Landing on May 28th. She discharged her supplies cargo. Wren went to work fitting the ship's hold for livestock, wool packs, fur packs and other sundry exports, such as hand-cut grass from the salt marsh. The grass would travel with the livestock for their benefit on board and arrival at Victoria.

Two men were also transferred with the cattle. Sandwich Islander Kahili and Mr. Wren were reassigned to Fort Victoria.

The livestock was loaded in the morning, allowing the schooner to prepare for afternoon departure with tide. Mr. Douglas, his family, Mr. MacArthur, and Father Lempit boarded the ship just after dinner. The schooner weighed anchor and was off. Apparently the American bull that Mr. Douglas bought at Ford's farm did not go to Victoria as planned. It had escaped from an enclosure over night and wandered away toward its favorite farm.

Governor Lane's message to the Indians about gunpowder and lead was delivered by Doctor Tolmie when Patakynum and his Snoqualmies camped on Kittson's Island. It was accepted with all the ceremony the Indians could bring. Tolmie heard their comments and replies, but suggested that the Indians be ready for a personal summons from the Governor.

The sheep shearing was continuing at a good clip producing 400 fleeces each day, most weighing nearly 6 pounds. The merino wool seemed the best, but the Chevriot and Leicester fleeces were as stout. The cross-bred animals produced fleeces weighing a little over 5 pounds on the average.

The *Cadboro* was back for a load of wool only a day before the chartered ship *Harpooner* arrived. She was carrying a contingent of 33 passengers. They were miners, settlers and some "mechanics". Tolmie entertained Captain Morice of the *Harpooner*, Captain Sangster of the *Cadboro*, and some Americans named Colonel Tayler, Mr. Lewis and Mr. Wallace, the brother of the one who had been shot. We can only imagine the conversation around Doctor Tolmie's elegant English dinner table.

Slocum, Linklater, Cowie, Kalama, Slugamas, Keava, Cush, Squally, Kahannui, a "gang" of Indian women, Lowe and Beinston were assigned to routine jobs repairing wagons, ploughing potatoes, weighing and pressing wool bales, clearing roads, hoeing, weeding, baling shingles, roofing the store, sweeping and clearing barns, clearing streams, at Sastuc, Yanalacows near Muck, McLeod's, Tenalquot, and at Tyrell's Lake. Whatever work they were doing it was difficult because of the smoky air. The Nisqually were burning the prairie grasses to clear away the dead grass and brush. This was an annual event that filled the air with smoke that hung in the still air. Winds could blow away the smoke, but made the fires less controllable. Calm days were best for burning grasses.

Two Sinahomish men were hired for some incidental work. On July 7th one was missing, but finally found dead. His partner, Joe, confessed to the murder. It seems they disagreed about something as they worked. Both decided to take a nap after the argument during the heat of the summer day. While sleeping Joe simply slit his friend's throat while he slept. There is no record of punishment.

Dr. Tolmie returned from a visit to Vancouver and Cowlitz only to leave again to help Mr. Chambers settle the estate of Joseph Heath. It was a two-day job, but finally the American tax system was satisfied. An auction was held on Wednesday, July 25, 1849, to liquidate Heath's estate. There was little work done that day as everyone, it seems, attended the auction. Prices were deemed "very good" but little was left for Heath's heirs after the taxes were paid. The exercise seemed to stimulate a need to count all of the Fort's cattle. Dr. Tolmie superintended the census taking at the Fort, until Mr. Tod and Tolmie left, again, for the Cowlitz.

John Ross was pretty badly hurt while setting up a corn shed. The Ross farm was part of the Establishment, but operated almost like private property, to occupy the land and prevent squatters from settling. The shed was being built of squared timbers. One piece of squared timber fell suddenly, slamming into Ross' leg just above the ankle. The leg bone was broken and quite painful. Slocum and six Indians completed the shed building job, even though Slocum was in mourning for his wife who died three days before. Ross' leg bone was set, splinted and a makeshift cast was set. He would never walk well again.

Cradles and carts had to be repaired because a large crew of about 60 Indians was hired to help the Fort men bring in the harvest. Oats, peas, corn, crops were ready at about the same time. It took many days of constant labor, with smoky hot weather. The oats were almost done, so some of the Indians were sent to break up the ground in the dried swamps. These would become farm fields the next season.

The new Indian Sub-Agent, Mr. Thorton, came to Nisqually from his office in Newmarket for the purpose of distributing some presents from the American government to various Indian Chiefs of the Sound. That day most were at Steilacoom pulling peas. Some were helping McLeod prepare the tobacco water for bathing lambs. The schooner was reported to be inward bound from Port Orchard.

The Indian Sub-agent, Judge Thorton, addressed the assembled representatives of the Scadgets, Sinahomish, Soquamish, Stichasamish and Nisqually people. The Chiefs and principle men were given blankets. Three Chiefs each got two three-point blankets; one also received a fathom of baize. About twenty others also received some baize. The next day the gifts were of a more moderate scale. Governor Lane had allowed only four hundred dollars for the gift giving budget. It was far from the amount the various treaties the previous Governor Stevens had negotiated. Judge Thornton had been accused of smuggled goods and selling liquor to the Indians along the Columbia, so there was some level of mistrust by Governor Lane.

In late August, with the wheat reapers advancing slowly, the artillery arrived. That is, Major Hathaway of a U.S. Artillery unit was assigned to the area. He was planning to set up an army post. Hathaway was accompanied by Mr. Lattie, of the HBC Marine Department. About dusk Captain Hill of the U.S. Artillery accompanied by several officers of his company arrived on the chartered barque *Harpooner*. Captain Morice of the *Harpooner* joined the party that stayed up until a late hour.

Major Hathaway proclaimed his intension of "surveying the river estuaries and harbors of the continental shore of Puget Sound." He needed a base from which to operate, so on August 24 Dr. Tolmie rode to Steilacoom as a guide for Hathaway and Captain Hill. He urged them to judge for themselves as to whether Steilacoom would form the best winter quarters for the troops. The number of buildings already erected impressed the Major, but he decided to engage S'Neitlam, the Scadgets Chief, to guide the survey of the shorelines. Captain Morice accompanied the Major on his survey.

The U.S. Army formally established Fort Steilacoom on August 27, 1849. Captain Bennett H. Hill commanded Company M of the First Artillery Regiment assigned to the new army post. The HBC negotiated a lease of PSAC property at Steilacoom for $50 per month.[234] This spot, one mile inland from a small bay north of the Fort Nisqually landing, was favored because there were existing buildings to become the winter quarters for the soldiers. The buildings were those constructed by Joseph Heath and used, however briefly, by the Red River settlers. The buildings were wooden shells of houses and log cabins. The troops soon added more buildings, at a total cost of $3,000.

The U.S. Army was soon making its presence known in the area on a regular basis. In October Fort Nisqually entertained visits from Lt. Dement; General Smith, Commander in Chief of the Pacific troops; Quartermaster Talmage, and Dr. A. I. Haden of the Steilacoom troops. Most visits were social calls. The Quartermaster ordered beef for the troops. That was business.

An account was set up and signed by Major Thornton for $421.26 for Indian presents and a second account for $20 for traveling expenses. Both accounts were counter-signed by Dr. Tolmie and sent under cover to Chief Factor Peter Skene Ogden at Fort Vancouver. Mr. Tod and Dr. Tolmie inspected the army officers' progress in moving to Steilacoom, and then offered any assistance that might have been required.

In the midst of the Americans moving in nearby, some British seamen were moving out. They seemed to have disappeared from the crew of the *Beaver*. Mr. Wright, the Chief Officer of the *Harpooner* arrived with Mr. Roderick Finlayson and Mr. Mowatt, Chief Officer of the *Mary Dare* and Mr. Joseph McKay and some other men. They were all in

---

[234] The rental fee of $600 per year was paid by the U.S. Government for 15 years. *Journal of Occurrences*, 1849.

pursuit of 8 seamen and one Canadian named Champagne. These men were runaways from the steamer and the *Mary Dare*.

Soon enough reports began to come in about strangers in the area. Mr. Ross reported that four white men were seen prowling about his place. Finlayson, Mowatt, McKay and Tolmie set out after the prowlers, but to no avail. Then the runaways were spotted at Steilacoom. Tolmie and Tod, with a posse of Indians, set out after them. Their intent was to reason with the men, to persuade them to return to their duties. The posse saw traces of the men but could not make contact. Word soon came that the Victoria runaways were seen on horseback at the Skookumchuck River on their way to Cowlitz.

The hunt for the missing men was apparently given up. Major Thornton, too, gave up finding a better locale than Steilacoom for his planned army post. Tolmie sent 30 three-point blankets to the soldiers at Steilacoom to be used as circumstances required. He suggested that the Americans would need to make gifts to the Snoqualmies for the shooting incident in May. It was common knowledge among the Nisqually that the Snoqualmies were coming to make a settlement for the deaths of three Indians—and now the Americans were in charge, so they were the responsible people in the Indian view. The death price would have to be paid, one way or another, peacefully or not.

The final settlement was typical of what had happened under HBC rules in years past. Nearly all of the Nisqually people engaged with the company were off to Steilacoom along with Tolmie and Tod. The settlement was concluded with six of the worst offenders being arrested and 80 blankets paid to various chiefs of the Snoqualmish tribe. The six offenders named were: Whyeek, Qullawout, Copass, Tahawat, Quillawowt, and Tatam.

With new American legal authority, the first full term of an American court was held at Fort Steilacoom on the third Monday in October, 1849. Chief Justice Bryan of the First Judicial Court of Oregon presided. The six Snoqualmie Indians were on trial for the death of Leander Wallace. Two Indians, Copass and Quillawowt, were convicted of the murder of Wallace and subsequently hanged at 4 PM, Wednesday, October 2, 1849. American frontier justice had arrived on the shores of Puget Sound.

Other accounts were settled at about this time, too. Captain Morice, perhaps with more knowledge about Company affairs than most, presented Dr. Tolmie with $11,000 to settle various accounts and different debts. In a few days Dr. Tolmie called all of the men in from their outstation assignments. John M. McCleod from Muck Creek, John Montgomery from Spanueh, Peter Wilson a carpenter, Edward Shearer sheep herder, and Mathew Nelson from Tenalquot, came to the understanding that their account balances had to improve. Tolmie laid down the law. He explained that he had just received orders from Mr. Douglas to raise wages to £15 for two men and to £20 for three of them, but bills for their outstanding balances up to the previous June had to be paid first. Tolmie told them he did not feel justified in granting the raises given the bills due. He also told them that if the Company was to be bought out (as the Treaty of 1846 stated) before their contracts expired they would all be paid in full whereby the Company would sustain the loss and damages. If they were to leave the service to the Company before the end of their individual contracts they would forfeit all unpaid wages.

The men were unanimous in rejecting the offer, each one unconditionally demanding $100 per month to be paid monthly or they would all leave the Company. They were using an American wage as an example. Tolmie replied that he had no authority to pay more or change the offer in any way. He dictated to them that their demand was dishonorable conduct. They were given to understand that leaving their posts before the end of their contracts would cause the loss of all unpaid wages. Their labor was very much needed at the peak of the harvest season. All five men gave Dr. Tolmie notice that they would return in three days to give up their responsibilities and any Company tools they had been issued.

On the appointed day all five men left the Company. In addition Mr. Moatt's contract ran out so he left the service of the Company too. He announced his intention to seek his fortune in the California gold fields.

The Nisqually Landing was pretty active in late October. The *Cadboro* discharged a load of sugar before it sailed for Newmarket with passengers. She was replaced the next day at the dock by the *Collooney*. Captain Sanster reported three from his crew had deserted over night. Dr. Tolmie agreed to board the *Collooney* for the short voyage to Newmnarket, in search of the deserters. Once in town they learned that the Company's most recent designees had joined with the three runaways from the *Cadboro* and the *Collooney*.

Dr. Tolmie returned to Fort Nisqually without recovering the deserters.

Dr. Tolmie shipped a load of shingles aboard the *Collooney*. Most of the men at the Fort helped in filling the ship with bales of shingles. Tolmie often bought the shingles from Americans who needed work for trade store credit. Typical prices of the prices paid for shingles was 10 cents per bundle. A bundle was defined as the number of shingles a man could carry on his shoulder. Dr. Tolmie sold the shingles in San Francisco during the California Gold Rush for a substantial profit; about seventeen cents per bundle. It was a relatively new aspect of the HBC enterprise on Puget Sound.

Other business included the sale of live cows. The Nisqually herd was prolific. Selling some made business sense. Some were butchered then sold as meat to the American troops. Others were sold on the hoof to growing American herds. Mr. Thomas Glasgow, the squatter close to the Fort, had paid for ten cows, their calves and two bullocks in the spring. The Fort had to deliver, it was already late October. The cattle were wild, and that is an understatement. Two Americans, Glasgow and Chambers, came to help the Fort cowboys round up the wild herd. It was a tough job. Around noon Ross was pressed for assistance. Mr. Jones of Newmarket came to purchase two more cows. He stepped in to help the round-up. Finally all of the cows and the two bullocks were roped and the cattle drive to Glasgow's farm began. The next day four of Glasgow's new cows were loose, and he was very annoyed. They returned to their favorite areas on Fort Nisqually grazing plains.

Adam Beinston may have felt his assignment—to shoot beef cattle, was the easier job. It probably was until his gun burst, lacerating his left thumb. Within three weeks Dr. Tolmie diagnosed Beinston with "alarmingly severe Traumatic Tetanus." The patient was becoming very weak. He wrote a Will in favor of his two sons and appointed Thomas Linklater executor of the will and guardian of the children.[235]

Glasgow was back at Fort Nisqually in a few days. He came to inform Dr. Tolmie that the Company should stay off his land which he claimed to commence at the Nisqually sawpit and running northward so as to enclose much of Sequalitchew Creek. He handed Tolmie a hand-written note to detail the claim. Tolmie refused to accept the paper. The Company Factor informed Glasgow that he was trespassing on the lands of the Puget Sound Agricultural Company. Glasgow's claim was probably, given the location described, the same property where the Nisqually Methodist Mission had stood 1839—1842. Perhaps it really was "American land," originally taken directly from the Indians before Fort Nisqually was moved up and inland to the prairie the year after the Mission was closed. Of course the Methodist Mission relinquished any land claim after the arson fire burned them out.

Two days later Thomas M. Chambers rode by the Fort toward Steilacoom where he proceeded to mark off a claim in his son's name on still more Company land. He included in this claim the excellent mill site at the mouth of Steilacoom Creek (today's Chambers Creek and Bay). Tolmie planned to set Chambers' mind concerning the illegal claim, too. The doctor searched for Chambers but the man was off in the woods tracing his claim. He could not, nor would not, be found.

The ship *Inez*, Captain Mosher, arrived at the landing. She was guided to shore by Glasgow. Captain Mosher sat with Tolmie for a couple of hours then spent the night with Glasgow. The boat crew was fed and put up for the night at Fort Nisqually. It seems the *Inez* was sent by Mr. Fruit in San Francisco to buy lumber and shingles from Col.

---

235 Beinston survived to eventually desert the Hudson's Bay Company in 1852. *Journal of Occurrences*

Simmons with Glasgow somehow participating in the business arrangement. The next day Tolmie took an aggressive stand against Glasgow. Tolmie told Glasgow in the presence of witnesses (Captain Mosher, Col. Simmons, Charles Ross, and Adam Beinston) that Glasgow was trespassing on Company land. Glasgow, in turn, warned against any further Company improvements to "his land."

The Sandwich Islanders were "neglecting their work." Dr. Tolmie investigated and found them and some soldiers drunk on the beach. They had discovered that the American ship brought in by Glasgow had a crew willing to traffic in liquor. Dr. Tolmie talked to the Captain of the *Inez*. Tolmie offered to pay Captain Mosher one dollar per head to transport 1,000 sheep to Victoria as freight. Mosher declined the generous offer. The next day Tolmie demanded the immediate and complete settling of accounts of the *Inez*, her captain and crew. Tolmie also sent a gift of three mutton carcasses to Captain Corser and the crew of the ship *General Patterson*, to be certain the *Inez* did not receive a gift, but witnessed one given.

Three Sandwich Islanders and their wives boarded the *Inez* as she weighed anchor and shoved off. Five days later they returned, having quit the *Inez* at Port Orchard. All three, Cowie, Kalama, and Keave'haccow, returned to work for the Company. The first day back they repaired a cart and built a new one to serve as its partner. They were no longer "neglecting their work."

By December 6, the soldiers had turned Heath's farm into a nearly complete military post, with a hospital, a storehouse, a guardhouse, a bake house, and two officers' quarters. The artillery soldiers simply bivouacked on the easily established parade grounds in front of the officers' quarters.

The arrival of the soldiers may have had something to do with the first United States coinage being produced in Oregon City. Soldiers had to be paid. The Oregon Exchange Company was authorized to mint $5 and $10 gold pieces. The coin had a beaver's image on the face. They were made of "natural gold and quite soft."

Dr. Tolmie handed out the Christmas Regale as usual. It was the same as the year before, except that some of the beef was a bit tainted, so all were warned to smoke-dry it right away. Christmas Day was spent quietly at Fort Nisqually for all hands except Mr. Tod who dined with the Army officers at Steilacoom

The New Year's Regale seemed to be an interruption. It was a poor work-day weather-wise, but Cowie was roofing the stable and Kalama was repairing a bateau. Again the Islanders were not neglecting their chores. About mid-day Tolmie passed out the treats.

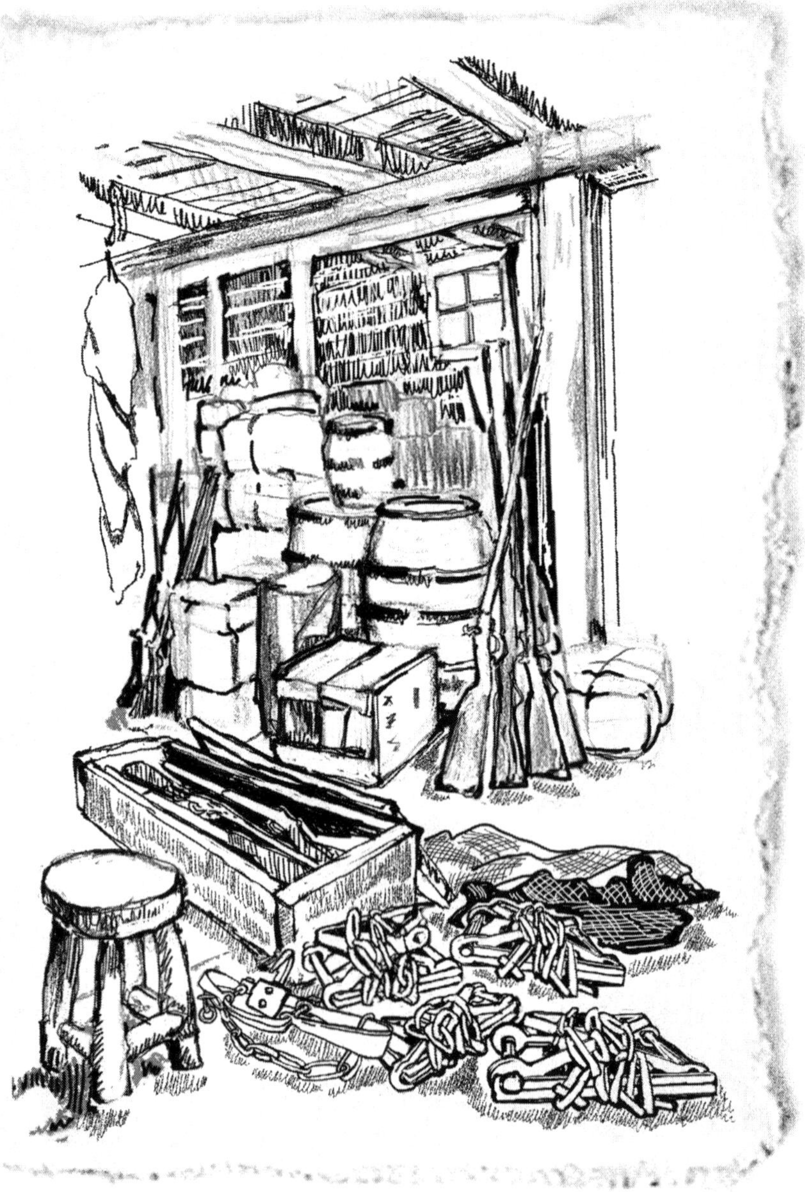

1850

DR. TOLMIE ASSISTED Mrs. Kalama in delivering a fine stout boy on January 15th. A few days later, the Mr. Kalama and the other Islanders were off to the Steilacoom forest to cut timbers for a log house 30 x 18 feet. After the baby's delivery, Tolmie visited the sick soldiers' hospital before he sailed for Victoria. Mr. Tod took charge for about a month during which time the *Journal of Occurrences* seems to have been neglected.

In Victoria, Tolmie surely heard talk of the changes in preferred headgear for fashionable gentlemen of London. It wasn't about the hat's height, nor was it the new collapsible versions known as chapeaux claques. Most gentlemen still clung to the time honored beaver hats, but in 1850, Royal Consort Prince Albert began wearing a top hat made of "hatters[236] plush," a fine silk shag material. Things changed quickly in men's fashions. It was a trend that would put a practical end to the North American beaver-pelt industry.

Tolmie had apparently overcome the old world tradition of racial superiority to see Native Americans as God's children, certainly, but still of a lesser human status than whites. Tolmie's diary mentions the marriage of " *half-breed woman*" to an HBC man as "...*the most prudent plan which could be adopted*..." after which he writes "*a wife is the only being to whom one could unreservedly pour out his soul, but one with whom could be enjoyed a sweet communion of mind is not to be met in this country.*"[237] At one time he lamented the necessity of a wife for a gentleman in the wilderness, where, there is a

---

236 Mad Hatters, a phrase made famous by Lewis Carroll's 1865 novel "Alice's Adventures in Wonderland" actually referred to the physical disorder hatters acquired after working too long with a mercury solution used in the felting process. Breathing mercury fumes caused lung damage, but also affected the nervous system and brain, eventually resulting in dementia, memory loss, paralysis and death. In the USA the disease was known as the Danbury Shakes, since most American top hats were manufactured in Danbury, Connecticut. Laws were eventually passed that required proper ventilation. Mad Hatter Disease, http://en.wikipedia.org

237 Tolmie Diary, Vol. 3, page 108 (January 2, 1834) as quoted by Stuart, Walter Henry, *"Some Aspects of the Life of William Fraser Tolmie"* Master of Arts Thesis in History, University of British Columbia, September, 1948, on microfilm at the University of Washington Library, Seattle, WA https://circle.ubc.ca/bitstream...UBC_1949_A8%20S78%20S6.pdf

decided lack of "polished female society."[238] Still, Jane Work, Métis daughter of an Irish fur trader and a Native American, won his heart.

In full view of the frontier peccadilloes of other fur traders, Tolmie remained a moral, single man for many years before requesting a furlough in 1850 for the expressed purpose to "get a wife which a farmer above all men requires."[239]

Upon his return from England, female attraction appeared in Tolmie's life in the form of Jane Work, the daughter of John Work. Jane was born at Fort Colville on Christmas Day, 1827, less than four years before Tolmie signed on with the HBC at age twenty-one. Tolmie gradually reduced his idealism and apparently any remaining racial superiority. In 1839 he wrote to the Reverend Jason Lee in Portland requesting that Jane Work be admitted to the Methodist School as he, Tolmie, had a "…peculiar interest in that young lady's education…"

Early in the year and above all else, Dr. Tolmie seemed concerned with the snow on the ground and the accounts-receivable from American customers. In late January, however, he remained in Victoria for approximately six weeks to visit John Work and his family. Tolmie was particularly interested in the young Jane Work, the daughter of Tolmie's host. During that festive time in Victoria, Tolmie planned his marriage to Miss Work. The Reverend Robert John Staines, ordained by the Church of England, and serving as Chaplain of the Hudson's Bay Company, officiated at the Tolmie-Work wedding ceremony on February 19, 1850.

Rev. Staines' parishioners were scattered from Fort Vancouver and Fort Nisqually to the south of the new international boundary, to all Company outposts north of that border. Reverend Staines also served the United States Garrison at Fort Steilacoom until his accidental death by drowning in 1854. The Church of England sent his replacement, who did not serve south of the border in American territory.

Doctor Tolmie left Mr. C. T. Tod in charge while being married in Victoria. When he returned to Fort Nisqually he found the place was suddenly in "hot water." Soon after his return in late February aboard the *Cadboro*, Tolmie welcomed the brig *Sacramento* which was now chartered to carry shingles from the Company to San Francisco. The cedar shingle business was a stellar success. Passengers were also aboard the *Sacramento*, but rumors of deserting American soldiers being stowed away on one of the ships were proven (temporarily) false, to the satisfaction of Lt. Osborne, U.S. Army, who searched the vessel with First Mate Dixon.

---

238 Ibid., p.111

239 Letterbook, W.F. Tolmie to Sir George Simpson, 10 March 1848, as quoted in Stuart, Walter Henry, Thesis, 1948.

More hot water, or perhaps "hot air," came from the honorable Samuel R. Thurston, Oregon Territorial Delegate to the United States Congress, who accused Tolmie of being a foreigner interfering in local Indian affairs during the Leander Wallace affair. Thurston objected to the fact that Tolmie had offered 80 blankets as a reward for the surrender of the Indians who shot Wallace. But Governor Lane had ordered Tolmie to do just that. The Indians recognized the blankets as HBC merchandise, then thanked Tolmie personally. The fact that Lane had made the order was lost to the Indians, and apparently to Thurston, as well. Thurston accused Tolmie of making a continuing effort to sway the Indians to the British "side" and told the Department of the Interior (Bureau of Indian Affairs) of his suspicions.

Tolmie formally protested the charge, with support from U.S. Army Captain Hill of Fort Steilacoom, stating that the blankets were purchased from, but not distributed by, Fort Nisqually. There was no other source of 80 blankets outside of the U.S. Army issues requisitioned from an eastern supply depot. Ordering, obtaining military command approvals, and transporting new army blankets would have taken weeks, perhaps months, and arrived much later in the year. The effectiveness of such a late distribution would have diminished the intent. The controversy seemed to disappear, but the anti-British political sentiment remained with most Americans. HBC blankets were large symbols of British presence when used as gifts.

Another twist in the story relating to Leander Wallace's death is the subsequent death of Nisqually Chief Lahalet. He may have been involved in the surrender of the six Snoqualmie accused of killing Wallace. Lahalet helped negotiate peace between the Nisqually and the Snoqualmie. The main ingredient for peace was established by the marriage of Lahalet's son to a daughter of a Snoqualmie Chief. If his son mistreated his new wife, it was an intertribal problem for which Lahalet was responsible as Chief[240] of the Nisqually. It was his duty and honor to protect his daughter-in-law from abuse.

The Snoqualmie Chief, Patkamin, originally came to Lahalet to check on the rumors of mistreatment of his daughter, who was Lahalet's wife. He brought the angry armed band of his people along to enforce that sacred marriage agreement. These marriages were essential to inter-tribal peace. During the confusion surrounding the gun fire at the gate, Lahalet may have helped Patkamin escape from inside the fort.

After the fracas at the gate, the Snoqualmies, who were suspected of killing Wallace, were brought in, tried in the American court, found guilty, and quickly hanged. This last set of events the Snoqualmies blamed on Lahalet. According to well established

---

240 Use of the title "Chief" is an American term not attributed to the Native Americans of Puget Sound in the author's experience.

tradition, he had to pay the death price, because the "marriage-peace treaty" had been broken by deaths of Snoqualmies.

The exact time and cause of Lahalet's death remains a mystery. Even the certainty of his burial place is unknown. Tolmie refers to Lahalet's demise as "the supposed effects of a carouse."[241] Today's politics might call this the "cover story." There is no reason to think the unusual timing of Lahalet's sudden death, and clandestine burial, was not revenge for his participation in the surrender of those two Snoqualmie convicted and executed by the American court for the death of Leander Wallace.

Oregon Territory was formed in 1848 when President Polk signed the Organic Act. Olympia's first official U.S. Post Office was opened in the town formerly called Newmarket. Oregon Territory included all of what now is Washington State and much more. The Oregon Provisional Government land ordinances remained in effect until Congress passed the Donation Land Act, which was signed into law by President Millard Fillmore on September 27, 1850. That law, sponsored by Oregon Territory Congressional Delegate Samuel R. Thurston, allowed married adult couples to claim a full square mile, and, after four years of occupancy, to receive a patent (ownership certificate) as a free gift of a generous nation.

Because wives could claim land, and because there was a "shortage" of eligible women, some very young (age 10 and up) girls became "brides." Parents allowed the arrangement to help a neighbor, or perhaps even accepted a quiet payment. It is presumed that some of the marriages were never consummated in any manner. Marriage licenses were not issued, required, or even available. Many of these "marriages" were never documented anywhere but the land office records, often without the "wife" ever appearing. There was actually very little legal authority of any kind, even after the place became an 'organized' United States Territory.

A total of 7,437 patents (land claims) were issued under the Donation Land Claim Act of 1850 before its expiration on December 1, 1855.[242] Oregon City area residents filed 5,289 of those claims. Clearly land seekers took full advantage of the law's allowance of

---

241 Carpenter, Cecelia Svinth, *Fort Nisqually, A Documented History of Indian and British Interaction*, Tahoma Research, Tacoma, WA, 1986.

242 Sumner, Esther, "You Can't Just Take Land...Can You?" Ancestry, September / October 2007.
"Squatters rights seem more like lore and legend than something legal (but) they are very much a fact of law today, just as they were 200 years ago. Squatter's rights are known legally as adverse possession, the act of taking title of owner-absent private land, provided certain conditions are met. These include living on the property for a specified period of time (as short as five years), openly remaining there while keeping others out, treating the land as if it were owned, and gaining access without breaking and entering. Author's notes.

"back dating" claims up to three years. Only 58 claims were granted in 1851, and only 117 in 1852. The land office received claims from 3,134 people qualified to receive certificates by virtue of residence in Oregon before December 1, 1850.

After the cutoff date, land was sold at $1.25 per acre with a limit of 320 acres in any one claim. Over the years the price was increased and the size of the plot reduced. The Homestead Act of 1862 replaced all of the Donation Land Claims laws with more stringent and precise legal language.

Captain Lafayette Balch sailed from Bath, Maine, reaching Puget Sound in 1850. He brought with him previously sawed lumber, which he used to erect on his donation land claim, the first building in what he named the City of Steilacoom. It was, in nearly every sense of the word, a prefabricated house. For a while it was the only house of any kind in Steilacoom.

John B. Chapman filed a claim adjacent to Balch's. Both men competitively encouraged settlement of Steilacoom. The name may have come from the Indian word Tchilac-cum meaning "pink flower."

Fort Nisqually was expanding again in 1850. The "new" granary was being erected.[243] The old granary was pulled down, and apparently some of the squared timbers of that earlier building were used in the "new" one. Often old, still serviceable, timbers were used in new configurations, showing the value of the squared timber with post and sill design. It is possible the floor planks were cut at Simmons' mill in Tumwater. Several entries in the *Journal of Occurrences* tell of men hauling planks from the beach. One can theorize that the planks were cut by 'machine' in Tumwater, lashed into a 'raft,' then floated with an outgoing tide to Sequalitchew Creek and the beach at Fort Nisqually. By December the new granary was nearly complete and in place. Only the flooring remained to be completed by Jean Baptiste Chalifoux, the Fort carpenter.[244]

As yields increased, additional storage space was needed for the agricultural products that had become such a large part of the business of PSAC at Fort Nisqually. The

---

243 The Granary is on the National Registry of Historic Sites and now stands at the reconstructed site of Fort Nisqually Living History Museum in Tacoma's Point Defiance Park. It is owned by the Metropolitan Park District of Tacoma. The particular building referred to is the oldest standing wooden structure in the Puget Sound region, and one of the oldest buildings in the state.

244 "At Fort Nisqually there wasn't a building, wall, water trough, or wool press that didn't bear the handiwork of J. B. Chalifoux." Watson, Bruce McIntyre, *A Biographical Dictionary of Fur Traders Working West of the Rockies, 1793-1858"* University of British Columbia, Kelowna, British Columbia, Canada, 2010, p. 257.

granary[245] was called Store No. 2 to differentiate it from the Large Store and the Beach House/Store. All were storage facilities and were augmented by several root cellars. Today we might call all of them warehouses. Grain, flour, potatoes and peas were stored in each of these buildings, along with an inventory of trade goods and recently purchased beaver pelts. All were used for the extensive PSAC import-export business.

In all of these buildings, barrels, kegs, crates, boxes, buckets, bags and packs were stacked to the rafters. Technically a "barrel" is just one size of cask. In cooper's language a barrel is a cask of 36 gallons. Smaller casks are the Kilderkin (18 gallons), the Firkin (9 gallons) and the Pin (41/2 gallons). Casks larger than a barrel include the Hogshead (54 gallons), the Puncheon (72 gallons), and the Butt (108 Galloons). All sizes were apparently utilized in transporting goods to and from Fort Nisqually.

The cooperage at Fort Langley was the likely source of all sizes of shipping-containers leaving the northwest. Some containers were paraffin lined, and some were charred to seal the interior. Some kegs had hinged tops, while others came with wooden stands to facilitate horizontal uses. Some had wooden spigots.

Fort Nisqually casks of the barrel size were primarily used for shipping processed meats. "Prime Pork" and flour are mentioned in 1854 accounts. Half barrels of dried apples and peaches, trapper prepared pelts, and kegs of ox chain, lead bars, garden tool heads, and cut nails were also shipped to Fort Nisqually in barrels. Often "country produce" is the journal entry for the filled casks. That term would presumably include wheat, rye, barley, beef, pork, mutton, butter, ox meat, peas and potatoes. All were produced in abundance at PSAC farms.

It is likely that the various storehouses were used as receiving stations as well. Incoming shipments were offloaded from the sailing vessels and stored until needed. Various trade items found in the journal lists at least 19 different items, including "brushes and shaving boxes, files, thimbles, combs, gunflints, trowsers, pewter, mirrors, etc."

Account books mention bags and bales of usually soft items such as clothing (which was wrapped around items like writing paper and single padlocks). Molasses was usually shipped in large casks, often with breakables in the molasses for protection. Window glass and dishes were literally shipped in the barrels of molasses. The molasses was warmed to make it more liquid, the fragile items were slipped into the thick substance. Then all of it was packed away. The molasses cooled, hardened and protected the fragile items. At the destination the molasses could be dissolved in hot water, which was

---

245 By definition a granary is a storehouse for threshed grain. In England the term "corn-house, root house, barley house" are all terms referring to an enclosure for storage of crops and produce. *English Agriculture in 1850-51*, Sir James Caird, Longman, Brown, Green, and Longmans, 1852 London.

captured to use in sweetening coffee or tea.

The account books mention "pieces" quite often. This term refers to the items gathered together to make an "outfit." Each piece was marked by year, destination, and inventory number. An item coming to Fort Nisqually might be marked:

49
FN#18

That shorthand means "in 1849, Box Number eighteen was destined for Fort Nisqually." Typically each piece weighed about 90 ponds, as that was the weight a man could carry over a portage easily. It was also a size that fit well, when matched, on each side of a pack horse or mule. This weight was also useful aboard ships. Accurate weight meant the cargo could be distributed evenly across the cargo hold of the ship. An unbalance load could spell disaster on the ocean or traveling overland.

Small scales were used to determine the weight of small items to be inserted into the pieces, but a steelyard or scale was used to establish the weight of the entire piece. It could also weigh heavy items weighing hundreds of pounds.

There were many Indians on the plains. Just north of what is now Parkland they gathered la camas roots and wild sunflower roots and seeds. They often dug a pit six feet across and three or four feet deep. After it was lined with stones, a fire was built in the cavity and kept hot for at least a day. With the ashes removed, the pit was quickly lined with ferns and the center filled with the gathered "la camas" roots. The root pile was covered with ferns and a layer of soil. After several days of steaming in the pit oven, the "kalse" became a sweet, juicy, and nutritious food. Most was packed away in baskets for the winter meals, that usually included clams, salmon, and dried berries for variety.

Sunflower roots were brewed to make strong liquor. Kinnikinnick leaves were dried, pulverized and mixed with tobacco for a "sensation similar to those produced by opium" according to the *Herald*. Dried gweduc (pronounced gooeyduck) was consumed in winter, also. Dried berries and dried salmon eggs were mixed to form a favorite winter dish, as were dandelion leaves, squelips (a wild plant like parsnips) and wapatos, or spay-koolts. Another favorite was the roasted bracken fern, beaten into a coarse, starchy meal which was mixed with salmon eggs and set aside to "ripen." It produced an odor decidedly undelightful, to most white people.

In 1850 the 267 soldiers (the number of men varied over time) and officers at Fort Steilacoom ate quite differently than the Indians. The Army purchased salt pork, fresh beef, and mutton from Fort Nisqually. It was sold in "rations" of 334 pounds of salt pork or 200 pounds of fresh beef or mutton. Each soldier was allotted a personal ration of 1¼ pound of salt pork, or ¾ pound of fresh beef. There is little mention of vegetables in the Army diet, but we can assume potatoes and bread were staples. These rations are somewhat equal to the food quantities Fort Nisqually men received.

Thomas Chambers built a grist mill on his claim, along what is now Chambers Creek. A small dam backed up water for a mill pond in the lower reaches of the creek. It was clearly in view of Fort Nisqually on Company land. Dr. Tolmie wrote letters to the Americans, Thomas Chambers, Thomas Glasgow, and many others, concerning their trespassing on Company land. He also wrote letters to Captain Hill, at Fort Steilacoom, and Governor Lane, in Olympia.

Tolmie wrote to John Chambers concerning the Company property that was sold at the Heath estate auction. Tolmie wanted compensation for Company things sold as if they were Heath's personal property. In question, too, was the debt Heath owed to the Company. At first Chambers was hesitant, then downright opposed, to any such dealings. He disdained discussions of the matter. He claimed that Judge Skinner told him that all his actions were legal in having officiated in the Heath estate sale. Chambers would have nothing more to do with the affair. He refused to put his statement in writing. He refused to let Tolmie write it out for him to sign. He refused to have witnesses hear his statement. Tolmie did convince Chambers that at least a letter to Heath's brother in England should be sent to explain the situation. To this Chambers did agree.

When Tolmie wrote a letter valuing the Heath property and requesting Chambers' signature, Chambers simply pocketed the paper without reading it. He offered to reply soon. Tolmie wrote out the details of the Chambers response, asking for a legal opinion of the validity of Chambers position from Chief Factor Peter Skene Ogden at Vancouver. Ogden agreed with Tolmie, but the American judge agreed with Chambers.

At the same time, the Company was realizing the tenuous nature of maintaining possession of Company farms at Tenalquot and Tyrell's Lake. The employee at Tenalquot, Thomas Linklater, was removed from his command after all the sheep had been removed from there to Victoria. The potatoes at Tyrell's Lake were a different matter. After the spuds were dug up, the fields were ploughed and wheat was seeded. Geography seems to have made the difference. Tenalquot was south of the Nisqually River, but Tyrell's Lake was north of the river. Perhaps Tolmie was simply consolidating the Company lands in a more "defendable" position between the Nisqually and Puyallup Rivers.

Company needs were met at Muck. The farm site center was moved a mile west (toward the Fort) and a new house built. A new dwelling house was built at Tlithlow, too. PSAC operations were not backing down to American encroachment.

HBC seemed to be doing the same sort of consolidations. Fort Vancouver was being phased out, in spite of the fact that the Board of Governors resided at Vancouver. A replacement of Dr. John McLoughlin, who retired in 1846, was not made because most of the fur trade had already moved north of the border (to Victoria) as prices declined in the European markets. There would be one last "British Huzzah" for the fur trade in American Territory, and that would be at Fort Nisqually in 1855.

At Cowlitz Farms, Edward Warbass filed a Donation Land Claim, laid out a town site, and named it after himself. Soon there was a store and a hotel among several buildings directly adjacent to Cowlitz Landing. Warbass became the U.S. Postmaster, but the name was changed to the historic Cowlitz Landing when the two competing villages merged. Warbass added the duties of County Auditor until 1856, and continued as Postmaster until 1858, when he left for the Fraser River gold rush.

Many American soldiers were ill in January, 1850. The weather was not kind to them. Dr. Tolmie called on the Army sickbay, in the absence of Dr. Haden, who had gone to Vancouver temporarily. Three inches of snow on the ground must have made the visits more of a chore.

The *Pleiades* took on 900 pounds of potatoes in exchange for 450 pounds of rice. It was a fair trade that benefited the ship's crew and the trade store by giving both a highly desired alternative food supply.

The *HMS Driver* arrived from Victoria with Governor Blanchard as passenger. He was at Fort Nisqually to purchase a cargo of cattle and sheep for the infant colony on Vancouver's Island. Dr. Tolmie entertained the Governor and the deck officers from the *Sacramento, Pleiades,* and the *Driver* at his tiny cottage. The main topic of discussion was the fact that two American soldiers had deserted the U.S. Army on board the recently departed *Cadboro,* just as Lt. Osborne had suspected earlier. It appeared to the Americans that the British had facilitated the deserters. The British were in a tight spot. The spot would get tighter.

Hiding stowaways on the *Cadboro* was easier than loading cattle aboard the *Driver.* Three attempts were made to "park" the cattle, with no satisfactory result, before the first of 85 head were finally on board. Tolmie was not there to supervise, as he was writing to Captain Hill regarding the garrison's deserters. Finally, the next day, a full complement of 800 sheep were loaded, and paid for, in time for a 4 pm departure for Victoria.

Three Islanders quit their jobs abruptly in March. First they refused their daily rations, then Cowie, Kalama, and Kewwa removed their personal things from the fort dwelling house, moving to Indian-style mat lodges outside the Fort. No reason was given for the sudden change of employment. Speculation is that the pay rate was in dispute. Contracts were signed and enforced, so HBC would not have raised pay rates, but Americans offered a higher rate without a contract or housing. The wage comparisons were probably at the heart of the disagreement.

Trade store cash flow seems to have been adequate in the spring of 1850. The Government Account, which referred to Fort Steilacoom purchases, took in $729. The *Pleiades* Account received $235. The *Contra* Account added another $144.46. The *Sacramento* and the *Orbit* also settled positive accounts, but lumber and shingle prices in California were depressed. Some ships from California were speculating in Newmarket with surplus goods. The *Cadboro* account seems to have had an outstanding balance due when a boat load of Indians arrived as passengers. They had been employed by the Company elsewhere, and now were assigned to Fort Nisqually. Tolmie immediately put them to work discharging the *Cadboro* cargo.

The one passenger on board the *Cadboro* was Mr. Edward Huggins. He was under contract for one year as a clerk and shop man.[246] A French Canadian, Louis Trudelle, one Orkney man, and two Englishmen were also added to the roster of workers at Fort Nisqually. With four new 'Gentlemen class' servants of the company, all seemed well for the moment at least.

Before the *Cadboro* could be completely offloaded of her cargo, Captain Hill, U.S. Army, arrived to seize the ship for non-payment of U.S. import duties. Captain Hill informed Dr. Tolmie that the ship would be detained until Mr. Dorr, the Customs Officer, arrived from Oregon City, about 150 miles away. Until his arrival, the ship would be formally seized.

Fully armed U.S. soldiers, commanded by Lt. Dement, took possession of the ship, even hauling down the British flag. Captain Sangster, Master of the *Cadboro*, protested the seizure. He was assisted by Mr. Denny, an American, who tried to assure the soldiers that the ship was prepared to pay the duties as soon as an official Custom House and Collector was established on Puget's Sound. There was not, at the time, any person properly authorized to do the customs business. The ship was moved to Steilacoom. Mr. Dixon, First Mate and Mahon, a Sandwich Islander cook, as well as the entire crew, were ordered off the *Cadboro* by Captain Hill. They were told to seek quarters from Dr. Tolmie.

Captain Sangster asked for assistance as he took inventory of the ship's rigging, sails, shore boats, anchors, oars, and other equipment. Huggins was sent to help, but was prevented from boarding. Armed soldiers told him he could not come aboard without orders from Captain Hill. Huggins needed an officially written note requesting the reason

---

246 Huggins lived at Fort Nisqually longer than any other individual, with the possible exception of his wife Letitia, who was Dr. Tolmie's daughter. Author's comment.

for boarding. Tolmie sent just such a note the next day. By afternoon, having not received a reply, Tolmie rode to Steilacoom to call on Captain Hill in person. He obtained a "drummer boy" as an escort and permission to board the ship to talk with her captain. After a few hours Tolmie and Sangster agreed it was best for both men to leave the ship as no harm could come to the Company's interests.

Only two days later, about 1 pm, April 19, Mr. Dorr and Captain Hill arrived at the fort. Tolmie offered wine and cake, which was consumed before the party adjourned to the beach storehouse. Once there, Captain Hill proceeded to confiscate all of the imported goods in the building. He took everything, from Victoria wheat to sea salt. He said he was uncertain about seizing the salt but would obtain full knowledge by the morrow. He was also uncertain about a keg that Tolmie said was nails made at Fort Nisqually. Hill broke the keg open, only to find nails. Hill agreed that some of the contents of the store should not be seized. He declined to take the flour, hoes, and lumber, as these were obviously locally produced. He did, however, seize the key to the door. Hill gave the key to Glasgow, as custodian, so there could be easy access should it be required.

Dr. Tolmie asked for the invoice and bill of lading,[247] but was told that there was no manifest, hence the Americans would keep the invoice and bill of lading. Tolmie could have a copy made at his own expense.

Mr. Dorr then read the instructions, which required him to seize any vessel found in violation of the U.S. Revenue Laws, in particular the *Cadboro* and the *Beaver*. He was empowered to enter and examine any building that he suspected of containing smuggled goods. At that point he demanded the keys to the Trade Store and the large storehouse. He seized the contents that had landed since the ratification of the Boundary Treaty in 1846. As a courtesy, and to avoid a gang of disgruntled Indians, Dorr allowed Tolmie to take some goods for the payment of Indian day laborers.

The next day all of the goods in the Trade Store were moved to the large store and a Customs House Seal was placed on the door. Tolmie left for Victoria to consult with Chief Factor Douglas about the "doings of the U.S. authorities at this place." James Sangster was left in charge. He signed to certify the copies of the inventory of the seized goods. Thomas Glasgow seems to have become an agent for the U.S., because he held the keys to at least three of the Fort's buildings and used one of the keys to further seize some barrels of coarse-ground flour, which was ignored the day before. Sangster protested that it was

---

[247] Bill of lading is a key document used in the transport of goods serving as a document of title, an important financial document generated by a shipper. It details the merchandise and releases the goods to a named party at the destination. It is a negotiable instrument, as a title and/or receipt. Author comment.

Nisqually wheat, not Victoria wheat, and was ground in Newmarket (now Olympia). It didn't matter to Glasgow. Sangster vowed to not send any more wheat to be ground by the Americans at Newmarket, because it could be seized on the same grounds. The remaining flour casks were sealed, with eight of them being allowed to the Fort because that flour was the due payment for previously mentioned Indian laborers. The full payment would not be made with the remaining available supplies.

Eben May Dorr, newly appointed customs inspector, was eager to perform his duties, not only at Fort Nisqually, but up and down Puget Sound. On April 22, Inspector Dorr seized the British ship *Albion* at Discovery Bay, on the northeastern tip of the Olympic Peninsula. It seems the *Albion* was harvesting trees to sell as ship spars, in violation of American revenue laws.

The 18 massive trees taken aboard the *Albion* were the initial efforts of the logging industry on the Olympic Peninsula.[248] Captain Brotchie, Master of the *SS Beaver* in the 1840s, had noted the abundance of straight, strong, and huge fir, cedar, and hemlock trees as he sailed around Puget Sound delivering supplies and people to and from Fort Nisqually.

In 1850 Captain Brotchie returned to Puget Sound as Supercargo[249] aboard the *Albion*. Brotchie had been in England, where he proposed to investors that a supply of spars, or masts, for British Royal Navy ships could be had for the taking. Commanded by Captain Richard O. Hinderwell, the *Albion* sailed into Discovery Bay with an assortment of trade goods for the Clallam Indians who lived there. Brotchie had clothing, knives, tobacco, metal files, fishhooks, needles, etc. to trade for permission to remove some trees with the assistance of Clallam workers who would also be paid in trade goods.

After a successful trading session, the ship's carpenter, William Bolton, selected at least 100 men for the project. Avoiding the largest trees, Bolton then surveyed the forest of trees like none he had ever seen before. Finally he selected 18 trees to cut down, dress, and load aboard the *Albion*. It took four months for the massive timbers to be felled and dressed. All the bark and branches were removed. Moving such massive trees, even cleaned of bark and limbs, was a back breaking and dangerous job, heavy on the manual labor. By April 22, the Clallam crew had successfully loaded 17 of the 18 spars on the *Albion*.

That very morning, Eben May Dorr appeared in a small boat with six armed U.S.

---

248 Morgan, Murray, *The Last Wilderness*, Viking Press, New York, 1955.

249 The Supercargo is the officer, or cargo owner's agent, on a merchant ship, who has charge of the cargo and its sale. A Supercargo sails from port to port with the vessel to which he is attached. He differs from a Factor, who has a fixed place for trading. Author comment.

Army soldiers from Fort Steilacoom. Dorr saw it his duty to stop the illegal trade that had begun before Congress had created his customs post, before Dorr was appointed to office, and before there were procedures developed to register entry into U.S. Territory. The British were engaged in illegal trade, as Dorr saw it.

The *Albion* was taken under armed guard to Steilacoom. A libel suit was filed in federal district court for Oregon Territory in Clark County. The ship and its contents were sold at a public auction for $1,450. Captain Hinderwell estimated the value at $50,000. No doubt the outcome of the trial added to the already strained relations between the Americans and the British in the Northwest.

The winning bidders at the auction broke open the ship's stores and treated the town of Steilacoom to a brandy and champagne party. Soon the *Albion* was sailed to San Francisco, where the cargo brought a good price, but the ship did not sell. There were already so many ships in the gold rush harbor that the *Albion* was finally sold as junk and scuttled along the San Francisco waterfront as fill. This action also prevented the British owners from paying the fines imposed by the American courts, thus redeeming her.

The ship's carpenter, Bolton, and three crew members settled near Fort Nisqually, where Bolton started a shipyard[250] on the shore near Day Island, in what is now the city of University Place.

Fort Nisqually continued to have problems with some neighbors. Thomas Glasgow was appointed United States Customs Inspector assigned to Port Nisqually. His job was to collect tariff fees on imported goods. Almost every item received by ship at Fort Nisqually was imported from Europe or Victoria. Glasgow constructed a cabin and a saw mill on the north side of Sequalitchew Creek, and was a squatter on company land.

Edward Huggins claimed that Glasgow was selling homemade liquor to the Indians and the soldiers. The Nisqually Indians did not get along well with Glasgow, but held their vengeance because he had married a Nisqually maiden upon his early arrival, then claimed a large piece of land at Sequalitchew Creek, roughly where the Nisqually Methodist Mission had been burned out by an arsonist.

Glasgow did not get along with Dr. Tolmie at all. The dislike stemmed from Glasgow's treatment of the Nisqually traditions, even their respect for the dead. Glasgow began to build his water-powered sawmill on Sequalitchew Creek. To do so, he needed to erect a dam. He proceeded to do so, in spite of the fact that many interred Indians were located in the very spot he would build the dam. Some were in shallow graves with just enough rock piled on to protect the bodies from marauding wolves, others were placed upright

---

250 Snowden, Clinton A., *History of Washington*, Vol. 2, pp. 447-448, The Century History Company, New York, 1909.

in canoes that were carefully placed in the crotch of trees for their eternal rest. Huggins was upset by the lack of respectful treatment that Glasgow gave these dead individuals. At least one Indian was beaten mercilessly to death by Thomas Glasgow. Huggins account continues…

> …one day in July, 1850, I was employed with a gang of (Indian) men… when we heard a great noise of people talking excitedly. Glasgow, bareheaded, ran into the fort and after him was a crowd of beach (Nisqually) Indians, some of them with large dagger-like knives in their hands, Glasgow came toward me and in an excited manner demanded that I protect him. He said the Indians had attempted to take his life but he had so far evaded them. One of the relatives of the man he had mistreated spoke up and charged him with murdering his relative and calling him a very bad Boston man who had not only killed a harmless Tillicum but had stolen and locked up Dr. Tolmie's goods…[251]

The Indians probably would have killed Glasgow on the spot had it not been for Huggins and Willie Young. They convinced the Indians that the consequences of killing an American were not worth the effort. Huggins advised Glasgow to apologize with a payment of goods to the offended family, then leave the country quickly.

Surprisingly, Glasgow did leave. He sold his valuable property, basically the timber he had cut, to Dr. Tolmie. Glasgow's next residence was on the other (south) side of the Nisqually River. There he abandoned his Nisqually wife and built a farm.[252]

Almost immediately another American claimed Glasgow's abandoned farm land. Levant F. Thompson, with the assistance of Lafayette Balch of Steilacoom, built a saw mill despite the repeated trespass warnings sent by Huggins on behalf of HBC and PSAC.[253]

The American navy steamship *USS Massachusetts* anchored off the beach store. Captain Leadbetter of U.S. Topographic Corps paid a visit to the Fort, cordially introducing himself to Dr. Tolmie. It was a pleasant interlude in the customs struggle, but still reinforced the American presence on Puget Sound.

By May 7 Tolmie had received a letter informing him that the *Cadboro* would be

---

[251] Carpenter, Ceceila Svinth, *Fort Nisqually, A documented History of Indian and British Interaction*, Tahoma Research, Tacoma, WA 1986

[252] Ibid., Glasgow's farm was destroyed by the Indians during the Puget Sound Indian wars. Glasgow found personal protection in a community blockhouse. Indians, still seeking revenge for the death of the Indian Glasgow had killed, burned his house and barn to the ground. Glasgow would surely have been killed had he been there at the time of the arson attack.

[253] Ibid, Thompson's sawmill was also destroyed by the Indians during the Puget Sound Indian Wars, because the mill and mill pond interfered with the Nisqually traditional burial grounds.

"liberated" on the presentation of a proper invoice and manifest of her cargo. Those papers were in the possession of Mr. Dorr, so it was a waiting game. He was in Oregon City again.

Four days later the U.S. transport schooner *Invincible,* Captain Wilcox, arrived to purchase some sheep. Tolmie took full advantage of the opportunity to send a letter to Mr. Secretary Barclay, Hudson's Bay Company Board of Governors in London (via California). Tolmie was calling in the 'big guns' of British politics, but used an American ship to deliver the mail.

Eight days passed before Mr. Dorr returned to Steilacoom. Tolmie went to him immediately with a request to release some of the necessary goods. Dorr gave Tolmie a written order addressed to Glasgow to allow some articles to be removed from bond. Tolmie had to sign a personal note and a receipt for the goods. He then picked up $6,400 out of the funds deposited at the Fort to pay the price of the bond. Glasgow finally allowed the withdrawal of the listed goods.

Chief Factor James Douglas arrived at Fort Nisqually in the forenoon of the 23rd of May. Douglas had a conversation with Dorr regarding the *Cadboro*. While they talked Douglas decided to take a canoe ride to Newmarket, but wanted his horses taken ahead so he would have them to continue on to Vancouver. He hired an Indian to deliver the horses. In trying to cross the Nisqually River at the more treacherous lower fjord, instead of at the middle crossing known as Tlalagwelmeen, two of the horse accidentally drowned. Douglas was quite upset and had to purchase more horses in Newmarket at high American prices.

While Dr. Tolmie was occupied with the customs issue, the young Mr. Huggins was gradually taking more responsibility. He saw to it that a flock of 2,642 sheep were clipped in the last five days of May, paying the shearers one blanket and one shirt each, and the washers one blanket each. He also had Jollibois and Trudelle dig a new "necessary" behind the main store. By the last week of June Huggins had counted 5,282 more shorn sheep, a grand total of 7,924 sheep hand-shorn in 32 days. The Daily Journal seems to project Huggin's own pride at the accomplishments.

The seven English and Canadian deserters were caught in June. Six agreed to return, but the seventh wanted to talk with Governor Douglas. It was the Canadian who wanted "terms" for returning. Eventually, all of them were returned to Victoria n Company terms, conveyed by Mr. Dixon, and some engaged Indians hired to guard the renegade white men. The Company's stern business was not conducted without a sense of irony.

At the end of June, there was a slight hint of excess labor at Fort Nisqually. At least quality labor was recognized. Mr. L. Leclair had been showing "great remissness." He was sent "about his business" as he was "altogether a good for nothing, disorganizing sort of fellow." It just happened that a fellow named Baptiste Chaulifoux came by the day before requesting to reengage with the Company for one year. Dr. Tolmie hired the always reliable Jean Baptiste Chaulifoux at £30 per annum and immediately put him to the task of completing the wool packs Leclair had neglected.

During the spring and summer months of 1850, Colonel[254] Isaac Ebey departed from Olympia to explore Puget Sound in search of farmland. He had arrived at Olympia on New Year's Day from the gold rush town of San Francisco. Exploring in a native canoe paddled by enterprising Indians, they came to a beautiful bay. In a letter to Colonel M.T. Simmons, Ebey relates:

> "The Powalp (Puyallup) is the first stream of any size falling into the bay north of the Nesqually (Nisqually) River. This stream falls into Powalp Bay a little south and east of Vashon's Island. This bay is beautifully situated, with abundance of good anchorage. It is surrounded, and to a considerable distance in the interior, by a body of low timber land, covered with a growth of cedar, fir, and maple timber. This charater [sic] of land continues to a considerable distance up this river. The soil will be found of first quality, with easy access to navigation. The river is rapid and of no great depth. Fine mill privileges exist here, with an abundance of good timber. Many good situations for farms are to be met with, where the removal of the timber is by no means as undertaking of serious moment. I know of no plains on this river near the bay. Where the wagon road from Walla Walla via Mt Rainier crosses this river, about thirty miles from the bay, fine rich plains are found, with soil that will not suffer by comparison with the best land in Oregon. Of their extent I am acquainted."

Ebey was writing about Commencement Bay, named so by Lt Charles Wilkes in 1841, when the United States Exploring Expedition surveyed much of what became Washington. Ebey also mentioned Dewmams (Duwanish) Bay and river, which eventually took the names Elliott Bay and Black River. Lake Washington is the name that survived, but Ebey named it Lake Geneva. Eventually Ebey settled on Whidbey Island. His first wife and two sons joined him there in 1851. Isaac Ebey died in 1857, but we will get to that bloody part of the story soon.

A year before Ebey's family arrived, on September 29, 1850, the U.S. Congress passed

---

254 Nearly all Americans in the PNW using the title "Colonel" were not military men in any sense of the word. They assumed the title to proclaim leadership along the trail or in the community. Their title had held in the same legal and military status as the Colonel of Kentucky Fried Chicken fame. Author comment.

the Donation Land Claim Law. It provided for one half section of land (320 acres) to be granted to male applicants over the age of 18 who were United States citizens, or declared intentions to become a citizen by December 1, 1851, and who had occupied and cultivated the land for four previous years. Married applicants could also claim 320 acres for the wife. Later the amount of land was reduced to 160 acres for each husband and wife.

People with mixed racial ancestry (Indian and American) could qualify, but Indians could not. The Indian title to the lands north of the Columbia River had not been extinguished by any treaty as yet, but that did not seem to matter to the Congress.

The law had a tremendous effect on the land and the people in the Puget Sound area. It was simple to make a declaration or two to become a land owner. Americans took full advantage of the opportunity, as did some British subjects. They simply declared their intention to become American citizens and staked[255] a claim. Several employees of Hudson's Bay Company and Puget Sound Agricultural Company did just that. Many claimed land that was clearly used by the Companies. Edward Huggins actually listed at least 70 names of people who "squatted" on Company land. They tried to take plots from upper Steilacoom, to American Lake, to Puyallup, to Flett's Prairie, to Spanaway, to Squally Bottom, to High Muck, to South Muck, to Clover Creek, to the edge of Fort Nisqually at (later) Dupont. All of these claims were filed between 1847 and 1853. Huggins sent letters to one and all defending the Company's property. Some people did abandon their effort, others did not. One of the most troublesome was still Thomas Glasgow, the U.S. Customs Inspector mentioned earlier.

The Indians were again burning the grasses of the plains in autumn, as was their custom. The practice cleared the grasslands of dried, combustible materials and exposed the camas plants to the crisp air of the fall and winter. The root of the camas plant was harvested after the blue flowers had bloomed. The fires caused tremendous air pollution by today's standards. September 27, 1850, may have been one of those smoke filled days on Puget Sound. It was the day the Donation Land Claim Act went into effect.[256]

It was also on just such a smoky day in September that a former British sailor named Carter came to the Trade Store. He confessed to killing a Company milk cow. He explained that his employer, an American named Luther Collins, of Nisqually Bottom, told him to kill the cow. Collins had lost three cows that wandered away from his farm to become mixed with Company herds. Collins simply wanted revenge and hired Carter to

---

255 To "stake a claim" meant to literally place wooden stakes in the ground at the corners of the land to be claimed. A written description of the land was sometimes useful, but most often useless, describing features such as trees that eventually died. Author's note.

256 Amendments to the DLC Act of 1850 modified the size of claims in 1853 and 1854.

do the dirty work. Carter brought two Americans, McAllister and Lowry, as witnesses. Apparently Dr. Tolmie compassionately offered no punishment to Carter. Collins was expected to pay for the dead beast.

Dr. Tolmie, the Chief Trader at Fort Nisqually, made a hand drawn map of the HBC land where the Puget Sound Agricultural Company operated. He documented where cattle and sheep herdsmen built hut-homes across the prairies, where future military bases would be built. As late as 1908 some of the herdsman's huts were documented by timber cruisers to still exist. Eventually a discharged Fort Steilacoom soldier, John Rigney, received a homestead claim of 640 acres in southern Pierce County. Rigney, an Irish immigrant, purchased more land, adding many hundreds of acres to his original farm.[257] Rigney's land stretched from Rigney Hill (at 74th and South Tacoma Way) to include vast reaches southward (including the western half of Joint Base Lewis McChord) to Spanaway Lake.

Near the center of that Rigney family claim, originally PSAC pasture lands, was a natural swampy lake. It was in a triangular area between two branches of Clover Creek and Morey Creek. Most of the area was grassy plains and prairie. The moderate temperatures (32°F–82°F) ensured year-round use. The terrain is generally flat, ranging for 200 to 800 feet above sea level. The Cascade Mountain Range is 25 miles to the east. Mount Rainier is 40 miles to the southeast of the claim. The strongest winds are generally from the southwest at 35-50 knots. Clover Creek drains the region, running generally northwest to Chambers Creek then to Puget Sound. Clover Creek originates in the East part of the area, picking up water from Spanaway (Spa-nu-eh) and Tule Lakes, then discharging into Steilacoom Lake, about two miles to the West and North. It was ideal natural grassland, choice for grazing farm animals.

As mentioned earlier, Dr. John McLoughlin and his Métis wife Margaret were shocked and saddened by the news of the death of their son, John, Jr. He was murdered by employees of HBC at Fort Stikine, in the far north. McLoughlin read the report of his superior, HBC Governor Sir George Simpson, and was disgusted. The report was presumptive in McLoughlin's view. It was marred by inconsistencies and seemed to protect the company and some employees rather than seek justice. McLoughlin decided to investigate the death of his beloved son himself, since there was no other legal authority. As HBC Chief Factor and head of the Board of Management of the Columbia Department, he convened what might be called a grand jury to investigate the "*life of an HBC*

---

257 Rigney sold 900 acres of his land to Pierce County, which built and opened Tacoma Field on June 10, 1929. On May 5, 1938 Pierce County passed the deed of the Tacoma Airport to the War Department. The Tacoma Airport then became McChord Field, and later McChord Air Force Base.

Officer taken with impunity by a group of subordinates."[258]

A group was assembled at Fort Nisqually for the proceedings. Included were Fort Nisqually Postmaster Angus McDonald, Chief Factor James Douglas, Chief Trader Donald Manson, Chief trader Captain William, H. McNeill, Captain James Scarborough, and company clerks: James Steel, Paul Fraser, and John O'Brien.

Testimony was taken and recorded over two days, clearly revealing that there had been a conspiracy by several people and a murder carried out. The transcript of the testimony was sent to HBC Secretary and Governor Archibald Barclay in London. His reply statement was a clear rebuke of Governor Simpson's earlier report. The Secretary and committee in London clearly saw the trumped-up story Simpson had sent.

Still, no one seems to have been punished. McLoughlin had the conspirators arrested and sent to Montreal for trial. The London committee censured McLoughlin, sensing that convictions were not likely. The London Directors eventually freed and paid the accused for the time they were under arrest. Some were rehired and sent back to McLoughlin's Columbia Department. It was the irreversible turning point in McLoughlin's life. Within four years he would retire, move to Oregon City, become an American, and resent HBC for the remainder of his life.

As the fall weather crept into the summer's smoky air, the outstation employees came to collect their rations for the last four months of the year. Some men, Charles Ross in particular, terminated their employment with the Company, only to hire on at another local (American) farm. Nevertheless, potato crops were dug, cleaned and stored, especially the Kidney potatoes, a special variety, "a rather scarce sort," of only 13 bushels.[259] One Kidney potato can have up to 15 'eyes' to be used as seeds for new crops.

Over 1,400 bushels of potatoes were harvested in October, as some wheat was planted. Mr. Charles Forrest of Cowlitz Farm came with Captain Fay of the *Orbit*. They were eager to make arrangements to transport a load of horses to Victoria for $7 per head. Tolmie's price was $12 per horse. Consequentially, Dr. Tolmie and Captain Fay would not accept the offer. Sheep skin dressing and wool packing occupied the men for much of the time, but other repairs were always in line. Chalifoux built a new ladder to reach the loft of the Trade Store. And someone had to dress the band of rams that were attacked by a

---

258 Anderson, Steve A., "McLoughlin's Grand Jury," Columbia, Washington State History Museum, Tacoma, Winter Edition, 2008-09.

259 Thin skinned Kidney potatoes are low in potassium, but have a high number of 'eyes' that, when planted correctly, produce an abundant crop. Today these potatoes are branded "Jersey Royal" and grown only on the Island of Jersey, which is just off the coast of Normandy, France, but officially a self-governing British Crown Dependency. Elsewhere this spud is called the international kidney potato. http://en.wkipedia.org/wiki/Jersy_Royals

scab infection. The peas and oats were harvested and the land cleared for a new season of crops. Wheat was sowed in several fields and pigs were brought in for fattening. When fattened and dressed the pigs weighed in at 235 to 270 pounds each.

Word arrived November 17 that Dr. Tolmie was urgently needed at Victoria for his medical skills. Governor Blanshard had taken suddenly ill and a physician was in need of immediate attendance. Dr. Tolmie and Mrs. Tolmie departed immediately in a large seagoing, Indian driven, express canoe.

The next day Dr. Haden of Steilacoom, Judge Strong of Newmarket, Marshall Meek, Mr. Simmons, and Mr. Strong, a brother to the judge, arrived at Fort Nisqually to speak with Dr. Tolmie. They formed an American delegation that wanted a complete animal census and complete evaluation of the HBC and PSAC property. There was no one available who could comply with the demanded task. The Americans were told politely, to stand off until Dr. Tolmie returned.

A few days later Mr. Tod was nearly killed in a routine canoe trip. His canoe was a complete loss, but he heroically saved a packet of mail destined for England. It seems a storm came up suddenly, so Tod directed his hired Indian paddlers to take the canoe closer to shore. The wind was blowing very strongly. Just as the canoe reached a "safe" spot along the shore a gust of wind toppled a tree which fell directly across the canoe, smashing it to pieces. Tod and the others on board were lucky to escape injury. The packet of letters was recovered from the wreckage then sent on its way by U.S. Military express.

It was gloomy, rainy, cold, and sometimes frosty when Chalifoux nearly completed work on the flooring for the new granary.[260] He collected his Christmas Regale,[261] along with the others, late in the day on Christmas Eve. A festive holiday ball was held at "Rossville" on Christmas Day. The following day several men were not at work. They "over exerted themselves at the Ball."

December 31 was a "rather bad day for work in consequence of serving out a regale" for New Year's Day according to the Fort Journal. It seems that 'calling in sick' on this holiday was a "tradition" for some workmen even in the 1850s.

---

260 This granary is the one now designated a National Historic Site at Fort Nisqually Living History Museum in Point Defiance Park, Tacoma, Washington according to Metro Parks Tacoma records..

261 A British choral tradition modified by gift giving on the western frontier during the fur trade era. The Company provided, as a Christmas gift, a package of meat, sugar, salt, etc., and often a stiff drink of rum to each of the primary employees (servants) of the Company. Workers were also given a day without work, excluding the necessary care of animals. Shine, Gregory P., "A General Time of Indulgence and Festivity" Vancouver "Columbian" Dec. 9. 2007.

1851

THE FIRST AMERICAN EDITION of Herman Melville's *Moby Dick* was published, but not yet read in the Puget Sound region. It was a story of a whaling ship captained by Ahab, who had lost a leg to a "white-headed whale with a wrinkled brow and a crooked jaw." While many of the Europeans and Americans who lived along the shores of the North Pacific had traveled by sea from their previous homes, the book would only gain wide interest decades later.[262]

Perhaps more was known in the Pacific Northwest about London's Great Exhibition of 1851. Some 13,000 exhibits demonstrated England's industrial supremacy for the 19th century world.

One of the world's oldest sports and game manufacturers commemorated the original croquet set first presented by the master wood turners at John Jaques Company, established in 1795. These croquet sets drew upon the unparalleled Jaques family craftsmanship. They used wood seasoned for three years after harvest. The set included mallets made from hardy English ash, bound with brass fittings. This is the same type of wood used by English longbows in the Middle Ages. Two mallets were made, one with rock wood heads, the other with hickory heads. These were made for professional competition, rather than leisure play. Intermediate mallets, made for shorter and younger players were inlaid with a boxwood sightline. The set included a canvas bag for two sets of handcrafted, 13-ounce wooden balls, winning pegs with eight colored stripes, boundary flags, eight colored clips, hoops, a smasher, a drill, ball markers, and a complete set of rules. The entire set, including the mallets, came in a stout oak storage chest. Croquet is a modern favorite of visitors at Fort Nisqually Living History Museum.

Industrial advances eased transportation difficulties in the Pacific Northwest, if only a bit. Old Oregon's first "real," purposely constructed road, opened for business to avoid the hazardous Cascades of the Columbia River. That deadly stretch of the river

---

262 Herman Melville August 1, 1819—September 28, 1891. *Moby Dick* was considered to be a failure at the time. His death sparked a renewed interest in the novel, vastly increasing its popularity.

was treacherous at best. Portage around the rapids was essential. The new Barlow Road took travelers considerably south to higher elevations (4,920 feet), around Mount Hood, through the heavily forested mountains before turning north to the Willamette Valley. It was by far the most harrowing 100 miles of the Oregon Trail, yet it saved innumerable lives that would have been lost in the dangerous Cascade river rapids.

As competition for the longer Barlow Road, a make-shift railroad was built on a six-mile-long route roughly parallel to the most turbulent rapids, the Cascades, of the river. In 1850 or 1851 a wooden tram was the first built parallel to the Columbia River. The Oregon Portage Railway employed a mule to pull a flat car to connect passengers and freight to the river steamers both upstream and down from the treacherous Cascades of the Columbia. Periodic flooding caused many delays as the roadbed was rebuilt. It was not the equal of the railroads of the East at that time period, but approached the quality of, perhaps 1830. The rails were wooden, but capped with iron on the load bearing surfaces. By 1850 all but the most backward eastern railroads were using iron rail, some had already switched to 'T' shaped steel rails. The technology of the Columbia River portage rail line was primitive, but it served the needs of the frontier traveler.[263]

The success of the 1839 PSAC contract with the Russian-America Fur Trading Company began to fall on hard times when gold was discovered in California. Farmers and laborers of both American and British origin departed Oregon and the Puget Sound area for the riches to be had south of the Spanish California border at the 42nd parallel.

The boundary Treaty of 1846 established northern limits that isolated the farms of Nisqually, Cowlitz and Vancouver from the British lands north of the 49th parallel. The 1847 crop failure around Puget Sound required PSAC farms at Forts Victoria and Langley to meet the requirements of the contract with the Russians.

Governor Tebebkov in Sitka recognized the abandonment of the Oregon Country for gold, the resulting short-fall of wheat production, and the subsequent entry into the market of Chilean wheat at exorbitant prices. He was unwilling to pay the Chilean price, but could not find enough available wheat. The Russian-American head office was surprisingly understanding of the situation confronting the PSAC.

When some American settlers returned to Oregon Country the PSAC farms and ranches were plundered, again, by these and other American squatters who simply took company land, livestock, and crops at will. Some Americans even moved into Company workers' homes. In this sense PSAC was a political failure because the British failed to

---

263 Schwantes, Carlos A. "The West the Railroads Made", *Columbia. The Magazine of Northwest History*, Spring, 2008, pp 24-31, Washington State Historical Society, Tacoma. The first steam locomotive operating in the Pacific Northwest was the "Oregon Pony" built in San Francisco in 1861.

defend the Company's legitimate International Treaty rights. But the company regrouped physically and economically on Vancouver Island, out of the reach of Americans. There Captain Langford of the 73rd Regiment became manager (1851–1861). He and his wife and five daughters resided at Langford Lake to operate the Esquimalt (First Nations transliteration of Ess-whoy-malth, the Place of Shoaling Waters) Farm of the PSAC, west of Victoria.[264]

Captain Langford did not entirely neglect his duties around the PSAC Esquimalt Farm. It was first built in 1850 as Viewland Farm, with Constance Cove Farm and Craigflower Farms added later. He seemed much more interested in performing as a genial country squire. He kept his house open for young officers of the Royal Navy who could make eligible husbands for his daughters. The Langford family was the first English family to immigrate to the English Colony of British Columbia. He, his wife, and five "good looking" daughters arrived in May, 1851. Langford (1809–95) returned to England in 1861.

On Whidbey[265] Island, unlikely settlers who had first met in New Orleans on their way to California gold fields founded Oak Harbor. New Englander and former Swiss Army officer Ulrich Freund and Norwegian shoemaker Zackary Toftezen named the place after the handsome stands of Garry Oak trees in the area. Dutch settlers, followed by Irish immigrants, provided the now deeply rooted traditions of the town. It would be a year before salty seadog Captain Thomas Coupe would settle on Penn Cove, the beginnings of Coupeville.

One of the first settlers on Whidbey Island was Dr. John Coe Kellogg—the "Canoe Doctor." He was once a prominent landowner at Red Bluff, later called Kellogg Point, now known as Admiralty Head on Whidbey Island. John and his wife Caroline built a cabin and a log hospital there in 1849. Kellogg was nearly as well known at the time as Isaac Ebey.

Isaac Neff Ebey's life story tells about settling on Whidbey Island. Called by Native Americans Tscha-kole-chy, it was re-named by Captain Vancouver in 1792 after Joseph Whidby, master of *H.M.S. Discovery*. Ebey, the Missourian, staked his claim in October, 1850, on the prairie along the island's western shore. He built a dock to service commercial boat traffic. Ebey was an attorney by schooling, but planted wheat and potatoes,

---

264 PSAC continued to operate successfully until nearly a century after its formation (1934), when it ceased to be listed on the London Stock exchange, following the sale of its last real estate holdings. Author's notes.

265 Historically spelled Whidby, It is the longest island in the continental United States by legal definition... Long Island, N.Y. isn't actually an island, a fact decided by the U.S. Supreme Court which declared in a 1985 boundary case that Long Island is a peninsula extending the coast line of the state. It is geographically 118 miles long, more than twice the length of Whidby, at 45 miles.

served in the territorial legislature, collected customs duties, and arbitrated disputes between whites and Indians. He apparently did not arbitrate well in the view of the Kake Indians of Alaska. Revenge was taken in 1857, as we shall see.

The *USS Massachusetts* confronted a group of Kake people camped near Fort Gamble and opened fire. The Kake had been in the decades-long habit of raiding the Puget Sound tribes for wives and slaves. The US Navy exercised typical "gunboat" diplomacy to stop the raids.

Fort Victoria was built in 1843 at the southern tip of Vancouver's Island. It had grown into a center of trade and commerce, primarily because of Hudson's Bay Company, but also because of the Royal Navy's presence a few miles away at Esquimalt. This navy base was the home port for the gunboats of the British Flying Squadron. There was a clear need for law enforcement in the rough and tumble town filled with fur traders, sailors, gold seekers, opportunists, and local Indians. Victoria Voltigeurs were formed and financed by the new colonial government and outfitted by the Hudson's Bay Company.

The Victoria Voltigeurs operated as a militia, or police force, from 1851 to 1858. This force was comprised of an eclectic group of individuals gleaned from the general population, but Scots commanded Voltigeurs. Among the troops were French-Canadians, Englishmen, Kanakas, Métis, and Cherokee. Their uniform consisted of a red stocking cap, a blue capote, and sash. They were armed with HBC trade guns, navy Colt revolvers, pocket revolvers, and single shot pistols. While the general population may have been raucous, Voltigeurs were trained and disciplined police and military men, who carried out their duties with dependable pride, with only the occasional turbulence.

Washington Territory had no counterpart of equal stature to the Victoria Voltigeurs. An artillery unit of the U.S. Army was stationed at Fort Steilacoom, but there was little in the way of civilian law enforcement beyond appointed county sheriffs and judges of a meager court system. There were endless land claims disputes after the boundary was set in 1846, and even after 1853, when territorial government civil courts were established.

The initial Oregon Territorial land survey (1851) set up the Willamette Meridian and base lines that would lead to the townships and ranges.[266] All land claims from that time forward were based on the survey. Roads and property lines are even today described on the basis of this original survey. Old Oregon was growing modern.

Olympia was growing, too. Town site proprietor, Edmund Sylvester, operated the Washington Hotel at the corner of 2nd and Main. It was the center of trade. Several stores were doing a booming business. George A. Barnes sold nails and oakum. Parker, Colter

---

266 The Willamette Meridian extends north beyond Fort Nisqually, about where Meridian Avenue is located in Pierce County today. Author's comment.

& Company sold food supplies along with sawed lumber. Other stores were operated by Kandall Company, A.J. Moses, and the Bettman Brothers. A United States Customs District of Puget Sound was established on February 14, 1851. Port Townsend and Port Angeles would challenge Olympia for the prized government office.

G.N. McConaha and J.W. Wiley were lawyers, H.A. Golsborough and Mike Simmons sold real estate. Olympia had a bakery, a livery stable, and, of course, a blacksmith shop. There were perhaps 100 people in this little town. Even the Methodists were back with a growing congregation. In May, Reverend Benjamin F. Close began holding services every Sunday in a small building at Barnes' store.

On the eastern shore of Puget Sound, on January 23, Port Steilacoom was founded by Captain Layfayette Balch. On August 23, John B. Chapman took a claim on adjoining land to form Steilacoom City. These rival towns were built only a mile apart, on separate claims. Informally they were known as upper and lower Steilacoom. They were also collectively known as Balch's Town. In 1851 the combined merchants in the two Steilacoom towns offered more merchandise than was then available from Olympia's merchants. Even with such vast merchandise choices, the supplies available at Fort Nisqually and Puget Sound Agricultural Company probably equaled that of the three towns combined. Of course, most of the merchandise at Nisqually was of British origin and, therefore, less desired by the prejudiced Americans. The Fort Nisqually Indian Trade store was rapidly becoming irrelevant, except for the singularly successful, but diminishing, fur trade.

Sergeant Hall of Fort Steilacoom was notified that the Army could no longer exchange pork for beef when ordering meat from Fort Nisqually. Dr. Tolmie had decided it was no longer beneficial to the Company bottom line to do so. He didn't specify a reason for his decision, but the practice was discontinued. Speculation says the habit of substituting less expensive pork for beef was for financial advantage, rather than culinary reasons. Fort Nisqually always had more mutton and beef than pork available

Two American settlers in the Nisqually bottom lands got into a personal disagreement. Soon knives replaced words as the weapon of choice and both were injured. George Shazer was severely cut and Robert Wilson required some degree of doctoring. Someone called for Dr. Tolmie. He treated both men, declaring Shazer to be in danger of losing his life. He had been cruelly cut, and hacked, by Wilson. Later both men worked under contract for the Company.

Dr. Tolmie took a canoe to the ship *George Emory* to present Captain Balch with a written notice to cease and desist in building improvements at Steilacoom on HBC and PSAC lands. Edward Huggins had delivered several notices to Balch, but they had been ignored. Tolmie assumed his personal presence would turn Balch's mind. He was wrong.

Balch replied that he would take no notice of the warnings and would continue his improvements. The Army continued improvements, too. They, however, acknowledged that it was PSAC land enclosed by an Army fence.

The Company's retreat on the cattle plains continued. Mr. Ross was hired to kill and butcher the long-horn cows at the rate of one per week. He would send the carcass, tallow, hides, hooves, and horns to the Fort. All of the cow parts were marketed locally or in London. Dr. Tolmie was determined to make a profit from these tough old animals.

More and more we see the Journal representing workers' pay in American currency. It was the currency in ascendancy. For example, 8 cents per bushel of potatoes hauled in was paid to one man, while £86.6.1 was due to J.M. McLeod a few days later. Then a week later the Fort paid a uniform rate of $1.00 per head of sheep hauled to Victoria aboard the Brig *Orbit*, Captained by Mr. Simmons. On another day Tolmie agreed to sell 2,895 feet of lumber at 7½ American cents per foot.

That outbound shipment of animals aboard the *Orbit* had 45 horses, 328 ewes, and a single ram. The potato crop yielded 997 bushels by early March. As the wild geese flew north the peas were planted, the sheepskins were packed for the packhorses, and another new building was put up. Mr. Walter Ross needed a house, so four men were sent to help him construct the dwelling. Other men were cutting a new water course to drain the swamps and low wetland near the Fort. Soon the land would drain and fields would blossom with wheat, peas, oats, and even grasses for the grazing animal stock.

In mid-April Lettitia Work traveled with Reverend Staines from Victoria for a short visit. Staines and Tolmie visited several towns and many of the Company outstations. One only speculates that Lettie was with Mrs. Tolmie at the Factor's House. As sisters, they were very close. Of course Mr. Huggins was sure to make his presence known to the young lady visitor. Lettitia Work did not return to Victoria with Reverend Staines. There was "talk" that Huggins and Miss Work were "sweet" on each other.

It was late in April that news was relayed to Fort Nisqually of the formation of more bureaucracy. Dr. Haden and Major Goldsboro of Fort Steilacoom provided the intelligence that a port of entry had been established at the City of Olympia. It was good news. Two days later Tolmie paddled a canoe three miles south of Steilacoom to visit Captain Sangster of the *Una*. She was anchored off shore waiting for the Customs Collector. Another three days would pass before the offloading of the *Una* could begin, with approval from the customs agent.

On April 24, 1851, Alfred A. Plummer and Charles Bachelder filed a claim for land at the mouth of Port Townsend. The Clallam Indians called the place Kah Tai, meaning to 'pass through' or "to carry." Soon Loren B. Hastings and Francis W. Pettigrove moved

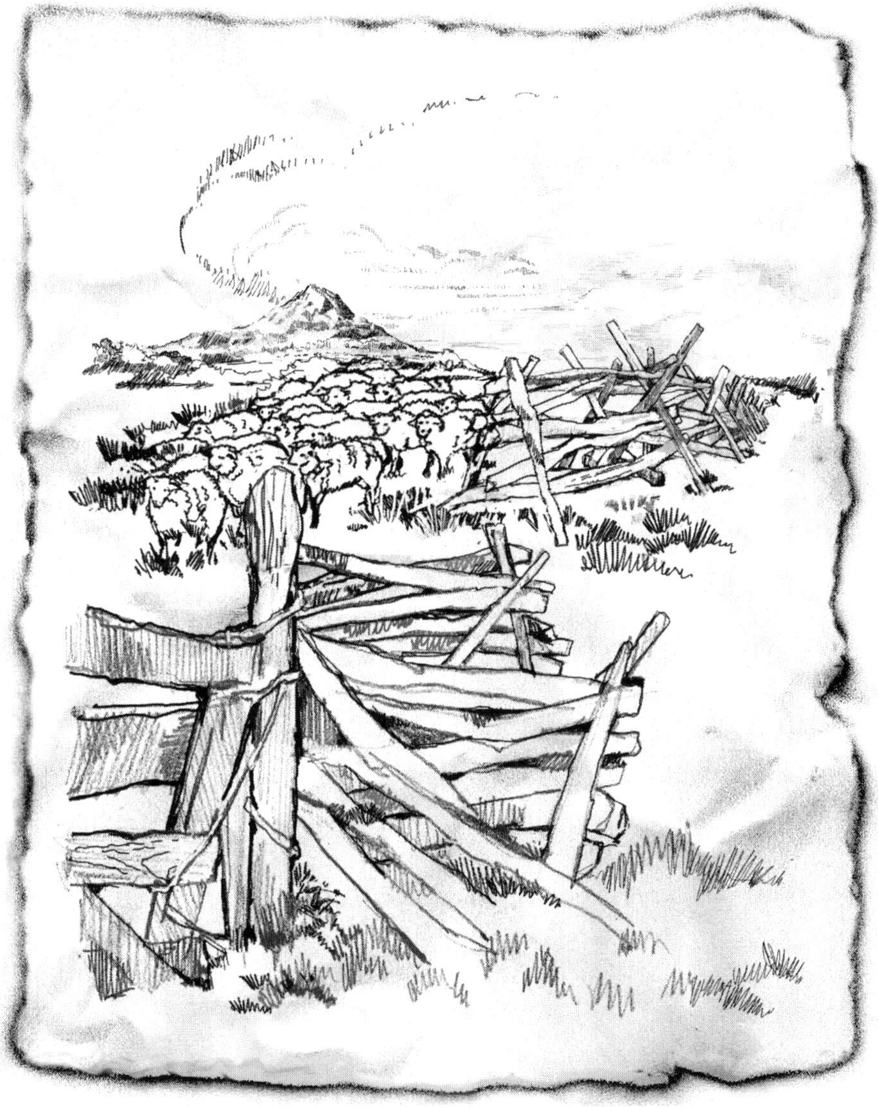

to Port Townsend. Together the men established a new town which they named after the bay on which it sat. The site had been recommended by Captain Lafayette Balch to Plummer, who was running a San Francisco hotel at the time.

A public meeting was called in Steilacoom on May 15, 1851. Dr. Tolmie was accused of being an agent of a foreign monopoly which was controlling land without the people to improve. Furthermore, Americans who made improvements on these lands received threats and warnings to leave. The meeting concluded with a resolution:

> *"Resolved, that we regard the Puget Sound Agricultural Society as being a system of fraud and pretext invented by the shrewd cunning of Englishmen of influence, who foreseen the policy influenced their government at setting of the boundary question, too urge as a proposition the donating themselves of a large scope of land."*[267]

Dr. Tolmie continued to remove farm animals to Victoria. It was a long project. Ship capacity for live animals was limited. The number of ships was also limited, as was the ability of Victoria to absorb the herds. But the animal removal continued. In May the *Una* took on 20 horses, 2 oxen, 100 wedders, and 305 gimmers. Then one of the squatters, Joseph Broshears, sent a letter to Dr. Tolmie advising him to remove the Company's cattle and horses from the part of the PSAC Round Plain. Broshears had simply seized the land without any legal authority.

As the shearing of sheep commenced, the men completed white-washing all of the Fort's buildings. The place was in top shape as the *Orbit* was loaded with 22 head of long horn cattle, 104 gimmers, plus the wool bales from 100 sheared sheep. As the ship set sail on a very warm day in mid-May, Dr. Tolmie was off to court concerning the Broshears land seizure.

In the Olympia court, Tolmie charged Charles Wren with stealing and branding a PSAC filly. He was accompanied by witnesses John Montgomery, Jean Baptiste, Jean Lapoitre and Edward Huggins. Later in the week, other Americans were given warnings about trespassing. Legal notices were delivered to Charles Wren, John McCleod, Lyman A. Smith, Thomas Chambers, B.L. Lamie, William Dougherty, John Bradley, Daniel Brownfield, and J. S. Broshears. All of them ignored the notices and the law.

On May 24th, a new type of "settler" arrived on the *Orbit*. The settler was Thomas Dean. He was a Brit hired by the Company in London to claim land for the Company at Tlithlow. He was also given the title of Bailiff. Other passengers of the *Orbit* were Mrs.

---

267 *Oregon Spectator,* June 5, 1851

Dean, the Dean's son George, John Thornhill, Mrs. Thornhill, W. Cross, W. Northover, Henry Barnes, and George Hayward. The men were all English, hired by the Company to work at Fort Nisqually, mainly securing Company lands. They were to be a "counter force" to the American settlers. HBC needed people to occupy land. Operating two thriving international business enterprises just was not enough to fend off the immigration of Americans into the area. British "settlers" seemed to be the solution. They were expected to occupy the land, thereby halting American incursions.

In June the clipping of sheep's wool occupied a great deal of time. About 2376 were sheared in short order. Some 1,659 head of sheep were sent to Victoria, along with several shepherds. Many bushels of potatoes were harvested, too. The Fort had been sending wheat to the Simmons mill in Olympia for some time, but the demand for the grinding service was increasing with more and more settlers. Sometimes there was a backup line a week long. Flour was occasionally scarce as a result of the less-than-timely processing.

The *U.S.S. Falmouth*, an American man-of-war, anchored off the landing after reporting at Steilacoom. The officers of the *Falmouth*, Captain Pearson and Purser Mr. Mason, visited with Dr. Tolmie, Mrs. Tolmie and Lettitia Work. In the evening they all rode out to Tlithlow for an evening of recreation on horseback.

The *Falmouth* departed for Olympia as Dr. Tolmie organized a sheep drive to Vancouver. A herd of 832 wedders were gathered, along with a gang of ten Indians to drive the sheep to Mr. Peter Skene Ogden, at Vancouver. Ogden was a member of the HBC Board of Management. The animals were being consigned to Ogden for ultimate sale to Americans in exchange for a shipload of farm equipment to be sent a few days later. By the Fourth of July the sheep were on their way, and Dr. Tolmie was in Olympia to witness the American celebration of the anniversary of their Independence from Great Britain. It must have been a grand celebration, for the good doctor didn't return until late on the night of the fifth.

The potato and oat harvests were in full swing by late July. The recently arrived Englishmen were assigned duties that had been Indian jobs. "English men and women hoeing potatoes," one entry reads. It is supposed that the labor was paying for the "extra" supplies needed by the families, but not included in the ordinary supplies issued to the workers.

On August 29, 1851, a convention was called to order at Cowlitz Landing. The plan of this convention was for settlers north of the Columbia to draft a memorial to Congress seeking a new territorial designation, separate from the Territorial Government of Oregon. Lawyer John Chapman wrote the resolution. Congress completely ignored it. The document severely criticized Hudson's Bay Company monopoly, but barely mentioned any political advantages in creating a new territory.

In August, when the men at Fort Nisqually were pulling peas, cutting and binding oats, carting firewood and hay, harvesting wheat, and otherwise "jobbing about" in the sometimes dense smoke from the prairie fires, five ships were reported on the Sound. None were destined for Fort Nisqually. All were American vessels bound for the new towns.

The *Cadboro* was spotted at Commencement Bay a day before it arrived at the landing with Mrs. & Mr. James Douglas, Head of the Columbia Department, since Dr. McLoughlin's retirement in '46. Along with the Douglas family was Mr. Henry Peers, the replacement for Mr. Roberts, who had just resigned from his duties at Cowlitz. While at Fort Nisqually, Douglas visited with Mr. Dean concerning his duties as bailiff for the Company, and determined that Thomas Linklater, Company Manager at Tenalquot, was no longer needed. Another man was sent to bring to the Fort the horses and tools that belonged to the Company, as the Company was prepared to completely abandon the outstation at Tenalquot. Linklater immediately filed a claim for the farm and land, declaring his American citizenship rights.

Dr. Tolmie was on the sick list in mid-September, along with William Northover and Chaulifoux. While intoxicated, Northover was injured when a powder horn exploded. Chaulifoux and Tolmie probably had influenza.

Two horses fared worse than the ill humans. The horses were dead. One, an old stud named "Turk," was found shot to death near (American) Dougharty's house at Steilacoom. The other was a young mare, also found shot dead, near Thomas Linklater's new claim. Dougharty and Linklater were the obvious suspects, but were never charged.

Captain Boland, of the sloop *Georgiana*, pulled up to the landing as the *Cadboro* was loading sheep and human passengers bound for Victoria. The captain convinced Mr. Douglas to let him carry some sheep, too. In all the two ships hauled another 150 wedders and rams, along with the Douglas family, and Jean Baptiste Jollibois and his family, to Vancouver's Island. Jollibois was also leaving the service of the Company for a farm he claimed north of Victoria. The *Georgiana* was soon back to carry eight oxen to Victoria.

On September 14, 1851 Luther M. Collins, Henry Van Asselt, Jacob Maple, and his son Samuel Maple arrived at the mouth of the Duwamish River (Ouvré's River) in search of a place to settle.[268]

On September 25, 1851 David Denny, John Low, and Lee Terry arrive at the mouth of the Duwamish River. They are greeted by the Luther Collins party. Low and Terry

---

268 HistoryLink.org www.historylink.org/essays/output.cfm?file_id=5390

selected land at Alki Point, then sent messages to Arthur Denny, an unsuccessful settler in the Willamette Valley, about their new claims. Arthur Denny organized a move for his family and those of Low and David Denny. The Denny party arrived on November 13, 1851, aboard the schooner *Exact*, to find the Low cabin still unfinished. By the following spring most of a disgruntled group numbering 20 people in four families plus four single individuals, relocated to the opposite side of Elliott Bay.[269]

The arrival of American settlers had some positive effects on the Establishment at Nisqually. In November Dr. Tolmie was told of the need for new wheels for the wagons. They had always been hand-made, or "country made" in the language of the time. This time, however, the Doctor went to a store in Steilacoom. He purchased two pair of seven-foot wagon wheels at $25.00 per pair. While he was there he also picked up a small hand truck, for another $35. For four days the Journal entry is quite clear about men hauling firewood.

Dr. Tolmie consulted with the Army Doctor, Haden, concerning the death of three Indians and the severe dysentery suffered by many others. Even Edward Huggins was ill with the prevailing complaint. After 15 days Huggins was better, and at sixteen days was back to work but still feeling effects of his bout with severe dysentery.

She was ill for only five days before Mrs. McPhail died of the same dysentery complaint. Her husband was also ill, but he finally recovered in about two weeks. Pere F. Jayoul, a Catholic Priest of the Mission of St Joseph in Olympia was called at the request of Charles Forrest, an employee at Cowlitz Farm. Forest came to Dr. Tolmie for treatment at the height of the dysentery outbreak. He was very ill. After ten days he asked for the priest. He wrote his last will, appointing James Douglas, Esquire, and Dr. Tolmie as executors.

Cowie and Chaulifoux built the coffins for Mrs. McPhail and Charles Forrest. It took the better part of two days to construct the enclosures for the deceased. All hands attended the burial service performed by Father Jayoul. They were buried outside the garden fence on the southeast side, a spot chosen by Charles Forrest before he died. Chaulifoux, Cowie, Gohome, and Keave'haccow spent the better part of four days building a proper enclosing fence around Forrest's grave, then Dr. Tolmie gave them the next day off.

John Ross decided to leave the Company. His cattle were the property of the Company, so he was ordered to drive the herd to the Fort. The Nisqually River was a major obstacle without considerable help. Dr. Tolmie sent a crew of Indians to do the job of cowboys. Ross had some Cowlitz people working for him, but when they learned he

---

269 Today the spot in downtown Seattle is called Pioneer Square. Author's comment.

was leaving the Company, they left him. Tolmie calculated the balance in the Ross account (trade store debt, cow sales, animal deaths, births, etc.) ending with a balance of 55 head for the Company and 25 head for Ross. There were another 30 head of cattle to be left at the farm.

December was a period of turmoil at Fort Nisqually. The brother of the U.S. Customs Collector for Puget's Sound arrived at Fort Nisqually with a friend, Mr. Miller, bright and early Monday morning, December 1, 1851. It seems that two Company ships had been seized at the Port of Entry. Two days later Dr. Tolmie confirmed the news. The *Mary Dare* and the *S.S. Beaver* were both in custody of the Customs Agent in Olympia. The *Mary Dare* was seized because there was a discrepancy in the weight of a single package sugar cask. The *S.S. Beaver* was seized because her manifest had entered ballast, while the ship carried none.

The crewmembers of both ships were not allowed off the vessels. The Fort sent a canoe-load of fresh beef and other food for the sailors. In all, more than six sides of beef were taken by Indian paddlers to the ships. The storehouse at Nisqually was overflowing with cargo to be delivered by the two ships. There were casks of tallow, bales of wool, and sundry other products of the Fort destined for ports around the world. More importantly, however, was some luggage on board the *Mary Dare*.

Passengers from Victoria were allowed to depart the ship at Nisqually, rather than take the slow trip to Olympia and return. Their luggage was still on the ship so as to pass through customs. The passengers, Mrs. Work and Miss Burney, were required to travel to Olympia to obtain possession of their luggage. It was apparently a newly instituted procedure, as this had never been required before. But then, Olympia was now an official American Port of Entry. Customs agents and officers were on hand to levy duties, inspect travelers' luggage, and control immigration. Being a Port of Entry also meant that exports of Olympia's first products, beer and oysters, could be expedited. Freshness was expected in Victoria and San Francisco.

Captain Stuart of the *Beaver* and Dr. Tolmie were busy all day writing dispatches to Victoria to explain the situation and ask for advice or instructions. After another trip to Olympia, the *Mary Dare* was released. She was sailed to Nisqually by the First Mate and crew, as the Captain was with Tolmie in Vancouver to consult the law concerning ship seizures.

While Tolmie was away, Huggins received a request to purchase 800 pounds of beef at seven cents per pound. Captain Balch in Steilacoom was planning to resell the beef in his market. Huggins told Balch that, without specific authority, he could not sell the meat at less than eight cents per pound, but could deliver the eight hundred pounds in two days. Balch accepted the eight cent price.

Then, with Tolmie still in Vancouver, Mr. Ross was out killing cattle, as his contract specified. As he pursued a wily old ox, his horse fell with its full weight on Ross' left leg, breaking it severely. Dr. Haden of the Army post at Steilacoom was sent for and attended the injury immediately. Ross spent the holidays with a broken leg, but was improving. Perhaps the cure came in a bottle of American brandy that was passed out for the 1851 Regales at Christmas and New Year's.

On December 11, 1851, the schooner *Robert Bruce* was intentionally set on fire by the ship's cook. The schooner burned to the water line in Shoalwater Bay (now Willapa Bay), where she was loading oysters for the lucrative San Francisco market. All crew were saved, but lost their belongings. These rugged individuals simply built cabins, named the brand new settlement Bruceville,[270] and went into the oyster-shipping business.

James Swan spent three years at Shoalwater Bay, as Willapa Bay was known in 1851. Swan wrote of his experiences in *The Northwest Coast, or Three Years Residence in Washington Territory*. It is one of the earliest books about life in Washington.

The so-called "C-Spring" Victoria Carriage was named for Queen Victoria. It became the most popular conveyance at the Crystal Palace Exhibition in London. That world's fair was attended by some six million visitors, many of whom used the wagonette body frame pioneered for Queen Victoria. It was popular because it allowed up to six passengers to sit facing each other along the sides of the carriage.

---

270 Bruceville was changed to Bruceport in a short time. See www.historylink.org

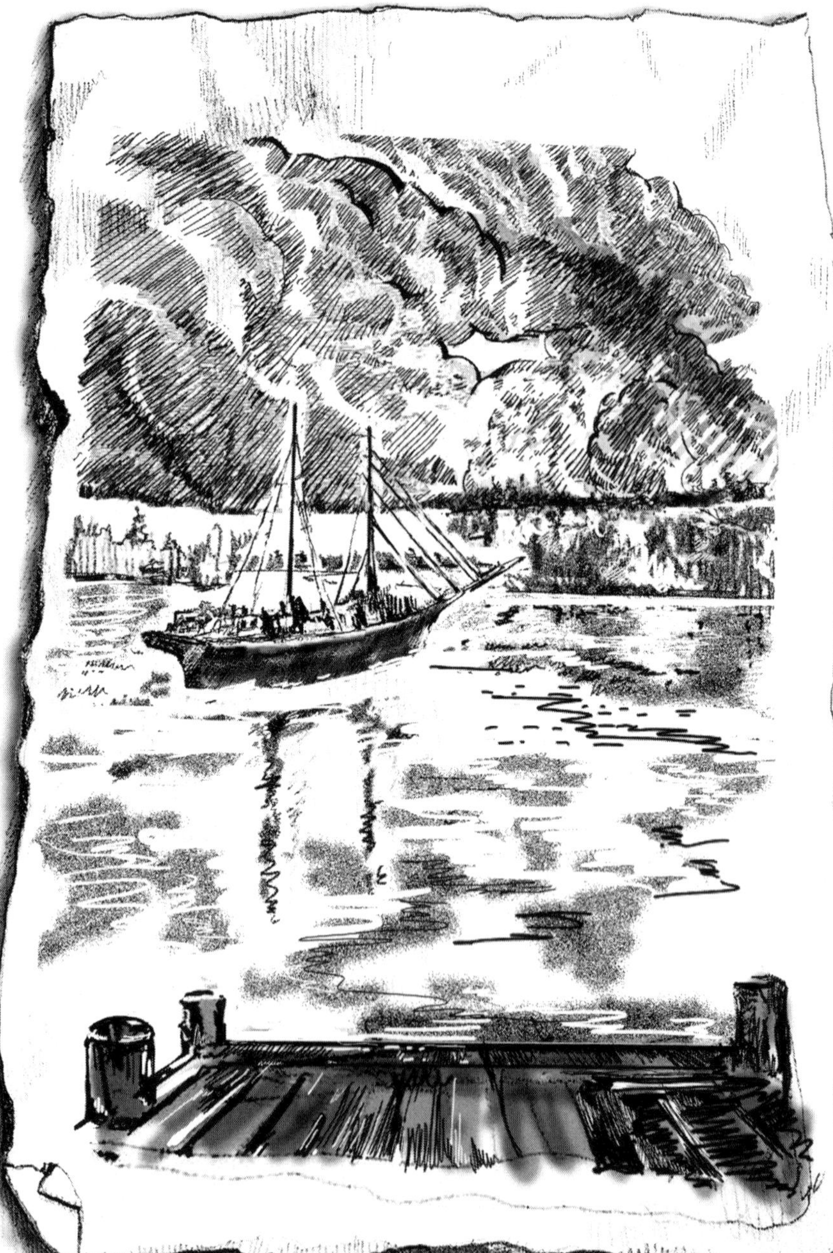

1852

IN FEBRUARY, 1852, Clement and Henry Studebaker, a blacksmith and foundry man, respectively, began manufacturing parts for freight wagons in South Bend, Indiana. Their brother, John, built wheelbarrows in Placerville, California. Soon all five Studebaker brothers were manufacturing and selling wagons and carriages for thousands of people traveling west on the Oregon Trail. It is interesting to note that there were also five Studebaker sisters.

On December 28, Asher Sarjent of Indiana sent a letter to his sons, Nels and Wils, in Olympia informing them that he was joining James Longmire and others to organize a wagon train to the soon-to-be Washington Territory.

A newly arrived American settler

> ...stopped all night at a frame tavern dignified by the name Olympia Hotel[271] and made inquiries about Stilacom [sic], where I had been asked to settle, and found there was some difficulty about title, it once having been a post of the Hudson's Bay Company, and reserved by them in our treaty with England. So I concluded to go no farther, at present, feeling the necessity for a little respite from my arduous journeying.[272]

It is doubtful that Edward Huggins and some Indian friends had such fine accommodations, or used a Studebaker cart on a short trip to Day Island.[273] Actually their hunting and

---

271 Owned by Edmund Sylvester, founder of Olympia, the building was merely a rustic cabin built by its owner according to George E. Blankenship "Lights and shades of Pioneer Life, by a Native Son" olympiahistory.org.

272 Johnson, Karen L. and Larsen Dennis M. *Yankee of Puget Sound, Pioneer Dispatches of Edward Jay Allen, 1852-1855*, WSU Press, Pullman, WA 2013

273 Day Island was named by Commander Charles Wilkes of the U.S. Exploring Expedition in the spring of 1841 for hospital steward Stephen W. Day travelling with the Expedition. There is, however, a persistent story that the island name is the result being an actual geographically-defined island only on the highest tides, which make it an unmistakable island. For many years residents celebrated the rare highest tide day with a boat and canoe parade around the tiny isle, often to the cheers of neighbors, according to Marcia Willoughby Tucker, Day Island resident, historian and author of *Day Island, A Glimpse of the Past*, Rhododendron Press, 1997.

fishing camp was at Crystal Creek[274] on the mainland across the shallow, on the island's eastern shore. Huggins wrote in March that the camp had been used for a long time.

> *Just a little before dark, we reached the usual encampment, a small streamlet, on the mainland at the north end of Days Island, called by the Indians 'Tuk-a-ma-lie' and from the large mound of shells there, it had evidently been a camping ground for centuries.*[275]

Indians from Steilacoom Creek and Wollochet Bay shared the encampment and duck-hunting grounds. They made seasonal trips to Day Island. The sand spit was a center of activity during duck hunting expeditions. In the half light of dawn or twilight, the Indians prepared a cedar bark net between two poles stuck in the sandy gravel beach. They hung a twelve foot long net from the poles. The net had a mesh large enough for a duck to poke its head through, but small enough to make it difficult to pull free. Later the duck hunters would startle the slumbering fowl, which then tried to escape but flew into the netting. The hunters quickly released the poles. The netting collapsed on the beach, where the hunters flogged the birds with sticks.[276]

Manufacturing came to the area that is now downtown Tacoma on April 1, 1852, when white settlement began in the heart of Puyallup tribal lands. Nicholas Delin, a Swedish carpenter, built his sawmill on pilings near the head of what is now Foss Waterway (located about where 23rd and Dock Streets are today). That new sawmill, the cutting edge of technology at the foot of Gallaher's Gulch (where South Tacoma Way begins at Pacific Avenue), became the first structure built by American settlers in what would someday be the City of Tacoma. Delin Creek ambled down the hillside gullies to the sea water. That water flow, impounded by a wood and earthen dam, along with the abundance of nearby trees on the hillsides, was enough for a young entrepreneur to speculate with a lumber business. Delin obtained the financial backing of Sam McCaw, Jacob Burnhardt, and William Sales to erect the mill. The logs were cut with a water-powered "Muley" saw.[277]

Delin claimed a total of 318 acres at the edge of extensive PSAC pastures called Puyallup Plain. Mill workers and fishermen began to populate the settlement. John Swan and Peter Rielly fished. Chauncy Baird operated a cooperage. Army veterans of the Mexican

---

274 Now in University Place, Washington. (Author comment)
275 Huggins, Edward, Seattle Times March 9, 1852, "*Perilous Trip for Fool.*"
276 Smith, Marion *The Puyallup-Nisqually*, p. 263, Columbia University Press
277 History Link, www.historylink.org/essays/output.cfm?file_id=5017. A Muley saw has a stiff blade that is not stretched at the gate, but whose motion is directed by clamps at the ends mounted on guide rails.

War (Jacob Kershner, Peter Runquist, and Carl Gorisch) took land claims and worked at the Delin mill, along with Scot Adam Benston.[278]

William and Eliza Sales came from England to build their family and a log cabin near the Delin sawmill. Their son, James, was the first white child born within the area that became Tacoma. James was born on October 20, 1853. The timing also makes James among the first whites born after the founding of Pierce County. The county was politically "born" only ten months before, on December 22, 1852.

Nicholas Delin, born in Sweden in 1817, came to the Puget Sound area from California in 1850, planning to partner with Col. Michael T. Simmons and Smith Hays, of Tumwater, to build a sawmill, but obtained other backers. Delin impounded two creeks with a ten-foot high timber dam at the mouth of a ravine later known as Gallagher's Gulch.[279] The water flow was harnessed to turn a wooden turbine wheel that Delin designed and built to drive the little mill. When operating at full speed under favorable conditions Delin and his crew were able to produce 2,000 feet of lumber in a day. It was the first industry at the head of Commencement Bay.

Delin's house was a few yards back of the mill, a little upland and facing the bay, near the south end of today's Foss Waterway. It was about 24 x 30 feet, one story and a half built of sawn boards standing vertically on end. The interior was finished with sawn cedar and hand-planned boards nailed horizontally. Nicholas and his brother Andrus built their own furniture and all of the cabinets. These were not simple "country-made" tables and chairs, as the Delin boys were skilled craftsmen. Contemporary observers declared the furniture to be "fine enough for a hotel!" Nicholas and Andrus were skilled craftsmen, indeed.

The little brig *George W. Emory*, Captain Trask commanding, sat at anchor in Commencement Bay while lumber was rafted out and loaded board by board over the stern. Delin cut nature's logs free of cost, bought logs others delivered to him for $6 each, and sold the sawn lumber for $20 per thousand board feet. The first cargo load of 350,000 feet of lumber was sold in San Francisco after delivery by the *George W. Emory*, providing Delin with a handsome $7,000 gross return.

It was not long until Jacob Burnhardt, Peter Judson, Chauncey Baird, and their

---

278 The thriving little settlement was evacuated during the Indian Treaty War of 1855-56. Subsequently Del Lin sold his mill to James L. Perkins for $3,500. Job Carr, celebrated as the First Tacoma settler, did not arrive until December 25, 1864. Carr's sons, Howard and Anthony, joined him in 1866.

279 The mill stood near the intersection of today's Dock Street at East "D" Street near Historic Puyallup Avenue. One creek probably drained the gulch that became South Tacoma Way. The other creek probably drained the gulch used today by the Tacoma & Eastern Railway west of McKinley Hill, and the one that drained through what is now Lincoln Bowl. Author Comments

families joined the Delin family in the new community, which was previously occupied only by a large Puyallup Indian long house, and two smaller ones.[280] Possibly five families occupied the three cedar longhouses, at what they called Gog-le-hi-te (where land meets water). It was an excellent fishing spot, opposite the original, natural, mouth of the Puyallup River.

This area at the head of the bay appears to have been the central village of the Puyallup Tribe of Indians, led by Chief Squatahan.[281] There were Indian longhouses along the western shore of the bay. Foss Waterway was called To-wad-sham (fording place) by these First People. The Puyallup River originally emptied into the waterway opposite the larger Indian village. Additional Puyallup Indian shelters were scattered upstream along the river through the valley and northward along the eastern shores of the bay as far as Redondo, dotting the beaches at Brown's Point, Dash Point, and Old Tacoma. A significant burial ground seems to have been where the Tacoma (later ASARCO) Smelter was built many years later, on nearly 100 acres at the southeastern shore of Point Defiance.[282]

The Territory of Washington established a Volunteer Militia, installing Brigadier General George Gibbs as the first commanding officer. Gibbs exercised his right to a Donation Land Claim of 320 acres by establishing his residence at Sastuc, where McChord Air Force base is today.[283] Gibbs' home was built less than ten miles from Fort Nisqually and the headquarters of the Puget Sound Agricultural Company. That land had been, since at least 1838, the site of the PSAC Sastuc Station where over 1,000 head of PSAC sheep grazed. Tolmie protested, with little success. This high ranking American squatter blatantly took Company land which had been in British possession for fourteen years.

Transportation was easy on the waters of Puget Sound. The Puyallup Indian villages

---

280 The Puyallup Village was located near the foot of 15th Street on the west shore of Foss Waterway. Author's comment.

281 Hunt, Herbert, *Tacoma, Its History and Its Builders, Volume I*, The J.S. Clarke Publishing Company, 1916, reprinted by the Tacoma Historical Society, Tacoma, WA, 2005.

282 The Tacoma Smelter was built by Dennis Ryan of St. Paul in 1888 at a cost of $209,000. William Rust took over the cash poor company, renaming it the Tacoma Smelting & Refining Company around 1890. Rust focused on modernizing the plant, changing its original emphasis on refining lead to the more profitable copper ore. By 1917 the smokestack was the tallest in the world, at 571 feet. Rust sold the smelter to the Guggenheim partners, who owned ASARCO, The American Smelting and Refining Company, for $5.5 million. Rust built the famous Rust Mansion on I Street and another home on Yakima Avenue. In 1983 the site became an EPA Superfund cleanup project, then redeveloped as the planned community "Point Ruston." The original human use for the site is believed to have been a Native American burial ground. Author's notes.

283 "A Chronological History of McChord Air Force Base" assembled by Robert D. MacDonald, Base Forester, 62 CES/DEEP

and many of the new settlers' homes along the shores of Commencement Bay were a relatively short canoe ride around Point Defiance to Fort Nisqually and Steilacoom City. Other Puyallup Indian villages were located along the river and in the valley that today bears the tribal name and means "twisting-turning" river."[284]

The romantic image of Oregon Country captured the imagination of the nation, beginning with Lewis and Clark, and gained popular momentum into the 1840s. But in 1852, Indiana was the "hot bed" of Oregon rhetoric. The state assembly even passed three resolutions urging the United States to take control of Oregon. The first resolution urged the government to take possession and organize a civil government. The second resolution was extremely anti-British. It demanded the United States defend Oregon "peaceably if we can, forcefully if we must."[285] The third and final resolution on the subject declared that the U.S. had a right to the land south of the 52nd parallel. It urged the United States to abrogate the joint occupation treaty of 1818.

Olympia's first newspaper began publishing on September 11, 1852. The "Columbian" lasted about a year. Much of the news it published was about the lack of government in Old Oregon. Indiana newspapers got into the territorial fray with editorials and articles demanding "no surrender" and immediate "action." Many articles proclaimed the fertility of the soil, but others called Old Oregon a "wasteland," while still demanding military intervention if certain demands were not met. All of this led to many Hoosiers migrating west for perfect health and easy wealth.

The newspapers advertised flour for $50 per barrel and potatoes for $2 per bushel. Certainly not bargain prices when compared to eastern state prices. In one of his letters to the *Pittsburg Dispatch*, Edward Jay Allen commented on prices:

> *Our beef cost us 16 cents per pound, potatoes $2.50 per bushel, turnips 12½ cents each. Our barrel of flour cost us $40, a barrel of salmon (cheapest thing in the country) is $15.... Our whole concern, including a canoe, and provisions sufficient to last us a month, cost $210, probably at home (in Pennsylvania) would only have cost $70.*

Much of the produce Edwards was purchasing originated at PSAC farms, but was retailed at Olympia stores. PSAC workers such as John McPhail did the farm work. But John McPhail had become quite troublesome to Dr. Tolmie and the others at Fort

---

284 Dr. James Hoard during several personal conversations. Author's notes.

285 Maben, Michael, "There is a Land in the Far Off West," *Columbia*, Winter 2006-07. Washington State Historical Society, Tacoma, WA.

Nisqually early in 1852. He was drunk, quarreling, and even fighting with some of the men when Tolmie declared him an "utterly worthless fellow." Other men were doing well. Chaulifoux, Thornhill, Barnes, Tapou, Cowie, and Keave'hacow were at their assigned duties every day in spite of the nearly incessant rain. A new stable was built. Firewood was cut and hauled. Wheat was winnowed. Fodder was fetched. Three beef cows were slaughtered for market and meals.

Heavy winter rain washed out many of the dirt roads, more correctly called trails. Deeper drainage ditches were dug to relieve the swamps and low areas of PSAC farms on the flat plains. The Nisqually River ran very high and became treacherous, but Tolmie risked his life as he made his way across the rain-swollen water hazard to Olympia to present Mr. Moses, the U.S. Customs Officer, with a bill. Tolmie demanded payment for goods purchased at the Trade Store by American Captain Balch Master of the *Damarascove*. The bill Tolmie delivered had to be left with Captain Stuart, as Moses was (conveniently?) not in town. It was another point of American annoyance for Dr. Tolmie, adding to the tension between the Brits and the new American authorities.

It was not long, however, before capitalist endeavor eased the long-standing problem of crossing the swollen Nisqually River. William Packwood requested and was granted a charter, by the Thurston County Commissioners, to operate a ferry across the Nisqually River in 1852.

News of events out of the local area included the unfortunate wreck of the *Georgiana* on the coast of the Queen Charlotte Islands (Haida Gwaii) which are northwest of British Columbia. Crew and passengers all survived only to be made prisoner-slaves of the Haida. A ransom of $1,800 was paid in HBC goods to free the hostages.

Also the *Suzanna* was wrecked off Cape Flattery (northwest tip of Washington State). She was driven by the power of the weather into the rocks. Again all passengers and crew were saved only to be captured, this time by the Makah. There is no mention of a ransom being paid, but the Indians did burn the ship to get the iron, copper and other metal pieces. The passengers and crew from both shipwrecks were finally rescued at the end of January by the American Captain Balch, Master of the *Damarascove*, and first citizen of Steilacoom City.

Other local news reported that Captain Balch suffered a break-in at his Steilacoom store. Several blankets were stolen. Indians were blamed, of course, without evidence. The weather was probably the motivation for the theft: the perpetrator was probably wet and cold. Miserably cold rain continued to fall, and the temperatures fell as well. Even the ink froze in Dr. Tolmie's ink reservoir.

As the rainfalls slowed, the frozen ground halted all plowing, but the roads were more passable without the mud. Tolmie returned to Olympia to seek out Moses for the payment of the bill left earlier. Moses offered to settle the bill by drawing on the United States Treasury, or by order on the Bank of San Francisco. He had written to both for instructions but had not yet seen a reply. Both money sources Moses mentioned would decline to pay any draft Moses might write. Tolmie still didn't get paid. His Fort Nisqually account books still showed a past due account for $1,839.90. He went to the Columbia River for instructions of his superiors at Fort Vancouver.

While Tolmie was absent, two Indian boys "borrowed" some horses for a nighttime run. They were caught and confined to the uppermost floor of the bastion. Three days later they were flogged and released.

On his return trip from Fort Vancouver, Tolmie was accompanied as far as Olympia by Judge Strong and some HBC lawyers. Tolmie was eager to collect the past due account from Moses, and wanted the American court in Olympia to agree.

There was also the matter of some American charges against the steamer *Beaver*. It seems the *Beaver* had offloaded three dozen scythes, while the manifest listed only one dozen. The extra scythes, according to Fort Nisqually records, were properly delivered by the *Mary Dare,* but that was a detail Mr. Moses seemed to ignore. Mr. Moses seized the *Beaver* and the beach store, but released the store when confronted with a copy of the written law. Tolmie complained of a half days' work being lost after Moses took all of the scythes. Tolmie called it a "foolish transaction." It was, at the least, frustrating intimidation by the American Customs Officer.

A few days later a secret note arrived at Fort Nisqually from the Company lawyers. In the note the lawyers advised Mr. Maire, Master of the *Beaver,* to quickly make his way to Vancouver Island (out of reach of American courts), as he was about to be arrested and personally charged with liability for the fines attached to the charges against his ship.

Dr. Tolmie wrote a letter to the U.S. Customs House after he discovered that some tobacco had also been seized from the *SS Beaver*. It seems that leaf tobacco was inadvertently retained on board at Victoria. The tobacco was sent for use as trade goods North of Latitude 49, but not offloaded at Victoria as planned. The *Beaver* proceeded to Nisqually with the *Mary Dare* in tow. The scythes and the tobacco were supposed to be on board the *Mary Dare*. There should not have been any charges against the *Beaver,* according to Tolmie's contention. The plan was for the cargo to be transferred to the proper ship for delivery to the proper places. Judge Strong, Mr. Moses and Dr. Tolmie finally reached an agreement that met the desires of all parties.

Mr. Work, his family, and Mrs. Ross departed as passengers aboard the *Mary Dare* to Victoria. Mrs. Ross intended to reside at Victoria near Mr. Work and his family. The cargo hold contained some tobacco and two dozen scythes all destined for points north.

A "grand meeting" was held at Steilacoom to discuss the conduct of Mr. Moses and Judge Strong in the seizure affair. It was generally agreed that Moses had done his duty by seizing the cargo and the ship. Most thought Moses deserved thanks from his fellow citizens. There was an allegation that Judge Strong had been bribed. Some very fierce sentiment against the Company was expressed. Balch, Hall, Chambers, and Bradley talked of confining the Company within a one-mile-square and killing all of the cattle found by Americans outside the prescribed mile. All of this rhetorical discussion came after Dr. Tolmie and Mr. Moses had come to a clear and distinct understanding, based on Judge Strong's ruling, that the goods in question should be sent out of the country, as had been done.

While the paperwork and hot words sailed between Olympia, Steilacoom, and Fort Nisqually, ships were sailing, too. The *Susan Stugis, Beaver,* and *Mary Dare* all carried huge cargos of goods from Fort Nisqually. Some 40,000 shingles (at $4 per 100), a storefull of dry goods, 59 beef quarters, 70 sheep, and more were shipped out. All hands were involved in loading the cargo. Fort Nisqually was clearly downsizing.

In less than a month the U.S. Sloop of War *Vincennes*, Captain Hudson, was lying at anchor at the Fort Nisqually landing. Within hours of landing, the Captain and officers were visiting Dr. Tolmie. The visit from today's perspective seems to have been a bit of "Gunboat Diplomacy." The U.S. seems to have sent a warship to observe an international dispute that was unsettling to the American population. Dr. Tolmie hospitably opened his home for the visiting officers, but undoubtedly made his political points as well.

After a few hours of visiting with the officers aboard the *Vincennes,* Tolmie had sold some 150 bushes of potatoes to the ship's mess for 60 cents per bushel. In another three days Tolmie had sold to the ship nine live hogs for ten cents per pound, and fed the Captain and officers in his formal dining room as a pleasant farewell. The *Vincennes* spent five days and nearly $200 with the "enemy" at Fort Nisqually. All of the supplies purchased by the *Vincennes* that week could have been purchased in Steilacoom or Olympia from American merchants. Perhaps the ship was on a "Goodwill Mission," rather than exerting "Gunboat Diplomacy."

Mr. Moses did not give up his procedural attacks on the British at Fort Nisqually. When the *Mary Dare* landed again, Customs Collector Moses drew out a form of affidavit to be sworn and signed at Victoria regarding some plows and the flour recently imported for use at Fort Nisqually. Dr. Tolmie instantly objected to the procedures, as there was already an affidavit for the goods mentioned. Moses responded that the affidavit was not "certified with an oath" at Victoria before sailing.

Meanwhile, Tolmie had the men deliver 1,200 pounds of beef and 25 barrels of flour to the Balch store in Steilacoom for resale to Americans. Beef sold at nearly twice the price of live hogs, and flour was $16 per barrel. Tolmie, with Captain Mouat along for the ride, collected something in the range of $640 from one slow-to-pay antagonistic American customer. A few days later, another 800 pounds of PSAC beef was delivered to Balch. Obviously Americans liked the Fort Nisqually meat, but preferred the "Balch" retail brand.

Some situations were not so good. The English contract laborers began demanding a wage increase. Soon some 400 wedder lambs died at Beinston's pasture. The weather was blamed, but lack of attention could also be blamed. Very cold temperatures and gale-force winds caused a great deal of suffering. Adam Beinston quit at the end of his contract to take an American land claim along the Puyallup River. Beinston was replaced by Mr. Northover, with wages set at £20 per annum, an increase for the position. Tolmie found 60 more lambs dead just before eight inches of snow fell. A horse named Kamboo died in his stall. The animal was opened to find his insides full of worms, so this animal's death was probably not due to the wage dispute or the cold weather. Chaulifoux and McPhail couldn't work because they were sick. Keave'hacow quit, taking a job with Mr. Chambers for more pay in American currency. Cross and Cowie were drunk and couldn't work.

Still, goods worth some $600 were purchased by Mr. Palmer of Port Steilacoom. It was necessary to provide a 20 per cent discount to get the sale. Captain Cooper ordered a full cargo of beef, but instead took a load of live sheep at 62½ cents per head. The men willing and able to work could not round up enough cattle for Cooper, so he accepted the sheep. Tolmie was pleased, as a sale was made.

Four Soquamish Indians in the trade store drew their knives without provocation. Huggins, with nerves of steel, chased the knife wielders out of the store with words alone. The daring robbers got away. Huggins probably decided against actually catching any of the armed thieves. Dr. Tolmie notified Mr. Starling, the American Indian Agent, of the incident. There were no apparent results.

Gold was discovered in the (Haida Gwaii) Queen Charlotte Islands northwest of British Columbia. Captain Balch sent his ship, but refused to take any of the Company's men, as he knew they were employed at Fort Nisqually. If the employees were to desert their employer, Balch would not be complicit. An American merchant fleet (*Franklin, G.W. Kendal, Leonora,* and others) did set sail to find a gold fortune after purchasing supplies at Fort Nisqually. Business was brisk at the trade store.

By April, the frogs were croaking and Americans were coming to the Fort to purchase supplies and have their wagons repaired. More reports of gold in the Queen Charlotte

Islands came when the *Exact* landed after a four month cruise. After loading provisions, she was off to the islands once more.

Just then three American soldiers assumed that Fort Steilacoom discharge papers meant they had a right to claim Company land. These squatters were relatively easy to handle. Their former commanding officers were asked to assist Tolmie in explaining the laws. The former soldiers were sent away by their former commanding officer.

The annual animal census of the Fort Nisqually was begun by counting the horses and loading a herd of cattle aboard an American vessel bound for Victoria. The sheep count was delayed as some Californian customers endeavored to make a bargain for a nice sized flock. There seems to have been no record of price for the animals the Californians wanted, but a ship named *Honolulu* took on 270 sheep, 453 quarters of beef, and some livestock for private individuals. Interestingly, the *Honolulu* immediately set sail in a fair wind bound for Victoria, not California.

By mid-April a new road was under construction. It would facilitate the loading of cattle at the Nisqually Landing. Drinking was a continuing problem among the men. McPhail, always listed first, was "troublesome," Barnes and Legg were "away drinking", so Dr. Tolmie took on more Indian workers. New oxen yokes were built, the horse cart was repaired, two ploughs were in the fields, fencing logs were brought in, and peas were sowed. The business of the Fort Nisqually fur trade post and Puget Sound Agricultural Company continued in spite of drunkenness, sickness, and labor-wage disputes.

More soldiers attempted to take claims, again near Sastuc. Notices were presented to Sergeant Jason Hall, R.M Hall, Christopher Mahon, Thomas Tolentire, John Withal, and C.W. Savage, informing them in writing that they were trespassers on Company lands. The U.S. Army sent Dr. Haden and Lieutenant Dement to Fort Nisqually the next day to discuss matters with Dr. Tolmie. The doctor and lieutenant suggested that legal efforts might find the solution the Company desired.

About this time, Mr. J. Chapman of Steilacoom City was engaged to survey PSAC lands. He was accompanied in his work by Huggins, Barnes, Dean, and six Indians. By the end of April more than thirty miles had been surveyed. It was arduous and fatiguing work, but not as difficult as building the new cattle road, which was completed about the same time.

A large cattle drive was organized. Several Indians and Company servants became cowboys to drive 50 head down the new road one day, then 20 head the second day, and another 17 the next. Reluctant wild cattle were killed, butchered on the spot, and immediately sold for meat to keep the herd moving along. The horns, hides, and hooves of the butchered animals were packaged for sale in London. A fourth cattle drive brought in another 22 head, still 109 head of cattle not enough for the *Honolulu* shipment. The live cattle were on board, but the ship's Captain was so unhappy with a short load that Dr. Tolmie had to pay him $100 for his loss. Certainly more cattle were available, if time were allowed to gather a herd, but the horses and men were spent, and the ship already delayed.

The *Honolulu* was expected to return for another shipload of live cattle, so a new 'cowboy' crew was sent to Tlithlow with Mr. Ross. They succeeded in bringing in a herd of about 21 cattle, in two efforts, for the next shipment.

Before they were finished with the cattle drive, the survey party suddenly appeared at the Fort. Their operations were halted by armed squatters, who would not allow them to proceed. The survey was about three-fourths complete when Chapman departed for the East. His incomplete map was somewhat distorted as well.

Months later, plans were made for the remaining survey crew to complete the map by working from Steilacoom City, behind Charles Ross' house, back toward the other side of the squatters. They commenced at the corner, one mile below Steilacoom, and finished at the point where the squatters had stopped them on the first of May.

Chaulifoux repaired the woolpress lever handle, aired out the furs, and beat them clean of dust and bugs. Tolmie negotiated a contract with Mr. W. Huntley of Steilacoom to purchase a beef carcass twice a week. Oats were brought in from Muck. Five milk cows were driven in to make butter. The Fort held an auction to sell the effects of the deceased Charles Forrest. There is no word on the circumstances of his death. New carts were built, fodder was carted to the stable, and firewood was stacked. "Jobbing" about the Fort continued.

There were more squatters and more land possession problems, but business continued. The U.S. Army sent notice of a surplus goods sale at Steilacoom Barracks. Dr. Tolmie attended the sale, purchasing several barrels of flour. It was a strategic purchase, preventing the flour from going to a competitor, and boosting available supplies at the Fort. No one knows how food stuff could be surplus at a remote Army post.

For several weeks Charles Ross and the cowboys were decidedly unsuccessful at driving significant numbers of cattle to the temporary cattle park at the Fort. Then Charles Wren brought in 7 large oxen. He was paid $4 each in cash for the delivery. Near the end of May seven more head were finally driven into the cattle park. Another 50 head came in as Dr. Tolmie headed to Olympia and another court date for the *Mary Dare* case. Altogether the *Honolulu* shipped another 105 head of cattle, along with 50 quarters of beef. Tolmie arrived back at Fort Nisqually in time to see the *Honolulu* off to Victoria again. It seems the court decided not to decide the *Mary Dare* case during that session.

At the end of May, Dr. Tolmie sold 600 head of sheep to a Californian at $5 per head.

Mr. Dean's error in leaving some rams with the band had turned a profit after all. The rams were ordered to be separated, or slaughtered, to keep the flock from growing so rapidly. The Californian came along at just the right time to keep the size of the flock at manageable numbers.

June was hot. Temperatures reached 92 early in the month. It was sheep shearing season. Hot dirty work any day, but hotter days made for even more difficult working conditions. The *Honolulu* was becalmed off Whidby Island, where Captain Thomas Coupe had just claimed land and settled in to become a gentleman farmer. Fort Nisqually men were hard pressed to find the cattle needed to complete a ship load for the *Honolulu*. The calm winds meant more time to gather the animals. John Ross agreed to sell his entire herd to the Company for $300. His herd of animals was also wild longhorn "Spanish" cattle. They were running wild on the plains, too, but at least they could be more easily found.

An American, Mr. Parker, came to the Fort to buy some shorn sheep. Tolmie negotiated a sweet deal for 1,000 head to be delivered to Cowlitz Farms. McPhail was the chosen herdsman, with four Indians as helpers. Parker selected several ewes to be washed and examined. Parker liked what he saw, made a partial payment and left for home. The sheep were to be delivered to the mouth of the Cowlitz. Three days later, McPhail sent word that he had crossed the now calmer Nisqually River with all 1,000 head, but that two Indian helpers had quit. He needed two replacements right away. The request was quickly met and five days later a report came in that said McPhail had been seen 12 miles from the Cowlitz. Only one animal had died. That was a remarkable feat for this kind of hard journey. Tolmie departed for Fort Vancouver and the mouth of the Cowlitz to settle accounts with Mr. Parker.

The good news did not carry over. The *Honolulu* was roped into the landing at Nisqually. She reported that on the last voyage 40 head of cattle had died in transit. It was a sparse load in the beginning, but Tolmie insisted it was a risk taken by the Super Cargo and buyer. The contract called for delivery of live cattle. Tolmie still had to deliver live cattle in the numbers the contract had specified. Under the contract, Tolmie took the risk. He was an additional 40 head short of the number needed.

While Tolmie was away in Olympia, the trade store took in $270 in brisk sales. The men packed 7,766 pounds of quality wool destined for the London auction markets. Three Company horses were shot and severely injured, probably by Americans. One did not recover from the ball in his chest. A squatter named Tollentire was the prime suspect, since the horses were found near his place on the Sustac Plain. A horse belonging to Montgomery was stabbed with a knife and a Company bull was shot dead on

Sustac Plain, the grassland immediately north of Nisqually plain.[286] Patchin, a Nisqually residing at Sustac, reported that he saw Tollentire fire at the Company's animals. Indian testimony was not allowed in American courts at the time.

Mr. Sales abruptly announced his intention to desert his contract with the Company. It seems Mr. Sales had a barrel of liquor in his house. He was selling to Indians, while working only 5 or 6 hours for the Company instead of the normal 10 hours. He was caught, and punished appropriately by Company standards. His booze was destroyed.

It must have been a good party celebrating American Independence in Steilacoom City. The town had been awarded the first United States Post Office in Pierce County. It opened officially on July 6, 1852. Dr. Tolmie went to town on the morning of the fifth (the fourth was a Sunday) to join the Independence Day Celebration party. He returned on the sixth with a "bad foot." There were no entries in the journal explaining the injury and none for the next two days.

Tolmie's negotiation skills were not harmed by the party or the mysterious injury. An American ship, *John Davis*, landed at Nisqually. Captain Plummer wanted to off-load 50 tons of cargo for the Catholic Bishop of Vancouver Island. He wanted the goods stored until Tolmie could arrange for further transport to the Bishop. Tolmie offered $450 for Plummer to take the Bishop's goods to Vancouver Island and bring back a full supply cargo for the Fort. Speculation says that certain Customs regulations could be avoided by this business arrangement. An American ship transporting goods for the British Bishop and returning with Fort Nisqually supplies might be missed by U.S. Customs agents.

Within a month, the *John Davis* was back at Nisqually with that cargo of supplies from Victoria, and Tolmie was in Olympia settling Customs business. While he was there, Tolmie mentioned to Mr. Moses, the Customs Agent, that the bill for $1,800 in goods supplied by Fort Nisqually to the *Damarascove* in January had still not been paid, but Tolmie received no reply.

On August 14th Dr. Tolmie, Mrs. Tolmie, the two sisters of James Burnie of the Cowlitz departed for Victoria. Thornhill went along as steward. Imagine the Indian Canoe loaded with the baggage for five passengers, all the food and overnight accommodations they would require, the finery needed for a servant to act as steward, and the crew of Indian paddlers with their required supplies, paddles, tents, food, etc. This party was of the "Gentleman Class" and as such would have been treated with near royal aid and assistance for every need real or imagined. Presumably tea was served at four.

---

286 Sastuc Plain might also be called American Plain, an extension of the much smaller Methodist Mission Plain. It is west of American Lake where North Fort Lewis is located today as part of Joint Base Lewis McChord. (Author comment)

The return trip was more eventful than the initial voyage. This time Dr. and Mrs. Tolmie traveled with Miss Work, Miss Anderson, and Master Anderson. Thornhill again served as steward. It was a tedious and stormy passage of seven days.

Tolmie's temper showed almost immediately upon his return. It seems that a sheep was stolen, killed and eaten by some vagabond Indians. Tolmie flogged them before he let them go the next morning.

A new property tax bill of $645.12 was paid under protest. The Pierce County assessment for real estate taxes amounted to $ 645.12 at the rate of 75 cents per acre on 244 square miles as shown on the recently completed Chapman survey map. James Douglas, HBC Manager at Fort Vancouver, was concerned. He protested,

> "By my calculations of the extent of the area, the rate of tax will not come to more than one half cent per acre or exactly $2.88 a square mile, a matter to which I call your attention lest there should be a mistake in your (tax) statement."[287]

There seems to have been no tax relief in spite of the obvious miscalculation by both sides.[288] Douglas continued

> ...I suppose according to the law, the sum would have been levied by execution (sale) of the Company's property, even if you (Dr. Tolmie) had not consented to pay the demand, you had therefore no alternative but to pay the sum under protest.[289]

A few days later all of the Englishmen at the Fort were sent to do road work, as required of all residents, for the new military road between Steilacoom and Olympia. All able-bodied men were expected to "subscribe" to donate funds, supplies, or labor for the work on the road designated by the Territorial Legislature in Salem. It mattered not that all of the roads had been initiated by Fort men and based on Indian trails long before the American settlers arrived. The early workers were granted no credit for the roads across the 161,000 acres of Company farm and ranch land that settlers used with impunity. It did not matter that these Englishmen were not American citizens. All that mattered was the required participation of ALL men in the area, except Indians.

287

288 At 75 cents per acre the tax would have been well over $120,000, while at one-half cent per acre the tax should have been $8,050. HBC paid the $645.12 as requested without further comment. (Author comment)

289 Unpublished letter Douglas to Tolmie, 14 Oct 1852.

Ross fell off his horse, breaking his arm. He was soon transferred to the new coal mines at Nanaimo on Vancouver Island. The flour in the beach store barrels turned bad; only one-third could be saved. Apparently the former Mate of the *Beaver* could not be saved either. He had very recently left the service, and while in a fit of intoxication, blew his brains out.

A pistol broke the jaw of a quarreling sailor on board the American ship *Persea*. Captain Brown brought the sailor to Dr. Tolmie for medical assistance, but quarreling was apparently more violent at Victoria. An Orkney man was shot dead near a saloon in the middle of town by quarrelsome Indians.

Two Americans and two Indians were apparently drowned on a short trip from Olympia to the Fort. Puget Sound is normally quite calm and smooth, but on occasion it can become treacherous, even in nice weather. In late November, normally gentle showers and winds apparently caused an incident on the water. Americans named Ellet and Davis, along with two Indians, were presumed drowned a week after their departure. The Fort Nisqually *Journal of Occurrences* reported, *"...no tidings have been received of them to the present."*

Production of oats at PSAC was less than expected, and less than needed for export, so Dr. Tolmie began making strategic purchases. He got 200 bushels from Charles Wren at $1.25 each, and another 100 bushels from Gravelle for $1.00 per bushel. All of the oats were shipped to Victoria.

The potato crop was smaller as well. Only 800 bushels were in by November. Flour prices were rising. At the mill in town a barrel was selling for $15, but the Fort was able to get $18. Perhaps quality makes the difference. Blanket prices were lowered to encourage trade. A three-point blanket was sold for $4 and a two-point was available for only $3 cash. HBC blankets were marked during production with straight woven lines, much like a modern bar code, to indicate the relative value of each individual item.

Perhaps Dr. Tolmie picked up a copy of Washington's first weekly newspaper, *The Columbian*, published on September 11, 1852, while he walked along busy Commercial Street in Steilacoom. The first edition must have been shared widely among the shops, saloons, and stables where Pioneer Orchard Park stands today. *The Columbian* reported that the little village on Elliott Bay named Seattle, would get its first United States Post Office on October 12, 1852 with Arthur F. Denny as postmaster.

Later in September *The Columbian* announced the arrival of a new Brevet Captain at Vancouver's Columbia Barracks. Ulysses S. Grant, later to gain fame in the Civil War and become President of the United States, brought his troops from San Francisco for a 15 month deployment. Grant was the regimental quartermaster for the 4th Infantry. During his tour of duty in the northwest, Grant began growing his iconic beard. His letters to his wife and children reveal the new growth just before he arrived in Washington Territory.

November saw a grand total of $2,200 in receipts at the trade store. Americans were becoming quite adept at purchasing at the trade store and reselling the same goods in Steilacoom and Olympia. Dr. Tolmie agreed to pay a commission of 7 percent to Major Goldsboro for selling Company goods. Mr. Cushman purchased three bales of three-point blankets at $6.00 each. He was planning to resell the blankets individually, of course.

Regularly scheduled canoe and wagonloads of beef carcasses were sent to Steilacoom and Olympia for the American butcher shops to cut and resell. Thirty-seven quarters of beef were delivered in Olympia just before Christmas. Another 2,500 pounds of meat was delivered just before New Year's Day, with 500 pounds of the total going directly to Customs Collector Moses. Presumably the meat sent to Moses was a payment of Customs Duties, not for personal use.

On Christmas day, with the thermometer reading 4°, Dr. Tolmie and Captain Mouat went to the Olympia Customs House to settle the *Mary Dare's* customs problems with Mr. Moses. Finally the issue was cleared. Tolmie, Mouat and all the Fort employees enjoyed a celebratory regale with dancing and singing in one of the stores. McPhail and Tawai were soon drunk and disorderly.

The most important change came to the region on December 22, 1852: the creation of Pierce County. The Oregon Territorial Legislature clipped off a portion of Thurston County to form Pierce, Island, Jefferson, King, Pacific, Lewis, and Clark counties. These were the original political subdivisions of Washington Territory when it was formed on March 2, 1853.

Pierce County, situated between the Nisqually and Puyallup Rivers, was named in honor of President-Elect Franklin Pierce, one of the last slave-holding Presidents. He was elected President of the United States in November, 1852, and served from 1853 to 1857. Thomas Chambers, William P. Dougherty, and Alexander Smith were the first Pierce County Commissioners. John Bradley was named sheriff. John M. Chapman became probate clerk.

On December 28 Asher Sarjent sent a letter from Indiana to his wife, Della, and their adult sons in Olympia. Sarjent informed Della, Nelson, and Wils Sarjent that an Oregon Trail wagon train was being organized with James Longmire and others. Della Sarjent's letter of February 1, 1853, tells of her anxiety in waiting for her husband to return to Olympia.[290] Sarjent became the pilot, or trail guide, for the Longmire Party.[291] It was son Nelson who told in a letter to the pioneers that the Naches Trail was becoming a "road" by workmen from Olympia and Steilacoom. Nelson exaggerated in the extreme.

---

[290] Emmons, Della Gould, *Nothing In Life Is Free, Through Naches Pass to Puget Sound*, The Northwest Press, Minneapolis, 1953. The Longmire Party departed Indiana on March 6, 1853, after James Longmire and others sold their farms in Fountain County.

[291] *The Columbian*, October 22, 1853.

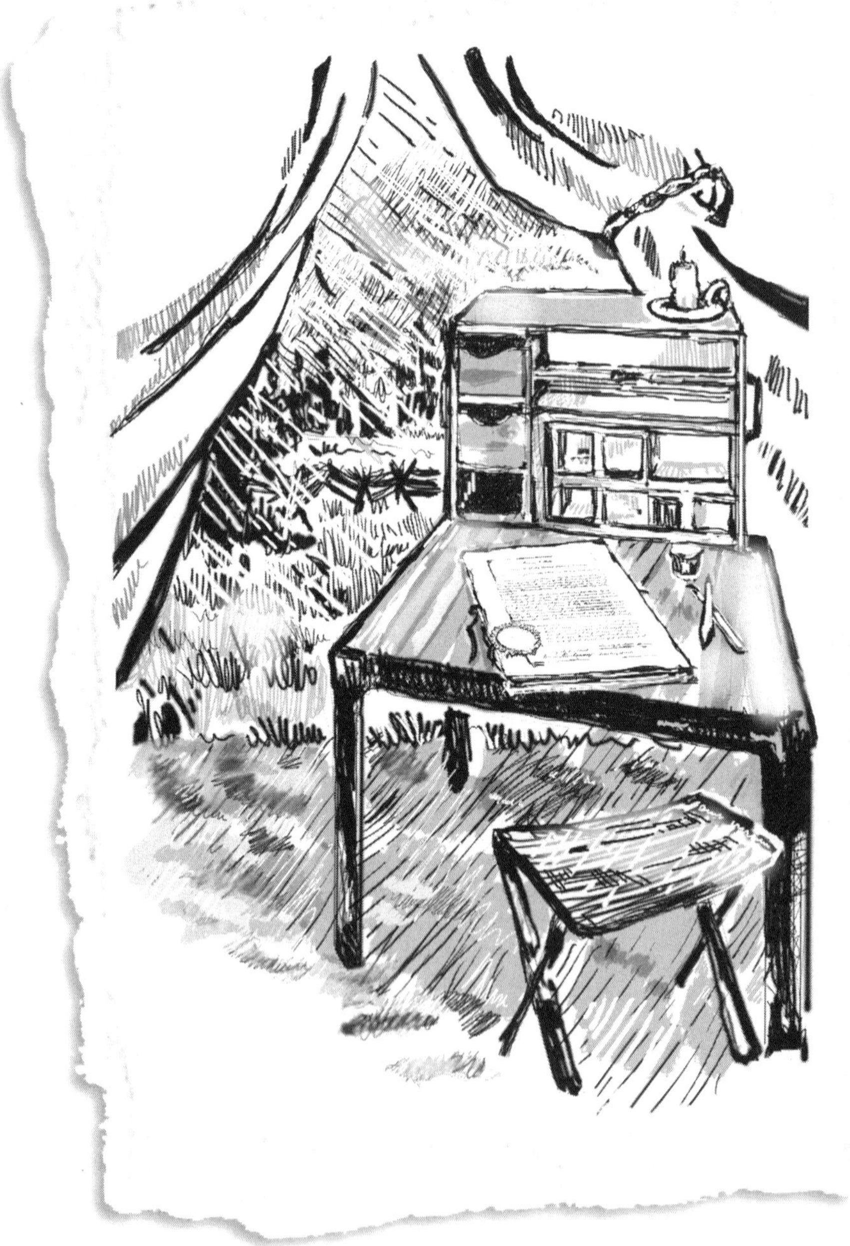

1853

THERE WERE AN ESTIMATED 4,000 non-Indian people living near Puget Sound as the Crimean War broke out between Russia and Turkey along the Black Sea. Britain would be involved in that war, while continuing operations of PASC at Nisqually. International politics created a situation whereby the British and Russians were enemies on the eastern side of the world, while continuing as trading partners through PSAC on the western side.

The first American wagon train to cross the Cascade mountain range (rather than follow the Columbia River to the Willamette Valley) carried immigrants who primarily settled in Steilacoom. The so-called Military Road was built initially by civilians along the centuries-old Naches Pass Trail. It had been in use from ancient times through the 1840s connecting Puget Sound and the interior. It was not much of a road. Even calling it a trail was generously picturesque.

Today modern adventurers occasionally attempt crossing the Cascade Mountains on the pioneer Naches Trail. Often these modern hikers are turned back by the Greenwater Bluff, which has been called a cliff. Even modern all-terrain vehicles, meandering off-trail logging roads, often make it only to Government Meadows, short of the actual apex of Naches Pass. Our forefathers faced much more difficult situations as they drove cumbersome, but powerful, ox teams towing wagons filled with a family's worldly possessions along an ancient Indian foot path leading westward toward Puget Sound from the Yakima Valley.

Edward Jay Allen, a native of Pittsburg, was the foreman of the crew organized in Olympia to open the Naches Road. After fording the Muck River and emerging on the Island Prairie, then on to Selquite Prairie, Cado Prairie, and Echo Prairie, Allen described the scenes he observed:

> ...we suddenly came upon another herd of wild cattle (belonging to the Hudson Bay Company,) which had been running wild cattle so many generations that they were as timid as buffalo. Such a scampering! Away, like the wind, passing not to look back, for shed of blood was quick on their track.

Allen's men were all set for a mass cattle killing when Allen offered a timely word to prevent a slaughter. The trail they were by then following cut overland directly from Fort Nisqually. Captain Wilkes had used the same trail in 1841. Theodore Winthrop had traversed the same 'road' only months before Wilkes. In 1848 the Naches Trail was described by Father Blanchet in his journal. This trail connected many of the HBC/PSAC ranches and pasture lands, where thousands of sheep and cattle had grazed for nearly sixteen years.

Funds were raised to pay for the supplies and labor required to build a Cascade Road wide enough for a wagon. Cash was sought from those who could not contribute sweat equity. Dr. Tolmie was a generous contributor. Not only did he provide cash, but he also donated provisions, "and other necessary material." The actual road construction began at John Montgomery's PSAC place near Spanaway Lake, the edge of Nisqually Plain.

Ten years earlier the eruption of Mt. St. Helens had played a part in developing this vast heard of cattle. The eruption sent toxic ash as far as Fort Vancouver, covering Columbia River pastures in a heavy sulphur-ash that threatened to kill the livestock. The Company was compelled to move the cattle to Nisqually, adding again to the PSAC operation. Allen seemed to be aware, and understand the legality, of the HBC possession of the land. He even directed the work crew to John Edgar's PSAC ranch before deeming the route feasible for work to begin.

The 1853 Longmire party of hardy pioneers heading for Puget Sound via Naches Pass reached Umatilla, Oregon, well east of the Cascade Mountains, as their provisions ran short. James Longmire reported that he "paid $40 in gold coin for (100 pounds) unbolted flour."[292]

Near Walla Walla, at the former mission of Marcus Whitman, the pioneers found a store known as Bumford and Broke. Prices were again very high. As an alternative source the pioneers purchased beef from Indians, who carefully sought payment for each piece as it was weighed.

The southern border of the U.S. changed as a treaty was signed to allow the U.S. purchase of 45,000 square miles of land from Mexico for $10 million in a deal known as the Gadsden Purchase. The treaty was not unlike the one made in 1846 concerning the northern border. In it, the U.S. agreed to purchase British land possessed by the HBC and PSAC along the shores of Puget Sound. By 1853 no payment had been made for the British property.

At its peak, England's HBC governed 1.5 million square miles of what are now Canada and the U.S. Pacific Northwest on behalf of a fewer than a hundred stockholders in

---

292 *Told by the Pioneers,* Tacoma Leger August 21, 1892, Reprint Olympia, 1937, 3 Volumes.

London, England. It was not the only company in the world doing exactly the same thing. Portugal, Spain, Netherlands, Russia, and France established colonies based on merchantile interests. The Royal Africa Company, the Dutch East India Company, the English East India Company, and many others, were all "stalking horses" for kings and parliaments. Judging those historic colonial enterprises against modern standards is called "cultural relativity" in sociology. Remember, Massachusetts and Virginia, homes of our most prestigious founding fathers, were founded by private trading companies licensed by kings, too.

On February 22, there was a change of the guard at U.S. Army's Fort Steilacoom. Lieutenant Dement was reassigned to return to the States from the Territory. He was replaced by Lieutenant William A. Slaughter. Captain George D. Hill and both sergeants R. Hall & A. J. Hall were replaced. Fort Steilacoom continued to be one of the most consistent and reliable customers of the HBC establishments, buying nearly all of the supplies the soldiers needed. A celebratory ball was held in early March for and by the soldiers during the change of command. All hands at Fort Nisqually were invited and most attended. Toward the end of March, a new company of 50 U.S. infantry men arrived at Steilacoom Barracks from Vancouver. Lieutenant Jones took command at the barracks.

Lieutenant William Slaughter, U.S. Army civil engineer, surveyed and platted the town of Steilacoom for merchant Captain Lafayette Balch.[293] Steilacoom became the first incorporated city in what is now Washington State by filing paperwork before any other town. It did not matter that the land was still British, under the Treaty of 1846, which required compensation to extinguish any British land claims.[294] It didn't matter to the British or Americans that aboriginal people (Steilacoom) still lived there, either. The Steilacoom Tribe is not recognized, even today, by the U.S. government.

In 1853 the first stagecoach operation in Washington Territory rumbled out of Monticello, near the mouth of the Cowlitz River, toward Olympia, the capitol of Washington Territory. It was a "mail line" route carrying the mail for the United States Postal Service, along with passengers and some light freight. It would be obsolete in 20 years, but was nearly a luxury to the people affected along that 90 mile route in 1853. The stage stopped every ten miles, or so, to change horse teams and give drivers and passengers a short period to relax.

American settlers around Puget Sound were troubled by the British land rules at Fort

---

293 The original map is in the archive collection at the Washington State History Museum, Ferry Building, in Tacoma.

294 That payment from the United States for the British land possession was still sixteen years in the future.

Nisqually in the midst of United States territory. At least 53 Americans had received letters of warning from Dr. Tolmie accusing them of trespassing on HBC/PSAC farm and ranch land.[295] It was, in fact, Pierce County, Washington Territory, U.S.A. However, the Boundary Treaty of 1846 established the border clearly granting the British businesses superior position concerning the real estate lands previously and continuously occupied by the HBC and the PSAC since 1833. Those land claims and improvements could only be legally extinguished by a cash settlement dually agreed to, and approved by, America's Congress, the British Parliament, the president, and the queen.

Here, dated September 13, 1853, is an excerpt from one of Tolmie's letters to James Douglas, Chief Factor of HBC:

> *I regret to inform you that squatters on Puget's Sound Agricultural Company's lands continue to increase in numbers, and are becoming bolder in their aggressions. Two men, deserted from the service—Barnes and William Northover—have taken claims in the vicinity of Tlithlkow, Mr. Dean's Stattion, and the latter of the two has built his house close to the four acre field of the Company's where there is now a crop of potatoes, he may not molest the crop, buty makes no secret of his intention of appropriating the field this autumn. Aubret and George Dean have recently.... established themselves on Company's lands near the Douglas River. One American has squatted close to Sastuck shepherd station in the north side of the plains and has enclosed his claim the buildings... (and) enclosures there. Early squatters have incessantly endeavoured... (and) doubtless induced many ignorant persons to join them. (Some lands) are considered fair game as well as all the encliosures at Tlithlow, or this palce, made since the date of the Boundary Treaty. From the foregoing statements you will perieve that our positon here is rapidly becoming worse, and that unless the proceedings of the squatters can in some way be checked, the business will soon be completely disorganized.*[296]

Tolmie recognized the legal community was American, as were the squatters. Neither group was inclined to accept the International Treaty at face value with so little to lose from British protest letters.

Trespassers and squatters regularly tried, and did, take land in the choicest spots, but all of it was British land between the Puyallup and Nisqually Rivers, the Sound and the

---

295 Oliphant, J. Orin "On the Cattle Ranges of the Oregon Country," University of Washington Press, Seattle, 1968.

296 *Fort Nisqually Correspondence Book*, 1852-1854 (B151/b2) HBC Archives of Manitoba, Canada, courtesy of email of Steve A. Anderson, transcriber January 2015, unpublished document.

Mountain foothills. The British enterprise, HBC was the largest corporation in the world, occupying 161,000 treeless acres of very desirable farm and ranch land in Pierce County alone. Simply put, the Hudson's Bay Company was here first, and chose the best land.

In 1853, believing the boundary line followed Rosario Strait, the deepest navigation channel closest to the mainland the HBC began to utilize the vast plains and prairies of the San Juan Islands. Belle Vue Farms of PSAC were established, with Charles John Griffin in charge of grazing sheep and pigs. Six years later (in 1859) an American, Lyman Cutler, moved to the island claiming farm land under the Donation Land Claim Act. Cutler found a large black pig rooting in his garden, eating his tubers. After several of these events, Cutler shot the pig and offered $10 for the dead animal. Griffin demanded $100, saying "It is up to you to keep your potatoes out of my pig." [297] Military forces were dispatched by both countries, and not fully withdrawn until 1874. During the ensuing years of confrontation and military bluster, local British authorities consistently lobbied London to seize back the Puget Sound region entirely, as Americans were busy with the Civil War.

Henry Yesler cut the first lumber in his new mill at the foot of what became Yesler Way, Seattle, on March 26, 1853. His land claim was well north of the HBC property. His lumber sold for $60 per thousand feet in the San Francisco market, in direct competition with Fort Nisqually shingles.

Levant F. Thompson and his wife Susannah Thompson acquired the old John Glasgow saw mill property on the north side of Sequalitchew Creek. Their donation land claim measured 157.3 acres of land surrounding the three-year-old water-powered saw mill. Glasgow had illegally squatted on HBC land, then deceptively sold his little business development to an unknowing and unaware Thompson, who purchased the stolen property. Of course, Dr. Tolmie sent a letter to Thompson and filed a court case, to little avail.

In Washington, D.C. the Congressional Committee on Territories met at the request of Oregon Delegate Joseph Lane. He wanted a report on the memorial referred to them the year before by the Oregon Legislature, urging the division of Oregon Territory. The committee reported a bill (H.R. 348) to the entire congress, passed on February 10, and signed by President Millard Fillmore on March 2, 1853. It created Washington Territory. News of the Congressional vote arrived at Olympia on April 25, 1853.

The Washington Territorial Legislature met for the first time at the Parker & Cole store in the Gold Building in Olympia. The second and third sessions of the legislature

---

297 Woodbury, Chuck, *"How One Pig Could Have Changed American History,"* Out West Newspaper as quoted by Wikipedia http://en.wikipedia.org/wiki/Pig_War

were held in the Masonic Building. In platting the town, Edmund Sylvester had set aside 12 acres for the capitol campus.

Even after the government of Pierce County was formed in 1853, much of the land in that county was still British owned. Local magistrates often ignored International Treaty Law to decide in favor of the increasing number of American settlers coming to claim their "legal allotment of 160 acres granted by Congress and the President of the United States." British legal ownership claims were most often simply ignored.

The wagon train led by James Longmire[298] and James Biles left the main Oregon Trail at Fort Walla Walla. Crossing the Columbia River in shifts took the afternoon and the night. Indians helped, when paid a pretty price. When the pioneer horses were half way across the swift and treacherous river, the helpful Indians formed a line, with the horses caught in the current. With very clear sign language the demand was made for more money to complete the crossing. "*I took out my purse*" James Longmire said in a narrative,[299] "*....to pay a hostage price.*"

Crossing the dry lands southeast of the Cascade Mountains the Indian guide for the Longmire Party considered himself cheated in a horse trade. Indignantly the guide deserted the wagon train near the mouth of the Yakima River. Without their Indian guide the pioneers were on their own without compass or landmark in a land where the natives were very opposed to the migratory invasion of their ancient homeland.

A band of Indians followed the wagon train for days, knowing the settlers had lost the trail. Scouts were sent out from the wagons to search for the elusive "road" that did not yet exist. Longmire set guards at night, while thoughts of massacre troubled the party. At Selah they met a Catholic priest, Father Herbonez, who directed them to the Wenas, which could lead them upstream to the Naches Road. The pioneers were still unaware that there really was no real wagon road. Just beyond the Wenas River they purchased thirteen bushels of potatoes from friendly local Indians.

The Columbian, on August 6, 1850, had a newspaper article concerning the Citizen's Road being built across Naches Pass.[300] Three years later the same paper found there was no road project, but there was. It had been abandoned (but wasn't), according to another erroneous report in April 23, 1853. However, Theodore Winthrop, also in 1853, described an elaborate wooden incline plane, a corduroy road, on the steepest pitches.[301]

---

298 Longmire departed from Shawnee Prairie, Indiana, on March 6, 1853.

299 *As Told by the Pioneers*, p. 129, Tacoma Leger, August 21, 1892, reprinted 1937.

300 Henry Sicade, in a letter dated June 23, 1929 said the word Naches was actually two Salish words "naugh" meaning rough, roaring turbulent, and "chez" referring to water or waters.

301 Winthrop, Theodore, *The Canoe and Saddle*, Binsford & Mort, Portland, undated reprint.

The wagon train headed into Selah Valley with a sketchy map, then found the Naches River[302] and followed it into the Naches Canyon. They were forced to cross the boulder strewn river 68 times before climbing to higher ground, blazing a wagon trail out of the foot path as they went. *"The whole party narrowly escaped starvation in the mountains and Sarjent (was) at great risk of his neck at the hands of immigrants."*[303]

The precipitous drop just west of the summit forced the pioneers to lower their wagons tied to ropes wound around a tree.

> *"The wagons could not be brought over the trail, so father killed three cattle, made ropes of the rawhide round and round in a continuous strip. These, with the ropes we had, were made fast to the wagons."*[304] *"Our teams could not go down the first hundred feet in the yokes, but unyoking them, we took them around singly on a sort of trail. We then rough-locked all the wheels and fastened a long rope to the hind axletree, the further end of which rope was wound several times around a tree, and by letting the rope out little by little, the wagon reached the place where it was level enough to again hitch the oxen to them."*[305]

It should be noted here that several sources dispute the claim of killing oxen at the Naches Trail to make ropes of their hides. Logic tells the story. It would have taken considerable time and provided dearly needed food, but is not likely as most reports declare the near total lack of sustenance. The two versions of the story do not match.

Only one wagon, owned by Daniel Lane, was lost on this steep cliff. The Lane family's worldly possessions were scattered, broken and muddied at the base of the cliff after traveling all those miles across the continent. The family soon settled in the Puyallup Valley.

The Lanes picked up what they could and continued with the emigrant train into late October. Everyone was nearly out of food and strength, but made snail-like progress each day. At the road builder's camp on the Puyallup, a dispatch was sent forward to Steilacoom. The road builders were offered potatoes *"confiscated from an Indian potato patch."* according to Robert More.[306] Col. Simmons of Olympia sent relief provisions that included 1,000 pounds of flour. It was about this time that Michael Simmons and George

---

302 Wilkes, of the U.S. Naval Exploration Expedition in 1841 called the Naches, the River Spipen.

303 Meeker, Ezra, *"Pioneer Reminiscences of Puget Sound,"* Lowman & Harford, Seattle, 1905

304 *Emmons, Deella Gould,* Nothing in Life is Free," footnote of Susan Isabel Biles Drew, MS. *"Crossing the Plains in 1853"*

305 Light, Erasmus .A., *"Crossing the Plains,"* Tacoma Leger, June 19, 1892, as noted in Emmons.

306 More, Robert, *Cutting of the Naches Pass'* in History of Enumclaw, compiled by Women's Progressive Club, undated

Bush were hired by Dr. Tolmie to build "claim houses" for the company. These four houses, and others, would be occupied by HBC employees to hold the PSAC property with a person on the site at every sheep station and cattle park.

When they finally reached the Puyallup River, the wagon train immigrants feasted on fall run salmon, then followed an HBC/Indian trail to Clover Creek and the Nisqually Plain. Arriving at Steilacoom City, they were given a royal welcome by Captain Balch as the first group to come directly across the Cascade Mountains to Puget Sound. The seventy[307] wagons carried 180 people in the train, who were added to the 513 citizens of Pierce County, a glorious 35% gain in white population overnight.

Neither the law, nor the international treaty with the authority of the U.S. Constitution, stopped the Americans at Fort Nisqually property lines. Andrew Byrd filed a claim for 159 acres[308] at the north end of a swamp, or marshland. Byrd formed a partnership with his brother Preston and Steilacoom merchant A. E. Light. The new company built a dam and a saw mill on the land.

The British and American Joint Commission Claims, volume 1, page 26 reads as follows:

> *The tract of land ...extending along the shores of Puget Sound, from the Nisqually River, on the one side, to the Puyallup River on the other, and back to the coast range of mountains, containing not less than two hundred and sixty-one (square) miles, or one hundred sixty-seven thousand and forty acres/"*[309]

That description of HBC land ownership takes in the western portion of Pierce County without exception. The Boundary Treaty of 1846 adopted this description. It was accepted and approved by both Britain and the United States political processes, but utterly rejected by the Americans who migrated into the area.

Fort Nisqually continued the wholesale transfer of animal herds and cargo to Victoria. The *Mary Dare* took on a full cargo of wool, furs, hides, and fodder for live animals, 94 quarters of beef, 13 Company horses, 3 privately owned horses, and a privately owned bull in early January. It was part of the continuing effort to reduce the herds and flocks at the Nisqually farms, as well as a money-making venture in transport.

---

307 Various sources claim 70 wagons others make it 35 or 80 wagons. This author is unable to determine the truth.

308 Byrd's claim was near what is now the corner of Steilacoom Boulevard and Phillips Road.

309 Caughey, James, British and American Joint Commission of the Hudson's Bay Company and Puget Sound Agricultural Company Claims, 10 April 1865, call number CIHM 64027 University of Alberta Libraries, Canada

Americans were moving into the Puget Sound area in increasing numbers. Two businessmen from Maine, Andrew Jackson Pope and William Talbot, built the Pope and Talbot lumber mill at Port Gamble in 1853. Their mill was far from PSAC lands, strategically located on a sheltered harbor with an abundance of trees in close proximity. Financial success was nearly guaranteed, as the market in San Francisco, and around Puget Sound was growing rapidly.

Four large iron boilers arrived at the Nisqually landing from San Francisco, aboard the *G.W. Kendall*. They were purchased by Mr. Lowe. He soon built the first steam powered mill to initiate the industrialization of the Puget Sound area in 1853.

American Captain Bonneville, on leave from the US Army, found himself dropped from the army rolls for a short period. He was soon reinstated and, by order of President Pierce, stationed at Vancouver Barracks. He was charged with keeping the peace with the Indians. Bonneville's command post stood uphill, just across the road from HBC Fort Vancouver. The location of the U.S. Army post was meant to make a statement, perhaps two statements. Americans were here to stay, and, at least by the height of the land, looked down on the British. But the Americans still had to pay for use of the British docks on the river.

The Fort Nisqually wild longhorn cattle were getting more difficult to capture or kill, so Tolmie raised prices for meat. That move increased the incentive to obtain the critters, and potentially increased profits. A complete carcass could be had for 10 cents per pound, with the Company retaining the hide, horns, and hooves for sale in London auction markets. The leather was considered to be "prime," and the horns and hooves could be melted and shaped in a plastic-like manner to manufacture several desirable items such as combs. One-half carcass sold for the new price of 11 cents per pound. One hind quarter was 12 cents per pound, and a fore quarter sold for 10 cents per pound. The demand for Fort Nisqually beef still ran high. Horses on the hoof sold for six blanket points per horse. The sale might involve several blankets to reach six points. A rather high price compared to the early years, when one horse could be purchased for a total of only four points. New pricing patterns sometimes required 13 blankets to reach an agreement.

The sheep business suffered through the winter, losing some 1,300 head to the severe weather and *"considerable neglect of the Shepherd, Adam Beinston,"* according to the Journal. The cattle herd was smaller by 893 animals, sold or transferred to Victoria. Four horses were lost along the road to McPhail's sheep park. Tolmie's written report to London was carried by a Mr. Logan, traveling with the Rocky Mountain Express. Logan also carried the accounts for Cowlitz and Victoria. Mr. Northover went along to handle the horses during the trip.

The brigantine *Mary Dare* brought the news from London. The winter of '53 was quite severe in the North Atlantic. During the months of November, December, and January, gales and rain lashed the coast of the British Isles. There were some 300 to 400 shipwrecks, with more than 250 lives lost. Farming and garden work had come to a standstill. Thousands of workmen and their families were destitute. A man with a job at the workhouse might earn a shilling, but have only two pence after housing costs were paid. Fort Nisqually and the Puget Sound Agricultural Company might have had their problems, but life seemed better after the news.

While the men squared timbers, melted tallow, and mended bags, they received from London via Victoria, dry goods and 50 barrels of salmon, 30 barrels of flour, and a huge quantity of grass seed. Dr. Tolmie purchased a new wagon in Olympia. It must have been a good buy, because about two weeks later he bought another light wagon to haul beef from the pastures to the Fort stores. About the middle of February, the *Mary Dare* shipped out, with a fair wind, 200 quarters of beef, 49 live horned cattle, 500 bushels of oats, 130 hides, and 7 barrels of tallow, bound for Victoria and Europe.

While Tolmie was gone from Fort Nisqually purchasing wagons, some men jumped the claim at the mouth of the Sequalitchew. They were encouraged by John Chambers who established his mill there earlier. The American squatters encroaching on Company land just as Chambers had, were moving ever closer to the Fort.

The encroachment didn't stop the Company from building new facilities. Another new farm was established at Muck. That new farm required 7,400 split cedar rails for fencing. Indian laborers were paid $10 in trade goods for splitting rails and building fences. Meanwhile the squatters at Sequalitchew, Mr. Thompson, and Mr. Rosencrants, were presented with formal written warning notices. Huggins, Thomas, and Aubrey Dean also presented written warnings to Hugh Hunter, Henry Chapman, John Sechy, and H. John for squatting on Company lands at various locations.

Mr. Dean recognized a half-tame ox as Company property while it was being driven, along with three or four other head, by some Americans. He inquired as to the ownership, and was told the animals all belonged to the Americans. Dean reported this to Dr. Tolmie.

In an edition of the *Weekly Columbian*, a notice was printed by L.A. Smith warning PSAC employees about driving cattle or shooting cattle on his land at Muck (which he had stolen from the PSAC). He concluded the notice with *"they must abide by the consequences."* It was a clearly worded threat from an American settler.

An ugly and sad tragedy occurred near the PSAC Spanueh House that summer of '53. Daytime temperatures were very hot. Comfort for some people was found in the numbing effects of alcohol. It was most often homemade, and very potent. Robert

Buchanan, a squatter farmer and discharged soldier from Artillery Company M, was drinking with another squatter named Hugh Hunter and an Indian named Wilcut. They began to quarrel, as drinking buddies sometimes do. Hunter, "driven to madness by the liquor", murdered Buchanan by stabbing him in the chest. Hunter then slashed Wilcut severely with the same knife. An Indian boy was found strangled to death in the same house. A few days later, Hunter apparently recovered from the effects of the alcohol. He realized the severity of what he had done. Hunter's frontier punishment was swift and severe. He blew his own brains out with his Army rifle. Though seriously slashed, Wilcut and his Indian friends borrowed a wagon from Fort Nisqually to haul the bodies back from Spanueh for proper burials.

Edward Huggins and Thomas Linklater delivered affidavits[310] before the Justice of the Peace in Olympia detailing the extent of Puget Sound Agricultural Company land previous to the Treaty of 1846. Dr. Tolmie had been required by the Territorial Lawyer General[311] to present such information in a timely manner. Several other people also made affidavits for the courts. American settlers Simmons, John Montgomery, Louis Latour, and John Edgar made their statements, also. The Lawyer General required the affidavits be only from people who had resided in the Puget Sound area prior to the signing of the treaty. Tolmie and Huggins were expecting something definite to be made known concerning the extent of the land claimed by the Company. The survey conducted earlier by John Henry Chapman (himself a squatter in Steilacoom) showed a farm and ranch operation of 15 miles square.[312] Still, a notice was presented to W. Sales, a squatter near Tlithlow.

The hard labor of running a farm and ranch continued, with all hands undertaking various tasks, except for the often drunk or the occasionally injured. Tolmie didn't let the contract with the U.S. Army expire. He and Lt. Slaughter, Quartermaster for the U.S. Infantry at Fort Steilacoom, negotiated a deal for the troops. Beef would henceforth be supplied by Fort Nisqually at 19 cents per pound, delivered.

One cow-hide was discovered to have the brand of Mr. Chambers on it. The animal was accidentally included in a "kill" for the beef. Another bull was found shot, the body left to rot, by a squatter named Smith at Muck. He claimed the bull was spoiling the

---

310 Affidavits are written (out of court) statements signed and sworn under oath as truthful for use in court.

311 Today the title is most often Attorney General.

312 This is a total area, considerably condensed from the area that was often calculated for the far flung Fort Nisqually—Puget Sound Agricultural Company farms and ranches. At the peak of operations, some 161,000 acres (251+ square miles) were in use, in what became Pierce and Thurston Counties.

breeding of his cattle. He announced he would continue to kill wandering wild animals that belonged to the Company herds. Apparently Dr. Tolmie ignored the threat. He went to Tlithlow to supervise the castrating of the lambs.

Towns around Puget Sound were springing up everywhere it seemed. On May 23, 1853 Arthur Denny and Dr. David Maynard filed a land plat for the Town of Seattle. Maynard came to the planning meeting drunk, declaring himself a sort of monarch. He wanted streets to follow the cardinal points of the compass. His opponents wanted streets to follow the shore line of Elliott Bay. The "Skid Road[313]" to Henry Yesler's saw mill divided the divergent grids. Seattle streets still suffer directional issues stemming from this disagreement.

In September, 1853, Michael T. Simmons filed a claim for 640 acres (near modern Shelton) on Hammersley Inlet, or as the Indians called it "Big Skookum." Simmons claim was near the home of John Slocum, who later formed the Indian Shaker Church. Adjoining Simmons property was 315 acres claimed by Alfred Hall. Wesley Gosnell filed for 248 acres, too. Gosnell and Simmons partnered in a saw mill on Gosnell's Creek. One report claims that they displaced a Sahehwamish Village of 300 inhabitants.[314]

The first American settlers to cross the Cascades on the Military Road were in the Longmire-Biles wagon train. Their most difficult journey is well documented in other places. Here we acknowledge the Longmire-Biles wagon train crossing what is now known as South Hill Puyallup on October 8, 1853, their difficult journey nearly complete.

That fall, Peter Judson filed a Donation Land Claim for 321 acres on Commencement Bay, just north of Nicolas Delin's sawmill. Judson, his wife Anna, and their sons Steven and Paul, along with an orphaned niece, Gertrude Weller, were members of the Longmire-Biles wagon party. Judson's claim amounted to 320 acres, and lay in the area where downtown Tacoma streets of South 7th to South 20th are today along the waterfront of Commencement Bay. The Foss Waterway shoreline was much closer to those streets 160 years ago.

At the 1853 Oregon Conference of the Methodist Church, Reverend Benjamin Close was appointed presiding elder of the Puget Sound District. His associate, Reverend William B. Morse was also assigned to Olympia. These two were the first clergy men assigned by the Methodist Church to the region since the Nisqually Mission was burned only a decade earlier. Circuit riders, a Methodist tradition since John Wesley's days, had been serving the area since 1852 when two itinerant preachers, Reverend Roberts and

---

313 A Skid Road is not a road at all. It is a planked water trough designed to float-push, or skid, entire logs downhill to a saw mill. It replaced the use of donkeys and oxen for moving heavy logs.

314 *Columbia Magazine*, Fall 2007, page 8.

Reverend James Harvey Wilbur, occasionally preached in Olympia.

Reverend Close, assigned to Olympia, preached in Steilacoom, Seattle, and Coupeville on Whidby Island as an itinerant circuit rider. Reverend Close recommended the appointments of Reverends E.R. Ames, Beverly Waugh, John F. DeVore, and David E Blaine to the regional conference area. With the arrival of these clergymen the Methodist Church returned after only a decade of absence from Puget Sound. It was a different emphasis than the Nisqually Methodist missionaries, but the same ambition: spirit and Christian authority.

On August 18, 1853 the Methodist Church assigned the Reverend John F. DeVore, D.D.,[315] and his wife to a congregation in Olympia. The parishioners had been meeting without the benefit of clergy. DeVore's ship arrived at Alki Point where they were met by Captain Balch and Dr. Webber representing the citizens of Steilacoom. To persuade Dr. DeVore to locate his new Methodist church in Steilacoom instead of Olympia, the good citizens of Steilacoom pointed out that Rev. B. Close, a Methodist Bishop had been preaching in Olympia since April, 1853. He was regularly conducting Sunday services in his new home in Olympia after taking the Oregon Trail overland route.

DeVore accepted the challenge to build a new Methodist congregation in Steilacoom, but only if enough pledges could be made to assure the construction of a proper church building. Balch and Webber immediately passed the hat to the locals at Alki and everyone on board ship. Ten days later, the first services were held on Sunday, August 28, 1853 in Steilacoom after a Methodist Episcopal Church congregation was organized.

During the year that followed, more Methodist congregations were developed at Salmon Creek and Alki (Seattle). In 1854 Port Townsend and Puyallup Methodist congregations were organized. The first Methodist settlers arrived just three years after the Nisqually Methodist Mission closed. The clergy reestablished an organized Methodist Church after an absence of only ten years.

The first quarterly Conference of the Methodist Church in the Pacific Northwest was held in Rev. DeVore's Steilacoom home on October 29, 1853. The minutes of that meeting state that,

> *"We have one Sabbath School with four teachers, 20 children, and 40 volumes in the library."*

Mrs. DeVore was in ill health at the time. Her sister, Evelyne Babb, soon came to care for her and became a charter member of that first congregation. It proudly built

---

315 Doctor of Divinity apparently granted by a Deacon of the Methodist Church

Steilacoom's "proper church building" less than nine months after the first services were conducted. On May 20, 1854, Dr. DeVore reported,

> "We have built the first church (building) in the (Washington) Territory, which cost us $2,300 and was dedicated on the 19th of March last."

The money was mostly raised in Steilacoom and the lumber was sawed at Clanrick Crosby's Tumwater Mill.[316]

A remarkable incident occurred in the construction of the first Methodist Church building in Steilacoom. DeVore, who later served as the Presiding Elder of the Puget Sound District of the growing Methodist Episcopal Church, was challenged by Captain Crosby to "actually do some work" (meaning physical labor) to build the church. DeVore asked the challenger to pay for all the lumber the preacher could haul from the mill site to the building site in one day. The challenge was accepted, with the assumption that the Good Doctor would actually move a small amount of sawn lumber.

Dr. DeVore was a clever man. He asked that all of the lumber for the building be sawn and stacked. With virtually no experience as a sailor DeVore built a raft of the lumber stack. He then proceeded to use the outgoing tide of Puget Sound to help float his raft of precious building materials from the Crosby Tumwater Mill to the Steilacoom waterfront. He single-handedly floated enough lumber to build the entire church! Other members of the church increased the lumber supply enough to build a parsonage, too. Crosby, it is said, never made such banter to a mere preacher again.

Among the church subscribers was Lieutenant Phillip Sheridan of Fort Steilacoom, who gave $10. In another ten years Sheridan would become one of the most famous men in the world, serving in the Civil War. Another subscriber to the church construction was Miss Babb who loaned $700 to the effort. The tiny church struggled financially during the Puget Sound Indian War. When the church was in danger of being sold to pay its debts, Miss Babb cancelled her portion of the debt, saving the church.

During the Indian War DeVore was the only preacher who did not seek safety away from home. One night his family slept at "the fort"[317] on account of an extraordinary alarm being raised about an Indian attack that never took place.

Mrs. DeVore died of complications of her long illness. Her sister, the second Miss

---

316 After 1847, Michael T. Simmons sold his gristmill and saw mill property, including all three waterfalls, to Clanrick Crosby, a recent settler who had been a sea captain from Maine. The Crosby House still stands as a historic monument open to the public. Clanrick was grandfather of Harry Lowe "Bing" Crosby, a singer and actor born in Tacoma.

317 Probably they were sheltered at Fort Steilacoom, but possibly Fort Nisqually.

Babb, was married at Vancouver to become the second Mrs. DeVore seven years after her arrival at Steilacoom.[318]

While Roman Catholic priests visited Puget Sound regularly, their flock didn't construct a Catholic chapel building until 1855 for the Fort Steilacoom "Irish Catholic soldiers." In 1864 that small chapel building was physically moved to Nisqually Street in Steilacoom. Soldiers deconstructed the building board by board, moved the lumber by wagon, and reassembled it[319]. Father Louis Rossi, the original Steilacoom priest, served there for six years.[320].

The gloomy weather of early June meant that few sheep were washed at Fort Nisqually. Tobacco was boiling (an ingredient of disinfecting slurry), oxen were hauling sawmill planks floated to the beach, and horse wagons were carrying fence rails for enclosing another large sheep park. Six Indians were sent to work on the new county road in the Squally bottom. One of the wild cattle was killed and carted to the Fort. The gloomy weather made preparing scythe handles a welcome indoor task, even when transplanting turnips and weeding oat fields needed manpower. Indians were pressed into doing the less desirable tasks. Dr. Tolmie went to Olympia to purchase advertising space to publicly caution people from taking any interest in land suddenly occupied by F. L. Thompson at Sequalitchew Creek. Tolmie would declare it was Puget Sound Company real estate.

By the 6th of June the gloomy weather was replaced with 98 degree days. With the favorable weather the sheep were washed. The animals were actually forced to swim through a *"very strong discoction [sic] of Tobacco water"* before being shorn. The wool was dried, pressed, and packed into 90 pound bundles. That day five bushels of barley seed was sown in the dry swamp farm, too.

---

318 Steilacoom Methodist Church operated until 1894 when the real estate was sold to pay the street improvement levy issued by the Steilacoom Town Marshall. A small portion of the land was deeded to the State Historical Society for a monument to commemorate the First Church in the state of Washington. The old church bell, which was also the first in the state, was placed on top of the monument. The records of this transaction were wrapped in asbestos, put in a box, and placed in a fireproof vault of the Methodist Church Archives at the University of Puget Sound library. Those archives are now at Wesley Gardens, in Des Moines, Washington.

319 Renamed the Church of Immaculate Conception, it was placed on the Register of Historic Places in 1974. It still stands, well over 150 years later.

320 The last resident pastor at Steilacoom was Father Peter F. Hylebos, who left in 1881 for Tacoma, according to *Town on the Sound, Stories of Steilacoom,* edited by Joan Curtis, Alice Watson, Bette Bradley, the Steilacoom Historical Museum Association, Steilacoom, WA 1988.

The old prairie land was overrun with sorrel,[321] so the land had to be plowed and re-plowed to rid the field of the sour weed. The wool gathering continued. By the end of the first week of June, 548 wedder lambs had been clipped and an entire band of wedder lambs marked (branded). "Wedder" appears to be a remark related to the breeding of ewes.

Wool shearing stopped completely with gale force winds and rain by mid-June. Horse wagons still went out for beef, but trade was dull in the Sales Shop until the severe weather ceased. One Kanaka, Kahannui, deserted when his credit was cut off because of too much debt. Captain James Bachelder[322] was confronted with the same problem. Bachelder offered $20 cash and a note for the remaining $70 of debt. The *Journal of Occurrences* said, "Mr. B. has a bit of the swindler about him."

Gohome was sent to the Wells & McAllister Mill for a raft of lumber, returning with 10,000 feet of lumber. The oxen team was employed hauling the planks from the beach. The planks were used to rebuild the dam used to impound water in Sequalitchew Creek for sheep washing. The Sales Shop agreed to sell 300 wedders to Mr. McArthur for $8 per head. Some 280 head were delivered to McArthur immediately, with the promise of the remainder in August. McArthur also agreed to take 20 rams to the Willamette Valley for exchange.

As June came to a close, the Fort again saw gloomy weather. This time the weather didn't stop the work. Two wagons were sent out for beef. Sheep were washed, clipped and branded. Three plows were at work. Green oats were cut to feed the horses. Horse teams were mining clay. A group of girls were hired to weed the garden. A new roof was built for the boilers, and turnip transplanting was continued.

A regular delivery of beef to American retail shops in Olympia and Steilacoom was set up in July. Dr. Tolmie was busy dealing with U.S. Customs concerning the *Alice*, which had only a few items shipped to Fort Nisqually. Later a canoe was sent to pick up the small shipment. The *Alice* passed Fort Nisqually late in the summer with a load of timber for Victoria. This activity had to be explained to the Customs House. Tolmie was also regularly dealing with Deputy Surveyor Mr. Hyde concerning the extent of PSAC property lines.

Some strange events were discovered in late July by Mr. Dean. He found 30 sheep

---

321 Sorrel has reddish-green whorled spikes which bloom in hot summer sun. Roots run deep, the ripe seeds are shiny brown. It grows easily around the world and is sometimes a food plant. HBC called it a weed.

322 James Bachelder was Master of the *George Emory* sutler at Fort Steilacoom, relocated to Port Townsend where he became a Justice of the Peace 3rd District, Washington Territory handling marriages, legal disputes, and land claims.

completely separated from the herd. Then, with a little effort, he discovered another 30 in a second hidden location. Further investigation revealed that Tapou had been developing his own business with animals stolen from the PSAC herd. He pretended to be doing the Company's business. It could have been a lucrative, if illegal, business. PSAC sold live sheep through regular means to Americans Hadley & Bailey for $3,258. The Americans happily received 344 animals of varying quality for the fee. Tapou was prevented from entering the black market for stolen sheep.

With oppressive temperatures approaching 95 degrees on July 24, Captain Howard arrived overland from Vancouver with Theodore Winthrop as a traveling companion. Howard was changing professions to commence mine work on a newly discovered coal deposit at Bellingham Bay.

Theodore Winthrop was a 25 year-old graduate of Yale University traveling on a lark through the "wild west." Winthrop found himself somewhat stranded in Oregon Country in May, 1853. He was traveling about the area with Captain Bonneville and a small detail of soldiers from the American Fort Vancouver. When the group reached The Dalles, Winthrop was diagnosed with smallpox. Bonneville left Winthrop behind to recover. He used the situation to travel to Puget Sound as he, perhaps, had planned to do anyway after wandering around the towns of Oregon. His ancestor, several generations earlier, was the first governor of Connecticut. Theodore had a gift for language that allows us to see some of what he saw in quite vivid detail. For example, Winthrop is credited with "originating the name Tacoma from some words claimed to have been spoken by the Indians as the name of the mountain."[323]

It should be remembered that many others had frequented the bay of the Puyallup River and seen the mountain on fishing expeditions prior to Winthrop's visit. John Swan and a man named Riley reportedly took two thousand large fish in one haul of their seine a few months earlier. Ezra Meeker claims to have fished there with Indians in June before Winthrop's September trip. The first American explorer was Captain Wilkes in 1841. None of the prior visitors mentioned in writing the name "Tacoma" for the mountain. Traditions say it was the Indian name for many years, perhaps centuries.

During 1853, the year that Pierce County was organized into a political jurisdiction, Winthrop described a number of small non-native settlements:

> **Astoria**—*"a cove of a few houses… not fitted for a town.*
>
> **Rainier**—*a small village . . growing up to meet the trade from Puget Sound.*

---

323 Meeker, Ezra, *Pioneer Reminiscences of Puget Sound, The Tragedy of Leschi,* Lowman and Hanford Stationery and Printing Co., Seattle, WA, 1905.

St. Helens—...*about 30 homes, at the proper head of navigation for large ships and likely to become the important point."*

Portland—*Up the Willamette, the farthest point to which vessels of any size can go, struggles along the river bank, a thriving place of 1,500 people, rescued from the forest.*

Salem—*"A village of less than one thousand people, on one of these exquisite plains. The streets are wide, and the original oak trees have been left about...*

Cowlitz Farms—*Rich with ripe grain. Over the trees that belted the river... rose graceful St. Helens... and the immense bulk of Tacoma (Rainier), the most massive of all—grand, grand above the plain!*

Monticello—*Deposited among the blood-sucking mosquitoes...*

Jackson Prairie—*... an old settler has a splendid farm.*

Mound Prairie—*Spotted with small mounds...fifty feet in diameter, and ten to fifteen feet high, covering an immense tract.*

Olympia—*A few houses make Olympia, a thriving lumbering village cleared from the woods, with stumps in the main street. Plenty of "ostend" oysters and large queer clams.*[324] *Low tide leaves a great mud flat...*

Victoria—*... looks beautiful in the sunny afternoon, with smoke just obscuring the rocky barren shores, and veiling the white houses of the village. Town lots of 66x132 feet sell at $50. Seventy-five town lots registered.*

Bellingham Bay—*... the Indian women admired my red whiskers.*

Port Townsend—*The bluff above Port Townsend is bold and fine.*

Squallyabasch— *euphonized to Nisqually, is six or seven miles from Fort Steilacoom....at a high bluff (with a trail inland) under the oaks.*

Fort Steilacoom—*An American army post one mile inland from Whulge. It was commanded by Major Leonard, was supplied with 500 pounds of beef each week by Fort Nisqually farms.*

Fort Nisqually—*A Hudson's Bay Company farm and station. Dr. Tolmie in charge, going to Vancouver Island tomorrow, invited me to go..*[325]

Only the last three listed were in Pierce County, but from this brief description of some of the towns and establishments in the region one gleans a sense of the growing

---

324 The geoduck "gooey duck" is known scientifically as *Panopea generosa* in the family *Hiatellidae*. It is native to Puget Sound waters. The shell ranges up to nearly six inches long, with a siphon or "neck" reaching 3 feet or more. It is a culinary favorite prized for is savory flavor and crunchy texture.

325 Winthrop, Theodore, *Canoe and Saddle, Nisqually Edition,* Binsford & Mort Publishers, Portland, Oregon, undated reprint.

American population in the area by 1853. Politics and population created Washington Territory and Pierce County in late 1852. While some settlers had arrived earlier, the fact of local government had not yet fully arrived near Fort Nisqually farms, fields and fur trade post until the first paperwork was done. The paperwork to form the first legally incorporated town in Washington Territory (Steilacoom) was still a year away.

Six years after Mike Simmons built the very first saw mill on Puget Sound (1847), Henry Yesler opened the first steam-powered saw mill on Puget Sound. Doc Maynard suggested the location should be called Seattle in 1853.

Cowlitz Landing ranked second to Monticello as the most important settlement on the Cowlitz River. The little town was six miles north of the present boundary of Lewis County. That would make it a little more than a mile south of the present town of Toledo. A complete description of the place in territorial days is not available, but we know it was the transfer point for all commerce north and south between Fort Vancouver and Fort Nisqually. All goods and travelers switched from boat to horse power, or visa-versa, at Cowlitz Landing regardless of their ultimate destination. Logic tells us it had the appearance of a thriving little town.

We know from Cowlitz Farms PSAC records that Cowlitz Landing had only a crude wharf and a blockhouse in 1849. Soon there was also a hotel, Carter and Pagett's general store, a tavern, and a few new farm homes nearby. Captain E.D. Warbass built a gristmill and sawmill in 1852. The landing was created to assist the canoes and bateaux as they ferried customers across the river. The village became a common meeting place.

The *Oregonian* breathlessly reported the Independence Day celebration of July 4, 1853 at Cowlitz Landing. An eyewitness account said, "*...we put powder into 13 large fir logs and touched them off at sunrise.*" Around noon they raised a "Liberty Pole" formed into a procession, marched, with music, to a dinner table set up on the banks for the river. After the meal, a second parade took all the people present to a speaker's platform where orators, readers, preachers, and young people all had a few words to compliment American independence.

In the fall of 1850 a rather uncertain stage coach service was initiated from Cowlitz to Puget Sound, but it was in 1853 when Rabbeson and Yantis organized a satisfactory stage line with regular service to Olympia. The first local mail service began in 1851, but U.S. Government mail delivery didn't begin until January 21, 1854, with Henry Windsor receiving the contract. He rode his mule 60 miles every day between Cowlitz and Olympia for eight years, assisted by Rice Tilley.

Mrs. Isaac I. Stevens, wife of the first territorial Governor of Washington gives us a more feminine view of Cowlitz Landing. The Governor and his wife were there in 1854.

Laura (Towne) Stevens described the accommodations in her diary:[326]

> *We walked ankle-deep in mud to a small log door, where we had a good meal. Here we found a number of dirty-looking men with pantaloons tucked inside their boots and so much hair upon their heads and faces (that) they all looked alike. After tea we were shown a room to sleep in, full of beds...*

The governor and Mrs. Stevens had traveled all day, sitting in one position on mats in the bottom of a canoe. Her diary continues:

> *I was so worn out with this novel way of traveling that I laid down on a narrow strip of bed, not undressed, all of my family alongside on the same bed. The governor sat on a stool nearby, and strange to say, slept through the long, dismal night.*
>
> *He had been shown his bed up through a hole on top of the shanty. He said one look was sufficient. Men were strewn as thick as possible on the floor in their blankets. The steam generated from their wet clothes, boots and blankets was stifling. One small hole cut through the roof was the only ventilation.*

The fall census of Washington Territory counted 3,968 citizens, but only 1,682 were voters. The tally did not include Indians as citizen, or women as voters. Pierce County had 513 settlers in spite of the legal title Hudson's Bay Company, Fort Nisqually, and the Puget Sound Agricultural Company held for the vast majority of the land.

Chalifoux began the fall hay cutting in early August. It was an attempt to forestall American theft of the hay, and to get it on the market first. Four loads were brought in the first day of the harvest. Five loads of hay and two of green oats came in the second day. Increasing the use of the animals increased the production. Soon three horse wagons and two ox wagons were bringing in the hay at the rate of five loads a day. The crew drying the hay was hard pressed to keep up. Some Indians were hired to haul potatoes from the field, too.

Several days were spent capturing wild young bulls and training them to the yoke after castration. Once caught the oxen were chained to trees until they were calm enough to feed. When feeding began, and castration was complete, the training of the now docile animals could begin. Finally the trained oxen were exported to Victoria for sale to colonists in great need of animal power.

---

326 Towne, Laura M. *Letters and Diary of Laura M. Towne: Written from the Sea...*, Riverside Press, 1912

On Saturday, August fifth, the dangers of frontier living hit home dramatically. Squatters blatantly shot and killed three Company horses on the Sastuc Plain. A fourth large cart horse later died of his wounds. A large number of Americans continued to search the plains for places to claim.

Seattle was not much more developed than Tacoma in 1853. Neither city actually or legally existed yet. The first settlers in what is now West Seattle arrived on September 25, 1851. John Low, David Denny, and Lee Terry sailed on Captain Robert C. Fay's ship to the Duwamish Head. Denny and Terry explored the area for three days before starting to build a log cabin on a Donation Land Claims at Alki Point. John Low returned to Portland to help organize the party of pioneers led by Arthur Denny. The schooner *Exact* with the complete Denny Party on board, arrived at Alki Point to find a single cabin still unfinished. The Denny party decided to locate across Elliot Bay, leaving only Terry and Charles Lee at the site originally selected on Alki Point. The Lees dubbed their place "New York" but they, too, gave up their settlement in the spring of 1852.

Coal was discovered near the south end of Lake Washington. The Duwamish Coal Company was formed by Leonard Felker and L.M. Collins. In a year they were shipping 300 tons of coal to San Francisco and by 1855 they were out of business because of poor management.

John Flett, one of the more outspoken of the former HBC Red River settlers, was residing in Southern Oregon when he witnessed the Rogue River Indian Treaty on September 10, 1853. It was signed near Table Rock, Oregon Territory, by Joel Palmer, Superintendent of Indian Affairs, and Samuel Culver, Indian Agent. Flett signed as a witness to the X marks made by the Indians and the U.S. government agents on several such treaties.

By 1859 Flett was back in Pierce County operating a large dairy farm a mile west of Rigney Hill,[327] east of Fort Steilacoom, which was the original central site of the Red River settlement in Pierce County.

In middle to late October, Dr. Tolmie was approached by an American named Boyce, who seemed interested in purchasing some sheep. The two men rode out to Tlithlow to inspect the sheep and arrange the purchase. It was a two-day effort on the part of Tolmie to close the deal, but Boyce bought a flock worth $1,500 American. The sale made all the difference, as the Sales Shop was very low in supplies. When the schooner *Alice* arrived with no new supplies for the Sales Shop, she was loaded with lumber for

---

327 Rigney Hill was approximately located at the intersection of 74th Street and South Tacoma Way. The Flett dairy was located near, but southward, from the 2005 location of the second Mount Tahoma High School campus.

Victoria, along with two men, Guillion and Thronhill, who were sent to Victoria to complete their contracts.

It was about this time that another American scam was discovered. It seems that two Americans were found skinning a cow near Treehatchie. Huggins and Legg rode out to "discuss" the matter with the Americans. They said the cow had been shot by Charles Wren, who was in turn commissioned by Mr. Asher Sargent. Sargent claimed that he had permission from Dr. Tolmie to kill as many as he pleased, then settle up afterwards. Of course no such permission was ever granted. The scam nearly worked that showery day.

As a result of the American rustlers' efforts, Tolmie ordered a load of 15 cattle be put down and loaded on the *Alice*. Another 15 live oxen were also loaded as "passengers" with Guillion & Thornhill. Kuphai and Wyamock were sent to tend the remaining cattle at Treehatchie. Tolmie immediately ordered the killing of PSAC cattle to preserve the meat for sale. Montgomery was sent with a team of men and wagons to bring back the meat for the sales shop or for consignment in Olympia butcher shops.

The annual September Indian fires burned the plains for days. The air was very smoky, limiting visibility to 200 yards on Sunday September 11, 1853. Emerging out of the thick smoke on September 13 was a newly discharged American soldier seeking work at Fort Nisqually. John Daly was hired for 30 Pounds per year. His first assignment was to cut logs for a new ox park. In two days Daly was repairing a bard door with the help of Chaulifoux. Soon Daly was building and hanging some gates and raising the height of the fences at the cattle park near the stables. Daly was then sent to build some cattle feeding troughs.

Young Mr. Daly was proving to be a good worker. He was put to work October 3rd through the 7th, bossing a crew, completing the permanent flooring in the loft of the large store. Daly completed the job in four days with the help of three men. Dr. Tolmie was very pleased with the work of this American, a former soldier at Fort Steilacoom. Next Daly was soon "jobbing" at the store according to the Journal.

On Monday October 24, Daly was put to work pulling down the old potato house to be replaced by a new office and dwelling house for the clerk. Chaulifoux assisted Daly in preparing timber for the new house. Oxen were used to haul in the logs. In early November, Daly, Gohome, Chaulifoux, and Squally were busy erecting the new house. Soon a man named M.D. Wooden was hired (at 30 Pounds per year) to work constructing the new house, as well. The new man seems to have been a finish carpenter. Daly and Wooden had been assigned that task for only a couple of days. Then they went to working installing window frames and floor boards. Chaulifoux and Daly built new "Necessaries" behind the new house, while some planks were brought up from the beach by an oxen team. The new clerk's house was ready for occupancy at Christmas.

A major medical advance in England allowed Queen Victoria to give birth to her seventh child, Leopold, after the administration of chloroform to ease her pain. These medical advances were probably a great topic of conversation at Fort Nisqually. Dr. Tolmie was probably at the center of any local medical discussion.

Dr. Tolmie's medical skills were tested again when another small pox outbreak hit Tlithlow very hard in early November. An Indian shepherd in the employ of the PSAC died on Nov, 8, 1853. A few days later, when the *SS Otter* sailed out of the Narrows, firing the customary signal cannon, a sailor's hand was shattered. Dr. Tolmie and Dr. A.I. Haden of Fort Steilacoom administered some of that new chloroform and operated on him immediately. Both medical men reported that Seaman Vine was soon 'doing well.' He was recovering quickly with Harber and Kuhai as his nursing attendants.

It was good that Vine was healing quickly. The doctors were scarcely done with the surgery when an emergency called them to the beach house, where an Indian, Kahannui, was on a violent drunken spree. When the doctors arrived they found he had been murdered. Within hours Kahannui's Indian wife hung herself while in a "fit of passion." The *Journal of Occurrences* does not reveal any direct connection between the murder and the suicide, but one does wonder.

The *SS Otter* loaded 35 bales of wool, 4 bales of fur, 138 quarters of beef, 163 boxes of cabbages, onions, and parsnips, as well as livestock from PSAC, and personal items for private individuals, before she sailed for Victoria with Seaman Vine on board.

On November 28, 1853, Governor Isaac Stevens proclaimed Olympia the capitol city of Washington Territory. Stevens also ordered the election of a legislature and called for a legislative assembly to convene in January, 1854.

Also in November, 1853, William Douglas, Chief Factor at HBC Fort Victoria, and Governor of the Crown Colony of Vancouver Island, decided to allow the Puget Sound Agricultural Company to occupy San Juan and Lopez Islands, of the archipelago west of Rosario Straits. Douglas was prompted by an American squatter claiming land on Lopez Island. Douglas was reinforcing the presumed border between the British Crown Colony of Vancouver Island and the American mainland Territory of Washington.

R.W. Cussans, an American citizen, had simply taken that tract of land on Lopez Island early in 1853. He had no legal right to do so. Cussans cut and squared some 30,000 board feet of lumber and made $1,500 worth of improvements to the property. Douglas compelled Cussans to apply for a British license and clear British customs in Victoria before he could sell his lumber. As a result Cussans was (economically) defeated in his attempt to occupy the San Juan Islands.

After Cussans departed the Islands, the only whites who occupied any of the islands west of Rosario Straits were some British subjects at the HBC fishing station built many years earlier. Under direct orders from Chief Factor Douglas, on December 15 a group of Kanaka herdsmen and HBC Agent Charles John Griffin took 1,350 sheep to establish Belle Vue [sic] Farm for the Puget Sound Agricultural Company on San Juan Island. Griffin would, as a consequence then, establish a British presence to reinforce the British possession of the San Juan Islands.

Griffin's was no small enterprise. In addition to the sheep, he brought seed for crops and other farm animals. At least four sheep stations were set up, first on the sweeping prairie of San Juan, at Oak Prairie (now San Juan Valley), near Roche Harbor, and at Friday Harbor.

While American settlers were increasing their numbers, the Indian population was still high in spite of measles and small pox outbreaks. William Lane, a settler who arrived in 1853, described the gathering he witnessed on the Nisqually Plains near Fort Nisqually:

> ...four to six thousand Indians from all over the Sound Country and from east of the mountains...congregated for horse races, gambling and Tamanamous. Their principle gathering place was about two miles southeast of American Lake...
>
> The Indians had great times at these gatherings. Some of their races were over a six-mile course...Their gambling was almost continuous and they wagered everything, even their (wives) and the last rags off their backs. The (women) gambled with marked beaver teeth...the men used disks cut from dogwood. In front of each player was a little 'nest' of cedar bark finely cut until it was almost like cotton. With disks (concealed) in their hands sunk in the 'cotton', move them about rapidly and mysteriously, while mumbling to Tamanamus. Then removing their hands from the bark...the opponent had to guess where the disks were. Hour after hour this went on. An Indian not infrequently would sit on his knees for eight or ten hours, or even longer, without once changing his position.[328]

Indians of the Puget Sound area played few athletic games. They did not wrestle, box, or race on foot. Both genders enjoyed swimming. Great crowds often swam together.

---

328 Hunt, Herbert, *Tacoma, Its History and Its Builders, Volume I*, The S.J. Clarke Publishing Company, Chicago, Illinois. Reprinted by the Tacoma Historical Society, Tacoma, WA 2005.

They loved boating, singing joyously as they paddled huge canoes. Several old settlers described the Indian's music as merrier than what they had heard in other places. Indian songs pervaded the whole country when groups traveled together in canoes, their paddle strokes accompanied by the songs.

A site in what is now South Tacoma was a favorite for Indian elk and deer hunters. They called the place "Cahk-hund."[329] It was east of where South Tacoma Way runs now and probably north of what is now 64th Street. Part of the area is now a well-used recreational park, while further north the Northern Pacific Railroad shops of the early 20th century have given way to a diversified industrial park. During their tenure the Indians built corral type traps of logs and brush in the swampy bogs where the elk and deer came for water and tender shoots. Once thus surrounded, with only one exit, the animals were easy targets. Hunting there on very rare occasions conditioned the animals to not fear the place.

The Indians had other traps to worry about. Disease, smallpox in particular, severely decimated the northwest Indian population several times. It was a European disease to which native North Americans had absolutely no resistance. The disease was also devastating to European populations, which did have some resistance, but certainly not immunity. While not wiping out entire European towns, smallpox did kill thousands in continental epidemics. European doctors and scientists studied the disease in efforts to develop some sort of defense. When a vaccination was found to be effective in 1840 it was made compulsory in Britain. Every subject of the crown was compelled to have a vaccination in 1853. Smallpox serum was injected subcutaneously, using the hypodermic syringe invented by Alexander Woods. The serum was not available for anyone in North America for many more years. It was ruled in 1905 that the State could require individual vaccinations for the common good.

The Indian Sales Shop at Fort Nisqually continued to operate the fur trade business even as it was becoming almost a sideline operation. In late August, Klikitat Chief An-Ouichi brought in $400 worth of furs to sell. One Klikitat, Queehen, son of Oriehl, was hired by Theodore Winthrop. He needed a guide to cross Naches Pass going eastward.

Americans 'jumped' (took over) part of the PSAC Sastuc Farm. Two deserters from the company jumped the potato patch near the old slaughter house. A new PSAC manager, Mr. Cheeseman, was sent to take charge at Sastuc, but little was done about the deserters. Dr. Tolmie petitioned the Pierce County government to build a road from Muck to Nisqually Beach. There was no immediate reply to the petition.

---

329 Ibid.

The Company farms operated by Mr. Dean and Mr. Fiandre were transferred from Company ownership to private claims, recorded in the names of Dean and Fiandre. The U.S. Government had purchased the Company's land rights during treaty negotiations, but the Company had not been paid. Converting PSAC land into private claims was deemed advisable, as several Americans had been talking publicly of jumping the farms Dean and Fiandre had been operating. Had the Americans done so, the Pierce County Courts could easily side with the claim jumpers, but officially recording the farms as belonging to Dean and Fiandre, the courts would protect the recorded owners.

Stern written legal warnings were presented in person to many squatters on Company lands by Mr. Dean and J.L. Moss representing the Puget Sound Agricultural Company. The recipients of the legal notices to vacate the properties were J.T. Hanson, H. Barnes, W. Northover, W. Sales, J. Montgomery, G. Dean, A. J. Byrd, A. Dean, L. Tibeault, and J.B, Deschamps. Dr. Tolmie filed copies of the notices in Olympia before departing by canoe for a visit to Mr. Ebey and his ailing wife on Whidby Island. After treating Mrs. Ebey, Tolmie crossed over to Victoria with the mail before returning to South Puget Sound. Upon his arrival back home the news was spread of the wreck of the new ship *Vancouver* on Point Ross, Queen Charlotte Island. The supplies from London destined for Fort Simpson were completely lost, but the crew was saved.

After serving a generous regale to his men, Dr. Tolmie rode in the rain to Steilacoom on December 24th. He was on a quest for an interview with the new governor regarding the status of PSAC and Fort Nisqually. A rumor had been circulating that Governor Stevens had the power to purchase the British company's property or confine the operations within certain limits.

Stevens reassured Tolmie that justice would be administered fairly. Then a letter was handed to Tolmie ordering the Hudson's Bay Company to cease trading with Indians after July 1, 1854. The letter actually meant nothing, as the Boundary Treaty had no such clause. So in response, Tolmie invited the Governor, Mr. Mason, Captain McClellan and their wives to a Christmas dinner celebration and dance at the Fort on Christmas Day. The party was held in the Tolmie's new house, clearly one of the finest in the region.

In far off Cuba, William Rufus King was very ill. He had been elected Vice President of the United States, with President Franklin Pierce (Democrat) ticket. King, the son of a North Carolina plantation and slave owner, became a lawyer and politician. King entered politics as one of the earliest Democrat party organizers. He was sixty-six when elected Vice President, before being diagnosed with tuberculosis. His oath of office was administered in Cuba, where he had gone seeking a cure. He died after an arduous two week return voyage to his own America. He expired the day after his arrival back home. King County, Washington Territory, was named for this Vice President who never served in that office.

[342]

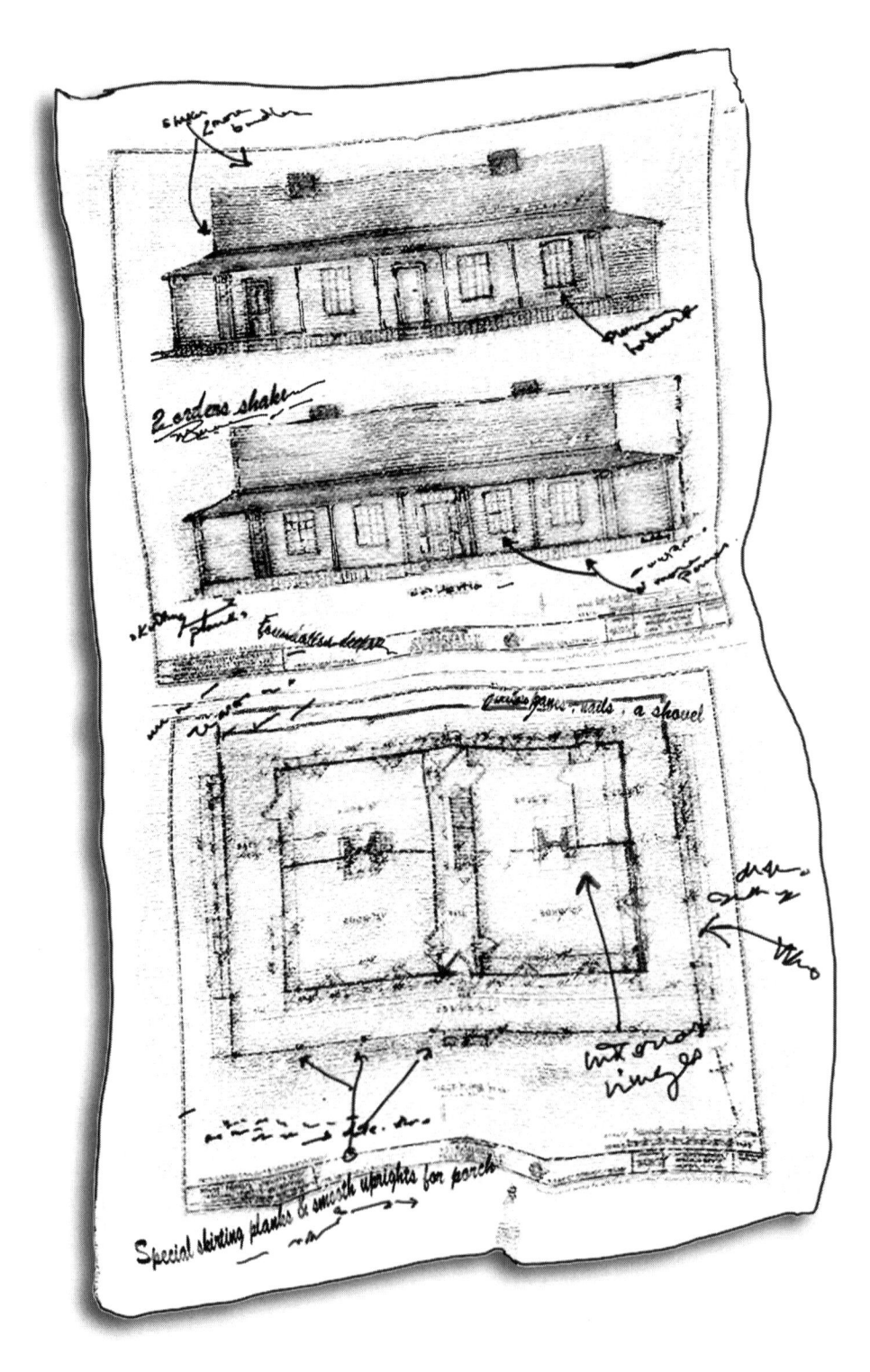

1854

THE *PIONEER AND DEMOCRAT* newspaper of Olympia reported that Britain and France had joined an alliance with Turkey, declaring war on Russia in the Crimean War. It was the first war covered by newspapers, because the speed of the press had improved by 1854. The British Hudson's Bay Company and Puget Sound Agricultural Company continued to honor contracts with the Russian American Fur Company during the war on the other side of the globe. The City of Steilacoom was formed by the merger of Steilacoom City and Port Steilacoom. It became the first city to be incorporated under the laws of Washington Territory.

Woodcutter crews providing fuel to the steamers on Puget Sound had cleared significant land on Anderson Island. The Island was a short canoe trip away from the new Steilacoom City. Michael Luar thought the land was attractive enough to homestead. As the first farm on Anderson Island, he could not have envisioned the island as a suburb, as it is today.

January opened with pleasant weather, but turned very cold by the 4th. Two inches of snow had fallen, along with the temperatures. According to the notes in The *Journal of Occurrences*, the thermometer said 24°. Soon, with a north wind blowing, the temperatures dropped to 5°. The creek froze over and the ice on Lake Sequalitchew was 6 inches thick. Twelve inches of snow lay on the ground. A few days later the temperature had eased to 8°, but 8 more inches of snow fell. It was not until late in January that the weather turned warmer and the snow began to disappear. Before they could thaw and spoil, all of the frozen vegetables were thrown to feed the pigs.

During the extreme cold weather, HBC blankets were literally flying out of the trade store. After a quick inventory, some questions were asked of a Kanaka named Kalama, who readily accused other Kanakas of stealing blankets, sugar, sheep, and cattle. A longtime employee of the Company, he accompanied Dr. Tolmie and Edward Huggins to Steilacoom to report the crime to Pierce County law enforcement authorities. Kalama agreed to testify as a witness.

In court, Kalama charged that his fellow Kanakas, Kuphai and Tamaru, took a total of 168 blankets between September 19th and January 3rd. Kalama listed 50 green, 50 scarlet, 18 more two-and three-point HBC blankets of various colors, and two large sacks of imported sugar. Kalama also claimed that some of the stolen blankets were freely distributed to friends, while others were used for horse trading. As the story unfolded, Kalama soon confessed to his own involvement with the heist, that included stealing two head of Company cattle and 12 head of Company sheep.

Faced with evidence of his personal involvement by expressing detailed knowledge of the illegal events, Kalama turned state's evidence to avoid prosecution. Tolmie was advised by Pierce County Justice Charles Bachelder to let the matter rest until Tamaru and Kuphai could be apprehended. Instead, Tolmie pressed the matter with the Justice, immediately swearing out charges against Tamaru and Kuphai.

A side note should be mentioned here. Kalama's testimony made it very clear that Justice of the Peace Charles Bachelder of Pierce County, Washington Territory, had purchased some of the stolen HBC cattle from the Kanaka Tamaru. It was illegal then, as now, to receive stolen goods.

Once that information was absolutely clear to the judge, the Pierce County Constable was summoned. Justice Bachaelder immediately issued warrants for the arrest of both Tamaru and Kuphai. The Justice ordered Tamaru, Kuphai, and all of the Kanakas who received the stolen HBC property, to each give the Company a horse as payment for their share of the villainy.

When confronted at Fort Nisqually, Kuphai readily confessed to his role, saying that he had assisted Tamaru in stealing the HBC goods and animals. Other Kanakas agreed that they had received stolen blankets from Tamaru. The suspect was reported to have gone to Cowlitz with the horses and other proceeds of his robbery. The Company was finally satisfied with the legal maneuvers only when the payment of horses was made. Justice Bachelder received no punishment for receiving stolen goods.

In Washington, D.C., the U.S. Treasury Department sanctioned the removal of the customs headquarters from Olympia to Port Townsend. Olympia residents were upset at the lost of this important government office, and the prestige attached to it, but Port Angeles, led by Victor Smith, made it a contest between Port Angeles and Port Townsend. This battle between two upstart towns seemed beneath the dignity of Olympians. As Olympians remained "above the fray", it became a vigorous and intense 'battle" to the point that threats of naval bombardment from Port Angeles caused Port Townsend to relinquish the government documents to Port Angeles temporarily.

The contest to claim the U.S. Customs Office was not over, as Port Townsend continued the struggle for the prize over the next decade. In a final showdown, the issue was settled by an act of Congress. On July 25, 1866, Port Townsend permanently gained the coveted office.

With the issue of the location of the U.S. Customs Office settled, Isaac Ebey, the U.S. Customs Collector, threatened in April to seize British property on San Juan Island for failure to pay American customs duties. Ebey also accused Charles John Griffin, an employee of the Puget Sound Agricultural Company, of molesting American property and disturbing the peace. Griffin had been a resident farmer and employee of the Company on San Juan Island since December 13, 1853. For assistance and protection, Griffin sent a message to Governor Douglas, who ordered a Union Jack be run up the Belle Vue [sic] farms flagpole. It was the opinion of Douglas that the San Juan Islands actually belonged to the British, under the 1846 Boundary Treaty.

In response to what he considered a provocation, Ebey sent his assistant, Henry Webber, to pitch a tent directly behind Griffin's cabin. Webber hoisted the Stars and Stripes. The next morning Griffin asked British Constable Holland to serve a warrant for the arrest of the American, Mr. Webber. Well-armed, Webber resisted arrest by the British Constable. Holland organized a posse of six men for assistance. Webber was still determined to resist arrest. The British posse backed off.

Governor Douglas confirmed the decision to at least delay Webber's arrest, but ordered that Webber be treated only as a U.S. citizen, not a U.S. government agent. Furthermore, Douglas said, Webber would be subject to British arrest if he should attempt to carry out any American government orders as a mere citizen. Ebey ordered Webber to just keep an eye on the HBC men, for which he would be paid $5 per day. Payment made Webber a U.S. government employee.

Henry Webber became friends with his close neighbor, Charles Griffin. Meanwhile, there were many diplomatic exchanges between London and Washington, D.C. over the issue until early 1855.

Meanwhile, at Fort Nisqually, Robert Daly continued detailed construction work on the clerk's house. Over thirteen thousand pounds of wool were shipped to England from Fort Nisqually as business activities continued. The sheep herds were so large that the grazing capacity of the plains was being exceeded, even though there were some 161,000 acres available. Doctor Tolmie, the businessman, realized the high demand for live sheep in the Willamette Valley would bring a good price for the Company animals.

Tolmie organized the first big sheep drive from Puget Sound, taking 3,600 head as far south as Eugene, in the Willamette Valley. Imagine the supplies, horses, herdsmen and sheep dogs necessary for such a trip. Selling small numbers of animals all along the way, the trip took four months, and proved very profitable. Old timers remember prices ranging from $100 to $125 per head in the Willamette Valley. At that rate it was nearly a 100% gross profit for Tolmie and the Company for the sale of what might be called surplus livestock.

Just imagine: 3,600 sheep at $100 brings $360,000 gross revenue. At $125 per head we get $450,000 gross revenue. It is difficult to reconcile these figures with those who claim that PSAC at Fort Nisqually was a 'failed' business of 'little or no consequence' to history. It seems clear that the British enterprise was substantial enough to create jealousies among American competitors.

Short horn cows sold for $250, and young bulls for $500 each. When American immigrants brought animals from the east over the Oregon Trail, Fort Nisqually had been in the cattle breeding business on Puget Sound for thirteen years.

Other areas in the region developed alternate economic endeavors. R.H. Espy and I.A. Clark, it is said, walked across the American Great Plains before they became friends, in 1854, with Chief Nahcati. The chief lived near the oyster beds of Willapa (Americans called it Shoalwater) Bay. This was a fortunate friendship, as it made possible the settlement of Oysterville, on the Long Beach Peninsula, near Leadbetter Point.

Oysters were plentiful, and became the center of the town economy. Each Willapa Bay oyster sold for a dollar gold coin in San Francisco. Steamships, depending on the tide, brought those gold coins to Oysterville in huge quantities in search of those delicious Willapa Bay Oysters. Since the town had no bank, and the overland trip to Olympia started with slogging through the mudflats to catch a stage coach, most Oysterville residents stashed their gold coins under their bedroom mattresses. It was alleged that Oysterville had more gold coins than any town on the west coast except San Francisco. In fact, the importance of Oysterville was displayed on the maps of the day. "Oysterville" was printed in larger letters than either Olympia or Seattle.

On February 8th, near Fort Nisqually, Edward Huggins, George Harber, and P. Lewgace presented legal warning notices to James Boyce and Richard Fiander, American squatters on the Company's farmland at Muck. Fiander was determined to stay on the Company land unless compelled to leave by the law. He also threatened to use the Company fence rails unless the Company moved them "forthwith".

On February 10, Dr. Tolmie presented Jessie Varner a squatter notice. Huggins was the witness required by the law. Thirteen days later William Legg, Company employee at Muck, came to the Fort proclaiming that Varner threatened him with personal injury. Huggins took Legg out to Muck to "more clearly see the affair." The next day Tolmie went to Steilacoom City to file a law suit against Varner, Boyce, and Fiander. Tolmie was joined in court the next day by Huggins, Brooks, Legg, and Legace, who were key witnesses for the Company. The case was continued to November.

When the case was finally heard in a Saturday session, all of the testimony and evidence favored the Company position, i.e., Legg was indeed physically threatened with bodily harm by Varner, but the Justice decided in favor of the squatters. The Company men were certain that the Justices were always willing to decide in favor of the squatters.

Legg and Young continued their work at Muck. It is interesting that they were expected to work without interruption from the American squatters, in spite of the legal ruling in favor of the Americans. In June the conflict came to a conclusion. William Legg, the company employee who was a witness against squatters, deserted from the service of the Company to become one of the squatters. He joined an American named Mosley to split the Company's Tlithlow Farm between them. Legg had the nerve to build inside one of the fenced enclosures, while Mosley took the other unfenced half. Huggins, Thomas Dean, and George Harber, all Englishmen, served warning notices to these new squatters.

Two days later, two calves were brought in from Tlithlow for slaughter. It was discovered that both had been shot, but not fatally, with Colt revolvers. It was clear evidence of the deadly and vicious actions of squatters.

The work at Fort Nisqually and Puget Sound Agriculture Company farms and ranches continued all through the spring and summer of 1854, with the almost monotonous regular tasks. Men continued caring for cattle, butchering and selling beef, sowing oats, herding sheep, feeding work horses, delivering mail to and from Victoria, hauling hay and grass, washing sheep, gathering potatoes, dipping and shearing sheep, packing wool, searching for stray horses, bringing in yearling calves for slaughter, and building the chimney for the clerk's house.

Robert Daly's work on the clerk's house was interrupted occasionally by his personal state of intoxication. He sometimes spent entire days in Steilacoom City[330] without much in the way of consequences. Daly may have been celebrating the completion of the carpentry work for which he was hired. Harber and Cowie were assigned to begin painting the new house. The exterior painting was completely finished in only seven days. Probably several others assisted Harber and Coiwie, as the *Journal* says "hands employed about the new house," but they may have been doing other work. Daly left the service of the Company on September 16th. Apparently the new house was sufficiently completed by then, so his carpentry skills were no longer needed. Or perhaps he just

---

330 Officially incorporated in 1854, the place gets its name from an adaption of "Tail-aKoom" or "Chilacoom" or "Chelakom" all examples of the Anglicized Native American village named Scht'leqem.

needed a drink, after receiving his final payoff.

Mrs. Sherwood Bonney opened the first public school in Pierce County during July, August, and September of 1854. That summer, blacksmiths at Hanson, Ackerman & Co. pounded out the first small change in iron and brass. Technically it was not government issued legal tender, but it worked to make financial exchanges easier. The coins were in denominations of 40 and 45 cents, and one dollar.

Money has a three part function. It serves as a means of exchange, a store of value, and a measure of value. This blacksmith coinage served in all of these categories, only because people agreed to use it for that purpose. Any material could have been used for the same purposes, but are generally less acceptable. Legal tender is money recognized by some government entity. It is actually no more valid than an alternate material used, and accepted, as money. So the Hanson/Ackerman coins became money. Wooden nickels have served the same purposes.

In late July, a scow, the *H. C. Page,* arrived from Victoria with K. M. Kennic, Agent for Puget Sound Agricultural Company farms on Vancouver Island on board. Kennic's mission was to pick up work oxen, cows, mares, geldings, two-year-old cattle, and a flock of sheep to be delivered on the scow to the PSAC farms on Vancouver Island. The complete transfer of Puget Sound Agricultural Company was still far off, but the intention was clear enough. PSAC was moving away from Fort Nisqually.

In August, 1854, carpenter Daly returned to work and agreed to serve the Company for one year on a contract that paid 40 Pounds Sterling. He commenced immediately to apply decorative wall paper[331] to the dining room, parlor, and bedrooms of the new clerk's house, with the help of George Harber.

As the new house was reaching completion, social guests were seen more frequently at the Fort. Among the visitors were U. S. Collector of Customs, Colonel Rey, and Reverend John DeVore, the Methodist Minister at Steilacoom, who baptized a son of the Tolmie's. Captain McLean, along with Captain Hawkins of Fort Steilacoom, delivered and collected the mail. Dr. and Mrs. Helmcken, Mrs. Douglas, her three children, and Miss Work, all of Victoria, stopped for a short visit. Captain and Mrs. Slaughter of Steilacoom stopped by as well.

In the autumn of 1854, nearly two years after his appointment as Governor of the Territory of Washington, Isaac Stevens prepared to write treaties for the Indians. He assumed, not as governor, but as Superintendent of Indian Affairs, all authority of the government to make treaties with foreign nations. He appointed the chiefs, as many

---

331 Purchase in San Francisco.

Salish tribes had no 'chief' as such. In this manner, Stevens selected with whom he would negotiate.

It is probably an understatement to say that Stevens was a well trained soldier, not a diplomat. He appointed a land surveyor, George Gibbs, to conduct a census of the Indians. Gibbs found only 893, all told, in nine tribes. Some counted only 15 members in the tribe, according to Gibbs' count. The census was, by all estimations, inaccurate by hundreds, if not thousands.

Stevens initially blocked out a basic treaty form with the aid of "Kentucky Colonel" Michael Simmons, the man Stevens appointed as Indian Agent because he had led a wagon train party to Budd inlet. The plan was to have the Indians sign whatever was presented to them. Period! With no changes or revisions from the first draft, the treaty was presented completely without any prior consultation, let alone any negotiations, with any Indians. A man was sent to notify the Indians of the council meeting to be held.

The ground selected for the treaty signing was on a small, partially wooded knoll on the right bank of the She-nah-nam, a creek known by white people as McAllister Creek, near the Nisqually River delta. The exact spot was about a mile upstream from the mouth of the creek, where fresh water mixes with the saltwater tides of Puget Sound. Medicine Creek, known as Squa-quid to the Nisqually, falls into the She-nah-nam about a mile above the treaty grounds. Medicine Creek actually is lost in the waters of McAllister Creek at that point, McAllister being the larger of the two. The larger creek is only about four miles long, with an astonishing volume emitting from a pure ground water spring. Nearby, the sandy shores were totally obscured by shells and other by-products of hundreds of Indian feasts over the many decades that they called this place home.

Every effort was made during the first day of the treaty council to create good feelings among the Indians. Rumors had already reached them that Stevens planned to move them all to the land of permanent darkness (Alaska). Stevens may have actually had a plan at one time to place all the Indians in a northern Puget Sound area. That plan was never formalized, nor presented. The winter weather was bad, and the Indians were not in a pleasant mood, even with the gift-giving efforts. It was, in their view, a poor substitute for a lavish Native American potlatch. Stevens saw some very stubborn opposition, especially from Leschi, who reportedly tore up the commission paper naming him a subchief and left the council grounds in an angry mood.

On the second day of the council, the Governor made some progress toward his goal when some of the appointed chiefs made their mark. None of them could read, or even reasonably understand the English language. Certainly few understood the far reaching significance of those words, even when translated to Chinook, a trade language totally unsuited for use with serious diplomatic nuances.

Stevens offered more presents and gifts. They were distributed on the third day in an effort to create a favorable impression, where previously there had been little the Indians could see as favorable. The opposite of Stevens' intended result was achieved when paltry gifts were allotted to non-chiefs. Each Indian attending the parley was given two yards of calico, or a yard or two of ribbon, etc. The gifts were too small to sew any useful garment. The gifts were insignificant, but the Indians were significantly insulted!

Somehow, Leschi's mark appeared on the Medicine Creek Treaty. There is no account of his ascent to the treaty. He did not attend after leaving on the first day of the council. Overwhelming testimony from both sides of the issue supports this fact of Leschi's opposition. Yet there is an 'X mark' adjacent to his name on the document. Official records, the minutes, of the Medicine Creek Treaty council long ago disappeared from government files in Washington, D.C. Indian Superintendent Stevens' garbled extracts of the proceedings conveniently suppress all reference to Leschi.[332]

On December 26, 1854, the Medicine Creek Treaty[333] reserved 1,280 acres of land along a steep high bank on the north side of the Nisqually River for the Nisqually tribe. Not only was it a tiny fraction of the Nisqually watershed land area they had "owned" since time immemorial,[334] it was impossible to catch fish there, farm like the whites expected, or even build any decent or substantial homes.

Signatures on the Medicine Creek Treaty show marks by sixty-two chiefs appointed by Stevens. Coast Salish clans did not have "Chiefs," as whites expected. The culture was organized differently. Names on the Treaty include the assigned head-men and delegates from Puyallup, Steilacoom, Squawksin, S'homamish, Stehchass, T'Peeksin, Squiaitl, Saheh-wamish, and Nisqually. Leschi of the Nisqually refused to sign, but an X appears beside his name on the signature page, placed there by an unknown person. Quiemuth, the older half-brother of Leschi, was not a signatory either. Both had been appointed

---

[332] Meeker, Ezra, *Pioneer Reminiscences of Puget Sound, The Tragedy of Leschi*, Lowman & Hanford Stationary and Printing Co., Seattle, WA, 1905.

[333] The last fir tree at Medicine Creek, where the Indian Treaty was signed, fell in December, 2006. The tree died in the winter of 1979, four years after an effort was made to gather seeds to plant in a grove of descendant trees on Indian Reservation lands thought-out the northwest. The descendant "treaty trees" seem to be flourishing.

[334] On January 20, 1856, a Presidential Executive Order enlarged the original Nisqually Reservation to 4,717 acres on both sides of the Nisqually River. In 1917, the U.S. Army condemned 3,353 acres of the Nisqually Reservation to expand Fort Lewis military reserve. See http://nisqually-nsn.gov The aboriginal Nisqually lived on more than 1,100,000 square acres of land before white people came to live here.

as "Chief" by Governor Stevens. The Nisqually Tribe did not consider either Leschi or Quiemuth as their political "Chief." Both men were respected business leaders of their community dealing as horse traders, but were afforded no political power by the tribe.

Among the non-tribal signers of the Treaty were: M.T. Simmons, Indian Agent, James Doty, Secretary of the Commission, C.H. Mason, Secretary, Washington Territory, and W. A. Slaughter.

The Treaty, with all of the flaws intact, was ratified by the United States Senate on March 3, 1855, and proclaimed law of the land on April 10, 1855, by the signature of President Franklin Pierce. During his campaign for election, Franklin Pierce, a Mexican War veteran, was accused of drunkenness and ridiculed as the "hero of many well-fought bottles".

Article one of the Medicine Creek Treaty required the Indians to cede, relinquish, and convey to the United States all their legal right, title, and interest in and to all lands and country occupied by them. It was very precise in describing the geographic points of the eastern side of the Puget Sound region of western Washington. Article two reserved "for the present use and occupation of said tribes and bands" certain tracts of land and a small island without a source of fresh water. All these tracts were surveyed and marked for exclusive use by Indians. Whites were not permitted to reside on those lands without permission of the tribe and the Indian Agent. All tribes and bands were allowed one year to move and settle on the reserved land tracts. Exceptions were allowed for the public convenience of roads to run through the reserved lands.

Article three granted the Indians the "right of taking fish, at all usual and accustomed grounds and stations" and to erect "temporary houses for the purpose of curing [fish]… hunting, gathering roots and berries, and pasturing their horses on open unclaimed lands."

In consideration, the United States, in Article four, agreed to pay the "sum of $32,500." The payment was to be spread over a twenty-year period. The President of the United States would determine, at his discretion, if there were benefits to expending the federal money.

Article five of the Medicine Creek Treaty "sweetened the pot," with an inducement allowing the Nisqually people to clear, fence, and cultivate the reserved lands. Then there was an extra inducement of $3,250, to be expended only at the direction of the President in a manner he alone could approve.

In Article six it was all taken back. The President was given the power to remove the Indians from the reservations, should he alone decide that "Indian welfare" needed to be promoted. The President could abandon the treaty at any time.

Article seven prohibited the use of the annuities to pay individual debts.

Article eight required the Indians to be friendly and to commit no depredations or be punished under the laws of the United States.

In Article nine, Indians were not allowed to use any alcohol. Article ten agreed to establish an agricultural and industrial school to be operated for twenty years for the free benefit of Indian students. The U.S. further agreed to furnish medicine, vaccinations, and a physician without cost to the Indians.

All Indian slaves were to be released and no others could be acquired under Article eleven. Foreign trade to and from Vancouver Island was prohibited in Article twelve. Article thirteen outlined the ratification process.

The entire treaty was, perhaps three hand-written pages in all, with the "marks" of the signatories following. There were nineteen white's signatures and sixty-two Indian marks attached to the treaty. Although Leschi's name was there and an "X" mark beside it, he denied signing the treaty, even later, while being tried and hung for a murder he did not commit.

With the Indian Treaties signed into law with the Constitutional Authority of every international treaty, settlers were eager to claim open land. After 1854, the land was no longer free to any settlers coming to Oregon or Washington Territory. The government-set price was established at $1.25 per acre, with a maximum limit of 320 acres allowed for any single claim.[335]

The treaty did not confine the Indians to the reserved lands in any manner. This fact was missed by a large majority of whites. Many Nisqually continued to work for the HBC at Fort Nisqually and serve the Puget Sound Agricultural Company. At this same time, the Oregon Territorial legislature created severe laws with obvious racial bias.

East of the Rockies, Americans were fighting over slavery, even before the Civil War began. The fight in 1854 was called "Bleeding Kansas." The issue was "slave state or free state." Oregon Territory had already decided it would not allow blacks to own property, but had not completely decided the slavery issue. The Oregon Organic laws were based on Iowa's legal code, simply because someone had carried the law book of Iowa all the way to Oregon. Much of it was simply adopted.

Washington Territory made no mention of Indian or black land ownership. After all, George Washington Bush, a black American, was already a prominent and established settler at Bush Prairie before the earliest white settlers arrived. Bush, in fact, helped many of the new arrivals with food and supplies at a time when they desperately needed assistance.

---

[335] Fort Nisqually and the PSAC held 161,000 acres under the Treaty of 1846. If valued at the congressionally assigned rate for settlers' purchase, the British land was worth about $201,000 plus the value of any buildings, fences, farms, ranches, etc.

It is possible that Bush helped Hugh Pattison establish, in 1854, the first plant nursery in Pierce County near Fern Hill, along what is now called (State Historical Road Number One) 84th Street.

On Wednesday, September 27, 1854, Puget Sound Agricultural Company hired George Palmer, a Negro[336], to serve as cook.[337] Palmer was not the first, last, nor only cook at Fort Nisqually. Over the years, many men held the position. According to an article in *Occurrences*,[338] Mathew Nelson, Richard Slocum, Adam Beinston, Richard Thornhill, W. Sales, Joseph Thibeault, and Indians named Cush, Weenaculneala, Gwakany, were employed as cooks at Fort Nisqually between 1833 and 1859. Others probably cooked at various times without being hired for that specific job

Palmer appears to have been the only Negro ever hired to work at Fort Nisqually. Huggins described him as from the West Indies. His duties were probably related to only food preparation. There were between twelve and twenty men employed at the Fort, so one must conclude that Palmer was probably on the job constantly. Meal preparation would have been limited to serving those unmarried men and families living inside the Fort. Men with families typically lived in homes outside of the palisades. Officers of the Company lived inside the walls with their families, as did the single men, i.e., the ones for whom a Company cook was hired.

Palmer seems to have done the job with satisfactory results, except for one incident. The U.S. Army confined Palmer in the Guard House at Fort Steilacoom for illegally selling liquor to the Indians. A Kanaka named Auoha substituted as cook for a time.

At Fort Nisqually, Robert Daly turned his carpentry skills to furniture making. When he was not drunk and absent from work, he built sofas for the new clerk's house. A man named Weller was employed to build bedsteads for Tolmie's new home, too.

In September Huggins took one man and a horse-drawn wagon to Tlithlow. Nearby Americans, Barnes and Northover, had settled on Company land and were pilfering Company fence rails. Huggins wanted to retrieve the fence rails for use at Tlithlow farms. Barnes and Northover, with guns drawn, would not allow Huggins to remove the Company's fence rails from land the Americans now occupied illegally. The next day Huggins went to Steilacoom to complain to authorities about Barnes and Northover. On the third day Huggins went again to Tlithlow, this time accomplishing his mission without incident. It was a small victory in a losing battle.

---

336 HBC Governor James Douglas, Prime Minister of British Columbia, was a Jamaican-Scot.

337 The first known Negro to settle near Puget Sound was George Washington Bush. He and four other American families settled near Budd Inlet and Bush Prairie, in Thurston County, WA.

338 "Kitchen Facilities at Fort Nisqually", Steve Anderson, *Occurrences,* Volume 8, Number 2, June, 1988.

In late September, the *SS Major Tompkins* arrived at Steilacoom City from San Francisco. The steamer was planning to run a regular route from Olympia to Victoria, landing at various intermediate ports carrying passengers, mail, and freight. This was, perhaps, the first of a number of competing ships that together would be called the Puget Sound "Mosquito Fleet."

One of the first voyages of the *SS Major Tompkins* was to tow the *Prince Albert*, a sailing barque, out of London, with supplies for Fort Nisqually. Captains Mannock and Mitchell of the *Prince Albert* were thankful for the power of the American steamship as they anchored at Nisqually landing. The *Major Tompkins* was also employed by Fort Nisqually. The good ship hauled 366 sheep to Victoria, as ordered by James Douglas, Esquire, and numerous times the officers of the steam ship purchased beef from the Fort. Captain Scranton, Master of the *SS Major Tompkins,* earned $600 towing other vessels up and down Puget Sound in 1854.

In early November the court case originally begun in February, charging Jessie Varner, Richard Fiandre, and James Boyce with squatting on Company land and threatening violence, was still not settled by the Justice in Steilacoom. Again Tolmie, Harber, Legace, and Legg attended court sessions in Steilacoom.

Tolmie was again in Steilacoom for the legal case charging Tamaru with thievery. Keave'haccow and Cowie were witnesses against Tamaru. Understandably, Tolmie's well used buggy was in the carpenter's repair shop before the end of the month.

During the fall months a new wash house was built, fields were stripped of potatoes and turnips, cattle were slaughtered for meat sales in the nearby towns, Fort Steilacoom, and to any and all passing ships. The fur trade was an ever smaller portion of the business at Fort Nisqually. Only two fur bales were shipped in all of December, 1854.

On the other hand, the Fort received 100 barrels of salt salmon from Fort Langley that same month. Sheep were dipped, wool was sheared, cattle hides and horns were bundled, while lumber was hauled, firewood cut and stacked, and livestock fed. Indian women thrashed the wheat, oats were cut, and pork was placed in barrels for rations at Tlithlow and Muck. Another new stable was constructed, as were some bookshelves for Dr. Tolmie's house. Daily life continued apace.

As December turned frosty, 69 quarters of beef were shipped to Victoria. Freight charges were only $10.00 per ton on the American *SS Major Tompkins*. Four-hundred bundles of wheat were used as payment for the use of two horse wagons and a team of oxen by Louis Latour, a company employee's son.

The slaughter house was busy, but not overwhelmed by any measure. The cattle were not scarce, but scared. Americans were out killing Company cattle as if the animals were wild beasts, unrelated to the ranch that had existed for years on the plains of Pierce County, long before it was agreed that it was to be American land. Company hunters found few, but continued to search, as the meat was in very high demand in the nearby towns. One wagon was out nearly every day in search of beef cattle, while one man seemed to always be employed in the slaughter house.

There was no mention in the Fort Nisqually business journal of a Christmas regale, or a Hogmanay celebration at the New Year. The weather was gloomy. The mood at Fort Nisqually seemed to match the seasonal Puget Sound weather.

On December 26, 1854, in heavy periodic rains on the muddy grounds of Medicine Creek, that treaty was presented to the indigenous people reserving a small, steep hillside far above the river for the Nisqually Tribe. All of the rest of the land in the Nisqually world was for settlers to take at will, with no cost.

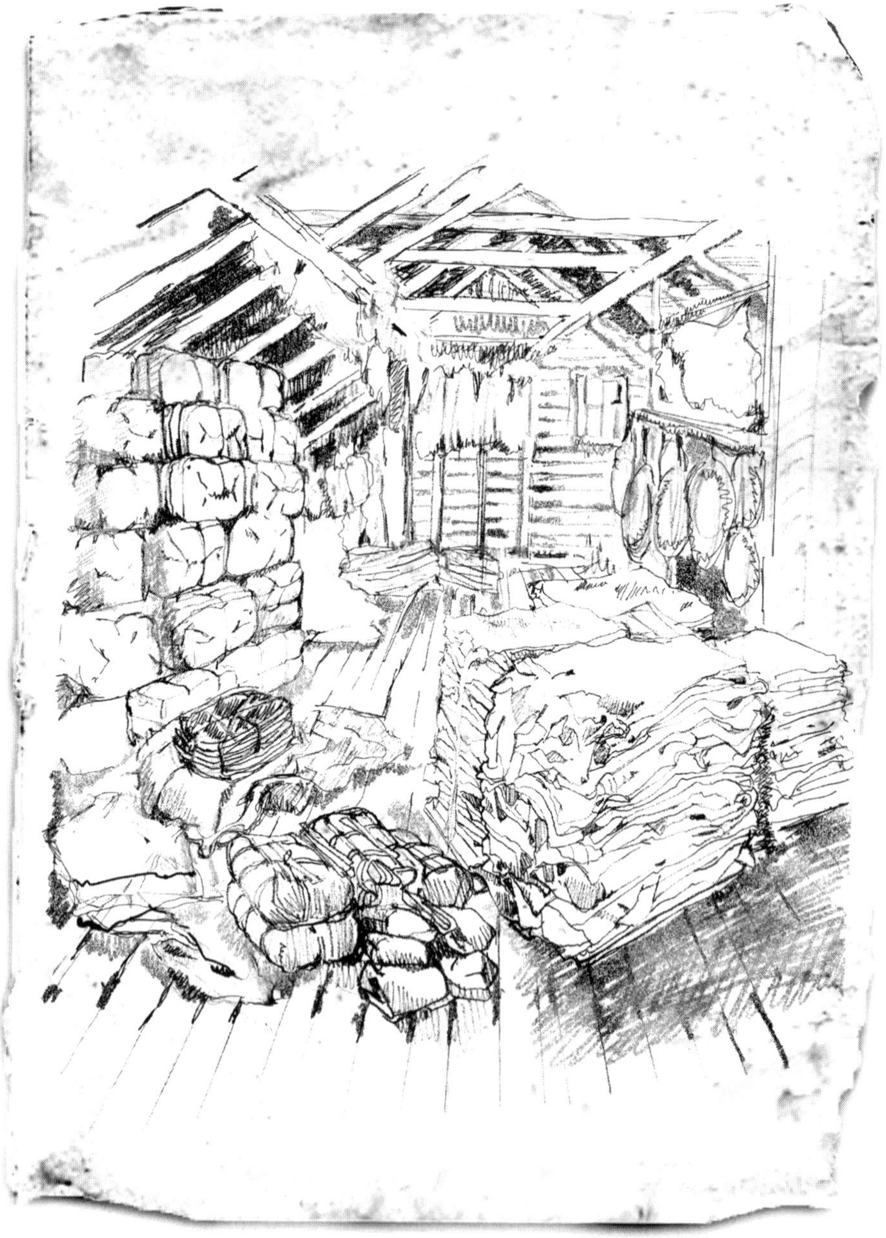

1855

THE CRIMEAN WAR continued in 1855, if only a little more hygienic because of Florence Nightingale's pioneering nursing. The Paris World's Fair was a great success. London installed the first sewers to quell the outbreak of cholera, and digging began on the Suez Canal. The Atlantic Ocean was crossed in record time by the first iron-hull steamer, this one of the Canard Line. It took only 9½ days to traverse from Europe to America, but little had changed around Puget Sound. The area was still a remote corner of the known world. Progress was celebrated by the settlers when the first public (tax supported) school in Olympia was opened.

Governor Stevens spent the winter and spring "negotiating" treaties to reserve land for Indian Tribes. The Point-No-Point Treaty was signed on January 26, 1856, only four days after the Point Elliott Treaty was signed. The Neah Bay Treaty was concluded on January 31, and the Mill Creek Treaty with the Walla Walla Indians was dated May 24, 1855. Other treaties were developed in rapid succession across the entire northwest, from the Pacific to the Rockies.

In the early part of the year, the San Juan Islands dispute became temporarily somewhat academic, as most Americans fled the islands in fear of a rumored northern Indian raid. The Islands were "all British," at least for a time. Part of the PSAC sheep herds were there at Bell Vue Farms. Northern Indians had been raiding Coast Salish villages in Puget Sound for eons, perhaps. While avoiding British establishments, they were hitting American settlers' camps, too. Their goal was to take slaves, firearms, pots and pans, and anything else not nailed down. Sometimes they wanted the nails, too. They were ruthless, even to the point of severing heads to take as trophies. U.S. military posts were set up at Bellingham Bay and Port Townsend. The northern Indians avoided attacks on British places because the Royal Navy had used "Gunboat Diplomacy" from the beginning of British explorations against hostile indigenous peoples around the world. It was easy for a British warship to level a coastal village with a cannon volley. It was nearly as easy to burn to the ground any inland village of hostile natives. The Indians, especially in what is now British Columbia, quickly learned the lessons taught by British violence, which the British always justified in the name of "keeping the peace".

The roster shows twenty-four men with a variety of ethnic backgrounds were employed at Fort Nisqually in January, 1855:

Dr. William Fraser Tolmie (Scotsman, Chief Factor)
Baptiste Chalifoux (Fr Canadian or Métis, laborer & carpenter)
Cowie (Kanaka laborer)
Bill (perhaps several men of the same name)
William Cheeseman (English farmer)
Cush (Indian)
Robert Daly (American soldier, then employee)
Dixon (English sailor on *Cadboro*, employee)
Roderick Finlayson, Jr. (English shepherd)
Alfred Gorridge (English? laborer)
Charles Gullion (Shepherd, then squatter)
Edward Huggins (English Clerk)
Frederick W. Kennedy (English clerk, son of a Doctor)
Keave'haccow (Kanaka laborer)
William Legg (American squatter, then employee)
Allan McIsaac (American squatter, then employee)
Henry Moar (Mour?) (English laborer)
John Montgomery (Scottish cattle herder at Spanueh. Spanaway's first settler)
Oniare (Métis employee)
Parkinson (Shepherd, later settler)
Charles Ross (Canadian farmer)
Simon (Indian horse breeder)
S'Hattol (Indian)
S'talol (Indian)
Squally (Indian)
Tapou (Kanaka shepherd)
Joseph Thibeault (Canadian, then squatter)
Richard Thornhill (English steward)
William Young (English farm manager)
James Venn (English farm manager)[339]

---

[339] This employee list, though researched, is not definitive. There could be more employees depending on the moment-in-time of any census. Workers were often hired for day labor. Men were frequently sent to other posts for short periods. This list could provide some measure of historical accuracy for reenactors, who could present an actual historic persona of Fort Nisqually in 1855.

1855

Steilacoom's first hometown newspaper hit the streets in May, 1855. It reported that there were two companies of the United States Army 4th Infantry stationed at Fort Steilacoom, one and a half miles from town, on the Military Road to Fort Walla Walla.

Along the Military Road (also called Byrd Road) only a mile or two east of Fort Steilacoom, Andrew F. Byrd and his partners built a saw mill in 1853. Near the sawmill Byrd's company constructed a grist mill and a slaughter house. He impounded the water of Chambers Creek with an earthen dam, so that a swamp at the edge of the creek was soon filled, forming a handsome lake. In due time, the lake would be named Steilacoom Lake. Byrd was in industrious and ambitious man, well-liked by his contemporaries and customers. Byrd promoted the ideas for a local school, library, more roads, and a Masonic Lodge.

Military Road went to the Puyallup Valley and beyond, after it passed directly in front of Byrd's Mill (in today's Lakewood), so it was natural that people began to call it Byrd's Mill Road, at least in that local section.[340] It was also called the "immigrant road," recognized as the Oregon Trail wagon trains began to come downhill from the Cascade Mountains. The Longmire–Biles wagon train was first to pass this way in 1853, after crossing the mountains on the Naches Pass Trail. It was the entire length of the road from Walla Walla to Steilacoom that was named as the Military Road. In the 20th Century it became, for a time at least, State Historical Road #1.

In February Tapou built a brick and clay cooking oven behind the Factor's new house. It was near the kitchen house. Tolmie ordered Daly, Keave'haccow, and Gohome to pull down a barn at Harry Dean's farm. An employee of Dean's refused to allow the operation. He threatened to shoot anyone laying a hand on the place. Later Huggins and Gorridge went to Dean's place and pulled the barn down before nightfall. Gorridge hauled the barn timbers back to the Fort with a crew of Indians and three wagons pulled by horses and oxen.

Daly was using a plane to smooth boards for the new house veranda when word came that the American *SS Major Tompkins* had been wrecked off Victoria during a nighttime squall. The loss was felt at Fort Nisqually because the men had come to rely on the regular schedule the ship had maintained. On the other hand, work never stopped. There was simply too much to do.

Spring plowing began, as new fences were installed and veranda planks were planed smooth. Spring wheat sales were so brisk that Tolmie purchased 24 bushels from Mr. L.A.

---

340 Byrd's Mill Road was said to be the only safe route out of the Puyallup Valley during the Puget Sound Indian War. Later it was the location and route of the never completed "Russian—American Telegraph Line." The line was proposed to extend to Europe by way of the Bering Strait and Asia.

Smith for $4.50 in trade goods. Other work continued. As an indicator of work accomplished in March 1855, we look at the numbers:

- 22 quarters of beef sold
- 160 bushels of potatoes opened
- 12 horses driven to Dominique's Prairie
- 64 bushels of oats delivered (75 cents per bushel)
- 17 sides of leather sent to Victoria
- 2 horses sold ($50 and $60 respectively)
- 2 potato pits dug
- 600 pounds of flour produced
- 100 hides sold
- 95 bushels of potatoes planted

The list doesn't include the wagons hauling dung day after day to fertilize the swampy potato and pea fields, or the wagon loads of firewood hauled into the place. There is little mention of the wagon loads of beef sold to the U.S. Army at Fort Steilacoom and the nearby civilian towns.

Soldiers' camp and garrison rations were issued, according to Hardee's 1855 Manual.[341] Meat rations in this official Army Manual allowed each soldier to have 12 ounces of pork or bacon, and 1 pound 4 ounces of beef. For every 100 soldiers there was an allowance of 15 pounds of peas. Fort Nisqually farms of the PSAC was contracted to provide these rations to Fort Steilacoom.

Additional soldiers' rations included soft bread or flour, and hard bread (hardtack) or corn meal. Every 100 soldiers shared green coffee or tea, sugar, vinegar, candy, soap, salt, pepper, molasses, and when practical, an additional 30 pounds of potatoes. Much of these rations were supplied by the British trading post, in competition with American merchants in Steilacoom City[342] and Olympia.

Tempers flared in early April. Robert Daly, showing a complete lack of disciplined leadership, whacked Oniare on the head with a Jack Plane[343] for some perceived infrac-

---

341 Hardee, William J. "Rifle and Light Infantry Tactics for the Exercise and Maneuvers of Troops When Acting as a Light Infantry or Riflemen," United States War Department, 1855.

342 Steilacoom City is the name adopted for the merged villages of Steilacoom and Port Steilacoom when the place became the first incorporated city in Washington Territory, 1853.

343 A Jack Plane is a medium sized general-purpose tool used by carpenters and joiners to smooth wood.

tion of Daly's rules. Oniare, in return, delivered a well-deserved walloping to Daly for his "intemperate and cowardly act."

April, May and June were no less busy. It was May when Huggins delivered the legal papers required by Pierce County and the Surveyor General of Washington Territory concerning the land claims of Puget Sound Agricultural Company. While Huggins was in Olympia, Tolmie was again in a Steilacoom court room for basically the same issue. In the month of May, Tolmie was in Olympia or Steilacoom, on the issue of land rights for at least ten days. In June, Mrs. Tolmie was suddenly quite ill. Dr. Potts, army surgeon at Fort Steilacoom, was called to her bedside on three consecutive days. After five days of illness, and another visit from Dr. Potts, Jane Work Tolmie's health was improving. Her other visitors included Lt. Nugent, Lt. Williams, and Mrs. Potts.

Some remarkable animals were slaughtered in June. One beef oxen weighed in at 618 pounds, while some 710 wedder sheep, one horse, and one stag bull were loaded aboard the *SS Otter* bound for Victoria. One man spent two full days butchering pigs. The pork was salted and packed in barrels. Another man spent the same time salting hides, packing them and the corresponding horns and hooves for eventual sale in London. The horns and hooves were probably destined to become combs, brush handles, powder horns, and glue.

Mr. Henry Newsham Peers, Manager of the Puget Sound Agricultural Company farms at Cowlitz, was at Nisqually for much of the summer. He assisted and supervised the arrival of supplies, including 40 bales of brown sugar, three barrels of crushed sugar, fifteen cases of candles, and, curiously, 10 bags of balls. Peers was needed at the Fort because, for at least part of the month Dr. Tolmie took his wife Jane, his sister-in-law Lettie Work, Mrs. Helmcken, Mrs. Douglas, and two of the children off to Victoria.

Every effort was being made to prepare before the horse brigade arrived in July. Until 1855 the "Fur Returns" were taken to Fort Vancouver or Fort Victoria, the two Company headquarter sites between 1824 and 1869, to be ultimately transshipped to London. For years the furs taken in at the coastal trade posts had been collected piecemeal at Fort Nisqually. For the trapper's year ending on May 31, 1855, all furs from the entire Columbia Department would be collected at Fort Nisqually. Transshipment would begin on Puget Sound, and from there be shipped to London's fur auctions.

The coastal merchant ship traders and the horse brigade trappers from the Rockies would descend on Puget Sound with the year's catch. While at Fort Nisqually, they would replenish their trade goods inventory for a new trading and trapping season. It was a decision made in light of the declining number of Americans and Indians trading for supplies at the Fort sales shop. The trade store simply had too much inventory, high quality trade goods, and not enough room for the merchandise on hand or about to arrive from Europe. Business is business. If the store needs to change practices for the customers' benefit, so be it. Fort Nisqually would change.

The story of HBC horse brigade coming to Fort Nisqually in 1855 was told by Edward Huggins.[344]

> "The Board of Management of Hudson's Bay Company's affairs, with headquarters at Fort Vancouver, Columbia River, had decided that the "Fur Returns' from the different posts, or trading establishments in Oregon and Washington Territory, for the accounting year ending May 31, 1855—which hitherto had been taken to Fort Vancouver—should this year, be taken to Fort Nisqually (which post is situated on Puget Sound, six miles south of Steilacoom, directly upon the road between Olympia and Tacoma) by way of the Cascade Range of mountains, through Naches Pass, and the supply of goods required by these posts, and servants, for the trade and wants of the ensuing year should be obtained at Fort Nisqually and freighted back by the horse that carried the furs."

The principle reason for making this order was because Fort Nisqually was overstocked with goods: the usual kind, required to carry on trade with the Indians, and a small selection of the finer goods, to satisfy the demands of the fast-increasing white population coming into the country to find employment at large saw mills and to take up land claims—farms—under the United States liberal land laws.

On the 27th of June, the Fort Nisqually Journal states:

> "We at Fort Nisqually made preparations for packing the goods for the interior posts long before the arrival of the Brigade of horses bringing furs. A small press was made by one of our Canadian carpenters. It was a primitive affair but answered all purposes. Its pressing power was the wedge and it made a compact, small bale. Each bale weighing about eighty pounds, two of which made a load for a horse and weighed 160 pounds, a load quite heavy enough for a common pony weighing for 700 to 1,000 pounds to pack over such roads and trails as are found in this mountainous country. Some of the goods couldn't be pressed and such were put in strong boxes. Shot and ball were put in rawhide casings, which (were) required to be strong enough to prevent loss en route.
>
> "Three French Canadians arrived at the Fort and presented an order from

---

344 Huggins, Edward, The Beaver, Summer, 1961, as reprinted in Fort Notes, The newsletter of Fort Nisqually Living History Museum, June 2008.

Mr. Angus McDonald, the officer in charge of Fort Colvile[345] for flour and other provisions for the use of the Brigade, which was in the mountain approaches and would probably arrive in about five days. They were correct in their prediction, for on the 2nd of July at about midday, I was startled to see a tall rather slim man ride into the Fort, dismount and walk towards the large house where he was met and kindly received by Doctor Tolmie. This was Angus McDonald of Fort Colvile, now in charge of the Brigade of upwards of 200 horses, most of them packed with furs[346], the result of the year's trade of Fort Colvile, Walla Walla, Boise, Hall, Okanogan, Nez Perce and the Snake Country.

"I had heard a great deal about MacDonald [sic] and was anxious to meet him, which desire was soon gratified, for Doctor Tolmie brought him to the packing room where I was working and gave me an introduction to him. He was a rather good looking man, about six feet in height, straight and slim, but is said to be very wiry and strong. He had a dark complexion, with long jet black hair reaching over his shoulders and a thick long very black beard and mustache. He wore a dressed deer skin over shirt and pants, a regatta rowing shirt and had a black silk handkerchief tied loosely around his neck He had black piercing eyes and a deep sonorous voice with a low rather monotonous manner of speaking. He was fond of telling Indian stories and legends, and would sometimes keep the audience entranced and spellbound, when walking slowly to and fro in the large Nisqually reception room, telling some blood curdling Indian story in which he had a conspicuous part. He could speak several Indian languages and had lived amongst the Blackfoot Indians and was full of interesting stories of adventure amongst that one time savage tribe. He was excessively fond of living the life of an aborigine and would much prefer to live in a tent or lodge than a house built in accordance with civilized plans. He was fairly educated. He read a great deal and was well up on the politics of the day. He was a good French linguist but his native tongue was Gaelic of the Scottish Highlands. He was very fond of singing or chanting in a deep, not by any means musical, voice, Gaelic songs and verses improvised by himself."[347]

"Sometimes Dr. Tolmie would join in, when he sang or attempted to sing, some old and well known Scotch ditty. The Doctor could talk and understand

---

345 Fort Colvile was upstream on the Columbia River and named for Andrew Colvile of the HBC Committee in London.

346 Typically a single horse carried two ninety-pound packs.

347 Huggins, Edward, as quoted in the June, 2006 *Fort Notes*, Pp 13-14, quoting from an article published in *The Beaver*, Summer Edition, 1961. Huggins is believed to have written the original account prior to 1870.

Gaelic although he wasn't a native Highlander, but came near being one, having been born in Inverness. The Doctor was very fond of music and although he was not a possessor of a voice like "Mario's" or Jean de Resche," he could sing a great variety of Gaelic songs. But as for MacDonald he was never tired of chanting Gaelic lines. I should think it was something kin to the late Signor Folis' voice, the great basso, when suffering from a very bad cold. The most astonishing thing about it was that "Mac" labored under the idea that he was a fine singer, and the possessor of a voice which only required a little training to be equal to any of the leading basso profudos [sic] of the day. He was married to either a Nez Perce or a Kalispel, the daughter of a leading chieftain, and had several children by her. One girl named Christine, who was said to be quite good looking, for a long time was the belle of Colvile.

"MacDonald was a staunch Briton, and was very plain spoken. In fact, he was sometimes offensively rude when talking to Americans. He made a visit to us during the San Juan difficulty....Not very long after his arrival, there came trotting into the Fort yard the first detachment of the Brigade, about 20 horses, all laden with packs of furs and in charge of two men. Detachments continued to arrive until upwards of 200 pack animals were inside the Fort yard and 25 men were in charge of them. There were also spare animals for packing and riding and not a few were packed with tents, cooking utensils and what little provisions remained. Unloading the animals immediately commenced, each detachment being attended to by the two men to whom its care belonged.

"The valuable lot of furs was turned over to me and I had 20 men selected to watch them. There was a lot of work to do with these furs, exposing them to the air, beating and getting them ready for making into larger bales for shipment to Victoria. Amongst the lot of furs received were a large number of foxes, Marten and Mink, small but valuable furs and strict watch had to be kept over them to prevent peculation by Indians. Sometimes even white men would be trying to get away with a Marten.

"Some of the furs had been slightly damaged in crossing the many rivers along the route, but I was surprised to see them open up in such condition as they did. To give some idea of the extensive character of the fur trade at the few posts in the Rocky Mountain district, and in a country not at all remarkable for prolific returns, I will give here a statement of the kinds of quantities of the furs now handling and just delivered by the pack train.

"1,200 Bear skins 250 of the Grizzlies; 200 Badgers; 2,500 Beaver; 350 Fisher, a beautiful fur scarce and hard to catch. It is something like a Marten, only very much larger, and a first class skin was worth here from $5 to $8 and in the

London market would fetch probably $20 tp $30); 12 Silver, 80 Cross Silver and 334 Red Foxes; 185 lynx (prime fur); 1,550 Marten; 575 Mink; 8,000 Musquash (Muskrat) 412 Land Otter; 580 Wolves (prime fur) and 45 wolverine.

"The men accompanying MacDonald were a cosmopolitan crowd. There were Scotchmen, French Canadians, Half-breeds, and Iroquois. The foreman a Scotch Highlander and when at home was in charge of a little trading post amongst the Blackfoot Indians. The Canadians were strong, wiry fellows, and amongst them were men who had been in the employ of the company for fifty years. The Iroquois or Half-breed Iroquois were the best looking men in the band. The handsomest and strongest amongst them was a Halfbreed Iroquois and French Canadian. He was very strong and agile, and being the champion athlete amongst his own people, he challenged our hands to run a foot race and other games requiring strength and endurance. Although amongst our staff were some strong and powerful fellows this Iroquois beat them all, and running a foot race he beat them badly."

Once all of the furs were collected, over 400 packs of trade goods (two packs per horse at eighty pounds each) had to be made up for the fur traders' next winter season. In addition, all of the survival supplies the trappers would need for a complete year in the mountains were to be packed at Fort Nisqually for each of the men, and often for their wives, too. Flour, dried meat, coffee, tobacco, gun powder, shot and ball, and every other need had to be anticipated and met. Some goods were pressed into ninety-pound packs; others were placed in wooden boxes, while still goods were loaded onto barrels. Often supplies were tied into strong rawhide casings to reduce losses and damages en route.

British called the gatherings "Brigade Encampments." The same sort of get-together was referred to by Americans as the annual (mountain man) "Rendezvous." With either name, these were often raucous affairs. The trappers sold their furs, paid their debts, and celebrated their bountiful riches by spending it all. They gambled, bought new things, drank excessively, gambled some more and drank even more, until there was nothing left of their hard-earned profits won during a year of extreme danger and hard labor. They were happy people, indeed, doing it "their way."

Edward Huggins was a storyteller with a sense of history. He was anxious to record the events of his surroundings for posterity, even when not many listened or cared. His letters, articles and stories, written during a long lifetime, tell us a great deal of what it was like beyond the pages of the official *Journal of Occurrences*.

During the 1855 Brigade Encampment at Fort Nisqually there were many friendly "competitions," often simply designed to separate a man from his money, but often as a manly challenge to reveal the superior human specimen. The braggart was expected. The "showoff" was sought out. The gullible were entertained. And the bets were placed on each and every challenge or contest. They ran long and short races, threw the hammer, put the stone, and aimed at targets with arrows, hatchets, knives, rocks and guns. And they fought. The Marquis of Queensberry was ignored. This was not the sport of boxing. This was fighting! If there were rules, no one admitted to know them. It was winner take all, down and dirty. Bare knuckles were the weapons, and alcohol was the fuel.

Boasting was expected to draw a challenge. It seems that a young Iroquois-French-Canadian boasted of his running speed. The Iroquois was named Edouard Pichette. He claimed absolute superiority without having run a race. One particular proper English gentleman at Fort Nisqually was repeatedly taunted by this fellow. Most of the men felt they would be humiliated in any footrace with the braggart Iroquois.

Edward Huggins, English gentlemen, reported on the 100-yard sprint contest between Edouard Pichette and an unnamed English gentleman.

After describing the opponent as big and barrel-chested, Huggins' tale goes on to tell of his attire.

> *"He wore a red silk belt around his waist over a pair of thin cotton drawers which showed his handsome, muscular legs to good advantage... he looked a fit model to satisfy any fastidious painter or sculptor."*

The opponent was identified only as "an Englishman." Huggins does not admit to his own participation, avoiding the braggart status he previously attached negatively to the Iroquois. He says, using third person language, that the Englishman stripped down to reveal a well-developed chest and powerful arms. He was after all the leading athlete in the local "games" of throwing, putting, and pitching.

The race was set. The Iroquois was cool and confident. His fellows, also confident, were willing to bet their last shirt, their last inch of tobacco, their last dram of rum, and even some future promises to pay. The race course began just west of the water gate, running 100 yards to Sequalitchew Creek, a smooth, slightly downward sloping path very familiar to Huggins.

Angus McDonald made the signal to start the race. The young Englishman jumped to an instant lead, increasing it until the 50 yard mark. Pichette then closed the gap to about three yards and continued to shorten the distance between the racers. To the intense disgust of Scotsman Angus McDonald, the Englishman won by four or five feet.

Huggins delights in his storytelling about the "howling and hurrahing" of those supporting bets on the Englishman and the demoralized expressions of the Canadian, Métis, and Indian supporters. The Nisqually Indians, Huggins says, celebrated with expressions of "silent jubilance."

Edouard Pichette earnestly begged for a rematch, which the Englishman wisely turned down. The Englishman was content to rest on his victory laurels. He had earned the reputation as the runner who defeated the Champion of the Rockies, then retired immediately, undefeated.

Many modern readers of Huggins story believe it was Huggins himself as the unnamed Englishman.

The Brigade Encampment continued with other activities and attractions. Dr. Tolmie offered a dance in the large store. It was a fine dance hall, about 60 feet by 30 feet when cleared of boxes, barrels, casks, and burlap bags. The rough floor seemed to not bother the dancers at all. Music was supplied by some Canadian fiddlers, lubricated with a liberal supply of whisky. Nearly all of the young Indian girls in the neighborhood were there, along with the country wives of nearly all of the Brigade men and the Fort men.

The Kanakas (Sandwich Islanders) employed by the Company were there. They too, danced. Huggins found some of their routine to be an unseemly performance in the presence of ladies. There is no word of the ladies objecting to the Kanakas dancing in a row, with a wild and monotonous chant, keeping time by moving their bodies with "great exactitude," as Huggins phrased it. There seemed to be less dancing and more posturing.

Mr. Thomas Dean, employed by the Company as Bailiff, originally sent out from London to supersede Dr. Tolmie, was a popular entertainer at the Brigade Encampment. He was a natural musician, a comic, a singer of songs in character, and "for a time, the life of the place," according to Huggins.

Dean made a tin whistle and offered a "Punch and Judy" show, as seen in London. His puppets were presented at McDonald's party. Probably none of the fur traders had ever seen such a show, or ever entered a theater. One stout old man, small in stature but very strong, upwards of 60 years old, was so delighted in the show that he laughed until he fell down, kicking his heels in the air in a burst of laughter so expressive that he became the delight of the show. Punch and Judy was performed repeatedly on the trails and in the camps for many years

By July 16, the horses had put on flesh and their backs had healed when the Walla Walla portion of the fur brigade was fully packed and prepared to depart Fort Nisqually for the hinterlands. The horses were fresh. Muscle and flesh had returned to their backs, which had healed up nicely. The men were rested. The party was over. The difficult work and life of a fur trader beckoned. Fifty-five horses and packs were headed back to the beaver dams.

The second contingent of the Brigade was loaded by July 25th. McDonald led the remaining 76 horses and men packed with goods toward Naches pass. They carried some 151 "pieces of goods" on their pack horses. This inventory was probably a total of over 12,000 pounds of supplies and trade goods. Fort Nisqually would learn the rest of the story after the Brigades reached journey's end, when Angus McDonald sent his report letter to Dr. Tolmie from Colvile.

The letter revealed that the Walla Walla party entered the foothills of the Cascades, ,where they waited for McDonald. They had learned of hostile Indians on the East side of the Cascades. McDonald's influence among the Indians was so great that he was able to gain safe passage through the hostile territory unscathed. He was admired with great respect by the Spokane, Nez Perce, Blackfoot, Kalispels, indeed all of the tribes between the Yakima Tribe and the Rocky Mountain Tribes. He was considered to be a great medicine man. Although Caucasian, a Scotsman to be more exact, McDonald's lifestyle and manner was almost entirely Indian. His Indian-like reputation and his nearly profound ability to talk in their many languages, helped gain permission to travel safely through the danger they posed to strangers. The joint pack train was carrying upwards of 20,000 pounds of valuable trade goods and supplies that any self-respecting Indian wanted. McDonald, the black-bearded Indian, made them understand that they wanted the goods only through fair trade.

Other travelers through the same mountain passes met with quite different treatment. The Puget Sound Indian Wars began slowly in Washington Territory. Indians on both sides of the Cascades were decidedly unhappy with the one-sided treaties forced upon them by Governor Isaac Stevens, representing the United States government.

The summer of 1855 saw a great deal of unrest, most of it based on news of violence east of the Cascades. On October 2, Dr. Tolmie wrote,

> "This part of the country in now greatly disturbed on account of false rumors of Indian hostilities. Yesterday the panic was great, but is now subsiding."

The situation was quite different only 26 days later. On October 28, three settler families living along the Green River were attacked. Nine white people were killed during the surprise attack. Their cabins were ransacked and burned. It was in quick succession that nearly all of the settlers were burned out of their homes along the lower Green, White, and Duwamish River valleys. While the entire Indian population was estimated at about 6,000 in the Puget Sound basin at the outbreak of the war, only an estimated 200 were actively hostile during the Puget Sound Indian War.

1855

Acting Governor Charles Mason called out the militia and requested soldiers from Fort Steilacoom and Fort Vancouver to pursue the enemy. Settlers from the Puyallup Valley fled their homes, seeking protection at Fort Steilacoom. The refugees overwhelmed the tiny military camp with possessions and livestock. Imagine the confusion of the sudden influx of frightened families.

Lieutenant William Slaughter led most of the soldiers. After several weeks of little success in his quest to engage the Indians in a traditional battle, Slaughter ordered his detachment to camp near Brennan's Prairie along the White River. On the evening of December 4, 1855, they were suddenly attacked. The casualty list was extensive, including three dead, among them Lt. Slaughter.[348]

Captain Charles Eaton was ordered to intercept any Indians traveling over the mountains from the areas of hostility in the Yakima Valley. Eaton and 19 men were headed toward Muck Creek from Olympia. They came upon Leschi's ranch where he farmed and raised cows and horses. Leschi was nowhere to be seen, even though his plow was standing idle in a field. Eaton's rangers helped themselves, literally stealing fifteen of Leschi's horses.

They next day, having seen no Indians, eight Rangers were sent back to Olympia for additional supplies. Soon some Indians were spotted fishing in the White River. They were not identified as warriors, but Eaton was concerned they could have posed a problem for the militia. Eaton took some Rangers to examine the condition of the road ahead. It would need some repairs if heavy traffic were to use the lowest, swampy areas across Connell's Prairie. At about four in the afternoon on October 27, 1855, a sudden volley of musket shots rang out. James McAllister fell, wounded with the first shot, and Michael Connell was fatally wounded.

The Rangers sought cover in Connell's house. Andrew Laws returned fire, killing one Indian, while the other Indians surrounded the house. Edward Wallace was wounded when a ricochet bounced into the side of his head during one of the frequent volleys from the Indians. Before daylight on the 28th the shooting stopped. The Rangers were certain they had killed seven Indians, but no bodies were ever found. That morning the Rangers made their way back to Fort Steilacoom unchallenged. By this time there was no doubt: the Puget Sound Indian War of 1855-56 had begun.[349]

At the outbreak of the war around Fort Nisqually, the Company's flock master and the men under him became frightened, demoralized, and refused to remain at their scattered

---

348 For a period of time after the Puget Sound Indian War the town known today as Auburn was in fact named Slaughter.

349 Eckrom, Jerry, *Remembered Drums*, Pioneer Press, Walla Walla, WA, 1989.

outposts on the exposed prairies of the 161,000 acres of farm and ranch land. Edward Huggins, the young Englishman working as a clerk close to Dr. Tolmie, volunteered to take charge of the far flung livestock branch of the Puget Sound Company's business. Dr. Tolmie and Huggins prevailed upon the cattle and sheep herdsmen to return to their traditional grazing grounds, with Huggins as their leader. Huggins remained in charge of this department for nearly five years with good success, according to his own reports. Even with the hostilities, and some expressed fear, all Fort men continued to be friendly with the Indians, the principle customers and regular employees of the Puget Sound Agricultural Company. In spite of the fear expressed by some HBC workers, American settlers accused Fort employees of aiding the Indian war efforts.

Most agree that the October 29 Indian attack on American settlers was in protest of the unfair and lopsided Medicine Creek Treaty written by Governor Stevens. Whatever the reason, Fort Steilacoom was overwhelmed by the civilian stampede seeking safety. Some 80 families arrived demanding protection. They had abandoned their farms in fear. Ironically, it was Abram Salitat, a Nisqually Indian, who warned the settlers of the potential attack. Some were well-prepared for exile, but most brought nothing with them. They all found that there was no housing for them at Fort Steilacoom, and no protection, for that matter. Fort Steilacoom was actually a converted farm without a defensive perimeter. Many soldiers, without barracks, regularly bivouacked on the grounds.

The Methodist preacher of Steilacoom City, Reverend John DeVore, fled to Olympia to write to his Oregon brethren. He told them:

> We hear nothing but the clangor of arms and the war whoop. We lie down at night after bidding each other farewell and resign ourselves into the hands of the God of battles, not knowing that we shall ever behold the light of another day.
>
> On the night of December 28, a Fort Steilacoom sentry spotted something moving in the shadows. He fired a single shot. He then observed someone dragging away a wounded person. A patrol was sent the following morning. They found a small trail of blood but no body.[350]

Edward Huggins later explained his role during the Puget Sound Indian War:

> After the outbreak of the Indian war in 1855, the exigencies of the company's business caused me to take charge of the live stock and farming part of the business, and in the fall of 1855 I moved to Muck Station, with a party of fifteen or twenty men—Englishmen, Canadians, and Kanakas. I remained at that station

---

350 Ibid.

until 1859. After the conclusion of the war (end of 1856), I continued to reside at Muck and had several Indians employed along with English, Canadian laborers, thus affording me a good opportunity of learning the comparative merits of each class, and I do not hesitate to say that I found the Indian laborer much superior as a workman to the English and Canadian workmen. The Indians made capital plowmen and cared for their horses much better than did the others; and, to cut the matter short, I would sooner have my Indian laborer than the white men I had with me during my five years of service as farm overseer at Muck. I had a few Indians who were good rough carpenters, and first rate axmen. I had three Indians who were, as farm workers in general, incomparably superior to any white men the company had employed.[351]

In November, Captain Hays and his Volunteer Militia confiscated three sacks of goods from some Indians. Later Hays accused seven Nisqually of hostile actions near Puyallup. The seven accused had actually sought refuge at Fort Nisqually. Dr. Tolmie spent the night with Hays' soldiers at John Montgomery's Spanaway farm, where the seven Nisqually were imprisoned. Within two days, Tolmie had convinced Captain Hays that the seven captured Indians were indeed innocent. All seven were released to return to Fort Nisqually.

In late November, part of the palisade was blown down by the wind. Four men spent the next full day repairing the damage. Some horses were missing. Men were sent to search for the animals, one of which seemed to be in the possession of a soldier who would not give it up. The news at Fort Steilacoom was far more serious than a missing horse. Lt. Slaughter and his men were surrounded by enemy Indians along the White River. One volunteer soldier had been killed and 38 horses stolen from Slaughter's troops. Captain Hays took a Company of Washington Volunteers to join the battle.

News came to Fort Nisqually on Saturday, December 8, that Lt. Slaughter and three soldiers had been killed, with four others wounded. The soldiers had taken up a position in an old log cabin with large gaps between the logs and a large fire in the center of the house. They did not post a watch or night guard outside the house. It was a very dark, night, enabling the Indians to creep, unseen to the walls of the house, and thrust their guns through the crevices. Slaughter was shot through the heart.

Dr. Tolmie, Mr. Huggins, and Mr. Greig, from Fort Nisqually, attended the funerals.

As the hostilities between Americans and Indians increased around lower Puget Sound, so, too, they were increasing in the San Juan Islands. The difference was the

---

[351] Meeker, Ezra, *Pioneer Reminiscences of Puget Sound, The Tragedy of Leschi*, Lowman & Hanford Stationery and Printing Co., Seattle, Wa, 1905.

Indians were not among the hostiles involved. American settlers and the British Navy were at odds. In October the Americans again ordered Charles John Griffin, the British shepherd of Belle Vue Farms on San Juan Island, to pay ($80.33) in back taxes. After refusing to pay, the Americans confiscated and "sold" forty rams at fifty cents to one dollar a head to themselves, the money going for the back taxes allegedly owed. The Americans tried to load the forty rams into a large Indian canoe for transport. The rams were not cooperative, of course. Some of the men were butted, the canoe tipped and the rams galloped off across the vast prairie.

Thirty-four sheep were finally aboard the *Vidette* the next morning before Griffin released the remaining herd from overnight pens. With the *S.S. Beaver* approaching the Islands, the British subjects felt more protected, but with so many animals already taken by the Americans, there were financial losses to Puget Sound Agricultural Company.

The British Ambassador claimed the Americans owed £650 for stealing 34 rams, £650 for 267 ewes and lambs, £500 for the hire of the *S.S. Beaver*, £1,100 for incidental losses, altogether about $15,000. The American government labeled the claim fraudulent and unfounded. The ambassador soon told Governor Isaac Stevens to back off. The border issue was not settled by the International Boundary Treaty of 1846. Nearly ten years later the San Juan Islands were still disputed territory, claimed by both nations, but occupied by PSAC Belle Vue Farms.

Most Pierce County settlers felt unable to plant crops in 1855 because of the Treaty War. They lost the entire season as farmers. Most lost their homes and possessions, too, as many were destroyed or looted by both Indians and soldiers. Even the old Glasgow saw mill was burned. It was within easy sight of Fort Nisqually on the north side of Sequalitchew Creek. After the war it was rebuilt and sold to Lafayette Balch, the founder of Steilacoom. During its twelve years of operation it became known as the Sequalitchew Mill, under a succession of owners.

During the Puget Sound Indian War most non-combatant white people gathered together, built block houses, or moved to the towns of Steilacoom and Olympia for protection. Many non-combatant Indian people were interred on Fox Island, where they were left very hungry. General stagnation of business was the norm, except for war-related enterprises. At least half of the able bodied male settlers volunteered for general military service. It was a way to keep busy and get paid. Others acted as home guards.

Some settlers, however, returned to their homes to plant crops and resume a frontier life. Leschi is often given credit for protecting those who did return to the Muck Creek farms. Governor Stevens called them "treasonable" settlers for accepting Leschi's protection and ignoring the official government edicts. Most of those who returned home were discharged HBC employees married to Indian women, and claiming some farmland. Much of the farmland they claimed was ancestral land the wives' parents had lived on. Stevens claimed these people aided the Indians, but no proof was ever presented. There seems to have been more assistance given by the Indians to farmers, than to the Indians by the U.S. Government treaty makers.

Late December was cold as the *SS Beaver,* sailing out of Victoria, landed at Nisqually with a new employee, Mr. William Atkinson, and the Peter and William Audrey families, on their way to Oregon. After a day or so of talking with Dr. Tolmie, both Oregon-bound American men had PSAC jobs.

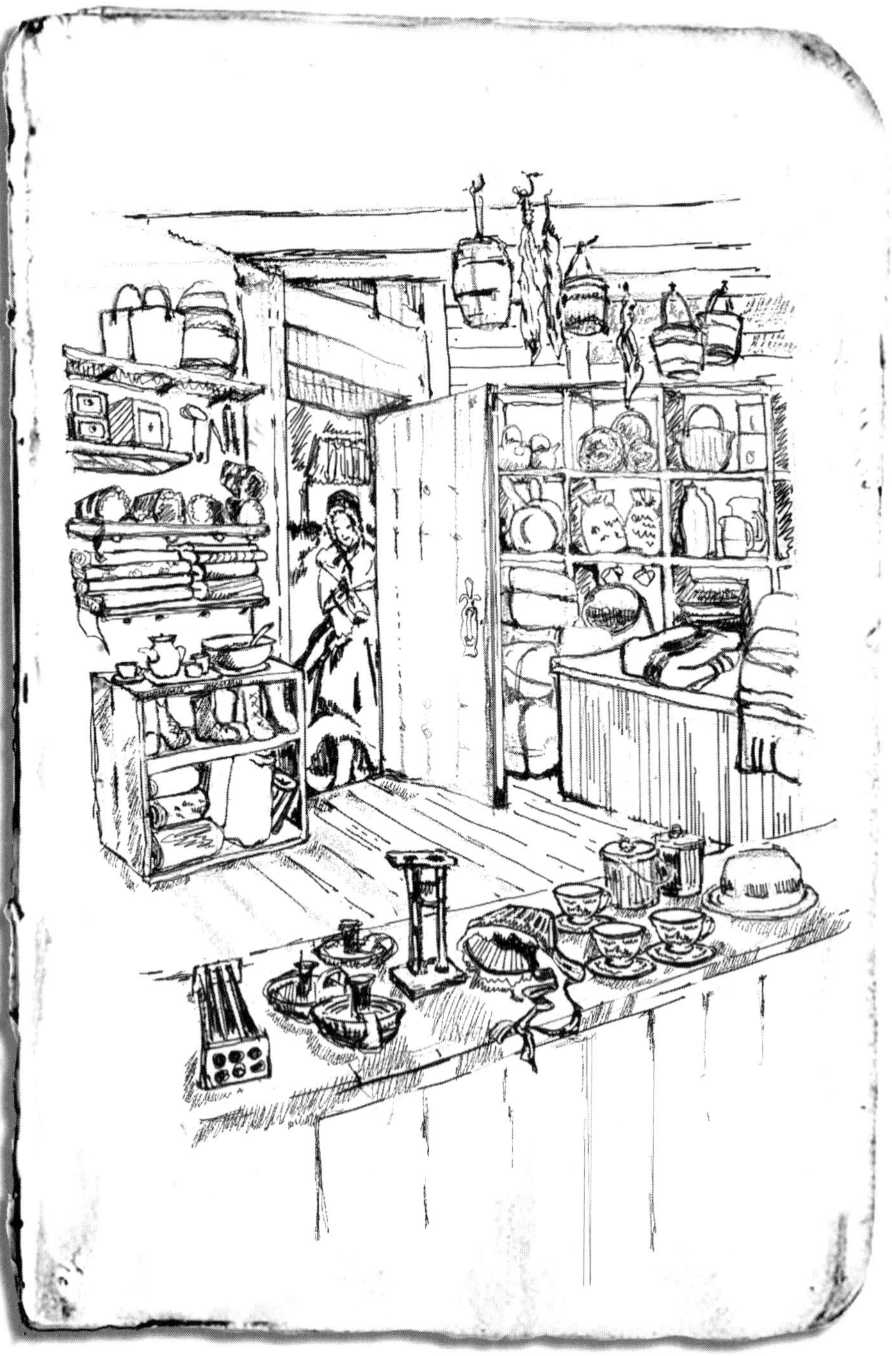

1856

THE WEATHER WAS generally mild, but snow was falling in early January when the *SS Beaver* pulled into Nisqually Landing. She came to load fuel wood, of course. Then regular commerce from Victoria was discharged and new cargo loaded over the next few days.

The Indian Treaty War continued sporadically. Many of the less hostile Indians had been interred in a miserable camp on Fox Island. All means of leaving the Island were removed in an effort to confine the people, mostly women, children, and the elderly. Food supplies, and the means of getting it, were scarce on Fox Island. The resulting situation further increased hostile feelings toward the Washington Territorial government. Dr. Webber, the recently appointed Indian Agent, was doing his best to keep the hungry crowd calm, when suddenly Leschi appeared on the Island. Leschi was at least the de facto leader of the hostile Indians.

Dr. Webber lost control of his assignment. Leschi came to induce the peaceful Indians to join him. They took John Swan, a man very friendly to the Indians, captive with no intention of harm, but to draw attention to their plight. Swan may have cooperated in the ransom plan. The Indians only sought the essential food supplies promised by the Indian Agent. News of the hostage-taking was sent to Fort Steilacoom and received by Captain Maloney. A contingent of soldiers was organized to respond to the kidnapping of Swan. To facilitate the passage of American soldiers to Fox Island, the Army requisitioned the nearly empty *SS Beaver* from the British.

With a contingent of soldiers on board, the *Beaver* chugged across Puget Sound, every soldier well-armed. Upon arrival at the island they discovered that the Indians were now armed as well. Any attempt to land the soldiers would be suicidal.

Normally, in a battle such as this, the ship would simply open fire with cannons to 'soften' the land based resistance, but the *Beaver* could not do that. Several years earlier the HBC had ordered Captain McNeill to remove the cannons, muskets, powder, shot and balls, along with any other heavy items, to increase the fuel efficiency of the ship.

The *SS Beaver* was totally incapable of defending herself, let alone attacking an enemy of another nation. Even if a cannon bombardment had taken place, the soldiers could not have landed. The *SS Beaver* carried no shore craft other than the Captain's gig, which was only large enough for two or three men.

The *Beaver* returned to Steilacoom. Embarrassed soldiers, their tails between their legs, demanded reinforcements, which they got in the form of the *Active*. It carried 100 soldiers and enough cannons to permanently destroy the Indian internment camp. Arriving at Fox Island a short time later, the *Active* discovered that Leschi and 40 of the formerly friendly Indians had escaped to the mainland after liberating John Swan. Some people at the time reported that the Indians actually swam across Puget Sound from Fox Island to the mainland near Day Island. Dr. Webber, the Indian Agent, was certain there were absolutely no canoes on Fox Island to aid the escape. Many Indians were, indeed, strong swimmers who could easily swim across the southern Tacoma Narrows, especially at a time of slack tide.

The *Beaver*, after returning to Fort Nisqually, returned to the task of loading cattle hides, hooves, and horns bound for the auction markets of London, after a stop at Fort Victoria. The beef associated with those hides went to Fort Steilacoom to feed hungry soldiers after the Fox Island "battle" that never happened.

A "battle" that did occur came from a marauding Canadian tribe of about 100 individuals who attacked Steilacoom City in a daring raid in 1856. It was actually more of a looting. The citizens of the town sought safety in nearby blockhouses. Nearly the entire potato harvest of the city was taken by the invaders. The looters were chased by American soldiers, who cornered them at Hood Canal, killing 27, including a chief.[352]

On February 5, 1856, John Muir, writing in the Sacramento Daily Union, warned of sawmills encroaching on Redwood forests. He also complained of smoke from "sheepmen's" fires and the danger of widespread wildfire. Despite John Muir's environmental complaint, the shepherds at Fort Nisqually continued to burn their fires on the American Plain, and across the entire 161,000 acres of PSAC land. Sheep were THE business of the place in '56.

During January and February, the Fort's work continued as usual. By the end of February the men had processed in one manner or another some 1,617 pounds of beef, 417 pounds of pork, 24 bushels of wheat seed, too-many-to-count loads of firewood, all while repairing carts, wagons, and winnowing machines, plus tending to the flocks of sheep, herds of cattle and horses, as well as their own families.

---

352 Ritter, Harry, *Washington's History, The People, Land, and Events of the Far Northwest*, West Winds Press, Portland,, OR, 2003. p. 57.

In March the reports were much the same, but with one clear exception. Soldiers were posted around Fort Nisqually for protection at night. These soldiers were certain they saw hostiles in the darkness. They fired their guns at regular intervals all night long from the safety of the openings in the bastion walls. Every morning a scout could find no traces of anyone having been out and about. Fort workmen were unwilling to work during the next day, having lost so much sleep. Still nine American soldiers patrolled for several nights, protecting the British compound from Indians who would have, mostly, been happy to get paid work.

About twelve miles southeast from the U.S. Army's Fort Steilacoom is Muck Creek. The creek's waters flow southwesterly, parallel to a timber belt about a mile to the east. Several men who were former HBC employees settled there with their Indian or Métis wives. They were all American citizens by this time. They spoke English and taught their Métis children English, too. It was an American settlement, although of foreign stock, often called Montgomery Station. The settlers there were named Wren, two Smith families, two Murray families, McLoed, and Gravelle. All of them volunteered the use of their horse and ox teams to the war effort against the Indians. They were comparatively well-to-do American farmers in an advanced settlement, but Governor Stevens called them "so-called neutrals." Stevens compelled them to live at Fort Nisqually while "our patriotic citizens live in blockhouses."

To enforce his prejudiced order, Governor Stevens on March 8, 1856 ordered Isaac W. Smith, Acting Secretary of Washington Territory, to take 20 men "to the settlement occupied by the French and other foreign-born settlers, and remove them to Fort Nisqually."[353] There was no legal authority for Stevens' actions.

Ezra Meeker continues the story: According to Meeker, Secretary Smith reported to the Governor that:

> *"The settlers of the PSAC could not be removed without danger to the large flocks of sheep under their charge…*
>
> *"Secretary Smith further reported that… it was necessary (to) wait the return of the horse teams and ox teams in order to remove the large families and household furniture. They will turn over to the Quartermaster and Commissary General such stock, provisions, and grain as they may not need for private use."*

There is a lot of meaning in that last sentence.

The volunteer soldiers had been dismissed and the hostile Indians were scattered.

---

353 Meeker, Ezra, *Reminiscences of Puget Sound, the Tragedy of Leschi*, Lowman & Hanford, Seattle, 1905.

The Army Regulars had completely occupied the area and planted garden crops at Muckleshoot by this time. The army controlled the entire "hostile zone" in and around Muck Creek, Montgomery Station, and had commandeered John Montgomery's farm at Spanaway. These PSAC men, American citizens, and Indian wives, had already lost their land, horses, oxen, and personal property, including their growing crops in the fields, by leaving them in an unnecessary rush to safety. A rush to safety ordered by Stevens.

Stevens claimed that the settlers had been ordered into towns (Olympia, Steilacoom, or Fort Nisqually) but they had remained, or returned, to their land in violation of his orders. This violation "caused them to be put in close confinement," in Steven's words.

Some settlers returned to their farms but were arrested and held as prisoners on the grounds that they had violated Stevens' order. They were held without due process of the law. No crime was ever charged. The Indians found themselves in the same situation. Stevens' orders were illegal, but because of his enormous power, he was never challenged.

American Ezra Meeker admits he personally violated the Governor's order. He looked after his own farm and animals in the Puyallup Valley. Meeker claims there were no hostile Indians in the vicinity. He says several other settlers did the same, but none were ever associated with Fort Nisqually or PSAC and were not arrested.[354] No independent news of the controversy has survived. Stevens' records were destroyed. Ezra Meeker said, "Such was the iron hand that ruled the Territory."

In 1856 the first newspaper in Pierce County, *The Puget Sound Courier*, was published in Steilacoom. It lasted about a year. The *Puget Sound Herald* was first issued on March 12, 1858 in Steilacoom, two years after the Stevens affairs.

Olympia's *Pioneer and Democrat* newspaper received generous support from what Meeker called the "Junta" government of Isaac Stevens. It published columns of support amounting to many pages over many weeks to strengthen Stevens' position.

A second newssheet in 1856; named the *Truth Teller*, was devoted to the dissemination of a different view and "suppression of humbug." It was edited by "Ann Onymous." Contributors of opinions to the *Truth Teller* signed their names, even as the editor was obviously not revealed. Dr. Tolmie and A.M. Kautz were among the correspondents to the alternative newspaper. Only four copies were known to remain in existence in 1905.

Indian Bob was not as safe as the settlers who had retreated to the safety of blockhouses and forts. Indian Bob was peacefully employed, along with several men, cutting firewood for Puget Sound Agricultural Company at the side of Military Road near Fort Nisqually. Indian Bob was unarmed except for the axe he used in his work. On May 21, 1856, he was shot dead, entirely without provocation or warning, as Maxon's Mounted

---

354 Ibid.

Rifle Company of Washington Volunteers passed by.

Dr. Tolmie wrote an angry letter to Colonel Casey at Fort Steilacoom protesting this attack on a peaceful individual employed by the PSAC:

> Ft. Nisqually, W.T.
> May 27. 1856.
>
> Colonel Casey, 9th Infantry, U.S.A.,
> Commanding Puget Sound District,
> Fort Steilacoom, W.T.:
>
> Sir—
> On the 23rd inst. I addressed you, detailing the circumstances of the murder at this place, on the 21st inst., of a friendly Indian by a passing volunteer, and have now to inform you what has subsequently happened in relation to that unfortunate affair.
>
> On the 22nd inst. I saw at Camp Montgomery Colonel B.F. Shaw, commanding the Northern Battalion of Volunteers, when I mentioned to him the murder that had been committed the day before. The Colonel thereupon requested me to return the following day, accompanied by witnesses able to identify the supposed murderer, and in reply to an inquiry on my part as to whether it would be safe to bring Indians to camp to testify against a volunteer, he stated that it would, and supported in his opinion by other officers, all agreeing that no one would sympathize with the perpetrators of such a foul and unprovoked murder as that to be investigated.
>
> I accordingly, on the 23rd inst., went to Camp Montgomery, accompanied by three white men, one Sandwich Islander and four Indians amongst them, able to substantiate all the statements set forth in my letter to you of the 23rd inst. reporting the murder. On our arrival at camp two companies of volunteers were paraded for inspection and in one of them the man Lake was recognized at a glance as the volunteer who had passed Ft. Nisqually about 2:30 P.M. on the 21st inst. His perturbed and guilty look while standing in line betrayed him to myself and others to whom he was personally unknown.
>
> I heard Colonel Casey then give orders to have Lake deprived of his gun and arrested, which I believe was done.
>
> Very soon after that a large number of volunteers tumultuously declared that Lake should not be molested. They spoke of murdering the Indian witnesses, and of lynching two persons they supposed had given information regarding

Lake's position in the line of volunteers paraded for inspection. They also, I am informed, spoke of shooting me, but as I remained with the Indians in front of Colonel Shaw's tent until the commotion had nearly subsided, I did not myself hear any threats uttered. Being at length called into the crowd to exonerate Dr. M.P. Burns of the volunteer force of having given information regarding Lake's position, I was lectured in a loud voice by one of the volunteers on the impropriety of bringing a charge against any volunteer at the suggestion or by the wish of their officers, for whom, Colonel Shaw and Governor Stevens included, he in emphatic terns said they did not care.

The last act of the volunteers that I witnessed was the getting of Lake into their midst and saluting him with repeated cheers.

Very respectfully, your obt., servant,

/signed/

WILLIAM F. TOLMIE.

PSAC and HBC had financially assisted in the prosecution of the Puget Sound Indian War by providing $40,000 in aid to the government of Washington Territory. Instead of gaining protection, their employees were attacked, and at least one killed, by the agents of the Territorial Governor.

On May 23, 1856, Dr. Tolmie, Atkinson, Kennedy, Dean, and J. Allard, along with Indians Charles, Guakany, Jack, Bill, and Molka, went to Montgomery's farm as witnesses to testify in the case of Indian Bob's murder. The culprit was soon pointed out by the others who were present at the time of the murder. Colonel Shaw ordered Private Lake placed under arrest. His fellows, all volunteers of Captain H.J.G. Maxon's Mounted Rifles, disapproved and began loading their firearms. It was a show of unmistakable opposition to the arrest. One was believed to have said, "Let's shoot the whole of the witnesses," and other threatening language.

With less than an hour of testimony, Colonel Shaw ordered Private Lake discharged from Maxon's Mounted Rifle Company and U.S. Army service. It was his only punishment. There were cheers from his friends and groans from those who wanted justice for murder. The witnesses were soon glad to return to the safety of Fort Nisqually.

Thirteen days later (June 6) the Mounted Volunteers killed some Fort Nisqually sheep and left them on the plains. The dead animals were discovered a day later, after wolves had a feast. At least one horse went missing after the Volunteers passed by the Fort, and more sheep were shot on the eleventh. By the end of the month many Nisqually employees were afraid to work.

History's final resolution to the Indian Bob murder case apparently came after 37 years had passed. Noted local historian James Wickersham filed a fact paper with the Washington State Historical Society on October 30, 1893. Wickersham wrote:

> *Colonel Shaw returned to Camp Montgomery while Maxon's company again turned south and east and went up the Nisqually to near the canyon, where they discovered a large fishing camp, and here murdered everyone—men, women and children.*[355] *But, Mr. Evans says, where is your record? Such as it is, is on pages 307-8 of Governor Stevens' War Message...*
>
> *"We (Maxon) continued our returning course next on the trail, being generally in a south and east direction. * * * * Again arrived at Michel prairie. * * * * Having no provisions, I have come to this place to await orders.*
> *Signed H.J.G. Maxon, Capt.*
> *Com'd'g Mounted Rifles."*
>
> *Now, read those eight asterisks and you have the massacre. The record is mutilated... When Governor Stevens printed his message... he found it too vile in this spot and cut out the account of the massacre ... it is not there and we must supply it....*
>
> *Robert Thompson... was present when Maxon's company attacked this camp and I quote.... him on this subject:*
>
> *I know about the killings of the Indians by Maxon's company on the upper Nisqually. They killed about fifteen to seventeen, maybe more.*
>
> *...Governor Stevens' war message is the order under which Maxon made his raid to the upper Nisqually. The last clause reads "all Indians found in your field of operations... are to be considered as enemies."*
>
> *...It meant kill every Indian you find. How well this was done appears from the eight asterisks in Governor Stevens' message.*

Wickersham indicted Governor Isaac Stevens for ordering the killing of "all Indians found in your field of operations"—including the peaceful woodcutter Indian Bob along

---

355 They murdered about thirty people, only two were men. All were unarmed, engaged in fishing.

Military Road. Governor Stevens' official messages came home to haunt him, at least in historical accounts. Isaac Stevens died in 1862 at the Civil War Battle of Chantilly.

Many years later Charles Prosch, the Steilacoom newspaper man, was quoted as saying:

> *It is not always agreeable to say things of the Indians, and not always grateful to say things of the whites. In contrasting them, but the most atrocious, fiendish and barbarous acts in the struggle herein briefly treated were those of our own people—the cruel, cold-blooded killing of the wife and six children of Chief Spencer, the killing and mutilation of Chief Peu-Peu-Mox-Mox and other deeds of similar character that we all know about but shrink from mentioning"*[356],

Sheep washing and shearing took most of the ink in the reports of June and July 1856 at Fort Nisqually. There were many pounds of sheep and beef slaughtered, butchered, sold, and eaten. Estimated total was around 3140 pounds for the beef and 167 head of sheep (including the animals killed by the marauding Maxon's Mounted Rifle Company).

World events continued, but were nearly oblivious to the struggles in the Puget Sound basin. Finally the Crimean War was over. Russia, England, and France signed the Treaty of Paris on April 29th, but the Second Anglo-Chinese War broke out on October 8th, when Chinese police boarded the British *Arrow* to arrest 12 Chinese crewmen on suspicion of piracy. The police lowered the ship's British flag. Some argue that the lowering of the flag was actually considered the more serious offense to the British.

Far north of Fort Nisqually, the Russian-American Fur Company outpost at Batzulnetas was attacked by First People in 1856. The occupying Russians called it a massacre, while the local people considered it liberation. All of the Russians at the outpost were killed. The site is just south of today's Salana, Alaska.[357]

Fort Nisqually buildings of the middle 1850s are the ones depicted today at modern day Fort Nisqually Living History Museum at Tacoma's Point Defiance Park. Paramount among the remaining structures is the Granary, rebuilt in 1851. It was never used as a living space, but is seen on the site plan drawn by Dr. Tolmie, Chief Trader, in 1847. He marked it "Store" as in storage or warehouse—a place for storing grains. Its function was broader, however. Goods from London could have been conveniently stored there after arrival, but before distribution to the Trade Store or "Sales Shop." Other goods, those leaving Fort Nisqually, also could have found a temporary home in the Granary on

---

356 Hunt, Herbert, and Kaylor, Floyd C. *Washington West of the Cascades, Vol 1,"* page 164, S.J. Clarke Publishing Company, Chicago, Seattle, *1917,* Prosch founded the "Puget Sound Herald" in Steilacoom. In 1868 Prosch bought the "Pacific Tribune," making it the first daily newspaper in WA Territory.

357 Salana was the last location where the United States offered homestead land in the 1980s.

occasion. These exports included salted beef, tallow, hides, horns, hooves, sheep's wool, several types of grains, and of course, the highly prized fur pelts.

Imported goods and exported items were packaged in three basic forms: barrels and kegs of all sizes and descriptions; boxes made of wood in equally diverse descriptions; and bundles, often made of burlap type materials to cover blankets, cloth, steel, tools, and other normal supplies.

Historians must, on occasion, make assumptions about a place like the Granary.[358] The building may be the oldest existing example of European structures remaining in the State of Washington. It was probably first erected about 1847, though much of the place was thoroughly rebuilt in 1851. There was another remodeling completed in the 1890s. The granary was never heated during the HBC warehouse period, but evidently had a stove installed sometime after Fort Nisqually became Huggins family homestead property. With good reason, historians suggest another use for the building, at some point in history, was probably a chicken coop. This building was at the heart of the complex, central to PSAC and HBC business enterprises for many years.

The granary had no electricity, of course, and no heating system in 1851, when it was built with timbers salvaged from older structures. Interior lighting was supplied by candles in lanterns and chamber sticks. There was an "office" area in the granary for a clerk, who kept the accounting records of the goods entering and leaving the premises. The windows were shuttered, in typical HBC style, for security from curious eyes and for weather protection. Window glass measuring 7"x9" was imported to the Columbia Department from 1825 through 1855 for use in buildings such as the granary. The casement styles are typical construction in the region and the time period. The frames were painted in standard HBC Spanish Brown colored lead-based paint. The building contained a steelyard (pronounced "still-yard") for weighing heavy barrels and boxes of goods. When used correctly, the steelyard could measure only the contents of a keg or box. The clever device could deduct the weight of the container and accurately report the weight of the contents of the container.

The "Case Lock" on the door today is typical of the ones used on HBC homes and stores. The 19th century terms were used for warehouses (a store), as opposed to dwelling houses and trade stores (retail shops).

Approximately 60% of the material of the granary is original, surviving several restoration projects and natural deterioration. It is believed to be one of very few remaining original examples of the standard "post-in-sill" or "French Canadian" construction

---

358 *Granary/Store,* pamphlet distributed by Metro Parks Tacoma in 1985 describing the Granary.

technology used nearly universally in the fur trade regions of North America. Logs were shaped using hand tools such as the adz, broadaxes, and whipsaws. There were no power tools in the mid 19th Century.

The fir and cedar beams used in the walls and the roof were no more than 10' long, allowing two men to erect the entire building in as little as a day, assuming that the logs were previously prepared for the final assembly. Fort Nisqually granary measures 32'x20', providing 640 square feet of usable storage space. It serves today as a standing example of the hard hand labor employed at the HBC trading post at Nisqually and so many other places on the North American continent in the nineteenth century.

Other buildings depicted at Fort Nisqually Living History Museum are from the same period of the 1850s. The trade store, blacksmiths' shop, the cook house, the men's dwelling, the large store, and the laborers' family dwelling are reconstructions based on the best research available, coupled with the modern resources and constraints, such as legally binding modern building codes.

During 1856 the work continued at Fort Nisqually in spite of the Puget Sound Indian War raging around the place. The sheep skins of butchered animals are bundled 50 to a pack. Cowhides were bundled the same way. By mid-March, the potatoes were going back into the ground in well-prepared fields. Dung was spread if the sheep were not naturally adequate in spreading it while penned overnight in carefully located folds.

Oxen were butchered at regular intervals, as were the "wild" cattle. The meat was most often sold to Fort Steilacoom and the American meat markets in Olympia and Steilacoom. The slaughterhouse, which was typically outdoors, could be a very busy place.

On one August day, Chalifoux, Rapjohn, Lagace, Edwards, McLeod, McFadden, Cooper, Dean, Charles, and Gwakany hauled oats, cleared a swamp, prepared fence poles, mended harnesses, marked animals for slaughter, killed a 585 pound ox, and six sheep.

The next day, under a very hot August sun, the same men continued their work, digging potatoes for their families and the Tolmie household. They also killed another sheep and melted the fat from all of the recent killed animals. The fat would be used as an ingredient in candles, soap, axle grease, and caulking for the scow.

Huggins sold 12 sheep for $60, and delivered them live to the beach where the buyer picked them up. Cush was of little help in driving the sheep down the steep road. He was drunk. Again! Another 440 pound ox was killed, along with six small wedders, before Huggins took a crew to Muck. Rapjohn took the beef to a Steilacoom market, while Gwakkany and Squadsup were cutting the tallow, rendered the day before, into blocks.

By the end of the first week of August the men had collected garden seeds, grubbed out a swamp for later planting, killed 16 more sheep, plowed a field, delivered 1500 pounds of straw to the Commissary at Fort Steilacoom, delivered mutton to Steilacoom, collected and delivered the incoming and outgoing mail for Captain Jones' ship bound for Victoria.

They also wasted half of one day taking a wagon to Steilacoom to buy lumber that was not ready to be delivered. It would not be ready for the crew to pick up for another four days. For some unknown reason the American sawmill workers did not complete Dr. Tolmie's order for 388 board feet lumber. Was it a delay designed to irritate the Brits, or simply a backlog of lumber orders at the very busy sawmill?

Latour and McFadden refused harvest work on Saturday afternoon, a typically busy day. Both men left employment with the company on Monday, August 11, 1856. Tuesday, without the two recently fired workers, the remaining crew brought in 175 pounds of flour, 204 pounds of shorts, 165 pounds of bran, 20½ bushels of wheat, plus all of the reaping, plowing, harrowing, slaughtering, dusting, and packing furs.

By the end of the month a great deal of work had been accomplished under the hot August sun. Some astounding numbers can be read from the Journals and account books of 1856. Fort Nisqually and Puget Sound Agricultural Company produced 5,363 pounds of beef, representing ten full grown animals. Almost all of the meat was sold to the Americans at Steilacoom City markets or to the soldier's commissary at Fort Steilacoom. The hides, hooves and horns were packaged for sale at the London auction houses. Additionally, 163 head of sheep were butchered. That meat was also sold to the Americans, for the most part. Nearly four hundred board feet of lumber was cut at the American sawmill, from logs hauled there by Fort employees. Over 1500 pounds of straw was produced, used, and then hauled out of the animal barns with the manure before being spread in the crop lands. Over four and one half tons of grain (wheat, bran, rye, and shorts[359]) were produced for local consumption and sale.

All of that work was accomplished while still maintaining a standard routine and caring for emergencies, such as rescuing a hapless ox found helplessly mired in the natural ditch that was Sequalitchew creek. Apparently, the ox wanted some relief from the hot August sun, and found the stream appealing, until it was so trapped that its life was in peril. Never fear, the skilled farmers at Fort Nisqually removed the animal from the little river by late afternoon. Another emergency seemed of strange origin. One of the fences burst into flame. Again, the fire was soon extinguished without the aid of professionally trained firemen or pressure water hoses.

---

359 Shorts are defined as a mixture of grains, sometimes coarse flour, often considered less crude than "middlings" which are fragments of outer skins of grain from the French term "remoulage demi-blanc".

Daily work included making oakum, axle grease, and cleaning everything. Salmon had to be salted before farm fields were looked after. On occasion, a horse had to be broken to the saddle or the plow. Swamps always needed to be cut clear of brush, ditched, or drained. Four or five days were spent repairing and caulking the little scow the men used for transport on Puget Sound. That scow was often rented to Americans for $2.00 per day. Fort Nisqually never missed an opportunity to make a sale.

That scow was most often employed hauling natural hay from the Nisqually River delta, or the Squally Marsh, as the records called the place. Fine natural grasses grew there, the sort of nutritionally valuable fodder needed for barn animals. The end of August was a perfect time to harvest nature's bounty of hay. With the entire complement of workers and 10½ tons of the dry grass on board the scow, Dr. Tolmie reported in the *Journal of Occurrences* that they got stuck in the mud. The weather was "splendid," he reported, but all were at the mercy of Puget Sound tides. They patiently waited on nature's clock, arriving home at sundown with all hands safe once again.

Someone was cutting firewood almost every day. And of course, the Indian Trade Store had to be operated. Customers, both Indian and American, expected nothing but the best from the emporium with the most comprehensive inventory in the region. The Fort Nisqually Indian Trade store was the 1856 version of today's most modern shopping mall.

On September 3rd, Dr. Tolmie went to Olympia with legal business concerning the encroachment of American squatters on company land. His absence seemed to be the opportunity that Chaulifoux, McPhail, Cush, and Jack needed to get drunk. Again! Chaulifoux worked in the blacksmith shop, however inefficiently. The others were out of commission until Tolmie returned the next day.

The second week of September saw HBC ship *Otter*, Captain Mowat, and the *Troncomalee*, at the Nisqually landing. Dr. Tolmie treated the officers from both ships to a day in Steilacoom, while the crewmen and fort employees hauled goods from the ships to the beach store, then reversed the process by taking 34 bales of sheep's wool to the ships. After a few days, the *Otter* was loaded with 30 beef cattle, 300 ewes, wool, and sundry supplies.

The last of the potatoes were pulled in late fall. They were stored in underground cellars situated strategically around the post. Other goods were taken to the Beach Store for export, or separated for local markets. Tolmie's kitchen garden proudly grew a 37 pound pumpkin.

During the late summer and fall, wheat and oats were brought in from the outstations. The crops were stored at the Fort and packaged for use or export. Hay was brought in by the ton from the farm operated by a Mr. Packwood. He had a claim just north of the Nisqually River in the large Squally Marsh. Packwood was paid in goods at the rate of $12 per ton. Hay was also being cut at all of the outstations. Wheat was threshed in the winter and promptly milled. Most often Fort Nisqually wheat and oats was ground at Chambers Mill, near Steilacoom.

While Tolmie was away purchasing cattle in Oregon, Edward Huggins took over the direction of the Fort and dealt with some of the legal problems in Steilacoom. It seems that Huggins hired a lawyer named Wallace and the two of them appeared before a Notary Public to file affidavits relative to some stolen horses. Later Huggins found the stolen horse at Gwinap's home. When confronted, Gwinap was willing to give up the stolen animals—when asked.

Huggins went out to visit the crew at Muck, where he had been in charge until called in to cover for the absent Dr. Tolmie. He found the men drunk. Grieg had not been with his sheep herd for two days. Thornhill was belligerent when Huggins sent him back to work. When ordered to leave the house, he refused. Huggins said:

> "...he would not go, defied me to make him leave the house, tried to put him out —when he struck me in the face—I gave him a good thrashing. Thornhill is a useless mess and is adept at swearing and lying."

Two days later Thornhill was paid off. Three days after that an "old Englishman named George" was hired to partner with Grieg at sheep herding near Muck Station.

Sheep and lambs were "dipped" in a tobacco liquor to kill vermin that inhabit the wool. In October, 1856 all hands assisted in the dipping of 1037 lambs from Willy's flock, 430 from Tapou's herd, and all but 150 from Moloch House, during a six day period. There was some concern that the rainy nights could counteract the application of the tobacco-based insecticide. Sheep dipping resumed later in the month, but was not completed until well into November.

While the October weather was less than desirable for sheep dipping, the task turned to pig slaughtering. Ten barrels of pork were salted. The individual animals weighed in at 235, 232, 188, and 144 pounds, respectively.

On a gloomy October 31st Huggins went to Steilacoom to pay, under protest, the land tax to Pierce County for Puget Sound Agricultural Company and the Hudson's Bay Company. The bill was for $1400.

Grain harvests were the major work assignments in November as one might expect, but the slaughter of cattle, sheep, and pigs continued, as well. Contracts for sale of the meat had been signed, so business continued as usual. Mr. Chamber purchased two barrels of butter weighing 217 pounds. The Puget Sound Indian War was having little effect on business at Fort Nisqually.

All was not well, however. On Monday, November 17th, when all hands were engaged in loading live cattle aboard the *Otter*, Mr. Dean, a tenant farmer at the PSAC farm at Tlithlow, came in to inquire about a letter he expected from England. Dean explained that he was anticipating a gratuity from Hudson's Bay House, London, for his work to improve the Company's business. He claimed that he was to be presented with a gratuity of 300 pounds sterling at the end of his term of contracted service. The reward was to compensate Dean for perseverance in making the Company more profitable and valuable under his charge.

Dr. Tolmie replied that Dean was to be paid only his salary, having in no manner bettered the Company business. However, Tolmie did offer a present of 100 pounds sterling, for which Dean would sign a receipt and vacate the Tlithlow Farm, leaving everything on it belonging to the PSAC. At first Dean accepted the terms, but upon reflection, decided not to not take the cash. He claimed Tolmie was, in fact, cheating him out of $1,000. He announced that he would claim the Tlithlow Farm as his own, under American land claims laws. Dean demanded that Huggins immediately remove from Tlithlow Farm all PSAC property. Huggins sent Grieg to Tlithlow to take charge the next day.

Huggins went to Tlithlow to talk with Dean, but the man was no longer there. Huggins put Grieg in charge and sent Smitkaynum to gather Dean's sheep. When Dean returned he refused to relinquish the chickens and turkeys, or to hand over the keys to the barn. Huggins broke it open to remove Dean's horses. While Grieg repaired the barn lock, Dean enlisted some neighbors to assist him in removing Company horses from the barn. Huggins defied him, put Dean's horses out instead, then locked the barn door. Dean then broke the repaired lock and returned his horses to the stables.

Huggins, accompanied by Grieg, went to Steilacoom, where he filed legal action against Dean. On the 26th, Huggins and Grieg were summoned to Steilacoom concerning the Tlithlow difficulty. Murdock McLeod was a witness in the case. Huggins and Grieg were both arrested for breaking open the barn and for keeping possession of the Tlithlow stable. They were tried immediately, found guilty, and fined $20 each. Dr. Tolmie filed an appeal with the 3rd Judicial District Court of Washington Territory regarding the Tlithlow situation.

Dean sent notice to Dr. Tolmie that Company wheat and rye had to be removed from the Tlithlow barns, as Dean was prepared to begin plowing. Mour quit his job with the Company, signing on with Dean for $20 per month. Dean took one yoke of oxen to Fort

Nisqually, where he stayed for dinner with Tolmie, then spent the night contemplating the dinner conversation. In the morning Dr. Tolmie purchased all of Dean's cattle.

Dr. Tolmie, well-armed for a court fight, took Huggins, Bastian, McLeod, Adam Beinson, and John Montgomery, with their signed affidavits, to appear before U.S. Commissioner T. M. Bachelder in 3rd District Court. Grieg spent the previous night at the Fort because Dean had threatened to shoot the driver and the oxen removing fence rails at Tlithlow. Furthermore, Dean said he would shoot any other person who persisted in working at Tlithlow. Dean had presented Grieg with a written notice to leave Tlithlow. The notice announced that rent would be charged on every building occupied by Company employees and material.

Grieg brought an ox wagon loaded with sheep skins, a plow, and a harrow. An Indian boy and Ambrose Skinner were sent to Tlithlow to search for cattle, but they found none.

A few days later Huggins, with the assistance of Grieg, brought some cattle and a beef carcass, weighing 424 pounds, from Tlithlow.

Dr. Tolmie, Edward Huggins, and Mr. Kennedy went to the court session in Steilacoom concerning Dean's complaint against Grieg. Complaints ranged from breaking the barn lock to sowing rye at Tlithlow on land plowed by Dean, after he had been warned to stop plowing. The American jury could not agree on a verdict. The trial was postponed for seven days. When the trial resumed, it was immediately postponed, this time for three more weeks.

Skip ahead to April, 1857. Huggins moved all of the breeding ewes from Tlithlow, replacing them with gimmer[360] ewes. This process ensured that lambs would not be born at the disputed Tlithlow Farm.

Skip ahead another month. Tolmie, Huggins, Kennedy, and Fiander were in court again for several days before Dean's suit against Grieg and Huggins for breaking the lock on the Company's Stable at Tlithlow was settled. The jury found both Huggins and Grieg not guilty. Dean sold his possessions at Tlithlow to John Chambers later in the month, forever ending the dispute. Tlithlow continued to be PSAC land.

Tolmie's law suit against Dean concerning the rye planting and plowing on Company land at Tlithlow was not settled, however. That suit would wait until the end of May, 1857, when the PSAC would prevail.

The blacksmith, Chalifoux, and others were busy as usual repairing carts, wagons, and Tolmie's carriage, while many miles of fences had to be repaired regularly. Winter gales often knocked over fences, and sometimes even the palisades fell. Thieves stole

---

360 A gimmer ewe is a weaned, but not sheared, female sheep between 6 and 15 months old that has not had her first lamb.

fence rails for firewood in winter.

Butchering resumed in earnest with the spring weather. Oxen, sheep, and beef were killed at an amazing pace, sometimes as many as 13 animals in one day. Once cut, the meat was salted, or "corned," to preserve it as long as possible. There was a regular transit of meat to the towns. Sales were good when the product was taken to the American markets. Retail buyers seldom visited the Fort, often speaking ill of the British. Apparently they were unaware of the British source of the meat they bought in Steilacoom markets and butcher shops.

Daily notation of sales dropped abruptly in late 1856. Consistent entries reveal "slow" or "dull" activity in the Sales Shop. There were many other sources of goods by this time, but the traffic to Fort Nisqually was probably depressed as much by the fears of the Puget Sound Indian War as American prejudice against the Company that was so friendly to the Indians. None of the men or property of Fort Nisqually or Puget Sound Agricultural Company were attacked by the Indians. Many were actually employed there. The Americans, perhaps prone to conspiracies, were almost totally convinced that Dr. Tolmie sold guns to the hostiles for the purpose of making war on the Americans. Of course many guns had been sold to the Indians over the years. Fur trappers, Indian or white, often needed weapons for self-defense in the wilds of the mountains. The guns Fort Nisqually sold were not weapons of war, but hunting tools.

Business was still brisk enough. Army contracts for provisions and other goods kept Fort Nisqually busy. Beyond the regular Army commissary requisitions, the Washington Territorial government was also ordering goods from Fort Nisqually. Some of the purchases were the result of the Indian Wars heating up in late 1855.

The Fort continued diversifying the Sales Shop inventory, too. Tolmie began wholesale purchase of sugar, coffee, and other domestic supplies from Allan Lowe and Co., of San Francisco. This procedure minimized the customs duties which were charged on items from Europe, while assuring more frequent delivery for eventual retail sales Most of the interior decorations, such as draperies and wallpaper, for Tolmie's new home, were purchased from Allan Lowe distributors in San Francisco. The home was built in 1854.

Even in 1856 there was the question of whether Indian leaders understood the document written by English speakers in a language the Indians could not read, and explained only in the Chinook trade jargon. The Treaty reserving land for the Native Americans was never presented in Salish or any other native tongue. The Nisqually were unhappy with the measly 1,280 acres of land reserved for them on a high, forested land, considerably east and upstream of their traditional Nisqually fishing areas. The Nisqually nation lost the use of 70 miles of the Nisqually River and 431 tributary streams, draining 515 square miles of territory (about 330,600 acres).

After a council meeting at Fox Island between Governor Stevens and noncombatant Indians who had been concentrated in the internment camp, the size and location of the Nisqually Reservation was changed. Suddenly the reserved land area increased to 4,700 acres of Nisqually River bottom land near the delta. The new reserved land at Mitsuckwie was of far better quality for farming and somewhat closer to great fishing waters. It was still only a tiny fraction of the Nisqually ancestral homeland.

Local news arrived at the Fort on November 19, that Queimuth died in Olympia the evening before. He was shot and stabbed by an unknown assailant(s) while sleeping inside the Governor's office. Governor Stevens had left the back door unlocked for access to the outhouse. There was no further mention of the murder in the Fort Nisqually Journals or the newspapers of the day. No one was ever charged with the crime.

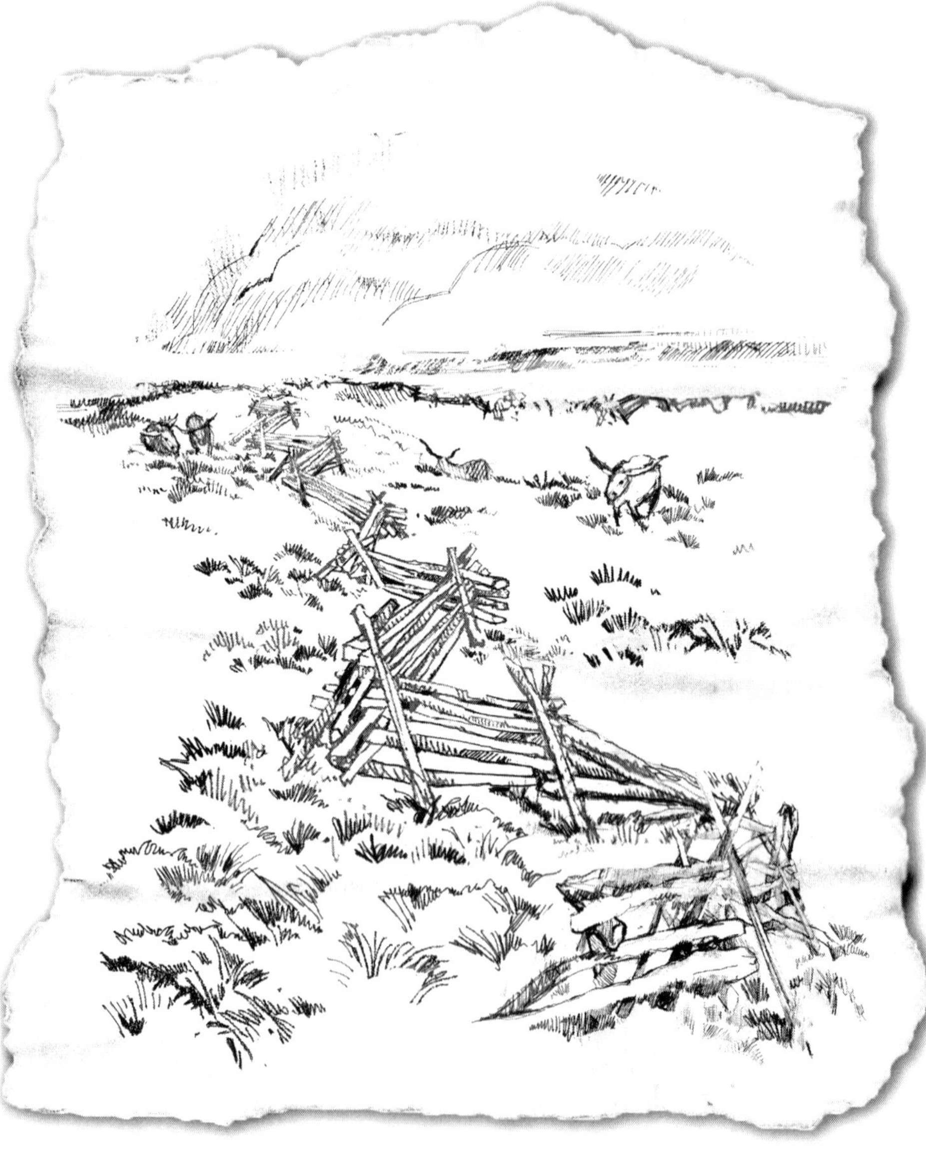

1857

THE BRITISH WERE having a time of it in India. The Bengal Army, which was made up of East Indian soldiers serving in the British Army, made what some see as a first attempt at national independence. In July many British women and children were murdered in a massacre during the East Indian Mutiny.

In spite of all this turmoil in the Empire, the British Monarch found time to declare Ottawa the capital of Canada.

Politics and politicians flourished in Washington Territory as well. Fayette McMullin succeeded Governor Isaac Stevens in Olympia. He was a Virginia congressman and continuing defender of slavery when appointed to the highest office in Washington Territory. Newspaper accounts say he took office "like wildfire," but actually he took no real political interest in the Territory or the people's concerns.

He was vexed by the same problems facing Stevens: Indian relations and geographic isolation from the seat of real power. The transcontinental railroad was years off, under the political conditions of the day, so McMullin recommended that the Oregon Trail be moved to the north. There it would follow the trail blazed by Isaac Stevens in 1853. His plan was never implemented. It never occurred to him that a second trail could have been developed.

Governor McMullin was also plagued by the murder of Whidbey Island settler Isaac Ebey by Indians from the British territory to the north. After some considerable bluster, McMullin acknowledged that the territory lacked any means to bring to justice or punish the perpetrators of the beheading, let alone prevent such an attack in the future. The press condemned him for "non-fulfillment of the promises which he voluntarily made."

The Governor did achieve a notable success in divorcing his first wife by using a legislative act. It was a scandal to be sure. Apparently there were no divorce statutes in the Territorial Code, so McMullin asked for a legislative act on the matter. The legislature complied as simply and directly as possible, granting the Governor exactly what he asked for—the divorce he sought—without the work of actually writing the statute language to make divorce legally possible for the general population in WA Territory.

McMullin is most often remembered as the Chief Executive who could have pardoned Leschi for the crimes he was accused of, but could not have committed, during the Puget Sound Indian War. Leschi, you will remember, was convicted on the basis of perjured testimony. He was scheduled for execution in 1858. A committee of regular army officers, and others, was organized to seek a pardon from McMullin. The governor listened to their case at Fort Steilacoom, examining the exculpatory evidence, and appeared to the officers to be convinced of the need for a pardon.

Back in Olympia, Governor McMullin was confronted by a demonstration of Stevens' supporters, who favored the immediate execution. McMullin suddenly reversed his earlier opinion by proclaiming "clemency as a gross violation of justice." He used strong language against the U.S. Army advocates favoring a pardon for Leschi. His action allowed Leschi to hang. He also demanded that the War Department transfer Fort Steilacoom Army officers for interfering with local civilian law and order. He was not successful in getting them transferred.

Henry Tolmie was born on January 23, in the Factor's House at Fort Nisqually. The Tolmie household already included Alec, William, John, and James. Newborn Henry made it five boys under five years old.

James Buchanan succeeded Franklin Pierce as President of the United States on March 4. Dr. John McLoughlin, a naturalized American citizen, died in Oregon City on September 3. He was not well-liked in his adopted American city, even as the "Father of Oregon."

As American settlement continued in Oregon and Washington Territory, Fort Nisqually area "squatters" continued to plague the company. Warning letters were delivered every time a settler tried to establish a claim on HBC or PSAC land. The Company began a legal land survey to establish the boundaries of their acreage on paper. Some settlers even objected to the survey. Six of them armed themselves and confronted the survey party. With guns in the mix, the surveyors stopped work. The Company called the six settlers a "mob" and accused them of "rebellion." The settlers probably did not think they were doing wrong, but had a belief that somehow the survey results would provide evidence against their claims. They may have been bolstered by cheap whiskey, no one knows.

John McCleod was one involved in the armed confrontation, but letters were sent to many settlers. Here is the wording of one nearly complete and surviving warning, presented to Thomas Hadley:

We hereby certify that a correct copy of the within notice was presented to T. Hadley by Mr. Wm. Greig this 6th day of April, 1857.

WILLAM GREIG,
ALFRED McNEILL.
AMBROSE SKINNER.
Nisqually, W.T. 12th March, 1857.

To Mr. Thomas Hadley.—Sir: I hereby warn you that, in cultivating and making other improvements on your present location in or near the———(Note: some letters are missing) entire precinct, Pierce County, Washington Territory, you are trespassing on the lands confirmed to the Puget's Sound Agricultural Company by the Boundary Treaty, ratified in July, 1846, between Great Britain and the United States of America.

Your Obed't Sert.,
W.F. TOLMIE
Agent Puget's Sound Agricultural Company

    The survey party halted their work temporarily but resumed at a later date, mostly in secret, sufficiently completing the platting in spite of the armed belligerents.

    More than once Dr. Tolmie, after legally complaining to settlers about stealing Company beef, was invited to socialize at dinner. Settler families made an effort to smooth hard feelings. Tolmie often accepted such offerings hoping to find direct evidence of cattle thievery. The pioneers often justified their actions by reminding Tolmie of the fact that the British cattle were, in the American view, wild animals, and therefore common property. That was a view Tolmie refuted often.

    Often at the family meal a good, old fashioned Methodist blessing was said over the food, giving thanks for the bountiful supply of the many good things of the world, and asking safe travel for the guest present. The settler would then, in true pioneer hospitality, cut a generous sized piece of beef roast for his guest, the actual owner of the meat. Tolmie, who was ever the polite gentleman, apparently never complained during these dinner parties.

    A bridge (Fourth Avenue) was built to link Olympia with "Marshville" (now Westside Olympia). The structure was a cantilevered wooden causeway over the mud flats that extended well into what is now Capitol Lake. Samuel Percival, a settler from Massachusetts, built the original Percival's Landing on the Olympia waterfront in the mid-1850s.

The Army continued to station guards at Fort Nisqually well into springtime. Col. Shaw and two men were there most nights. Ostensibly, the soldiers were there to keep the peace that might have been disrupted by angry Indians, but the anger may actually have come from American settlers. Indians continued to be employed by the HBC, and they were the Fort's most loyal customers. Work about the place continued without interruption. In May at least 4,550 pounds of butchered beef and 70 sheep carcasses was sold. In the grain department the totals were even more impressive: some 5,600 pounds of grains were processed for human and animal consumption.

On Tuesday, April 21st Mr. A.G. Dallas, Esquire, Director of Hudson's Bay Company, and Mr. Munro, accountant for the PSAC, arrived at Fort Nisqually from London via Fort Vancouver. Dr. Tolmie led the visitors on a tour of the Company's stations at Kullkullee, Dominque's Prairie, S'Gukgwas' place, Cowie's, Muck, Elk Plain, the Nisqually Reservation at Mitsuckwie, and returned by Squally Road.

The Factor of Fort Nisqually again took his distinguished visitors to Muck a few days later to see the huge sheep herds there. They returned to Muck later in the week, as well. At least a portion of the Director's and Accountant's visit was recreational. Dallas, Munro, and Tolmie were joined by Mr. Peers of Cowlitz on a fishing excursion at Gordon's lake. Tolmie also took his guests hunting wild cattle on at least one occasion.

The "big wigs" from London finally completed their inspection of PSAC and HBC farms. Tolmie, Peers, Dallas and Munro boarded the *Otter* bound for Victoria on May 6th. There is no doubt the party met Mr. Frost, American Collector of Customs for Puget Sound District, as he debarked from the *Otter* at Nisqually Landing that same day. Frost was bound for Cowlitz on official business.

Tolmie was back in court in May. He had filed a law suit to prevent Dean from planting rye on Company land at Tlithlow. The case lasted for several days, during which several company employees (Huggins, Bates, and Fiander) also testified. The jury was in disagreement, so the case was again put off.

June, July and August were typically productive months. Most of the work was entirely routine and quite profitable. Class and G. Daniels came in from Muck needing medical attention. Class had a dangerous cut on his neck and Daniels had cuts on his head, and his face was badly bruised. The two men had been drinking, and disagreeing, then started fighting. One used a knife, the other stones, which caused the cuts and facial bruises.

Interestingly, Chalifioux may have been the final victim of the drunkenness. Huggins went to Muck to supervise the fighters' return to work. Once there he found Chalifoux drunk for four days and scarcely doing any work. Huggins discharged Chalifoux two days later. He was back on the job in early 1858.

In October at Fort Nisqually Clerk Edward Huggins married Lettitia Work, daughter of John Work of Victoria, and sister of Jane Work Tolmie. Dr. Tolmie's right hand man became his brother-in-law, and a son-in-law of the venerable Chief Factor John Work. Huggins was also destined to become Tolmie's successor at Fort Nisqually and PSAC.

Huggins provided the punch for the reception that followed the wedding ceremony. He also hired a fiddle player for the exorbitant sum of $20 for the evening. That fiddle player, Mose Spicer, was a "little drunk at first but he sobered up" according to the diary of Lieutenant August Kautz (October 22, 1857). Kautz was among the large party from Fort Steilacoom and Steilacoom City, who attended the reception.

Among the guests from Fort Steilacoom were Lt. David McKibben and Lt. Arthur Shaff, who drove to the ceremony in the roomy army ambulance. Both men consumed at least their share of the punch and became quite inebriated. Other guests had been invited from Victoria. Among them was Miss Maryann Reed, who would lodge in Steilacoom City until her return home. After the dancing and partying, Lt. Shaaff and Lt. McKibben offered to drive Miss Reed, to the boarding house in Steilacoom. During the short trip, Shaaf attempted to kiss Miss Reed, but she refused him. At Fort Steilacoom Miss Reed mounted a horse to complete her journey, but Shaaf insisted on accompanying her down the hill and through the woods. Maryann set off on horseback alone before Shaaf was mounted. Mr. Sam McCaw realized what was happening and quickly went after the two young people. Somehow Shaaf was thrown from his horse, landing behind a log. Completely embarrassed, he returned to his officer's quarters alone. Sam McCaw escorted Maryann to her rooming house. The rest of the story is that Sam had been Maryann's original escort to the wedding.

On a more serious note, the *SS Fairy* burst her boiler just off the Sequalitchew Landing. In a letter written many years after the incident, Huggins says Dr. Tolmie was called to attend to the injured passengers. As it turns out, only one passenger was seriously burned. No one was killed and the little steamer did not sink.

The wedding party was nearly crashed by Charley Daniels, Jim Reilly and a third unnamed man. They forced their way into the house to see the fiddler, Mose Spicer. Lieutenant Schaaf and McKibben "nearly had a serious row with them." They were escorted from the party without a fight, but they retaliated by slashing the mule harness in the stable. The Army men had some difficulties at their time of departure because of the cut up leather and their own liberal use of the available punch (or was it the wine and rum?)

One can only speculate about a honeymoon trip. It seems that Edward and Letitia, the wedding couple, remained at Fort Nisqually, while three of Letitia's sisters, her parents Mr. and Mrs. John Work, Dr. Tolmie, his wife and children, and Mr. Finlayson all boarded the *Constitution* for the voyage to Victoria.

An interesting engineering accomplishment was completed in 1857 at what is now Steilacoom Lake. An American settler, Andrew Byrd, took a claim along the creek that drained American Lake. His claim included some low, swampy land that proved perfect as the large holding "pond" for the water backed up by his earthen dam at the outlet. His dam impounded the water that was used to power the Byrd Grist Mill. The pond is known today as Steilacoom Lake, and is surrounded by many luxury homes and pricey real estate. The Byrd Grist Mill was soon a profitable operation on the upland side of Fort Steilacoom, a little west of the site where Leschi was soon to be hanged.

News from the Oregon-California Trail said that on September 11, some 120 men, women and children were killed, slaughtered actually, by Paiute Warriors and Mormon militiamen at Mountain Meadows, Utah. It was an act of religious intolerance and unreasoning hatred attributed to religious zealots, something rarely seen on the shores of Puget Sound.

In November, 1856, a Kake Indian couple, who had survived the 1851 U.S. Navy gunboat attack near Fort Gamble, inquired of an Isaac Ebey farmhand on Whidbey Island if his employer was "Hyas Tyee"—that is, an important man or chief. The worker generously replied that his boss was indeed an important fellow. On August 11, 1857, a night raiding party of Kake warriors returned to shoot Ebey, taking his severed head as a trophy for their homeland.

There is little doubt that the Kake warriors were actually looking for Dr. Kellogg that fateful night. The Canoe Doctor was on a house call. Ebey was an important sacrificial substitute, as well as the object of revenge for the attack by the *USS Massachusetts* in 1851.

A thrashing machine is mentioned for the first time in November. There is no mention of purchase, but the records show "all hands putting up the thrashing machine" on November 25th, when six bushels of wheat were thrashed. Some 60 bushels of wheat were trashed the next day, while the job was finished on the third day. One thousand pounds of flour came back from the Steilacoom mill that week.

Business was good in 1857. Dr. Tolmie purchased a new buggy in Steilacoom.

The year closed with a violent storm on December 30. Heavy rains flooded the creeks and rivers of the Puget Sound area. The ground around the Fort turned to deep mud. Over at Fort Steilacoom, the not-quite-finished house being constructed for Colonel Casey, his wife Abby, son Ned and daughters Abby and Bessie, was devastated when the storm's high winds blew the partially completed roof and the rafters to the ground.

1858

IN JANUARY the efforts to save Leschi from execution became intense. Dr. Tolmie, Col Simmons, Lt Kautz, and Mr. Clark went to the Nisqually Reservation to induce an Indian living there to confess that he was the one who shot A.B. Moses at the outbreak of the Puget Sound Indian War of 1855. It was the crime Leschi was accused and convicted of committing. The Indian would not confess to anything that would save Leschi and implicate himself.

On February 19, 1858, Leschi was hanged on a crude wooden gallows built less than a mile east of Fort Steilacoom and close to Andrew Byrd's new Lake Steilacoom Grist Mill. His first trial had ended in a hung jury. At the second trial, held by the Supreme Court of Washington Territory, he was found guilty of murder, Leschi said:

> "... I have supposed that the killing of armed men in wartime was not murder... I deny that I had any part in the killing (of Colonel Benton)...as God sees me, this is the truth."[361]

About 300 people gathered around the gallows to witness the execution. His hangman and executioner, Charles Grainger, is quoted as saying at the time:

> "...I felt then I was hanging an innocent man, and I believe it yet."[362]

It was the first case of capital punishment in Washington Territory. Leschi was found guilty of murdering Colonel Abram Benton of the Territorial Volunteer Militia, serving with the United States Army at Fort Steilacoom.[363]

In March the long postponed trial Dean had brought against the Company for back

---

361 History link, www.historylink.org/essay/output.cfm?file-id=5145.

362 Ibid.

363 Chief Leschi was exonerated by a Historical Court of Inquiry on December 10, 2004. Chief Justice Gerry Alexander, of the Washington State Supreme Court, presided in a Special Session held in Tacoma at the Washington State History Museum.

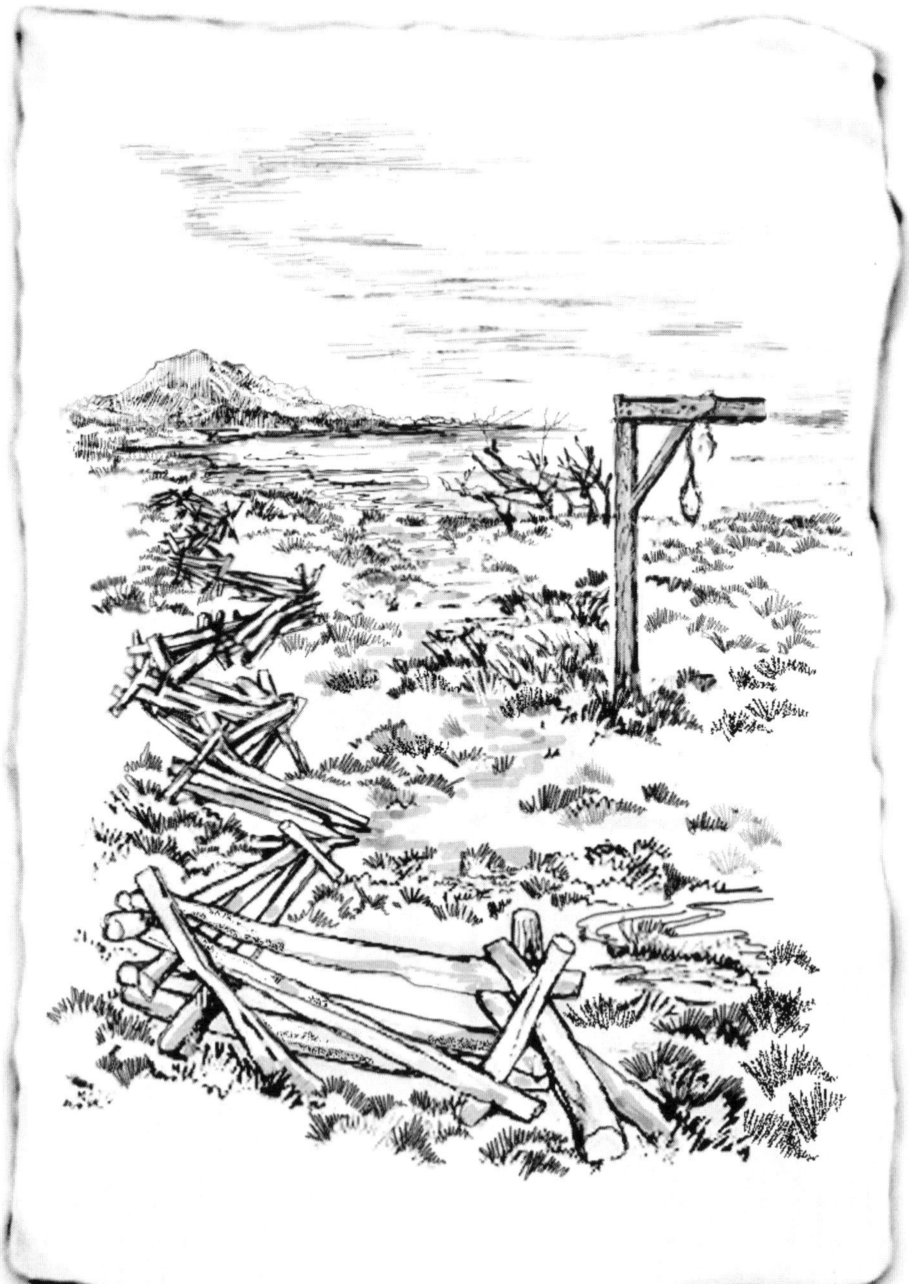

salary was decided by a jury verdict in favor of the Company. Mr. Dean was not happy.

A gold discovery was made along the upper Thompson River in British Columbia which began affecting Fort Nisqually in April. Seventy miner's packs were prepared for the gold seekers. Hawaiian employees Kalama and Keave'haccow were joined by Englishman Gale, who collected their pay, settled their accounts, and were off to seek their fortunes digging for gold.

Flour was abundant at the Steilacoom flour mill in April. Mr. Work inquired as to the price and was told $17.50 per barrel. Three days later, when Mr. Kennedy arrived to purchase the flour he had inquired about, the price had dropped to $15.00 per barrel. Delivery of the flour aboard the *Wild Pigeon* from Olympia to Nisqually Landing was an additional 50 cents per barrel.

In comparison, Fort Nisqually beef was selling at 10 to 12 cents per pound. Sheep on the hoof sold for 12½ cents per pound. Live Sheep exchanged for cattle were calculated at 15 cents per pound.

In May, Indians living in the village near the Fort (Jack, Cush, Gohome, Myak, and his wife, along with some Snoqualmie friends), obtained some illegal liquor. Soon a fight broke out among the drinkers. Gohome got his gun and shot a Snoqualmie Indian dead. Friends of the dead man inflicted serious and severe knife wounds on Gohome's shoulder and arm. Myak's wife was also stabbed in the breast.

About daybreak, four friends of the dead man crept to Jack's house. They saw Cush through a window and shot him. Cush did not die, but the wound was intended to be mortal. The Snoqualmies fled into the woods. Apparently there was no other punishment for the killer or those who retaliated with such vengeance. Dr. Tolmie treated the wounded, while the Snoqualmie buried the dead man with a traditional ceremony.

Englishman George B. Roberts related his plight, in the face of American settler depredations. Roberts was born in Aldborough, Suffolk. After three years at the Greenwich Royal Naval School he was apprenticed to the *Ganymede* headed for the Columbia River. At Fort Vancouver he became the overseer of nearly 200 laborers. In 1858 Dr. Tolmie arranged for Roberts to take charge at the PSAC Cowlitz Farm. Roberts was to continue the farming operation and keep the buildings in good repair until the British claims were settled. Roberts wrote his *Recollections*:

> "I took possession unopposed, and all went well until my hay was put up in cocks, when here came a lot of fellows, armed with rifles, and carried it all off. One of these was the justice (of the peace) so my lawyer recommended changing the venue. The jury decided that they knew nothing of treaties, and of course, I

had all the expense to bear...The judge was a federal appointee, and in theory independent, but liable to be unseated at any time and returned to the people whom he had offended...I leave to your imagination the state I was kept in.... sometimes my windows at night were riddled with shot, my fences set upon, and in dry weather set on fire. It was an immense effort to unseat me, and cheat the government of these lands...all the clamor was against the PSAC for nothing else."[364]

Another individual and his family provides another example of the importance of family ties during the HBC years on Puget Sound. Pierre Legace (a Métis of Kalispell and French-Canadian ancestry) was a trusted and loyal employee of the HBC for most of his life. He held several positions at numerous posts throughout the Columbia District over the years. As a relative of both Dr. Tolmie and Edward Huggins (their wives were sisters of the Legace Family), and a brother-in-law of John Work, Pierre and his sons were often placed in authority positions at various outstations operated for the PSAC. On May 5, for example, Pierre was sent to Ashland Farm.

Today we still do not know the exact location or dimensions of the Ashland Farm, but we do know it was along Muck Creek, somewhere between the satellite farms at Kul-kul-hee, and S'Gukoguas. Those were part of the extensive and complex company farms interspersed with native Nisqually villages located on Back Squally Creek, near today's Roy, Washington. Ashland was originally established by Dominique Farron as an HBC farm on the west side of the present day town of Roy. It was later claimed by Frank Goodwin. Still later it became the homestead of Gregg/Spence families, with fence lines changing with each possession.

The 1860 Federal Census for Pierce County lists Pierre Legace and his family, including Peter Legace [sic] age 50, Charles Legace (age 21), Peter Legace, Jr. (age 19), wife Milo (Amelia, age 19), and daughters Rosalie (age 21) and Susan (age 2 months).[365] They were probably all living in close proximity to, if not actually on, the original Ashland Farm property.

Native Americans held a major "potlatch" in November, 1858, to receive the payment promised by the U.S. as compensation for the land ceded to the government. The *Steilacoom Herald* reported on the festivities:

---

364 Roberts, George B., *Recollections* cited in Bancroft, Herbert Howe, *History of Washington, Idaho and Montana*, San Francisco, The History Company, 1890, p. 42.

365 For more on Pierre Legace see "Pierre Legace: Life of an Extraordinary Hudson's Bay Company Man" by Drew W. Crooks, *Occurrences, The Journal of Northwest History during the Fur Trade"* Summer 2009, pp 7-13, Fort Nisqually Living History Museum, Tacoma, WA.

The Indians belonging to the reservations at Nisqually, Puyallup and Squax-in received their annuities (from the U.S.) at Puyallup on the twenty-third instant. Colonel Simmons, and his staff of subagents, and his clerk, Mr. Armstrong delivered the goods amounting in value to $3,600.

A large body of Indians was present, and from appearances they considered the whole affair in the light of a grand feast, got up to promote good feeling and fellowship between the 'Reds' and 'Whites'. And good feeling there certainly was.

In the evening a dance was held. Colonel Simmons ("Old Mike") danced with a "dusky beauty of some fifty years and two-hundred-fifty pounds" according to the newspaper that decided the annuity payments (made by the Federal Government under fulfillment of the Medicine Creek Treaty) were "most excellently and most satisfactorily managed."

The amount paid was clearly not more than two dollars per person, though the treaty held that teach individual should receive five dollars each. Some families received only a relatively small amount of green baize fabric and calico cloth. The discrepancy was explained away when the Indian Agent told the Indians that the census had under calculated their population. Even when the U.S. numbers were incorrect, and admitted to be in error, no effort was ever made to increase the total allotment to the individual amounts specified in the Medicine Creek Treaty. Congress was never even asked to consider such an adjustment to a "settled" issue.

The *Herald* editorial told of that shortfall: *"It was only another case of the Indian getting the short end."*

The U.S. Lighthouse Board purchased ten acres on Whidbey Island from Dr. John Coe Kellogg, the first settler at what was then Red Bluff. A square-tower, two-story Cape Cod style beacon house was erected.[366]

Gold was discovered along the upper Fraser River, British Columbia. The "rush" was on again. This time most of the hoards of gold seekers trampled Victoria. It is said that on one day some 10,000 people arrived in that city by ships from all along the west coast.

Sometime during 1858 John Bennett, a Scot coal miner living at S-yah-whom (Sehome neighborhood of Bellingham today) planted English holly. That easy-to-grow plant developed into a huge industry by 1938, which supplied about half of the Christmas holly used in the 48 states, Hawaii, and China. Much of the English holly production of western Washington was packaged for railroads and international ships sailing from Tacoma.

---

[366] The flame in the sentinel was lit in January, 1861 by William Robertson, a retired sea captain. In 1897 the place became a coastal artillery installation.

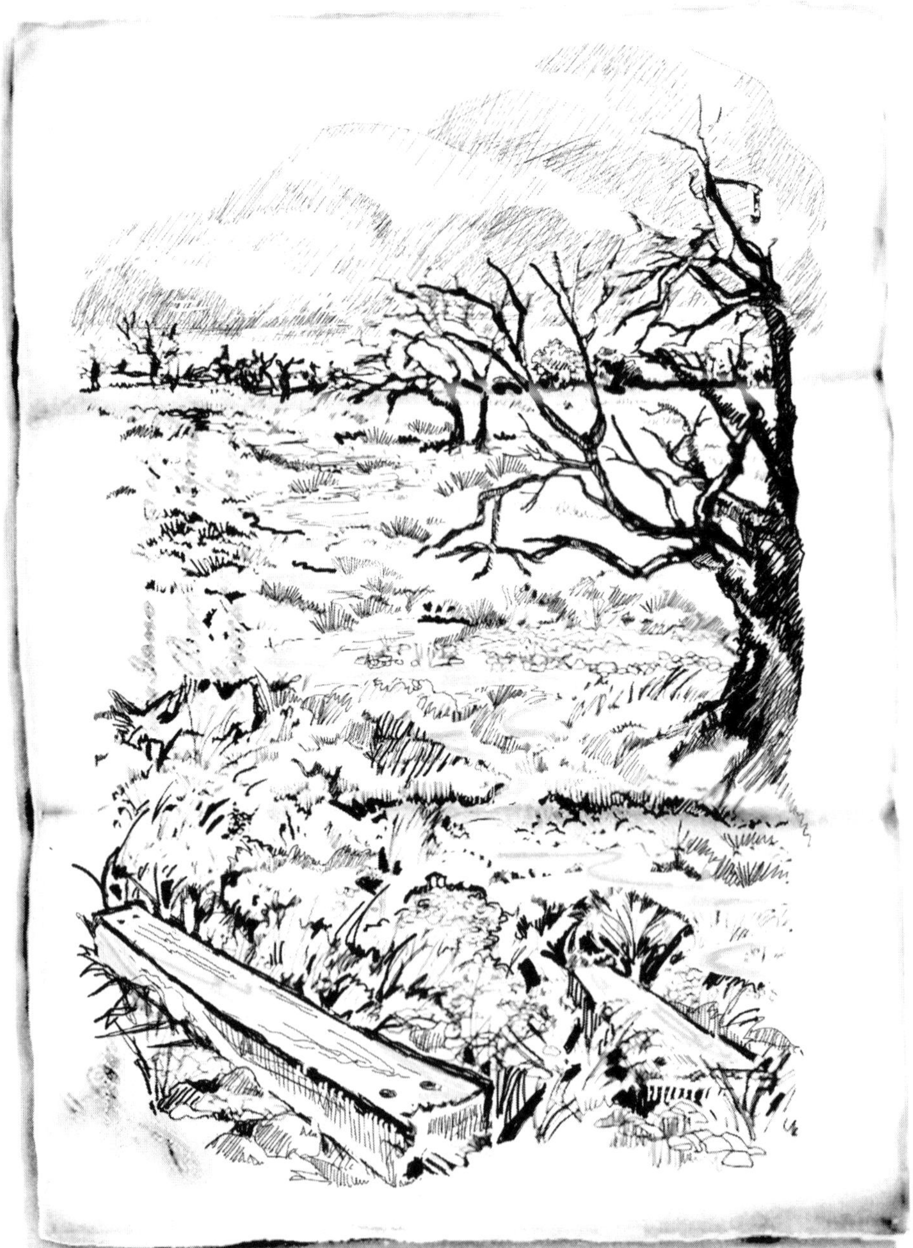

1859

IN 1859 a young explorer named Paul du Chaillu emerged from Africa with evidence proving the existence of an animal that seemed more mythical than real. It was the low land gorilla, and upon its discovery, it was considered to be man's closet's relative. But the story doesn't stop there. It was the center of the biggest issue of the time—the debate on Darwin's theory of evolution had begun.

Other world news included the first successful commercial oil well being drilled near Titusville, Pennsylvania. The big news on the west coast was different. In mid-March the people of Portland heard that President James Buchanan had signed the legislation making Oregon the 33rd state of the union.

Buchanan had actually signed the document on February 14th. It took a full month for the breaking news to be delivered to the news readers of Oregon. The official copies of the statehood document traveled across the continent in the fastest mode possible. It went by stagecoach to St Louis, then across the desert southwest, then north to San Francisco. From there the papers were casually taken aboard the steamship *Brother Jonathan*, which was delivering important cargo to Portland.

Oregon statehood meant the creation of Washington Territory was necessary because the portion of the Old Oregon Country north of the Columbia was not included in the new state. Ignoring the presence of the British corporations nearby, there was a concerted political effort to make Olympia, with the most Americans, the capitol of the new territory instead of Vancouver, which had the taint of British history. To secure the votes needed to accomplish the goal of assigning Olympia as the capitol, legislators offered the territorial university to Seattle, and the territorial penitentiary and the Customs House to Port Townsend. Tacoma got the Washington State History Museum and, twenty-four years later, the transcontinental railroad President Lincoln proposed. Steilacoom, the first incorporated city in the territory, got the State Hospital for the Insane. For the most part, the political maneuvers failed, but the university was placed in Seattle, while the prison went to Walla Walla. The Capitol was established in Olympia. Port Townsend, in a second effort to obtain political largess, eventually lost even the federal Customs House.

In Pierce County, Steilacoom to be exact, the County Auditor's office burned to the ground, unfortunately taking all county records collected from the earliest territorial days. Some were disappointed that all of the legal documents concerning the furor over Leschi's trials and execution were forever lost, only fourteen months after his controversial hanging. More importantly, in the historic long run, Pierce County documents dealing with Hudson's Bay Company land holdings were (conveniently?) lost. The HBC still had their own documents, which were of little interest to Pierce County officials.

Port Townsend turned to industry and religion, building a saw mill, a grist mill at the mouth of Chimicum Creek, a Catholic Mission, and an Episcopal church. The Methodists were not far behind in constructing a church. A Methodist clergyman won the race to be first in town. Reverend John F. DeVore is said to be the first ordained minister to hold Christian religious services in many other places around Puget Sound. He paddled his canoe from Steilacoom one fine Sunday morning, only to find "the boys" engaged in a spirited (not spiritual) poker game at Port Townsend. DeVore broke up the sinful gambling, strongly inviting the men to his Sunday service. He rolled up his sleeves to give a boxing lesson to one of the card sharks who tried to belittle his cloth.[367] He was a convincing preacher, and an effective puncher.

America's Independence Day rated top billing in the *Puget Sound Herald* published in Steilacoom by Charles Prosch. It was a "modern" celebration in 1859. The U.S. warship *Massachusetts,* commanded by Brigadier General W. S. Harney, fired off a gun at sunrise. The general and his officers landed and rode to Fort Steilacoom on proud steeds. Many local citizens accompanied the navy parade. At noon, a proper thirty-three gun salute[368] was fired. The Fort Steilacoom troops were mustered and drilled by Colonel Casey.

The Steilacoom citizen's celebration was led by the Library Association at the Methodist Episcopal Church. Frank Balch read the Declaration of Independence. Reverend Sloan presented a patriotic address. In the evening the Steilacoom Library Association held a grand ball and supper. Presumably the Methodists ate a typical church supper, but maintained their serious decorum by abstaining from dancing.

Early in the year Dr. Tolmie began the task of permanently establishing his family's new home in British territory. His Cloverdale farm was thriving with absentee ownership, but Dr. Tolmie ordered construction of a substantial stone and timber dwellinghouse. By July the family had moved. Cloverdale was probably the first stone house in

---

367 Welsh, William d., *A Brief Historical Sketch of Port Townsend,* Crown Zellerbach Corporation and the Port Townsend Chamber of Commerce, 1941.

368 In honor of the 33 United States existing at the time. A gun salute in ancient times was to demonstrate all weapons were rendered ineffective for battle.

Victoria. It was built along the lines of a Scottish farm house, with spacious, old-world atmosphere. The family counted six children. One can assume it was a grand place, with the knowledge that Cloverdale was much later utilized as a rooming house.[369]

After the revelry of the American Independence Day Celebration in 1859 there was truly no doubt the Americans had taken control of the Puget Sound region. The Boundary Treaty settled the legal issue in 1846. The Territory of Washington established local government in 1853. The last Hudson's Bay Company fur brigade rendezvous was held at Fort Nisqually in 1855. The final transfer of the last livestock was completed in early 1859. It was time for fur trader and Factor, Dr. Tolmie, to move on after 16 years at Fort Nisqually and Puget Sound Agricultural Company helms.

Change was clearly noted on June 30. The Hudson's Bay Company steamer *Beaver* arrived with passengers and no furs. Mr. Harding, Doctor Tolmie, and Tolmie's two eldest sons were the only passengers. Harding was reassigned to work at Fort Nisqually and soon Dr. Tolmie would be reassigned as well. This voyage of the *Beaver* was intended to collect another fifty head of cattle for Victoria. The next day all hands were employed in loading the powerful little steamer. Along with the cattle herd, some 43 sheep and Dr. Tolmie's horse (and buggy?) were on board when the steamer departed.

On Tuesday, July 26th the passenger-friendly HBC steamer *Otter* arrived at the roadstead to transfer Dr. Tolmie and his family to his new company assignment at Victoria. Upon departure, the fully loaded steamer carried Tolmie and his family, along with a contingent of 48 PSAC cattle. So much for human comfort, the animals needed a ride, as well.

Before he left Fort Nisqually this last time, Dr. Tolmie went to Steilacoom at the request of his friend and colleague Edward Huggins. At the County seat, with Tolmie as a witness, Huggins officially declared his intentions to become an American citizen. Just as others had been reassigned by the Company or their church (McDonald, Anderson and Kittson of HBC; Reverend Richmond, Teacher Chloe Clark, carpenter William Willson of the Methodist Mission: Father Blanchet of the Roman Catholic Church; and numerous servants of the Company). Tolmie was sent to a new position at another place, but Huggins stayed for the rest of his life.

Doctor Tolmie was moving to his own estate at Cloverdale. He had accumulated at least three parcels of privately owned farmland totaling 682 acres[370] in addition to the

---

369 "Historic Home of Pioneer Family Opens its Doors," The Victoria *Daily Colonist*, Sunday, November 14, 1929, p. 15.

370 Tolmie had three "farms" at Cloverdale. The smallest measured only 99 acres, but the other two were 272 acres and 311 acres, respectively. The PSAC operated on five nearby parcels that measured 213; 605; 606; 610; and 630 acres, for a total of 2,666 acres for the huge international agricultural business on Vancouver Island and in London, England.

several PSAC farms and ranches that he managed as Chief Factor on Vancouver and other nearby islands.

It was the end of an era. For eleven more years Fort Nisqually would wait for the ultimate closure that could only come when the U.S. Congress completed the financial purchase of the 250 square miles of HBC/PSAC real estate. The buyout was clearly delineated thirteen years earlier in the Treaty of 1846, but artfully delayed for twenty-four years by the American Congress.

Upon Hudson's Bay Company's transfer of Dr. Tolmie to Fort Victoria, Vancouver Island, Huggins took charge of the entire business at Fort Nisqually. He was technically still under the direction and supervision of his absent brother-in-law and good friend, Dr. Tolmie. Huggins moved his home from the plains near Muck Creek into the former Factor's House. In the next few years Huggins consolidated and concentrated the old 250 square mile trading post, farms, and ranch land into about 1,000 close-in acres. But Huggins also expanded the grazing stations on those nearby plains. John McLeod was put to work pulling logs out of the woods for a new sheep station at a manageable distance from the house.

In the summer of 1859, some sixteen American settlers drifted from the gold diggings along the Fraser River in British Territory to the San Juan Islands. The boundary issue flared again when a pig was shot. The question was over national control of the archipelago between the U.S mainland and the British Vancouver Island. The British had been occupying San Juan for years with Belle Vue Farms, a part of Puget Sound Agricultural Company. In 1846, the British had succeeded in defeating every attempt made by American squatters to occupy the (British named) Arro Islands. Yankee timber men were warned off, but American fishing stations were established on San Juan's western shore.

PSAC was legally incorporated and listed on the London Stock Exchange in 1838, but in essence begun in 1824 as a practical means of feeding and clothing HBC employees in the old Columbia Department. It had grown into a corporate entity that combined furs, wool, mutton, beef, lumber, cattle, sheep, and fish into an international economic export force on the Pacific Rim. Products were shipped from Puget Sound to Russian America (Alaska), China, Spanish California, and other points, including Europe, specifically England. The Company was the realization of Alexander MacKenzie's words when he wrote of his epic journey across Canada to the Pacific in 1793.[371]

In 1859 Americans were claiming farm land in the San Juan Islands, too. It was an affront almost impossible to bear by some Brits.

Belle Vue Sheep Farm Home Prairie, part of Puget Sound Agricultural Company

---

371 Belle Vue Sheep Farm at www.nps.gov/sajh/historyculturebelle-vue-sheep-farm.htm

in 1853, had some 1,369 sheep grazing on San Juan Island. By 1859 the flock had grown to 4,500 along with 40 cattle, five yoked oxen, 35 horses, 40 hogs, including several high-quality Berkshire breeding boars, and 80 acres of fenced crop lands. The British agriculture company had 19 employees assigned to Belle Vue farms. There were also some 19 British settlers on San Juan Island.

There were no Americans at all until 1859, when 400 PSAC sheep were stolen. Thirty-five breeding rams were taken at gunpoint by the American sheriff to satisfy Customs Duties. Eleven British settler farms were listed as Stubb's, Fraser's, Droyen's, Blake's, Chandler's, along with PSAC sheep pens at New Station, Limestone Station, John Bull Station, Porte L'Enfre, Little Mountain on Oak Prairie, and Longacres. At Home Prairie a large vegetable garden was planted, while split-log rail fences were erected, along with typical and substantial French-style "post and sill" cottages and barns.

A road of sorts was cleared by Cowichan employees of PSAC. It was a rough track running along the center of the 16½ mile-long island and connecting the English Camp to the U.S. Army post (1959-1872). Cowichan Road[372] later became known as Military Road after American soldiers improved the track. Many of the side roads lead to pastures already occupied and named by the British before Americans arrived. Today much of the area is forested, while it was nearly all prairie grasslands with oak tree clusters in the 19th Century.

News of the growing tension in the San Juan Islands reached the east coast in record time, because the old burro trail across Panama had been replaced by a 48-mile long rail road. Ships were sent from each coast with the assurance that a train would carry the mail immediately across the isthmus. A letter could actually reach the opposite coast in 25 days. The speed of mail service would not improve again until the telegraph, Pony Express Service (1860), and a transcontinental stagecoach line that began operations in 1859.

At the peak of the hostilities, in July 1859, there was a formidable military force on each side. The British sent the Royal Navy, the fleet opposing American army forces, consisting of five formidable warships: the *Ganges, Tribune, Pleyades, Satellite,* and the *Plumper.* They carried a total of 167 big guns, ranging in size from small one-man pivot guns to 32 pounders and even some 68 pound cannons. The ships' armaments were manned by Marines, Sappers[373], and Miners[374], along with other Navy personnel totaling

---

372 Cowichan (Military) Road bisects the Mitchell Hill portion of San Juan Island National Historic Park. Rip-rap rock placed by HBC laborers is still visible there, as are wagon-wheel ruts from those days. Many other roads follow sheep paths.

373 A sapper is a soldier responsible for building and repairing roads and bridges (a combat engineer).

374 A miner replaces explosives.

2,140 fighting men. It was an astonishing display of fire power.

The Americans set up Camp Picket,[375] officially known as Military Post San Juan Island. The garrison consisted of 471 men and 18 officers from Companies B, D and M of the U.S. Artillery; plus Companies A, C and D of the 4th US Infantry; and Companies D and H of the 9th U.S. Infantry. The Americans also had some officers and men of Company A, U.S. Engineers. The *US Massachusetts* brought eight 32 pound cannons to shore. The big guns were situated in an earthen redoubt of irregular shape extending for 425 feet. It was 25-feet wide, with a parapet 20-feet thick. This redoubt was surrounded by a ditch 20-feet wide and eight-feet deep. None of the military installations were needed until a large black pig was killed.

Squatters were plaguing PSAC shepherd Charles John Griffin on San Juan Island. Some 16 Americans, former gold diggers from the Fraser River, settled on San Juan Island. Griffin, like Huggins at Nisqually, needed sufficient acreage to graze huge herds of HBC sheep. The trespassing Americans were carving the land into conveniently sized subsistence farms. Griffin appealed to Governor Douglas of the Royal Colony of British Columbia for help. He wanted the Americans, particularly Lyman Cutler, removed from the British island. Cutler built a three-sided fence to hold the pig out. It gave Griffin's hog completely free access to Cutler's potato patch on the fourth side nearest Cutler's pig house.

A single gunshot on June 15, 1859, brought the United States and Britain to the brink of war. Lyman Cutler, the American squatter, shot his British neighbor's hog as it rooted around in Cutler's kitchen garden. This single-shot execution occurred on San Juan Island, which was claimed by both countries, but occupied almost exclusively by the British. Cutler was a Kentuckian. The "railback[376]" Berkshire boar was owned by Charles Griffin, an employee of the HBC-PSAC who worked at Belle Vue Farms, established in 1853, six years earlier.

Cutler offered to pay for the dead pig, but recoiled at the price. Griffin demanded $100, equivalent to about $2,000 today by some accounts. British authorities threatened to arrest Cutler, so he called for U.S. Army help.

This incident had fallen directly into the stew that had been brewing for years. The boundary was established in 1846, but was not completely drawn on maps. The San Juan Archipelago sits between Haro Strait and San Juan Strait. The Americans wanted the boundary

---

375 Named for Captain George Edward Picket, Commander of Company D, 9th U.S. Infantry garrison at San Juan Island 1859. In 1856 he built Picket House, now the oldest house in Bellingham.

376 Railbacks are Berkshire pigs, a rare breed that originated in Berkshire County, England, still renowned for rooting for food. In 2008 fewer than 300 breeding sows were known to exist according to Wikipedia, The Free Encyclopedia. http://en.wkipedia.org

to follow the westerly body of water. The British wanted the other easterly passage.

This squabble turned more serious when General William Harney, U.S. commander of the Department of Oregon, and James Douglas, Governor of the Royal Colony of Vancouver Island, got involved. On July 27 Harney sent 66 soldiers commanded by Captain George Pickett[377] to the island. Governor Douglas countered with a British warship. The Americans escalated their forces. By September they had 461 soldiers and 14 cannons dug in on the island. The British fleet included several thousand men ready to storm the beaches. Douglas asked the navy to land the Royal Marines. British officers politely refused the request.

President James Buchanan sent General Winfield Scott, commander of the U.S. Army, to calm things down. For a time both countries agreed to joint occupancy of the islands. But both sides agreed to allow an uninterested third party, Kaiser Wilhelm I of Germany, to decide the fate of the scenic islands. The Kaiser ruled in favor of the United States on October 21, 1872. The only casualty in the Pig War was, indeed, a pig,[378] and the United Sates gained more territory from the British 96 years after The War for Independence.

In September, Dr. Tolmie returned to Fort Nisqually to help select 180 sheep for a California purchaser, a Mr. Davidson. Once the herd had been selected, Huggins, Tolmie, and Davidson drove the flock southward as far as Steilacoom, where Tolmie boarded the steamer *Julia* for his trip back to his new home at Cloverdale, near Victoria.

Even though political settlement had been made between the Americans and the British, the financial aspects were lacking. The Oregon Treaty of 1846 between the British and the U.S. government firmly established the boundary and provided for a payment of $650,000 to the Hudson's Bay Company: $250,000 of that total was for PSAC alone.

Huggins would wait for the government check until 1869, fully 24 years after the Boundary Treaty was ratified and signed, binding the government to the required payment with the authority of the United States Constitution. Even then it would take two years to make the first payment, and two more years to settle the boundary at San Juan Island.

---

377 Pickett was a Confederate General at Gettysburg only four years later.

378 Beyer, Rick, *The Greatest War Stories Never Told from Military History to Astonish, Bewilder, and Stupefy*, Lexington, 2006. Also, Murray, Keith, *The Pig War*, Washington State Historical Society, Tacoma, 1968. Also, Peck, William A. Jr., *The Pig War, Journal of a Soldier*, Edited by C. Brewster Coulter and Bert Webber, Webb Research Group, Medford, Oregon, 1993. Also see Richardson, David, *Pig War Islands*, Orcas Publishing Company, Eastsound, WA, 1971 and 1990.

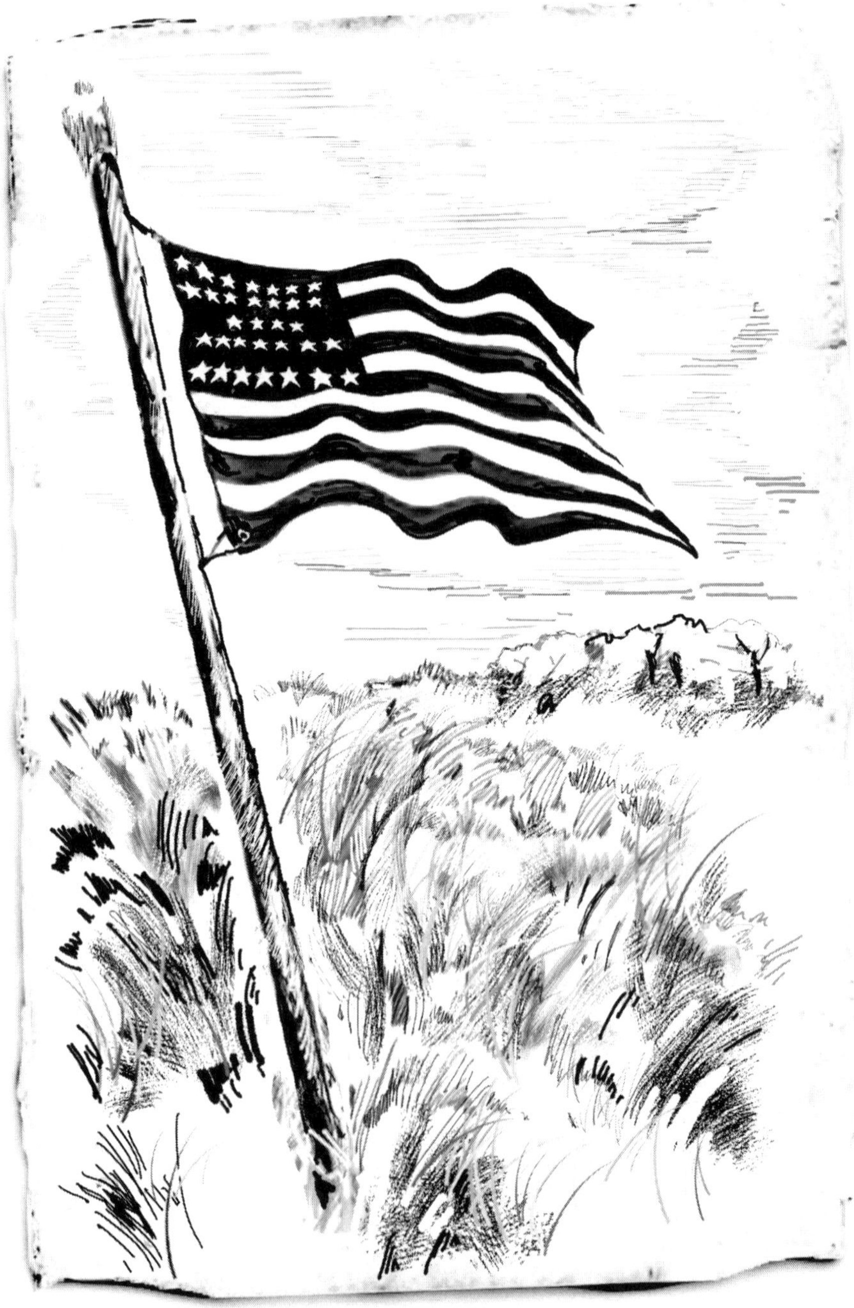

1860 - 2014

THERE IS NO KNOWN PROCEDURE to precisely calculate today's value of the goods produced at Fort Nisqually by PSAC in any given month, and certainly not for the entire 40-year span of operations. However, if we assign an arbitrary value we can gain a bit of understanding of the relative importance of the HBC, Fort Nisqually, and PSAC operations. Historical records show that at one particular time PSAC mutton sold for 12½ cents per pound, while lamb meat sold for 15 cents per pound. By assigning an "equal value" to all 18,483 different things produced (i.e. crops, skins, furs, fence rails, repairs, etc.) as numerated in the journals, and decide they all sold for 15 cents per pound, we find a "monetary value" of $2,772.45. That's not bad when the average working wage was typically less than a dollar for a long summer work day, and in the earliest days, only £15 Sterling per year.

By placing that arbitrary value as a monetary value, we can extrapolate that PSAC was a very successful business operation, indeed. While some historians have suggested that Fort Nisqually operations were "of no consequence" because it lacks a continuing contemporary legacy, others point to the legacy of people, descendants of those early men and women of the fort. Many of those descendants live among us today.

There is also the business legacy that survived, by moving completely to Vancouver Island. The PSAC was listed on the London Stock exchange from 1838 through 1934. For nearly 100 years the company paid regular dividends to shareholders, finally closing the books after selling the final piece of real estate in the 20th century, as the City of Victoria developed.

Sir George Simpson, Governor of the HBC, fought to protect his vision for HBC and PSAC, while losing his ability to see. He fought against the forces of change until he died in 1860, just after hosting a visit from the Prince of Wales (later Edward VII) in Montreal.

Fort Vancouver along the Columbia River was completely abandoned to the Americans, but Fort Nisqually hung on for years, under the direction of HBC Clerk Edward Huggins and his wife Lettitia Work Huggins. Fort Nisqually's vast land of ranches and farms formed a "British island" in Pierce County, Washington Territory, until 1870.

That "British Island" consisted of about 250 square miles of land stretching from the Cascade foothills to Puget Sound shores, and from the Puyallup River to the Nisqually River. It belonged to the British by a tacit agreement with the Indians for trading purposes. Finally, three years after the United States had purchased Alaska from the Russians in 1867, the American Congress appropriated the funds to comply with the Boundary Treaty of 1846.

1852
Nicolas Delin constructed a sawmill at the head of Commencement Bay on April first.

1853
James Sales, the first child of European descent was born in Tacoma to William and Eliza Sales. William worked at the Delin sawmill.

1861
While a transcontinental telegraph was completed in October, the news still arrived in Oregon and Washington Territory only after a steamship or stagecoach, dispatched from San Francisco, arrived at the post office in Portland. Puget Sound was still days away.

1862
Measles broke out among the Northwest Indians again. The white population was mostly concerned with the potential spread of the disease to their own communities.

1863
Fort Steilacoom Army Chapel was moved to the town of Steilacoom by Roman Catholics, who renamed the building "The Immaculate Conception Mission Chapel."

The beautiful building, recognized around the world as the United States Capitol, with its massive dome, was substantially completed and finally crowned with the bronze Statue of Freedom bolted on the top on November 30, 1863.

America was eighty-seven years old. Fort Nisqually was thirty, and still a British enclave, doing business in Pierce County on Puget Sound ten years after Washington Territory was established.

In the San Juan Islands, during the early stages of the Pig War, the American and British military men got along quite well. Captain Lyman Bissell of the American troops and Captain George Bazalgette, his British opponent, organized a track meet and joint banquet to celebrate American Independence Day, July 4, 1863. Later that summer, at least 100 men and women from Victoria visited the soldiers of both sides for a huge picnic on San Juan Island.

1864

Congress chartered the Northern Pacific Railway Company to connect Puget Sound and the Great Lakes by rail, as the second transcontinental railroad.

Job Carr filed a claim for 168 acres of land at Shubahlup ("sheltered place") on the shores of Commencement Bay. Carr was speculating that the western terminus of the new railroad would be at deep-water Commencement Bay. Tacoma was selected on July 14, 1873 as the western terminus, as Job Carr had hoped. The final leg of the NPRR line was across the prairie of South Tacoma, which was PSAC land only three years earlier.

The first telegraph message from California reached Portland on March 5, 1864. The news was only 20 hours old! The Wells Fargo stagecoach carried the news, parcels, and passengers north from Portland to Puget Sound the next day.

The U.S Army (one company of regular army infantrymen) was assigned to the San Juan Island's Camp Pickett[379] through 1864. They were ordered to protect American citizens and rebuff all British attempts to keep the San Juan Islands as British territory. A dispute was over a portion of the boundary. Was it north or south of the San Juan Islands? A Joint Occupation Agreement was signed on March 31, and not extinguished until 1872, when Kaiser Wilhelm I of Germany, the arbitrator, awarded the island group to the U.S., thus ending the twelve-year-long Pig War.[380] The settlement effectively expelled the British from Puget Sound. All that remained was the required compensation outlined in the original Boundary Treaty.

1865

The United States played a waiting game between 1846 and 1870, clearly hoping to dictate a settlement and acquire the British property rights without compensation. A commission was organized to inquire into the worth of the British property, beginning in 1856. Dozens of witnesses before the Joint Commission gave appraisals and depositions concerning American depredations. Simon Plomondon testified of Americans helping themselves to the Company crops, animals, barns, fences, and even houses whenever it suited them. James E. Williamson, an American butcher, testified that many of the

---

379 Camp Pickett was named for George Pickett, U.S. Army Captain in charge at San Juan until he resigned his commission to join the Confederacy. He led the suicidal charge at the Battle of Gettysburg.

380 There were only two major conflicts in the Pig War. One was the prohibition of liquor sales to Indians by civilians on both sides. The area was awash with whiskey that was untaxed by either country. Both countries wanted that revenue, of course. The other dispute was about land ownership. The HBC owned and occupied Belle Vue Farms on at least twenty acres of prime pasturage. American settlers had squatted on that land.

Company's cattle were slaughtered by Americans as a common practice. In fact, Williamson bought many of the Company's cattle that were killed by Americans for resale in his shop. Williamson continued, *"there were but two or three in the county that did not kill the cattle. They were very poor shots."*[381] Dr. Tolmie claimed the value of stolen cattle and horses came to $180,000.[382]

Fourteen volumes of testimony and statements led to an award to the British of $650,000, which was paid only after several more disagreements. On July 10, 1848, Sir George Simpson, on behalf of the Hudson's Bay Company, let it be known to Congress that the company was willing to sacrifice its rights for $1,000,000. In 1849 the Legislature of Oregon Territory sent memorials to Congress resisting PSAC efforts insisting that the Company had enclosed lands to which it had no right. In 1854 the Washington Territorial Governor complained that the Company claimed the right to fell timber, graze on large tracts of unenclosed pasture and prairie land with immense herds of cattle and flocks of sheep. PSAC sheep flocks numbered 12,000 and cattle were counted at 10,000 head.

As early as 1863 President Lincoln had presented to Congress an agreement for ratification to settle the Treaty. Lincoln recommended an appropriation to carry out the provisions of the treaty. In 1864 Lincoln again mentioned the British claims, this time in his fourth State of the Union address to Congress. In 1868 President Johnson reiterated the proceedings of the Joint Commission of the British claims. No congressional action was taken.

1866

The Hudson's Bay Company won the contract to carry the United States mail between San Francisco and Victoria. Captain William Mouat was given command of the *Labouchere* on 15 Feb to be refitted for passengers and mail service. Mouat sailed on 14 April in a thick fog. The *Labouchere* struck the rocks off Point Reyes. Mouat gave the order to abandon ship, but 18 men were left after all available lifeboats were launched. Mouat ordered rafts to be built. Before the ship sank all hands were rescued by the sailing ship *Andrew*.

1867

On March 30, Russia offered to sell Alaska to the United States for $7.2 million. Final approval of Congress came on October 18, 1867. The check was issued on August 1, 1868.

Father Francis Xavier Prefontaine was assigned as Seattle's first resident Roman Catholic priest, thirty-five years after the first Protestant resident clergyman, Dr. John

---

381 Green, Frank L., *Captains, Curates, and Cockneys: The English in the Pacific Northwest*, Washington State Historical Society, Tacoma, 1981.

382 IBID

Richmond, was assigned to Nisqually. Richmond, his wife and four children, along with William Willson and his wife, teacher Chloe Clark Wilson, operated the Nisqually Methodist Mission from 1839 to 1842.

1868

Fort Steilacoom was abandoned by the U.S. Army on April 22, 1868. The land became the site for Fort Steilacoom Asylum, renamed Western State Hospital for the Insane, Washington State Hospital, and finally simply Western State Hospital in 1915.

John W. Ackerson built the (Old) Tacoma Mill on Commencement Bay in October, only four years after Job Carr set up a cabin on a 168 acre claim as the first permanent settler after the Indian Treaty War. Carr's claim eventually became Old Town Tacoma. Nichols de Lin constructed a sawmill at the head of Commencement Bay on April 1, 1852.

1869

On May 10, 1869, the *Jupiter,* a wood-burning locomotive from the west, and *No. 119,* a coal-burning engine from the east, met at the Last Spike Ceremony at Promontory Summit, Utah. Leland Stanford and Thomas Durant drove the last spike in the world's longest railroad. The telegrapher wrote: "Promontory to the country: Bulletin: DONE." That simple message was already understood at Fort Nisqually and the Puget Sound Agricultural Company.

Edward Huggins' long ten-year wait was about to end. Congress finally got around to funding the buyout of Hudson's Bay Company land and improvements in the U.S. south of the Oregon Treaty boundary line. The Fort Nisqually tract of 167,000 acres and the Cowlitz Farm tract of 3572 acres were originally valued at $5,449,936.67 when presented to the Joint International Commission. The total payment for Fort Nisqually and the Puget Sound Agricultural Company improvements was only $650,000, paid in two installments in 1871 and 1872.

Those payments ended British land ownership of Puget Sound area farms and ranches operated by PSAC for forty years (1832 -1872). The settlement allowed the NPRR to lay a line of tracks to the water's edge across the prairies (Lakewood, Fort Lewis, South Tacoma) on a route now called "The Prairie Line Trail," through the University of Washington (Tacoma) and downtown Tacoma.

The Territory of Washington claimed unpaid real estate property taxes (from 1853 to 1859) to be deducted from the total authorized payment to the HBC, but the federal government ignored the local politician's belated claim. Paying local taxes was not part of the treaty and could not be justified legally under any circumstances. The Company had never been legally assessed. The news was received around Puget Sound in mere hours by telegraph, but the confirming documents still needed five days travel time to cross the continent to the State capitol.

1870

The government check to purchase the HBC British lands in Pierce County was issued, more than three years after the check that purchased Alaska from the Russians.

1871

On February 21, 1871, Congress appropriated a partial payment of $350,000 in gold coin for the British property remaining in Pierce County, Washington Territory.

1872

The second installment of the awarded payment for British property in Pierce County, Washington Territory, was made on May, 24, 1872. Pierce County sought $50,000 for real estate taxes on the land, but the Commissioner of Internal Revenue, J.W. Douglas, ruled that no taxes had been legally assessed on Puget Sound Agricultural Company land up to the time of the award, therefore PSAC received the full payment of $350,000. Edward Huggins, by then a naturalized American citizen, represented HBC, PSAC, and Fort Nisqually in the legal proceedings. Huggins immediately filed a claim for the land he had lived on for over twenty years. He sold the land in 1909, after working the land since 1849. During his life Huggins also served as Pierce County Auditor and as director and vice-president of the National Commerce Bank of Tacoma.

Alaska was purchased from Russia in 1867. The United States paid $7.2 million for the new territory, five years before it paid the British $650,000 for Pierce County.

1873

Northern Pacific Railway Company made impressive strides to reach Tacoma on July 14, but the company went bankrupt on September 18. The national Panic of 1873 engulfed the country and nearly paralyzed the railroad, but on December 16, the first steam train arrived in Tacoma across the Prairie Line tracks laid on former PSAC pastures. Tacoma was declared the City of Destiny, exporting coal to fuel steam engines of all railroads.

Between 1874 and 1880 Tacoma would become not only the western terminus, but the site of one of the largest railroad shop complexes for building and repairing heavy railroad equipment on the (former PSAC) prairie at South Tacoma.

The Hudson's Bay Company conserved its paradise. It moved its cattle and sheep at intervals to encourage new grass growth. In later years, the (American) settlers took no such precautions and very close grazing destroyed the grass roots. A less valuable and thinner forage usurped the soil. Then came the army of trees. Until then there were almost no fir trees, save occasional patches of oaks, to break the vistas of Mount Tacoma.

1909

After living on the (PSAC) land for over fifty years and becoming an American citizen, Edward Huggins sold his homestead, the Old Fort Nisqually and Puget Sound Agricultural Company land, to the industrial giant *Eleuthere Irenee. du Pont de Nemours* and Company, for the manufacture of smokeless gunpowder and dynamite. The du Pont Company products were used by industries such as mining, road, and railroad construction, and of course the military.

1933

Two original buildings at Fort Nisqually were saved by local and federal workers with relief agency connections. The 1851 granary and the 1854 factor's house were saved and moved to Point Defiance Park, overlooking the Tacoma Narrows of Puget Sound. Major restoration and replication of Fort Nisqually has been undertaken in the years since. The original site of Fort Nisqually was 100 years old when it was abandoned, but is now a National Archaeological Conservancy site.

PSAC moved to Vancouver Island (1870) but, until 1934, continued to operate for nearly one hundred years. PSAC farms were located in what is now Victoria. The history of 40 years of doing business at the original headquarters site (Du Pont) is reflected in the Fort Nisqually Living History Museum in Point Defiance Park, a Metro Parks Tacoma facility. Two original buildings, the Factor's House and the Granary, are original, with repairs and restoration. All other buildings at the Museum are replicas, built from original construction plans, but with modern amenities in some cases. All are deemed handicapped accessible and fire safe, under modern legal requirements.

1934

The Puget Sound Agricultural Company, with no assets and no operations, ceased to be listed on the Register of the Joint Stock Companies of the London Stock Exchange.[383] Former farm and ranch land on Vancouver Island had become urbanized. There was, in fact, more value in the land than in the farm business on that land.

Fort Nisqually was moved.[384] The *Tacoma Times* and the *Tacoma News-Tribune* of September 4, 1934, each had front page stories and illustrations of a great event of the

---

[383] Coyle, Brian, "The Puget's Sound Agricultural Company of Vancouver Island 1847-1857, Unpublished thesis. Department of History, Simon Fraser University, November, 1977.

[384] "Not the same Puget, Not The Same Fort Nisqually" www.journals.lib.washington.edu/index.php/whq/article

previous day. For two years the Young Men's Business Club of Tacoma had sponsored the removal of old Fort Nisqually buildings to Point Defiance Park in Tacoma. The dedication ceremonies were the culmination of an unusual celebration of Labor Day.

The ceremonies consisted of an elaborate and spectacular parade through the streets of Tacoma and a dedication of the old buildings on the new site. W.P. Bonney, Secretary of the Washington State Historical Society, gave the historical background of the fort. Other participants included representatives of prominent pioneers.

An old American flag, taken down from Fort Steilacoom in 1868 was presented to, and saved at, the Ferry Museum. That American flag, of course, had nothing to do with the British Fort Nisqually which flew an HBC Union Jack, but the old pioneers were happy to put their stamp on it. For many years, until 1980, Fort Nisqually Museum flew an American flag, in spite of historical accuracy.

1943
Fort Nisqually, at the reconstructed site in Point Defiance Park, publicly celebrated the centennial of the second historic site at Dupont, WA.

1980
Steve A. Anderson was hired by Metro Parks Tacoma. Steve began a Living History Program, as Fort Nisqually's historic buildings became the focus of local history.

1990
Melissa McGinnis was hired by Metro Parks Tacoma. Melissa expanded the Fort Nisqually Living History program with a large cadre of volunteers.

1999
The "*Dr. Jerry V. Ramsey and Elaine Perdue Ramsey Endowment Fund for Fort Nisqually Living History Museum*" was established by a generous donation from Jerry and Elaine. The permanent endowment fund is managed in perpetuity by the Greater Tacoma Community Foundation (GTCF). Annual cash grants are awarded to Fort Nisqually Foundation for any purpose, except salaries, supporting Fort Nisqually Living History Museum.

2002
Historic Factor's House was restored with state and federal grants, along with local fundraising efforts.

2007

Metro Parks Tacoma bond issue request was approved by the voters of Tacoma. Money was made available to build the Large Storehouse replica, as well as the Men's Dwelling replica. Serving a dual purpose of replicating the exterior of original homes of workers, the interior became a gift shop and interpretive center. The largest building at the original fort site was a two-story storage facility. Today the replica provides programming space for current events.

2008

The Men's Dwelling House (Interpretive Center and Gift Shop) and the Large Store (Meeting Hall, Administrative Offices, Research Library, and Curatorial Storage) were constructed. The exteriors of these buildings match the original design (in appearance) of the structure from history. The Fort Nisqually Living History Museum Research Library received a significant cash grant from the Ramsey Endowment Fund. The Ramseys also donated a rare and nearly complete set of "Bancroft's Works," a substantial thirty-nine volume history of the west, published in 1883 by A.L. Bancroft & Company, Publishers, San Francisco, CA. Not only the contents, but the actual books, are historic.

2009

The new Dwelling House and Large Store were opened to the public with a grand celebration.

2013

The Granary was fully protected and refurbished under federal and state guidelines for historic preservation and earthquake safety standards.

APPENDIX: PART ONE

The following excerpt comes from a History Commentary written by Richard Rhodes for *Columbia, the Magazine of History,* published by the Washington State History Museum. The original commentary appeared in the Fall, 2006 edition, specifically concerning the preservation of the B Reactor at Hanford, WA, but aspects of the article apply generally to all historic preservation.

> *Why preserve the physical remains of the past? Why are the Declaration of Independence and the United States Constitution maintained in elaborately sealed cases lowered at night into expensive bomb proof vaults when there are perfectly readable copies around? Why preserve Williamsburg? Why Fort Walla Walla?*
>
> *The answer is not necessarily mystical, but it is philosophical.*
>
> *We preserve what we value of the physical past because it specifically embodies our social past. However weightless and invisible social reality might be—all the vast interconnections and communications we share together and with our forebears, all our records, experiences, photographs, poems, paintings, inventions, celebrations and styles… is anchored in physical objects…extending deep into the physical world of landscapes, buildings, documents, machines, and artifacts. Finding meaning in the preservation and contemplation of those physical objects is not merely sentimental, because the meaning is not merely an add-on. Physical facts and social facts can and do occupy the same place at the same time.*
>
> *When we lose parts of our physical past we lose parts of our common social past as well. Anyone who has lost a wedding ring… knows what I mean. The uniqueness informs the purpose and justifies the expense of historic preservation.*
>
> *There were log cabins everywhere in rural and frontier America, but only a few witnessed the birth of poets or presidents [or opened a territory for a new culture].*
>
> *[We do not] often preserve places where we did things we were ashamed of, except to educate future generations and to memorialize and commemorate the victims.*

APPENDIX: PART TWO

The following list and the brief descriptions of Hudson's Bay Company trading posts in the Columbia Department west of the Rockies, and are excerpted from *Frontier Forts & Posts of the Hudson's Bay Company* by Kenneth E. Steele, published by Hancock House, Surrey B. C. Canada, 1943, revised in 2006.

These establishments did not all exist at the same time. Some were used for very brief periods, while others developed into permanent towns and cities. Some individual stores continue operations today. All are historic, even if not officially listed by accrediting agencies.

Fort Alexandria—Named for Alexander McKenzie, on the west side of the Fraser River (near Quesnel)

Fort Babine—Originally Kilmaurs, on a point 80 miles from the southeast end of the Lake Babine

Barkersvill Post—Now a thriving town in the Caraboo, with a world class Heritage Site

Bella Coola Post—Near the entrance of the Bella Coola River

Belle Vue Farm—1500 acres (PSAC) sheep ranch and farm on San Juan Island

Black River Post—Seventy miles from Laird River, ninety-five miles from Dease Lake

Fort Berens—A subsidiary of Fort Kamloops on the eastside of the Fraser at Lilooet

Fort Chilcotin—At the confluence of the Chilcotin and Chiko Rivers near Alexis Creek

Fort Colville—Columbia River upstream from Kettle Falls, now under Lake Roosevelt

Fort Conconolly—Northern end of Bear Lake near the outlet of the Skeena River

Cowlitz Farms—Sixty-six miles north of the Columbia at the east end of the Cowlitz River Landing (PSAC)

Fort Dallas—A design that never opened; plans terminated when Fort Berens closed.

Appendix: Part Two

Dease Lake Post—Northeast shore of the lake, moved five times (AKA Laketon Post, Porter's Landing)

Fort Durham—Near Taku River and Russian American Territory, opened 1840 -42

Fort Esquimalt—Esquimalt Harbor, fur cargo transfer and tall ship supply docks

Frances Lake Post—on the north shore of Frances Lake, Yukon

Fort Fraser—On Fraser Lake, established by Simon Fraser in 1806

Fort George (Fort Astoria)—On a rocky outcropping at the mouth of the Columbia River

Fort George (Fraser River) Confluence of Nechako and Fraser Rivers, later downriver

Glenora Post—12 Miles downriver of Telegraph Creek, Stikine River, then at Teslin Lake

Fort Grahame—Upstream from Finlay Forks, at confluence of Parsnip and Peace Rivers

Fort Halket—West branch of the Laird River, later Buffalo River, near Reindeer River

Hazelton Post—Hagwilget on the forks of the Skeena and Agwilget (Buckley) Rivers

Herschel Island Post—Pauline Cove, an Arctic Sea Island, then Shingle Point, then Tuktuk

Fort Hope—Henry Newsham Peers built, at Brigade Trail end, at Hope, B.C.

Hudson Hope Post—AKA Rocky Mountain House Portage, moved 3 times on Peace R.

Fort Kamloops—at Lake Kamloops, moved several times, then to Thompson River

Kitwanga Post—AKA Gitwanggak, near the railway station at Kitanga

Kootenay House Post—On Lake Windermere, then at Toby Creek & Columbia River

La Pierre's Post—On the right bank of the Bell River, Yukon; moved four times

Fort Langley—Junction of Salmon & Fraser, moved near Langley Farm (and town)

Little Post—A cabin only, E. side of North Thompson River, outpost of Fort Kamloops

Lower (Laird) Post—Laird River one mile above Dease River, two miles S. of Yukon

Manson Creek Post—150 miles north of Fort St. James on Manson Creek

McDame Creek Post—(Sylvester's Landing) 75 Miles north of Dease Lake

Fort McLeod—First white settlement west of the Rockies, at north end of McLoed Lake

Fort McLoughlin—Eastside of Campbell Is. at a Bella Bella village known as Waglisla

Nanaimo Post—(Sne-my-mo or Snuneymuxw) Coalville Town, E.side Vancouver Island

Fort Nelson—80 miles north of the forks of the Laird River. Destroyed by Beaver Indians

Fort Nez Perce—AKA Ft. Walla Walla, confluence of Columbia & Walla Walla Rivers

Fort Nisqually—current day Dupont, WA, along Sequalitchew Creek on the eastern shore of Puget Sound. A replica with two original historic buildings is at Fort Nisqually Living History Museum in Point Defiance Park, Tacoma, WA

Fort Okanogan—On Okanogan River ½ mile upstream from Columbia River confluence.

Osoyoos Post—Near the narrows of Osoyoos Lake, 18 miles from Fort Similkameen

Fort Pelly Banks—on the Yukon River, men nearly starved after a fire destroyed it

Perry Creek Post—A single "cabin" NW of Cranbrook produced a large amount of gold

Quesnel Post—at the mouth of the Quesnel River, it replaced Alexandria

Rampart House Post—On the Porcupine River near Fort Yukon in USA territory

Fort Rupert—Northeast end of Vancouver Island at Beaver Harbor

Fort Shepherd—(Fort Pend d'Oreille) on west bank of the Columbia at Pend d'Oreille River.

Fort Simpson (Nass River)—Built to keep the Americans out, moved to Portland Canal

Fort Simpson—North shore Port Simpson Harbor, 40 miles from Nass & Skeena Rivers

Fort Similkameen—In the valley of the same name, a few miles north of USA border

Fort St. John—(Rocky Mountain House) on the Peace River upstream of Moberly River

Fort St James—(Stewart Lake Post) HQ for the Caledonia District

Spokane House—Spokane Falls, ten miles NW of Spokane, WA, on Little Spokane River

Fort Stager—In the Kisiox Valley near town of Hazelton at Skeena and Kisiox Rivers

Fort Stikine—four miles from the mouth of the Stikine, later at Ft. Wrangell

Stoney Creek Post—On banks of Stoney Creek, five miles from Nookli and Tachic Lakes

Telegraph Creek—On the north Bank of the Stikine at Raspberry Creek (Cla-aka-heen)

Teslin Lake Post—on Teslin Lake at Second Street Teslin City

Fort Vancouver—100 miles up the Columbia on North shore—HQ for Columbia Dept.

Vernon Post—In the Okanagan Valley at present day Vernon

Fort Victoria—(Fort Camosun & Fort Albert) at southeast end of Vancouver Island

Fort Ware—Mile-and-a-half upstream from White Water River on the Finlay River

Wild Horse Creek Post—(Stud Horse Creek) in the East Kootenay Region

Westwold Post—(Frenchman's Prairie) 40 miles southeast of Kamloops

Fort Yale—At the head of navigation of the Fraser River.

Fort Yukon—(Youcan) on the Yukon River above the Porcupine (Rat) River

APPENDIX: PART THREE

1833 HBC Servants at Fort Nisqually, including an account of livestock

1. Pierre Charles—Hunter/trapper
2. Archibald McDonald—Chief Trader, AKA "Black Eagle" to the Indians
3. James Rindale—Cooper
4. William Ouvrie—Trapper
5. Dr. William Fraser Tolmie—Physician
6. James Murray Yale—Trader, Plus Four horses, four oxen,

1847 HBC/PSAC Servants at Fort Nisqually (after Boundary Treaty of 1846)

1. Isaac Bastien
2. Adam Beiston
3. Cowie
4. John Edgar
5. Ehoo
6. Kahanniu
7. Keavahaccow
8. Louis La Doux
9. Louis La Tour
10. Thomas Linklater
11. Jacob Low
12. John Macleod
13. Murdo MacDonald
14. John Montgomery
15. Napahay
16. Matthew Nelson
17. Walter Ross
18. Richard Slocum
19. Joe Tapou
20. William F. Tolmie
21. Charles Wren
22. W. F. Tolmie

1852 HBC/PSAC Servants
at Fort Nisqually (Before WA Territory was established)

1. Barnes
2. Beiston
3. Chalifoux
4. Cowie
5. Cush
6. Fiande
7. Gohome
8. Hatal
9. Huggins
10. Keavahaccow
11. Linklater
12. McPhail
13. Montgomery
14. Northover
15. Rabasca
16. Ross
17. Sales
18. Slogomas
19. Squally
20. Thornhill
21. Tolmie
22. Young

1854 Pierce County Census
Showing only non-native PSAC employees. Indians were not originally counted.

1. Andrew Burge, 25, Farmer, Des Moines, Iowa
2. Edward Huggins, 22, Clerk, London
3. Kalama, Kanaka
4. Keavakow, Kanaka
5. Lowie, Kanaka
6. William Legg, 21, Farmer, Berkshire, England
7. Charles Ross, (Métis)
8. W.F. Tolmie, 33, MD, Scotland

1860 Pierce County Census (Showing only PSAC employees

1. Issac Bastien, 41, Canada
2. Andrew Burge, 31, Missouri
3. Edward Huggins, 28, Merchant, England
4. Perish La Gacey, 48, Farmer, Washington Territory
5. Joseph LeGrarde, 32, Farmer, Red River
6. William Legg, 28, Farmer, England
7. Joseph Teboe, 43, Farmer, Canada

APPENDIX: PART FOUR

Puget Sound Agricultural Company Place Names from Fort Nisqually "*Journal of Occurrences*"* These places are shown on the map included in this book by small squares or triangles.

American Plain—pasture, Horse Racing
Ash (Ashland) Farm; Oats, Potatoes
Auser's Place—Farm; various crops
Bursts—Beef Cattle Pasture
Back Plain (Back Squally Plain)—Cattle
Bolton's Prairie—Pasture
Canadian Plain—Pasture
Cattle Burn—Pasture
Cooper's House—Farm—various crops
Couri's—Sheep Pasture
Cowie's Muck—Pasture
Daniel's—Sheep Pasture
Dean's—Dairy Farm, various crops
East Field—Farm and Pasture
Elk Plain—Farm and Pasture
Field # 1—Various Crops
Field # 2—Potatoes & Peas
Field # 3—Potatoes & Peas
Field # 4—Potatoes & Peas
Four Lakes—Cattle Pasture
Large Field # 5—Various crops
Long Plain—Pasture
Grand Prairie—Tenino, Cattle Pasture
Gravell's—Farm; Potatoes, Peas
Grieg's—Farm; Potatoes, Peas
Gordon's Lake—Pasture

Hadley's—Cattle Pasture
Heatherly's—Cattle Pasture
Heath's—Farm/Ranch
Kahimin's—Oats & potatoes
Kitchen Garden—Fort Nisqually
Kul-Kul-illa-Hee—Horse Pasture/breeding
Large Potato Patch—Four Acres
Le Shuou—May be the same places as Kul-Kul-illa-Hee
Mahon—Cattle, Mostly Steers
Macleod's—Merino Sheep Breeding
Maroon Lake—Sheep Pasture
Mission Plain (American Methodist)—Farm, School
Morrison—American Farm Purchased by PSAC
Molock House—Oats, Straw, Potatoes
Montgomery's Farm—Crops, Sheep, Cattle, Butcher
Mound Prairie—Cattle Pasture
Muck Station (House)—2,000 Sheep (30 miles of farmland)
Nisqually Farm—Potatoes, Peas
Old Spanaway—Sheep Pasture
Packard's—American sawmill, Sold cedar boards

[430]

Red House Mound—Pastures
Parrish—Cattle, Oxen, Steers, Breeding Station
Red Pines—Forest
Round Plain—Pasture
Salt Marsh—Pasture
Siluchogwas Farm—Oats, Potatoes
Skookumchuck—Beef Cattle Pasture
Southwest Farms—Potatoes, Cabbage
Spa-nu-eh—Sheep Pasture
Spotsisichth Lake—Cattle
Steilaacoom Plain—Pasture
Squally Plain—Pasture
Tlithlow—Sheep Pasture
Tuc-Hast-Chu—Pasture & Farm
Tweatchie—Farm
Wilson's Farm (American)

Old Fort—Farm & Pastures
Puyallup Plain—Pasture
Sil-uth-os-twas—Indian Oat Farm
South Plain—Pastures
Sastuc—Merino & Leicester Sheep
Spanaway—Pastures
Squally Lake—Cattle
Suiqulroot—Indian, Sheep Ranch
Steilacoom Farm
Steilacoom Plain
Tenalquot—Farm/pasture
Wyatchie Farm—Pasture/potatoes
Yam Hill—Horses
Yelim—Cattle
Yelmor—Mares
Young's House—Farm

* It is possible that some named locations have been missed in this compilation. Occasionally places were called by two names, or the names changed. PSAC farms and ranches gradually became "American" as squatters took the land. Some properties were legitimately American and often did business with PSAC. A few places were named after Indians who were valuable employees of PSAC. Exact locations are not revealed to protect current occupant's privacy rights.

Index

49th parallel 39, 212, 217, 219, 220, 228, 234, 284
1833 HBC Servants 428
1847 HBC/PSAC Servants 428
1852 HBC/PSAC Servants 429
1854 Pierce County Census 429
1860 Pierce County Census 429

A

aboriginal battle 23
aboriginal homes 2
accountant 396
Account Ledgers 68
Ackerson 417
Acting Secretary 377
Active Cove 95
Adams, John Quincy 35
Adams-Onis Treaty 27
Administrative Offices 421
Admiralty Head 285
Admiralty Inlet 51, 159
Alaska xii, 2, 12, 14, 17, 18, 20, 27, 39, 120, 135, 138, 145, 153, 156, 191, 192, 195, 211, 217, 286, 349, 382, 408, 414, 416, 418
Albion 4, 274, 275
Alexander Baranov 191
Alexander Caulfield Anderson 111, 144
Alexis Creek 424
Alice 263, 329, 330, 335, 336
Allard 238
Allen 297, 301, 316
Alleyne Fitzherbert 163
Allyn 8
American vi, vii, xii, 1, 2, 4, 5, 6, 7, 11, 14, 15, 16, 17, 18, 19, 20, 21, 22, 23, 26, 27, 28, 31, 32, 39, 40, 42, 43, 44, 45, 47, 48, 54, 59, 63, 65, 68, 69, 74, 80, 81, 85, 86, 88, 89, 90, 98, 105, 106, 107, 108, 110, 111, 112, 114, 115, 120, 121, 122, 124, 125, 126, 127, 128, 130, 131, 133, 135, 136, 138, 139, 141, 142, 143, 144, 145, 151, 152, 153, 154, 155, 156, 157, 159, 164, 165, 166, 167, 169, 170, 171, 172, 173, 174, 175, 176, 177, 178, 179, 181, 182, 183, 184, 188, 189, 190, 191, 194, 195, 196, 197, 199, 202, 203, 205, 206, 207, 208, 209, 211, 213, 215, 216, 217, 218, 219, 220, 221, 222, 223, 224, 225, 226, 228, 231, 232, 234, 235, 236, 237, 238, 240, 243, 246, 247, 248, 250, 251, 252, 254, 255, 256, 258, 259, 260, 261, 263, 264, 265, 266, 270, 271, 272, 274, 275, 276, 277, 279, 281, 282, 283, 284, 287, 288, 291, 292, 293, 294, 295, 297, 298, 300, 302, 303, 304, 305, 306, 308, 309, 310, 311, 312, 315, 317, 319, 320, 322, 323, 324, 325, 326, 330, 331, 332, 333, 334, 335, 336, 337, 338, 343, 345, 346, 347, 349, 352, 353, 354, 355, 357, 358, 359, 360, 370, 372, 373, 375, 376, 377, 378, 382, 384, 385, 386, 388, 389, 390, 394, 395, 396, 398, 401, 407, 408, 409, 410, 414, 415, 418, 419, 420, 425
American Farm Purchased by PSAC 430
American flag 32
American Fur Company 65
American Lake 11, 130, 164, 166, 167, 195, 279, 309, 398
American pioneers 127, 130
American Plain 164, 166, 174, 226, 430
Americans vii, 5, 18, 25, 28, 39, 40, 45, 50, 63, 80, 89, 93, 97, 105, 106, 107, 126, 127, 128, 130, 135, 144, 151, 155, 159, 161, 166, 171, 174, 175, 177, 183, 188, 189, 191, 192, 205, 206, 207, 208, 209, 211, 212, 213, 215, 218, 219, 221, 223, 226, 228, 229, 232, 234, 237, 238, 239, 240, 250, 252, 254, 255, 257, 258, 259, 260, 265, 270, 271, 272, 273, 274, 275, 278, 279, 280, 282, 283, 284, 287, 290, 291, 304, 305, 308, 311, 312, 318, 319, 322, 323, 324, 331, 335, 336, 339, 340, 346, 347, 352, 353, 354, 357, 361, 364, 365, 371, 372, 385, 386, 390, 405, 407, 408, 409, 410, 411, 413, 415, 426
American settlers vii
America Richmond 143, 157, 166
Ames 327
Anawascum 96, 100, 117
Anawiscum 101, 103
Anderson ix, 14, 69, 72, 114, 144, 145, 156, 157, 158, 163, 175, 206, 240, 241, 242, 281, 310, 343, 353, 407, 420
Anderson, Steven A. ix
Andrew 35, 107, 123, 141, 157, 213, 238, 322, 323, 359, 363, 369, 398, 399, 416, 429
Anglo-American Convention 27
Anglo-Russian treaty 27
Ann Onymous 378
An-Ouichi 339
Arcadia 8, 9
archeologists 12
Army vii, 17, 37, 105, 131, 155, 157, 166, 203, 207, 234, 250, 251, 257, 261, 264, 265, 269, 271, 272, 275, 285, 286, 287, 288, 293, 295, 298, 306, 307, 317, 323, 325, 350, 353, 359, 360, 375, 377, 378, 380, 390, 393, 394, 396, 397, 399, 409, 410, 411, 414, 415, 417

[433]

Army Regulars 378
Arrow 382
Artic Sea Island 425
Ash (Ashland) 430
Ashland Farm 402
Aspin Field 220
Astoria 17, 19, 22, 121, 164, 229, 235, 331
Astor, John Jacob 17
Astor's Pacific Fur Company 33
Atkinson 373, 380
Aucock 114
Auctions at Garraway's Coffee House 18
Audrey 373
August Ludlow Case 159
Auoha 353
Auser's Place 430

B
Babb 327, 328, 329
Babillard 79
Babine 424
Bachelder 288, 330, 344, 389
Back Plain 430
Back Plain (Back Squally Plain) 430
Back Squally Plain 430
Bahia de la Asuncion de Nuestra Senora 3
Bailey 110, 148, 149, 150, 153, 331
Baillie 216, 226
Baird 298, 299
Balch 206, 267, 276, 287, 290, 294, 302, 304, 305, 317, 322, 327, 372, 406
Ball, John 47
Bancroft's Works 421
Baptiste 24, 38, 40, 41, 69, 72, 73, 98, 114, 244, 267, 278, 290, 292, 358
Barkersvill Post 424
Barlow Road 284
Barnes 286, 287, 291, 302, 306, 340, 353, 429
Bastain 222, 223
Bastien 429
Bastien, Isaac 428
Bastien, Issac 429
Batzulnetas 382
Bazalgette 414
Bear Lake 424
beaver 5, 10, 20, 21, 26, 27, 51, 55,
56, 58, 59, 66, 71, 72, 76, 78, 79, 80, 91, 96, 97, 110, 113, 121, 135, 141, 190, 238, 240, 241, 244, 247, 261, 263, 268, 367, 362, 365
Beaver (ship), see *S. S. Beaver*
beaver fur trade 5, 135
Beaver Harbor 426
beaver hat 10
Beaver, Rev. 182
Beinson 389
Beinston 243, 255, 260, 261, 305, 323, 353
Beiston 429
Beiston, Adam 428
Bella Coola River 424
Belle Vue 105, 319, 338, 345, 372, 408, 410, 415, 424
Belle Vue Farms 105, 319, 372, 408, 415
Bell River, Yukon 425
Bell Vue Farms 357
Benjamin Louis Eulalle de Bonneville 37
Bennett 257, 403
Benston 299
Benton 399
Bernier 25, 131, 216
Big Skookum 326
Biles 320, 321, 326, 359
Birnie 131, 216
Bissell 414
Black Eagle 428
Black Lake 12, 161
Black River 12, 24, 25, 161, 278, 424
Blaine 327
Blake 409
Blanchet 82, 98, 131, 134, 139, 143, 238, 316, 407
Blanshard 282
Bodega 3, 31
Boland 292
Bolton 274, 275
Bonaparte, Napoleon 19
Bonneville 37, 47, 202, 323, 331
Bonney 28, 30, 348, 420
Borgeau 114
Boulanger 221, 222
Boundary set vi
Boundary Treaty 127, 137, 208, 220, 228, 273, 318, 322, 340, 345, 395, 407, 411, 414, 428
Bourshaw 56

Boyce 335, 346, 354
Bradley 240, 290, 304, 312, 329
Brakenridge 161
Brigade vii, 21, 154, 190, 362, 363, 364, 365, 367, 368, 425
Britain xii, 2, 19, 23, 27, 32, 33, 34, 113, 141, 188, 189, 217, 218, 228, 229, 247, 291, 315, 322, 339, 343, 395, 410
British vi, vii, ix, xi, xii, 2, 16, 18, 22, 25, 26, 28, 32, 34, 37, 39, 40, 42, 43, 44, 49, 54, 59, 74, 77, 86, 89, 93, 105, 106, 121, 123, 124, 126, 127, 128, 135, 137, 145, 151, 153, 155, 156, 157, 159, 163, 164, 165, 171, 172, 175, 176, 177, 178, 186, 188, 189, 190, 191, 192, 194, 197, 205, 207, 208, 210, 211, 212, 215, 216, 217, 219, 220, 225, 228, 229, 232, 233, 235, 237, 238, 239, 240, 247, 251, 252, 254, 257, 263, 265, 266, 267, 271, 272, 274, 275, 276, 277, 279, 281, 282, 284, 285, 286, 287, 291, 300, 301, 302, 304, 305, 309, 315, 316, 317, 318, 319, 320, 322, 323, 324, 337, 338, 340, 343, 345, 346, 352, 353, 357, 360, 365, 372, 375, 377, 382, 390, 393, 395, 401, 403, 405, 406, 408, 409, 410, 411, 414, 415, 416, 418, 420
British Columbia xii, 123, 267
British Columbia, Canada 93, 155
British company land xi
British Parliament xii, 318
Brits 202, 207, 208, 302, 385, 408
Brooks 347
Broshears 290
Brotchie 104, 108, 274
Brother Jonathan 405
Brown 12, 50, 55, 56, 69, 72, 73, 75, 205, 268, 300, 311, 383
Brownfield 240, 290
Bryant 44, 74, 252
Buchanan xii, 325, 394, 405, 411
Budd Inlet 7, 8, 9, 199, 218, 243, 353
Buffalo River 425
Bull, John 114, 116, 207
Burge, Andrew 429
Burley Lagoon 8
Burnhardt 298, 299
Bursts 430
Bush 127, 143, 170, 175, 239, 322,

Index

352, 353
Byrd 322, 340, 359, 398, 399
Byrd Grist Mill 398

C

Cadboro 52, 54, 58, 64, 70, 104, 171, 233, 243, 248, 254, 255, 259, 264, 271, 272, 273, 276, 277, 292, 358
Cado Prairie 315
Cahk-hund 339
Calamity Bay 95
California 2, 3, 4, 14, 17, 18, 27, 39, 47, 91, 93, 103, 104, 107, 108, 114, 117, 124, 137, 151, 153, 154, 159, 170, 171, 176, 177, 186, 187, 191, 195, 196, 211, 213, 215, 216, 220, 228, 231, 235, 237, 246, 259, 272, 277, 284, 285, 299, 306, 398, 408, 411, 415
Camp Picket 410
Canada xii, 7, 14, 19, 26, 45, 52, 63, 73, 95, 105, 125, 135, 143, 153, 155, 173, 211, 212, 231, 267, 316, 322, 393, 408, 424
Canadian 25, 43, 66, 68, 69, 70, 73, 81, 102, 114, 120, 125, 128, 130, 131, 133, 137, 139, 143, 153, 173, 174, 175, 185, 205, 211, 217, 221, 258, 272, 277, 358, 362, 365, 366, 367, 371, 376, 383, 402
Canadian North West Company 120
Canadian Plain 430
Can-La-Fer-Quoy 85
cannon-fire 34
Canoe Doctor 285, 398
Cape Disappointment 3, 4, 31, 222, 229
Cape Flattery 4, 71, 72, 75, 157, 302
capital punishment 399
Captain Cook 4
Captain George Vancouver 16
Carbon River 8
Carol Ann Johnson ix
Carter 148, 279, 333
Cascade 1, 15, 21, 38, 40, 55, 60, 103, 106, 111, 124, 136, 152, 160, 161, 190, 249, 280, 284, 315, 316, 320, 322, 359, 362, 414
Cascade Mountains 1, 15, 21, 38, 40, 55, 60, 103, 106, 111, 124, 136, 152, 160, 161, 190, 249, 315, 316, 320, 322, 359

Cascades 1, 3, 12, 13, 16, 126, 144, 156, 164, 175, 190, 200, 241, 283, 284, 326, 368, 382
Case, Augustus L. 164
Case Inlet 159
Case Lock 383
Cathalamet 216
Catholic 47, 65, 98, 130, 131, 132, 133, 134, 141, 143, 157, 178, 183, 185, 195, 239, 252, 293, 309, 320, 329, 406, 407, 416
Catholicism 130
Cayuse 236, 246
Cedar Canoes 89
Cerro Nevada de Santa Rosalia (Mount Olympus) 3
Chalifoux 85, 267, 281, 282, 334, 358, 384, 389, 396, 429
Challicum 112
Chamber 388, 406
Chambers 9, 10, 15, 24, 197, 218, 238, 239, 240, 256, 260, 270, 280, 290, 304, 305, 312, 324, 325, 359, 387, 389
Chambers Creek 9, 10, 15, 24, 260
Champagne 258
Champoeg 106, 222
Chandler 409
Chapman 267, 287, 291, 306, 307, 310, 312, 324, 325
Charles, Pierre 50, 51, 52, 53, 54, 56, 58, 63, 64, 69, 72, 73, 96, 100, 428
Chatham 16
Chaulifoux 278, 292, 293, 302, 305, 307, 336, 386
Chechellis 58
Cheeseman 339, 358
Cheetwoot 218
Cheezer 239
Chehalis River 12, 160, 161
Cherokees 157
Cherouze, Pere 241
Chet-teh 9
Chief 23, 24, 25, 49, 50, 54, 55, 56, 57, 58, 62, 63, 69, 70, 72, 74, 76, 78, 79, 81, 85, 86, 87, 105, 112, 113, 114, 118, 120, 121, 125, 126, 130, 137, 142, 145, 160, 161, 176, 187, 188, 192, 208, 209, 218, 238, 244, 249, 250, 251, 252, 254, 257, 258, 265, 270, 273, 277, 280, 281, 300, 337, 338, 339, 346, 351, 358, 382, 394, 397, 399, 408

Chief Kitsap 23, 24
Chief Schanewah 25
Chilacoom 34, 347
Chilalucum 57
Chilcotin and Chiko Rivers 424
Chimicum Creek 406
China 80, 104, 403, 408
Chinook 5, 7, 17, 22, 23, 42, 48, 73, 132, 134, 160, 188, 192, 222, 349, 390
Chloe 143, 146, 148, 150, 151, 157, 167, 172, 179, 181, 206, 407
Choctaw 184
Christmas Holly 403
Christopher Columbus 16
Chute River 97
City of Destiny ix, 39, 170
Civil War xii, 122, 203, 220, 311, 319, 328, 382
Clallam 274, 288
Clark 8, 17, 32, 37, 39, 115, 120, 128, 143, 148, 150, 151, 157, 167, 179, 181, 206, 275, 301, 312, 346, 399, 407
Clark's Creek 8
Clark, William 32
Clasits 115
Clatsop 5, 17, 115, 182
Clay Creek 8
Cle-cat-tats 113
Clement 95, 297
Close, Reverend Benjamin 326, 327
Clover Creek 9, 10, 279, 280, 322
Cloverdale 406, 407, 411
Coalville Town 426
Coiwie 347
Cold Spring 220
Cole Creek 8
Collins 238, 239, 279, 292, 335
Collooney 259
Colonel Casey 379, 398, 406
Colt 85, 286, 347
Columbia xi, xii, 2, 3, 4, 5, 6, 7, 16, 17, 22, 23, 25, 28, 31, 32, 33, 34, 37, 38, 39, 44, 48, 65, 66, 68, 72, 82, 88, 89, 90, 93, 97, 98, 100, 104, 105, 107, 108, 115, 116, 120, 121, 123, 124, 126, 127, 136, 139, 142, 152, 153, 155, 157, 159, 160, 161, 164, 165, 166, 170, 171, 172, 175, 176, 177, 178, 179, 182, 183, 185, 188, 189, 190, 192, 199, 203, 205, 206, 213, 216, 217, 219,

[435]

220, 223, 225, 229, 237, 242, 251, 256, 263, 267, 279, 280, 281, 283, 284, 285, 291, 292, 298, 301, 302, 303, 305, 311, 315, 316, 320, 326, 353, 358, 361, 362, 363, 383, 401, 402, 403, 405, 408, 410, 413, 423, 424, 425, 426, 427
Columbia Department xii, 25, 28
Columbia Rediviva 5
Columbia River xi, 3, 4, 5, 6, 7, 16, 17, 22, 24, 25, 28, 32, 33, 34, 37, 38, 39, 44, 48, 65, 82, 90, 93, 100, 104, 115, 124, 126, 142, 157, 164, 165, 170, 171, 172, 175, 176, 179, 182, 183, 188, 189, 199, 203, 205, 206, 216, 225, 237, 251, 279, 283, 284, 303, 315, 316, 320, 362, 363, 401, 413, 424, 425, 426
Columbia, the Magazine of History 423
Colvile, Andrew 123, 363
Colville 34, 95, 143, 264, 424
Colvos Passage 161
commander 3, 31, 163, 410, 411
Commencement Bay 59, 60, 159, 163, 170, 278, 292, 299, 301, 326, 417
Commissary General 377
Commissioner 389, 418
Company vi, xii, 18, 19, 26, 28, 30, 32, 33, 39, 42, 43, 44, 45, 48, 53, 55, 62, 64, 65, 66, 68, 73, 74, 77, 81, 83, 86, 87, 90, 91, 95, 97, 100, 101, 102, 103, 105, 108, 111, 121, 124, 126, 127, 131, 135, 136, 137, 138, 143, 144, 153, 154, 159, 160, 163, 167, 170, 171, 174, 176, 177, 178, 183, 184, 187, 189, 190, 191, 192, 195, 196, 199, 200, 203, 205, 208, 210, 219, 220, 221, 222, 225, 226, 228, 237, 240, 241, 243, 246, 247, 248, 251, 252, 257, 258, 259, 260, 261, 264, 270, 272, 273, 275, 277, 278, 279, 280, 281, 282, 283, 284, 286, 287, 288, 290, 292, 293, 294, 300, 303, 304, 305, 306, 309, 310, 312, 315, 316, 317, 322, 323, 324, 325, 326, 329, 331, 334, 335, 337, 338, 340, 343, 344, 345, 346, 347, 348, 352, 353, 354, 361, 367, 369, 371, 372, 378, 382, 385, 387, 388, 389, 390, 394, 395, 396, 399, 402, 407, 408, 410, 411, 415, 416, 417, 418, 419, 421, 424, 430
Concomly 188

Conconolly 424
Congress xii, 65, 128, 157, 170, 188, 220, 228, 236, 246, 265, 266, 275, 278, 279, 291, 318, 320, 345, 403, 408, 414, 416, 417, 418
Connell 369
Connell's Prairie 369
Constance 225, 285
Constitution 322, 398, 411, 423
Contra 272
Cook, James 4, 31
Cook, Nelson 221, 232
Cooper 305, 384
Cooper's House 430
Copass 249, 258
Cormorant 225, 227, 229, 238
Cossack Harbour 95
Coulter Creek 8
Counties of Washington State xii
country wife 68, 146
County Auditor 271, 406, 418
Coupe 285, 308
Coupeville 285, 327
Couri's 430
Coweeman 222
Cowichan 13, 23, 409
Cowie 100, 255, 261, 271, 293, 302, 305, 347, 354, 358, 396, 428, 429, 430
Cowlitz xi, xii, 25, 42, 58, 77, 81, 82, 87, 99, 100, 101, 105, 106, 113, 115, 120, 124, 125, 126, 131, 136, 137, 142, 145, 160, 161, 173, 174, 175, 182, 187, 189, 197, 206, 208, 212, 216, 217, 218, 220, 221, 226, 231, 234, 235, 238, 244, 248, 250, 251, 254, 256, 258, 271, 281, 284, 291, 292, 293, 308, 309, 317, 323, 332, 333, 344, 361, 396, 401, 417, 424
Cowlitz Farms 81
Cowlitz Landing (Toledo, WA) 25
Cowlitz Portage 25
Cowlitz Prairie 25, 81
Cowlitz River xi, 25, 77, 81, 82, 100, 145, 160, 175, 189, 212, 220, 235, 238, 317, 333, 424
Cowlitz tribe 25
Cowltiz 101
Craigflower 285
Cranbrook 426
Cree 82
Creek 7, 8, 9, 10, 11, 12, 15, 24, 38, 47, 51, 57, 58, 62, 86, 98, 121,

127, 130, 138, 157, 158, 159, 174, 192, 194, 197, 198, 220, 227, 249, 258, 260, 267, 270, 275, 280, 298, 319, 326, 327, 329, 330, 349, 350, 357, 359, 366, 369, 372, 377, 378, 402, 408, 425, 426, 427
Crescent Valley Creek 8
Crosby 328
Crystal Creek 298
Culver 335
Curatorial Storage 421
Cush 255, 353, 358, 384, 386, 401, 429
Cussans 337, 338
Cussass 249, 250
Customs Collector 288, 294, 304, 312, 345
Customs House 273, 303, 312, 330, 405
Customs Officer 272, 302, 303
Cutler 319, 410

D
Dallas 396, 424
Daly 336, 345, 347, 348, 353, 358, 359, 360
Damarascove 302
Daniels 396, 397, 430
Darwin's theory 405
Dauphine 114
Davidson 411
Davy Crocket 85
Day Island 9, 275, 297, 298, 376
Dean 290, 292, 306, 308, 324, 330, 340, 347, 359, 367, 380, 384, 388, 389, 396, 399
Dean's 291, 359, 388, 389, 430
Dease Lake 424, 425
Dease River 425
De Chutes 56
Declaration of Independence 169, 406, 423
De Lin 8, 128, 298, 299, 300, 326
Dement 257, 272, 306, 317
Demers 98, 131, 132, 134, 138, 139
Denny 272, 292, 311, 326, 335
Deschamps 340
Deshutes 199, 232
DeSmet, Father Pierre-Jean 131
DeVore 327, 328, 348, 370, 406
Director 123, 242, 396
Discovery 16, 17, 32, 115, 128, 157, 274, 285

Index

Discovery Bay 32, 274
Dixon 264, 272, 277, 358
Dodd 223
Dokibatt 15
Dolin, Eric Jay 26
Dominique 69, 100, 360, 402
Dominque's Prairie 396
Donation Land Claim 155, 266, 271, 279, 300, 326
Donation Land Claim Act 266, 279
Donkey Creek 8
Dorr 272, 273, 274, 277
Doty 351
Dougherty 240, 290, 312
Douglas 31, 41, 49, 145, 166, 187, 217, 220, 222, 233, 252, 254, 255, 258, 273, 277, 292, 310, 337, 338, 345, 361, 410, 411, 418
Douglas, David 41, 49
Dr. Jerry V. Ramsey and Elaine Perdue Ramsey Endowment Fund 420
Droyen 409
Dr. Tolmie vii, 23, 49, 50, 51, 52, 86, 88, 91, 136, 189, 197, 198, 202, 221, 223, 224, 225, 228, 229, 233, 234, 239, 241, 242, 243, 246, 248, 250, 251, 252, 254, 256, 257, 258, 259, 260, 261, 263, 264, 270, 271, 272, 273, 275, 276, 277, 278, 280, 281, 282, 287, 288, 290, 291, 292, 293, 294, 301, 302, 303, 304, 305, 306, 307, 309, 310, 311, 312, 316, 318, 319, 322, 324, 325, 326, 329, 330, 332, 335, 336, 337, 339, 340, 343, 346, 354, 361, 363, 367, 368, 370, 371, 373, 378, 379, 380, 382, 385, 386, 387, 388, 389, 390, 395, 396, 397, 398, 399, 401, 402, 406, 407, 408, 411, 416
du Chaillu 405
Dungeness 23, 72, 247
Dungeness Spit 23
Dunn, John 114
Duntze 225, 226
DuPont 7, 47, 121, 248, 279
du Pont Company 419
DuPont Creek 7
Durant, Thomas 417
Durham 425
Duwamish 2, 8, 15, 23, 24, 57, 72, 116, 237, 292, 335, 368

Duwamish and White River Valleys 2
Duwamish River 8, 24, 57, 116, 292, 368
Dwelling House 421

E

Eagle 37, 80, 104
earthquake 2, 3, 50, 55, 112, 421
Eaton 239, 369
Ebey 278, 285, 340, 345, 393, 398
Echo Prairie 315
Edgar 158, 199, 208, 220, 221, 228, 234, 316, 325
Edgar, John 208, 428
Edward Piper 108
Edwards 110, 153, 301, 384
Egyptian Pyramids 18
Ehoo 428
Eilowhallis 220
Eld Inlet 9, 161
Elee-ay-nay 114
Eliza 32, 37, 85, 247, 299
Eliza Spaulding 85
Elk Plain 11, 77, 105, 121, 195, 396, 430
England 4, 10, 18, 26, 33, 48, 49, 72, 74, 75, 82, 89, 91, 104, 116, 122, 124, 125, 127, 128, 131, 145, 152, 158, 173, 176, 185, 188, 200, 206, 211, 213, 215, 216, 225, 234, 242, 248, 264, 268, 270, 274, 282, 283, 285, 297, 299, 316, 337, 345, 382, 388, 408, 410, 429
English 4, 6, 16, 18, 19, 27, 31, 32, 42, 43, 44, 48, 53, 59, 66, 69, 74, 75, 114, 124, 125, 126, 128, 132, 133, 134, 151, 154, 156, 159, 165, 168, 174, 175, 190, 194, 195, 199, 207, 211, 215, 216, 225, 226, 238, 255, 268, 277, 283, 285, 291, 305, 317, 349, 358, 366, 371, 377, 390, 403, 409, 416
English explorers 4
Episcopal 166, 327, 328, 406
Espy 346
Esquimalt Harbor 225, 425
Europeans, first 3
European ix, 5, 10, 16, 17, 18, 20, 21, 22, 34, 38, 42, 48, 55, 68, 79, 80, 81, 86, 90, 93, 104, 125, 130, 138, 146, 154, 161, 166, 174, 176, 217, 218, 222, 224, 271, 339, 383
Europeans 7, 10, 13, 17, 21, 22, 26, 27, 30, 38, 41, 45, 55, 117, 215, 254, 283

European traders 34
Evans 381
Everett, John 247
Exact 220, 293, 306, 335
explorers 3, 5, 16, 17, 24, 61, 131, 161

F

Factor 62, 63, 69, 70, 72, 74, 86, 87, 105, 120, 121, 125, 137, 145, 176, 187, 209, 229, 251, 252, 254, 257, 260, 270, 273, 274, 277, 280, 281, 288, 337, 338, 358, 359, 394, 396, 397, 407, 408, 420
Falls of the Willamette 28
Falmouth 291
Farms 105, 125, 126, 138, 152, 216, 218, 244, 251, 271, 285, 308, 332, 333, 424, 431
Farnham 134
Farron 69, 402
Father de la Sierra 3
Fay 281, 335
Federal Department of Indian Affairs 35
Felice Adventurer 4
Ferrelo, Bartlome 31
Ferry Museum 420
Fiande 429
Fiander 346, 389, 396
Fiandre 340, 354
Fidalgo, Salvador 4
Fillmore 266, 319
Finlay Forks 425
Finlay River 427
Finlayson 74, 108, 174, 240, 257, 258, 358, 398
First American vi
First Artillery Regiment 257
First Creek 8
first immigrant home and lumber mill 8
First Nations 188, 285
First People 3, 4, 6, 10, 13, 21, 43, 44, 209, 238, 300, 382
Fisgaurd 226, 227, 229
Fisguard 198
fishing station 9, 338
fish spawning rivers 2
Flett 173, 175, 206, 279, 335
Flying Fish 164
Forrest, Charles 216, 217, 281, 293, 307
Fort vii, ix, xi, 7, 9, 11, 19, 22, 23,

24, 27, 28, 32, 33, 34, 37, 38, 39, 40, 42, 43, 44, 45, 47, 48, 49, 51, 52, 53, 54, 55, 56, 57, 58, 59, 60, 62, 63, 64, 65, 68, 69, 70, 71, 72, 73, 74, 75, 76, 77, 78, 79, 80, 81, 82, 83, 85, 86, 87, 88, 89, 90, 91, 93, 95, 96, 97, 98, 99, 100, 101, 102, 103, 104, 105, 106, 107, 111, 112, 113, 114, 116, 117, 118, 120, 121, 124, 126, 127, 128, 130, 131, 132, 133, 134, 135, 136, 137, 138, 139, 141, 142, 143, 144, 145, 146, 153, 154, 155, 156, 157, 158, 159, 160, 163, 164, 165, 166, 172, 173, 174, 175, 176, 177, 178, 179, 181, 182, 183, 185, 186, 187, 188, 189, 190, 191, 192, 194, 195, 197, 198, 199, 200, 202, 203, 205, 206, 208, 209, 211, 215, 216, 217, 218, 219, 220, 221, 222, 223, 224, 225, 226, 227, 228, 229, 231, 232, 233, 234, 236, 237, 238, 239, 240, 241, 242, 243, 246, 247, 248, 249, 250, 251, 252, 254, 255, 256, 257, 258, 259, 260, 261, 264, 265, 266, 267, 268, 269, 270, 271, 272, 273, 274, 275, 276, 277, 279, 280, 281, 282, 283, 286, 287, 288, 290, 291, 292, 293, 294, 300, 301, 303, 304, 305, 306, 307, 308, 309, 310, 311, 312, 316, 317, 319, 320, 322, 323, 324, 325, 328, 329, 330, 331, 332, 333, 334, 335, 336, 337, 338, 339, 340, 344, 345, 346, 347, 348, 350, 352, 353, 354, 355, 358, 359, 360, 361, 362, 363, 364, 365, 366, 367, 368, 369, 370, 371, 372, 375, 376, 377, 378, 379, 380, 382, 383, 384, 385, 386, 387, 388, 389, 390, 391, 394, 396, 397, 398, 399, 401, 402, 406, 407, 408, 411, 413, 414, 417, 418, 419, 420, 421, 423, 424, 425, 426, 427, 428, 429, 430, 431
Fort Astoria 32, 33, 34, 39, 120, 121, 425
Fort Berens 424
Fort Boise 117, 222
Fort Camosun & Fort Albert 427
Fort Colvile 55, 222, 363
Fort Colville 34
Fort George 22, 121, 164, 216, 222, 425
Fort Hall 141, 222
Fort Kamloops 424
Fort Lake 11
Fort Langley 24, 27, 38, 40, 48, 49, 56, 71, 72, 75, 86, 87, 89, 104, 126, 135, 137, 232, 268, 354, 425
Fort Laramie 65
Fort Lewis 9, 105
Fort Nez Perce 33
Fort Nisqually vii, ix, xi, 7, 24, 25, 39, 43, 48, 51, 62, 64, 70, 72, 73, 75, 76, 80, 81, 82, 86, 87, 95, 98, 101, 104, 106, 111, 113, 121, 124, 126, 127, 128, 130, 131, 134, 135, 136, 137, 143, 144, 145, 155, 156, 160, 164, 176, 182, 187, 189, 190, 206, 209, 211, 218, 220, 221, 229, 232, 235, 237, 238, 239, 240, 241, 242, 246, 247, 252, 260, 267, 268, 270, 275, 281, 287, 292, 294, 304, 305, 306, 309, 323, 330, 338, 345, 352, 353, 354, 355, 361, 362, 371, 382, 387, 390, 397, 407, 413, 417, 419, 420, 426, 428, 429, 430
Fort Okanogan 32, 33, 34, 222, 426
Fort Pend d'Oreille 426
Fort Ross 191, 192
Fort Simpson 48, 51, 64, 88, 93, 103, 104, 114, 135, 189, 190, 340, 426
Fort Spokane 33
Fort Steilacoom vii, 225, 251, 317, 348, 359, 361, 369, 385, 397, 398, 406, 417
Fort Stikeen 177
Fort Umpqua 98, 222
Fort Vancouver 22, 24, 27, 28, 33, 34, 37, 76, 90, 93, 107, 120, 143, 177, 178, 188, 217, 220, 229, 236, 250, 251, 323, 362
Fort Walla Walla 33
Fort William 34, 39
Four Lakes 430
France 32, 281, 343, 382
Frances Lake 425
Franklin 235, 305, 312, 340, 351, 394
Fraser 24, 33, 40, 48, 49, 50, 52, 64, 86, 89, 124, 135, 185, 187, 189, 190, 216, 263, 271, 281, 358, 403, 408, 409, 410, 419, 424, 425, 427
Fraser Lake 425
Fraser River 24, 33, 40, 48, 86, 271, 403, 408, 410, 424, 425, 427
French 19, 22, 25, 27, 30, 32, 37, 42, 43, 48, 66, 68, 69, 70, 114, 131, 133, 137, 139, 174, 175, 185, 216, 217, 233, 272, 286, 362, 363, 365, 366, 377, 383, 385, 402, 409
French Canadian 25
Frenchman's Prairie 427
French voyageurs 22
Freund 285
Friday Harbor 338
Frontier Forts 424
Ft. Wrangell 426
fur actions 18
fur ships 18
Fur Trade Monopoly 20
fur trade post 19, 22, 144, 172, 189, 222, 233, 251, 306, 333
Fur Trader 14, 38, 52, 63, 68, 89, 135, 187, 189
fur traders vi, 10, 21, 22, 25, 27, 31, 34, 37, 38, 41, 42, 59, 64, 73, 76, 77, 88, 127, 130, 131, 136, 141, 146, 151, 154, 174, 190, 192, 264, 286, 365, 367
Fur Trading Company 284

G
Gale 401
Gallagher's Gulch 298, 299
Gamble 286
Ganges 409
Ganymede 48, 59, 104, 216, 401
Garfield, James 218
Gentleman 48, 53, 55, 56, 57, 60, 66, 68, 73, 89, 138, 143, 199, 309
geologic record 2
George Colvocoresses 161
George Emory 287, 330
George Simpson 19, 22, 66, 74, 87, 95, 105, 123, 137, 145, 172, 176, 210, 264, 280, 413, 416
George W. Emory 299
Georgiana 292, 302
Gibbs 300, 349
Gig Harbor 8, 9, 15
Gitwanggak 425
Glasgow 48, 55, 205, 237, 254, 259, 260, 261, 270, 273, 275, 276, 277, 279, 319, 372
Glen Cove 8
Glenora Post 425
Global climate 2
Gobar 131, 216
Gog-le-hi-te 300
Gohome 249, 252, 293, 330, 336,

[438]

Index

359, 401, 429
Goldsboro 288, 312
Gonzales, Don Juan 3
Goodwin 402
Gordon 242, 243, 396
Gordon's Lake 430
Gorisch 299
Gorridge 358, 359
Gosnell 326
Governor vi, 18, 19, 22, 66, 87, 95, 105, 120, 123, 124, 126, 172, 203, 211, 217, 220, 228, 250, 252, 255, 256, 265, 270, 271, 277, 280, 281, 282, 284, 333, 337, 340, 345, 348, 349, 351, 353, 357, 368, 369, 370, 372, 377, 378, 380, 381, 391, 393, 394, 410, 411, 413, 416
Governor Simpson vi
Governor Stevens 351
Grahame 425
Grainger, Charles 399
Granary 267, 268, 382, 383, 421
Grand Prairie 430
Gravelle 311, 377
Gravell's 430
Gray, Robert 4, 5, 16, 23, 31, 32, 120, 164
Gray's Harbor 12, 24, 30, 32, 160, 161
Gray, W. H. 183
Great Britain 33, 218
Great Emigration 188
Greater Tacoma Community Foundation 420
Green River villages 8
Greenwater River 16
Gregg 402
Greig 371, 395
Grenville Bay (Grays Harbor) 3
Grieg 387, 388, 389, 430
Griffin 319, 338, 345, 372, 410
Guillion 336
Gullion 358
Gunn 114
Gwakany 353, 384
Gwakkany 384
gwiduhg 11
Gwinap 387
G.W. Kendal 305, 323

H

Haden 257, 271, 282, 288, 293, 295, 306, 337
Hadley 331, 394, 395

Hadley's 430
Hagwilget 425
Haida 4, 88, 93, 302, 305
Halket 425
Hall 115, 141, 157, 231, 287, 304, 306, 317, 326, 363, 421
Hamilton 128
Hammatt 74
Hammersley Inlet 9, 326
Hancock 235, 424
Hanson, Ackerman & Co 348
Harber 337, 346, 347, 348, 354
Hardee's 1855 Manual 360
Harding 407
Harney 406, 411
Haro Strait 410
Harpooner 255, 257
Hastings 288
Hatal 429
Hathaway 171, 172, 257
Haus 114
Hawaiian Islands 34
Hawaiians 34, 42, 43
Hawkins 348
Hays 299, 371
Hazelton 425, 426
Hazelton Post 425
HBC (Hudson's Bay Company) vi, xi, xii, 7, 18, 19, 21, 22, 24, 25, 26, 27, 28, 33, 34, 37, 38, 39, 41, 42, 43, 44, 49, 52, 53, 56, 57, 58, 59, 61, 62, 63, 64, 66, 68, 69, 70, 71, 72, 73, 74, 77, 78, 79, 80, 81, 82, 85, 86, 87, 88, 89, 91, 93, 95, 97, 98, 99, 100, 101, 104, 105, 106, 107, 108, 111, 114, 116, 117, 118, 120, 121, 122, 123, 124, 125, 126, 127, 131, 133, 134, 136, 137, 138, 139, 141, 143, 144, 145, 146, 151, 153, 154, 155, 158, 159, 164, 166, 171, 172, 173, 174, 175, 176, 177, 178, 181, 183, 184, 185, 186, 188, 189, 190, 192, 196, 197, 198, 199, 202, 205, 206, 207, 208, 210, 215, 216, 217, 218, 219, 221, 222, 223, 228, 232, 233, 234, 236, 237, 238, 242, 257, 258, 259, 263, 264, 265, 271, 272, 276, 280, 281, 282, 286, 287, 291, 302, 303, 310, 311, 316, 317, 318, 319, 322, 323, 330, 335, 337, 338, 343, 344, 345, 352, 353, 362, 363, 370, 373, 375, 377, 380, 383, 384, 386, 394, 396, 402, 406, 407, 408, 409, 410, 413, 415, 417, 418, 428, 429

HBC blankets 26
HBC Board of Governors 33
HBC Columbia Department Board of Management 33
HBC Servants at Fort Nisqually 428
H. C. Page 348
Heath vi, 157, 158, 197, 198, 199, 202, 206, 208, 209, 221, 224, 225, 227, 238, 239, 242, 248, 251, 256, 257, 261, 270
Heatherly's 430
Heath's 198, 199, 239, 248, 256, 270, 430
Heceta, Bruno 31
Helmcken 348, 361
Henderson Inlet 8
Henrietta Pillefier 82
Herald 225, 241, 269, 378, 382, 402, 403, 406
Herea 69
Heritage Site 424
Her Majesty the Queen xii
Heron 55, 56, 57, 69, 73
Herron 49, 50, 54, 55, 56, 57, 58, 59, 62, 63, 70, 71, 72, 73, 79, 85, 86, 95, 146
Herschel Island Post 425
Hezeta 3, 4, 5
Hezeta, Bruno 3
Hill 11, 77, 134, 188, 191, 251, 273, 280, 299, 317, 326, 335, 353, 409
Hill, Captain 257, 265, 270, 271, 272, 273
Hill, Captain Bennett H. 257
Hinderwell 274, 275
HMS Driver 271
HMS Inconstant 251
H.M.S. Pinafore 216
Hoh 3
Holland 345
Holth-nuh-mish 113
Home 9, 90, 93, 115, 243, 407, 408, 409
home school method 15
Honolulu 306, 307, 308
Hood Canal 29, 34, 50, 159, 164, 376
Hope Post 425
Horn Creek 9
Horses 15, 82, 211, 227, 323, 431
Howard 299, 331
Hudson xi, xii, 5, 18, 19, 20, 22, 23, 24, 25, 30, 33, 34, 37, 39, 42, 44,

[439]

47, 48, 49, 58, 66, 73, 93, 106, 110, 122, 123, 124, 126, 127, 130, 138, 142, 153, 170, 171, 172, 174, 176, 183, 186, 187, 188, 190, 197, 200, 206, 208, 210, 212, 213, 219, 223, 228, 243, 260, 264, 277, 279, 286, 291, 297, 304, 315, 319, 322, 332, 334, 340, 343, 362, 387, 388, 396, 402, 406, 407, 408, 411, 416, 417, 424, 425

Hudson's Bay Company xi, xii, 5, 18, 19, 20, 22, 23, 24, 25, 30, 33, 34, 37, 39, 44, 47, 48, 49, 58, 66, 73, 93, 106, 122, 123, 124, 126, 127, 138, 142, 153, 171, 172, 173, 174, 176, 183, 186, 187, 188, 190, 206, 208, 210, 212, 213, 219, 228, 260, 264, 277, 279, 286, 291, 297, 319, 322, 332, 334, 340, 343, 362, 387, 396, 402, 406, 407, 408, 411, 416, 417, 424

Hudson's Bay Fur Trade Horse Brigade 110

Huggins vii, 156, 248, 249, 272, 275, 276, 277, 279, 287, 288, 290, 293, 294, 297, 298, 305, 306, 324, 325, 336, 343, 346, 347, 353, 358, 359, 361, 362, 363, 365, 366, 367, 370, 371, 383, 384, 387, 388, 389, 396, 397, 402, 407, 408, 410, 411, 413, 417, 418, 419, 429

Huggins, Edward 429

Hunter 324, 325, 428

Huptickynum 251

Hyqua 101

I

Ice Age glacier 1

Idaho 33, 37, 141, 185, 215, 246, 402

Independence Day 165, 166, 167, 309, 333, 406, 407, 414

Indian vii, 2, 3, 5, 8, 17, 21, 22, 24, 25, 26, 27, 35, 42, 43, 50, 52, 57, 58, 59, 63, 65, 66, 68, 69, 71, 73, 75, 77, 79, 80, 81, 82, 85, 86, 87, 88, 89, 91, 93, 95, 96, 97, 99, 100, 101, 102, 103, 105, 111, 112, 114, 115, 116, 117, 120, 125, 127, 128, 130, 131, 133, 134, 137, 138, 146, 151, 152, 157, 161, 164, 167, 172, 174, 175, 179, 181, 183, 185, 187, 189, 190, 197, 198, 199, 200, 203, 207, 208, 209, 215, 216, 217, 218, 222, 223, 224, 226, 227, 232, 234, 236, 238, 240, 242, 243, 244, 248, 254, 255, 256, 257, 258, 265, 266, 267, 271, 273, 274, 276, 277, 279, 282, 287, 291, 294, 297, 299, 300, 303, 305, 306, 308, 309, 310, 315, 320, 321, 322, 324, 325, 326, 328, 331, 332, 335, 336, 337, 338, 339, 348, 349, 350, 351, 352, 354, 357, 358, 359, 363, 367, 368, 369, 370, 372, 373, 375, 376, 377, 378, 379, 380, 381, 384, 386, 388, 389, 390, 393, 394, 398, 399, 401, 403, 417

Indian Agent 335, 375, 376

Indian Bob 378, 381

Indian fur traders 22

Indians vii, 5, 6, 9, 10, 12, 16, 17, 21, 23, 24, 25, 26, 28, 37, 38, 41, 42, 43, 44, 50, 51, 52, 54, 56, 57, 58, 59, 60, 61, 62, 63, 68, 70, 73, 75, 77, 78, 79, 80, 81, 82, 86, 88, 93, 95, 97, 98, 99, 100, 101, 103, 104, 110, 112, 113, 115, 117, 118, 123, 130, 131, 132, 134, 137, 139, 144, 151, 158, 159, 161, 164, 165, 166, 167, 168, 171, 174, 175, 183, 185, 187, 194, 198, 199, 200, 202, 203, 207, 208, 209, 211, 215, 216, 222, 223, 224, 232, 235, 236, 237, 238, 239, 240, 241, 244, 248, 249, 250, 252, 254, 255, 256, 258, 260, 265, 269, 272, 273, 274, 275, 276, 277, 278, 279, 286, 288, 291, 293, 298, 300, 302, 305, 306, 308, 310, 311, 316, 320, 323, 326, 329, 331, 334, 335, 338, 339, 340, 348, 349, 350, 351, 352, 353, 357, 359, 361, 362, 363, 364, 365, 367, 368, 369, 370, 371, 372, 373, 375, 376, 377, 378, 379, 380, 381, 382, 390, 391, 393, 396, 401, 403, 414, 415, 426, 428, 429, 431

Indian Treaty War vii

Indian War 369, 399

Inez 260, 261

Inside Passage 12, 89, 145, 177, 225

International Boundary Treaty 219, 225, 372

Invincible 277

Iroquois 42, 43, 68, 100, 114, 130, 131, 133, 365, 366

Isabel 104, 321

Isabella 85, 104, 188, 208

J

Jackson 37, 47, 65, 81, 107, 157, 213, 323, 332

Jackson, President 37, 47, 65, 108

James Douglas 82, 95, 108, 125, 137, 145, 176, 186, 187, 188, 209, 217, 220, 277, 281, 292, 293, 310, 353, 354, 411

Japanese written records 2

Jason Lee 79, 82, 127, 128, 135, 147, 148, 170, 181, 182, 194

Jayoul 293

JBLM 9, 41, 155, 242 Jesuit 98, 131

Job Carr 128, 299, 417

John Davis 309

John Flett 173, 175, 335

John Jacob Astor 17, 32, 33, 39, 120

John McKee 73, 75

John McLoughlin 22, 28, 34, 79, 90, 95, 98, 105, 108, 111, 120, 122, 124, 145, 174, 178, 187, 188, 189, 194, 219, 271, 280, 394

Johnson, Carol Ann ix

Joint Commission 177, 322, 415, 416

Joint Commission Claims 322

Joint International Commission 417

Joint Occupancy Treaty of 1818 18, 28, 34, 128

Joint Occupancy Treaty of 1821 28

Joint Occupation Agreement 415

Jolie Prairie 22

Jollibois 277, 292

Joseph Heath 157, 197

Journal of Occurrences 24, 52, 55, 72, 77, 99, 134, 145, 148, 209, 277, 282, 288, 293, 323, 336, 347, 362, 402, 411, 430

Juan de Fuca 31, 211

Judson 299, 326

Julia 411

"Junta" government 378

Jupiter 417

K

Kachet 58

Kahannui 255, 330, 337, 428

Kahili 255

Kahimin's 430

Ka'I 114

Kaiser Wilhelm I 411, 415

Kake 286, 398

Kalama 248, 252, 255, 261, 263, 271, 343, 344, 401

Index

Kalama, Kanaka 429
Kamloops 425, 427
Kanaka 34, 43, 55, 66, 69, 70, 75, 330, 338, 343, 344, 353, 358
Kanakas 43, 54, 68, 175, 176, 216, 233, 286, 343, 344, 367, 370
Kautz 378, 397, 399
Keava 255
Keavahaccow 428, 429
Keavakow, Kanaka 429
Keave'haccow 261, 293, 302, 305, 354, 358, 359, 401
Keh-cuis-duts 9
Kellogg 285, 398, 403
Kendrick, John 31
Kennedy 358, 380, 389, 397, 401
Kennewick Man 1
Kennic 348
Kershner 299
Kettle Falls 33, 424
Kewwa 271
Kigarney 95, 103
Kilmaurs 424
King Charles xii, 18
King, William Rufus 340
Kisiox Valley 426
Kitanga 425
Kitchen Garden 430
Kittson 69, 73, 74, 76, 77, 78, 79, 80, 81, 82, 86, 95, 96, 97, 99, 100, 101, 102, 103, 104, 105, 111, 112, 113, 115, 116, 117, 118, 121, 126, 127, 128, 130, 132, 134, 136, 138, 139, 143, 144, 255, 407
Kittson, Alexander 85
Kitwanga Post 425
Klallune 113
Klickitats 238
Kli-ki-tat 190
Klikitat 339
Kootemai Post 222
Kootenay 98, 425, 427
Kooteney Post 143
Kul-Kul-eh 105
Kul-kul-hee 402
Kull-kullee 396
Kuphai 336, 344
Kwod-kwool-Mashel Creek 7
Kyumpt Harbour 95

L

laborers 43, 48, 57, 59, 63, 66, 68, 77, 116, 117, 137, 188, 216, 218, 221, 273, 274, 284, 305, 324, 371, 384, 401, 409
Labouchere 416
Lachelet 59, 60
La Doux, Louis 428
Lady Washington 31
La Fleur 114
Laframboise 110, 154
Lagace 384
La Gacey, Perish 429
La Grande Bish 80
La-ha-let 62, 70, 95, 113, 114
Lahalet 30, 61, 224, 238, 239, 240, 249, 250, 265, 266
La-Ha-Let 77, 85, 86, 101
Laird River 424, 425, 426
Lake Babine 424
Lake Charlton 11
Lake Kamloops 425
Lake Squally 220
Lake Steilacoom Grist Mill 399
Laketon Post 425
Lake Windermere 425
Lambert 221
Lamie 240, 290
land ceded 402
Land Claims 194, 209, 267, 335
Lane 250, 252, 255, 256, 265, 270, 321, 338
Lane, Joseph 246, 319
Langford 285
Langley 24, 72, 73, 75, 101, 221, 284, 425
La Pierre's Post 425
Lapoitre 290
Large Potato Patch 430
Large Store 268, 421
Lashima 60
Latour 116, 221, 222, 224, 385
Latour, Louis 114, 325, 354
Lattie 257
Lausanne 142, 150, 170
Leafy Cape 3
Leclair 277
Lee, Jason Reverend 37, 65, 79, 107, 120, 121, 135, 144, 147, 150, 170, 182, 194, 264
Legace 347, 354, 402
Legacie 402
Legg 306, 336, 346, 347, 354, 358, 429
Legg, William 347

LeGrarde, Joseph 429
Leonora 305
Le Pain 103, 114, 116
Leschi vii, 7, 114, 126, 161, 202, 331, 349, 350, 352, 369, 371, 372, 375, 376, 377, 394, 398, 399, 406
Le Shuou 430
Leslie 121, 122, 127, 128, 131, 133, 134, 136, 143, 146, 147, 148, 149, 206
Leslie, Reverend David 120, 122, 127, 147, 206
Lewgace 346
Lewis xii, 9, 11, 17, 30, 32, 37, 39, 41, 77, 100, 105, 115, 120, 121, 128, 143, 155, 156, 157, 166, 242, 246, 250, 263, 280, 301, 309, 312, 333, 350
Lewis, Meriwether 17, 32
Lhussich 221
Lieutenant 143, 203, 241, 306, 317, 328, 369, 397
Lighter 145
Lilooet 424
Lincoln 65, 122, 184, 299, 405, 416
Linklater, Thomas 239, 243, 248, 255, 260, 270, 292, 325, 428, 429
Little Post 425
Living History Museum ix, 42, 71, 81, 155, 186, 267, 282, 283, 362, 382, 384, 402, 419, 420, 421, 426
Living History program 420
Llama 44, 74, 75, 76, 86, 87, 88, 89, 93, 103, 104, 108
Logan 323
London x, 16, 18, 19, 26, 33, 41, 43, 48, 49, 59, 73, 89, 90, 95, 102, 105, 107, 113, 120, 122, 123, 126, 130, 137, 138, 145, 152, 154, 155, 173, 176, 178, 185, 187, 189, 195, 197, 210, 212, 213, 215, 217, 218, 226, 228, 242, 243, 248, 252, 263, 268, 277, 281, 283, 285, 288, 290, 295, 306, 308, 317, 319, 323, 324, 340, 345, 354, 357, 361, 363, 365, 367, 376, 382, 385, 388, 396, 407, 408, 413, 419
long house 11, 300
longhouses 8, 13, 38, 300
Longmire 15, 297, 312, 313, 316, 320, 326, 359
Longmire Trail 15
Lopez 337
Loriot 107, 108

[441]

Louisiana Territory 32
Louis La Tour 428
Louwala-Clough 163
Low 292, 332, 335
Lowe 254, 255, 323, 328, 390
Lowie, Kanaka 429
Low, Jacob 428
Lowry 280
Luar 343
Lucier 221, 222
Lughkynum 78
Lushootseed 3, 7, 11, 30, 48

M
MacArthur 254
MacDonald 300, 363, 364, 365, 428
MacDonald, Murdo 428
MacKenzie 408
Macleod, John 428
Macleod's 430
Macrae, John 223
Mad Hatters 10, 263
Mahon 272, 306, 430
Maire 303
Makah 3, 4, 71, 75, 80, 302
Mallard Hallow 220, 222
Maloney 375
Manifest Destiny 5, 39, 105, 121, 165, 166, 170, 174, 188, 207, 220, 235
Mannock 354
Manson 281, 425
Manson Creek 425
Maple 292
Margaret Smith 146
Maroon Lake 430
Martinez, Estevan 32
Mary Dare 257, 294, 303, 304, 307, 312, 322, 324
Mashel 7, 11, 12, 13, 15, 38
Mashel and Nisqually Rivers 7, 13
Mashel River 38
Mason 8, 30, 291, 340, 351, 369
Mason Creek 8
Massachusetts 37, 59, 65, 134, 146, 252, 276, 286, 317, 395, 398, 406, 410
material culture 5, 14
Maxon 378, 380, 381, 382
Maxon's Mounted Rifle Company 379, 380, 382
Maynard 326, 333

McAllister Creek 7
McAllister 252, 280, 330, 349, 369
McCaw 298, 397
McClellan 340
McCleod 224, 258, 290, 394
McCormick, Cyrus 35, 65
McDame Creek Post 425
McDonald 14, 38, 40, 48, 49, 50, 52, 53, 54, 55, 73, 75, 82, 95, 116, 144, 206, 223, 281, 363, 366, 367, 368, 407
McDonald, Archibald 38, 47, 50, 55, 73, 428
McFadden 384, 385
McGinnis, Melissa 420
McIsaac 358
McKay 56, 257, 258
McKenzie, Alexander 34, 78, 424
McKibben 397
McKie 50, 55, 56
McLeod 63, 154, 158, 221, 228, 232, 240, 244, 255, 256, 288, 384, 388, 389, 408, 425
McLoed 221, 377, 425
McLoughlin 22, 25, 28, 34, 37, 38, 44, 48, 51, 53, 64, 65, 73, 74, 75, 82, 87, 88, 90, 95, 106, 107, 108, 111, 120, 121, 122, 124, 125, 138, 139, 165, 173, 177, 178, 182, 189, 194, 199, 217, 219, 225, 232, 280, 281, 292, 426
McLoughlin, John 34
McMillan, James 24
McMullin 393, 394
McNeill vi, 44, 71, 74, 75, 82, 86, 87, 88, 89, 93, 95, 103, 104, 108, 111, 114, 118, 145, 146, 157, 158, 163, 177, 184, 197, 251, 281, 375, 395
McPhail 293, 301, 305, 306, 308, 312, 323, 386, 429
Meares, John 4, 31
Measles 5, 414
Medicine Creek 7, 9, 126, 349, 350, 351, 355, 370, 403
Medicine Creek Treaty 7, 9, 126, 350, 351, 370, 403
Meek 141, 236, 252, 282
Meeker, Ezra 202, 228, 251, 321, 331, 350, 371, 377, 378
Meridian 286
Methodist 37, 38, 65, 79, 82, 86, 107, 108, 120, 121, 122, 127, 128, 130, 131, 132, 133, 134, 135, 136, 138, 142, 143, 144, 146, 148, 149, 150, 151, 157, 159, 164, 165, 166, 170, 171, 174, 179, 181, 182, 184, 185, 188, 189, 192, 194, 195, 198, 199, 206, 216, 217, 226, 235, 237, 248, 260, 264, 275, 309, 326, 327, 328, 329, 348, 370, 395, 406, 407
Methodist Church 127, 131, 132, 171, 181, 184, 206, 237, 326, 327, 328, 329
Methodist Mission 37, 65, 79, 82, 107, 108, 120, 121, 122, 127, 128, 130, 133, 135, 136, 143, 146, 149, 150, 151, 157, 165, 170, 171, 174, 179, 181, 182, 184, 189, 192, 194, 206, 216, 226, 237, 248, 260, 275, 309, 327, 407
Methodist Missionaries 37, 86, 107, 121, 135, 142, 143, 144, 150, 157, 181, 185, 188, 194, 198, 199, 206, 207, 248
Methodists 122, 127, 128, 130, 131, 132, 133, 134, 149, 151, 157, 165, 173, 174, 175, 183, 194, 195, 206, 287, 406
Metís 42, 43, 47, 68, 69, 70, 95, 125, 157, 175, 185, 264, 280, 286, 358, 366, 377, 402
Metro Parks 282, 383, 420, 421
Milbanke 64, 87, 88, 93, 95
Milbanke Sound 87, 93
Military Post 410
Military Road 315, 326, 359, 378, 382, 409
Millar's Lake 220, 221
Mill Creek Treaty 357
Miller 294
Minter Creek 8
Mission Plain (American Methodist) 430
Missions 47, 122, 130, 135, 166, 171, 182, 183, 194, 217, 235
Mitchell 50, 52, 63, 135, 354, 409
Mitsuckwie 391, 396
Mit-suk-we 7
Mit-suk-wie (Medicine) Creek 9
Moar 358
Moberly River 426
Modeste 131, 205, 216, 225, 226
Molock House 430
Montgomery 155, 221, 223, 226, 228, 308, 336, 340, 377, 378, 379, 380, 381, 429, 430
Montgomery, John 155, 158, 208, 209, 222, 258, 290, 316, 325,

[442]

Index

358, 371, 378, 389, 428
Monticello 317, 333
Morey Creek 280
Morice 255, 257, 258
Mormon militiamen 398
Morrison 430
Morse, Reverend William B. 326
Moses 287, 302, 303, 304, 309, 312, 399
Mosher 260, 261
Mosquito Fleet 354
Moss 340
Mouat 305, 312, 416
Mound Prairie 430
Mounted Volunteers 380
Mount Hood 284
Mount Olympus 3, 31, 160
Mount Rainier 2, 12, 16, 61, 62, 77, 163, 280
Mount Rainier collapsed 2
Mount Sierra de Santa Rosalia 31
Mount Tahoma 42, 62, 335
Mour 358, 388
Mowat 100, 103, 386
Mowatt 257, 258
Mr. Lewis 155, 255
Mt Olympus 31
Mt. Rainier xi, 16, 30, 59, 63, 163, 192
Mt. St. Helens 163, 316
Muck 7, 11, 12, 15, 121, 156, 195, 198, 220, 227, 228, 255, 258, 270, 279, 307, 315, 324, 325, 339, 346, 347, 354, 369, 370, 372, 377, 378, 384, 387, 396, 402, 408
Muck Creek 12
Muckleshoot 8, 15, 25, 232, 378
Muckleshoot People 8
Muck Station (House) 430
Mud Bay 8, 24
Muir 376
Munro 396
Murdock 221, 388
Murray 10, 38, 210, 274, 377, 411, 428
Murray Creek 10
Myak 401

N

Naches 15, 21, 313, 315, 316, 320, 321, 339, 359, 362, 368
Naches Pass 15
Naches River 16
Naches Trail 21, 313, 315, 316, 321
Nahcati 346
Nahwitti 95
Nanaimo Post 426
Napahay 428
Narcissa Whitman 85
Narrows 16, 337, 376, 419
Nass 74, 95, 426
Native American 4, 15, 153, 208, 300
Native Americans 3, 14, 16, 38, 42, 43, 58, 86, 101, 133, 151, 161, 166, 174, 207, 215, 232, 238, 263, 265, 285, 390, 402
Native people 16, 163, 191
Neah Bay 4, 32, 357
Neah Bay Treaty 357
Nechako and Fraser Rivers 425
Negroes 38
Nelson 221, 232, 248, 258, 312, 353, 426
Nelson, Matthew 428
Nereide 104, 108, 117
Neride 137
New Albion 4
New Archangel 89, 191, 203, 222
Newell 141
Newmarket vi, 170, 223, 238, 239, 243, 256, 259, 260, 266, 274, 277, 282
New Muck 105
Nez Perce 33, 37, 79, 85, 98, 134, 141, 152, 222, 363, 364, 368, 426
Nezsqually 30
Nishga 89
Nisqually vi, vii, ix, xi, 6, 7, 8, 9, 10, 11, 12, 13, 14, 15, 16, 17, 20, 21, 23, 24, 25, 26, 27, 28, 30, 33, 34, 38, 39, 40, 42, 43, 44, 47, 48, 49, 50, 51, 52, 53, 54, 55, 56, 57, 58, 59, 60, 61, 62, 63, 64, 68, 69, 70, 71, 72, 73, 74, 75, 76, 77, 78, 79, 80, 81, 82, 83, 85, 86, 87, 88, 89, 90, 91, 92, 93, 95, 96, 97, 98, 99, 100, 101, 102, 103, 104, 105, 106, 111, 113, 114, 116, 117, 118, 120, 121, 124, 125, 126, 127, 128, 130, 131, 132, 133, 134, 135, 136, 137, 138, 139, 143, 144, 145, 146, 150, 151, 152, 153, 154, 155, 156, 157, 158, 159, 160, 161, 163, 164, 165, 166, 168, 170, 171, 172, 173, 174, 175, 176, 177, 178, 179, 181, 182, 183, 184, 185, 186, 187, 189, 190, 192, 194, 195, 197, 198, 199, 200, 202, 203, 206, 208, 209, 210, 211, 215, 216, 218, 220, 221, 222, 223, 224, 225, 226, 227, 228, 229, 231, 232, 233, 234, 235, 237, 238, 239, 240, 241, 242, 243, 246, 247, 248, 249, 250, 251, 252, 254, 255, 256, 257, 258, 259, 260, 261, 264, 265, 266, 267, 268, 269, 270, 271, 272, 273, 274, 275, 276, 277, 278, 279, 280, 281, 282, 283, 284, 286, 287, 288, 291, 292, 293, 294, 298, 300, 301, 302, 303, 304, 305, 306, 307, 308, 309, 311, 312, 315, 316, 317, 318, 319, 322, 323, 324, 325, 326, 327, 328, 329, 330, 332, 333, 334, 336, 337, 338, 339, 340, 344, 345, 346, 347, 348, 349, 350, 351, 352, 353, 354, 355, 358, 359, 360, 361, 362, 363, 365, 366, 367, 368, 369, 370, 371, 372, 373, 375, 376, 377, 378, 379, 380, 381, 382, 383, 384, 385, 386, 387, 388, 389, 390, 391, 394, 395, 396, 397, 398, 399, 401, 402, 403, 407, 408, 410, 411, 413, 414, 417, 418, 419, 420, 421, 426
Nisqually Deity 15
Nisqually Express 101
Nisqually Farm 430
Nisqually Glacier 12
Nisqually House vi
Nisqually or Puyallup Tribes 10
Nisqually Reservation 350, 396
Nisqually River 7, 11, 17, 33, 38, 209, 221, 277, 302, 350, 390, 391, 414
Nisqually villages 12
No.119 417
Nootka 4, 31, 32
Norman Morrison 226, 248
North America 1, 2, 4, 5, 18, 19, 20, 27, 31, 48, 90, 152, 164, 176, 177, 183, 188, 203, 206, 210, 212, 215, 339, 384
North American Indian legends 2
Northern Battalion of Volunteers 379
Northover 291, 292, 305, 323, 340, 353, 429
North Pacific 4, 44, 88, 89, 90, 91, 136, 155, 157, 283
North West Company 19, 33, 143
North West Fur Company 32

[443]

Nuamish 58
Nuckalkat 60, 61
Nueva Galicia 3
NWC 95

O

Oak Harbor 285
O'Brien 281
Occurrences 24, 58, 71, 73, 79, 99, 113, 114, 116, 118, 128, 148, 220, 222, 223, 227, 229, 240, 257, 260, 263, 267, 311, 330, 337, 343, 353, 365, 386, 402, 430
Ogden 33, 74, 143, 154, 174, 177, 219, 236, 257, 270, 291
Ogden, Peter Skene 33
Oh-qua-mish 79
Ojibwa 82
Okanogan 1, 363, 426
Okanogan River 426
Old Fort 100, 211, 431
Old Fort Cemetery 100
Old Muck 105, 220
Old Spanaway 430
Old Town Tacoma 417
Olympia 7, 24, 91, 161, 207, 218, 223, 237, 266, 270, 274, 278, 286, 287, 288, 290, 291, 293, 294, 297, 301, 302, 303, 304, 307, 308, 309, 310, 311, 312, 315, 316, 317, 319, 321, 325, 326, 327, 329, 330, 332, 333, 336, 337, 340, 343, 344, 346, 354, 357, 360, 361, 362, 369, 370, 372, 378, 384, 386, 391, 393, 394, 395, 401, 405
Olympic plate 1
Oniare 358, 360
Orbit 272, 281, 288, 290
Orchard 50, 256, 261, 311
Oregon vi, vii, xii, 5, 14, 15, 18, 27, 28, 32, 33, 37, 39, 40, 41, 44, 45, 58, 65, 76, 79, 82, 89, 91, 98, 106, 107, 108, 111, 115, 117, 120, 121, 122, 127, 128, 130, 134, 135, 141, 142, 144, 146, 147, 148, 149, 151, 153, 155, 157, 159, 164, 166, 170, 171, 172, 174, 176, 177, 178, 179, 181, 182, 183, 184, 185, 186, 188, 189, 194, 199, 203, 205, 206, 209, 210, 211, 212, 213, 215, 217, 218, 219, 225, 228, 229, 235, 236, 237, 240, 243, 246, 258, 261, 265, 266, 272, 275, 277, 278, 281, 283, 284, 286, 290, 291, 297, 301, 312, 318, 319, 320, 326, 327, 331, 332, 335, 346, 352, 359, 362, 370, 373, 387, 393, 394, 405, 411, 414, 416, 417
Oregon Country 27, 33
Oregonian 333
Oregon Trail 15, 37, 65, 76, 122, 134, 142, 153, 174, 188, 219, 235, 236, 284, 297, 312, 320, 327, 346, 359, 393
Oriehl 339
"Orphan Tsunami" 2
Orting 8
Osborne 264, 271
Osceola Mudflow 2
Osoyoos Lake 426
Osoyoos Post 426
Otter 91, 365, 386, 388, 396, 407
Ouvré, Jean Baptiste 24, 38, 40, 41, 48, 56, 72, 120, 292
Ouvrie, William 428
Owhyhees 116
Owyhee 66, 114
Oyster Bay 8, 9
Oysterville 346

P

Pacific xii, 1, 2, 3, 4, 7, 8, 9, 12, 17, 18, 19, 27, 31, 32, 33, 39, 41, 51, 74, 85, 86, 87, 88, 89, 90, 91, 93, 104, 115, 127, 128, 136, 144, 161, 164, 168, 170, 172, 185, 188, 190, 197, 209, 211, 212, 215, 219, 220, 226, 235, 237, 257, 283, 284, 298, 312, 327, 339, 357, 382, 408, 416
Pacific Coast xii, 12
Pacific Fur Company 19, 32, 33
Pacific Northwest 1, 3, 4, 7, 41, 85, 93, 104, 115, 185, 197, 209, 211, 220, 235, 237, 283, 284, 327, 416
Pacific Ocean 2, 18, 27
Packard's 430
Packwood 239, 302, 387
Pagett 333
Paiute Warriors 398
Paleilah 77, 220, 224
Palmer 305, 335, 353
Pambrun 142
Pandora 225, 241, 242, 243
Paquet 221
Paragon 88
Parker 286, 308, 319
Parkinson 358
Parkland 9, 11, 77, 121, 269
Parrish 44, 209, 431
Parsnip and Peace Rivers 425
Patakynum 249, 250, 252, 255
Patchin 309
Patkamin 265
Pattison 353
Pauline Cove 425
Payallipa 58
Peacock 161, 164
Pearson 291
Peers 226, 361, 396, 425
Peers, Henry 216, 292
Pelly 123, 426
Pend d'Oreille River 426
Penn Cove 285
Percival 395
Perez 3, 31
Perry 426
Persea 311
Pettigrove 288
Peu-Peu-Mox-Mox 382
Pichette 366, 367
Pickett 411, 415
Pierce vii, xi, xii, 28, 30, 40, 77, 78, 100, 111, 137, 138, 166, 170, 181, 206, 208, 220, 242, 280, 286, 299, 309, 310, 312, 318, 319, 320, 322, 323, 325, 331, 332, 334, 335, 339, 340, 343, 344, 348, 351, 353, 355, 361, 372, 378, 387, 394, 395, 402, 406, 414, 418, 429
Pierce County vii, xi, xii, 28, 30, 40, 77, 78, 100, 111, 137, 166, 170, 181, 206, 208, 220, 242, 280, 286, 309, 310, 312, 318, 319, 320, 322, 331, 332, 334, 335, 339, 340, 343, 344, 348, 353, 355, 361, 372, 378, 387, 395, 402, 406, 414, 418
Pierre Jean de Smet 98
Pig War 411, 414, 415
Pillar Rock 222
Pin, Joseph 114
Pioneer and Democrat 343, 378
Pleiades 271, 272
Pleyades 409
Plomodon 25, 73, 77, 79, 80, 81, 82, 216, 238
Plomondon 25, 69, 100, 106, 131, 235, 415
Plummer 288, 309
Plumper 409
PNW 31, 74, 104, 278
Point Defiance 71, 81, 155, 267, 282, 300, 301, 382, 419, 420, 426
Point Elliott Treaty 357

Index

Point Fosdick 16
Point Grenville 31
Point-No-Point Treaty 357
Point Roberts 89
Polk 76, 211, 213, 215, 217, 220, 235, 237, 243, 246, 266
Pony Express Service 409
Pool-yal-lap 97
Pool-yal-laps 113
Pope 157, 323
Poplar Park 220
Porcupine (Rat) River 427
Porcupine River 426
Porpoise 157, 159, 163, 164
Portage Railway 284
Port Angeles 247, 287, 344
Porter's Landing 425
Port Gamble 323
Portland 8, 44, 106, 148, 209, 264, 320, 332, 335, 376, 405, 414, 415, 426
Port Townsend 287, 288, 327, 330, 344, 357, 405, 406
Port Townshend 50, 86
potlatch 14, 101, 349, 402
Potts 361
Prefontaine 416
Presbyterian 133, 134, 182, 185
President xii, 4, 35, 37, 47, 65, 76, 107, 108, 157, 170, 184, 211, 213, 217, 220, 228, 235, 237, 243, 246, 266, 311, 312, 319, 320, 323, 340, 351, 394, 405, 411, 416
President Andrew Jackson 35
President of the United States xii, 4, 311, 320, 340, 351, 394
Prince Albert 141, 145, 263, 354
Prince of Wales 413
Private Lake 380
Prosch 382, 406
Protestant 130, 183, 185, 416
PSAC vii, ix, xi, xii, 25, 81, 102, 105, 106, 111, 116, 117, 118, 120, 121, 122, 123, 124, 125, 126, 130, 136, 137, 138, 154, 155, 158, 159, 173, 175, 176, 177, 188, 190, 192, 195, 196, 198, 199, 202, 208, 209, 210, 215, 216, 218, 219, 220, 221, 222, 223, 225, 228, 234, 239, 240, 242, 243, 247, 248, 250, 254, 257, 267, 268, 270, 276, 280, 282, 284, 285, 287, 290, 298, 300, 301, 302, 305, 306, 311, 316, 318, 319, 322, 323, 324, 330,

331, 333, 336, 337, 339, 340, 346, 348, 352, 357, 360, 372, 373, 376, 377, 378, 379, 380, 383, 388, 389, 394, 396, 397, 401, 402, 407, 408, 409, 410, 411, 413, 416, 418, 419, 424
PSAC employees 429
Puget, Peter 16, 17, 24, 32, 42
Puget Sound ix, xi, xii, 1, 2, 3, 4, 5, 7, 10, 11, 12, 15, 16, 17, 21, 23, 24, 25, 27, 30, 32, 34, 38, 39, 40, 41, 45, 47, 49, 50, 51, 63, 72, 77, 78, 80, 81, 86, 90, 91, 97, 100, 102, 105, 108, 111, 117, 120, 121, 124, 126, 127, 128, 130, 131, 132, 135, 136, 137, 142, 143, 144, 145, 151, 152, 154, 157, 159, 161, 163, 164, 166, 169, 171, 172, 173, 174, 176, 177, 183, 185, 187, 189, 190, 191, 195, 197, 199, 202, 203, 206, 207, 208, 210, 211, 215, 219, 220, 222, 225, 226, 228, 232, 234, 237, 246, 247, 248, 251, 257, 258, 259, 260, 265, 267, 274, 276, 278, 279, 280, 283, 284, 286, 287, 290, 297, 299, 300, 306, 311, 313, 315, 316, 317, 319, 321, 322, 323, 324, 325, 326, 327, 328, 329, 331, 332, 333, 334, 337, 338, 340, 343, 345, 346, 347, 348, 349, 350, 351, 352, 353, 354, 355, 357, 359, 361, 362, 368, 369, 370, 371, 372, 375, 376, 377, 378, 379, 380, 382, 384, 385, 386, 387, 388, 390, 394, 396, 398, 399, 402, 406, 407, 408, 414, 415, 417, 418, 419
Puget Sound Agricultural Company xii, 39, 77, 81, 102, 105, 111, 126, 127, 135, 136, 137, 144, 171, 176, 177, 187, 189, 190, 191, 195, 208, 210, 219, 220, 222, 226, 228, 237, 247, 251, 260, 279, 280, 287, 300, 306, 322, 324, 325, 334, 337, 338, 340, 343, 345, 348, 352, 353, 361, 370, 372, 378, 385, 387, 390, 407, 408, 417, 418, 419
Puget Sound Agricultural Company Place Names 430
Puget Sound Indian War 368
Puget Sound waterways 12
Puget's Sound vi, 86, 123, 159, 165, 172, 176, 213, 218, 219, 272, 294, 395, 419
Puget's Sound Agricultural Company vi, 123, 176, 213, 395, 419
Punta de los Martires (Martyrs

Point) 3
Puyallup 7, 8, 9, 10, 11, 15, 23, 25, 40, 42, 54, 59, 60, 61, 62, 77, 78, 105, 144, 155, 220, 223, 232, 234, 242, 270, 278, 279, 298, 299, 300, 305, 312, 318, 321, 322, 326, 327, 331, 350, 359, 369, 371, 378, 403, 414
Puyallup-Nisqually group 10
Puyallup River 8, 11, 60, 300
Puyallup River Valley 15

Q

Quallawowt 258
Quartermaster 9, 257, 325, 377
Quartermaster Harbor 9
Quay-aye-mal 85
Queehen 339
Queen Charlotte Islands 12, 93, 302, 305, 306
Queimuth 391
Quenelle 100
Quesnel 424, 426
Quesnel River 426
Quiemuth 350
Quileute 3
Quillawowt 249
Quillhiamish 60, 61
Quilliash 62
Quimper, Manuel 32
Quinalt 3, 4
Qullawout 258
Qunasapam 224, 238

R

Rabasca 429
Rabbeson 235, 237, 333
Rada de Bucareli 3
Rampart House Post 426
Ramsey, Elaine Sigrid Perdue ix
Ramsey Endowment Fund 421
Rapjohn 384
Recollections 401, 402
Red Bluff 285, 403
Red House Plains 220
Red Pines 431
Red River 125, 172, 173, 174, 175, 177, 181, 182, 185, 197, 198, 206, 257, 335
Reed 397
Reilly 397
Reindeer River 425
Reiter, Darlyne ix

[445]

Relief 164
Rendall 56
Research Library 186, 421
Reservation 156, 350, 391, 399
Revilla, Don Cristobal 3
Revolutionary War 4
Rhodes 423
Richmond 142, 143, 144, 150, 157, 159, 165, 166, 167, 168, 169, 170, 171, 172, 173, 174, 177, 179, 181, 182, 183, 184, 194, 199, 206, 216, 407
Richmond, Francis 143, 179
Richmond, John P. 142, 151, 169, 170, 179, 184, 206
Richmond, Reverend Doctor John 166
Rielly 298
Rigney 280, 335
Riley 331
Rindale, James 50, 54
Robert Bruce 295
Roberts 89, 131, 216, 217, 244, 246, 250, 292, 326, 401, 402
Robillard 221
Roche Harbor 338
Rocky Mountains xii, 18, 27, 32, 134, 141, 181, 243
Roderick 174, 240, 257, 358
Roman Catholics 414
Rosario Strait 319
Rosario Straits 337, 338
Rosencrants 324
Ross 191, 199, 208, 209, 218, 231, 234, 238, 254, 256, 258, 260, 261, 281, 288, 293, 295, 303, 307, 308, 311, 340, 358, 429
Ross, Walter 428
Round Plain 220, 226, 242, 290
Royal Charter in 1670 xii
Runquist 299
Rupert 18, 19, 125, 426
Russia 18, 27, 104, 154, 191, 315, 343, 382, 416, 418
Russian xii, 17, 18, 19, 27, 39, 48, 74, 81, 89, 90, 120, 124, 126, 135, 136, 137, 138, 145, 154, 171, 172, 177, 178, 190, 191, 192, 195, 196, 203, 211, 213, 215, 217, 219, 222, 225, 284, 343, 359, 382, 408, 425
Russian Alaska 17
Russian America xii, 18, 136, 138
Russians 4, 18, 27, 40, 74, 124, 135, 136, 138, 176, 177, 190, 191, 192, 196, 203, 219, 247, 284, 315, 382, 414, 418
Russian Territory 27
Ryan 51, 300

S
Sacajawea 32
Sachal 161
Sacramento 91, 108, 110, 153, 154, 264, 271, 272, 376
Sagogetsta 114
Sagohanenchata 73
Sahaptin 7
Sa-heh-wamish 350
Sahehwamish 326
Sahehwamush or Sahewabsh 9
Sah-saps 113
sailing ship named Vancouver 34
Salana 382
Sales vii, 218, 298, 299, 309, 325, 330, 339, 340, 353, 390, 429
Salish 3, 6, 7, 14, 15, 30, 38, 41, 42, 79, 86, 98, 131, 249, 320, 349, 350, 357, 390
Salitat 370
Samuel Spaulding 85
Sanders 221
Sandwich Islanders 42, 43, 54, 66, 138, 163, 261, 367
San Francisco 90, 91, 108, 117, 137, 164, 172, 177, 186, 195, 229, 232, 235, 246, 259, 260, 264, 275, 278, 284, 290, 294, 295, 299, 303, 311, 319, 323, 335, 346, 348, 354, 390, 402, 405, 414, 416, 421
Sangster 218, 229, 234, 248, 255, 272, 273, 288
San Juan xii, 1, 32, 105, 138, 226, 319, 337, 338, 345, 357, 364, 371, 372, 408, 409, 410, 411, 414, 415, 424
San Juan Islands 1, 32, 138, 226, 319, 338, 345, 357, 371, 372, 408, 409, 414, 415
San Juan Strait 410
San Roque 3
Santiago 3
Sargent 336
Sarjent 297, 312, 321
Sastuc 195, 220, 233, 255, 300, 306, 309, 335, 339, 431
Sastuck 10
Sastuc Station 300

Satellite 409
Savage 306
Sawamish 9
Saw-aye-waw-mish 113
Saw-wham-mish 113
Scadgets 251, 252, 256, 257
Scarborough 188
Scarborough, James 114, 188, 281
Scock-se-nate-mish 113
Scott 231, 411
Scranton 354
Sea Gull 164
Seal Harbour 95
Seattle 16, 135, 147, 150, 202, 228, 263, 293, 298, 311, 318, 319, 321, 326, 327, 331, 333, 335, 346, 350, 371, 377, 382, 405, 416
Sechy 324
See-yat 112, 113
Segeass 250
Selquite Prairie 315
Sequalitchew vi, 6, 7, 11, 12, 13, 14, 16, 20, 21, 24, 25, 30, 33, 38, 40, 41, 47, 51, 57, 58, 62, 78, 86, 100, 116, 121, 127, 130, 138, 150, 157, 158, 159, 167, 170, 192, 194, 249, 260, 267, 275, 319, 324, 329, 330, 343, 366, 372, 385, 397, 426
Sequalitchew Creek 7, 11, 12, 24, 158, 159
Sequalitchew Lake 11
Sequalitchew village 11
Servants 43, 125, 428
settler 81, 100, 128, 155, 157, 173, 175, 188, 206, 207, 208, 210, 226, 240, 290, 293, 297, 299, 324, 328, 332, 338, 352, 358, 368, 393, 394, 395, 398, 401, 403, 417
settlers vi, vii, 10, 16, 24, 25, 43, 47, 79, 80, 82, 108, 111, 122, 125, 126, 127, 128, 142, 143, 165, 166, 171, 172, 173, 174, 175, 177, 181, 183, 188, 189, 190, 196, 197, 198, 202, 203, 205, 206, 207, 208, 210, 215, 216, 217, 218, 219, 222, 223, 228, 232, 234, 237, 238, 239, 246, 247, 248, 251, 252, 255, 257, 284, 285, 287, 291, 293, 298, 301, 310, 317, 320, 325, 326, 327, 333, 334, 335, 338, 339, 352, 355, 357, 368, 370, 372, 377, 378, 394, 395, 396, 408, 409, 415
Settlers squat vii
S'Gukgwas 396
S'Gukoguas 402

[446]

Index

S'Gukugwa-Muck Creek 7
S'Gukugwas 105
Shaaff 397
Shaff 397
Shaker Church 326
Shaman 69
shaman power 7
S'Hattol 358
Shaw 379, 380, 381, 396
Shazer 287
Shearer 239, 258
Shee Atka 191
Shelton at Munson Point 9
Shelton Inlet 8, 9
She-nah-nam 7, 349
She-ne-wah 25
Sheridan 328
Shingle Point 425
Shoalwater 295, 346
Sho-dab-dab 7
S'homamish 350
Shoots River 56
Sicade, Henry 28, 320
Siluchogwas 431
Sil-uth-os-twas 431
Silvan Boutgeau 73
Silvin Bourgeau 68
Similkameen 426
Simmons 127, 143, 170, 175, 199, 206, 207, 221, 226, 232, 251, 261, 267, 278, 282, 287, 288, 291, 299, 321, 325, 326, 328, 333, 349, 351, 399, 403
Simmons, Michael Troutman 206, 207
Simon 25, 69, 73, 77, 79, 81, 100, 131, 213, 216, 235, 238, 358, 415, 419, 425
Simpson vi, 19, 23, 74, 95, 123, 124, 151, 172, 176, 177, 178, 228, 281, 426
Simpson, George 19
Sinahomish 85, 101, 175, 192, 232, 240, 241, 243, 248, 255, 256
Sinclair 163
Sin-ne-tee-aye 113
Sinnohmish 101
Sin-no-oh-mish 79
Sin-no-whom-mish 113
Siskiyou Trail 153, 154
Sitka 89, 90, 126, 135, 136, 137, 154, 172, 177, 190, 191, 203, 222, 284
Sitschahlabsh at Budd Inlet 7

Si-yah-ish-soot 85
Skagit 9, 238, 240, 244
Skagit family 9
Skalatchet 79
Skatcutxat (Mud Turtles) 22
Skate Creek 13, 38
Skay-waw-mish 113
Skeena and Agwilget (Buckley) Rivers 425
Skeena and Kisiox Rivers 426
Skeena River 424, 426
Skene 33, 74, 143, 154, 174, 177, 219, 236, 257, 270, 291
Skeywamish 249, 250
Skinner 270, 389, 395
S'Klallam 23, 33, 34, 56, 58, 63, 72, 78, 113, 115, 118
Skookumchuck 258, 431
Skookumchuck River 258
Skthon-la-tum 117
Skwai-aitl 9
Skykomish 249
Skywamish 240
Slacum 107, 108
Slaughter 158, 317, 325, 348, 351, 369, 371
slaughterhouse 384
Sloan 406
Slocum 153, 222, 235, 239, 248, 255, 256, 326, 353
Slocum, Richard 428
Slogomas 429
Slugamas 255
Smith 7, 42, 146, 150, 217, 218, 221, 240, 257, 290, 298, 299, 312, 324, 325, 344, 360, 377
Smith, Levi L. 237
Smith, Levi Lathrop 218
Smitkaynum 388
Snake River 33, 97, 143
S'Neitlam 244, 251, 252, 257
Sne-my-mo or Snuneymuxw 426
Snohomish 25, 237
Snoqualmie 8, 202, 237, 238, 249, 250, 251, 258, 265, 266, 401
Snoqualmie People 8
Snoqualmies 57, 240, 249, 250, 251, 252, 255, 258, 265, 401
Snoqualmish 258
Snoquamick 240
Snoquamie 58
Snoquamish 70, 233
Sonora 3

So-qua-mish 80, 112, 113
Soquamish 58, 112, 250, 254, 256, 305
Sou-cat 102
South Bay 7
South Prairie Creek 8
South Puget Sound Native American 7
South Sound 41, 51, 62, 86, 242, 250
Southwest Farms 431
Spain 3, 18, 27, 31, 32, 33, 104, 163
Spanaway 9, 10, 11, 77, 121, 155, 156, 158, 195, 198, 209, 220, 233, 279, 280, 316, 358, 371, 378, 431
Spanaway Lake 9, 10, 11, 195
Spaneuh 158
Spanish vi, 3, 4, 17, 18, 19, 27, 31, 32, 39, 40, 45, 75, 93, 107, 108, 111, 117, 124, 131, 153, 177, 186, 191, 195, 215, 222, 223, 239, 246, 247, 284, 308, 383, 408
Spanish California 17, 18
Spa-nu-eh 9, 10, 195, 220, 280
Spa-n'eh 431
Spanueh 105, 258, 324, 358
Spaulding 37, 85, 98
Spence 402
Spencer 382
Spicer 397
Spokan 79
Spokane Falls 426
Spokane House 32, 34, 143, 426
Spokane River 426
Spootsylth Lake 167
Spotsisichth Lake 431
squabble 223, 250, 411
Squadsup 384
Squalitchew 7, 16, 17, 42, 57, 86, 275
Squalitchew Creek 7
Squalli-absch 13, 38
Squally 28, 29, 30, 244, 254, 255, 279, 329, 336, 358, 386, 387, 396, 402, 429, 430, 431
Squallyabasch 332
Squally Lake 431
Squa-quid 349
Squatahan 300
squatter 260, 275, 300, 308, 325, 337, 346, 358, 410
squatters 125, 240, 247, 256, 284, 306, 307, 318, 324, 340, 346,

[447]

347, 386, 394, 431
Squatters 266, 290, 335, 408, 410
squatting 324, 354
Squawksin 350
Squaxin 15, 25, 54, 58, 218, 232, 403
Squiaitl 350
S.S. Beaver 89, 90, 91, 93, 95, 103, 104, 111, 112, 115, 118, 145, 155, 156, 157, 159, 163, 177, 178, 184, 187, 190, 221, 222, 227, 235, 239, 257, 273, 274, 294, 303, 304, 311, 363, 372, 373, 375, 376, 407
SS Fairy 91, 397
SS Major Tompkins 354, 359
SS Otter 91, 337, 361
Stager 426
Staines 264, 288
S'talol 358
Stanford, Leland 417
State Historical Society 170, 284, 301, 329, 381, 411, 416, 420
State Hospital for the Insane 405, 417
State of the Union address 416
Steamship Beaver vi, 45
Steel 158, 281
Stehchass 350
Stehrsasamish at Tumwater Falls 8
Steilacoom vii, 9, 10, 11, 15, 24, 25, 41, 71, 77, 144, 157, 158, 174, 185, 197, 198, 206, 221, 225, 226, 227, 228, 232, 239, 240, 242, 248, 251, 256, 257, 258, 260, 261, 263, 264, 265, 267, 269, 270, 272, 273, 275, 276, 277, 279, 280, 282, 286, 287, 288, 290, 291, 292, 293, 294, 295, 298, 301, 302, 304, 305, 306, 307, 309, 310, 311, 312, 313, 315, 317, 321, 322, 325, 327, 328, 329, 330, 332, 333, 335, 336, 337, 340, 343, 346, 347, 348, 350, 353, 354, 359, 360, 361, 362, 369, 370, 371, 372, 375, 376, 377, 378, 379, 382, 384, 385, 386, 387, 388, 389, 390, 394, 397, 398, 399, 401, 402, 405, 406, 407, 411, 414, 417, 420, 431
Steilacoom Band 10
Steilacoom City 287, 343, 397
Steilacoom Creek 15
Steilacoom Farm 431
Steilacoom Lake 11, 359, 398
Steilacoom Library Association 406

Steilacoom Plain 431
Steilacoom River 10
Steilacoom villages 10
Stevens 256, 333, 334, 337, 340, 349, 350, 357, 370, 372, 377, 378, 380, 381, 382, 391, 393, 394
Stevens, Isaac 126, 203, 337, 348, 368, 372, 378, 381, 382, 393
Stikine 177, 217, 221, 280, 425, 426
Stikine River 217, 425
St. James 425
St James (Stewart Lake Post) 426
St. John (Rocky Mountain House) on the Peace River 426
St. Martin 116
Stoney Creek 426
Stouddard 118
Strait of Juan de Fuca 23, 31, 51, 72, 157, 225, 234, 247
Strong 34, 56, 231, 282, 303, 304
Strong People 34
Stuart 124, 263, 264, 294, 302
Stubb 409
Stuck 8, 25, 220
Stuck River 8
Studebaker 297
Subjects of the King of England 18
Sublette, William 65
Suiqulroot 431
sulphur friction match 24
Su-nook-que-le-mish 113
Suquamish 23, 241, 244
Surveyor 330, 361
Susan Stugis 304
Sustac Plain 308
Sutherland 247
Suzanna 302
Swahsinamish 223
Swan 295, 298, 331, 375, 376
Swan, James 295
Sylvester, Edmund 218, 237, 286, 297, 320
Sylvester's Landing 425

T

Tacoma ix, xii, 8, 11, 16, 39, 40, 41, 47, 57, 59, 61, 62, 77, 81, 121, 128, 130, 152, 155, 168, 170, 171, 186, 210, 246, 251, 266, 267, 276, 280, 281, 282, 284, 298, 299, 300, 301, 316, 317, 320, 321, 326, 329, 331, 332, 335, 338, 339, 362, 376, 382, 383, 399, 402, 403,

405, 411, 416, 417, 418, 419, 420, 421, 426
Tacoma Historical Society ix, 170, 300, 338
Tahawat 258
Tahi 50, 55, 69
Tai 69, 73, 75, 288
Takhoma 16, 163
Tak-o-bet 163
Taku River 425
Talbot 323
Talley Richmond 179, 206
Talmage 257
Tamaru 344, 354
Tamattutaiah 221
Tapou 302, 331, 358, 359, 387
Tapou, Joe 428
Tatam 258
Tebebkov 284
Teboe, Joseph 429
Tekatat 60
Telegraph Creek 425, 426
Tenalquot 195, 220, 248, 255, 258, 270, 292, 431
tenant farmer 114, 123, 124, 126, 127, 128, 131, 133, 134, 135, 136, 138, 139, 145, 149, 152, 158, 173, 185, 206, 216, 247, 260, 264, 284, 417
Territorial government 375, 390
Territorial land survey 286
Territory vii, xii, 27, 32, 65, 128, 134, 184, 203, 208, 212, 218, 236, 243, 246, 266, 271, 275, 286, 295, 297, 300, 312, 317, 318, 319, 328, 330, 333, 334, 335, 337, 341, 343, 344, 348, 351, 352, 360, 361, 362, 368, 377, 378, 380, 388, 393, 394, 395, 399, 405, 407, 408, 414, 416, 417, 418, 425, 429
Territory of Oregon vii
Terry 292, 335
Teslin Lake 425, 427
The Columbian 251, 311, 313, 320
The Governor and Adventurers of England Trading in the Hudson Bay 18
The Little Emperor 19
the Mountain that was God 4
The War for Independence 411
Thibeault 250, 254, 353, 358
Thom-mas-chum 113
Thompson 33, 276, 319, 324, 329, 381, 401, 425

Index

Thornhill 291, 302, 309, 310, 336, 353, 358, 387, 429
Thornton 256, 257, 258
Thronhill 336
THS ix
Thuanok 58
Thurston xi, 30, 138, 207, 265, 266, 302, 312, 325, 353
Tibeault 340
Tilithlow 220
Tilley 333
Tlingit 191
Tlithlow 9, 10, 105, 195, 270, 290, 291, 307, 325, 326, 335, 337, 347, 353, 354, 388, 389, 396, 431
tobacco-slurry 138, 200
Toby Creek 425
Tod 256, 257, 258, 261, 263, 264, 282
Toftezen 285
Tolentire 306
Tollentire 308
Tolmie vii, 48, 49, 50, 51, 52, 53, 54, 55, 56, 57, 58, 59, 60, 61, 62, 63, 64, 87, 88, 99, 100, 124, 135, 174, 185, 187, 189, 190, 192, 198, 199, 202, 203, 206, 216, 218, 220, 223, 224, 225, 226, 228, 229, 234, 240, 242, 246, 249, 255, 256, 257, 258, 259, 260, 261, 263, 264, 265, 266, 270, 272, 273, 276, 277, 281, 282, 287, 288, 290, 291, 292, 293, 294, 295, 300, 302, 303, 304, 305, 306, 307, 308, 309, 310, 312, 323, 324, 325, 329, 330, 335, 336, 337, 340, 344, 345, 346, 348, 353, 354, 358, 359, 361, 363, 370, 371, 384, 386, 387, 388, 389, 390, 394, 395, 396, 397, 406, 407, 408, 411, 429
Tolmie, Dr. William Fraser 428
Tolmie, William F. 428
Toot-sehts-awh'lh 7
Totten Inlet 8
Totten Island 9
Towne 334
T'Peeksin 350
trade blankets 26, 40
Trade Blotter 55, 68, 209, 238, 241, 250
trade goods 20, 21, 22, 26, 40, 43, 48, 50, 52, 54, 58, 68, 70, 73, 77, 101, 115, 120, 185, 198, 248, 268, 274, 303, 324, 360, 361, 365, 368

Trader 22, 49, 54, 55, 56, 57, 58, 69, 70, 73, 76, 79, 87, 89, 112, 118, 126, 127, 130, 132, 142, 208, 218, 240, 280, 281, 382, 428
trade store 48, 52, 53, 57, 59, 66, 78, 79, 80, 85, 194, 210, 232, 236, 243, 244, 246, 252, 259, 271, 294, 305, 308, 312, 343, 361, 383, 384
Trade Store 54, 126, 144, 166, 198, 221, 229, 239, 240, 252, 273, 279, 281, 302, 382, 386
trading posts xii, 20, 22, 33, 44, 95, 105, 178, 189, 190, 424
trading system 14
Trask 299
Treaty of 1846 173, 205, 208, 220, 228, 259, 284, 317, 318, 322, 325, 352, 408, 411, 414
Treaty of Florida 33
Treaty of Ghent 33, 40
Treaty War vii, 299, 372, 375, 417
Treehatchee 105
Treehatchie 336
Tribune 134, 155, 210, 382, 409, 419
Troncomalee 386
Trudelle 272, 277
Truth Teller 378
Tsatsal 161
Tscha-kole-chy 285
Tse-alum 9
Tuc-Hast-Chu 431
Tuchoma 63
Tule 280
Tumwater 8, 170, 199, 206, 207, 226, 232, 238, 267, 299, 328
Tumwater Falls 8
Tun-sind 103
Turner, Nat 35
Turnip Park 220
Tyee 73, 192, 398
Tyrell's Lake 255, 270

U

Una 288, 290
United States xii, 4, 6, 9, 16, 17, 18, 19, 27, 32, 33, 37, 39, 47, 99, 104, 105, 107, 125, 128, 157, 158, 159, 169, 171, 172, 179, 188, 194, 202, 205, 207, 210, 218, 219, 220, 228, 231, 234, 235, 238, 243, 246, 251, 261, 264, 265, 266, 275, 278, 279, 285, 287, 301, 303, 309, 311, 312, 316, 317, 318, 320, 322, 340, 351, 352, 359, 360, 362, 368, 382, 394, 395, 399, 406, 410, 411, 414, 415, 416, 418, 423
United States Congress xii
Unites States and Great Britain 34
Upper Chehalis 8, 9
Upper Chehalis villages 8
US vii, 2, 17, 33, 35, 39, 65, 86, 91, 107, 108, 110, 128, 131, 155, 163, 164, 166, 170, 172, 188, 194, 207, 210, 215, 220, 226, 228, 234, 235, 236, 242, 251, 252, 257, 264, 265, 266, 271, 272, 273, 274, 276, 277, 278, 279, 282, 285, 294, 297, 302, 303, 304, 306, 307, 309, 316, 317, 321, 322, 323, 325, 330, 333, 335, 340, 344, 345, 350, 353, 357, 373, 377, 380, 389, 394, 402, 403, 406, 408, 409, 410, 411, 414, 415, 416, 417
USA border 426
US Army vii, 188, 251, 252, 265, 360
US Army Corps of Discovery 17
US Artillery 410
USA territory 426
US Engineers 410
US House of Representatives 35
US Infantry 410
US Lighthouse Board 403
US Navy gunboat attack 398

V

Valerianos, Apostolos 31
Van Asselt 292
Van Buren, Martin 35
Vancouver xi, 1, 4, 12, 13, 16, 22, 23, 24, 27, 28, 32, 33, 34, 37, 38, 39, 42, 44, 47, 48, 49, 50, 51, 52, 54, 55, 58, 59, 62, 63, 65, 72, 73, 74, 75, 76, 77, 79, 80, 81, 82, 85, 86, 87, 88, 89, 90, 93, 95, 97, 99, 100, 101, 103, 104, 106, 107, 116, 117, 120, 121, 123, 124, 126, 128, 135, 138, 139, 142, 143, 145, 150, 153, 155, 160, 163, 172, 173, 174, 176, 177, 178, 185, 187, 188, 189, 197, 199, 205, 211, 216, 217, 218, 219, 223, 225, 226, 229, 231, 232, 234, 236, 250, 251, 252, 256, 257, 264, 270, 271, 277, 282, 284, 285, 286, 291, 292, 294, 295, 303, 308, 309, 310, 311, 316, 317, 323, 329, 331, 332, 333, 337, 340, 348, 352, 361, 362, 369,

[449]

396, 401, 405, 407, 408, 411, 413, 419, 426, 427
Vancouver, Captain George 4, 16, 32, 163
Vancouver Island xi, 1, 23, 72, 93, 225, 309, 337, 348
Varner 346, 347, 354
Vavasour 210, 211, 212
Venn 358
Vernon Post 427
Victoria 23, 72, 89, 91, 113, 116, 123, 138, 141, 155, 156, 177, 187, 188, 189, 208, 219, 221, 223, 225, 226, 227, 232, 239, 240, 243, 244, 247, 251, 252, 254, 255, 258, 261, 263, 264, 270, 271, 273, 275, 277, 281, 282, 284, 285, 286, 288, 290, 291, 292, 294, 295, 303, 304, 306, 307, 309, 311, 322, 323, 324, 330, 334, 336, 337, 340, 347, 348, 354, 359, 360, 361, 364, 373, 375, 376, 385, 396, 397, 398, 403, 407, 408, 411, 413, 414, 416, 427
Vidette 372
Villages 6, 7, 23
Vincennes 157, 158, 164, 165, 169, 304
Vine 337
Vizcaino 31
Vogt Creek 8
volcanic activity 1
Voltigeurs 143, 286
Volunteer Militia 300, 371, 399
volunteer soldiers 377
Voyage of Discovery 17
Voyageurs 22, 66

W

Waglisla 426
Wailatpu 98, 188, 232, 235
Walker 47, 97, 100, 142, 179, 184
Wallace 250, 251, 252, 255, 258, 265, 266, 369, 387
Walla Walla 15, 33, 37, 39, 98, 141, 143, 235, 278, 316, 320, 357, 359, 363, 367, 368, 369, 405, 423, 426
Wapato Creek 8
Wapato Lake 11, 77
Warbass 271, 333
War (of 1812) 33
Warre 210, 211, 212
warships 172, 409
Washington vii, xii, 1, 2, 3, 4, 5, 15,

16, 19, 23, 24, 30, 31, 32, 33, 37, 41, 47, 71, 81, 82, 100, 105, 120, 123, 125, 135, 143, 151, 156, 157, 160, 161, 170, 186, 188, 202, 203, 207, 208, 215, 225, 235, 239, 240, 242, 244, 246, 248, 252, 263, 266, 275, 278, 281, 282, 284, 286, 295, 297, 298, 300, 301, 302, 311, 312, 317, 318, 319, 328, 329, 330, 333, 334, 335, 337, 341, 343, 344, 345, 348, 350, 351, 352, 353, 360, 361, 362, 368, 371, 375, 376, 377, 379, 380, 381, 382, 383, 388, 390, 393, 394, 395, 399, 402, 403, 405, 407, 411, 414, 416, 417, 418, 420, 423
Washington Coastline 2
Washington, D.C 203
Washington, General George 4
Washington State 3, 170, 399, 405
Washington State History Museum 242, 281, 317, 399, 405, 423
Washington Territory vii, xii, 317, 319, 333, 393
Waugh 327
Webber 327, 345, 375, 376, 411
Weekly Columbian 324
Weenaculneala 353
Weller 326, 353
Wells 330, 415
Wells Fargo stagecoach 415
Wenas 320
Wesley 107, 127, 131, 132, 182, 326, 329
Western State Hospital 225, 417
Westwold Post 427
Whidbey 34, 50, 78, 237, 285, 393, 403
Whidbey Island 34, 50, 78, 237, 393, 403
Whidby 50, 62, 72, 249, 278, 285, 308, 327, 398
Whitehorn 168
White River 2, 8, 369, 371
White "Stuck River" 25
White Water River 427
Whitman 85, 98, 134, 141, 182, 188, 219, 232, 235, 236, 246, 316
Whitman Massacre 235
Whulge 6, 10, 13, 15, 16, 17, 20, 23, 25, 42, 174, 332
Whyatchie 158, 220, 224
Whyatchie Farm 158
Whyeek 258

Wickersham 381
Wilbur 327
Wilcox 277
Wilcut 325
Wild Pigeon 401
Wilkes vi, 74, 86, 157, 158, 159, 160, 161, 163, 164, 165, 166, 167, 168, 169, 170, 171, 172, 185, 188, 189, 207, 226, 278, 297, 316, 321, 331
Willamette 28, 65, 73, 80, 98, 106, 107, 108, 110, 111, 120, 122, 127, 135, 141, 142, 146, 148, 151, 153, 154, 165, 172, 173, 174, 181, 185, 189, 194, 196, 198, 217, 219, 221, 235, 284, 286, 293, 315, 330, 332, 345
Willamette River Valley 65, 217
Willapa 295, 346
William and Ann 104
Williams 100, 103, 110, 153, 361
Williamson 415
Willson 121, 122, 127, 128, 130, 133, 134, 135, 136, 138, 143, 146, 147, 148, 149, 150, 151, 157, 167, 179, 181, 199, 206, 216, 407
Wilson's Farm 431
Wilson, William Holden 120
Wimahl 5
Windsor 143, 333
Winthrop 316, 320, 331, 332, 339
Wirsing, Dale ix
Wiscum 209, 220, 222
Withal 306
witnesses 261, 270, 280, 347, 354, 379, 380, 415
Witney, Thomas Empson 26
Wollochet Bay 9, 16, 298
Work John 24, 25, 33, 34, 86, 87, 88, 89, 96, 118, 120, 156, 174, 220, 264, 288, 291, 294, 303, 310, 348, 361, 396, 397, 398, 401, 402, 413
Work-McMillan's brigade 25
world's longest railroad 47, 417
Wren 234, 240, 241, 249, 250, 252, 254, 290, 307, 311, 336, 377
Wren, Charles 428
Wright 257
Wunch 238
Wyamock 336
Wyaseo 113
Wyatchew Lake 158
Wyatchie Farm 431

[450]

Index

Wyeth 37, 59, 106
Wyeth, Jarvus 37
Wynter 234

Y

Yac-kah-mah 113
Yakaama 117
Yakama 21, 103, 238, 241
Yakima 7, 77, 126, 152, 161, 175, 176, 190, 300, 315, 320, 368, 369
Yam Hill 431
Yanalacows 255
Yanatacow 243
Yantis 333
Yelim 431
Yelmor 431
Yelm Prairie 208
Yelm (Yellem) Prairie 9
Yesler 319, 326, 333
Youcan 427
Young 53, 66, 106, 107, 108, 110, 155, 276, 336, 347, 358, 420, 429, 431
Young, Ewing 106, 110, 111, 153
Young's House 431
Yo-wahisa-Clear Creek 7
YTanatacow 114
Yukon 425, 426, 427
Yukon River 426, 427

The author, JERRY V. RAMSEY, PH.D., earned his BA at the University of Puget Sound, Tacoma (1967), a Master's degree at the University of Washington, Seattle (1971), and a Doctorate at Columbia Pacific University in San Rafael, California (1985). He taught at all levels (pre-school to graduate), in public schools, universities, and learning centers for 30 years.

Ramsey is a skilled teacher, public speaker, history re-enactor, and radio announcer. His voice has been recorded for historic sites, commercials, public service announcements, and the popular swing music shows "Remember When" and "The Big Band Broadcast" heard on several radio stations.

Left: Dr. Dale Wirsing, V.P of Tacoma Historical Society. *Right*: The author, Jerry V. Ramsey. Photo by Ron Karabaich, Old Town Photo, Tacoma.

He is currently a volunteer at Tacoma History Museum and at Fort Nisqually Living History Museum. He has received many awards, including the coveted Murray Morgan Award for significant achievement in preserving and communicating local history. His published works include many magazine, newspaper, newsletter, and journal articles as well as two books: *A Curriculum for High School Economic Geography and History* and *A Fur Trade Era Anthology*.

In *Stealing Puget Sound, 1832-1869* Ramsey exposes the little known political tension between the first British settlers and the Americans who crossed the Oregon Trail fifteen years later. The British legal ownership of the precious land of the Puget Sound region was confirmed by international treaty. The well known "Pig War" was a direct result of the 'squeeze' aggressive Americans settlers put on the British owners.

Ramsey used primary source letters and journals, plus some secondary materials, to document and reference historical accuracy. The book remains comfortably readable, but challenges 'politically correct' history.

The Illustrator, CAROL ANN JOHNSON, earned her BFA in Printmaking at Syracuse University, New York. She lived and created in Hawaii for 25 years and has been active in cultural, artist, and community organizations in Gig Harbor, WA for 18 years. Johnson brings together the experience of over 45 years as an Artist in her award winning Fine Arts, Book Illustrations, and Graphic Art skills.

In this book, *Stealing Puget Sound, 1832-1869*, the artist drew great inspiration form the author's depth of knowledge and meticulous descriptions of the times. In a style similar to sketches by trappers and travelers of the time, images on weathered paper, the illustrations herein show both careful attention to accuracy and a sense of the period of history.

COLOPHON

This book was designed by Kathryn E. Campbell of Gorham Printing, located in Centralia, Washington. The interior text pages are set in 11-point Adobe Devanagari. Digital toner-based printing and perfect binding was also accomplished by Gorham Printing. Interior page paper is 60# white Lynx opaque, and cover stock is white 12pt C1S with gloss lamination.